survey of

Operating Systems

Seventh Edition

Jane Holcombe

SURVEY OF OPERATING SYSTEMS, SEVENTH EDITION

Published by McGraw Hill LLC, 1325 Avenue of the Americas, New York, NY 10019. Copyright ©2023 by McGraw Hill LLC. All rights reserved. Printed in the United States of America. Previous editions ©2020, 2017, and 2015. No part of this publication may be reproduced or distributed in No part of this publication may be reproduced or distributed in any form or by any means, or stored in a database or retrieval system, without the prior written consent of McGraw Hill LLC, including, but not limited to, in any network or other electronic storage or transmission, or broadcast for distance learning.

Some ancillaries, including electronic and print components, may not be available to customers outside the United States.

This book is printed on acid-free paper.

1 2 3 4 5 6 7 8 9 LWI 27 26 25 24 23 22

ISBN 978-1-264-13681-0 (bound edition)
MHID 1-264-13681-1 (bound edition)
ISBN 978-1-264-37396-3 (loose-leaf edition)
MHID 1-264-37396-1 (loose-leaf edition)

Portfolio Manager: *Wyatt Morris*
Product Developers: *Alan Palmer*
Marketing Manager: *Dean Karampelas*
Content Project Managers: *Maria McGreal, Rachael Hillebrand*
Buyer: *Laura Fuller*
Content Licensing Specialist: *Sarah Flynn*
Cover Image: *sdecoret/Shutterstock*
Compositor: *Straive*

All credits appearing on page or at the end of the book are considered to be an extension of the copyright page.

Library of Congress Cataloging-in-Publication Data
Names: Holcombe, Jane, author.
Title: Survey of operating systems / Jane Holcombe, Charles Holcombe.
Description: Seventh edition. | New York : McGraw Hill LLC, [2023] |
  Includes index.
Identifiers: LCCN 2021049845 (print) | LCCN 2021049846 (ebook) | ISBN
  9781264136810 (bound edition : acid-free paper) | ISBN 9781264373963
  (loose-leaf edition) | ISBN 9781264374489 (ebook)
Subjects: LCSH: Operating systems (Computers)
Classification: LCC QA76.77 .H65 2022 (print) | LCC QA76.77 (ebook) | DDC
  005.4/3—dc23/eng/20211020
LC record available at https://lccn.loc.gov/2021049845
LC ebook record available at https://lccn.loc.gov/2021049846

The Internet addresses listed in the text were accurate at the time of publication. The inclusion of a website does not indicate an endorsement by the authors or McGraw Hill LLC, and McGraw Hill LLC does not guarantee the accuracy of the information presented at these sites.

mheducation.com/highered

About the Author

JANE HOLCOMBE was the tech support person for a small financial planning company, a role she was assigned at a time when technology was about connecting specialized terminals to expensive industry-specific systems across telephone lines. These systems were limited in the reports they generated, and far from user-friendly. Her job was to research the emerging technologies of the time, including desktop PCs and local area networks. Jane would often discover bookmarked technical magazines on her desk, along with a note from the boss instructing her to check out the articles and research how to move their accounting and contact management systems to PCs. After months of research and after consulting with various experts, she oversaw the move of the accounting and contact management functions to IBM PCs connected via a local area network (LAN). The network was slow, and the software for accounting and contact management required memorizing keystrokes for each function. However, the boss was pleased with the ability to make quick changes to the reports these systems generated—something not possible with the old, mainframe-based systems. This project showed Jane the potential of personal computing in business.

She learned that one roadblock to bringing PCs into business was the lack of knowledgeable PC support staff. So, her next project was a career move, as she created appropriate courseware and co-founded a company that presented technical PC and network support courses nationwide.

Later, she sold her interest in the training company and returned to independent technical consulting and instruction, acquiring experience and certifications for desktop and server operating systems. Today, as a technical writer, she draws on this background as well as her continuing exploration of new technologies.

About the Contributors

This book was greatly influenced by the comments, suggestions, and feedback from the following group of dedicated instructors. To them I give my heartfelt thanks.

Reviewers

Tim S. Baron	*Schoolcraft College*
Nancy Woodard	*Moraine Valley Community College*
Chris Johnson	*South Piedmont Community College*
Jason Boyer	*Reedley College*
Janelle Arruda	*Bristol Community College*
Skip Russell	*Southern New Hampshire University*
Perry Kivolowitz	*Carthage College*
Andrew Collins	*Springfield Technical Community College*
Scott Rhine	*Lake Land College*
Kasia Taylor	*Anne Arundel Community College*

Audrey Styer	*Morton College*
Karen Henry	*New Mexico State University Grants*
David Harris	*Benedictine College*
Robert Doyle	*NMSU/Dona Ana Community College*
David Reva	*Kalamazoo Valley Community College*
Walter Schilling	*Milwaukee School of Engineering*
Christie Hovey	*Lincoln Land Community College*
Charles R. Whealton	*Delaware Technical Community College*
Marc Forestiere	*Fresno City College*
Cameron Spears	*Hillsborough Community College*
Shane Knighton	*Central Georgia Technical College*
Nary Subramanian	*University of Texas at Tyler*
Randy Gambill	*Wilkes Community College*
Anita Laird	*Schoolcraft College*
Mark Mahoney	*Carthage College*

Acknowledgments

When Alan Palmer, Senior Product Developer, notified me that McGraw Hill Higher Education had approved the seventh edition of the Survey of Operating Systems, I carefully reviewed the content in the last edition and created a suggested Table of Contents that Alan sent to appropriate instructors, along with a survey for them to complete. The results of this survey helped me create the outline for the seventh edition.

As with previous editions, knowledgeable peer reviewers scrutinized each chapter, providing invaluable feedback on the relevancy and accuracy of the content. I can't imagine writing a book like this without these technical reviews.

I thank every member of the talented team of people at McGraw Hill who ensured the book's integrity. They include Wyatt Morris, Alan Palmer, Maria McGreal, and Mithun Kothandath from Straive. I particularly want to thank Wyatt and Alan for their unstinting support, professionalism, and patience. I love the design of this edition and greatly appreciate the expertise of the members of the production group who all worked hard to make the book look wonderful. Creating and laying out the many elements of this complex book design was a huge task, and they handled it skillfully.

I appreciate all who worked so hard to make this book what it is.

Thank you!

About This Book

Important Technology Skills

Information technology (IT) offers many career paths, leading to occupations in such fields as PC repair, network administration, telecommunications, Web development, graphic design, and desktop support. To become competent in any IT field, however, you need certain basic computer skills. This book will help you build a foundation for success in the IT field by introducing you to fundamental information about popular desktop and mobile operating systems, a needed basis for working with all types of computing devices.

Try This!
exercises reinforce the concepts.

Warnings and Notes create a road map for success.

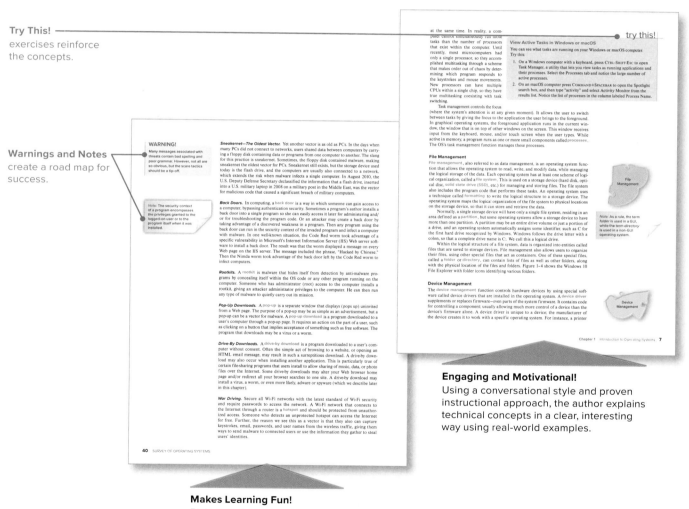

Engaging and Motivational!
Using a conversational style and proven instructional approach, the author explains technical concepts in a clear, interesting way using real-world examples.

Makes Learning Fun!
Rich, colorful text and enhanced illustrations bring technical subjects to life.

Effective Learning Tools

The design of this colorful, pedagogically rich book will make learning easy and enjoyable and help you develop the skills and critical thinking abilities that will enable you to adapt to different job situations and troubleshoot problems.

Jane Holcombe's proven ability to explain concepts in a clear, direct, even humorous way makes this book interesting and motivational, and fun.

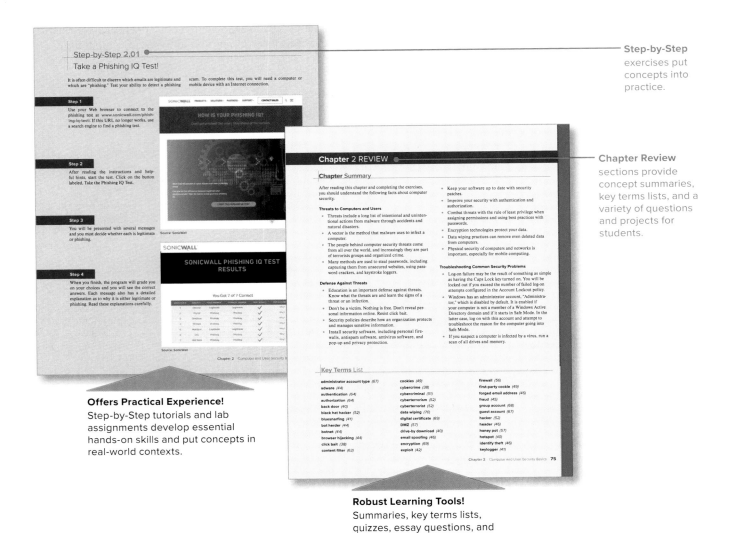

Step-by-Step exercises put concepts into practice.

Chapter Review sections provide concept summaries, key terms lists, and a variety of questions and projects for students.

Offers Practical Experience!
Step-by-Step tutorials and lab assignments develop essential hands-on skills and put concepts in real-world contexts.

Robust Learning Tools!
Summaries, key terms lists, quizzes, essay questions, and lab projects help you practice skills and measure progress.

Each chapter includes:

- **Learning Outcomes** that set measurable goals for chapter-by-chapter progress.
- **Four-Color Illustrations** that give you a clear picture of the technologies.
- **Step-by-Step Tutorials** that teach you to perform essential tasks and procedures hands-on.
- **Try This!** sidebars that encourage you to practice and apply the concepts in real-world settings.

- **Notes** and **Warnings** that guide you through difficult areas.
- **Chapter Summaries** and **Key Terms Lists** that provide you with an easy way to review important concepts and vocabulary.
- **Challenging End-of-Chapter Tests** that include vocabulary-building exercises, multiple-choice questions, essay questions, and on-the-job lab projects.

New to *Survey of Operating Systems,* Seventh Edition

General changes in this Seventh Edition:

- The Sixth Edition's Chapter 4, *Windows 7,* is removed. Some of the content that applies to Windows 10 has been updated and appears in *Windows 10,* now Chapter 4 and other content was moved to *Supporting and Troubleshooting Windows,* now Chapter 5.
- Chapter 11, *File Management in the Cloud,* previously only offered as online content, has been added to the textbook with revisions.
- In addition to reviewing and updating the content from the Sixth Edition, the author tightened the text throughout, improved the flow, and removed topics that are no longer relevant.
- Finally, the exercises, figures, and illustrations are updated to support learning.

Chapter 1 Introduction to Operating Systems

- This chapter now includes an introduction to cloud computing.

Chapter 2 Computer Security Basics

- Discussion of certain security features of Windows and macOS were moved from this chapter to the Windows and macOS chapters.

Chapter 3 Desktop Virtualization

- Coverage of both Windows XP Mode and Windows Virtual PC on Windows 7 were removed from this edition.
- The chapter now includes an explanation of the Hyper-V Quick Create utility as well as a related Step-by-Step exercise.

Chapter 4 Windows 10

- Content has been updated and enhanced with topics from the previous Windows 7 chapter that apply to Windows 10.

Chapter 5 Supporting and Troubleshooting Windows

- Content and images have been updated with topics from the previous Windows 7 chapter that apply to supporting and troubleshooting Windows.
- The chapter now includes two additional Learning Outcomes: *Manage Local Accounts* and *Manage Local Data Files.*

Chapter 6 Apple macOS on the Desktop

- The author removed the Learning Outcome titled *macOS History and Versions.*

- The chapter now addresses features of macOS on the new M1 Macs and MacBooks.
- A new Learning Outcome has been added on local file management.

Chapter 7 Linux on the Desktop

- This chapter compares distributions of Linux from two sources: Ubuntu and Raspberry Pi.

Chapter 8 Chromebooks and Chrome OS

- This chapter now includes content on troubleshooting and repair of Chrome OS using two important tools: the Diagnostics app and Powerwash.

Chapter 9 Connecting Desktops and Laptops to Networks

- Text and images were updated as needed in the chapter.

Chapter 10 Mobile Operating Systems

- Text and images are updated throughout the chapter.

Chapter 11 File Management in the Cloud

- This chapter was added to the textbook, in part, to explain the connection between cloud storage and your local operating system. It also serves as an aid to understanding the options for working with cloud storage from desktop or mobile devices.

Chapter 12 Windows 11 (online only)

- In the fall of 2021, Microsoft introduced Windows 11. At that point, the seventh edition of Survey of Operating Systems was in production, and it was too late to add a Windows 11 chapter to the textbook. Knowing that instructors and students would need this content, the author created and submitted a Windows 11 chapter in time for the editorial and production teams at McGraw Hill to publish an online chapter. The Instructor Supplements for this chapter are included with the Supplements for the complete textbook.

Contents

1 | Introduction to Operating Systems   1

2 | Computer and User Security Basics   37

3 | Desktop Virtualization   79

4 | Windows 10   105

11 | File Management in the Cloud   399

- The typical microcomputer also has some form of storage, such as a hard drive, and it has at least one means each for input and output.

Firmware

Each computer device you use has special software resident in integrated circuits called firmware containing small programs for providing basic communications between the operating system and the hardware.

- System firmware contains program code that informs the processor of the devices present and how to communicate with them.
- Most components and peripheral devices that connect to a computer (such as the video and network adapters, USB ports, and digital cameras) have their own firmware for providing basic communication between the operating system and the component.

Although you may never be aware of the firmware on a mobile device, on an older PC or laptop you may see evidence of the system and other firmware performing tests of the hardware. Carefully, watch the screen as you power up the computer, as shown in Figure 1-1. More recent computers may show a message only if there is a serious problem with the computer.

Today's Computers

The miniaturization of computers led to computers being built into all types of machinery, including vehicles, aircraft, and appliances. Computers touch our lives 24/7, and each has some form of operating system.

Servers. A server is a computer that provides one or more services to other computers over a network. What services do servers provide? A file server stores data files for network-connected users. If a server has one or more printers connected to it that it shares with users on the network, it is a print server. We call a server doing both tasks a file and print server; even though it sounds like two services, they combine into one service.

Other services include messaging services (email and fax), Web services, and many others. It takes specialized software to provide each type of server service, and complementary client software to request each type of service over a network. A computer on the user end of these services is a client. Today's client computers include the PCs, laptops, tablets, and smartphones discussed in this book. A server can offer multiple services at the same time while also being a client to other servers.

A desktop or laptop computer can act as a server for a few network clients. However, a server to which hundreds or thousands of clients must connect requires much more capable hardware to provide more storage, faster processing, and faster network access. It also requires specialized software, beginning with the operating systems. There are versions of Windows, Apple macOS, Linux, and UNIX especially designed as servers. The hardware for a high-quality server can run into the tens of thousands of dollars and upward, versus the much lower cost of a consumer-grade PC at a few hundred dollars.

> *Note:* The focus of this book is on using common desktop, laptop, and mobile operating systems. Therefore, it does not include details of server operating systems. It also does not discuss the operating systems in the various devices included in the Internet of Things (IoT).

```
Phoenix — Award BIOS v6.00PC

Copyright (C) 1984-2003, Phoenix Technologies, LTD


Main Processor : AMD Athlon (tm) 64 X2 Dual Core Processor 3000+

Memory Testing : 1720000K OK
```

FIGURE 1–1 An example of a firmware start-up message on an old PC.
Source: Phoenix Technologies Ltd.

A typical laptop.
Charts and BG/Shutterstock

A MacBook laptop.
Dzmitry Kliapitski/Alamy Stock Photo

Apple iPhone smartphone.
Alamy Stock Photo

Desktops and Laptops. A desktop computer, often called a personal computer (PC), is a computer designed to spend its useful life in one location—on a desk. A typical desktop computer consists of a box containing the main components, a display screen, a keyboard, and a pointing device (mouse). The box and the display screen may be combined into one case—referred to as an all-in-one.

A laptop computer has a flat screen and a keyboard, each integrated into a panel with a hinge holding the two together and allowing you to close the laptop and slip it into a case for easy portability. There are many sizes and types of laptop computers. Laptops are often used as portable replacements for desktop PCs.

The common operating systems for desktops and laptops are Apple's macOS (previously named OS X) for Apple brand desktops and laptops, Microsoft Windows, and Linux for other brands of PCs and laptops, the Chrome OS for Chromebox system units that are essentially PCs that come configured with the Chrome OS, and the Chrome OS for the Chromebook laptops. There are several manufacturers who offer these systems, but Google does not provide Chrome OS as a separate consumer product.

In this book, we use the term personal computer (PC) for a desktop computer running Windows or Linux and Mac for the Apple iMac desktop computers as well as the MacBook laptop computers. Both types of Apple computers run macOS.

Mobile Devices. Mobile computing in the 21st century has evolved from two branches of the technology tree: the telephony branch and the personal computing branch. Today's mobile devices only remotely resemble their awkward ancestors because today's devices are remarkably tiny and powerful, more like fictional Star Trek communicators than any 20th-century phones or computers. The versatility and widespread consumer appeal of today's mobile devices exceed the extraordinary imagination and vision of Star Trek creator Gene Roddenberry, at least in their use by consumers. Perhaps no one could have predicted five decades ago how tiny and powerful computing and communicating devices would become, and that they would be so common that individuals would insist on using their personal mobile devices at work, leading to a practice called bring your own device (BYOD).

Microcomputers today include a long list of devices that don't have *computer* in their name, including mobile devices. A mobile device has all or most of its electronic circuitry, such as the microprocessor, controllers, and memory, on a single microchip. This is known as system-on-a-chip (SoC). Mobile devices use wireless technologies and include a wide variety of products ranging from single-purpose computers to multifunction mobile devices. Some mobile devices run proprietary OSs, while others run scaled-down versions of desktop OSs. A mobile device commonly stores its OS in firmware, as an embedded OS.

The most popular mobile devices are smartphones. A smartphone works as a cell phone, but also lets you connect to the Internet, view your email, and install and run a variety of apps for entertainment, education, and work. Modern smartphones have high-quality touch screens. Examples of smartphones are Apple's iPhones and various models by Motorola, Nokia, HTC, Samsung, LG, and others. Examples of operating systems designed specifically for use on smartphones include Google's Android and Apple iOS.

Another very popular type of mobile device is a tablet. A tablet has a touch screen and no integrated keyboard. It is larger than a smartphone and more portable than a laptop. There are many lines of tablet products, such as the Apple iPad, Microsoft Surface, Samsung Galaxy, Google Nexus, Sony

Xperia, and Kindle Fire. Based on your preferences and needs, you can purchase a tablet with one of these OSs preinstalled: iPad OS, Microsoft Windows, or Android.

Internet of Things. And lastly, microcomputers exist in devices belonging to the Internet of things (IoT). These are devices we don't normally think of as computing devices. They include kitchen appliances, thermostats, utility meters, components in automobiles, light bulbs, and industrial control devices. They are not necessarily mobile, but they communicate on networks, often the Internet. IoT devices are increasingly used in industrial automation, connecting wirelessly, or via Ethernet, to automation networks.

Functions of Microcomputer Operating Systems

When using her PC at work or her Mac at home our friend Brianna spends much of her time in a specific application, such as a word processor, a graphical drawing program, or a Web browser. However, she must also perform tasks outside of these applications, beginning with the simple task of logging onto the computer, launching an application, and managing files. Since each type of computer requires different skills to complete tasks, she wants to gain a better understanding of the OSs to perform better on the job and be more comfortable working with the different computers. She wants to learn what an OS is and what functions it performs, which we describe in the following sections.

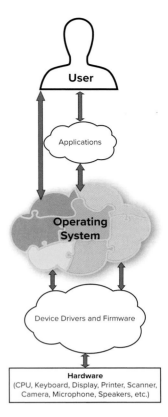

A simplified model of a user interaction with a computer.

The Big Picture

When a computer is turned on an operating system starts up (or "boots up," a derivation of the expression "lifting yourself by your own bootstraps"). Its main component, the kernel, remains in memory while the computer is running, managing low-level (close-to-the-hardware) OS tasks.

When a programmer, also known as a "developer," writes an application, he or she designs the application to interact with the operating system and to make requests for hardware services through the operating system. To do this, a programmer must write the program to use the correct commands to request operating system services. The operating system, in turn, interacts with the hardware on behalf of the application and fulfills the requests. Here is a simplified illustration of the interaction between the user and the hardware, managed by the operating system and various drivers and firmware. The operating system performs the following functions: user interface, job management, task management, file management, device management, memory management, and security. These functions are described next.

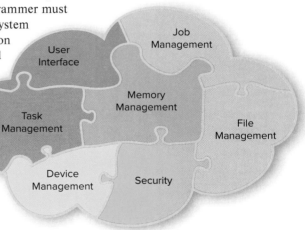

The functions of an operating system.

User Interface

The user interface (UI) is the software layer, sometimes called the shell, through which the user interacts with the OS. The UI includes the command processor, which loads programs into memory, as well as the many visual components of the operating system (what you see when you look at the display).

Command-line Interface. On a computer running Linux (without a graphical shell), this visual component consists of a character-based command line that requires text input. This is the command-line interface (CLI). Windows and macOS both have an optional CLI that runs in a window. Figure 1–2 shows the Windows 10 Command Prompt for the user janeh: white characters against a black screen, with a blinking cursor waiting for you to type a command at the keyboard. A cursor in a CLI is merely a marker for the current position where what you type on the keyboard will appear. Only a limited set of characters can display on the screen.

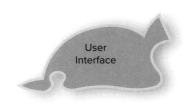

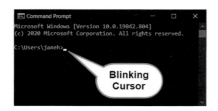

FIGURE 1–2 The Windows Command Prompt.
Source: Microsoft Corporation

To become proficient at working in a CLI, you must memorize the commands and their modifiers and subcommands.

Graphical User Interface. Apple's macOS, Microsoft's Windows, and even mobile operating systems each provides an information-rich graphical user interface (GUI), fully integrated into the operating system. It is through this GUI that you communicate with the OS and the computer. The GUI offers menus and small graphical icons that allow you to use a pointing device to select programs to run and to perform many other tasks, such as opening a word processor file.

Although you do not have to memorize commands, working within a GUI does require learning the meaning of the various graphical pieces that make up the GUI and how to navigate among them to access your programs and data. In addition, you must learn how to activate a program so that you can get your work or play done. Figure 1-3 shows the Apple's macOS GUI. Notice the graphical components, such as the bar at the bottom containing icons for starting apps. In a GUI, you move a graphical pointer around using a pointing device—usually a mouse, trackball, touch pad, or touch screen. The pointer allows you to select or manipulate objects in the GUI to accomplish tasks. For example, to delete an item in macOS drag it into the Trash, shown on the bottom right of Figure 1-3. By contrast, in a CLI, you would type a command such as "delete report.txt."

Note: Although Linux traditionally had a CLI, most current versions of Linux for the desktop come with both CLIs and GUIs.

Job Management

Job management, also known as process scheduler, is an operating system function that controls the order and time in which programs run. Two examples of programs that may take advantage of this function are a scheduling program that schedules other programs to run on a certain day and time, and a print program that manages and prioritizes multiple print jobs.

Task Management

Task management is an operating system function found in multitasking operating systems. Multitasking implies that a computer is running two or more programs (tasks)

FIGURE 1–3 The macOS GUI.
Source: Apple Inc.

at the same time. In reality, a computer cannot simultaneously run more tasks than the number of processors that exist within the computer. Until recently, most microcomputers had only a single processor, so they accomplished multitasking through a scheme that makes order out of chaos by determining which program responds to the keystrokes and mouse movements. New processors can have multiple CPUs within a single chip, so they have true multitasking coexisting with task switching.

try this!

View Active Tasks in Windows or macOS

You can see what tasks are running on your Windows or macOS computer. Try this:

1. On a Windows computer with a keyboard, press CTRL-SHIFT-ESC to open Task Manager, a utility that lets you view tasks as running applications and their processes. Select the Processes tab and notice the large number of active processes.

2. On an macOS computer press COMMAND+SPACEBAR to open the Spotlight search box, and then type "activity" and select Activity Monitor from the results list. Notice the list of processes in the column labeled Process Name.

Task management controls the focus (where the system's attention is at any given moment). It allows the user to switch between tasks by giving the focus to the application the user brings to the foreground. In graphical operating systems, the foreground application runs in the current window, the window that is on top of other windows on the screen. This window receives input from the keyboard, mouse, and/or touch screen when the user types. While active in memory, a program runs as one or more small components called processes. The OS's task management function manages these processes.

File Management

File management, also referred to as data management, is an operating system function that allows the operating system to read, write, and modify data, while managing the logical storage of the data. Each operating system has at least one scheme of logical organization, called a file system. This is used on a storage device (hard disk, optical disc, solid-state drive (SSD), etc.) for managing and storing files. The file system also includes the program code that performs these tasks. An operating system uses a technique called formatting to write the logical structure to a storage device. The operating system maps the logical organization of the file system to physical locations on the storage device, so that it can store and retrieve the data.

File Management

Note: As a rule, the term *folder* is used in a GUI, while the term *directory* is used in a non-GUI operating system.

Normally, a single storage device will have only a single file system, residing in an area defined as a partition, but some operating systems allow a storage device to have more than one partition. A partition may be an entire drive volume or just a portion of a drive, and an operating system automatically assigns some identifier, such as C for the first drive recognized by Windows. Windows follows the drive letter with a colon, so that a complete drive name is C:. We call this a logical drive.

Within the logical structure of a file system, data is organized into entities called files that are saved to storage devices. File management also allows users to organize their files, using other special files that act as containers. One of these special files, called a folder or directory, can contain lists of files as well as other folders, along with the physical location of the files and folders. Figure 1–4 shows the Windows 10 File Explorer with folder icons identifying various folders.

Device Management

The device management function controls hardware devices by using special software called device drivers that are installed in the operating system. A device driver supplements or replaces firmware—even parts of the system firmware. It contains code for controlling a component; usually allowing much more control of a device than the device's firmware alone. A device driver is unique to a device; the manufacturer of the device creates it to work with a specific operating system. For instance, a printer

Device Management

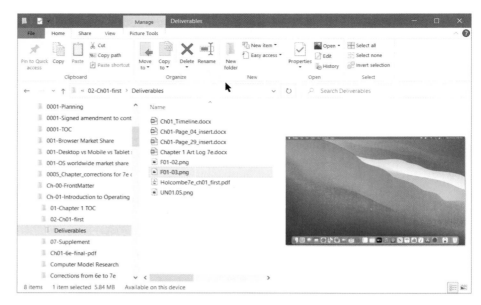

FIGURE 1–4 The File Explorer app in Windows 10.
Source: Microsoft Corporation

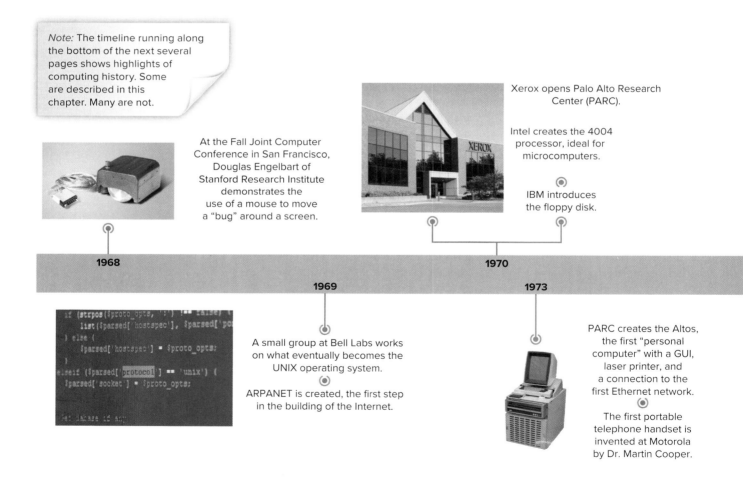

Note: The timeline running along the bottom of the next several pages shows highlights of computing history. Some are described in this chapter. Many are not.

At the Fall Joint Computer Conference in San Francisco, Douglas Engelbart of Stanford Research Institute demonstrates the use of a mouse to move a "bug" around a screen.

Xerox opens Palo Alto Research Center (PARC).

Intel creates the 4004 processor, ideal for microcomputers.

IBM introduces the floppy disk.

1968

1970

1969

1973

A small group at Bell Labs works on what eventually becomes the UNIX operating system.

ARPANET is created, the first step in the building of the Internet.

PARC creates the Altos, the first "personal computer" with a GUI, laser printer, and a connection to the first Ethernet network.

The first portable telephone handset is invented at Motorola by Dr. Martin Cooper.

or video adapter may come with separate device drivers for Windows, macOS, and Linux. OSs today are plug-and-play (PNP), which makes them intelligent enough to detect an installed or connected device and automatically search for and install the needed device driver.

Memory Management

Memory management is an operating system function that manages the placement of programs and data in memory, while keeping track of where it put them. Modern operating systems use a scheme for making optimal use of memory, even allowing more code and data to be in memory than what the physical RAM used as system memory can hold. However, if you have insufficient memory for the type and number of apps you use, you may notice your computer slowing down. Adding more memory to a computer will usually allow you to run applications faster. However, there is a limit to how much RAM you can physically install in a computer, and there is also a limit to how much memory each operating system can use.

Memory Management

Security

The built-in security features of an operating system provide password-protected authentication of the user before allowing access to the local computer and may restrict what someone can do on a computer. This protects the computer and the data it contains from unauthorized access. For example, Rachel is the accounting clerk in a small company. She has confidential information on her computer, and she doesn't want others to access the information stored there. Rachel can set up her computer to protect the data. Security is a large topic—one that would take many books and weeks

Security

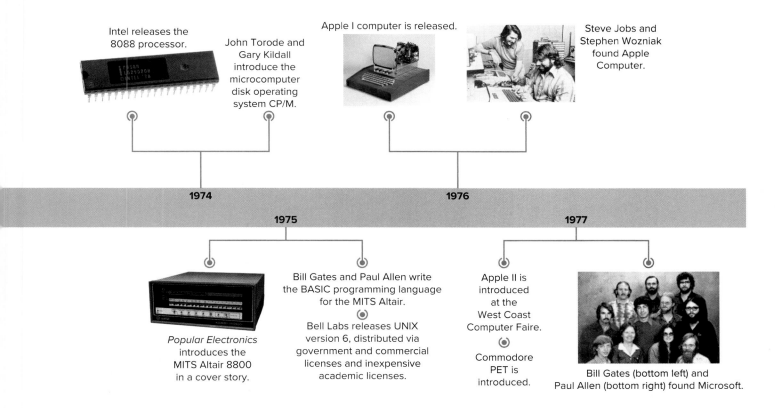

Intel releases the 8088 processor.

John Torode and Gary Kildall introduce the microcomputer disk operating system CP/M.

Apple I computer is released.

Steve Jobs and Stephen Wozniak found Apple Computer.

1974

1976

1975

1977

Popular Electronics introduces the MITS Altair 8800 in a cover story.

Bill Gates and Paul Allen write the BASIC programming language for the MITS Altair.

Bell Labs releases UNIX version 6, distributed via government and commercial licenses and inexpensive academic licenses.

Apple II is introduced at the West Coast Computer Faire.

Commodore PET is introduced.

Bill Gates (bottom left) and Paul Allen (bottom right) found Microsoft.

of your time to really master—but to go much farther in this book without addressing computer security would be foolish, so Chapter 2 is devoted to computer security basics. There you will learn about threats to computers and the steps you can take to protect yourself from threats.

LO 1.2 | Yesterday's Operating Systems

The complex operating systems you see on your desktop, laptop, and mobile devices didn't just magically appear one day. They evolved through many small steps over several decades. An operating system as a separate entity didn't exist in the early years of digital computing (defined roughly as from World War II into the 1950s). At that time, each computer was dedicated to a single purpose, such as performing trajectory calculations for weapons or mathematical analysis for a science lab. Each program included operating system functions as well as the main function of the computer.

In those early days, the "user" was a government agency, research institute, or large business. Each organization ordered a computer to meet their needs, as narrow as they may seem today. By the mid-1960s, as data storage on disk systems became more common, we needed operating systems to manage these disks and to perform other common system-level routines. As new technologies emerged, computers became more capable, leading to the need for a separate underlying operating system.

In this section, we explore the history of present-day computing devices and their operating systems. We start with UNIX, arguably the oldest OS still in use today. Its beginnings predate microcomputers.

UNIX—The Operating System for All Platforms

UNIX has a longer history than the other operating systems described in this book, and it is still in use today. In fact, Apple's macOS is a certified UNIX operating system.

Note: The MITS Altair 8800 was an important predecessor to the Apple II, TRS-80, and PET computers. It was featured in a cover article of the January 1975 issue of *Popular Mechanics;* it was not for everyday use. The input method was switches that you flipped to program it, and the result of these efforts (the output) was a pattern of blinking lights. The Altair 8800 gave Microsoft founders Bill Gates and Paul Allen their very first sale of a ROM-based interpreter for the BASIC programming language.

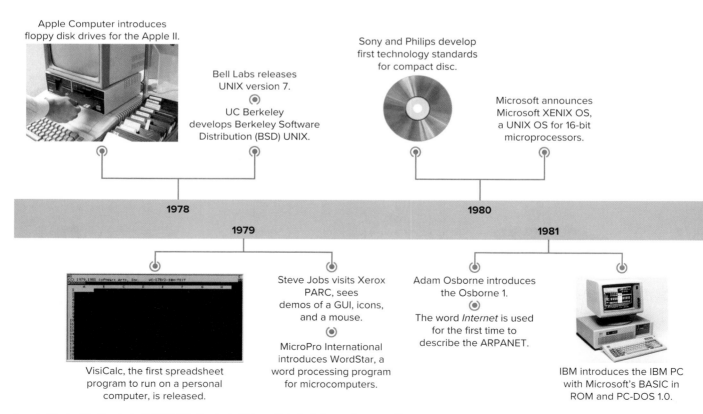

Apple Computer introduces floppy disk drives for the Apple II.

Bell Labs releases UNIX version 7.

UC Berkeley develops Berkeley Software Distribution (BSD) UNIX.

Sony and Philips develop first technology standards for compact disc.

Microsoft announces Microsoft XENIX OS, a UNIX OS for 16-bit microprocessors.

1978

1980

1979

1981

VisiCalc, the first spreadsheet program to run on a personal computer, is released.

Steve Jobs visits Xerox PARC, sees demos of a GUI, icons, and a mouse.

MicroPro International introduces WordStar, a word processing program for microcomputers.

Adam Osborne introduces the Osborne 1.

The word *Internet* is used for the first time to describe the ARPANET.

IBM introduces the IBM PC with Microsoft's BASIC in ROM and PC-DOS 1.0.

Angelo DAmico/Shutterstock, ANATOL/Shutterstock, Visicorp/Paladin Software, Bettmann/Getty Images

UNIX grew out of an operating system developed for an early Digital Equipment Corporation (DEC) computer and went through several generations of changes before it emerged from the Bell Labs Computing Science Research Center as UNIX version 6 in 1975, a portable operating system for minicomputers and mainframe computers. A portable operating system is one that you can use on a variety of computer system platforms, with only minor alterations required to be compatible with the underlying architecture. Minicomputers and mainframe computers allowed multiple remote users to connect and use the computer's resources, and UNIX supported the time-sharing and multitasking features that made this possible.

The University of California at Berkeley licensed UNIX, modified it, and distributed it to other schools as Berkeley Software Distribution (BSD) version 4.2. Later versions followed. The schools paid licensing fees to Bell Labs. Students and others improved on and added to UNIX, freely sharing their code with each other. This tradition still prevails today with such versions of UNIX as FreeBSD, NetBSD, OpenBSD, and OpenSolaris. Commercial versions of UNIX today include AIX, OpenServer (derived from SCO UNIX), and HP/UX.

UNIX is still used on very large computer systems and less commonly on Intel desktop systems, as well as on a variety of midsize computers. Versions of UNIX run on many of the world's Internet servers. Most versions of UNIX also offer several different user interfaces. Some use character

try this!

Research the History of UNIX

Learn more about the UNIX operating system.
Try this:

1. Point your browser to **opengroup.org/unix**.

2. Look for UNIX: An Innovative History. There is also a link to the UNIX Infographic that summarizes the history up to just a few years ago.

3. Browse through the OpenGroup website to learn more about what is currently happening with UNIX.

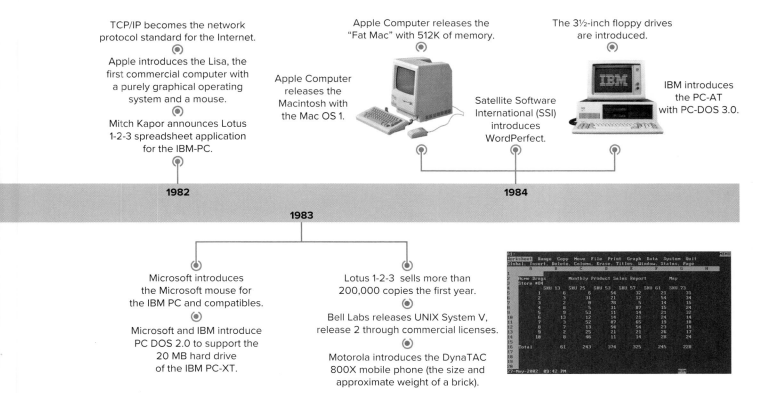

TCP/IP becomes the network protocol standard for the Internet.

Apple introduces the Lisa, the first commercial computer with a purely graphical operating system and a mouse.

Mitch Kapor announces Lotus 1-2-3 spreadsheet application for the IBM-PC.

Apple Computer releases the Macintosh with the Mac OS 1.

Apple Computer releases the "Fat Mac" with 512K of memory.

Satellite Software International (SSI) introduces WordPerfect.

The 3½-inch floppy drives are introduced.

IBM introduces the PC-AT with PC-DOS 3.0.

1982

1984

1983

Microsoft introduces the Microsoft mouse for the IBM PC and compatibles.

Microsoft and IBM introduce PC DOS 2.0 to support the 20 MB hard drive of the IBM PC-XT.

Lotus 1-2-3 sells more than 200,000 copies the first year.

Bell Labs releases UNIX System V, release 2 through commercial licenses.

Motorola introduces the DynaTAC 800X mobile phone (the size and approximate weight of a brick).

INTERFOTO/Alamy Stock Photo, Twin Design/Shutterstock, Convergent Technologies, Unix system

mode, like the traditional shells, such as the Bourne shell and the C shell. Others use a graphical interface such as GNOME or KDE. As mentioned earlier, Apple's macOS operating system has a graphical user interface, but it is based on a version of UNIX.

Even fierce UNIX advocates do not see UNIX taking over the desktop any time soon. However, it is very secure and stable.

The Evolution of Desktop Operating Systems

The miniaturization of computer components inevitably led to the evolution of desktop operating systems available to consumers.

Small Steps

Operating systems evolved through many small steps over several decades, some in the form of technical advances and others in evolutionary changes in how people used computers, especially as they saw the need to use computers as multipurpose devices. The "user," at first a government agency, research institute, or large business, would define the computer's purpose at any given time by the program chosen to run. In the 1950s, some early "operating systems" managed data storage on tape for mainframe computers, but it was much more common for application programmers to write system I/O routines (the stuff of today's OSs) right into their programs. By the mid-1960s, as disk systems became more common on large computers, we needed operating systems to manage these disks and to perform other common system-level routines.

The computer enthusiasts who bought the earliest microcomputers of the 1970s, such as the MITS Altair 8800, were infatuated with the technology. What we now consider slow CPU speeds, very limited memory, clumsy I/O devices, and lack of software was exciting and new technology at the time. Enthusiasts would network with like-minded people, have informal meetings and discussions, and then gather in

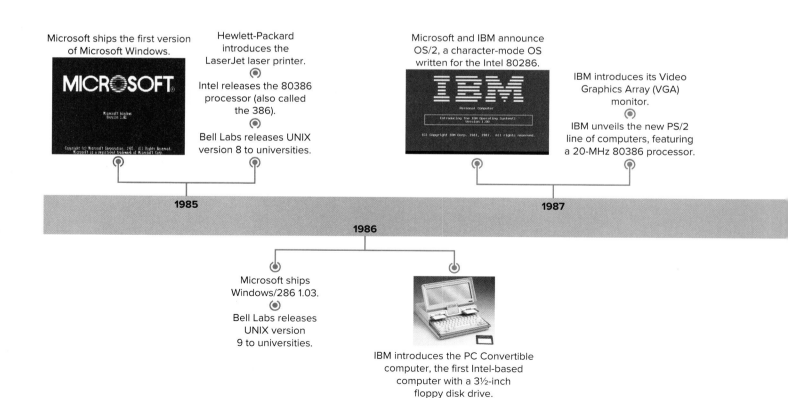

Microsoft ships the first version of Microsoft Windows.

Hewlett-Packard introduces the LaserJet laser printer.
Intel releases the 80386 processor (also called the 386).
Bell Labs releases UNIX version 8 to universities.

Microsoft and IBM announce OS/2, a character-mode OS written for the Intel 80286.

IBM introduces its Video Graphics Array (VGA) monitor.
IBM unveils the new PS/2 line of computers, featuring a 20-MHz 80386 processor.

1985

1987

1986

Microsoft ships Windows/286 1.03.
Bell Labs releases UNIX version 9 to universities.

IBM introduces the PC Convertible computer, the first Intel-based computer with a 3½-inch floppy disk drive.

Sources: Microsoft Corporation, IBM Corporation, Science & Society Picture Library/Getty Images

self-help groups and form clubs such as the Home Brew Computer Club in California's Silicon Valley. They shared their techniques for creating hardware and programming language software for these computers. Almost every one of these early microcomputers exceeded the expectations of their makers and users, but before long, and for a variety of reasons, most of the early entrepreneurial companies and their products disappeared.

Early Apple Computers and Their OSs

In 1976, Steve Jobs and Stephen Wozniak—two friends working out of a garage—founded Apple Computer, based on their first computer, the Apple I. Their real notoriety began in 1977 when they introduced the Apple II at the West Coast Computer Faire in San Francisco. This created interest in the brand, and the addition of disk drives in 1978 made it a sought-after product for the technically adventurous consumer. The OS for the Apple II did not have a GUI interface—this first appeared in later Apple computers.

The Killer App for the Apple II. For a microcomputer to truly become a successful, widely accepted product—used in businesses as well as by hobbyists—it had to be a tool that performed an important task; it had to have an application that many people needed enough to purchase a computer. We call that application a killer app.

One such killer app was VisiCalc, an electronic spreadsheet program introduced in 1979 for the Apple II computer (running the Apple OS). Before microcomputers and programs like VisiCalc, people created spreadsheets manually, on large grid-printed sheets of paper. Consider one scenario: the manager of a small retail store would enter a column of numbers—say, sales for one product in the store—day-by-day for a month. Then he would add up the daily columns to get the total sales for that product for that month. The next column was for the next product, and so on. The process was tedious and error prone, but very valuable to the manager of the store. VisiCalc automated this

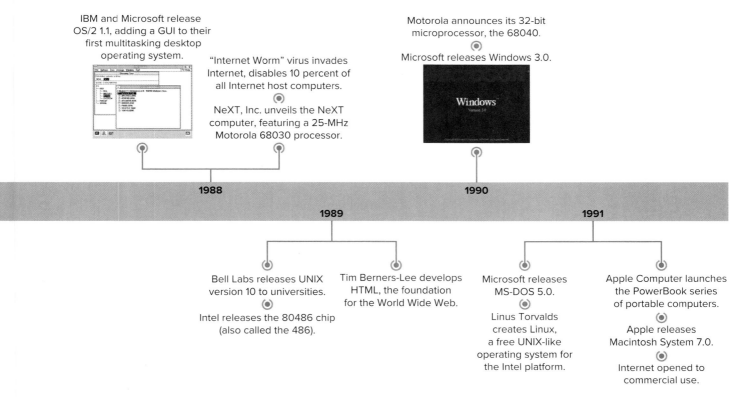

IBM and Microsoft release OS/2 1.1, adding a GUI to their first multitasking desktop operating system.

"Internet Worm" virus invades Internet, disables 10 percent of all Internet host computers.

NeXT, Inc. unveils the NeXT computer, featuring a 25-MHz Motorola 68030 processor.

Motorola announces its 32-bit microprocessor, the 68040.

Microsoft releases Windows 3.0.

1988

1989

1990

1991

Bell Labs releases UNIX version 10 to universities.

Intel releases the 80486 chip (also called the 486).

Tim Berners-Lee develops HTML, the foundation for the World Wide Web.

Microsoft releases MS-DOS 5.0.

Linus Torvalds creates Linux, a free UNIX-like operating system for the Intel platform.

Apple Computer launches the PowerBook series of portable computers.

Apple releases Macintosh System 7.0.

Internet opened to commercial use.

Sources: IBM Corporation and Microsoft Corporation

thankless job, remembered the formulas for the calculations, and allowed people to recalculate a whole column of numbers after changes were made.

VisiCalc gave people a reason to buy a personal computer, contributing to the success of the Apple II. However, as the 1980s arrived, Apple failed to come out with a successor to the Apple II in a timely fashion.

The Lisa Computer—a Pretty Face with No Apps. In 1982, Apple introduced the Lisa, the first commercially available computer with a purely graphical operating system—and a mouse. However, this computer was not the needed successor to the Apple II because it lacked something very important for consumers—applications. It was not successful.

try this!

Watch Old TV Commercials for the IBM PC and Lotus 1-2-3

It has been over 30 years since the introduction of the IBM PC in 1981 and the killer app Lotus 1-2-3 in 1983. See how these products were introduced to the public in TV advertisements. Try this:

1. Point your browser to **http://mentalfloss.com/article/48627/lotus-1-2-3-three-decades**
2. Read the article and watch the first two videos. Some of us can verify the accuracy of the portrayal of office workers at the time (except for the singing and dancing part).
3. The third video is no longer available.
4. The fourth video reviews the history of Lotus 1-2-3 with great clips of the news coverage and events and people behind the product.

Apple Macintosh and the Mac OS. Apple's Macintosh computer, released in 1984, overshadowed the Lisa and marked the beginning of consumer excitement and the near-cult following of the Apple computer products. The Macintosh came with Mac OS System 1, a GUI operating system that used a mouse. Apple improved the Mac OS over the years to include many easy-to-use features. Most importantly, there were soon plenty of apps for this computer.

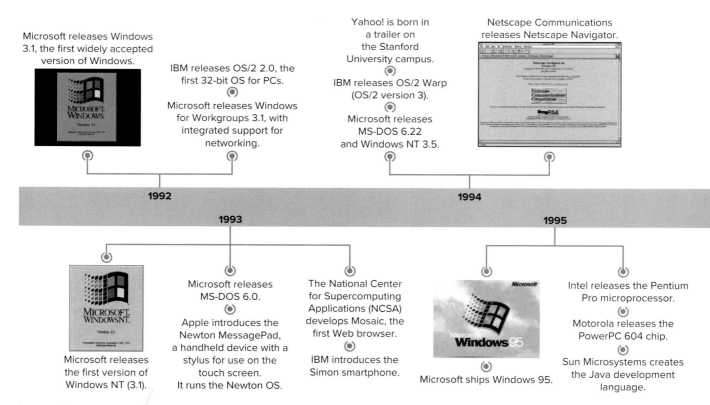

Microsoft releases Windows 3.1, the first widely accepted version of Windows.

IBM releases OS/2 2.0, the first 32-bit OS for PCs.

Microsoft releases Windows for Workgroups 3.1, with integrated support for networking.

Yahoo! is born in a trailer on the Stanford University campus.

IBM releases OS/2 Warp (OS/2 version 3).

Microsoft releases MS-DOS 6.22 and Windows NT 3.5.

Netscape Communications releases Netscape Navigator.

1992

1993

1994

1995

Microsoft releases the first version of Windows NT (3.1).

Microsoft releases MS-DOS 6.0.

Apple introduces the Newton MessagePad, a handheld device with a stylus for use on the touch screen. It runs the Newton OS.

The National Center for Supercomputing Applications (NCSA) develops Mosaic, the first Web browser.

IBM introduces the Simon smartphone.

Microsoft ships Windows 95.

Intel releases the Pentium Pro microprocessor.

Motorola releases the PowerPC 604 chip.

Sun Microsystems creates the Java development language.

Sources: Microsoft Corporation, Netscape Communications Corporation, Microsoft Corporation, Microsoft Corporation

The final release of the classic Mac OS family was Mac OS 9, introduced in 1999. In 2001, it was replaced by a completely new operating system—Mac OS X, based on UNIX. This is the OS on the Apple desktop and laptop computers currently in use, although Apple officially changed the name to macOS in 2016. We will use this latest name throughout the book to refer to the OS for the Apple Mac.

Note: In the years after its introduction, thousands of applications were written for PC DOS (and MS-DOS), but Lotus 1-2-3 (spreadsheet), dBase (database management), and WordPerfect (word processing) were the de facto business standards at the end of the 1980s. All contributed to the mass adoption of PCs at work, at school, and at home.

The IBM PC

IBM introduced the IBM PC in 1981, taking advantage of the void left by Apple, who had not introduced a true successor to their Apple II. The IBM PC far exceeded IBM's sales forecast of a quarter of a million units during its predicted five-year product lifetime. According to one account, IBM took orders for half a million computers in the first few days after introducing the IBM PC. The early enthusiasts bought it despite the roughly $5,000 price tag for a typical configuration. The IBM logo on the product implied that it was a serious business computer, inspiring business users to buy it.

IBM PC DOS. The selection of an OS for the IBM PC came from a fateful series of events. IBM representatives visited Microsoft, then a fledgling software company, with two objectives. Acquire a BASIC interpreter to install in firmware on their PCs and find an OS that would start up from disk (diskette at first). IBM subsequently licensed Microsoft's BASIC interpreter and installed it in the firmware of the IBM PC.

When the IBM folks talked to Bill Gates about providing an OS, he sent them to another company, Digital Research, the creators of the then-popular CP/M OS. Digital Research refused to sign a contract with IBM, so the IBM guys went back to Bill Gates. Consequently, Microsoft bought an OS from another company, and this was the basis of the first version of the IBM PC Disk Operating System (DOS).

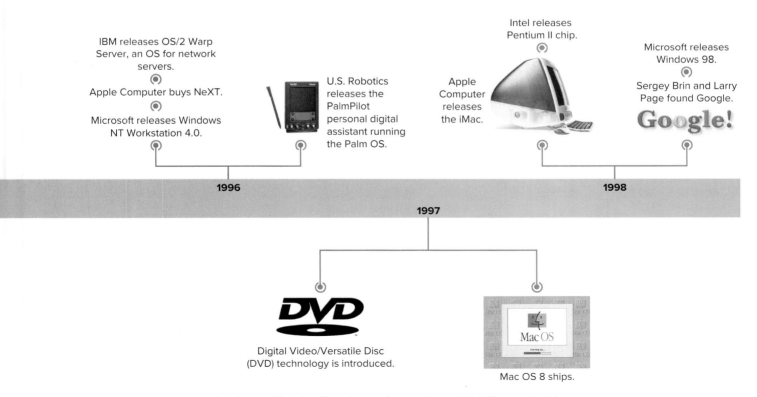

IBM releases OS/2 Warp Server, an OS for network servers.

Apple Computer buys NeXT.

Microsoft releases Windows NT Workstation 4.0.

U.S. Robotics releases the PalmPilot personal digital assistant running the Palm OS.

Intel releases Pentium II chip.

Apple Computer releases the iMac.

Microsoft releases Windows 98.

Sergey Brin and Larry Page found Google.

Google!

1996

1997

1998

Digital Video/Versatile Disc (DVD) technology is introduced.

Mac OS 8 ships.

Science & Society Picture Library/Getty Images, Bloomberg/Getty Images, Sources: Google LLC, Philips, and Apple Inc.

The Killer App for the IBM PC. While VisiCalc, the killer app for the Apple II, was still an important app, it did not take full advantage of the increased memory in the IBM PC. The IBM PC still needed a killer app. That app was a spreadsheet app that ran on the DOS operating system and used all the 640 KB of memory available to software (OS plus application) on the IBM PC. This new app was Lotus 1-2-3, which was noticeably faster than VisiCalc and had additional features, including database functions and a program for creating graphs from the spreadsheet data.

PC DOS versus MS-DOS. PC DOS was the version for IBM computers. MS-DOS refers to the several versions of DOS developed by Microsoft and licensed to non-IBM PC manufacturers. "DOS" in both names stands for "disk operating system." DOS did not have the more advanced capabilities of today's OSs. It was single-tasking, with no support for virtual memory, no native GUI, and no built-in security function. While it could use much more memory than the OSs that preceded it, DOS had very limited memory support compared to the OSs developed since then to support our much more advanced computer hardware.

DOS had a text-mode command-line interface that required users to remember cryptic commands and their subcommands to perform file management functions and to launch DOS applications. Figure 1–5 shows a good example of how cryptic DOS was.

PC DOS 1.0 supported single-sided 5.25-inch floppies. After that, each major version of DOS was released to support new disk capacities. MS-DOS 6.22 was the last widely used version of that OS. Some forms of DOS are now available from third-party sources, but the need for this type of OS is dwindling.

OS/2

In 1987, Microsoft and IBM introduced their jointly developed Operating System/2 (OS/2), intended to replace DOS. However, it required a much more advanced and expensive computer than DOS required, had very limited support for DOS apps, and lacked a killer app.

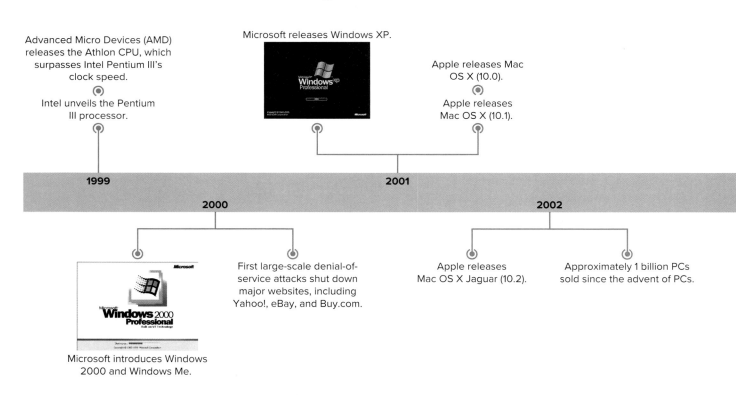

Advanced Micro Devices (AMD) releases the Athlon CPU, which surpasses Intel Pentium III's clock speed.

Intel unveils the Pentium III processor.

Microsoft releases Windows XP.

Apple releases Mac OS X (10.0).

Apple releases Mac OS X (10.1).

1999

2000

2001

2002

Microsoft introduces Windows 2000 and Windows Me.

First large-scale denial-of-service attacks shut down major websites, including Yahoo!, eBay, and Buy.com.

Apple releases Mac OS X Jaguar (10.2).

Approximately 1 billion PCs sold since the advent of PCs.

Source: Microsoft Corporation

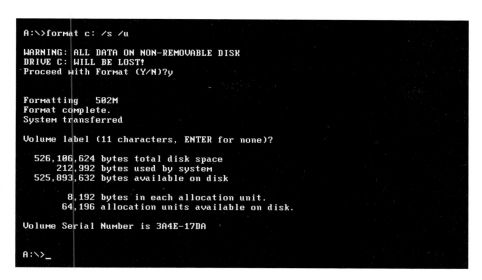

```
A:\>format c: /s /u

WARNING: ALL DATA ON NON-REMOVABLE DISK
DRIVE C: WILL BE LOST!
Proceed with Format (Y/N)?y


Formatting   502M
Format complete.
System transferred

Volume label (11 characters, ENTER for none)?

  526,106,624 bytes total disk space
      212,992 bytes used by system
  525,893,632 bytes available on disk

        8,192 bytes in each allocation unit.
       64,196 allocation units available on disk.

Volume Serial Number is 3A4E-17DA


A:\>_
```

FIGURE 1–5 The MS-DOS prompt showing the Format command and the resulting output to the screen.
Source: Microsoft Corporation

Note: Although OS/2 was not a success in terms of sales, an April 2, 2012, article in Time magazine by Harry McCracken, "25 Years of IBM's OS/2: The Strange Days and Surprising Afterlife of a Legendary Operating System" reported that OS/2 was still used on some New York City subway system servers and on some supermarket checkout systems.

In 1994, IBM introduced OS/2 Warp, an improved version of OS/2 with a GUI. After about 18 months, IBM retreated from the battle for the desktop and targeted sales of OS/2 Warp to the high-end server market. It never rivaled Windows or UNIX in terms of sales. In 2003, IBM announced it would not develop future versions of OS/2, and in December 2004 IBM sold its PC division to China-based Lenovo Group. OS/2 support was discontinued in 2005.

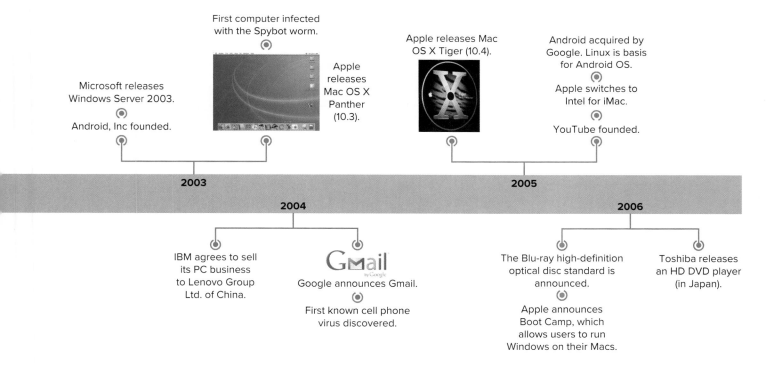

First computer infected with the Spybot worm.

Microsoft releases Windows Server 2003.

Android, Inc founded.

Apple releases Mac OS X Panther (10.3).

Apple releases Mac OS X Tiger (10.4).

Android acquired by Google. Linux is basis for Android OS.

Apple switches to Intel for iMac.

YouTube founded.

2003

2005

2004

2006

IBM agrees to sell its PC business to Lenovo Group Ltd. of China.

Google announces Gmail.

First known cell phone virus discovered.

The Blu-ray high-definition optical disc standard is announced.

Apple announces Boot Camp, which allows users to run Windows on their Macs.

Toshiba releases an HD DVD player (in Japan).

Sources: Microsoft Corporation, Apple Inc., Kim Kulish/Corbis/Getty Images, Google LLC.

Microsoft Windows

Microsoft Windows is an OS with a GUI. It began life in 1985 as a simple GUI shell on top of MS-DOS. Since then, it has evolved into a more advanced OS, dominating the desktop for much of its life. Windows' fate is tied to the PC. Therefore, as more people use mobile devices for many of the functions previously assigned to PCs, PC sales have declined. Windows computers have also faced tough competition in the K-12 education market, where Apple iPads and Chromebooks are important tools for students. Following is a brief look at the various Windows versions.

Windows 1 through 3. In 1985, when the first version of Windows appeared, it consisted of a primitive GUI by today's standards, balanced precariously on top of MS-DOS. The GUI code was separate from the OS code. It was slow and had a flat look—you couldn't lay one graphic on top of another. The ability to overlap graphical elements, such as windows and icons, did not show up until a later version.

Note: The success of a new version of any OS depends heavily on its ability to run old applications.

In 1990, Microsoft introduced Windows 3.0, which supported capabilities contained in the Intel processors in the latest PCs. The most important feature of Windows 3.0 was that it would run DOS apps better than previous versions, so that you could keep your old DOS apps, while gradually moving to the expanding number of Windows apps. Windows 3.0 still had its quirks, but for the first time, IT managers saw a potential GUI replacement for DOS as the desktop OS of choice.

In the spring of 1992, Microsoft brought out a minor upgrade, Windows 3.1, which many organizations adopted as the standard desktop OS. The fact that Microsoft's entire suite of productivity applications was also available in versions for Windows 3.*x* helped encourage adoption.

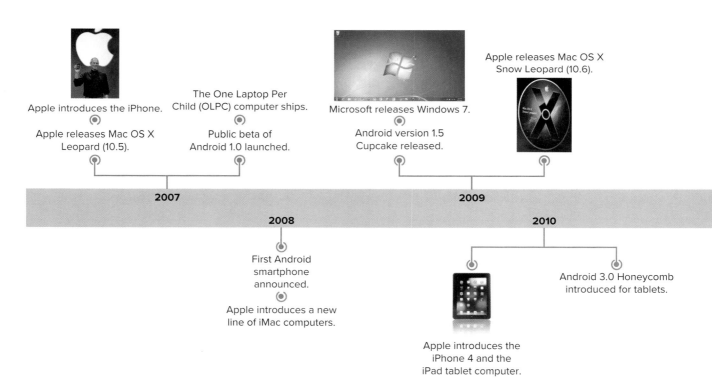

Apple introduces the iPhone.

Apple releases Mac OS X Leopard (10.5).

The One Laptop Per Child (OLPC) computer ships.

Public beta of Android 1.0 launched.

Microsoft releases Windows 7.

Android version 1.5 Cupcake released.

Apple releases Mac OS X Snow Leopard (10.6).

2007

2009

2008

2010

First Android smartphone announced.

Apple introduces a new line of iMac computers.

Android 3.0 Honeycomb introduced for tablets.

Apple introduces the iPhone 4 and the iPad tablet computer.

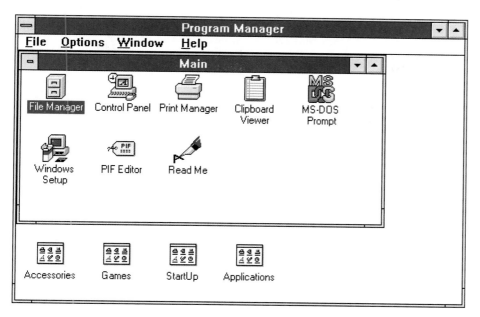

FIGURE 1–6 The Windows 3.1 desktop.
Source: Microsoft Corporation

Figure 1-6 shows the Windows 3.1 desktop. Notice that there is no task bar at the bottom of the screen, just the Program Manager window (the main window) containing the Main window as well as shortcuts to other windows.

Windows for Workgroups. DOS and Windows OSs through Windows 3.*x* included only the operating system functions. If you wanted to connect to a network, you added a network operating system (NOS) on top of your installed OS.

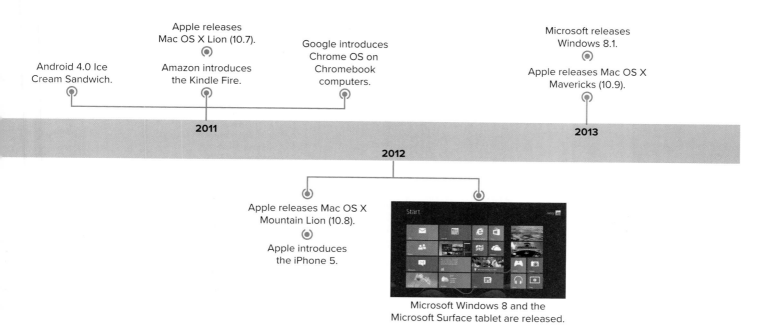

Source: Microsoft Corporation.

This separate network operating system might be from 3COM or Novell, or it might be Microsoft's LAN Manager NOS, developed in the late 1980s. You had to install the correct client software for the type of network and servers to which you connected.

Beginning in October 1992 with Windows for Workgroups 3.1, Microsoft included both the client and server software in all of its Windows OS products. This enabled peer-to-peer networking, meaning desktop computers could act as servers to their peers. This worked well in a small work group environment of 10 or fewer computers. Windows for Workgroups 3.1 was followed a year later by Windows for Workgroups 3.11, with some improvements. It was still a GUI running on top of MS-DOS.

Windows NT. Because it had the same user interface as Windows 3.1, Windows NT was introduced in 1993 as Windows NT 3.1. That was where the similarity ended. It was a server operating system, which included server protocols in its integrated network support. Furthermore, unlike Windows 3.x and Windows for Workgroups, the GUI did not sit on top of DOS but was an entirely new operating system.

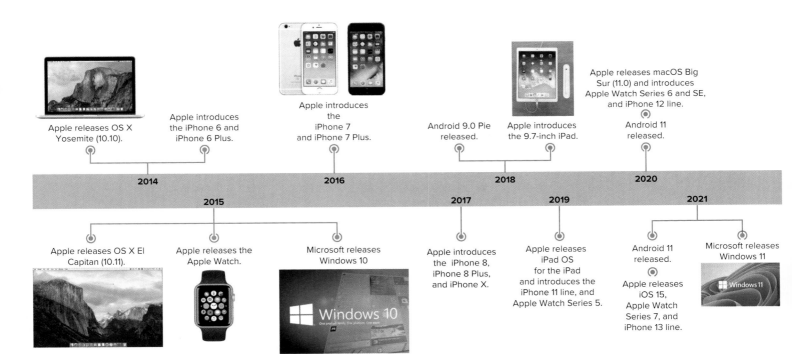

Apple releases OS X Yosemite (10.10).

Apple introduces the iPhone 6 and iPhone 6 Plus.

Apple introduces the iPhone 7 and iPhone 7 Plus.

Android 9.0 Pie released.

Apple introduces the 9.7-inch iPad.

Apple releases macOS Big Sur (11.0) and introduces Apple Watch Series 6 and SE, and iPhone 12 line.

Android 11 released.

2014   2016   2018   2020

2015   2017   2019   2021

Apple releases OS X El Capitan (10.11).

Apple releases the Apple Watch.

Microsoft releases Windows 10

Apple introduces the iPhone 8, iPhone 8 Plus, and iPhone X.

Apple releases iPad OS for the iPad and introduces the iPhone 11 line, and Apple Watch Series 5.

Android 11 released.

Apple releases iOS 15, Apple Watch Series 7, and iPhone 13 line.

Microsoft releases Windows 11

Alexey Boldin/Shutterstock, Aleksey Boldin/Alamy Stock Photo, Zeynep Demir/Shutterstock, BCFC/Shutterstock, mama_mia/Shutterstock, alexeyboldin/123RF, fotogigi85/123RF, olegganko/Shutterstock, Microsoft

With Windows NT, Microsoft introduced the New Technology File System (NTFS) with an entirely new logical structure for storing files. This file system uses a transaction processing system to track changes to files, so that it can roll back incomplete transactions. It also includes several other features, including file compression, file encryption, file and folder security, and indexing. NTFS is the default file system in the current versions of Windows.

Windows NT 3.5, released in 1994, was the first Windows OS to have separate editions: Windows NT Workstation and Windows NT Server. They used the same kernel and interface, but the Server version had enhancements and components that were needed only on a network server. The Workstation version was a robust desktop operating system targeted to corporate and advanced users.

In 1996, Microsoft introduced Server and Workstation editions of Windows NT 4.0, which had a GUI similar to that of Windows 95 as well as other improvements and enhancements to the OS.

Note: The acronym *NTFS* is the preferred usage when talking about the file system first introduced in Windows NT. The longer name for it, the "New Technology File System," is rarely used.

Windows 95. Windows 95, released in 1995, was a continuation of the Windows 3.*x* model with the graphical environment simply "sitting" on top of the DOS operating system. It did have some improvements in the operating system, including the GUI, which made it the most popular microcomputer operating system up to that time.

Windows 98. Windows 98 was an evolutionary development in the Windows desktop operating system, including improvements in both visible and under-the-hood components. It offered more stability than its immediate predecessor, and it was less likely to stop in its tracks just when you were about to complete that book order on Amazon. Figure 1–7 shows the Windows 98 desktop. Its biggest drawback was lack of security.

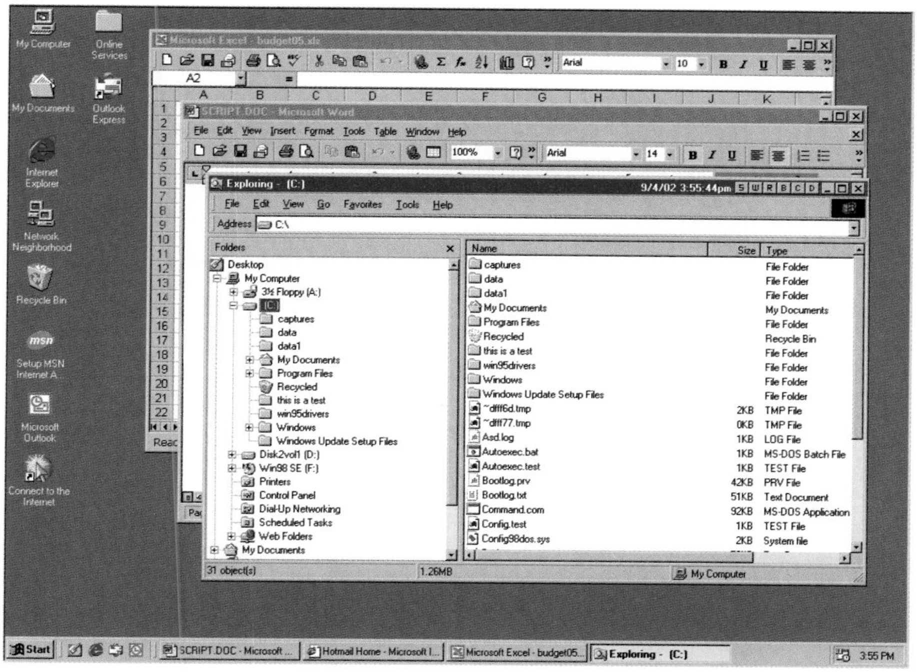

FIGURE 1–7 The Windows 98 desktop with open windows.
Source: Microsoft Corporation

The Windows XP Start Menu.
Source: Microsoft Corporation

Windows Me (Millennium Edition). Windows Me (Millennium edition), introduced in 2000, targeted the home market, especially the home game user. It was essentially Windows 98 with improved music, video, and home networking support. Windows Me was not an OS that organizations adopted.

Windows 2000. In 2000, Microsoft introduced the Windows 2000 family of OS products, which brought together the best of Windows 98 (the GUI) and Windows NT. Windows 2000 was available in several editions that covered OS needs from the desktop (Windows 2000 Professional) to the enterprise server. Figure 1–8 shows the Windows 2000 desktop.

Windows XP. In 2001, Microsoft introduced Windows XP, intended only for the consumer desktop, not for the corporate environment.

There were several Windows XP editions, but the three most common were Windows XP Home edition, Windows XP Professional, and Windows XP Media Center. All were 32-bit OSs, had the same improved GUI, and shared many of the same features, but only Windows XP Professional included several important network- and security-related features. Additionally, Microsoft offered Windows XP 64-bit edition, which supported only 64-bit software and was limited to computers with the Intel Itanium processors.

The Windows XP desktop was very different from that of Windows 98. Figure 1–9 shows the Windows XP desktop with several open windows.

Support for Windows XP Service Pack 3 (SP3) and for the 64-bit version with Service Pack 2 ended in April 2014, per Microsoft's published policy, the Microsoft Support Lifecycle.

Windows Vista. Microsoft released the first retail edition of Windows Vista early in 2007. Seen more as an upgrade of Windows XP, it included improvements in how Windows handles graphics, files, and communications. The GUI had a new

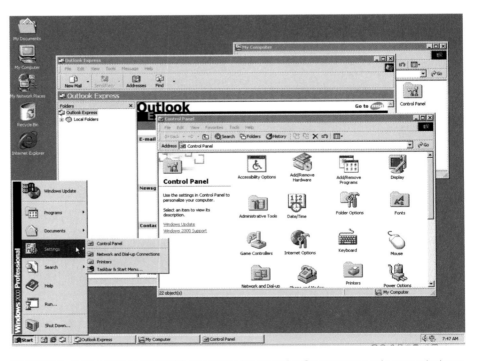

FIGURE 1–8 The Windows 2000 desktop showing the Start menu and open windows.
Source: Microsoft Corporation

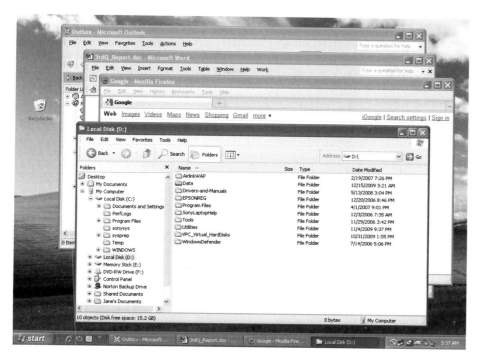

FIGURE 1–9 The Windows XP desktop with open windows.
Source: Microsoft Corporation

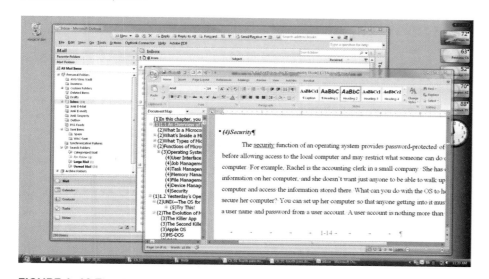

FIGURE 1–10 The Windows Vista desktop showing the transparent windows of the Aero feature.
Source: Jane Holcombe/Microsoft Corporation

look (see Figure 1–10). It also had a feature called Aero, which included translucent windows, live thumbnails, live icons, and other enhancements to the GUI. Windows Vista was not widely adopted due to problems with speed as well as high hardware requirements. Mainstream support for Windows Vista ended in April 2012.

try this!

Are You Running 32-bit or 64-bit Windows?

If you have a Windows computer handy, see if it is running a 32-bit or 64-bit version. Try this:

1. Open the Windows 10 Start menu and select *Settings* (the gear icon) to open the Settings app.
2. Select *System*.
3. Scroll down and select *About*.
4. The System Type field will say "32-bit Operating System" or "64-bit Operating System."

Windows 7

Released in October 2009, Windows 7 included several improvements correcting the shortcomings that kept Windows Vista from being widely accepted. Windows 7 was faster than Windows Vista in several ways, from starting up, to going into and out of sleep mode, to recognizing new devices. Windows 7 introduced a redesigned desktop (see Figure 1-11) with a new taskbar with many new features of its own, such as jump lists.

Windows 8 and 8.1

Windows 8, released in October 2012, came with better security and improved wireless connectivity as well as support for some newer hardware, such as USB 3.0 ports and improved touch screen support for simultaneous multiple touches and gestures.

The most controversial changes to Windows 8 were to the GUI, or rather GUIs. The default GUI, centered around the Start screen shown in Figure 1-12, is a departure from the Windows 7 desktop with its three-dimensional look. Objects in this new GUI appeared flat, without shading and borders so that they would not take up extra screen space on PCs, laptops, and tablets. The Windows 8 Start screen contained tiles representing apps. Each tile could show active content, such as newsfeeds, stock quotes, slideshows, and more, depending on the tile's app.

The second Windows 8 GUI, a modified version of the Windows 7 desktop (without the Start menu) had a very flat look to it in spite of having overlapping windows. Figure 1-13 shows the Windows 8 desktop. In 2013, Microsoft released an update to Windows 8—Windows 8.1—with changes to the Start screen and the desktop that they hoped would satisfy critics of the Windows 8 GUIs.

Although Windows 8 came after Windows 7, it never sold sufficiently to match the market share achieved by Windows 7 (or Windows XP). This was despite the changes made in Windows 8.1.

FIGURE 1–11 The Windows 7 desktop.
Source: Microsoft Corporation

FIGURE 1-12 The Windows 8 Start screen.
Source: Microsoft Corporation

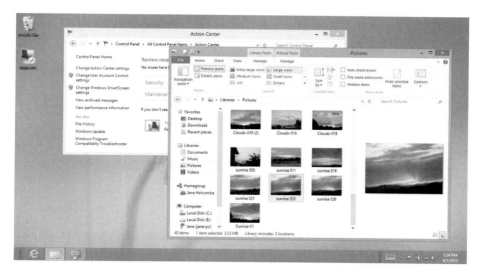

FIGURE 1-13 The Windows 8 desktop.
Sources: Jane Holcombe/Microsoft Corporation

LO 1.3 | Today's Desktop Operating Systems

Today's desktop microcomputer operating systems include Windows 10, macOS, Chrome OS, and Linux. All of these OSs are multiuser/multitasking operating systems, with support for virtual memory and security.

Table 1-1 summarizes the current desktop OSs covered in later chapters of this book, listing the publisher, platform, and types of applications that you can run natively on each OS. The following sections contain brief descriptions of the operating systems that are detailed in chapters in this book, as well as an overview of what is known about the next version of Windows. As this book goes into production, Microsoft has announced, but has not yet released, Windows 11.

FIGURE 1–14 The Windows 10 desktop as it appeared in 2015.
Source: Microsoft Corporation

TABLE 1–1 Summary of Current Desktop/Laptop Operating Systems

Desktop/Laptop OS	Company	Platform	Applications Supported
Windows 10	Microsoft	Intel/Microsoft	DOS, 16-bit Windows, 32-bit and 64-bit Windows applications
macOS	Apple	Intel or M1/Apple Mac and MacBook	Mac applications
Linux	Various	Intel	UNIX/Linux applications
Chrome OS	Google (Alphabet)	Intel	Chrome Web Store apps and Android apps via Google Play

Windows 10

In 2015, Microsoft introduced Windows 10, with a modified Start menu and many other features. Figure 1-14 shows the Windows 10 desktop as it appeared in 2015. The following is a short list of Windows 10 features:

- A new Start menu.
- Windows Hello biometric authentication using facial features or fingerprint.
- The Cortana personal assistant.
- The Microsoft Edge browser (replacing Internet Explorer).
- Universal apps that run on all Windows 10 systems.
- The Xbox app that brings game features to Windows 10.
- Support for multiple desktops within the GUI.

Further, for a period of one year after its introduction, Windows 10 was available as a free upgrade to consumers running Windows 7 Service Pack 1 (SP1) or Windows 8.1 Update on PCs, laptops, and tablets. Learn more about Windows 10 in Chapter 4.

Windows 11

During the summer of 2021, Microsoft announced Windows 11 and released it in a phased rollout to existing Windows 10 computers beginning October 5, 2021.

Because this was too late to include a chapter on Windows 11 in this textbook, a separate online chapter is available from McGraw-Hill with the Instructor Supplements. Windows 11, like Windows 10, will continue to evolve. Below is a brief overview of Windows 11.

Windows 11 Hardware Requirements

The hardware requirements for Windows 11 rule out many existing Windows 10 PCs that do not include some of these features, especially the features involving firmware needed for hardware-assisted security. Many security threats attack computers before an operating system is in control. Windows 11 requires hardware level security from the moment a device is turned.

Note: To check out the Windows 11 specifications go to https://www. microsoft.com and search on "windows 11 specifications."

Upgrading to Windows 11

Microsoft offers free upgrades to Windows 11 from Windows 10, but the upgrade depends on the existing computer meeting the minimum system requirements. If existing PCs do not meet these requirements, individuals and businesses can opt to stay with Windows 10, which will be supported until October 2025.

Using Apps in Windows 11

Microsoft upgraded the Microsoft Store with new features, including an option for third-party developers to sell their desktop apps through the Store. They also announced that they were working with Amazon and Intel on an Android subsystem for Windows to allow Android apps to run on the Windows 11 desktop. This was not available in the October 2021 release.

The Windows 11 GUI

The Windows 11 GUI is more evolutionary than revolutionary, but it is pleasant to view and work with. Many GUI features received the software equivalent of a new coat of paint achieved through new color themes, rounded corners on windows and dialog boxes, and a three-dimensional look to most windows icons and other graphical elements. Let's take a closer look at a few GUI features.

Taskbar, Start Menu, and Search. The first thing you will notice are the shortcuts centered on the taskbar, as shown in Figure 1–15. As a result, the Start button is no longer snugged up against the far left and opens a large Start menu, also in 1–15.

FIGURE 1–15 The Windows 11 desktop with the Start menu open.
Source: Jane Holcombe/Microsoft.

The Search feature is improved, and is handy to find apps, features, utilities, and more without several clicks or taps. Settings has undergone a reorganization and has some new options.

Snap Layouts. When working with several open windows on the desktop, Windows 11 Snap Layouts let you organize your windows. Begin with several windows open, then hover the cursor over a window's maximize button and select a layout from those offered. There are presently six layouts for two to four windows, and once you select one, the open windows snap into position. You can also use Snap Layouts across multiple Windows Virtual Desktops.

Widgets. Microsoft removed live tiles from the Start menu but added a Widgets pane that opens on the left side of the desktop when you select the new Widgets button, located on the taskbar. Widgets are tiny apps that give you quick information about topics such as weather, sports, the stock market, your photos, and news headlines.

Apple macOS

Whereas the Linux and Microsoft OSs are available to install on hardware from many manufacturers, the Apple Inc. strategy has been to produce proprietary hardware and software for better integration of the OS and the hardware. They do not license macOS to run on other manufacturers' computers. This has historically resulted in a higher price for a Mac than for a comparable PC. For several years, beginning in the mid-1990s, Macintosh computers used the Motorola PowerPC chip with an architecture enhanced for graphics and multimedia. Between 2005 and 2020, the Apple Mac line of computers were Intel-based. In 2020, Apple introduced new MacBook models that included their M1 processor, previously found in their mobile devices. Beginning in 2021, their iMac desktops include the M1 processors.

The Apple OS that was introduced in 2001 was a revolutionary change from the previous Mac OS 9 because Apple based it on NextStep, an OS with a UNIX kernel. Until macOS, the Macintosh OSs were strictly GUI environments, with no command-line option. The new macOS, with its UNIX origins, gives you the option of a character-based interface, but most users will happily work solely in the GUI (see Figure 1–16). Learn more about macOS and its features in Chapter 6.

Linux

Linux is an operating system modeled on UNIX and named in honor of its original developer, Linus Benedict Torvalds. He began it as a project in 1991 while a student at the University of Helsinki in his native Finland. He invited other programmers to work together to create an open-source operating system for modern computers. They created Linux using a powerful programming language called C, along with a free C compiler developed through the GNU project called GNU C Compiler (GCC). Linux has continued to evolve over the years, with programmers all over the globe testing and upgrading its code. Linus Torvalds could not have predicted in 1991 how well accepted the new operating system would be over 30 years later.

Note: A distribution is also called a "distro" or "flavor."

Linux is available in a variety of distributions, and it can be modified to run on nearly any computer. A distribution is a bundling of the Linux kernel and software—both enhancements to the OS and applications, such as word processors, spreadsheets, media players, and more. The person or organization providing the distribution may charge a fee for the enhancements and applications, but cannot charge a fee for the Linux code itself. Many distributions are free or very inexpensive.

Linux natively uses a command-line interface, and Figure 1–17 shows an example of a Linux directory list at the command line. Windows-like GUI environments,

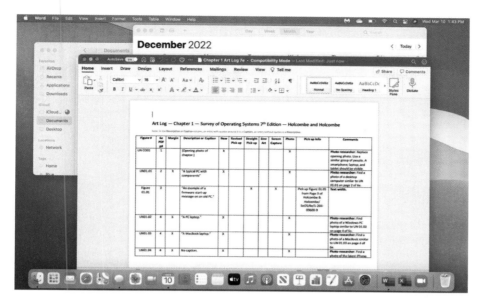

FIGURE 1–16 The macOS desktop with open windows.
Source: Jane Holcombe/Apple Inc.

```
[cottrell@localhost ppp]$ ls -l
total 56
-rw-------    1 root     root          78 Feb 27 17:09 chap-secrets
-rw-r--r--    1 root     root         927 Apr 14 12:38 firewall-masq
-rw-r--r--    1 root     root         825 Apr 14 12:38 firewall-standalone
-rw-r--r--    1 root     root           0 Apr  8 09:08 ioptions
-rwxr-xr-x    1 root     root         310 Dec 26  2000 ip-down
-rwxr-xr-x    1 root     root        3564 Mar 20 22:17 ip-down.ipv6to4
-rwxr-xr-x    1 root     root         362 Dec 26  2000 ip-up
-rwxr-xr-x    1 root     root        5745 Mar 11 17:42 ip-up.ipv6to4
-rwxr-xr-x    1 root     root         918 Mar 11 17:43 ipv6-down
-rwxr-xr-x    1 root     root         918 Mar 11 17:43 ipv6-up
-rw-r--r--    1 root     root           5 Feb 27 17:09 options
-rw-------    1 root     root          77 Feb 27 17:09 pap-secrets
drwxr-xr-x    3 root     root        4096 Jul  5 15:02 peers
-rw-r--r--    1 root     root          93 Apr 14 12:38 pppoe-server-options
[cottrell@localhost ppp]$
```

FIGURE 1–17 A Red Hat Linux directory listing (the ls command).
Source: Red Hat Inc.

called shells, are available that make it as accessible to most users as Windows or macOS. Learn more about Linux in Chapter 7.

Chrome OS

In the last three decades, computer-based work has gradually migrated away from our desktop computers and local networks to the cloud. We access cloud-based apps for online learning, completing projects and labs, submitting papers, collaborating with coworkers and fellow students, and for taking exams. At home, we connect to online services for entertainment, managing our finances, and much more. Recognizing this movement, Google created Chrome OS, an operating system based on a Linux kernel with a GUI based on the Chrome Web browser. Of course, Chrome is also its default browser.

At first, it wasn't taken seriously by many professionals because it was not much more than a Web browser, but Google has continued to improve the Chrome OS. Today, several manufacturers offer laptops, desktops, and tablets dedicated to the Chrome OS (see Figure 1-18).

FIGURE 1–18 The Chrome OS GUI.
Source: Google LLC

LO 1.4 | Today's Mobile Operating Systems

Mobile computing today has followed the trajectory of all computing, thanks to the miniaturization of components and new technologies. And like PCs, mobile devices became more desirable thanks to apps. However, don't look for a single "killer app" for mobile devices. Rather, the most popular mobile devices are those with a large number of compelling apps. Also, unlike the early PCs, today's mobile devices are very personal devices used for social interaction and entertainment as well as for work- and school-related tasks.

Of the mobile OSs featured in this book, Apple licenses theirs only for use on Apple mobile. Google allows manufacturers to use Android, but may require that certain Google apps and features be included. They license it for free under the Android Open Source Project. This helps hold down the cost of Android smartphones.

Before exploring mobile devices and their operating systems, consider one of the driving forces behind the wide adoption of mobile devices: cloud computing.

Cloud Computing

One of the biggest changes in how we work and manage our personal data is our dependency on cloud computing. For a basic understanding of cloud computing, let's start by defining terms.

Cloud Basics

We would not be talking about cloud computing without the existence of internetworks. An internetwork is a network of networks. The Internet, arguably the most famous internetwork, spans the entire world. For decades, the Internet has been represented in diagrams by a cloud, an image that evolved to hide the complexity. There are millions of privately owned internetworks, secured behind firewalls and accessed by authorized users. Such a private internetwork is an intranet.

The term *cloud* evolved to encompass all the services offered over the Internet and on intranets, such as storage and apps that run from remote servers. Cloud computing is the use of those services, regardless of their actual location. The simplest and most common cloud-based service is data storage, called cloud storage. Cloud storage services are provided by many sources for all sizes and types of data storage needs. In Chapter 11, File Management in the Cloud, we delve into cloud storage and how to manage your data in the cloud from various devices.

Note: The iPod Touch runs iOS, but we are not covering this device. With its small screen and NO cell phone support, it is simply a digital music player with tablet features.

Multiple-Choice Quiz

1. Which of the following operating systems cannot be licensed to run on a PC?
   a. macOS
   b. Windows 10
   c. Windows 7
   d. Linux
   e. Windows 8

2. Which of the following is a small electronic component made up of transistors (tiny switches) and other miniaturized parts?
   a. Peripheral
   b. Integrated circuit (IC)
   c. Tablet
   d. Mouse
   e. Vacuum tube

3. Introduced in 1983, this application program became the "killer app" that made the IBM PC a must-have business tool.
   a. Microsoft Word
   b. VisiCalc
   c. BASIC
   d. PC DOS
   e. Lotus 1-2-3

4. Which of the following is not available as a desktop operating system?
   a. Chrome OS
   b. macOS
   c. Windows 10
   d. Linux
   e. iOS

5. Which of the following is a computer input device? Select all correct answers.
   a. Mouse
   b. Printer
   c. Keyboard
   d. RAM
   e. ROM

6. On a network, the primary purpose of this type of computer is to allow users to connect over the network to save and access files stored on this computer, as well as to print to printers connected to this computer.
   a. Desktop computer
   b. File and print server
   c. Tablet
   d. Laptop
   e. Smartphone

7. Which acronym describes technology in which all or most of a device's electronic circuitry is on a single microchip?

   a. IoT
   b. UI
   c. RAM
   d. SSD
   e. SoC

8. macOS is built on NextStep, an OS based on what kernel?
   a. Linux
   b. UNIX
   c. DOS
   d. Windows
   e. Chrome OS

9. In the 1950s, a typical computer end user would have been a _____.
   a. computer gamer
   b. medical doctor
   c. politician
   d. government agency
   e. secretary

10. What acronym describes networked devices that contain microcomputers but are not thought of as computing devices, such as refrigerators, automobile components, light bulbs, and industrial control devices?
    a. IoT
    b. RAM
    c. NTFS
    d. SSD
    e. SoC

11. Which of the following accurately describes the overall trend in computing during the past 70-plus years?
    a. Toward physically larger, more-powerful computers.
    b. Toward physically larger, less-powerful computers.
    c. Toward physically smaller, less-powerful computers.
    d. Toward physically smaller, more-powerful computers.
    e. Toward physically smaller, single-use computers.

12. When working with a mobile device, if you touch an area of screen that requires text input, the OS will display this for your use.
    a. Help screen
    b. Virtual keyboard
    c. A Bluetooth button so that you can connect a keyboard
    d. CLI
    e. Screen gestures

13. Using this type of wireless network connection when browsing the Internet with a smartphone or tablet can save you data fees.
    a. Bluetooth
    b. Wi-Fi
    c. USB
    d. Cellular
    e. Ethernet

14. What file system is the default for current Windows OSs?
    a. iOS
    b. IC
    c. RAM
    d. NTFS
    e. SSD

15. Which of the following is a technology you would use to connect your smartphone to a wireless headset?
    a. Bluetooth
    b. Wi-Fi
    c. USB
    d. Cellular
    e. Ethernet

Essay Quiz

1. Describe the benefit to programmers of having an operating system when that programmer is creating a new application.

2. Based on your own observations, do you believe there are more differences or more commonalities among the different operating systems across devices: PCs, laptops, tablets, and smartphones?

3. Review the timeline provided in this chapter and select an event that you believe is the most significant event and give a reason for your choice.

4. Briefly describe the difference between a private cloud service and a public cloud service.

5. In general terms, describe a mobile OS's use of a device's accelerometer.

Lab Projects

LAB PROJECT 1.1

Pick a typical day for you, and create a journal of all the interactions you have with computers from the time you wake up in the morning until you go to bed at night. *Hint:* Even a gas pump contains a computer.

LAB PROJECT 1.2

If you use both a desktop (or laptop) computer and a mobile device, describe the similarities and differences you notice in working with the GUI on each device. If you do not use both types of devices, find someone who does (classmate or other) and interview that person for this project. Create a report of these results to submit to your instructor or to use in a discussion of results with your classmates.

LAB PROJECT 1.3

Poll classmates or coworkers to determine how they use their mobile devices. Are they primarily entertainment devices? If so, describe why this is the case. How many people polled used a mobile device as a primary computer? In that case, what tasks did they perform on the mobile devices? Were there tasks they preferred to do on a desktop or laptop? Create a report describing the results and be prepared to discuss with other students who completed this project separately.

2 Computer and User Security Basics

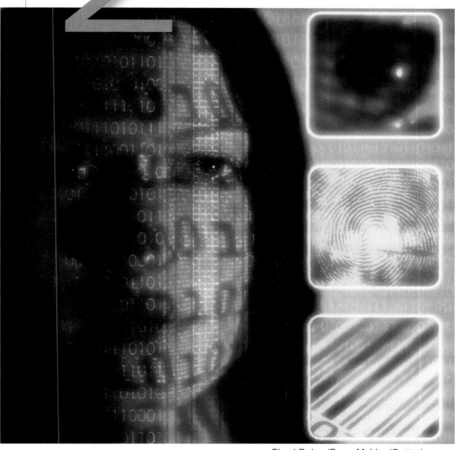

Chad Baker/Ryan McVay/Getty Images

Why do operating systems include security features? Why do we need to apply security patches to operating systems? Why has computer security become a multibillion-dollar business worldwide? Why? Because it's dangerous out there! And, as you will learn in this chapter, "out there" seems to be everywhere, because no place or technology is safe from threats. That includes the Internet, corporate intranets, desktop and laptop computers, cell phones, tablets, other mobile devices, and all your Internet-connected entertainment and environmental controls in your house. Here you'll learn about the threats, and the methods, practices, and technologies for protecting your computer systems.

In this chapter, we first attempt to instill a healthy dose of paranoia in your mind so that you avoid inviting malware and becoming victims of scams, and we identify methods for securing your computing devices. Then, in later chapters, you will learn how to implement OS-specific security. 🕸

LO 2.1 | Threats to Computers and Users

What are you risking if your computer or mobile device is not secure? The short answer is that you risk your identity, the work you have created, your company's integrity, and your own job if you are responsible for loss of the company's equipment or data. Today, government regulations, such as the Sarbanes–Oxley Act or the Health Insurance Portability and Accountability Act (HIPAA), require that organizations protect certain personal information, such as health and personal financial data. The consequences to an organization that does not comply with these regulations, or that experiences a breach of security involving such data, can be very severe.

We'll begin the long answer with an overview of common threats and how they gain access to computers. Many of the threats described are severe enough to be considered cybercrimes. A cybercrime is illegal activity performed using computer technology.

Malicious Tools and Methods

We call software threats malware, a shortened form of "malicious software." This term covers a large and growing list of threats, including many that you no doubt know about, such as viruses, worms, Trojan horses, or spam. But have you heard of pop-up downloads, drive-by downloads, war driving, bluesnarfing, adware, spyware, back doors, spim, phishing, or hoaxes? Read on and learn about the various types of malware and their methods of infecting computers and networks.

Malware is a huge industry that targets all computing devices, with the greatest growth in malware targeting mobile devices.

Vectors

A vector is a method that malware uses to infect a computer. While some malware may use just a single vector, multivector malware uses an array of methods to infect computers and networks. Let's look at a few well-known vectors.

Click Bait. Click bait is content in an email, a Web page, a social networking page, or within any online app, that is designed to lure you to click on it and its associated link in order to open a Web page or run a video. Click bait may simply be the link itself in an email or a headline or photo containing just enough information to make you curious so that you will click on the link.

Social Networking. Social networking is the use of social media, which is any service (Internet-based or other) that provides a place where people can interact in online communities, sharing information in various forms. Community members generate social-media content. A social networking site is a website that provides space where members can communicate with one another and share details of their business or personal lives. Facebook is a very popular social networking site. LinkedIn is a social media site for professionals who use it for business contacts. Twitter (Figure 2–1) allows users to send and receive short text messages (tweets) of up to 280 characters.

We see social media as a vector for malware and social engineering (defined later in this chapter) as well as a rich source of personal information. We are horrified to see the personal details that people reveal on Facebook and Twitter, and recent developments have shown that our personal data is being harvested through social media activities, as well as that of our contacts. Thousands of companies profit from the use of our data collected during a variety of online activities without our knowledge, and without our receiving any real compensation. This activity is called "surveillance capitalism" by Harvard Business School professor Shoshana Zuboff.

Email. Some malware infects computers via email. The simple act of opening an email containing a virus can infect a computer.

FIGURE 2–1 The Twitter Log in page.
Source: Twitter Inc.

Regardless of the email client you use, clicking on a link in an email message can launch malware from a website.

Malicious Code on Websites. Some malware infects computers by lurking in hidden code on websites. An unsuspecting user browses to a site and clicks on a link that launches and installs malware on their computer.

Trojan Horses. A Trojan horse, often simply called a Trojan, is both a type of malware and a vector. The modern-day Trojan horse program gains access to computers much like the ancient Greek warriors who, in Virgil's famous tale (the epic poem *The Aeneid*), gained access to the city of Troy by hiding in a large wooden horse presented as a gift to the city (a Trojan horse). A Trojan horse program installs and activates on a computer by appearing to be something harmless, which the user innocently installs. It may appear as just a useful free program that a user downloads and installs or a video, but it is a common way for malware to infect your system.

Although it is hard to fit all threats into tidy categories, we consider threats similar to the "Complete a Quick Survey" exploit to be a Trojan because it appears to be something harmless, tempting you to comply. If you complete the survey it may take some action, such as pretending to scan your computer for problems, but the results will be bogus, offering to fix the problems it claims to find and asking for payment. A threat that causes you to take action out of fear is scareware.

Searching for Unprotected Computers. Still other malware searches throughout a network for computers that do not have the latest security updates and/or do not have real-time antimalware installed. The malware can then install itself.

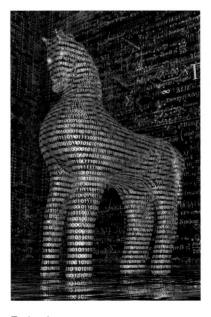

Trojan horse
posteriori/Shutterstock

Sneakernet—The Oldest Vector. Yet another vector is as old as PCs. In the days when many PCs did not connect to networks, users shared data between computers by carrying a floppy disk containing data or programs from one computer to another. The slang for this practice is sneakernet. Sometimes, the floppy disk contained malware, making sneakernet the oldest vector for PCs. Sneakernet still exists, but the storage device used today is the flash drive, and the computers are usually also connected to a network, which extends the risk when malware infects a single computer. In August 2010, the U.S. Deputy Defense Secretary declassified the information that a flash drive, inserted into a U.S. military laptop in 2008 on a military post in the Middle East, was the vector for malicious code that caused a significant breach of military computers.

Back Doors. In computing, a back door is a way in which someone can gain access to a computer, bypassing authentication security. Sometimes a program's author installs a back door into a single program so she can easily access it later for administering and/or for troubleshooting the program code. Or an attacker may create a back door by taking advantage of a discovered weakness in a program. Then any program using the back door can run in the security context of the invaded program and infect a computer with malware. In one well-known situation, the Code Red worm took advantage of a specific vulnerability in Microsoft's Internet Information Server (IIS) Web server software to install a back door. The result was that the worm displayed a message on every Web page on the IIS server. The message included the phrase, "Hacked by Chinese." Then the Nimda worm took advantage of the back door left by the Code Red worm to infect computers.

Rootkits. A rootkit is malware that hides itself from detection by anti-malware programs by concealing itself within the OS code or any other program running on the computer. Someone who has administrator (root) access to the computer installs a rootkit, giving an attacker administrator privileges to the computer. He can then run any type of malware to quietly carry out its mission.

Pop-Up Downloads. A pop-up is a separate window that displays (pops up) uninvited from a Web page. The purpose of a pop-up may be as simple as an advertisement, but a pop-up can be a vector for malware. A pop-up download is a program downloaded to a user's computer through a pop-up page. It requires an action on the part of a user, such as clicking on a button that implies acceptance of something such as free software. The program that downloads may be a virus or a worm.

Drive-By Downloads. A drive-by download is a program downloaded to a user's computer without consent. Often the simple act of browsing to a website, or opening an HTML email message, may result in such a surreptitious download. A drive-by download may also occur when installing another application. This is particularly true of certain file-sharing programs that users install to allow sharing of music, data, or photo files over the Internet. Some drive-by downloads may alter your Web browser home page and/or redirect all your browser searches to one site. A drive-by download may install a virus, a worm, or even more likely, adware or spyware (which we describe later in this chapter).

War Driving. Secure all Wi-Fi networks with the latest standard of Wi-Fi security and require passwords to access the network. A Wi-Fi network that connects to the Internet through a router is a hotspot and should be protected from unauthorized access. Someone who detects an unprotected hotspot can access the Internet for free. Further, the reason we see this as a vector is that they also can capture keystrokes, email, passwords, and user names from the wireless traffic, giving them ways to send malware to connected users or use the information they gather to steal users' identities.

Some people actively seek out unsecured Wi-Fi networks, a practice called war driving. A war driver moves through a neighborhood in a vehicle or on foot, using a mobile device equipped with Wi-Fi wireless network capability and software that identifies Wi-Fi networks. The software detects the level of security (or lack of) on each detected Wi-Fi network.

Note: A less-dramatic term for "war driving" is "access point mapping."

Using an unsecured hotspot can expose you to threats. If you need to be inspired to secure your Wi-Fi network, check out the Internet, where numerous websites describe how to war drive, as well as how to protect your data from theft. There are war driving videos on YouTube, as shown in Figure 2-2.

Bluesnarfing. Similar to war driving, bluesnarfing is the act of covertly obtaining information broadcast from wireless devices using the Bluetooth standard, a short-range wireless standard used for data exchange between devices. Bluetooth devices have a range of from 10 centimeters to 100 meters, depending on the power class of the device. Using a smartphone, a bluesnarfer can eavesdrop to acquire information, or even use the synchronizing feature of the device to pick up the user's information—all without the victim detecting it.

Password Theft

A password is a string of characters that you enter, along with an identifier, such as a user name or email address, to authenticate yourself. If someone steals your passwords

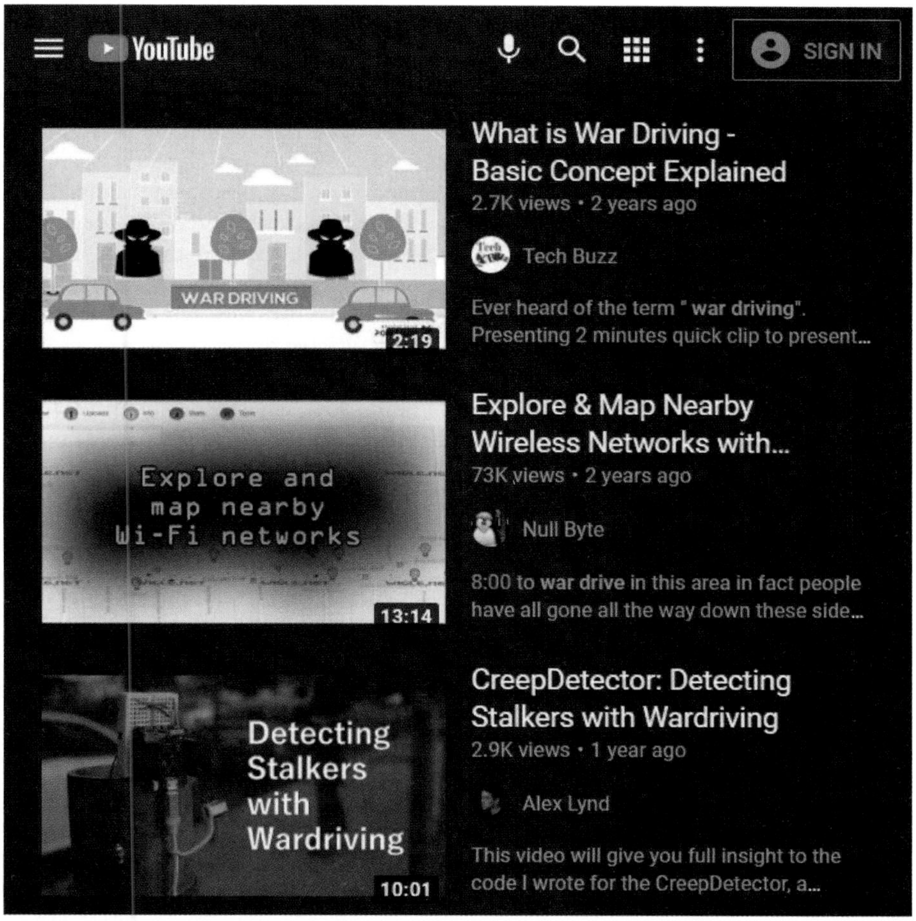

FIGURE 2–2 Online videos show examples of war driving.
Source: YouTube

they can gain access to whatever you thought you were protecting with the password. Stealing passwords is theft with intent to break into computers and networks.

Stealing Passwords through Websites. There are numerous programs and techniques for stealing passwords. One commonly used technique is to invade an unsecured website to access information unwitting users provide to the site, such as user names and passwords, and such personal information as account numbers, Social Security numbers, birth dates, and much more.

Stealing Passwords with Password Crackers. Another technique used for stealing a password is a program called a password cracker. Some password crackers fall into the category of "brute-force" password crackers, which simply means the program tries a huge number of permutations of possible passwords. Often, because people tend to use simple passwords such as their initials, birth dates, addresses, and so on, the brute-force method works. Other password crackers use more sophisticated statistical or mathematical methods to steal passwords.

Stealing Passwords with Keystroke Loggers. A method for stealing passwords, as well as lots of other information, is the use of a keystroke logger, also called a keylogger. This is either a hardware device or a program that monitors and records every keystroke, usually without the user's knowledge. In the case of a hardware logger, the person desiring the keystroke log must physically install it before recording. Some models are Wi-Fi enabled. When properly configured, a Wi-Fi keystroke logger can send reports on captured data via email, and the owner can also remotely access the keystroke logger. Without a network connection, a hardware keystroke logger must be physically retrieved to access the collected data.

A software keystroke logger program does not require physical access to the target computer but simply a method for downloading and installing it on the computer. This could occur through one of the vectors described earlier in this chapter. Once installed, such a program can send the logged information over the Internet via email, or using other methods, to the person desiring the log.

Some parents install keystroke loggers to monitor their children's Internet activity, but such programs have the potential for abuse by people with less-benign motivations, such as stalkers and identity thieves. A simple Internet search of "keystroke logger" will yield many sources of both hardware and software keystroke loggers. See Figure 2–3. The latter are now the more common.

Zero-Day Exploits

We call a malware attack an exploit when it takes advantage of some vulnerability in our computers or networks. Experts are constantly discovering these vulnerabilities and attempting to stay ahead of the bad guys with appropriate defense techniques. However, sometimes someone finds a software vulnerability in an operating system or application that is unknown to the publisher of the targeted software, and someone devises a way to exploit that vulnerability. We call this unknown exploit (often a virus) a zero-day exploit, and it is very difficult to protect against such a threat.

WARNING!

There are password crackers for every operating system, every type of computing device, and all the social networking services in use today. Learn more when you search on the key words "password cracker" using your favorite search engine.

try this!

Learn about Password Crackers

Research password crackers. Try this:

1. Open a browser and enter the key words "password cracker."
2. Do not select a result, but carefully scroll through the results.
3. Skip all results marked as Ads.
4. Skip results offering downloads.
5. Select a result from an informational site, like Wikipedia, but double-check that the URL is correct (in the case of Wikipedia it must contain wikipedia.org in a position close to **https://**. For the English version the correct URL begins with "**https://en.wikipedia.org**").
6. Read the article, noting the types of password cracking tools available and be prepared to discuss what you have learned.

Note: Advanced keystroke loggers may also capture screenshots of all activity on a computer.

Note: Two major flaws (or bugs) were revealed in Intel and AMD microprocessors, named Meltdown and Spectre. Exploits that take advantage of these flaws take over computers at the lowest, most vulnerable level.

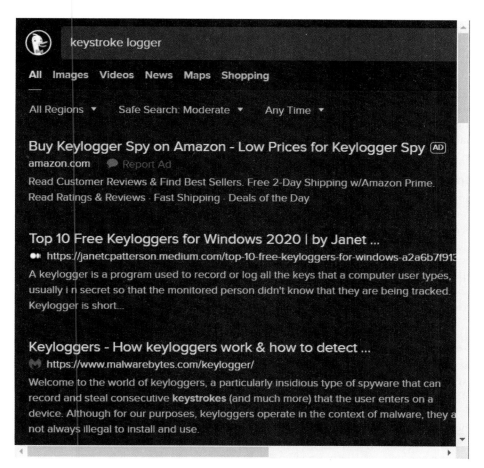

FIGURE 2–3 Search on "keystroke logger" to learn more about the devices and software available.
Source: DuckDuckGo.com

Viruses

While, in the broadest sense, "virus" is a term used for all malware, technically, a virus is one class of malware: a program installed and activated on a computer or mobile device without the knowledge or permission of the user. A virus often attaches to a file, such as a Microsoft Word document, and replicates as you copy or share the infected file. Like a living virus that infects humans and animals, a computer virus can result in a wide range of symptoms and outcomes. Loss of data, damage to or complete failure of an operating system, or theft of personal and financial information are just a few of the potential results of computer virus infections.

Worms

Like a virus, a worm is a program installed and activated on a computer without the knowledge or permission of the user. But a worm replicates itself on the computer, or throughout a network. In other words, a worm is a network-aware virus that does not require action from the unwitting user to replicate, and it can have a similar range of outcomes. The Netsky and MyDoom worms caused chaos and loss of productivity just by the huge amount of network traffic they generated. The typical worm resides in a single file that it replicates onto multiple machines. However, the Nimda worm changed all that by inserting its code into other executable files on the local drive of each machine to which it replicated itself, making it difficult to locate and remove the worm.

> *Note:* "In the wild" is a term frequently used to describe the overall computing environment, including private networks, and Internet and all other public networks. "In the zoo" refers to a controlled and isolated environment where viruses can be analyzed during the development of patches. This type of environment is also called a "sandbox."

> **WARNING!**
>
> A worm can replicate itself via Bluetooth, infecting mobile devices when people are in crowded public places, such as sports bars. Turn Bluetooth off when not in use and when in close proximity to strangers.

Botnets and Zombies

A botnet is a group of networked computers that, usually unbeknown to their owners, are infected with programs that forward information to other computers over a network. A bot, short for robot, is a program that acts as an agent for a user or master program, performing a variety of functions—for both good and evil. An individual computer in a botnet is a zombie because it mindlessly serves the person who originated the botnet code. A bot herder is someone who initiates and controls a botnet. Botnets have grown to be one of the biggest threats on the Internet.

Spyware

Spyware is a category of software that runs surreptitiously on a user's computer, gathers information without the user's permission, and then sends that information to the people or organizations that requested it. A virus may install Internet-based spyware, sometimes called tracking software or a spybot, on a computer. Spyware can be used by companies to trace users' surfing patterns to improve the company's marketing efforts; it can be used for industrial espionage; it is used by law enforcement to find sexual predators or criminals (with appropriate legal permissions); and it is used by governments to investigate terrorism.

Adware

Adware is a form of spyware that collects information about the user in order to display targeted advertisements to the user, either in the form of inline banners or in the form of pop-ups. Inline banners are advertisements that run within the context of the current page, just taking up screen real estate. Pop-ups are a greater annoyance, because they are ads that run in separate browser windows that you must close before you can continue with your present task. Clicking to accept an offer presented in an inline banner or a pop-up may trigger a pop-up download that can install a virus or worm.

Browser Hijacking

We received a call the other day from Dave, a finance officer at a large farm implement company. Every time he opened his browser, the home page pointed to a site advertising adware removal software. This is an example of browser hijacking, a practice that has been growing. Some unscrupulous people do this so that their website will register more visitors and then they can raise their rates to advertisers.

Dave was able to reverse this by changing the default page in settings, but it was very annoying. He was lucky; hijackers can make it very difficult to defeat the hijack by modifying the registry (a database that stores configuration settings in the Windows OS) so that every time you restart Windows or your Web browser the hijack reinstates.

try this!

Research Spam Statistics

Find out the latest bad news on the amount of Internet email identified as spam. Try this:

1. Open your Web browser and connect to your favorite search engine.

2. Search on the words "spam statistics." For a more targeted search include the current year in your search string.

3. Review the results and select a link that appears to give actual statistics on spam occurrences for Internet email users. Discuss the results with your classmates.

Spam and Spim

Spam is unsolicited email, often called junk email. This includes email from a legitimate source selling a real service or product, but if you did not give the source permission to send such information to you, it is spam. Too often spam involves some form of scam—a bogus offer to sell a service or product that does not exist or tries to include you in a complicated moneymaking deal. We call spam perpetrators spammers, and spam is illegal. Spam accounts for a huge amount of traffic on the Internet. Some corporate network administrators report that as much as 60 percent of the incoming email traffic is spam.

Spim is an acronym for spam over instant messaging, and the perpetrators are spimmers. A spimmer sends bots out over the Internet to collect instant-messaging screen names, and then a spimbot sends spim to the screen names. A typical spim message may contain a link to a website, where, like spam, the recipient will find products or services for sale, legitimate or otherwise.

Social Engineering

Social engineering is the use of persuasion techniques to gain the confidence of individuals—for both good and bad purposes. People with malicious intent use social engineering to persuade targeted people to reveal confidential information or to obtain something else of value. Social engineering is as old as human interaction, so there are countless techniques. Following are just a few categories of computer security threats that employ social engineering.

Robocalls. An unwanted and annoying call from an unknown source trying to extract either money or information from you is a robocall. These calls are often automated, thus, the prefix "robo" (for robot) in the name. They are illegal and use spoofed phone numbers. It is hard to believe that people are persuaded by the claims of these callers, but they use many social engineering tactics to persuade the victim to pay money or at least answer questions so that they can gather information. The first federal law against robocalls was created in 2019, but more needs to be done with both laws and technology to stop robocalls. The Federal Communications Commission (FCC) publishes guides on their website to educate consumers about the threat of robocalls. Learn more about robocalls by pointing your browser to **www.fcc.gov** and entering "robocalls" in the search box at the top of the page.

Fraud. Fraud is the use of deceit and trickery to persuade someone to hand over money or other valuables. Fraud is often associated with identify theft (discussed later), because the perpetrator will falsely claim to be the victim when using the victim's credit cards and other personal and financial information.

One form of fraud is ransomware, a type of scareware that threatens to do damage or lock a user out of a computer unless the user pays a "ransom." There is no guarantee that your data will be unencrypted once the payment is made. A more frightening variation of ransomware claims that the victim has been observed in an illegal act, such as distributing child pornography, and threatens to report this to the authorities unless the victim pays a ransom. Ransomware may require payment through an online payment system, such as bitcoin.

> *Note:* The brief reference to bitcoin does not begin to define this complex entity—both a new type of money as well as a network for paying with bitcoins.

Phishing. Phishing is a fraudulent method of obtaining personal and financial information through Web page pop-ups, email, and even paper letters mailed via the postal service. Think of the metaphor of a fisherman preparing and casting his bait in an ocean full of fish. Even if only one in a hundred fish take the bait, he is statistically likely to have many successes. A phishing message ("bait") purports to be from a legitimate organization, such as a bank, credit card company, retailer, and so on. In a typical phishing scenario, the email or pop-up may contain authentic-looking logos, and even links to the actual site, but the link specified for supplying personal financial information will take recipients (the "phish") to a Web page that asks them to enter their personal data. The Web page may look exactly like the company's legitimate Web page, but it's not.

While the typical phishing attack casts a wide net by sending out millions of messages, some phishing attacks are more targeted. We call these spear phishing, and the target of a spear-phishing attack is usually one that has a high probability of delivering a very valuable return. Such an attack may come in the form of a message with a greeting that includes your name and content that includes some of your personal information. If you work in a large organization, the attack may have language that seems to come from a coworker, detailing department information or referring to a recent meeting. The source of the message may actually be your coworker's valid address if the attacker managed to hijack the email account. Or it may be a forged email address. Someone forges an email address by modifying the sender's address in the email message's header—the information that accompanies a message but does not appear in the message. We also call this type of forgery email spoofing.

Be very suspicious of email requesting personal or financial information. Legitimate businesses will never contact you by email and ask you for your access code, Social Security number, or password.

WARNING!

Phishing (and spear phishing) are just old-fashioned scams in high-tech dress.

Note: This type of hoax is also known as an imposter scam.

Hoaxes. A hoax is a deception intended either for amusement or for some gain with malicious intent. Hoaxes take many forms. One example is an email message appearing to be from someone you know claiming she took an unplanned trip to London where she was mugged in the subway. The email address looks legitimate, but when you respond, you receive a message from someone else stating that your friend is now in jail and needs bail money. Sounds outlandish? We received such a message, but we were suspicious and called our friend who reported that she was safe at home and that several other of her friends had responded to the message and received the plea for money.

Enticements to Open Attachments. Social engineering is also involved in the enticements to open attachments to emails. Called "gimmes," you find these enticements either in the subject line or in the body of the email message. Opening the attachment then executes and infects the local computer with some form of malware. A huge number of methods are used. Sadly, enticements often appeal to the less-noble human characteristics such as greed (via an offer too good to be true), vanity (physical enhancement products), or simple curiosity (with a subject line that appears to be a response to an email from you). These enticements may appeal to people's sympathy and compassion by way of a nonexistent charity or by fraudulently representing a legitimate charity.

Identity Theft

Identify theft occurs when someone collects personal information belonging to another person and uses that information to fraudulently make purchases, open new credit accounts, and even obtain new driver's licenses and other forms of identification in the victim's name. There are many ways not directly involved with computers for thieves to steal your identity. However, the use of computers and mobile devices for social networking and purchasing has greatly expanded the scope of this type of crime, turning it into a huge business involved in the theft of large numbers of persons' data from large databases. These criminals sell such identity information for pennies per record. Several websites maintained by the U.S. government offer valuable information for consumers who wish to protect themselves from identify theft. A starting place is

Step-by-Step 2.01

Take a Phishing IQ Test!

It is often difficult to discern which emails are legitimate and which are "phishing." Test your ability to detect a phishing scam. To complete this test, you will need a computer or mobile device with an Internet connection.

Step 1

Use your Web browser to connect to the phishing test at **www.sonicwall.com/phishing-iq-test/**. If this URL no longer works, use a search engine to find a phishing test.

Step 2

After reading the instructions and helpful hints, start the test. Click on the button labeled, Take the Phishing IQ Test.

Step 3

You will be presented with several messages and you must decide whether each is legitimate or phishing.

Step 4

When you finish, the program will grade you on your choices and you will see the correct answers. Each message also has a detailed explanation as to why it is either legitimate or phishing. Read these explanations carefully.

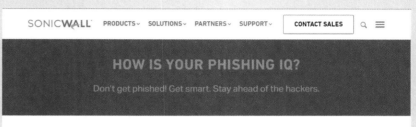

Source: SonicWall

You Got 7 of 7 Correct

QUESTION #	SUBJECT	YOUR ANSWER	CORRECT ANSWER	TEST RESULT	EXPLAIN ANSWER
1	Chrome	Legitimate	Legitimate	✓	Why?
2	PayPal	Phishing	Phishing	✓	Why?
3	OneDrive	Phishing	Phishing	✓	Why?
4	TD Bank	Phishing	Phishing	✓	Why?
5	HubSpot	Legitimate	Legitimate	✓	Why?
6	DHL	Phishing	Phishing	✓	Why?
7	ANZ Bank	Phishing	Phishing	✓	Why?

Source: SonicWall

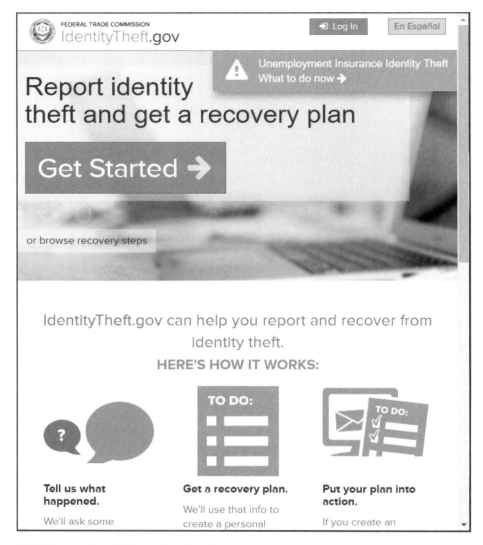

FIGURE 2–4 The FTC Identity Theft Web page.
Source: Federal Trade Commission

the website **www.idtheft.gov** (see Figure 2–4); it includes steps to take if you have been a victim of identity theft. Connect to this website in the Try This.

try this!

Learn More About Identity Theft

Learn more about identity theft and what to do if you are a victim of identity theft. Try this:

1. Open your browser; enter **www.idtheft.gov** into the address box. The actual URL is **www.identitytheft.gov**, but the shorter version works and is easier to type.

2. This site, shown in Figure 2–4, gives clear step-by-step instructions for what to do if you are a victim of identity theft.

3. Notice that you can print out each checklist.

4. For prevention tips, direct your browser to **ftc.gov/idtheft**. This is also a link found on the bottom of the **IdentityTheft.gov** page accessed in the previous steps.

Exposure to Inappropriate or Distasteful Content

The Internet, and especially the World Wide Web, is a treasure trove of information. It is hard to imagine a subject that cannot be found somewhere on the Internet. However, some of this content may be inappropriate or distasteful. To some extent, only an individual can judge what is inappropriate and distasteful; however, there are circumstances in which certain content harmful to some individuals—such as young children—is considered a threat.

Invasion of privacy by shoulder surfing.
Troy Aossey/Getty Images

Invasion of Privacy

One can also view many of the threats discussed so far as invasions of privacy. Protecting against privacy invasion includes protecting your personal information at your bank, credit union, online and brick-and-mortar retail stores, fitness centers, and any organization in which you are a customer, member, or employee. All steps you take to make your computer more secure also contribute to the protection of your privacy. Don't forget physical security and the ability of people to gather information by shoulder surfing, which entails reading information off your screen while you work on your computer in a busy office or public location.

Misuse of Cookies

One form of privacy invasion involves the misuse of something called cookies. Cookies are very small files a Web browser saves on the local hard drive at the request of a website. The next time you connect to that same website, it will request the cookies saved on previous visits—often giving you the convenience of automated log-ins to each site. Cookies are text files, so they cannot contain viruses, which are executable code, but they may contain the following:

- User preferences when visiting a specific site.
- Information you may have entered into a form at the website, including personal information.
- Browsing activity.
- Shopping selections on a website.

Users are not overtly aware of the saving and retrieving of cookies from their local hard disk, although most good websites clearly detail whether or not they use cookies and what they use them for. You can find this information in the privacy statement or policy of the site. Cookies are accessible by the website that created them, or through some subterfuge of the website creator. A cookie contains the name of the domain that originated that cookie. A first-party cookie is one that originates with the domain name of the URL to which you directly connect. A third-party cookie refers to a cookie

WARNING!

From now on, when you browse the Web, look for links to the privacy statement or site policy at each website you visit.

Guard against computer theft.

that originates with a domain name beyond the one shown in the current URL. An ad embedded in a Web page—often called banner ads—can use cookies to track your Web surfing habits, and third-party cookies play a part in this type of tracking, making third-party cookies less desirable than first-party cookies.

Computer Hardware Theft

Good security includes something as simple as locking doors, keeping hardware locked away from prying eyes and sticky fingers. That's obvious. What may not be obvious to you, especially if you use a laptop as your principal computer, is what happens if someone steals your computer. You would be astonished at how many computers, especially laptops and mobile devices, are stolen each year, and unless your computer has been properly secured, and all the data backed up, there goes your business information, your data files, your financial information, your address book, everything! Although a large percentage of computer thefts occur just so the thief can sell the hardware quickly and get some quick cash, an increasing number of thieves are technically sophisticated and will go through your hard drive looking for bank account, credit card, and other financial data so they can steal your identity.

Accidents, Mistakes, and Disasters

Accidents and mistakes happen. We don't know of anyone who hasn't accidentally erased an important file, pressed the wrong button at the wrong instant, or created a file name he can't remember. Disasters also happen in many forms. Just a few are fires, earthquakes, and weather-induced disasters such as tornadoes, lightning strikes, and floods. Predicting such events is imperfect at best. The principal way to protect against accidents, mistakes, and disasters is to make frequent, comprehensive backups. You can make backups of an entire hard drive using programs that make an image of the drive, or you can use programs that back up your critical data files on a periodic basis. Organizations that have a lot of valuable data even make multiple backups and keep copies off-site. Then, in case of fire, flood, earthquake, or other natural disaster that destroys not only the on-site backups but also the computer, they can still recover.

Keeping Track of New Threats

We cannot begin to cover all the methods currently used to victimize computer users. However, various organizations work to keep track of these threats, counter them, and inform the public. The Federal Trade Commission (FTC) Bureau of Consumer Protection is one such organization. It maintains a website (www.ftc.gov/bcp/), shown in Figure 2-5, containing a list of documents about various consumer issues and threats. These documents are worth reviewing from time to time to learn about new threats. This site also posts the latest related news and hosts a blog.

The People Behind the Threats

The people behind computer security threats are as varied as their motivations. They come from all walks of life and are scattered all over the globe. The umbrella term for a person who breaks laws using computer technology is cybercriminal. Other terms further define the people behind these threats.

Computer accidents are common.
Mikael Damkier/Shutterstock

Organized Crime

Organized crime is a growing source of these threats. Organized crime cartels exist in every major country in the world, with certain areas notorious for their homegrown crime organizations. Organized crime specialists work at stealing bank account login information and also are the source of many fraud attempts and money laundering via online shopping.

FIGURE 2–5 The FTC Bureau of Consumer Protection website.
Source: Federal Trade Commission

Cyberterrorists

Terrorists cause destruction without regard to its effect on humanity. Terrorists of all types have embraced cybercrime as a method by which individuals can wreak havoc on victims worldwide without putting themselves in physical danger. Such an attack is cyberterrorism, and a person who carries it out is a cyberterrorist.

Hackers

As any group of people engaged in similar endeavors grows and matures, it develops a set of terms and participant competency rankings. For years, the term "hacker" has been used, particularly by the press, to mean someone who uses sophisticated computer programming skills to invade private computers and networks to cause havoc, steal passwords, and steal identities and money. But the people who work to invade computer systems actually fall into several classifications describing their actions. For instance, in some circles, a hacker is someone with a great deal of computing expertise, a white hat hacker. Like the classic good cowboy who wore a white hat in old westerns, a white hat hacker is not a cybercriminal and only explores computer system weaknesses for the purpose of making systems more secure, an activity considered to be ethical.

Hacker.
Den Rise/Shutterstock

Crackers

A cracker is a member of a group of people who proudly call themselves hackers, but are regarded as black hat hackers. This again harks back to the old cowboy westerns in which the bad guys wore black hats. They may be after financial gain or simply get a kick out of causing damage after breaking into computers and making phone systems do things they aren't supposed to do (the latter is called phone phreaking). White hat hackers call these people "crackers" and want nothing to do with them because being able to break security doesn't make you a hacker any more than being able to hot-wire a car makes you an automotive engineer. The basic difference is this: white hat hackers build things and look for vulnerabilities in order to improve security; crackers break into systems illegally and do harm.

Script Kiddies

A script kiddie is someone who lacks the knowledge to personally develop a security threat, but uses scripted tools or programs created by others to break into computer systems to cause damage or mischief. The name implies enough knowledge to run computer scripts or programs.

Click Kiddies

A click kiddie is similar to a script kiddie, but with even less knowledge than a script kiddie, requiring a GUI to select and run a hacking tool. A click kiddie browses the Web, searching for sites that make it even easier by providing forms the click kiddie can fill out, enter a target IP address, and click to initiate an attack. Such sites provide the additional benefit of anonymity to the perpetrator.

Packet Monkeys

Packet monkeys are similar to script kiddies and click kiddies in that they need to use programs created by others to perform their attacks. They typically have little understanding of the harm they may cause, and their exploits are often random and without a purpose other than the thrill of trying to get away with something. Hackers call packet monkeys "bottom feeders."

Packet monkeys create denial-of-service attacks by inundating a site or a network with so much traffic (data packets) that the network is overwhelmed and denies service to additional traffic.

LO 2.2 | Defense Against Threats

No simple solutions exist to the damaging and mischievous threats that lurk on the Internet and on private networks, but doing nothing is not an option. We need to make our best efforts to thwart these threats, even if we cannot deter a determined and skilled invader. Most people do not have the necessary skills, motivation, or access to sophisticated tools, so implementing basic security will keep the majority out. Here are some basic defensive practices that you can apply in operating systems to avoid being a victim.

Education

This chapter may be just the beginning of your education about how threats, such as viruses, get access to computers and networks and how your own behavior can make you vulnerable to such threats as identity theft. Beyond understanding how these things can happen, also be actively alert to signs of a virus or that someone is using your credit cards or using your identity to obtain credit for themselves. Then you can take steps to defend against threats and recover from damage from threats.

Be suspicious of anything out of the ordinary on your computer. Any unusual computer event may indicate that a virus, some sort of browser hijack, or other form of spyware, adware, and so on has infected your computer. Signs to look for include:

- Strange screen messages.
- Sudden computer slowdown.
- Missing data.
- Inability to access the hard drive.

the-lightwriter/Getty Images

Similarly, unusual activity in any of your credit or savings accounts can indicate that you are a victim of identity theft, including:

- Charges on credit accounts that you are sure you or your family did not make.
- Calls from creditors about overdue payments on accounts you never opened.
- Being rejected when applying for new credit for reasons you know are not true.
- A credit bureau reports existing credit accounts you never opened.

Keep yourself informed by checking out reliable sources. ZDNet publishes articles on many technology topics. Just one of their regular security columns is the Zero Day blog, which gives an overview of the latest security-related news. Another good site for keeping up with security news is **www.schneier.com**.

Along with education about threats comes paranoia. However, if you use a computer at home, work, or school, and are on a network and/or the Internet, a touch of paranoia is healthy. Just don't let it distract you from your day-to-day tasks. Take proactive, responsible steps, as we outline here.

Paranoia 101: Don't Be a Victim

One important tool is a healthy skepticism (with a touch of paranoia) whenever you are online. Tech companies like Facebook, Google, and Amazon earn billions of dollars from your data without your permission and without compensation to you. Our goal here is to make you more aware of what you are giving away so that you can look for ways to avoid revealing too much about yourself.

Note: The use of your personal data hurts the economy because these tech companies, especially Facebook and Google, have relatively few employees, and therefore put very little back into the economy in the form of wages.

Nothing Is Free

Nothing is free, especially when it comes to online services, such as email and social media. Do you have a free email account with Google, Yahoo, Apple, or Microsoft? It isn't free. You are paying for it with your personal data. Some providers claim to use only the metadata. This is the data attached to the email identifying the source of the message and its destination. That data alone tells providers a lot about you and those with whom you communicate. Others don't stop at the metadata, but also scan the content of your email. Both types of data are used to target you with advertisements and other messages.

try this!

Social Media Data Breaches

Learn about the latest news involving personal data gathered through social media. Try this:

1. Open a Web browser and enter the search string, "social media data breach."
2. Skip the results that are clearly advertisements. In most browsers, ads are at the top of the list of results and identified by "Ad."
3. Look for links to recent articles and read several articles.
4. Discuss your findings, including any recent breaches and developments in laws to protect against data breaches or misuse of personal data.

Stay Safe and Connected: Avoid Illegal Online Activities

You may be thinking, "I don't do anything illegal online," but maybe your neighbor does. The author recently received an email from her Internet service provider (ISP) with the subject line "Illegal Downloading of Movies!—FBI WARNING." Before reading the message content, she simply shrugged her shoulders and thought, "I don't do that, so it doesn't affect me." However, once she read the message, she realized that she could be affected by others' behavior. The FBI tracks the illegal downloading of copyrighted materials, such as movies. Her ISP had received a notice of violation from the FBI that this activity was detected through the ISP's Internet connection. It is unclear at what point this ISP would be shut down by the FBI, but the threat was there. The email to customers included a reminder that this activity is against the Terms of Service we had agreed to, and that the ISP would terminate customers who violate it.

What Can You Do to Protect Yourself?

Look for security and privacy controls for your accounts. This includes email, social media, and any online service. Also, be more aware of free services, and consider if you truly need those services. If you decide you do, investigate purchasing an equivalent service. For instance, if you "rent" your own domain name, you can then pay for a hosting service to host your email. This has the added benefit of allowing you to have several email accounts linked to that domain name.

Freeze Your Credit. The most effective way to protect yourself against identity theft is to freeze your credit reports through each of the three major credit bureau: Equifax, Experian, and Transunion. This prevents anyone (including you) from opening a new account. You will need to temporarily unfreeze your account with each of these agencies whenever you plan to open a new credit account, but that is easy to do. To learn more, point your browser to https://www.ftc.gov/. When the site opens enter "freeze" in the search box. From the search results, select the article titled "What to Know about Credit Freezes and Fraud Alerts." Read the information under the topic "Credit Freezes" and then click the link to "three credit bureaus." Use the contact information on the resulting page to contact each one and freeze your credit.

Avoid Revealing Personal Information. Consider behavior modification. Your own behavior can make you vulnerable to data mining as well as to scams. Anytime you play a computer game online, enable apps within social media, or respond to online surveys (within social media or otherwise), you are providing data for someone, regardless of the security and privacy settings you may have for your various accounts. This is because you are voluntarily offering clues to your likes, dislikes, hobbies, friends, family connections, and more. It may be hard to resist responding to a simple question like, "What was your first car?" or "Do you remember this _____?" This second is usually accompanied by a photo of some obsolete tool or kitchen utensil. Responding to these questions adds more data points to the great database(s) in the cloud. Consider what you are revealing about yourself before you decide to participate in these services, survey, or games.

Resist Click Bait. Among all the distractions competing for our attention, click bait may be the most difficult to ignore, but you must try if you do not want to reveal more about yourself to persons unknown to you or risk inviting a malware infection.

Government Regulations

Slowly, governments are gaining some understanding of the threats to individuals and governments from the vast amounts of personal data collected without our permission or compensation. The European Commission's General Data Protection Regulation (GDPR) is one attempt to protect user data within the European Union (EU), as well as personal data exported from the EU. The United States Congress lags behind these efforts, but some legislation is in process.

Security Policies

Every organization should have a set of established security policies describing how they protect and manage sensitive information. Security policies define data sensitivity and data security practices, including security classifications of data, and who (usually based on job function) may have access to the various classes of data. For instance, a security policy may state, "Only server administrators and advanced technicians may access the server room, and must not give access to any other individuals." Security policies should also describe the consequences of breaking policy rules.

Security policies should exist in both document form and software form. For instance, at work or school, if you are logging into a network with a central login, such

WARNING!
A credit freeze is free or may require a one-time fee in some states. However, credit monitoring, which each service will offer under a different name, is often a fee-based service with ongoing charges. A credit freeze is preventative, while credit monitoring is after-the-fact, informing you that someone has opened an account in your name. You decide if you want any of the fee-based products.

Note: If you participate in social media in order to keep up with friends and family, consider adopting a "look, but don't click" approach.

Note: Password complexity requirements may state that a password must include a combination of both lowercase and uppercase alphabetical characters, numerals, punctuation, and math symbols.

as a Microsoft domain, administrators may configure the servers to enforce a password policy that accepts only strong passwords. How they define a strong password depends on the settings selected, such as minimum password length or complexity. In addition, they may require that you create a new password every month, and that you cannot repeat any of the previous 10 passwords.

Windows has security policies implemented from the domain level on the computers as well as on the users that log on to the domain. Windows also has a local security policy that affects the local computer and users, but can be overridden by domain policy when the computer and user are logged on to a Windows domain. The Local Security Policy console shown in Figure 2–6 allows an administrator to set local security policy. This is an advanced task.

Firewalls

A firewall is either software or a physical device that examines network traffic. Based on predefined rules, a firewall rejects certain traffic coming into a computer or network. The two general types of firewalls are network-based hardware firewalls and personal software firewalls that reside on individual computers. We recommend that you always have a reliable personal firewall installed, even if your computer is behind a hardware firewall. An attack can be from another computer behind the firewall, and that is when your personal firewall becomes your last line of defense between your computer and the world. Let's look at these two general types of firewalls.

Network-Based Firewalls

A network-based firewall is a hardware device designed to protect you against the dangers of having an unprotected connection to the Internet. It sits between a private network and the Internet (or other network) and examines all traffic in and out of the network it is protecting. It will block any traffic it recognizes as a potential threat, using a variety of techniques. Your ISP and most corporations employ hardware firewalls, expensive and specialized devices manufactured by companies such as Cisco, Palo Alto Networks, Fortinet, and others, and these sophisticated firewalls require highly trained people to manage them. Such a firewall probably protects the network at work or at school.

At home or in a small office, most people have a consumer-grade hardware firewall that comes in a small device that performs many of the same functions performed by a more professional-grade firewall. The most common name for these devices is broadband router or cable/DSL router. They combine the function of a firewall, a router (a device that "routes" traffic from one network to another), an Ethernet

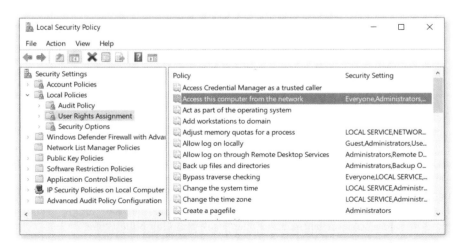

FIGURE 2–6 The Windows Local Security Policy console.
Source: Microsoft Corporation

switch, and a wireless access point all in one small box. This inexpensive device can handle the traffic of just a few computers, while the more serious devices employed by ISPs and large organizations can handle thousands of simultaneous high-speed transmissions. The consumer-grade devices now come with the "one button" configuration that automatically configures a simple connection to the Internet, with the latest security turned on. You can access the built-in Web page of your wireless access point to make manual changes to the settings. Figure 2-7 shows the Web page of an ASUS Wireless Router.

The firewall administrator configures a firewall to allow traffic into the private network or prohibit traffic from entering the private network based on the types of computers residing within the private network, and how they will interact with the Internet. If all the computers on a private network are desktop computers that connect to the Internet to browse Web pages and access FTP sites, the firewall protecting the network has a simple job. It simply blocks all in-bound traffic that is not the result of a request from a computer on the internal network; it matches incoming traffic with previous outgoing traffic that made requests that would result in incoming traffic. Then, when you connect to a website, outgoing traffic from your computer to the website requests to see a page. That page comes to you as incoming traffic and a firewall will allow it through based on your initial request.

If the private network includes servers that offer services on the Internet, then the firewall must allow initiating traffic to come through, but it does not allow all incoming traffic through. In this case, an administrator configures a firewall to allow incoming traffic of the type that can only communicate with the internally based servers. The various types of traffic include email, Web, FTP, and others. Each type of traffic has a certain characteristic the firewall can recognize. Figure 2-8 shows a firewall protecting a network containing both servers and desktop computers (shown as clients).

A network professional would look at the simplified example of a firewall shown in Figure 2-8 and immediately talk about setting up a DMZ, named for a wartime demilitarized zone. In networking, a DMZ is a network between a private (inside) network and public (outside) network. An organization puts any servers that offer services to the Internet in the DMZ.

Note: A server created as a decoy to draw malware attacks and gather information about attackers is called a **honey pot**. A honey pot may be located outside a corporate firewall, within a DMZ, or inside the corporate network.

FIGURE 2–7 The Web page of an ASUS Wireless Router's configuration utility.
Source: ASUSTek Computer Inc.

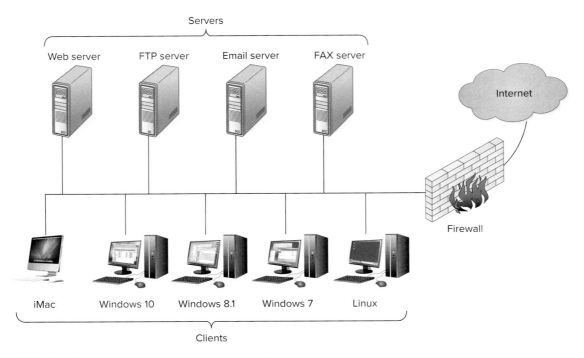

FIGURE 2–8 A private network protected by a firewall.

Personal Firewalls

Because many attacks come from within a private network, personal firewalls have become standard. The Windows Defender Firewall is included in Windows. macOS comes with a firewall, and there are many third-party firewalls for Windows, macOS, and Linux. There are two places where you can configure the Windows Firewall. One is the Windows Defender Firewall Control Panel, shown in Figure 2–9. Using the links in the pane on the left, you can make changes to the Firewall.

A more advanced configuration tool is Windows Defender Firewall with Advanced Security, a Microsoft Management console shown in Figure 2–10. Access this tool by clicking on Advanced Settings in the Windows Defender Firewall Control Panel.

Note: If a third-party firewall is installed, the Windows Defender Firewall will be disabled and the applet will show you a message stating. These settings are being managed by vendor application *name of firewall.*

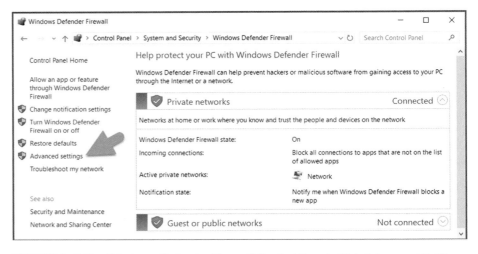

FIGURE 2–9 The Windows Defender Firewall Control Panel. Click Advanced Settings to make changes.
Source: Microsoft Corporation

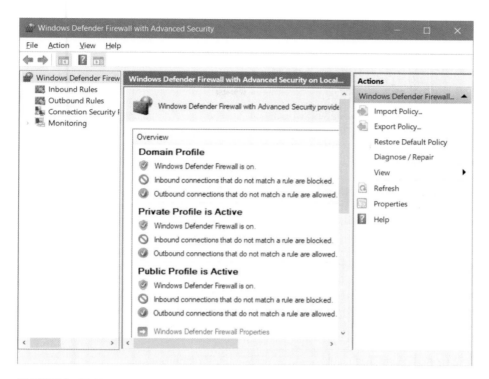

FIGURE 2–10 Windows Defender Firewall with Advanced Security.
Source: Microsoft Corporation

Security Software

A logical progression through the appropriate defense against computer security threats would have us look at authentication and authorization at this point. However, because we include activities that require that you access the Internet, we will first talk about the comprehensive security software that should be in place before you connect to the Internet. This does not mean that security software is more important than authentication and authorization. They are all important pieces of every security defense strategy.

Comprehensive security software may come in one bundle of software from one source, or it can be separate software from many sources. The pieces should include (at minimum) a personal firewall, antivirus software, anti-spam software, and an email scanner. Figure 2–11 shows the console for Bitdefender with security components and various tools for managing the security package. The following sections will describe security components included with common security software.

Antispam Software

A spam filter is software designed to combat spam by examining incoming email messages and filtering out those that have characteristics of spam, including certain identified keywords. In an organization with centralized network and computer management, spam filter software installed on central mail servers can remove spam before it gets to a user's desktop. Network administrators may use Internet-based spam filtering services that block spam before it reaches the corporate network.

Individuals connected to the Internet from home or in small businesses are often on their own when it comes to eliminating spam. Luckily, many email clients, such as Microsoft Outlook, offer spam filtering. Without a spam filter you must sort through your own email to find and delete the spam. Spam filters are not perfect—they can filter out legitimate messages, while allowing some spam messages through. For this reason, most spam filters require some configuration on the part of the user using

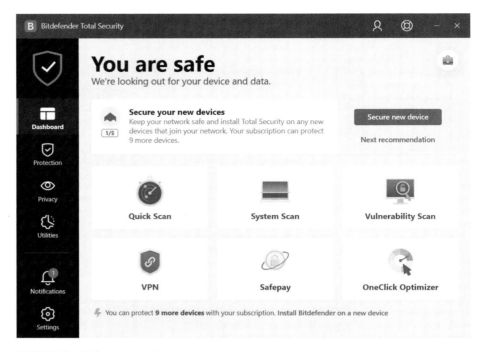

FIGURE 2–11 Security software with many bundled components.
Source: Bitdefender

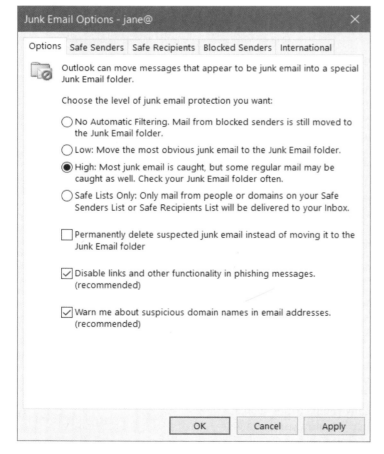

FIGURE 2–12 The Outlook Junk Email Options page.
Source: Microsoft Corporation

rules or filters that will automate the process of removing spam from known sources. And the user will still often need to review a list of suspected spam messages. Figure 2–12 shows the Microsoft Outlook Junk Email Options dialog box with several tabbed pages of settings that allow you to configure the spam filter.

Antivirus Software

An antivirus program can examine the contents of a storage device or RAM looking for hidden viruses and files that may act as hosts for virus code. Effective antivirus products not only detect and remove viruses, but they also help you recover data that has been lost because of a virus. To remain current, they require frequent updating as to the virus threats to watch for. An antivirus program includes an antivirus engine (the main program) and a set of patterns of recognized viruses, usually contained in files called definition files. Retailers of antivirus software commonly charge an annual fee for updates to the antivirus engine and the definition files. There are excellent free services for home users. One example is AVG antivirus from GRIsoft. Software companies that offer free security software usually also offer a feature-rich commercial version to which you can upgrade for a fee. The free version gives you a chance to see if you like using it before you put out any money. Once installed, most antivirus programs will automatically connect to the manufacturer's website and check for these updates.

Pop-Up Blockers

Many free and commercial programs are available that effectively block various forms of adware, especially pop-ups, which are the easiest to block and the most annoying because a pop-up advertisement appears in its own window and must be closed or moved before you can see the content you were seeking. A program that works against pop-ups is a **pop-up blocker**, and all major Web browsers now have built-in pop-up blockers.

We have found a few websites where blocking all pop-ups has blocked much of the content we were seeking. In that case, we may configure the pop-up blocker to make an exception for that site. You can enable the pop-up blocker feature for the Microsoft Edge browser in Settings, Site Permissions. Turn on the pop-up blocker for the Google Chrome browser by opening Settings, Privacy and Security, Site settings, Content Settings. The Pop-ups setting is one of many listed there, as shown in Figure 2–13.

To configure the pop-up blocker in Firefox, open Options and select the Content tab, where you will find the setting to turn the pop-up blocker off or on. You can also open the Exceptions dialog for Firefox, and add any website where you wish to enable pop-ups.

Note: The most important browser settings are often a few layers down in the Settings dialog for that browser. Be sure to explore these settings.

Note: We will explore and compare browser settings in Chapter 9.

Privacy Protection and Cookies

Web browsers and security programs offer privacy protection options. In Microsoft Internet Explorer, you can configure privacy settings, through the Internet Options dialog box, accessible from either the Control Panel or the Tools menu in Internet Explorer. This is also where you determine how Internet Explorer handles cookies. The settings range from "Block all cookies" to "Allow all cookies," with a variety of settings in between. Experiment with the settings by choosing one and then spending some time browsing the Internet. The balance here is between the convenience of cookies for automated login to frequently accessed sites and the risk of an invasion of privacy. We recommend that you allow first-party cookies for the convenience (explained earlier) and block third-party cookies because the tracking methods often associated with third-party cookies are an invasion of privacy.

Family Sharing and Microsoft Family

The feature for protecting children from inappropriate content in Apple products is Family Sharing. Family Sharing offers many protections. Figure 2-14 shows the initial Family Sharing setup screen. With a Microsoft account you can take advantage of a similar service called Microsoft family. Both the Apple and Microsoft services allow

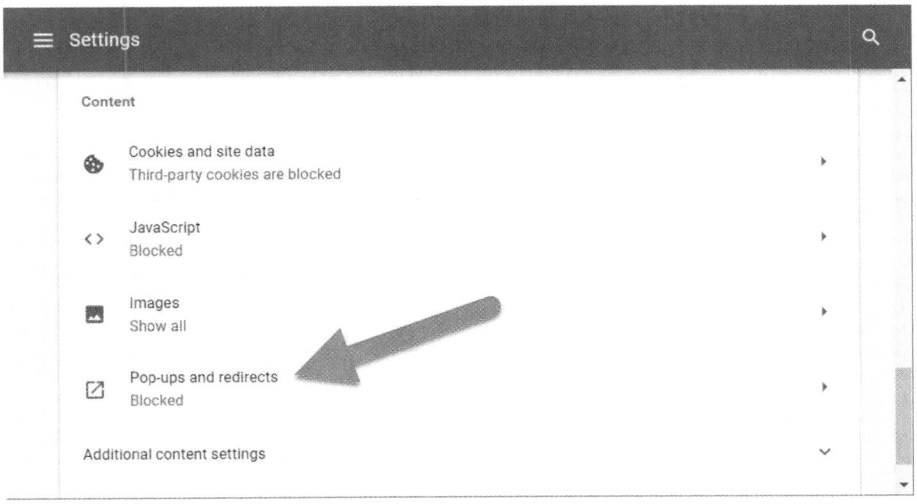

FIGURE 2–13 The Chrome Pop-Up Blocker setting.
Source: Google Chrome

FIGURE 2–14 Apple's Family Sharing setup screen.
Source: Apple Inc.

you to either create new accounts for family members or invite someone with a Microsoft or Apple account to join your family. You can protect children in your family by creating activity reporting, screen time limits, and content restrictions.

Content Filtering

You can use software that blocks content, called a content filter, to enable protection from inappropriate or distasteful content. A common type of content filter used on the Internet is a Web content filter, a software program designed to work with a Web browser either to block certain sites or to allow only certain sites. As with most types of software, you can find both free and commercial versions of Web content filters on the Internet. In fact, you may already have a Web content filter in your Web browser that you only need to enable and configure.

Many services are available on the Internet to evaluate website content and give each site ratings based on such parameters as language, nudity, sex, and violence. A content filter may use one or more of these rating services, and allow the administrator to choose the rating level to permit or exclude. Not all websites are rated, so if you enable a Web content filter, you will also have to decide what it should do in the event the user connects to an unrated site.

Software Updates

You should be sure to keep your operating system and applications up to date with security patches. Microsoft

try this!

View the Windows Update History

You can see the update history on your Windows computer. Try this:

1. In Windows 10 open *Settings* and select *Update & Security*.
2. In *Windows Update* select *View update history*.
3. Updates are organized under *Feature Updates, Quality Updates, Driver Updates, Definition Updates,* and *Other Updates*.
4. Scroll through the various updates and then close the page.

continues to update their software for several years and Windows automatically checks for the updates that plug security holes that malware perpetrators exploit. Windows keeps a list of all the updates installed on your computer, as shown in Figure 2–15.

Authentication and Authorization

One of the first defenses against threats is authentication and authorization by a security system built into the operating systems on your local computer and on network servers. The OSs surveyed in this book support authentication and authorization. In fact, Linux, Windows, and macOS require it.

Consider this scenario. After you, as the administrator, have set up an account for Rachel in accounting she must enter her username and password when she logs on to her computer. Before giving her access to the computer, security components of her operating system will verify that she used a valid user name and password. This validation of the user account and password is authentication.

A recently hired part-time clerk, Kirsten, works at night entering accounts payable information into Rachel's computer. To allow Kirsten to also log on to Rachel's computer, you can create a new user account for Kirsten. Although only Rachel and Kirsten can log on to this computer, Rachel does not want Kirsten to be able to access the payroll information, also stored there, because this is private information. What might you do to help Rachel with this problem? One thing you could do (if her operating system supports it) is to set up Rachel's computer so that she can assign special permissions to the files and folders on her hard disk, giving each user account the level of permission it needs. For instance, one of Kirsten's tasks is to add accounting information to the accounts payable files, so you could give Kirsten's account the authorization that will allow her to write to the files in the accounts payable folder.

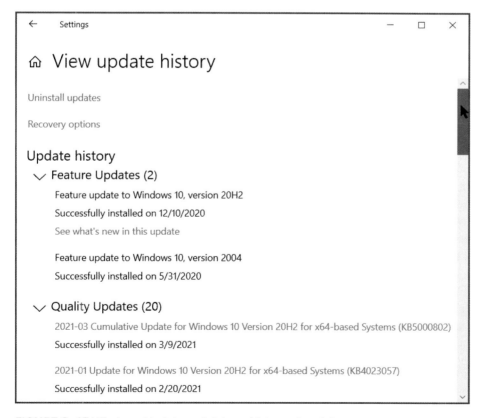

FIGURE 2–15 Windows Update maintains a history of updates.
Source: Microsoft Corporation

You will not give Kirsten's account access to any of the other folders, and you will only give Rachel's account full control of the folders that she needs to use.

Authentication

Note: There are several authenticator apps by Google, Microsoft, Apple, and others.

Authentication is the verification of who you are. Authentication may be one-factor, two-factor, or even three-factor. One-factor authentication is your use of a user name and password as you log on to your computer. In this case, you are authenticated based on something you know—your user name and password. One type of two-factor authentication involves the use of something you know plus something you have, referred to as a token. If you use a cash card at an ATM, you are familiar with two-factor authentication, because the something you know is your PIN (personal identification number) code, while the token is your cash card. Another type of two-factor authentication, common with many online services today, requires your authentication with a username and password followed by the service sending a one-time authentication code via a method you previously agreed to, such as a text message to your smartphone or the use of an authenticator app. For even more security, consider three-factor authentication, adding biometric data, such as a retinal scan, voice print, or fingerprint scan to the token and password.

Automatic Login

Right about now you're thinking that we're wrong about Windows and macOS requiring authentication. Your computer is running the latest version of Windows or macOS but you don't have to enter a username or password to access your desktop and all your personal settings and data. So, obviously, you are not authenticated. Right? Wrong! Windows, macOS, and Linux always require authentication, but each has a feature called automatic login that the OS installation program system turns on under certain circumstances, such as when you bring home a PC or Mac that you just bought in a retail store. Automatic login authenticates anyone who powers up your computer using the same credentials, and they have access to everything that you normally do. You should never enable automatic login on a computer at school or at work.

Authorization

Authorization determines the level of access to a computer or a resource (files, folders, printers, and so on) to an authenticated user. Authorization includes authentication plus verification of your level of access to a computer or resource, including permissions and/or user rights. When you connect to a shared folder on your LAN, the security system of the computer hosting the folder will perform authorization, authenticating you and verifying that your account has some level of access to the folder. This level of access is called a permission. Permission describes an action that you may perform on an object. An example of a permission found on a file system is the read permission that allows reading of the contents of a file or folder, but by itself it does not allow any other action on that file, such as deleting or changing it. Another component that affects level of access is a user right. A user right defines a system-wide action that a user or group may perform such as logging on to a computer or installing device drivers.

Passwords

WARNING!

A blank password (literally no password) or one written on a sticky note and kept handy near a computer provides no security. Always insist on nonblank passwords, and do not write down your passwords and leave them where others can find them.

The most common method of authentication is the use of a password and an identifier, such as a user name. A password is an important piece of the security puzzle. Don't take your password for granted. In fact, password should be plural, because you should use a unique password for every account, and you should put a great deal of thought into creating passwords that truly help you protect yourself. This is important because, secure authentication is your basic defense against an invasion of your privacy, and your password is central to having secure authentication. Most experts recommend using passwords that are at least eight characters long and that contain a mixture of numbers, letters (both uppercase and lowercase), and nonalphanumeric characters.

It's easy to guess passwords that use common words—such as the name of a pet—and therefore they offer little in the way of real security.

Establish a method for creating strong passwords—whether it is some scheme that you think up or software that helps you create these passwords. Begin by thinking of a phrase that is easy to remember such as: "I love the Boston Red Sox." Then take the first letter of each word in that phrase and string the letters together. In our example, the result is: iltbrs. Now turn it into a more complex password by capitalizing some of the alpha characters and inserting numbers and other symbols between the letters: i-l,T.b+r-s. If this meets the minimum password requirements, you have a password. Now, the trick is to remember this password without the use of sticky notes!

A great alternative to "do-it-yourself" password creating is to use password management software. A password manager will create strong passwords, remember them for you, and even insert the correct password when you need it. Secure the password manager itself with a single strong password. Use a single password manager, such as Dashlane or LastPass, to manage the passwords across all your devices. You can also use your browser as your password manager. Figure 2–16 shows the passwords settings page for Microsoft Edge.

Use unique and complex passwords.
Zmeel Photography/iStockphoto

Best Practices with Passwords and Accounts

You may actually have habits that make you vulnerable to identity theft or another type of attack on your computer, data, or personal information. Consider the following questions:

- Do you have too many passwords to remember?
- When you have an opportunity to create a new password, do you use your favorite password—the one that you use everywhere?

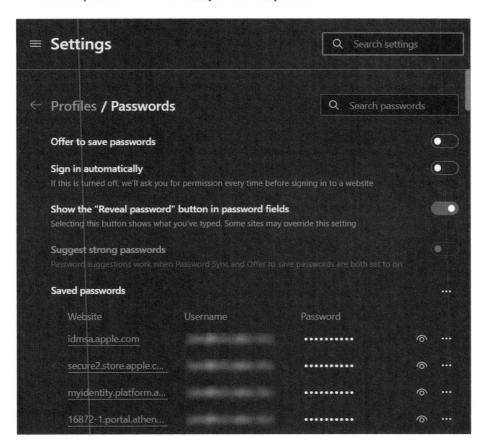

FIGURE 2–16 The passwords settings page for the Microsoft Edge browser.
Source: Microsoft Corporation.

- At school or work, do you have your password written on sticky notes or your desk calendar?
- Have you used the same password for more than a few months?

If you can answer yes to any of these questions, you are at risk! And the risk is not only with your password. Because many websites allow you to provide a user name to use when you log in, you may also be reusing the same user name and password combination. Now a hacker doesn't even have to guess your account name.

Create Strong Passwords. A strong password is one that meets certain criteria, and these criteria change over time as hackers create more techniques and tools for discovering passwords. An administrator should have a password that is a minimum of 15 characters long. Additionally, a strong password includes a combination of letters, numbers, and other symbols, as allowed by the security system accepting the password. Common sense requires that your personal password should be easy for you to remember, but difficult for others to guess.

Always use strong passwords for the following types of accounts:

- Banks, investments, credit cards, and online payment providers.
- Email.
- Work-related accounts.
- Online auction sites and retailers.
- Sites where you have provided personal information.

Avoid Creating Unnecessary Online Accounts. Many websites ask that you create an account and join, but what are the benefits of joining? Why do they need information about you?

try this!

Get Help Creating Passwords

There are programs that will help you create passwords. While we strongly recommend that you come up with your own method to create and remember strong passwords, it is helpful to see some strong passwords. Try this:

1. Open your browser and connect to your favorite search engine. Search on "random password generator" (without the quotation marks).
2. Select a password generator from the results list and experiment.
3. For instance, the password generator at **www.randomlists.com/random-password** allows you to define the password rules and then, after you click the Generate Password button, it will generate a password that complies with the rules.
4. Try creating a password, but do not use one you generated in this fashion. Rather, devise your own scheme for creating secure passwords. Then you are more likely to remember your password.

Don't Provide More Information Than Necessary. Avoid creating accounts with websites that request your Social Security number and other personal and financial information. Avoid having your credit card numbers and bank account information stored on a website. Although it's not easy to do online, you can do this with a merchant in person: If asked for your Social Security number, ask these four questions:

1. Why do you need it?
2. How will you protect it?
3. How will you use it?
4. What happens if I don't give it to you?

You may have to make a decision as to whether to do business with that merchant if you don't receive satisfactory answers.

Security Account Basics

A security account is an account that can be assigned permission to take action on an object (such as a file, folder, or printer) or the right to take some action on an entire system, such as install device drivers into an operating system on a computer. A security account may identify a single entity (individual or computer) or a group of entities. Security accounts exist in security databases, such as those maintained by UNIX or

Linux systems, macOS desktop and server OSs, and Windows server and desktop operating systems.

User Accounts

All operating systems discussed in this book have robust security that begins with using user and group accounts and the requirement to log in to the computer with a user account. The most common type of security account is an individual account, called a user account, assigned to a single person. In the security database on each device, a user account contains, at minimum, a user name and password used to authenticate a user. Depending on the structure of the security accounts database, a user account may contain additional identifying information. Typically, a user account will include the user's full name, a description, and a variety of other fields including email address, department, phone numbers, and so on.

Built-In User Accounts

Each OS has a very special, very privileged built-in account—a super user—that can perform virtually all tasks on a computer, from installing a device driver to creating other security accounts. In Windows this privileged built-in user is Administrator, and it is disabled by default. In those operating systems with their ancestry in UNIX, such as macOS and Linux, root is the most powerful user account, as it is in UNIX. We'll discuss these accounts in the appropriate chapters.

At the other end of the privilege spectrum, we have a guest account, found in Windows, macOS, and Linux. This account is the least privileged and is disabled by default in Windows. If this account is enabled, a stranger can log in with the account (usually with no password), but cannot see anyone else's files and cannot make changes to the system.

Standard versus Administrator Accounts

Linux and the versions of Windows and the other operating systems featured in this book all have the notion of types of user accounts. In Windows, a standard user account is for an "ordinary" user without administrator status. A Windows child account is basically a standard account with the additional restrictions applied through Microsoft family. A user logged on with a standard account can change their password and other personal settings, but cannot change computer settings, install or remove software and hardware, or perform other system-wide tasks. In contrast, a user logged on with an account that is an administrator account type can perform system-wide tasks that affect the overall operating system and other users. For example, an administrator can create new users, change user settings, install applications and operating system components, install hardware (and the drivers for that hardware), and access all files on a computer. Ignoring the built-in, but disabled, Administrator account, the first account created in any of these systems must be an administrator account type, and then you may use this account to create additional accounts. When an administrator creates a new account, the default type is Standard.

In macOS, there is a check box in the Accounts dialog for a user: the "Allow user to administer this computer" check box, shown in Figure 2–17. If this is checked, the user account is an administrator account; if it is unchecked, the account is a standard account. As with the Windows administrator accounts, a macOS administrator account can install programs and do a range of system-wide tasks. A macOS standard user is limited much as a Windows standard user is.

The administrator type of account in Linux includes the all-powerful root, and some other accounts, but the standard account type is not as clear. For instance, "standard user" is the term used to describe the long list of accounts some distributions will create automatically if you choose a special installation. Since this includes the root account and others with a wide range of permissions, it is not the same as the standard type of account used in Windows and macOS.

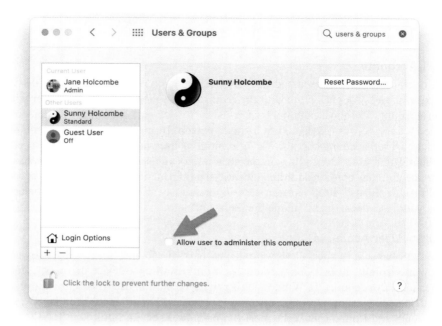

FIGURE 2–17 Select this check box to change a standard user to an administrator in macOS.
Source: Apple Inc.

Group Accounts

A group account is a security account that contains one or more individual accounts, and, in some security accounts databases, may contain other groups. Group accounts allow us to manage resources for multiple users and make administration of accounts much easier. Group accounts exist in the security accounts databases of all the OSs discussed here— some are built in and privileged users can create others. We will concern ourselves only with those groups that exist in the security accounts database on a desktop computer and not with the security accounts that exist on a network server, such as a Windows Domain Controller. We call the accounts on a desktop computer local user and group accounts. The built-in local groups in Windows include Administrators, Users, and Guests, but other groups are created for various services and applications as they install into Windows. Figure 2–18 shows the Local Users and Groups node of the Computer Management console, an advanced tool for managing users and groups in Windows.

Computer Accounts

Computers (and sometimes devices) may also have security accounts within a security accounts database maintained by a network server, such as in a Microsoft Windows Active Directory domain. This means your computer actually joins a domain before you, as a user, can log on to the network. When this occurs, new group accounts appear in the accounts database on your desktop Windows computer as it integrates into the domain. The details of this relationship are beyond the scope of this book, but be aware that this is the case if your computer is part of a Windows Active Directory Domain. How could this affect you? If you bring your personal laptop to the office, you will not be able to log on to the corporate network in the same way that you do from your desktop until an administrator makes your computer a member of the domain. If it's not desirable to join your personal laptop to the network, there are other methods to give you access to the corporate network.

Best Practices When Assigning Permissions

The most important practice in assigning permissions to accounts in any operating system is to use the rule of least privilege. Give permissions to each user or group that allows

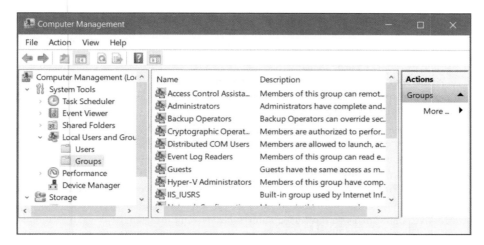

FIGURE 2–18 The Local Users and Groups node in Computer Management showing all groups on the local Windows 10 computer.
Source: Microsoft Corporation

each user the amount of access required to complete assigned tasks, but do not give users more access than required. Thus, the user has the least privileges necessary to function.

Encryption

Encryption is the transformation of data into an unreadable format (cipher text) that you can decrypt (decipher) only by using a secret key or password. A secret key is a special code used to decrypt encrypted data. You can encrypt data you are sending over a network. In addition, you can encrypt data files that are stored on a local computer or network server. Encryption protects sensitive or valuable data and only someone who knows the password or holds the secret key can decrypt the data back to its original state. The secret key may be held in a digital certificate (also called a security certificate, or simply a certificate), which is a file stored on a computer.

Encrypting Network Traffic

Without being aware, you participate in encrypting network traffic when you do online banking or shopping. Look at the address line and you will see the protocol prefix "http" replaced by "https." This means that you are now using Secure HTTP (HTTPS), which encrypts the communications between you and the bank or e-commerce server. HTTPS uses the Secure Sockets Layer (SSL) security protocol. For this encryption method, the user certificates contain identifying information used for verifying the holder of the certificate (your bank or the online retailer), including the holder's public key for use in encrypting a message for the user. Only the user holds the private key to decrypt the message. Your Web browser and its security protocols manage it all for you. If the browser detects a problem with a certificate as a page is loading, you will receive a warning that a website's security certificate is invalid. You should not continue loading the page and should block this website via your browser's security settings.

Encrypting Files

Encryption is very useful for data stored on a laptop or in professional settings, where data theft is a concern. In later chapters we will explore data encryption options.

Data Wiping

When you move computers from user to user or remove a computer from service within an organization and sell it or give it away, you should remove the data on the computer. This goes beyond a simple delete operation, because there are many methods for "undeleting" such files. To be sure that a determined person will not access your old files, you must remove them completely. The permanent removal of data from a storage device is data wiping.

A reformat of the hard drive is one method, but it's not truly very secure, and it's a problem if you wanted to keep the operating system and programs on the disk. Another method is to use data wiping software that uses an algorithm for writing over an entire drive volume, or just those portions of a drive that contain data—whether it has been deleted or not. You can perform data wiping on any storage media that is rewritable, including hard drives, optical drives, and solid-state storage. Both free and commercial data wiping programs will do the trick for most purposes. Such programs are available for all storage types. Those written for hard drives can take advantage of a government-approved ability built in to newer hard drives—Secure Erase. You cannot recover data once you have used such a data-wiping program.

Physical Security

Physical security of computers and networks is yet another huge topic that we can only touch on here. Physical security for desktop computers and networks includes limiting who has access to the building or room in which the desktop computers or network servers reside. Physical security is part of a school or other organization's security policy, and that policy must define its implementation. Small organizations often simply rely on the trustworthiness of their employees—with mixed results—while larger organizations implement formal physical security protection. This can include a mode of identifying someone trying to get entry to a building or room. This mode can be a guarded entrance with confirmation of a person's credentials, key card access, or a variety of other methods depending on the security needs of the organization.

Security for Mobile Computing

In addition to the practices outlined above as defenses against threats, special considerations are required when traveling with laptops or other mobile computing devices. We will discuss specific security options for mobile devices in Chapter 10.

LO 2.3 | Troubleshooting Common Security Problems

Most problems have a simple cause, and that is as true with security problems as it is with most computer-related tasks. Therefore, when troubleshooting any problem, you should first ask yourself, "What is the simplest (dumbest?) thing that could cause this problem?" The second question should be, "What has changed?" These two questions will keep you from going off in a panic looking for a high-tech solution before at least considering one or more simple solutions. In this section, we discuss some common security problems we have encountered and our recommended solutions.

Troubleshooting Log-On Problems

There are certain nearly universal log-on problems. They include the following.

Caps Lock Key Turned On

Everyone does it! You're in a hurry, and when you type in your user name and password, you don't notice the placement of your hands and one or both of them are incorrect. You receive an error message indicating that the user name or password is incorrect, as in Figure 2–19. No problem; you type it in again, but don't notice that you have the Caps Lock on. Some operating systems, including Windows, will warn you of this, but other operating systems will not. Therefore, be careful about the placement of your hands and ensure that Caps Lock is off before entering your user name and password.

Too Many Log-On Attempts

On a bad day, like your first day back at work after a vacation, you may try several times before you enter the password correctly. If you're logging on to a corporate network, it is counting all these tries and you may exceed a limit on the number of log-on attempts. This limit is part of account policies, a set of rules established by a server administrator. Exceeding the number of log-on attempts (account lockout threshold) may result in your user account being locked out of the computer and the network for a period of time (account lockout duration), and you will see a message similar to that in Figure 2-20. There is usually a third parameter used for account lockout duration: the period of time after which the counter for the number of log-on attempts resets to zero.

If a message like this appears when you are trying to log on to a network at school or work, you will have to call an administrator for help. An administrator may be able to override the lockout so that you can try again. Type carefully this time!

If no administrator is available, you will have to wait for the account lockout time to expire. An administrator configures these settings, usually to comply with a company's security standard (see Figure 2-21). So, it could be a matter of minutes, or it could even be days! Although at the time it can be a huge inconvenience, this is your protection against password crackers, who may need to make many tries before they guess the correct password.

FIGURE 2–19 Log-on error message.
Source: Microsoft Corporation

FIGURE 2–20 Log-on lockout message.
Source: Microsoft Corporation

FIGURE 2–21 The Windows Account Lockout policy, with settings for lockout duration, threshold, and a period of time after which the counter resets.
Source: Microsoft Corporation

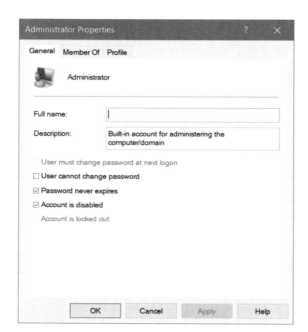

FIGURE 2–22 The Properties dialog box for the Administrator account shows it is disabled by default.
Source: Microsoft Corporation

Using the Administrator Account in Troubleshooting

Windows has an administrator account, named Administrator. It is disabled by default, as shown in Figure 2–22. The Administrator account is enabled if your computer starts in Safe Mode and if the computer is not a member of a Windows Active Directory domain. In this case, you can log on with this account and attempt to troubleshoot the reason for the computer going into Safe Mode.

Troubleshooting a Suspected Malware Attack

If you suspect a computer is infected by a virus and you have an antivirus program installed, first use it to run a scan of all drives and memory to see if you can discover and remove the virus. If this does not discover a virus but you are still suspicious, or if you do not have an up-to-date antivirus program installed, you can connect to one of many websites that offer free online scans. An online virus scanner does not fully install, so it should not conflict with your installed security software. Just one example of such a scanner is Housecall, found at **housecall.trendmicro.com**. This scanner is by Trend Micro, which also offers a commercial security suite.

Step-by-Step 2.02

Perform an Online Virus Scan on a PC or Mac

Try one of the online virus scanners. These steps require either a Windows computer or a Mac with a Web browser and a connection to the Internet. Use the online scanner at Trend Micro, or one recommended by your instructor.

Step 1

Open your browser and connect to **housecall.trendmicro.com**. Ensure that you are at this website, and were not redirected to one of the many download sites that entice you to download and install questionable software.

Step 2

On the Trend Micro HouseCall page, select the button for the OS you are using. Then respond to the prompts to download the Housecall Launcher app. With Windows you may be prompted to select a location for the file. We recommend the local Downloads folder. In macOS it will automatically be saved in the Downloads folder.

Source: Trend Micro Incorporated

Step 3

If you are using a Mac, skip to Step 4. On a Windows computer, when the download is complete, open the location and double-click to start the Housecall Launcher. It starts the installation process. If a User Account Control message displays, click the Yes button to continue. Skip to Step 5.

Step 4

On a Mac the file is a disk image, "Housecall.dmg." Click this to open the dialog shown here. Drag the HouseCall icon to the Applications folder. Then launch it from the Applications folder. Respond to the prompt to Open the app and then provide your password to allow the installation.

Source: Trend Micro Incorporated

Step 5

In both Windows and macOS, respond to the prompts for the licensing agreement until the app opens.

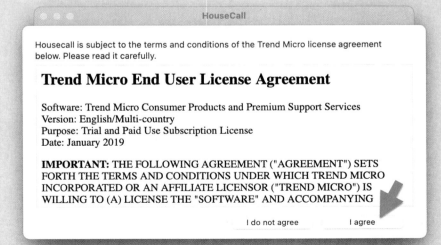

Source: Trend Micro Incorporated

Step 6

Follow the on-screen instructions to run the scan. The Windows House-Call is shown here, and the macOS version is shown below it. Select the Scan Now button.

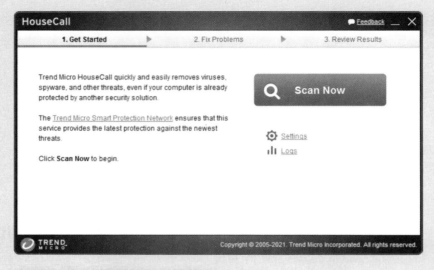

Source: Trend Micro Incorporated

Step 7

When finished, the results dialog box displays. Both the Windows and macOS versions are shown here. Close the window after viewing the results.

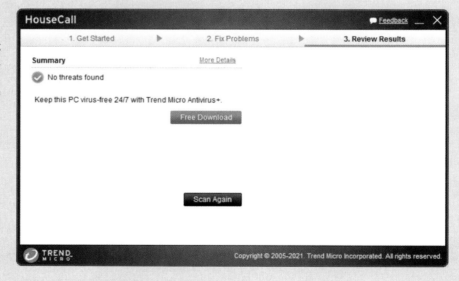

Source: Trend Micro Incorporated

Chapter Summary

After reading this chapter and completing the exercises, you should understand the following facts about computer security.

Threats to Computers and Users

- Threats include a long list of intentional and unintentional actions from malware through accidents and natural disasters.
- A vector is the method that malware uses to infect a computer.
- The people behind computer security threats come from all over the world, and increasingly they are part of terrorist groups and organized crime.
- Many methods are used to steal passwords, including capturing them from unsecured websites, using password crackers, and keystroke loggers.

Defense Against Threats

- Education is an important defense against threats. Know what the threats are and learn the signs of a threat or an infection.
- Don't be a victim. Nothing is free. Don't reveal personal information online. Resist click bait.
- Security policies describe how an organization protects and manages sensitive information.
- Install security software, including personal firewalls, antispam software, antivirus software, and pop-up and privacy protection.

- Keep your software up to date with security patches.
- Improve your security with authentication and authorization.
- Combat threats with the rule of least privilege when assigning permissions and using best practices with passwords.
- Encryption technologies protect your data.
- Data wiping practices can remove even deleted data from computers.
- Physical security of computers and networks is important, especially for mobile computing.

Troubleshooting Common Security Problems

- Log-on failure may be the result of something as simple as having the Caps Lock key turned on. You will be locked out if you exceed the number of failed log-on attempts configured in the Account Lockout policy.
- Windows has an administrator account, "Administrator," which is disabled by default. It is enabled if your computer is not a member of a Windows Active Directory domain and if it starts in Safe Mode. In the latter case, log on with this account and attempt to troubleshoot the reason for the computer going into Safe Mode.
- If you suspect a computer is infected by a virus, run a scan of all drives and memory.

Key Terms List

administrator account type *(67)*	cookies *(49)*	firewall *(56)*
adware *(44)*	cybercrime *(38)*	first-party cookie *(49)*
authentication *(64)*	cybercriminal *(51)*	forged email address *(46)*
authorization *(64)*	cyberterrorism *(52)*	fraud *(45)*
back door *(40)*	cyberterrorist *(52)*	group account *(68)*
black hat hacker *(52)*	data wiping *(70)*	guest account *(67)*
bluesnarfing *(41)*	digital certificate *(69)*	hacker *(52)*
bot herder *(44)*	DMZ *(57)*	header *(46)*
botnet *(44)*	drive-by download *(40)*	honey pot *(57)*
browser hijacking *(44)*	email spoofing *(46)*	hotspot *(40)*
click bait *(38)*	encryption *(69)*	identify theft *(46)*
content filter *(62)*	exploit *(42)*	keylogger *(41)*

keystroke logger *(41)*	secret key *(69)*	third-party cookie *(49)*
malware *(38)*	Secure HTTP (HTTPS) *(69)*	token *(64)*
password *(41)*	Secure Sockets Layer (SSL) *(69)*	Trojan horse *(39)*
password cracker *(41)*	security account *(66)*	user account *(67)*
password manager *(65)*	shoulder surfing *(49)*	user right *(64)*
permission *(64)*	social engineering *(45)*	vector *(38)*
phishing *(45)*	social media *(38)*	virus *(43)*
pop-up *(40)*	social networking *(38)*	war driving *(41)*
pop-up blocker *(61)*	spam *(44)*	white hat hacker *(52)*
pop-up download *(40)*	spam filter *(59)*	worm *(43)*
ransomware *(45)*	spear phishing *(46)*	zero-day exploit *(42)*
robocall *(45)*	spim *(45)*	zombie *(44)*
rootkit *(40)*	spyware *(44)*	
scareware *(39)*	standard user account *(67)*	

Key Terms Quiz

Use the Key Terms List to complete the sentences that follow. Not all terms will be used.

1. A/an _____ defines what a user or group can do to an object such as a file or folder.

2. Programs on a website may send very small text files called _____ to a Web browser, along with a request that the Web browser save the file on the user's computer.

3. Unsolicited email, usually sent to market a service or product (legitimate or otherwise), is called _____.

4. _____ occurs when someone collects personal information belonging to another person and uses that information fraudulently to make purchases, open credit accounts, and otherwise pose as the victim.

5. In Windows, a/an _____ defines a system-wide action a user or group may perform, such as logging on to a computer or installing device drivers.

6. _____ includes authentication, plus determination of a person's level of access to a computer or a resource.

7. _____ is a form of fraud that threatens to do damage or lock a user out of a computer unless the user makes some form of payment.

8. _____ is verification of who you are.

9. A parent wanting to protect a child from inappropriate Web content may use a/an _____.

10. A person or program with administrative access can install malicious code as a/an _____, which hides itself from detection within the operating system.

Multiple-Choice Quiz

1. What is the name for the defining rules and practices for protecting and managing an organization's sensitive information?
   a. Firewalls
   b. Security policies
   c. Security software
   d. Content filtering
   e. Antivirus

2. This type of annoyance appears uninvited in a separate window when you are browsing the Web and can provide a vector for malware infections.
   a. Inline banner
   b. Pop-up
   c. Spam
   d. Adware
   e. Back door

3. What may be the single most important action you can take to protect yourself against identity theft?
   a. Changing passwords frequently
   b. Using an antivirus
   c. Installing an ad blocker
   d. Freezing your credit
   e. Avoiding illegal online activities

4. This term describes unsolicited messages received via instant messaging.
   a. Spam
   b. Spyware
   c. Zombie
   d. Spim
   e. Bot

5. You open your browser and, rather than pointing to your home page, it opens to a Web page advertising adware removal or antivirus software. You reconfigure the browser to point to your home page, but when you restart the browser, it again points to the wrong Web page. This behavior is a symptom of what type of malware?
   a. Spyware
   b. Worm
   c. Browser hijacking
   d. Keystroke logger
   e. Trojan horse

6. What type of malware installs on a computer without the knowledge or permission of the user, and replicates itself on the computer or throughout a network?
   a. Virus
   b. Utility
   c. Worm
   d. Scam
   e. Spim

7. What term is used for a seemingly harmless program that has malicious code hidden inside?
   a. Worm
   b. Trojan horse
   c. Antivirus
   d. Optimizer
   e. Cookie

8. What utility or feature of a browser is used to inhibit the annoying windows that open when you are browsing the Web?
   a. Content filter
   b. Firewall
   c. Antivirus
   d. Spam filter
   e. Pop-up blocker

9. Strange screen messages, sudden computer slowdown, missing data, and inability to access the hard drive may be symptoms of what?
   a. War driving
   b. Spam
   c. Encryption
   d. Virus infection
   e. Fraud

10. This device sits between a private network and the Internet (or other network) and examines all traffic in and out of the network it is protecting, blocking any traffic it recognizes as a potential threat.
    a. Router
    b. Firewall
    c. Bridge
    d. Worm
    e. Keystroke logger

11. After several failed log-on attempts, a message appears stating that your account was locked out. This is the result of exceeding this setting in Account Lockout policy on a Windows computer.
    a. Password length
    b. Account lockout threshold
    c. Account lockout duration
    d. Maximum password age
    e. Password complexity requirements

12. This type of malware conceals itself within the OS code and gives someone administrative access to a computer.
    a. Rootkit
    b. Pop-up download
    c. Drive-by download
    d. Worm
    e. Hoax

13. What is the term used to describe the use of persuasion to gain the confidence of individuals?
    a. Hoax
    b. Fraud
    c. Phishing
    d. Social engineering
    e. Enticement

14. What term describes the action of a password cracker that simply tries a huge number of permutations of possible passwords?
    a. Keystroke logging
    b. Brute force
    c. Statistical analysis
    d. Mathematical analysis
    e. Phishing

15. This military term is a protective network located between a private network and a public network.
    a. Firewall
    b. VPN
    c. IP packet filter
    d. Encrypted authentication
    e. DMZ

Essay Quiz

1. Explain automatic log-in and why you should not allow it in a situation in which you require security.

2. Consider the following statement: My neighbor illegally downloading movies can affect my Internet access. Elaborate on this statement, describing why it is true, and why your neighbor's activity may put you at risk.

3. Why should you disable the Guest account?

4. In your own words, describe why the use of Internet cookies can be an invasion of privacy.

5. Differentiate between permission and user right.

Lab Projects

These Lab Projects ask you to research various topics. In your answers, please provide links to websites you discovered that support your essay or project responses.

LAB PROJECT 2.1

Research identity theft/fraud to answer the following questions.

① What is the estimated cost of identity theft/fraud in the United States in a recent year? What is the trend compared to previous years?

② Identity theft can involve computers, but in many cases, computers play only a small part in identity theft. Find a recent article on an identity theft ring and describe how the thieves operated.

③ Share your findings with others in your class and compare the information you found.

LAB PROJECT 2.2

Research the latest malware threats. Many organizations, including antivirus vendors and security services, post information on the Internet about the latest malware threats. Use an Internet search engine to research the latest threats, which you may find at one of the top security software manufacturers, such as McAfee or Symantec. Using the information from one of these sites, make a list of five current threats and research each to learn more about it. Briefly describe each threat and how you will use security software or behavior to defend your computer from each one.

LAB PROJECT 2.3

Organizations require trained specialists to keep their computers and networks secure. One way prospective employers can determine how much someone knows about security is by requiring job applicants to hold certain appropriate security certifications that require study, experience, and passing exams. Find and research a security certification and give a brief description of this certification, including the organization that is behind this certification, who should seek it, what domains (topics) are included in the exam, and the job titles this certification would apply to.

3 Desktop Virtualization

Source: Microsoft Corporation

Learning Outcomes

In this chapter, you will learn how to:

LO **3.1** Describe the various types of virtualization used in everyday computing and ways you might use desktop virtualization.

LO **3.2** Enable Hyper-V, a desktop virtualization feature of Windows. Use two methods to create a virtual machine in Hyper-V and create a virtual switch for network connections for VMs.

LO **3.3** Download and install the free Oracle VirtualBox hypervisor and create a virtual machine in VirtualBox.

When a software company such as Microsoft is developing new software, before it is released to the public, they make it available in beta form to people outside of the company to test. One way to get to know a new OS is to take advantage of the opportunity to try it out, but not all of us have an extra computer to use for such testing. That is when desktop virtualization comes in handy, letting you run Windows or Linux in a special environment on your computer, while keeping your existing operating system intact. The Chapter 3 opening image, above, shows Ubuntu Linux within a virtual machine in Windows 10.

In this chapter, we explore the exploding phenomenon of desktop virtualization and prepare you to install the desktop OSs described in this book into virtual machines. This will save you the cost and physical desktop space for multiple computers. ✺

LO 3.1 | Virtualization Overview

In this section, we define virtualization and many of the terms associated with it, describe its background, and discuss how it has led to the virtualization of desktop operating systems.

Virtualization Is Everywhere

Virtualization is the creation of an environment that seems real, but isn't, and today it seems like virtualization is everywhere. There are many types. You can spend time in a virtual world, such as Second Life (Figure 3–1). A virtual world often lets a user select an animated computer-generated human, an avatar, to represent them within it. People use virtual worlds in online training, marketing of products, and in games of many types. When a virtual world includes three-dimensional images and involves other senses, giving the participant a feeling of actually being present in that time and space, we call it virtual reality (VR).

Augmented reality (AR) is different from virtual reality, although the lines are sometimes blurred. Augmented reality involves viewing something in real time through a camera or other device while the image (or other input) is digitally modified. AR can involve any of the senses. AR technology is finding its way into gaming, retailing, job training, and education.

In the post-2020 world, more and more in-person meetings and events have moved online. To the author's left-brain thinking we are simply doing more things remotely, not "virtually." The word virtual in all its forms implies that these meetings and events are not quite real. They are real! This usage has been embraced by many, and therefore enters the American English lexicon as the correct usage. So, I will mourn what I believe is the correct usage of virtual along with the many American English grammar rules that have been tossed aside in recent decades.

Many organizations use storage virtualization in which client computers can utilize many networked hard drives as though they are one. Network engineers work with network virtualization involving a network addressing space that exists within one or more physical networks, but which is logically independent of the physical network structure. Then there is server virtualization, in which a single machine hosts multiple servers, each of which performs tasks as independently from the others as separate

Note: Pokemon GO is a very popular augmented reality (AR) game that brings out both the excitement and dangers presented by the distraction of using augmented reality games in public places.

FIGURE 3–1 Create an account, select an avatar to represent you in Second Life, then explore this virtual world where you can interact with others in a variety of destinations.
Miaa Rebane/Linden Research, Inc.

physical machines would. Companies that provide low-cost web hosting services can create a separate virtual web server for each customer.

With only a small leap from these we come to desktop virtualization, the virtualization of a desktop computer into which you can install an operating system, its unique configuration, and all the applications and data normally used by a single person. This virtual desktop may reside on a server, allowing a user to access it over a network from a computer with specialized client software, or it may exist on the local computer.

Each individual virtual environment in both server virtualization and desktop virtualization is a virtual machine (VM)—the software emulation of all hardware with which an operating system must interact. But wait, there's more! There is application virtualization, in which a user connects to a server and accesses one or more applications rather than an entire desktop environment. This chapter is devoted to today's desktop virtualization, but first we will look at the past.

Your (Great?) Grandparent's Virtual Machines

Today's virtual machines have a long pedigree: They can trace their roots back to the 1960s when mainframe computer manufacturers, such as IBM, added the ability to create multiple separate environments on a single computer. A user connected using a dumb terminal that was little more than a keyboard and display with a connection to a host computer (mainframe or minicomputer) with little or no native processing power (hence the term *dumb*).

A dumb terminal connected to the host computer, sending keystrokes and displaying the keystrokes and responses on the display. During a single terminal session, a user connected to a discrete area on the host called a partition. The partition to which each user connected was not like today's virtual machines, but was an area where the user had access to programs and data. After the advent of the IBM PC in the 1980s, a PC configured to emulate a dumb terminal often replaced the dumb terminal.

For years, this model prevailed for those organizations that wished to have a central system where all the programs and data resided, with the individual users connecting from whatever served as a terminal. The 1990s implementation of this model included servers or minicomputers running terminal services to which users connected nearly seamlessly to partitions from their desktop PCs using terminal client software. These were not, however, virtual machines because the entire hardware and operating system environment was not part of the partition to which users connected. They did not have a fully configurable desktop operating system, such as Windows, to work with beyond their application and data.

A 1970s-era computer terminal.
Bill Johnson/The Denver Post/Getty Images

Today's Virtual Desktops

Today connect to a virtual desktop from your local computer to a server on which the virtual environment resides or by using locally hosted virtual machine. We will briefly discuss the server-based model and then look more closely at options for virtual machines on your desktop computer.

Server-Based Virtual Desktops

In the past few decades, many large organizations have adopted the thin client for their desktop users. A thin client is a dedicated terminal or a PC with terminal client software. In either case, a thin client usually lacks such common peripherals as expansion

Note: Thin clients are the modern day dumb terminals.

slots and optical drives. The purpose of a thin client is to connect to a server, allowing the user to work in a server-hosted environment. When that environment provides the entire OS experience and the working applications, it is a virtual machine. This virtual machine may reside on a server and be accessed by a client computer (thin or not), or it may reside on a desktop computer. One term for hosting and managing multiple virtual desktops on network servers is virtual desktop infrastructure (VDI). Today, VDI applies to any server product that provides virtual desktop support.

Local Virtual Desktops

When desktop virtualization resides on a desktop computer, the interactive user (the one sitting in front of that computer) can switch between the host OS (the operating system installed directly on the computer) and a guest OS (the operating system installed within a VM). Figure 3–2 shows Windows 7 running in a virtual machine on a macOS desktop. If the computer has enough processing power, RAM, and disk space, it may simultaneously run multiple virtual desktops.

Type I and Type II Hypervisors

A hypervisor, also called a virtual machine monitor (VMM), is the software layer that manages underlying hardware allocated to one or more virtual machines. Hardware virtualization allows multiple operating systems to run simultaneously on a single computer. A hypervisor normally emulates a computer separate from the underlying computer, using a virtual processor compatible with that of the underlying machine— mainly either an Intel processor or an AMD processor.

There are two types of hypervisors, Type I and Type II. A Type I hypervisor— called either a native or a bare-metal hypervisor—can run directly on a computer without an underlying host operating system. A Type II hypervisor runs within a host operating system as an additional software layer.

Type I hypervisors first appeared on high-powered servers. At the time, desktop computers lacked the hardware support in the processors and firmware required for virtualization of some hardware. Of course, desktop computers became more powerful, and Type I hypervisors are available from the major hypervisor manufacturers—notably Citrix, Microsoft, Oracle, and VMware. These companies offer a selection of products that centrally manage desktop virtual machines, delivered to the desktop (laptop or PC) over a network.

Whatever hypervisor you use, you will find more and more organizations deploying server-based virtual machines that are the users' everyday work environment.

<aside>
Note: In 2020, Apple began the transition from Intel technology to their own ARM chips, referred to as M1 Macs with Apple Silicon. Currently, there is no software available for running Intel-based Windows in virtual machines on the new Apple Silicon Macs. This may change in the coming months. The screenshot in Figure 3-2 shows Windows 7 running in a VM on an Intel Mac.
</aside>

<aside>
Note: The two desktop hypervisors included in this chapter are Windows Hyper-V, a Type I hypervisor, and Oracle VMware, a Type II hypervisor.
</aside>

FIGURE 3–2 A Windows 7 client OS running in a virtual machine in macOS.
Source: Microsoft Corporation

The reason for this is easier central management of the operating systems and user environment.

You have several choices for hypervisors for desktops, but today some of these run only on computers with hardware-assisted virtualization features, which means they require a computer with either the Intel Virtualization Technology for x86 (Intel VT-x) or AMD Virtualization (AMD-V) architecture extensions, which improve the performance of virtual machines on the host. Some hypervisors, such as the one that comes with Windows 10, require even newer features.

The appropriate desktop hypervisor depends on both the hosting OS and the desired guest OSs. Once you select a hypervisor, work through the following tasks.

1. Prepare the host computer:
   - Select a computer that is not important for your everyday work.
   - Confirm that the computer's hardware and operating system meet the minimum requirements for hosting the hypervisor you intend to install.
   - Back up your hard drive.
   - Remove any conflicting software.

2. Install the hypervisor, such as Oracle's VirtualBox hypervisor.

3. Create a virtual machine, selecting from a list of guest OSs that the hypervisor supports.

4. Install the guest OS. This normally requires the full retail version of the OS. You may also use a compatible precreated virtual machine. You must have a legal license or a trial version for each guest OS. The guest OS can be installed directly from a physical disc (CD or DVD) or from a bootable ISO file, which is an image of the contents of a CD or DVD.

5. Install appropriate utilities for the guest OS, if provided by the hypervisor publisher.

6. Finally, once you have an OS installed into a virtual machine, you need to realize that the guest OS and host OS are sharing the same physical hardware, and the mouse and keyboard aren't easily shared. Normally, you give a VM control of a mouse by moving the pointer into the VM and clicking inside the guest window. The virtual machine captures the mouse and keyboard, giving the VM the focus. To release the mouse and keyboard, simply move the cursor outside the VM window and click or tap. Another way to release the mouse and keyboard from VM control is with a host key, a key or combination of keys. If a hypervisor will not release the mouse and keyboard from a VM, look for the name of the host key in the border of the window surrounding the virtual machine. Figure 3–3 shows the bottom right border of a VirtualBox window in Windows 10. The host key is the Right Ctrl key.

Note: If your computer's documentation indicates that the processor supports virtualization but a hypervisor requiring this fails to install due to lack of support, look in the documentation for the computer for instructions on enabling this feature.

Note: If you decide to install two or more different hypervisors on a single host system, do not try to run different hypervisors at the same time.

Major Hypervisor Sources

The major hypervisor manufacturers are Citrix, VMware, Parallels, Microsoft, and Oracle. There are other players in the field, described in articles and reviews in technical publications and websites. A short list of hypervisors that are free to individuals includes Windows Hyper-V, VMWare Workstation Client, VMWare Fusion Player for Mac, and Oracle's VirtualBox.

LO 3.2 | Enabling and Configuring Windows Hyper-V

You have several options—either fee-based or free—for running Linux, DOS, or Windows on a Windows desktop computer. At this writing you cannot run any version of macOS in a VM on a Windows PC, due to licensing issues. We do not expect this to change. The good news is that you can run versions of Windows, Linux, and even FreeBSD (a UNIX-like OS) in a Hyper-V VM. The list is somewhat shorter than the list of client OSs supported by VirtualBox, which we explore later in this chapter.

FIGURE 3–3 Look at the bottom of the VirtualBox VM window to learn what key or combination of keys is the host key.
Source: Oracle Corporation

Learn how to enable Hyper-V and create a virtual machine. Then configure a virtual switch to connect the virtual machine to an external network. Finally, use Hyper-V's Quick Create wizard to create virtual machines with Windows or Linux automatically preinstalled.

Enabling Hyper-V in Windows 10

Windows Hyper-V is a Type I hypervisor. This characteristic of Hyper-V is not apparent because you enable it from within Windows, but the host, or parent OS itself, runs in a virtual machine separate from the client VMs that you create. It is based on the Hyper-V hypervisor found on Windows Servers. Hyper-V includes the Windows To Go Virtual Hard Disk (VHD) feature that allows you to create a virtual hard disk (VHD) on a USB drive, take it to another computer, and boot from it.

Windows Hyper-V is only available in the Pro and Enterprise editions of Windows 10. It requires at least 4 GB of RAM (more is better) and a CPU with the **Second-Level Address Translation (SLAT)** feature found in many Intel and AMD CPUs. To check if your Windows 10 computer supports Hyper-V, open System Information, scroll to the bottom of the System Summary, and look for four items that begin with "Hyper-V." If the Value column contains a Yes, that feature is available.

If you have the Windows 10 Pro or Enterprise edition, enable Hyper-V as described in Step-by-Step 3.01, an exercise that walks through enabling Hyper-V and creating a virtual machine.

> *Note:* The Microsoft Windows Server versions of Hyper-V have more advanced capabilities for hosting server operating system clients.

Step-by-Step 3.01

Working with Hyper-V in Windows

In this hands-on exercise, you will enable Hyper- V in Windows. Then you will create a new virtual machine.

To complete this exercise, you will need the following:

- A desktop or laptop with the Pro or Enterprise edition of Windows 10 installed, with all current updates.
- To be logged in with a user account with administrator privileges.
- Sufficient installed RAM to support the existing programs and the addition of Hyper-V. We recommend a minimum of 8 GB of memory.
- A reliable and fast Internet connect.

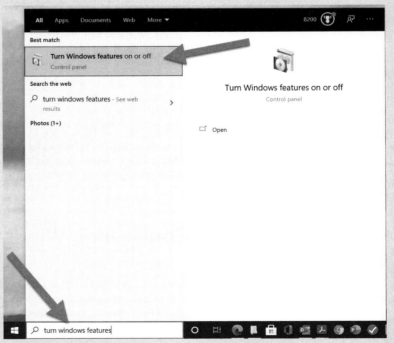

Step 1

From the Windows 10 desktop, enter the following in the Taskbar Search Box: **turn windows features**. From the results, select **Turn Windows features on or off**. This will open the Windows Features Control Panel dialog box.

Source: Microsoft Corporation

Step 2

The Windows Features Control Panel dialog box shows a list of available features. Some features have multiple selectable components, indicated by a plus sign to the left of the check box by the feature. An empty box indicates that it is not enabled. A check in a box means the feature is enabled. If Hyper-V is not enable, click the checkbox to enable it as well as the Hyper V Management Tools and the Hyper-V Platform. Then click OK.

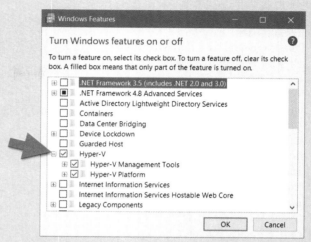

Source: Microsoft Corporation

Step 3

Follow the progress as Windows locates the required files and makes changes to the system. Watch for the message that Windows has completed the changes and click **Restart now**.

Step 4

After the restart, sign in and click the Start button. The Hyper-V Manager will appear in the list of programs under **Recently added** unless it was previously enabled. In that case, you will find it in the **Apps** list under **Windows Administrative Tools**. Click it to start the Hyper-V Manager.

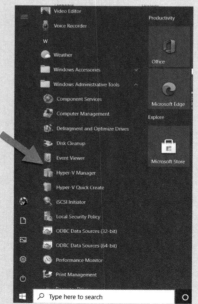

Source: Microsoft Corporation

Take a moment to familiarize yourself with the Hyper-V Manager. On
the left, below the Hyper-V Manager
node, is the name of the host computer. The middle pane contains
Virtual Machines (once created), as
well as Checkpoints and Details of
those VMs. A Checkpoint is a saved
"snapshot" of a virtual machine at a
single point in time. The pane to the
right contains actions you can take.
If your Hyper-V Manager shows different options, you may have a different version than the one in the
example.

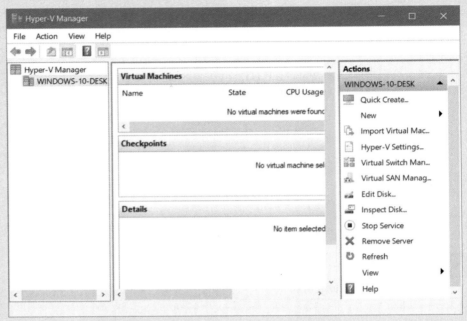

Source: Microsoft Corporation

A Hyper-V shortcut is added to the Windows Administrative Tools folder in the
Apps List, but this is not as convenient
as launching it from a pinned shortcut
on the Taskbar. With the Hyper-V Manager window open, locate the shortcut
for the running app on the taskbar and
right-click it. Then select the option Pin
to taskbar.

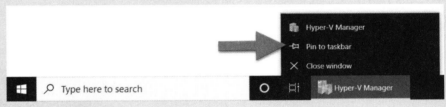

Source: Microsoft Corporation

Step 7

Return to the Hyper-V Manager window. Under Actions select New. From the pop-up menu, select Virtual Machine to start the New Virtual Machine Wizard.

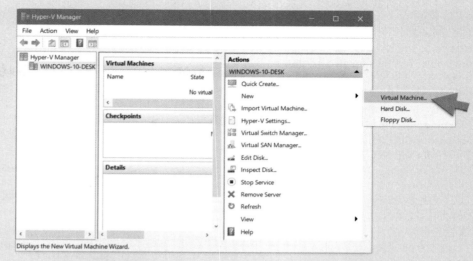

Source: Microsoft Corporation

Step 8

In the New Virtual Machine Wizard, take time to scroll through the items on the left, reading the explanation for each item in the right pane. Do not select any options while viewing these items. Then select Finish to quickly create a virtual machine with the default settings for the items listed in the left pane.

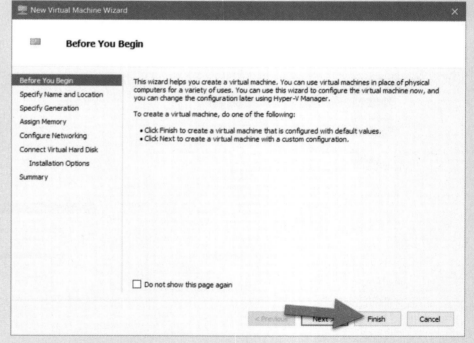

Source: Microsoft Corporation

Step 9

Return to the Hyper-V Manager window. The VM you created is shown in the Virtual Machines list in the middle pane. Because you used the defaults, it is named New Virtual Machine. Scroll down the list of actions in the right pane to see the actions for the New Virtual Machine.

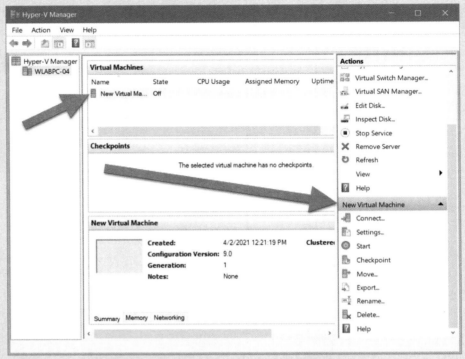

Source: Microsoft Corporation

Step 10

To rename a virtual machine, click on it and type a new name. Consider naming this virtual machine with your initials plus a number. Later, when you install a client operating system into the virtual machine, simply rename it so that it is easily identified, such as using the OS and version of that OS. You now have a virtual machine into which you can install an operating system. Now you are ready to install an operating system into the new virtual machine.

Source: Microsoft Corporation

Source: Microsoft Corporation

Connecting a Virtual Machine to a Network

In the physical world a switch is a device that connects multiple computers (and other devices) in a network, reviewing the packets of data and sending each packet to the correct device on that network. Hyper-V uses a virtual version of this device, a virtual switch, to connect VMs to a network. The three types of virtual switches are external, internal, and private. An external virtual switch gives the VMs connected to it access to a physical network. An internal switch allows the connected VMs to access other VMs connected to that switch as well as to the physical computer, but not to a physical network. A private switch allows communication among the VMs connected to that switch, but not to the physical computer or physical network.

Hyper-V includes an internal switch named Default Switch. New virtual machines can connect to this switch, but in order to give a virtual machine access to the external network (and to the Internet), you need to create a new switch of the external type, and then connect the VM to that switch. Step-by-Step 3.02 walks through the tasks required to create a virtual switch and to connect a VM to that switch.

Step-by-Step 3.02

Creating a Virtual Switch for Hyper-V VMs

In this hands-on exercise, you will create a new virtual switch using Hyper-V Manager.

To complete this exercise, you will need the following:

- A desktop or laptop with Windows 10 Pro or Enterprise edition installed and with Hyper-V enabled, as a result of completing Step-by-Step 3.01.

- To be logged in with a user account with administrator privileges.
- Sufficient installed RAM to support the existing programs and the addition of Hyper-V.

Step 1

From the Windows 10 desktop, open Hyper-V Manager. In the Actions list, click on Virtual Switch Manager.

Source: Microsoft Corporation

Step 2

In the Virtual Switch Manager, choose the type of switch and then click Create Virtual Switch.

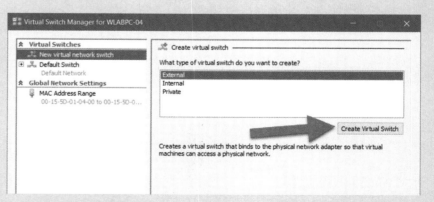

Source: Microsoft Corporation

Step 3

In the Virtual Switch Manager, locate the Name field in the right pane, select the entire name, and overwrite it with a new descriptive name. After changing the name of the switch, click the OK button that will become active at the bottom of the pane.

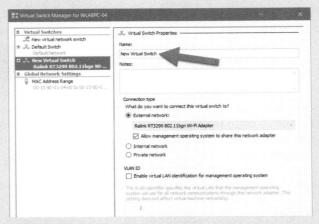

Source: Microsoft Corporation

Step 4

In our example, we used the name "Connect to Internet" because we selected the External network type, which connects to the host computer's external network, which, in turn, is connected to the Internet. Any virtual machine connected to this virtual switch will connect to the Internet.

Source: Microsoft Corporation

Step 5

Now connect a virtual machine to the virtual switch. Open Hyper-V Manager. In the Virtual Machines pane, click on the virtual machine you created in Step-by-Step 3.01. Under Actions, note that the actions for the host computer are at the top, and the actions for the selected virtual machine are next. In the Actions for the virtual machine click Settings.

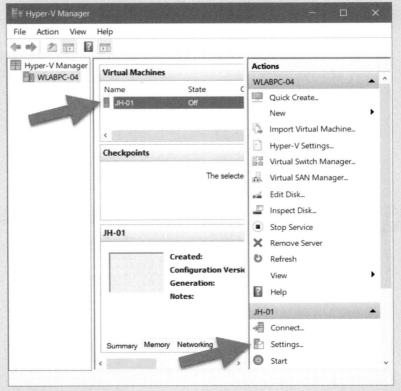

Source: Microsoft Corporation

In the Settings dialog for the virtual machine, click on Network Adapter under the list of Hardware on the left. Then, in the right-hand pane, click on the drop-down box under Virtual switch and then click on the switch you previously created and click the OK button.

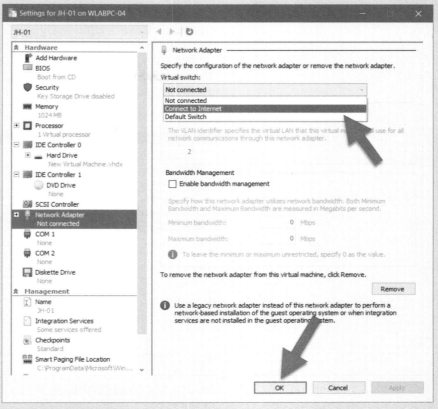

Source: Microsoft Corporation

The Virtual Machine Connection window will open. Our virtual machine is turned off, and we have not yet installed an operating system into this virtual machine. You are now ready to install an operating system into a virtual machine. In the coming chapters, you may use this virtual machine to install one of the operating systems you will study. For now, close this window.

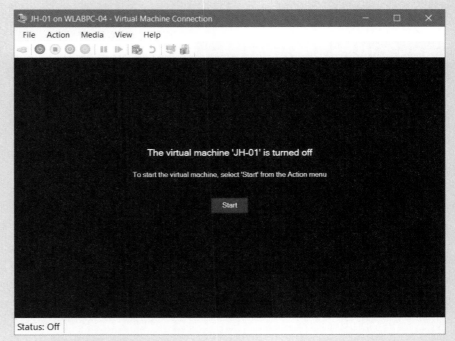

Source: Microsoft Corporation

Using Hyper-V Quick Create

One handy Hyper-V utility is Quick Create, which allows you to create and launch a virtual machine with an operating system pre-installed. The Quick Create options are shown in Figure 3–4. You can launch Quick Create from Windows Administrative Tools in the apps list or from within the Hyper-V Manager. Step-by-Step 3.03 provides the steps to use Quick Create.

FIGURE 3–4 Create Virtual Machine will create a virtual machine with an OS preinstalled.
Source: Microsoft Corporation

Step-by-Step 3.03

Using Quick Create in Hyper-V Manager

In this hands-on exercise, you will use the Hyper-V Manager's Quick Create option to create a new virtual machine.

To complete this exercise, you will need the following:

- A desktop or laptop with Windows 10 Pro or Enterprise edition installed, with all current updates.
- To be logged in with a user account with administrator privileges.

- Sufficient installed RAM to support the existing programs and the addition of Hyper-V. We recommend a minimum of 8 GB of memory.
- A reliable and fast Internet connect.

Step 1

From the Windows 10 desktop, open Hyper-V Manager. Open the **Action** Menu and select Quick Create.

Source: Microsoft Corporation

Step 2

In the **Create Virtual Machine** wizard scroll down to one of the Ubuntu options and click on the **More Options** button on the lower right. Then notice the **Network** option on the bottom left. The Default Switch normally does not have access to an external network. You can choose to connect the new VM to another switch at this point or wait and do it in **Settings** for the new VM. When you are ready, click the **Create Virtual Machine** button.

Source: Microsoft Corporation

Step 3

Follow the progress as the image is downloaded, a virtual hard drive is created, and the VM is configured.

Source: Microsoft Corporation

Step 4

When this message displays, you can click the **Connect** button to open the VM connected to the network selected in Step 2 or you can click **Edit Settings** to modify the settings for this virtual machine before starting it.

Source: Microsoft Corporation

The VM for Ubuntu opens. It is connected, but the operating system has not been started. For now, close the open window. We will start this virtual machine in Chapter 7 when studying Linux.

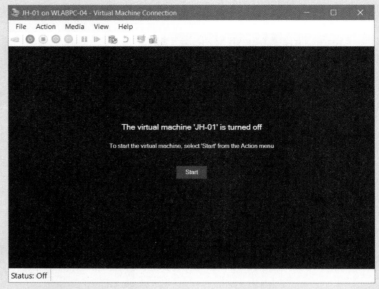

Source: Microsoft Corporation

Removing Hyper-V

Because Hyper-V is enabled through the Windows Features Control Panel, you need to remove it the same way. Locate the Hyper-V node shown in Step 2 of Step-by-Step 3.01 and click to clear the check box, and then click OK. The Windows Features dialog box will display progress information while it initiates the change, and then it will display a message stating that it needs to restart to complete the changes. Click the Restart Now button, and it will make changes as it shuts down and again when it restarts Windows.

LO 3.3 | Virtual Machines in Oracle VirtualBox

Note: VirtualBox is free Open Source Software, available under the terms of the GNU General Public License (GPS). Oracle, a for-profit company with many cloud-based products, supports the free VirtualBox hypervisor with professional oversight.

Oracle VirtualBox is a free Type II hypervisor available in versions for a variety of host operating systems including Windows, Linux, Oracle Solaris (a version of UNIX), and macOS. It supports as guest OSs versions of Windows, Linux, UNIX, and DOS. Figure 3–5 shows Windows 10 running in VirtualBox in macOS on a Mac with the Intel chipset. Step-by-Step 3.04 describes how to download and install Oracle VirtualBox.

FIGURE 3–5 Windows 10 running in VirtualBox on a macOS host.
Source: Microsoft Corporation

Step-by-Step 3.04

Installing Oracle VirtualBox

Using a file you will download or a file provided to you by your instructor, install Oracle VirtualBox. The instructions provided are for installing it into Windows 10. To complete this exercise, you will need the following:

- A computer running an operating system supported by VirtualBox.

- A computer that meets the hardware requirements for the version of VirtualBox you will install.

- The user name and password of an administrator account for this computer (even if you have logged on as an administrator, you may need these credentials to install new software).

- A broadband Internet connection.

Step 1

Open the browser and type "**virtualbox.org**" in the address box. You may need to scroll down on this page to find the large download button shown here. The version number will be newer than shown. Click on the Download button.

Source: Oracle Corporation

Step 2

Click on Windows hosts. Your browser will prompt you to open or save the executable. In the Microsoft Edge browser, a prompt displays at the bottom of the window. Click Open to run the installation program. A progress bar displays while the file is downloaded. When the download is complete, click **Open**.

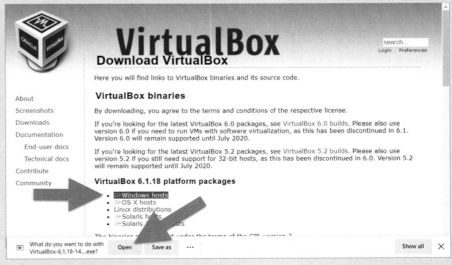

Source: Oracle Corporation

Step 3

When the Oracle VM VirtualBox Setup Wizard displays, click Next to continue.

Source: Oracle Corporation

Step 4

The next page of the Wizard is labeled **Custom Setup**. Unless your instructor tells you otherwise, do not make any changes, but click the **Next** button to continue setup using default options.

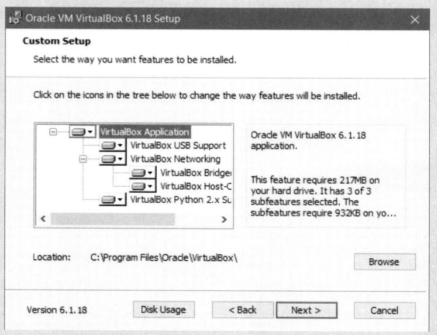

Source: Oracle Corporation

Keep the selected options and click **Next** to continue.

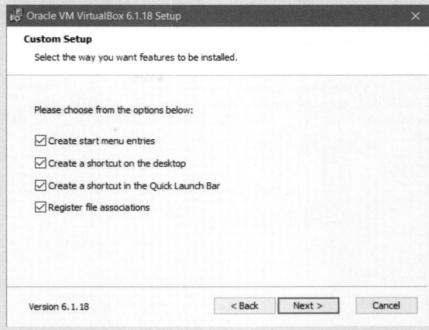

Source: Oracle Corporation

Note the warning. As it states, the network connection will temporarily disconnect. This disruption is normally so brief that you should not notice it. Click Yes to continue.

Source: Oracle Corporation

Step 7

Up to this point, the Setup Wizard was preparing for the installation. The installation begins after you click the **Install** button. If a **User Account Control** dialog appears (here or in later steps), click **Yes** to continue.

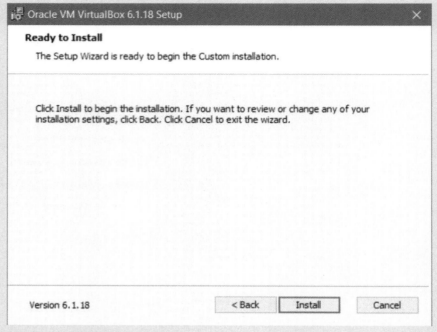

Source: Oracle Corporation

Step 8

The progress bar displays as the Install continues.

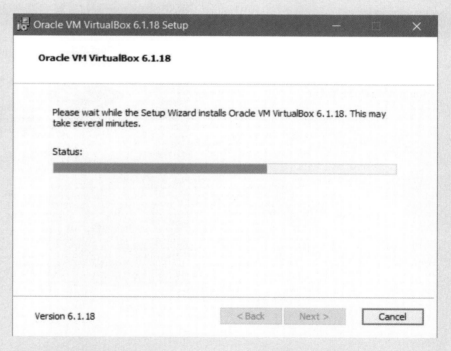

Source: Oracle Corporation

Step 9

The Windows Security dialog box may display when a device driver is installed into the host OS. Click **Install** to proceed.

Source: Oracle Corporation

Step 10

The installation continues...

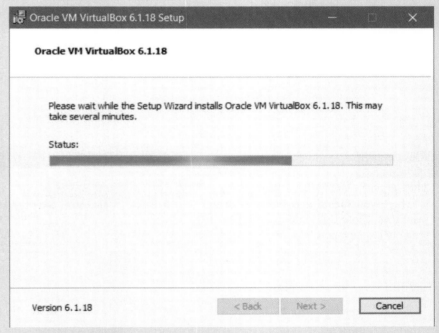

Source: Oracle Corporation

Step 11

When this dialog displays, the VirtualBox hypervisor is installed. Click **Finish** to open the Oracle VM VirtualBox Manager.

Source: Oracle Corporation

Step 12

The Oracle VM VirtualBox Manager is where you create and manage virtual machines. Close this window until you are ready to create a new VM.

Source: Oracle Corporation

Chapter Summary

After reading this chapter and completing the exercises, you should know the following facts about desktop virtualization.

Virtualization Overview

- There are many types of virtualization today, such as virtual worlds, virtual reality, storage virtualization, network virtualization, server virtualization, and desktop virtualization—the subject of this chapter.

- Virtualization had its roots in the dumb-terminal/mainframe systems of the 1960s and the terminal service/terminal client systems of the 1990s.

- You can host today's virtual desktops on network servers or on individual PCs.

- A hypervisor, or virtual machine monitor (VMM), is the software that emulates the necessary hardware on which an operating system runs.

- A Type I hypervisor (a "bare-metal hypervisor") runs directly on a computer without an underlying host operating system.

- A Type II hypervisor requires a host operating system.

- The major sources of hypervisors are Citrix, VMware, Parallels, Microsoft, and Oracle.

Enabling and Configuring Windows Hyper-V

- There are both commercial and free hypervisors for running Linux, DOS, or Windows in a virtual machine on a Windows desktop computer.

- Hyper-V is the Type I hypervisor included with Windows 10 Pro and Windows 10 Enterprise editions.

- Hyper-V has more rigorous hardware requirements than other desktop hypervisors, requiring at least 4 GB of RAM and a CPU with the Second-Level Address Translation (SLAT) feature.

- Enable Hyper-V through the Windows Features Control Panel.

- Remove Hyper-V by deselecting it in the Windows Features Control Panel.

Virtual Machines in Oracle VirtualBox

- Oracle VirtualBox is a free hypervisor. It runs on several hosts including versions of Windows, Linux, and macOS. Create VMs in VirtualBox for a variety of client OSs.

Key Terms List

application virtualization *(81)*

augmented reality (AR) *(80)*

avatar *(80)*

desktop virtualization *(81)*

dumb terminal *(81)*

guest OS *(82)*

host key *(83)*

host OS *(82)*

hypervisor *(82)*

ISO file *(83)*

network virtualization *(80)*

Second-Level Address Translation (SLAT) *(84)*

server virtualization *(80)*

switch *(88)*

storage virtualization *(80)*

terminal client *(81)*

terminal services *(81)*

thin client *(81)*

Type I hypervisor *(82)*

Type II hypervisor *(82)*

virtual desktop infrastructure (VDI) *(82)*

virtual machine (VM) *(81)*

virtual machine monitor (VMM) *(82)*

virtual reality (VR) *(80)*

virtual switch *(88)*

virtual world *(80)*

virtualization *(80)*

Key Terms Quiz

Use the Key Terms List to complete the sentences that follow. Not all terms will be used.

1. The software layer that emulates the necessary hardware on which an operating system runs in a virtual machine is a/an _____.

2. Viewing something in real time through a camera or other device while the image is digitally modified is an example of _____.

3. Many organization use _____ in which many networked hard drives are seen as one by the client computers.

4. _____ is the creation of an environment that seems to surround the participant and feels real.

5. When you run a desktop OS within a hypervisor, it is called _____.

6. In the 1960s, a/an _____ was the very simple interface device to a mainframe computer.

7. In the 1990s, people often used _____ software on a PC to connect to applications on a specialized server or minicomputer.

8. A/an _____ is a low-cost PC, usually without such common peripherals as expansion slots, and optical drives, and is used to allow a user to connect and work in a server-hosted environment.

9. In desktop or server virtualization, the software emulation of all hardware with which an operating system must interface is a/an _____.

10. Second Life is an example of a/an _____.

Multiple-Choice Quiz

1. In which type of virtualization does a user connect to a server and work within a program, without an entire virtualized desktop environment?
   a. Storage virtualization
   b. Application virtualization
   c. Terminal services
   d. Thin client
   e. Virtual world

2. What term describes the hosting and management of multiple virtual desktops on network servers?
   a. Thin client
   b. Terminal services
   c. Minicomputers
   d. Virtual desktop infrastructure (VDI)
   e. Partitioning

3. Which of the following does not run within a host OS?
   a. Type II hypervisor
   b. Type I hypervisor
   c. Windows 10
   d. Linux
   e. macOS

4. What hypervisor, described in this chapter, is a "bare metal" hypervisor?
   a. Windows 10
   b. Terminal client
   c. Thin client
   d. Oracle VirtualBox
   e. Hyper-V

5. What type of hypervisor requires a host OS?
   a. Type II
   b. Type I
   c. Type A
   d. A bare-metal hypervisor
   e. A dual-boot hypervisor

6. What Hyper-V tool will create a VM and preinstall a client OS you select from a list?
   a. Virtual Switch Manager
   b. Hyper-V
   c. Start
   d. Settings
   e. Quick Create

7. Which of these is a free hypervisor that runs on Windows, macOS, and Linux OSs?
   a. Hyper-V
   b. Windows Virtual PC
   c. Oracle VirtualBox
   d. Apple Boot Camp
   e. Windows XP Mode

8. Which acronym stands for a feature of many Intel and AMD CPUs required by Microsoft's Hyper-V?
   a. AR
   b. SLAT
   c. VMM
   d. VDI
   e. VR

9. Which of the following is a free hypervisor that will allow you to run a Windows guest on an Intel-based Mac?
   a. Desktop virtualization
   b. Terminal client
   c. Oracle VirtualBox
   d. SLAT
   e. Hyper-V

10. Which of the following will release the mouse from the control of a virtual machine?
    a. Guest key
    b. Host key
    c. Host OS
    d. VDI
    e. Terminal service

11. Which of the following is synonymous with hypervisor?
    a. Terminal service
    b. Bare metal

c. Virtual hard drive

d. Virtual machine

e. Virtual machine monitor (VMM)

12. You have created a virtual machine using Hyper-V. What will you need to connect the machine to a network?

a. VirtualBox

b. Virtual switch

c. Avatar

d. Network virtualization

e. Thin client

13. What legal issue must you consider when installing a guest OS into a hypervisor?

a. Copyright of guest OS

b. Antivirus

c. Licensing of guest OS

d. Guest key

e. Supplying security credentials

14. Using Oracle VirtualBox, which UNIX OS can you run as a client OS?

a. Solaris

b. SLAT

c. OS/2

d. Linux

e. DOS

15. What type of virtual switch, as defined by Hyper-V, will give a VM access to a physical network?

a. Private

b. Type I

c. Internal

d. External

e. Type II

Essay Quiz

1. Describe in your own words how a "virtual meeting" using Zoom or some other service differs from an in-person meeting. What do you see as the advantages and disadvantages of each type of meeting?

2. Describe a feature of Hyper-V that allows you to take a virtual machine to another computer on a common small handheld device.

3. Explain why an IT person would want to use a hypervisor on a desktop computer.

4. Provide a reason why you would not run macOS in a virtual machine on a Windows computer.

5. You would like to run a side-by-side comparison of running a Linux client OS in Hyper-V versus Oracle VirtualBox. Describe how you would do this comparison, including the computer resources and OS you would need.

Lab Projects

LAB PROJECT 3.1

Find out how virtualization is being used in an organization in your area. Arrange an interview with an IT manager, network engineer, or other knowledgeable IT staff person from an organization in your area. Consider approaching someone at a regional hospital or medical clinic because privacy laws require that they meet certain minimum standards in IT, and they often have the best IT staff in a community. Ask if they are using virtualization, and if so, what type. What are their future plans for virtualization? Report your findings to your classmates.

LAB PROJECT 3.2

If you installed a hypervisor on your computer, find another one that will run on your OS. Install the second hypervisor and attempt to open the virtual machines created for the first hypervisor. Compare the similarities and differences. Will the new hypervisor work with the virtual machines you created with the first one? Decide which one you prefer working with. If it is the second, then keep it; if you preferred the first one, uninstall the second.

LAB PROJECT 3.3

Research the latest desktop hypervisors. Browse the Internet using the key term *desktop virtualization* and watch for recent articles and news releases. Consider turning on Google alerts using this key term. Watch the number of alerts you receive over a few days.

4 Windows 10

Source: Microsoft Corporation

Learning Outcomes

In this chapter, you will learn how to:

LO **4.1** Select a Windows 10 edition and the method of installation, and then install and configure Windows 10 on a laptop or PC.

LO **4.2** Perform appropriate postinstallation tasks to prepare Windows 10 for everyday use.

LO **4.3** Practice working with the new features of the Windows 10 GUI.

LO **4.4** Manage local security in Windows 10.

Windows 10 was released in July 2015 as a cross-platform OS, designed to provide the same user interface (UI) across all their devices—PCs, laptops, tablets, and smartphones. Windows 10 may be the last official Windows version, as Microsoft has stated that they will continually upgrade and add features to this OS rather than release separate versions at intervals as they have done over nearly four decades. Keep in mind as you progress through this chapter that what is true today may not be true by the time you read this book. We hope to get you started with the basics of the operating system so you can continue to learn and use new features as they appear in Windows on your devices. ✳

LO 4.1 | Installing Windows 10

Perhaps you plan to purchase a new computer with Windows 10 preinstalled, or like many of us, you might decide to upgrade the operating system on your existing Windows PC or laptop.

In any event, you need to decide which edition of Windows 10 you will use and how to migrate data from your old computer or installation of Windows to Windows 10. Additionally, you may want all your old settings to apply in the new installation. Therefore, we begin by describing the Windows 10 editions, move on to reviewing the system requirements for Windows 10, and then consider how you might upgrade from

Windows 7 or Windows 8. Before installing Windows 10, decide how to sign in to the OS and take some necessary steps before installing it onto an older computer. After all this preparation, install Windows 10.

Windows 10 Editions

Note: Another edition, Windows 10 IoT Core, comes preinstalled on small, inexpensive mobile devices that fall into the Internet-of-Things (IoT) category.

Windows 10 comes in several editions. The Education Edition—for school staff, administrators, teachers, and students—is only available through academic Volume Licensing. And Microsoft has multiple levels of Enterprise Editions, also only available through Volume Licensing.

Retail Editions are available to any individual. Two of these, Windows 10 Home and Windows 10 Pro will run on almost any consumer-grade PC or laptop, while a third edition, Windows 10 Pro for Workstations will only run on very high-end PCs. It is aimed at people who require high-performance systems with more than two physical processors and up to six TB of RAM. The remainder of this chapter describes installing, configuring, and securing Windows 10 Home and Windows 10 Pro on PCs and laptops. Table 4–1 compares selected features of these two editions.

Windows 10 Home

Windows 10 Home Edition runs on PCs, laptops, and tablets and is aimed at consumers who do not need some of the premium features of Windows 10 Pro. Most consumer-level Windows computers come with Windows 10 Home pre-installed.

Windows 10 Pro

Windows 10 Pro runs on PCs, laptops, and tablets. The features that set it apart from Windows 10 Home include the ability to join a Microsoft Windows domain, support for file encryption, Group Policy Management for Windows domains, and the Hyper-V host described in Chapter 3.

System Requirements

The minimum hardware requirements to install Windows 10 on an Intel- or AMD-architecture computer are very modest, and you will want much more RAM and disk space than the minimum described if you plan to install several programs and store

TABLE 4–1 Comparison of Selected Features in Windows 10 Home and Pro Editions		
Features	**Windows 10 Home**	**Windows 10 Pro**
Maximum physical RAM memory	4 GB in 32-bit OS 128 GB in 64-bit OS	4 GB in 32-bit OS 512 GB in 64-bit OS
BitLocker & BitLocker To Go		✔
Continuum	✔	✔
Cortana personal digital assistant	✔	✔
Domain Join support for joining a Windows domain		✔
Encrypting File System (EFS) on NTFS volumes		✔
Group Policy Management for Windows domain		✔
Hyper-V client	✔	✔
Hyper-V host (64-bit OS only)		✔
Microsoft Edge Web Browser	✔	✔
Windows Apps	✔	✔
Virtual Desktops	✔	✔
Windows Hello biometric login	✔	✔
Works on PCs, tablets, and laptops	✔	✔

data locally. Fortunately, even today's budget-level computers come with hardware that far exceeds the requirements for Windows 10, so we do not expect you to have a problem with the minimum requirements. Having said all that, here are the minimum system requirements:

- 1-GHz or faster processor or a 1-GHz system on a chip (SoC) (such as in a mobile device)
- Minimum 1-GB RAM for 32-bit Windows 10 or 2-GB RAM for 64-bit Windows 10
- 16 GB available hard disk space for 32-bit Windows 10; 20 GB for 64-bit Windows 10
- DirectX 9 graphics device with Windows Display Driver Model (WDDM) 1.0
- 1,024 × 600 minimum screen resolution (1,366 × 768 recommended)
- Internet access

Further, a multitouch-capable touchscreen, touchpad, or touch mouse is required if you wish to take advantage of Windows 10's multitouch support that senses several simultaneous touch gestures.

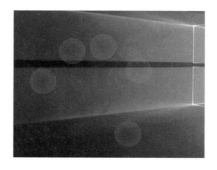

A touch screen on a Windows 10 PC showing the author's five simultaneous touches.
Source: Microsoft Corporation

Upgrading to Windows 10

Upgrading to Windows 10 is an easy decision for many because the system requirements are modest, and the previous versions of Windows are no longer supported. The actual upgrade installation is also smoother and faster than for previous versions. An upgrade is an installation of an OS installed directly into the folders in which the previous version was installed, preserving preferences and data. In this section, we discuss the free upgrade and the possible downside to upgrading.

Free Upgrade to Windows 10

Windows 10 was released July 29, 2015, and for a period of one year after that date it was a free upgrade for many existing installations of legally licensed and updated Windows 7 and Windows 8.1. A Windows 7 computer required Service Pack 1 (SP1) installed to qualify for the free upgrade to Windows 10. A Windows 8 computer had to have Windows 8.1 Update 1 installed. A qualifying computer also had to have Windows Update configured to download and install updates automatically.

The Downside to Upgrading

When upgrading an existing system to Windows 10, some features are removed. You should understand this ahead of time and consider if these are features you will miss. For instance, Windows Media Center is removed by Windows 10 Setup. While Media Center was included in certain editions of Windows 7, it was a feature you would have paid for if you added it to Windows 8 or 8.1. Here is a list of those features that we know are removed, along with a few remarks:

- Windows Virtual PC with Windows XP Mode
- Windows Media Center
- Windows 7 Desktop gadgets
- The ability to disable automatic Windows Update for Windows 10 Home
- Solitaire, Minesweeper, and Hearts games (Setup installs a new version of Solitaire. Minesweeper is a free app at the Windows Store. Several non-Microsoft versions of Hearts are also free.)
- Support for USB floppy drive driver (if present)
- The Windows Live Essentials OneDrive app (Rather than being a separate app, in Windows 10 OneDrive is integrated into File Explorer.)

Preparing to Install Windows 10

Before installing any operating system, there are preparation tasks—some requiring simple decisions, others requiring action beforehand.

Update Windows

Open Settings, Windows Update and ensure that your Windows installation is up to date.

Back Up Your Data

If you are doing an in-place upgrade, your data and settings will be preserved, but you should still back up any important data stored on that computer before upgrading. If, like many people, you save your data to the cloud using a file-storage service, such as Dropbox or Microsoft's OneDrive, then you may consider that file storage to be your backup. Or you may use a cloud-based backup service that is separate from the cloud-based file-storage service you use for saving your working files.

Be sure to review your storage situation and determine if you need to take extra steps to back up your data before upgrading.

Update Firmware

If you are planning to use an existing computer with a functioning operating system installed, we suggest a rather advanced task for those who don't mind challenges: Update the system firmware while the previous OS is intact. This is especially important on a computer that is several years old because a firmware update may make the difference between using all the computer's features with the new version of Windows versus experiencing instability problems, such as the system hanging up when you try to shut down. Some manufacturers install update-manager software that checks for and downloads drivers and firmware, in which case, your system may be up to date. Otherwise, you may need to do a little searching for the computer model on the computer manufacturer's site to see if there are any firmware updates for that model. Then, follow the manufacturer's instructions for updating the firmware.

Acquire Updated Drivers

As with firmware updates, your existing computer may have a utility installed by the manufacturer that checks for updates to the system drivers for that model computer. Over time, these utilities have morphed into full-blown marketing apps for the manufacturer, but the updating function is useful because it may ensure that you have the latest drivers for the installed OS, and they may be acceptable to Windows 10. Windows 10 Setup will check your system to ensure that it has current device drivers. If Windows 10 does not have new drivers and the previously installed drivers are incompatible, Setup may install a generic driver, providing there is a reasonably compatible driver. If Setup issues an error message, you may need to acquire an updated Windows 10 driver. Alternatively, if Setup installed a generic driver, you may still need to install an updated driver from the manufacturer to take advantage of all of a device's features.

Understand Microsoft Product Activation

Microsoft Product Activation (MPA) is an antipiracy tool that ensures you are using your software per the software license. One important change in the Windows 10 activation process is that you do not have to manually enter an alphanumeric string of characters called a product key during activation because Windows 10 comes "pre-keyed" and will automatically provide the key to Microsoft during the activation process. The product key only works with one instance of the Windows 10 product.

If there is no Internet connection, it will try to activate the product key once the computer is connected. If it fails to activate after several tries, a message will display with instructions on how to manually activate the product—usually via telephone. In more recent updates to Windows 10 Microsoft added the Activation option under Update & Security in the Settings app. You can now upgrade a Windows 10 edition using this option.

Choose How to Sign In to Windows 10

Decide ahead of time how you will sign in to Windows 10. Your choices are to sign in to Windows 10 with (1) a local account that exists only on the Windows 10 computer, (2) a Microsoft account, or (3) a Windows Active Directory account if your computer is a member of a Windows Active Directory domain (at work or school).

Signing In with a Local Account. When you install Windows it creates a local account, but you can sign in using either a local account or a Microsoft account. If you use a local account, it only gives you access to local resources; you will need to sign in separately to any Microsoft services you use. Figure 4–1 shows a Sign-In screen for a local account. This account has not been customized with a picture, which you can do at any time after you install Windows 10.

Signing In with a Microsoft Account. A Microsoft account (MSA) is a free account with Microsoft that gives the subscriber access to Microsoft services, such as **Outlook.com**, Messenger, OneDrive, and Xbox LIVE. If you use an MSA, the Sign-In screen will display the name and the email address associated with your MSA. We prefer to use the MSA because this one sign-in gives you access to the local computer as well as to your Microsoft services. Then you can access all your data across other devices and services, and you can synchronize your settings on other Windows 8.1 and Windows 10 devices that use the same sign-in. Learn more about syncing your devices in the section titled *Postinstallation Tasks.*

You can use your existing MSA, create one ahead of time by going to the Microsoft site, or wait and create a new MSA during Windows 10 installation. Figure 4-2 shows the MSA sign-in page for Windows 10.

Signing In with a Domain Account. If your computer is running Windows 10 Pro, Windows 10 Enterprise, or Windows 10 Education, it can join a Microsoft Active Directory Domain (based on Windows Server), and you will be required to sign in

FIGURE 4–1 The initial Sign-In screen for a local account. Personalize it with an image.
Source: Microsoft Corporation

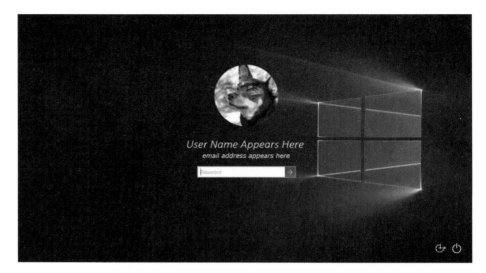

FIGURE 4-2 The Sign-In screen for a Microsoft account, personalized with an image of the author's pet.
Source: Microsoft Corporation

using a domain user account. In this case, you may not be involved in the installation of Windows or selection of the account at all but have a fully configured computer delivered to your desk. You will then enter your domain credentials, as instructed by a domain administrator.

Prepare to Install into a Virtual Machine

If you have a hypervisor installed on a lab computer and plan to install Windows 10 into a virtual machine, you will need to first create a VM for the installation (as described in Chapter 3), and then ensure that the virtual machine will boot from the drive containing the Windows 10 Setup files. By default, virtual machines in all the hypervisors discussed in Chapter 3 will connect to a computer's physical DVD drive as a virtual DVD drive and can boot from that drive at startup. Therefore, if you have a Windows 10 DVD, insert it into the host computer's DVD drive before starting the VM. At startup, the VM will boot into the Setup program. If the Windows 10 files are in an ISO image file, change the DVD settings for that virtual machine to point to the location of the ISO file before starting the VM, and then restart the VM and follow the prompts. Figure 4-3 shows the Client Hyper-V DVD Settings configured to use the ISO image file located in the Downloads folder of the host computer.

Installing

If you purchase Windows 10 online as a full retail product or as an upgrade from Windows 7 or Windows 8.1, you can do either a Web-based install or a more conventional Windows Setup install that you can do from a download from the Microsoft Store or from a USB drive purchased at the Microsoft Store, online or at one of the physical store locations.

Web-Based Setup

Microsoft's online Web-based setup is quick and combines the more traditional Windows Setup program with the features of the former Windows Upgrade Advisor and the settings and data migration tools used by previous versions of Windows. Web-based setup requires very little interaction and is very fast. If you select this option, follow the on-screen instructions to install it.

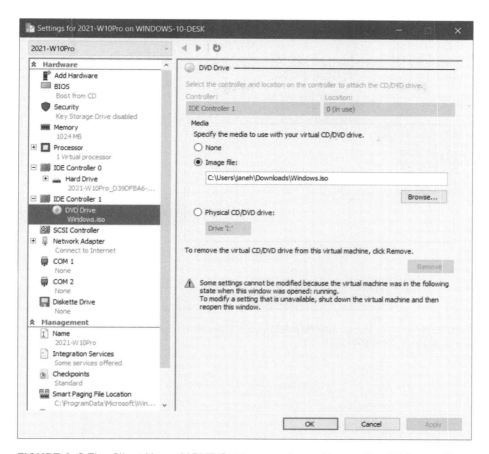

FIGURE 4–3 The Client Hyper-V DVD Settings configured to use the ISO image file located in the Downloads folder.
Source: Microsoft Corporation

WARNING!

A clean install will delete anything currently stored on the drive you select for the installation.

Bootable Media.

The retail editions of Windows 10 are no longer available directly from Microsoft on DVD. You can purchase Windows 10 on USB or as a download. When installing or upgrading online, you have the option to use the Windows Media Creation Tool to create bootable media (USB flash drive, DVD, or ISO file) from a download. Figure 4–4 shows Windows 10 Setup option to create installation media. If you choose USB flash drive, have the drive available to create on the machine you are using for the download. If you select DVD or ISO file, it will be downloaded and you can use it to create a bootable DVD or save it on a hypervisor host computer to use to install the OS into a VM.

Beginning Windows Setup.

Once you have the media, you can either boot your computer from it (a clean install) or, if upgrading, first sign in to your Windows computer and insert the disc. If it does not automatically run setup, open Windows Explorer or File Explorer (⊞+E), browse to the disc, and double-click the Setup file.

Step-by-Step 4.01 will walk you through the steps for a clean install of Windows 10 from bootable media. An upgrade can also be done from bootable media. When you start the installation, the **Windows Preinstallation Environment (Windows PE)** starts. Windows PE is a scaled-down Windows operating system that supports the Windows Setup GUID, collecting configuration information.

Note: Exercise 4.01 requires a computer that can boot from either a USB or a DVD drive. If your computer fails to do this, change the boot order setting in the computer's system settings. The actual steps for doing this vary by manufacturer. For instructions, do an online search using your computer model name and the key words "boot order."

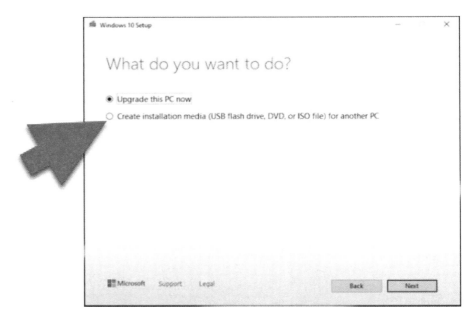

FIGURE 4–4 Select *Upgrade this PC now* or *Create installation media*.
Source: Microsoft Corporation

Step-by-Step 4.01

Installing Windows 10

In this hands-on exercise, you will do a clean installation of Windows 10 from bootable media. To complete this exercise, you will need the following:

- A personal computer (desktop or laptop) compatible with Windows 10, with at least the recommended minimum hardware and configured to boot from DVD or other media, and (ideally) an unpartitioned hard disk (disk 0, the first hard disk). Alternatively, you can install into a virtual machine you have prepared before beginning the Windows 10 installation (see Chapter 3 and the section in this chapter titled "Preparing to Install into a Virtual Machine").

- The Windows 10 DVD or other bootable media.
- If you plan on using a local account for sign in, you need to decide on a user name and password for that account.
- If you plan to use a Microsoft account, you need the email address and password for that account. If you do not have one, you can create a Microsoft account during the Setup process.
- If you are doing a clean install on a computer using a Wi-Fi router, be prepared to select the network and provide the password, when prompted.

Step 1

Insert the bootable media containing the Windows 10 installation files and boot the computer. Watch the screen for instructions to boot from the optical or USB drive. A plain black screen will briefly flash, followed by a black screen with the message: "Windows is loading files . . . " while the Windows Preinstallation Environment is loading and starting. The Starting Windows screen signals that Windows PE is starting and will soon load the GUI for Windows 10 setup.

Step 2

On the first Setup screen, select a language, time and currency format, and keyboard or input methods and click Next.

Source: Microsoft Corporation

Step 3

On the next screen, click Install now. Setup will start.

Source: Microsoft Corporation

Step 4

When the Activate Windows page displays enter the product key. If you are upgrading, select **I don't have a product key**.

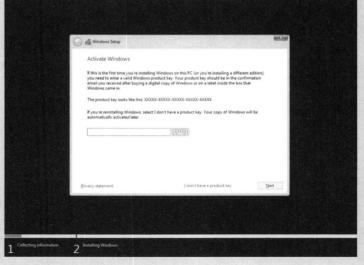

Source: Microsoft Corporation

Step 5

When the license screen appears, read the Microsoft Software License Terms, then click to place a check in the box labeled "I accept the license terms" and click the Next button.

Step 6

On the screen after the license screen you are asked, "Which type of installation do you want?" Select Custom if you are not upgrading and want to perform a clean installation.

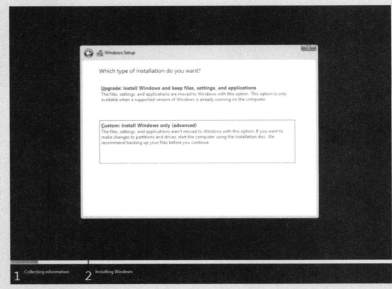

Source: Microsoft Corporation

Step 7

On the next screen, you select the target drive for the installation. Anything currently stored on the drive you select will be deleted. If Windows 7 or Windows 8 was previously installed on the system on which you are doing a clean installation, this screen will show two partitions on the drive. Select a partition, and click Next.

If you are installing into a virtual machine or onto a clean hard drive without a previous installation of Windows, there will be only a single partition. Select it and click Next.

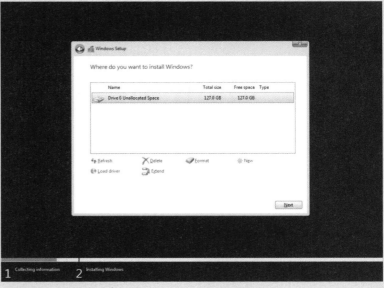

Source: Microsoft Corporation

Step 8

Windows 10 Setup will now go through the installation phases. It may restart several times and return to this page that displays progress with a green check by each completed phase.

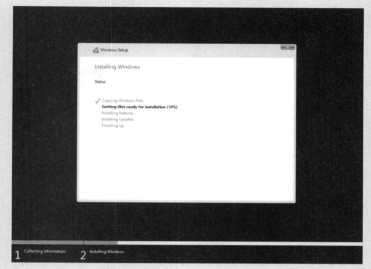

Source: Microsoft Corporation

Step 9

A screen with the Windows logo in the center and a progress animation over the words "Getting ready" displays. Eventually, a screen displays requesting the region information, as shown here. Select your region and click Yes. Respond to the following screens for keyboard layout and move to Step 10.

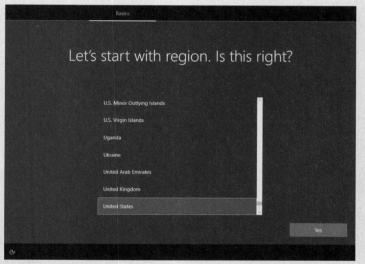

Source: Microsoft Corporation

Step 10

After a delay while Setup configures your system, this screen will display asking, "How would you like to set up?" Your response to this screen depends on your situation. In a classroom lab, you will probably select "Set up for an organization." At home, you will select "Set up for personal use." Select one of the choices; then click Next.

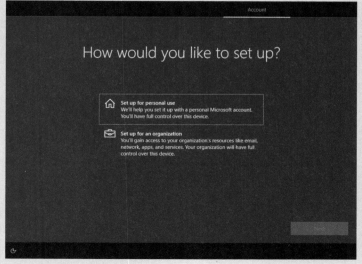

Source: Microsoft Corporation

Step 11

After another wait, a Sign-In screen opens. The actual screen depends on your choice in Step 10. If you selected "Set up for an organization," then you will follow the screen prompts and enter your credentials for signing in to the organization's network.

If this is your own computer and you do not need to sign in to a Windows domain, sign in with a Microsoft account or create a local account.

For this exercise, we will sign in with a Microsoft account. If you wish to do that, enter the email address associated with your Microsoft account in this screen. Click **Next** and on the next screen enter your password for this account. Then proceed to sign in with that account.

Alternatively, if you want to create a new Microsoft account, click on **Create account** and follow the instructions.

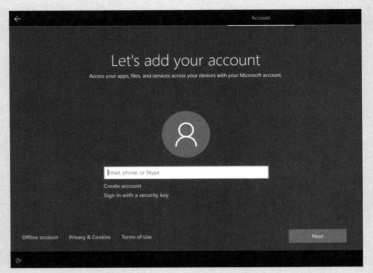

Source: Microsoft Corporation

If you wish to create and sign in with a local account, click the **Offline account** button at the bottom left. In all cases, follow the prompts on each screen. If you are not prompted to select a Wi-Fi network, skip to Step 13 when prompted to create a PIN.

Step 12

You will not see this screen if installing on a computer with a wired connection or into a virtual machine that is connected to a virtual switch with access to the Internet. If you are doing a clean install on a computer using a Wi-Fi router, be prepared to select the network and provide the password, when prompted.

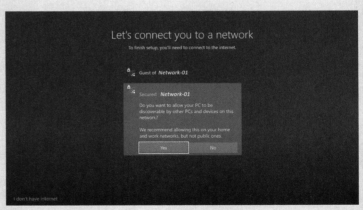

Source: Microsoft Corporation

Step 13

After signing in, you will be prompted to create a personal identification number (PIN) for this computer. Select Create PIN and type the new PIN in the two boxes. To create a more secure PIN, consider making it at least six characters long and including letters and symbols (after checking the box). Be sure to memorize this PIN!

Source: Microsoft Corporation

Source: Microsoft Corporation

Step 14

Continue through the Services pages, beginning with Privacy. Notice that all the privacy options are turned on by default. Consider keeping the privacy settings and moving on. On some pages, you will want to select the **Skip for now** button. When the OneDrive page displays, select **Only save files to this PC** unless your instructor gives you other instructions. On the **Cortana** page select **Not now**.

Source: Microsoft Corporation

Step 15

Setup will take several minutes to prepare your computer, and then you will sign-in. At this point, you will be prompted to explore new features, including those in the browser Microsoft Edge. When you close the open windows, the Windows 10 desktop displays.

Source: Microsoft Corporation

LO 4.2 | Postinstallation Tasks

You will need to do some tasks soon after installing Windows 10. In earlier versions of Windows, installing security software would have been at the top of the list, but Windows 10 comes with Windows Security enabled during setup. We will look at Windows Security later in this chapter. Your postinstallation tasks may include installing drivers, running Windows Update, and backing up Windows and your data files. But first, take a few minutes to familiarize yourself with the new GUI so that you can do these postinstallation tasks.

Get Acquainted with the GUI

There is only one Windows 10 GUI, but it does have two modes: Desktop and Tablet. In Desktop mode, it opens with the Recycle bin shortcut on the upper left and a taskbar with Start button along the bottom. A shortcut is an icon that represents a link to an object, such as a file or program. Activating a shortcut (by clicking on it) is a quick way to access an object or to start a program from any location. This section is a brief introduction to some of the features that you may need to work with when you do the postinstallation tasks. They include keyboard shortcuts, the Start menu, the File Explorer file management tool, and the Edge Web browser.

Keyboard Shortcuts

Note: Check out the Microsoft document *Keyboard shortcuts in Windows*, found by searching on "keyboard shortcuts" at https://support.microsoft .com.

A keyboard shortcut is a key combination or a key-mouse combination that initiates an assigned action, saving you several mouse, keyboard, or touch actions. Windows 10 supports most of the keyboard shortcuts included in previous versions, as well as a few new ones. Throughout this textbook we provide special notes, pointing out some of our favorite keyboard shortcuts. Many of them take advantage of the Windows key ⊞ located near the bottom left of most keyboards or as a special physical button on some tablets or on the Microsoft Touch Mouse.

The Windows 10 Start Menu

Note: A menu icon consisting of three horizontal lines is commonly called a hamburger icon. You will find this icon in Microsoft Windows and various Google settings and apps.

Click or tap the Start button (on the far left of the task bar) to open the Start menu. In Figure 4-5, the Start menu is in Desktop mode, covering a portion of the Desktop. This is how the Start menu appears on a computer with a keyboard attached. Scroll vertically to see more tiles on the Start menu.

FIGURE 4-5 The Windows 10 Desktop with the Start menu open on the left.
Source: Microsoft Corporation

Click or tap Start again to close the Start menu. Microsoft calls the Start menu simply "Start," but in this book, we will continue to use the term "Start menu." After its absence in Windows 8 and 8.1, the Start menu returned by popular demand, combining a selection of features from the Windows 7 Start menu and the Windows 8 Start screen along with new or improved features that change as Microsoft continues to update Windows 10.

User Tile and Quick Links. In the left column of the Start menu is the User tile for the currently signed-in user, with an optional picture. What we called a shortcut on the Start menu in Windows 7 is now called a Quick link. This is not exactly like the Windows 7 Start menu, but it does have a Quick link that opens the Power menu containing options to shut down, restart, or put Windows into Sleep mode. Double-click the Power Quick link to open the Power menu shown in Figure 4–6. To make room for touch, the Quick links and tiles become larger on a tablet, and menu choices are spaced farther apart. You can launch programs from Quick links, from tiles on the Start menu, from links pinned to the Taskbar, and from the All Apps list, which we look at next.

All Apps. In recent updates to Windows 10, the All Apps list appears by default on the Start Menu, providing a sorted list of installed apps, as shown in Figure 4–5. Hover the mouse near the border between the All Apps list and the tiles to see the vertical scroll bar on the right side of the Apps list, as shown in Figure 4–7. Drag the scroll bar up or down to browse through the list. Folder items have a drop-down button to the right that opens a list of the contents of that folder. Earlier installations of Windows 10 did not display the All Apps list by default but had an All apps Quick link above the Windows icon that would open the list on the Start menu.

Start Menu Settings. To explore options for personalizing the Start menu, open the Start page in Settings, as shown in Figure 4–8. Experiment with turning settings off and on to suit the way you work.

File Explorer

Another feature to check out before beginning your postinstallation tasks is File Explorer, the Windows 10 file management utility. This renamed and updated replacement for Windows Explorer first appeared in Windows 8. Microsoft has made more changes in the File Explorer UI in Windows 10, but nothing that should keep you from finding your way around if you are experienced with previous versions of Windows. Even the File Explorer shortcut on the taskbar (Figure 4–9), while updated somewhat, is recognizable. In Figure 4–10 notice the ribbon containing menu buttons near the top of the window and the list of Quick links under Quick access on the left. When browsing your folders, select one you open frequently and click the Pin to Quick Access button on the left side of the ribbon. Briefly acquaint yourself with File Explorer by selecting it from the taskbar and browsing the folders.

Lock Screen

The Lock screen is a screen that prevents you from accidentally triggering some action that you did not intend to occur on a device with a touch screen. The classic example is "pocket dialing" someone on a smartphone while the phone is in your pocket. By default, the Lock screen displays under certain conditions including: when you first start up your computer, after a period of inactivity, when you choose Lock from the User tile, or when you use the Windows Key+L shortcut.

Note: Later in this chapter, learn about the special user interface mode for tablets: Tablet mode.

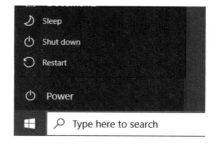

FIGURE 4–6 The Power menu options.
Source: Microsoft Corporation

Note: Later in this chapter, we will use the features of the Start menu's search box (now occupied by Cortana) to get help, find apps and settings, and access the other features of Windows 10.

FIGURE 4–7 Notice the scroll bar on the right side of the All Apps list.
Source: Microsoft Corporation

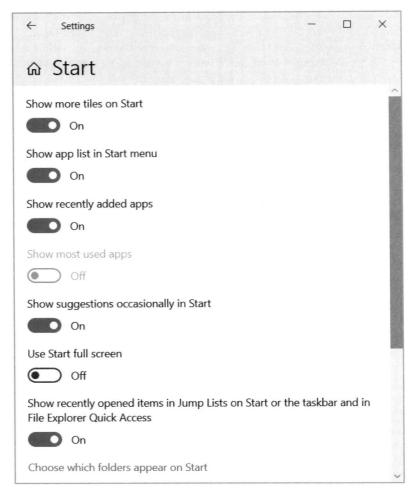

FIGURE 4–8 The Windows 10 Start Settings.
Source: Microsoft Corporation

FIGURE 4–9 The File Explorer
shortcut on the taskbar.
Source: Microsoft Corporation

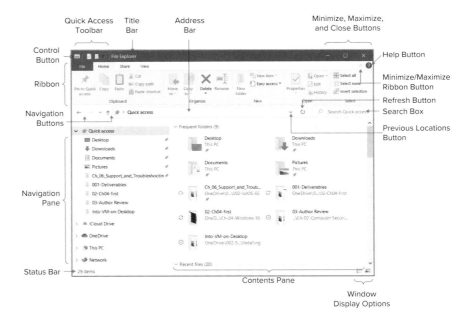

FIGURE 4–10 The Windows 10 File Explorer file management tool.
Source: Microsoft Corporation

Microsoft Edge

The last feature we will preview before discussing the postinstallation tasks is the Windows 10 Web browser, Microsoft Edge. This is an alternative to the decades-old Internet Explorer (IE).

Launch Microsoft Edge from its taskbar icon, shown in Figure 4–11. Notice the clean look of the Microsoft Edge window in Figure 4–12. This image shows the Microsoft Edge browser in dark mode, which may be easier to read.

Install and Troubleshoot Drivers

Windows Setup detects your hardware devices and installs appropriate drivers. If Setup detects a noncritical device that does not work with one of the available drivers, you may be prompted to provide the driver files, or setup may quietly install a generic driver that works with a device, but doesn't take advantage of all its features. Or you may have a noncritical device that simply does not work after Windows 10 is installed. Therefore, one postinstallation task is to watch for error messages and devices that do not seem to function properly and install updated drivers. You have some choices for this that we will explore next.

Install Updated Drivers from Manufacturers

If you were prepared to install new drivers during setup, but did not have an opportunity to install them, then immediately after setup check for problems with the installed drivers in the form of error messages or a component not functioning properly. If you see such symptoms, install those drivers that you prepared ahead of time. In most cases, when manufacturers supply a compatible driver, it comes as an executable. If you downloaded the driver file, it will normally be in your Downloads folder, or you may have the driver file on an external device. In either case, open File Explorer, locate the file, and double-click it to run the driver setup. If the driver file is not an executable file, the manufacturer will provide other instructions for installing the file.

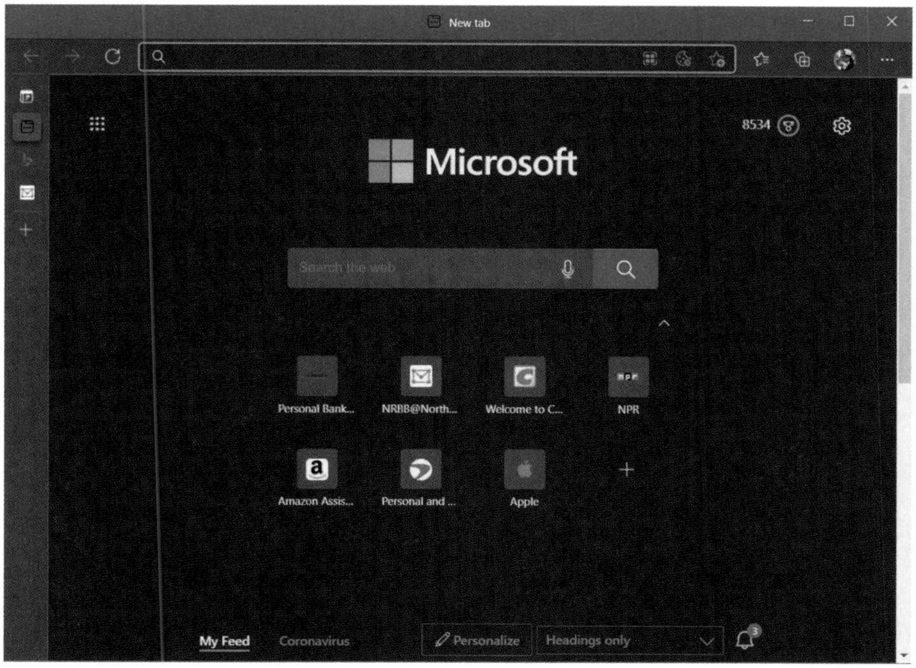

Note: Learn More about Edge and other browsers in Chapter 9, Connecting Desktop and Laptops to Networks.

Note: Microsoft Edge is a Windows app, which means that it runs in Windows 10 on all devices, adjusting itself for the various screen sizes. Take a closer look at Windows apps later in this chapter.

FIGURE 4–11 The Microsoft Edge shortcut is pinned to the taskbar by default.
Source: Microsoft Corporation

FIGURE 4–12 The Microsoft Edge browser window.
Source: Microsoft Corporation

Troubleshoot Drivers with Device Manager

We recommend that you troubleshoot driver problems with Device Manager, a Control Panel applet that displays the list of hardware and the status of each device. Familiarize yourself with this utility before you have problems. In Step-by-Step 4.02, use Device Manager to look for problem drivers in the new Windows 10 installation and to correct problems, if necessary.

Step-by-Step 4.02

Using Device Manager in Windows 10

In this exercise, you will open Device Manager to detect and resolve driver problems in Windows 10. To complete this exercise, you will need the following:

- A computer running Windows 10, preferably with a mouse and keyboard.
- You should be signed in with an administrator account, which you are if you are signed in as the user created during Windows 10 Setup.
- An Internet Connection will allow Device Manager to search online in Steps 6 and 7.

Step 1

In the Start menu's Search box, type "device manager." In the search results list, click on Device Manager, shown here at the top of the list.

Another way to open Device Manager is to use the ⊞+x shortcut to open the Power User Menu, and then select Device Manager.

Source: Microsoft Corporation

Notice that the name of your computer displays at the top of the contents pane in Device Manager. Below that the devices are arranged in nodes. If Device Manager detects a problem with a device, the node will expand to show the device, along with a yellow error icon. In this example, no errors were detected, but we clicked on the Mice and other pointing devices node to expand it and to learn more about the detected pointing devices. Notice that the mouse was detected, as well as the built-in touchpad (Lenovo Pointing Device).

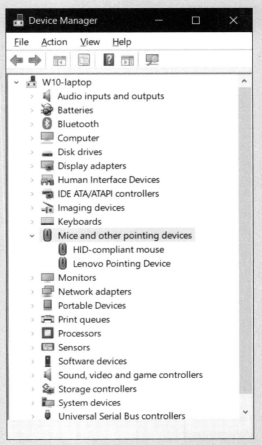

Source: Microsoft Corporation

If Device Manager shows an error for a device, double-click that device. If there is no error, select a device, as we did, and double-click it to open the Properties. The box below Device Status shows that this device is working properly. If there is a problem, an error message appears here. How you would troubleshoot a problem depends on the error. Device errors are often caused by the driver. Click the Driver tab to see your options for managing the driver.

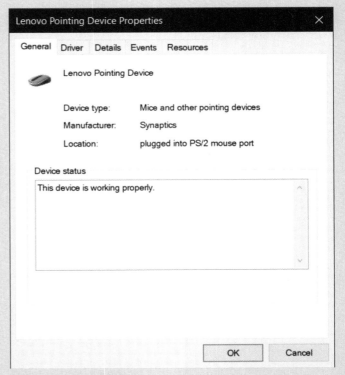

Source: Microsoft Corporation

The Driver page has several buttons for managing drivers. Click on the Driver Details button.

Note: In this example, the driver is several years old, running in the latest version of Windows 10. The device is still functioning well on this laptop, so there is no need to replace the driver.

Source: Microsoft Corporation

The Driver File Details page shows the location and name of the driver file. There may be more than one file, as shown here. Click OK to close Driver File Details and return to the Properties dialog box.

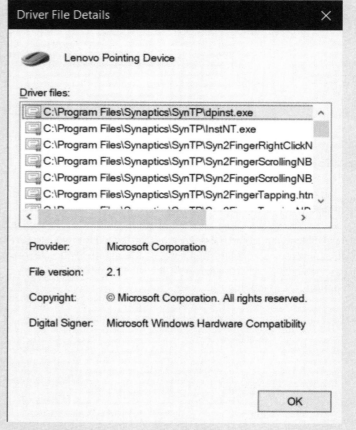

Source: Microsoft Corporation

Step 6

Back on the Driver page of the Properties dialog box, click the Update Driver button. On the Update Driver Software Page, click the top option titled *Search automatically for drivers* and follow the instructions.

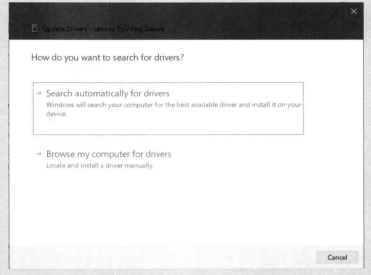

Source: Microsoft Corporation

Step 7

A message and progress bar displays while Windows searches for a driver on your local computer and on the Internet.

Step 8

In our example, Windows determined that the best driver was already installed, displaying this message. If this is the case on your computer, click the Close button to return to the Properties dialog box where you can click the OK button to end the exercise. If a message displays that a driver is being downloaded or installed, follow the instructions and when it completes, click the OK button to close the last dialog box.

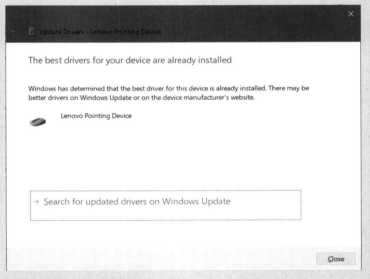

Source: Microsoft Corporation

If you update a device driver, then the Properties for that device shows that the Roll Back button is live. Click the Close button to end the exercise.

Source: Microsoft Corporation

If you upgrade a driver and then have problems with the device, or if Windows becomes unstable immediately after a driver upgrade, open the Properties dialog box for the device and use the Roll Back Driver button to remove the new driver and restore the old driver. The last two buttons on the Driver tab of the Properties dialog box for a device, Disable and Uninstall, trigger drastic measures that you would not normally take without advice from a very knowledgeable person.

Personalize Windows 10

After just a few minutes of using a new installation of Windows, you will feel the need to make it your own with your own preferences. Perhaps you want to change the size of icons on the desktop and taskbar or change pictures on the Lock screen, Desktop, or Sign-In screen. And we all have our own color preferences, which you can configure for the taskbar and windows. Begin by tweaking display settings, and then move on to the other ways to personalize Windows 10.

Tweak Display Settings

The Desktop context menu is one way to access Display settings. A context menu is a menu that displays when you right-click (or press on) an object in Windows. Not all objects have context menus, but many do. Open the Desktop context menu by right-clicking an empty area of the Desktop. On a touch screen, open this menu by pressing an empty area of the Desktop, holding until a small square appears, then quickly lifting your finger. Figure 4-13 shows the Desktop context menu as it displays using the first method, while Figure 4-14 shows this menu after using a touch screen action. Notice that they are identical menus, but the second one allows space for touch actions. From the context menu select Display settings. In Windows 10, this opens the Display page of the Settings app where you change settings to suit how you work. Figure 4-15 shows the Display settings. Since Windows 10 was first released,

Note: If you are using Windows 10 in a virtual machine, you will be able to view the Display settings but not change them.

FIGURE 4–13 The Desktop context menu resulting from right-clicking on the Desktop.
Source: Microsoft Corporation

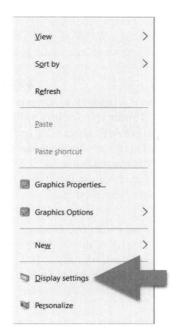

FIGURE 4–14 The Desktop context menu on a touch screen resulting from pressing on the Desktop.
Source: Microsoft Corporation

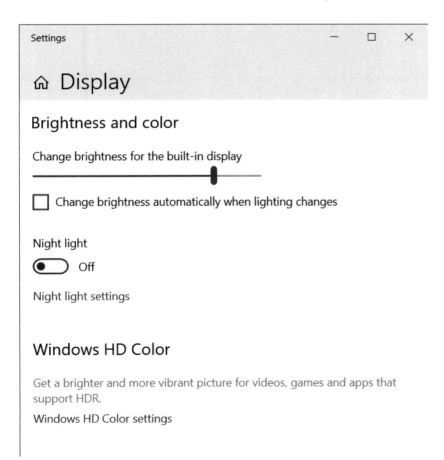

FIGURE 4–15 The Windows 10 Display settings.
Source: Microsoft Corporation

Microsoft has made several changes to Settings, so you may see different options. The Display settings on a Windows tablet will include orientation options (portrait or landscape). Scroll through the settings and select those options you would like to change.

Identify, Detect, and Connect to Displays. If you have multiple displays, the Display settings will show the displays as shown in Figure 4-16. Click on the Identify button. A number will appear on each display connected to your computer (see Figure 4-17). This is very helpful when you have multiple displays, so that you can select which display is the main display, the one that will show the Sign-In screen and will be the primary screen for the Desktop. Click Connect to a Wireless Display to initiate a connection with a wireless display.

Change the Size of Items on the Desktop. The Scale and Layout setting gives you some control over the size of displayed items; on the desktop computer, with 23 inch displays, the choices were 100%, 125%, 150%, or 175%, but on the laptop this was limited to either 100% or 125%. The default is 100%, and if you change it, you will need to sign out and sign in again for it to take effect.

Orientation and Lock Rotation. The Orientation setting allows you to change the orientation from landscape (normal on desktops and laptops) to Portrait, as well as both of these orientations reversed, or "flipped." You normally will not change this setting. On a tablet, the Orientation setting will be grayed out, because sensors in a tablet will detect when you physically rotate the device and change the orientation without modifying these settings. Sometimes when using a tablet you want the tablet to stay in one orientation, even as you physically rotate it. For that reason, tablets have the setting Lock rotation of this display.

Brightness Level. A Windows 10 laptop or tablet will automatically dim the screen when running on battery or, if the device has ambient light sensors, it will brighten the screen when it detects bright light. If a laptop dims the screen to an unacceptable level, even when it is plugged into an outlet, turn this setting off, and manually set the brightness level to the highest setting. Experiment with this setting. The setting that allows Windows to automatically adjust brightness works very well on most tablets. Look for the Night light settings, which allow you to change the color temperature at night from blue to a warmer color.

Resolution Settings. Scroll down to the resolution settings, which should be at the recommended setting on any modern flat-screen display, as this is the native resolution determined by the display's design.

Ease of Access

Windows includes Ease of Access settings to make Windows more accessible for all types of needs. The Ease of Access and Power buttons, shown here, are on the bottom right of the Sign-In screen so that you can change some Ease of Access settings at sign-in. At this writing, the best place to find a complete list of Ease of Access settings or links to related settings is in Control Panel. In the Start menu, Search box type "Ease of Access," and click or tap the result titled Ease of Access Center to open the Control Panel, as shown in Figure 4-18. There is a long list; some settings are out of view, and you can scroll down to see them.

Configure Windows Update

Windows 10 is configured for automatic updates by default. In fact, in both retail editions, Windows 10 Home and Windows 10 Pro, updates are mandatory.

Note: The actual settings will depend on the type of computer and the Windows 10 feature updates installed.

The Ease of Access button (left) and the Power button.
Source: Microsoft Corporation

In Windows 10 Pro, you can defer upgrades that would add new features. Deferred upgrades will keep new Windows features from downloading and installing for several months.

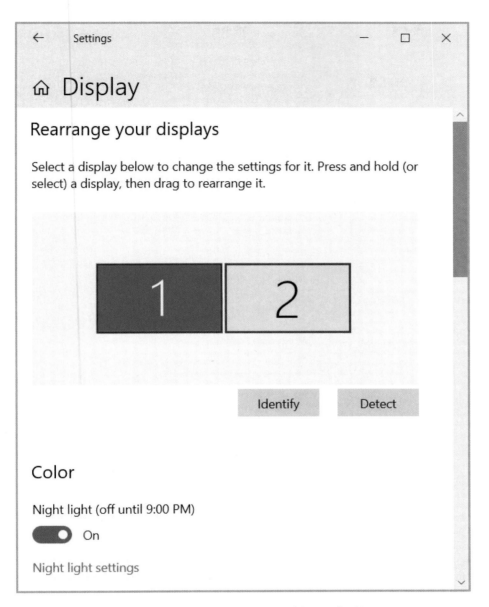

FIGURE 4–16 The Display settings on a computer with two displays.
Source: Microsoft Corporation

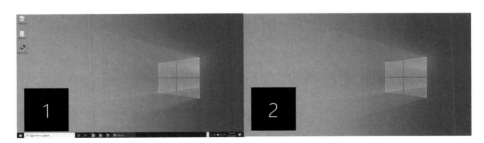

FIGURE 4–17 The result of selecting the Identify button on a dual-display computer.
Source: Microsoft Corporation

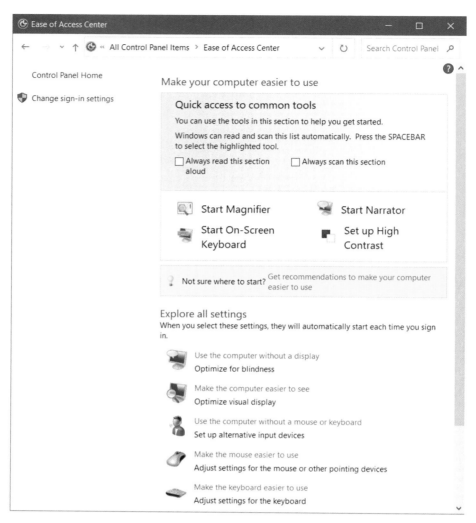

FIGURE 4–18 The Ease of Access Center in Control Panel.
Source: Microsoft Corporation

Note: The keyboard shortcut ⊞+I opens Settings.

However, you should manually trigger updates soon after the installation to ensure that your installation is completely up to date, and to help resolve any remaining driver issues. Additionally, we recommend configuring Windows Update to update all your installed Microsoft software, not just Windows components. Step-by-Step 4.03 walks through the steps for using Windows Update, available through the Settings GUI.

Step-by-Step 4.03

Configuring and Using Windows Update

In this Step-by-Step, you will open Windows Update from the Windows Settings GUI, configure Update to update other Microsoft software, and check for more updates. To complete this exercise, you will need the following:

- A computer running Windows 10 Pro.
- You should be signed in with an administrator account or have the user name and password of an administrator account for the computer.

Open Start and select the Settings gear icon to open the Windows 10 Settings GUI. Alternatively, open Settings with the keyboard shortcut ⊞+I. Notice the grouping of settings into categories. Locate and select the Update & Security category. Then click on Windows Update.

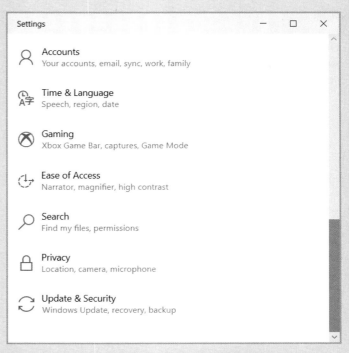

Source: Microsoft Corporation

To see what choices you have for configuring Windows Update, scroll through the options. Shown here are the first two pages of options. To see what updates have been installed click on View update history. Scroll down and select Advanced Options to see other important updates.

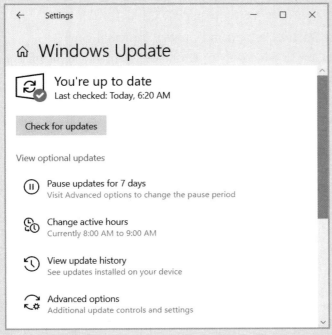

Source: Microsoft Corporation

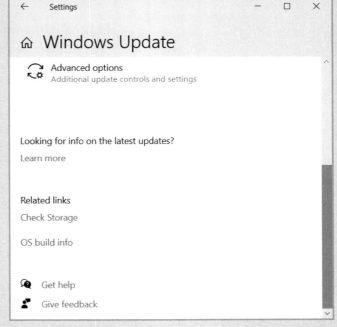

Source: Microsoft Corporation

Step 3

On the Advanced Options page, ensure that installed Microsoft apps are kept up to date by enabling **Receive updates for other Microsoft products when you update Windows**.

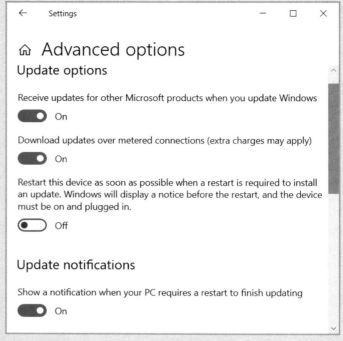

Source: Microsoft Corporation

Step 4

When you are done with Update settings return to the main Settings page using the back arrow at the top left of the title bar, or simply click the close (x) button on the top right to exit from Settings.

Remove Unwanted Software from a Factory Installation

If you purchase a computer with Windows 10 preinstalled, the first time you turn on your new computer you will go through the personalization tasks to configure your sign-in and to customize the Desktop. This Microsoft feature is the Out of Box Experience (OOBE), the last phase of the Windows installation. Then, when you arrive at the Desktop, you may find software installed by the manufacturer that you do not wish to use. Manufacturers received a lot of bad press several years ago for some of the "junk" software, referred to as bloatware, that was preinstalled. Since then, new computers we have worked with have not had as much junk software, although we still find software that we simply do not use.

This preinstalled software falls roughly into two categories: trial software from various software publishers and free utilities provided by the manufacturer and labeled with the manufacturer's name.

Trial software is free to use for a period of time, usually 30 days. At the end of that time, the trial software will cease to function unless you pay a fee to activate it. The two most common types of trial software are security, such as McAfee Antivirus, and productivity, such as Microsoft Office. When you launch one of these, it states that it is trial software and the length of the trial period. They also remind you before the trail period expires. What you choose to do about these trial apps depends on your own preferences and needs.

Apps installed by the computer manufacturer can usually be identified by the manufacturer's name in All Apps. Figure 4-19 shows the software installed by the manufacturer Lenovo. You may want to wait until you are more familiar with these apps before removing any.

When you decide to remove an app, open All Apps and scroll through the list to locate the app. You may need to open a folder, as in the case of Lenovo Reach, listed in Figure 4-19. Once you locate the app, right-click on it to bring up the context menu, shown in Figure 4-20. Then select Uninstall.

Migrate or Restore Data

Your next task is to migrate or restore local data from a previous installation. If you did an in-place upgrade, your data should be intact, but if you did a clean installation, you may have a data backup to restore.

If you are migrating data from a Windows 7 computer and backed up the data with the Windows 7 Backup and Restore utility before installing or upgrading, you are in luck because Windows 10 can do a restore from a Windows 7 backup. The Backup and Restore utility from Windows 7 is included in the Windows 10 Control Panel. Figure 4-21 shows this Backup and Restore utility. If you have files to restore from another installation, **select the option Select another backup to restore files from**.

Back Up Data and the System

Windows 10 includes both the Windows 7 Backup and Restore utility, and a File History tool for automatically backing up your local data. You should configure these, or a third-party backup utility, soon after installing Windows 10.

Use Backup and Restore (Windows 7) to Back Up Files

Microsoft returned the Windows 7 Backup and Restore utility to Windows 10, and you can choose to use this to back up your data from any location on your local computer to the backup media of your choice.

Turn on File History

If you store your data files on the local hard drive, you will want to turn on File History. File History will automatically back up files in your Libraries, Desktop, Contacts, and Favorites. Therefore, you will need to save your files in those locations. It also backs up any OneDrive files that are available offline. File History is not turned on by default; if you have a spare external drive connected to your computer or if you can back up to a network location, turn on and configure File History by opening Settings, selecting Update & Security. In Update & Security select Backup. On the Backup page, shown in Figure 4-22, turn on **Back up using File History**. When you first turn it on, you will be prompted to select a location. Once File History is turned on it works automatically, not only saving files as they change, but saving versions of each file, so that you can restore a file to a certain day and time.

Create a System Image Backup

If you installed Windows 10 from bootable media, you already have the means to reinstall or repair the OS, if necessary, using the bootable media. In the case of a new computer with Windows 10 preinstalled, look for some program from the manufacturer

FIGURE 4–19 The All Apps list showing software installed by the computer manufacturer Lenovo.
Source: Microsoft Corporation

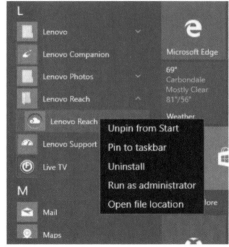

FIGURE 4–20 To remove an app, right-click on it, and select Uninstall.
Source: Microsoft Corporation

try this!

Use Backup and Restore (Windows 7)

Backup Windows 10 with the Windows 7 Backup and Restore utility. Try this:

1. In the Start Search box type "Control Panel."
2. From the search results list select Control Panel.
3. In the All Control Panel Items pane click Backup and Restore (Windows 7).
4. In the Backup and Restore (Windows 7) Control Panel, shown in Figure 4-21, select Set up Backup, following the prompts to create a backup.
5. When you are finished, close the Backup and Restore window.

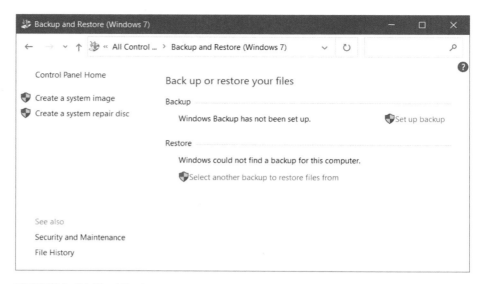

FIGURE 4–21 The Windows 7 Backup and Restore option in Control Panel.
Source: Microsoft Corporation

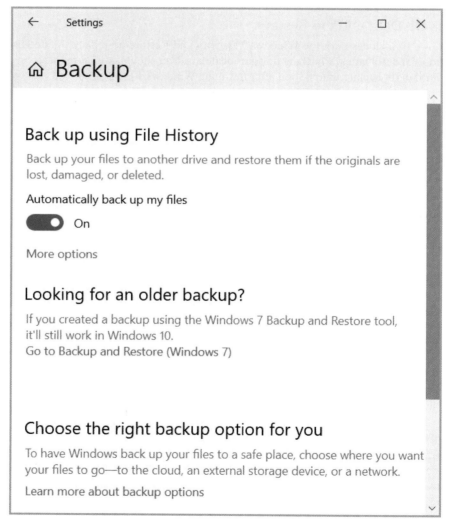

FIGURE 4–22 Turn on **Back up using File History** on the **Backup Settings** page.
Source: Microsoft Corporation

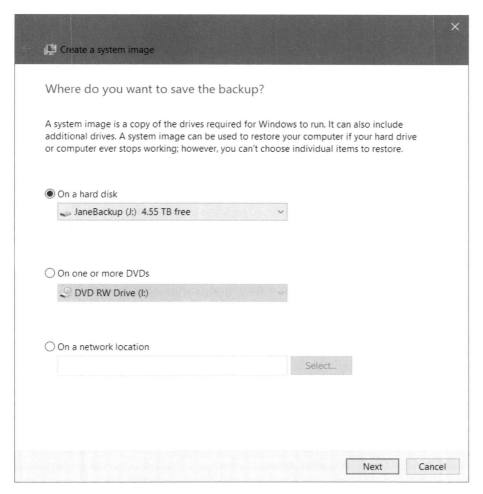

FIGURE 4-23 Create a system image.
Source: Microsoft Corporation

for creating an image of the factory-installed software in case you need to return the computer to its original state. Or you can create a system image. To do this open Control Panel. From the All Control Panel Items page select Backup and Restore (Windows 7). On that page, select Create a system image. This opens the page shown in Figure 4-23. Here you can create a System Image backup that you can use to restore Windows if it becomes irreparably damaged.

LO 4.3 | Working with Windows 10 Features

Microsoft releases frequent updates to Windows 10, adding features along with bug fixes and security patches. In the past, they brought out new versions every three years or so, which meant that they held most features back until they could present them bundled in a new version. Now they are moving away from that practice, relying on incremental changes made through Windows Update, and adding features when they have them ready to release.

The Windows 10 GUI Modes

Earlier we introduced the Windows GUI, and now we will look at it more closely. When you start up Windows 10 on a PC or laptop, the Desktop strongly resembles the Windows 7 Desktop, clear of clutter, just showing the taskbar with the Start button and other features, and the Recycle bin shortcut near the top left. As you use your computer, you may add other objects to the Desktop or taskbar. Microsoft has changed the look of many of these objects, but not so much that you wouldn't recognize them.

The Start menu contains Quick links and is customizable, letting you add or remove links to various folder locations such as Documents, Downloads, Pictures, Music, and Videos. The Start menu also highlights new apps right after they are installed, and contains the alphabetical list of installed apps. Next, explore the two modes of the Windows 10 GUI: Desktop and Tablet.

Desktop Mode

When you open the Start menu in Windows 10 in Desktop mode, the Start menu covers only a portion of the Desktop, as shown back in Figure 4-5. Desktop mode also displays apps windowed so they are easier to move around with a keyboard and mouse (or touchpad). You can use screen touch gestures in Desktop mode, but the Desktop GUI is not as convenient for touch screen use as is Tablet mode. In Desktop mode, the Start menu contains a column along the left with your most used items at the top. Near the bottom are Quick links for Settings and Power, topped off with the User tile. In addition, out to the right are groups of live tiles. A **live tile** is a rectangle on the Windows 10 Start menu that works like a shortcut or quick link to launch a program. The "live" part of the name refers to a tile's ability to display active content related to the app, without launching the app.

Tablet Mode

When Windows 10 wakes up on a tablet without an attached keyboard, the Start menu automatically opens in **Tablet mode** (full screen) to work better with a touch screen. In this mode, all your apps run full screen. To switch between Desktop mode and Tablet mode on a Windows 10 desktop or laptop, simply click or tap the Action Center icon in the Notification area on the right of the taskbar (Figure 4-24), or use the keyboard shortcut ⊞+A. When the Action Center opens (Figure 4-25) tap or click Tablet mode. Figure 4-26 shows the Start menu in Tablet mode. Notice that the taskbar remains on the bottom of the screen without the shortcuts of pinned and open apps seen in Desktop mode. The column of Quick links is on the left and the Apps list does not display. The third Quick link from the top opens the All Apps list, full screen. In Tablet mode, a Back icon, in the form of a left-facing arrow, appears on the left of the taskbar. Click or tap this to go back to the last open app.

FIGURE 4–24 The Action Center icon is on the taskbar.
Source: Microsoft Corporation

Note: The keyboard shortcut ⊞+A opens Action Center.

Note: Action Center opens on touch devices with an edge gesture: a swipe from the right-side of the screen.

FIGURE 4–25 Open Action Center and select Tablet mode.
Source: Microsoft Corporation

FIGURE 4–26 The Windows 10 Start menu in Tablet mode.
Source: Microsoft Corporation

Selecting Tablet mode from the Action Center may only turn it on temporarily. Depending on the computer and other variables, the next time you restart a computer with keyboard attached it will go back to the default Desktop mode. Learn more about personalizing Windows 10 in Step-by-Step 4.04.

Continuum

Continuum is a feature that is ideal for anyone working on a two-in-one device—a tablet with a detachable keyboard. With the keyboard attached, Windows 10 will display Desktop mode. Detach the keyboard and the Continuum feature automatically changes to Tablet mode on the fly, converting the Start menu and open apps to full screen. Touch gestures let you move through the open apps. In addition, the Continuum feature enables a Windows 10 Mobile device to connect to monitors and keyboards.

try this!

Turn On Tablet Mode at Startup

Even if you have an attached keyboard, you can have Tablet mode enabled every time Windows 10 restarts. Try this:

1. Open Settings by either of two methods: select Settings from the Start menu or use the keyboard shortcut, ⊞+I.
2. In Settings select Personalization, and then select Start.
3. Enable the option "Use Start full screen."
4. Close out of settings, and the Start menu will open full screen at Startup.
5. To return to Desktop mode at Startup, return to the Start page in Settings and disable the option "Use Start full screen."

Step-by-Step 4.04

Personalize the Windows 10 Desktop

The Windows 10 Desktop is more than just the Start menu, although that is an important feature. In this exercise, you will customize the Start menu To complete this exercise, you will need:

• A PC or laptop running Windows 10.

Step 1

Open Settings | Personalization | Start.

Step 2

On the Start page scroll down and click or tap "Choose which folders appear on Start."

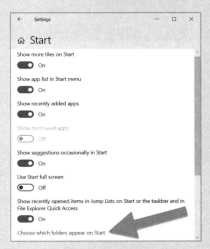

Source: Microsoft Corporation

Step 3

Scroll through the list and select a folder to appear on Start. We selected the Downloads folder.

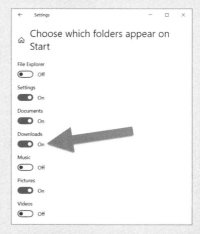

Source: Microsoft Corporation

Step 4

Close Settings and open Start to confirm that the folder you selected was added.

Step 5

Customize the Desktop. Open Settings again and return to the Personalization page. Select Background. The background can be a picture, solid color, or a slideshow. As you choose different options, the Preview (at the top) changes.

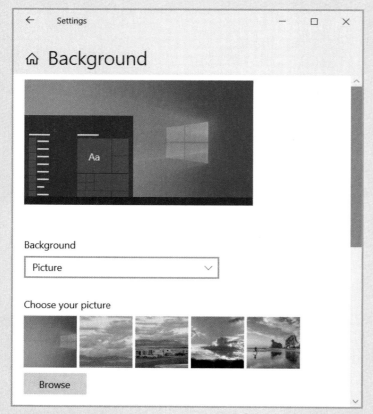

Source: Microsoft Corporation

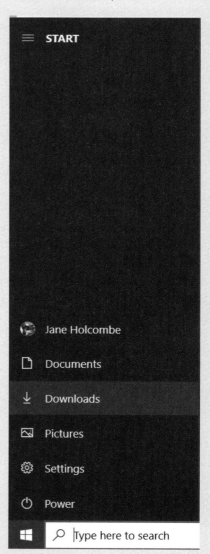

Source: Microsoft Corporation

Step 6

Click on the box labeled Picture in the Step 5 example, and it will open to three choices: Picture, Solid color, and Slideshow. If it was not already selected, select Picture. You can select a different picture from the choices shown or browse to select a personal picture. The Preview reflects your changes, as shown here.

Source: Microsoft Corporation

Step 7

Change the fit of the picture on the Desktop by scrolling down and clicking or tapping the box under Choose a fit. This opens a list of fit treatments that temporarily cover up other settings. The choices include Fill, Fit, Stretch, Tile, Center, and Span. Experiment with different fits and see how they change the picture on the Desktop. Select one that you like.

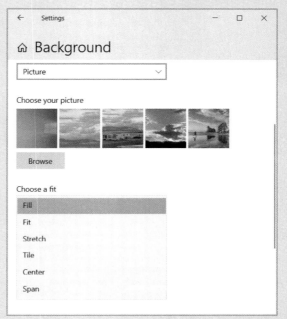

Source: Microsoft Corporation

Step 8

Now return to the Personalization page and select Colors. This opens the Colors pane. Click the box under **Choose your color** to open a menu that currently lists **Light, Dark**, and **Custom**. Experiment with the options. Choosing Light or Dark will turn defaults for both Windows mode and app mode to that choice. Choose **Custom** if you want a different mode (Light or Dark) for Windows and apps. You can still select the colors you want.

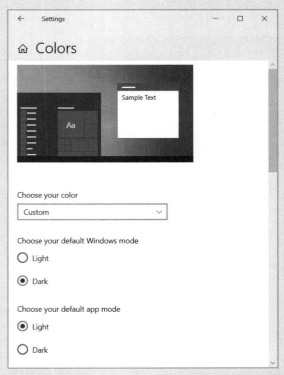

Source: Microsoft Corporation

Choose an accent color and add color to the Start menu, taskbar, and Action Center. You can also turn on or turn off the transparency of Start, taskbar, and Action Center. We prefer to have transparency turned off.

Experiment with other Personalization options, such as choosing a picture for the Lock screen and selecting apps to appear on the Lock screen. When you have completed the changes you want, exit from Settings and return to the Desktop.

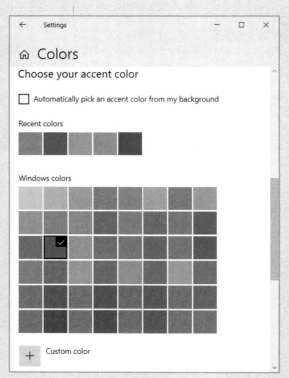

Source: Microsoft Corporation

FIGURE 4–27 The Cortana shortcut.
Source: Microsoft Corporation

FIGURE 4–28 Cortana's Home page.
Source: Microsoft Corporation

Getting Started with Cortana

Cortana is a personal assistant and an intelligent search system that searches the Web, your computer or device, and any cloud storage you use from that computer. It also learns about you, not by spying but by paying attention to things you permit Cortana to watch.

Communicating with Cortana

Interact with Cortana in several ways. To get started click or tap the Cortana icon (Figure 4-27). If you have not configured Cortana, the first time you click this shortcut it will open to the **Sign in to Cortana page**. If you do not wish to sign in and use Cortana, click the close button at the top right of this dialog. If you do want to use Cortana, click the **Sign in** button and follow the prompts. After that, click the Cortana shortcut to open the Home page where Cortana keeps pertinent information for you. If you have a working microphone on your computer, click or tap the microphone icon on the bottom right of the Ask Cortana box, and start talking to Cortana. With either action, Cortana will display results, as shown in Figure 4-28. Cortana also displays a configurable set of information for you as she learns more about you.

Select What Cortana Learns about You

From the Cortana menu open Cortana Settings, shown in Figure 4-29. Then select Privacy (Figure 4-30). This is where you tell Cortana the things you want it to know about you and what it can use to learn more. Move the mouse pointer to the right edge to activate the scroll bar, indicating that there are more items listed below.

Cortana can help you with many everyday tasks involving your installed apps, such as creating a play list, or creating an email. Cortana can go online to track a package based on information in an email. As Cortana learns, it will make appropriate suggestions and give reminders via posts on its Home page. Providing a notice or other information in anticipation of a need is called a predictive notification, a feature long available in Google Now. This requires some history, but you can configure just how much of your life is revealed to Cortana. Need a little cheering up? Ask Cortana to tell you a joke. Then prepare yourself for a corny joke.

Note: The autocorrect in apps for both PCs and mobile devices is another example of a predictive technology.

Hey Cortana

The voice activation option, Hey Cortana, was introduced in Windows Phone 8.1 and made available in Windows 10 for those devices that support voice input. This takes some training of the app by the user to ensure that Cortana responds to the voice query. You can either type your query or talk, and in both cases, you do not need to remember a syntax, but ask questions as you would if talking to or texting with a person.

Using Apps in Windows 10

When working on the Desktop in Windows 10, you will find your apps behaving much like traditional Windows apps did in Windows 7. Launch an app from the Apps list and then pin it to the taskbar or create a shortcut on the Desktop. The author's favorite feature of the taskbar shortcuts for apps is the Jump list that displays when you right-click on an app's shortcut. This list includes recently opened items, such as files, folders, and websites. Simply click one to open the app with that item loaded. Windows 10 introduced apps that display on any Windows 10 PC, laptop, or tablet. Your old Windows apps will still work in Windows 10.

Windows Store Apps versus Windows Desktop Apps

For Windows 10, Microsoft invested a large amount of effort into the notion that an application should be written once and run on many platforms—universally, so to speak. Therefore, Windows 10 introduced the Universal app that runs in Windows 10 on PCs and across all the devices this operating system supports, including conventional PCs and laptops as well as tablets.

Microsoft replaced the term Universal App with Windows Store App. This is an app that conforms to the different screen sizes and other features, such as input type (e.g., keyboard and mouse versus touch screen), making the switch automatically. In Figure 4-31 the Windows Store App, Photos, is full screen in Tablet mode. Just a few features of its windowed, Desktop mode, are missing—mainly the Minimize,

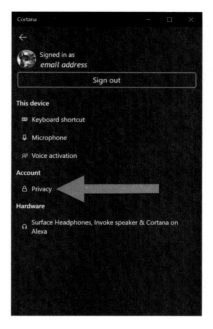

FIGURE 4–29 The Cortana Settings.
Source: Microsoft Corporation

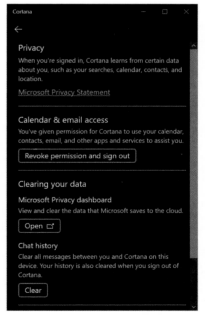

FIGURE 4–30 The Cortana Privacy page.
Source: Microsoft Corporation

FIGURE 4–31 A Windows Store app, Photos, full screen in Tablet mode.
Sources: Microsoft Corporation

Maximize, and Close Buttons normally at the top right of a windowed app. The Tablet mode task bar appears on the bottom, omitting the task bar shortcuts for pinned and open apps.

Windows 10 also supports legacy Windows Desktop apps. They only run in Windows on PCs and laptops.

Task View

Windows 10 Task view lets you quickly view all your open apps. Access Task view by clicking or tapping the Task view icon located to the right of the Cortana shortcut on the taskbar (Figure 4–32). It opens with large thumbnails for each open app, as shown in Figure 4–33.

Virtual Desktops

Windows 10 includes a feature that has long been available in OS X and Linux: support for multiple Desktops—Microsoft calls it Virtual Desktop. This is a great way to

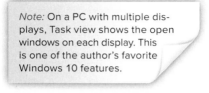

FIGURE 4–32 The Task view icon on the taskbar.
Source: Microsoft Corporation

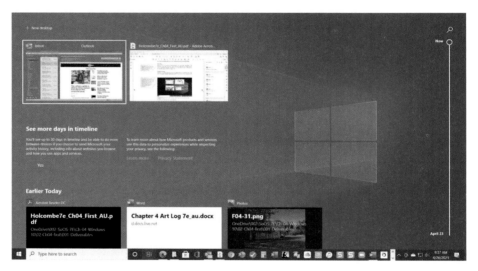

FIGURE 4–33 Task view.
Sources: Microsoft Corporation

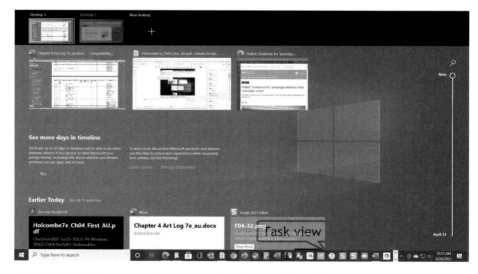

FIGURE 4–34 Task view showing the tiles for two Virtual Desktops.
Sources: Microsoft Corporation

group your projects. For instance, on your home PC you could create a new Desktop while working on personal finances with Windows for Quicken, Excel, a calculator app, and your personal banking website open in one Desktop. Then you could also open a second Desktop where you work on a genealogy project. Task view, as shown in Figure 4–34 displays tiles at the top of the screen for two separate Desktops. From Task view simply click or tap to select a Desktop. When working in a Virtual Desktop, switch to other active Virtual Desktops by using the shortcut keys **Ctrl+⊞+left arrow** and **Ctrl+⊞+right arrow**.

Microsoft Store

The Microsoft Store, Figure 4–35, is available from the Windows 10 Start menu. It requires an Internet connection and a Microsoft account. This one store provides Microsoft apps and services. It offers games, music, movies, and TV.

Be aware that many apps, especially games, have in-app purchases that can be quite expensive. You will need to configure a payment method for within the Store, and it will ask for an account password with each purchase—even with in-app purchases. You do not need a payment option to download and install free apps.

The Store Settings page, shown in Figure 4–36, has an option for automatically updating apps. This is turned on by default, and we recommend keeping this setting. This is also where you can control whether or not the Live Tile shows products. Scroll down to **Manage your devices**. Click this link to open a page in your Microsoft account settings where you can manage the devices on which you install apps. You may download apps and games from the Microsoft Store on up to 10 devices.

The Try This! walks you through installing a free app from the Windows Store.

try this!

Install a Free App from the Store

If you are signed in with a Microsoft account and have an Internet connection, browse for free apps at the Windows Store. Try this:

1. From the Start menu or the Taskbar tap or click the Store tile.
2. Enter a search string into the Search box or scroll through the selections and click those that interest you. Look for a free app.
3. Follow the on-screen instructions to download and install the app.

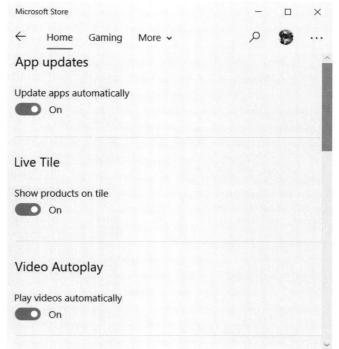

FIGURE 4–35 The Microsoft Store Home page.
Source: Microsoft Corporation

FIGURE 4–36 The Store Settings page.
Source: Microsoft Corporation

Changing the User Picture

In the left column of the Start menu the User tile displays the name and image associated with your account. Click or tap the User tile to open the menu shown in Figure 4-37. From this menu, you can change your account settings, lock the screen, or sign out. The Try This! describes how to change your account picture in Windows 10.

FIGURE 4-37 The User menu.
Source: Microsoft Corporation

try this!

Change Your Account Picture

Would you like to personalize your account picture? You can easily use an existing photo or take a new picture with your computer's camera. Try this:

1. Click or tap the User tile and select Change account settings.
2. This opens the Accounts pane in Settings. This page shows your present picture (or lack of one).
3. Click the Browse button and browse for a picture to use or select the Camera to take a picture.
4. Once you select a picture, return to the Accounts page where the new image will replace the previous one. Close the Settings window. The new picture will display on the Start menu and on the Sign-In screen.

LO 4.4 | Securing Windows 10

By default, Windows 10 installs with the most critical security features enabled. If your Windows computer is on a corporate (or school) network, the organization will centrally manage it, including securing it from a variety of threats. A term for software and hardware designed to be used and managed by large organizations is enterprise computing. This also applies to all the jobs and abilities available in an enterprise environment.

A computer that is not managed by an organization depends on the knowledge of the user/owner for its overall management and maintenance. Security implemented solely on a desktop or laptop computer is local security. In this learning objective, you will learn about features and tools available to you on your personal desktop. We will also briefly describe some of the enhanced security features of a computer that is part of an enterprise that implements Microsoft servers and security.

Windows 10 S Mode

Windows 10 S Mode began life as a separate Windows 10 edition (without the "mode" designation) intended for the education market. When in S Mode, a Windows 10 PC can only install apps from the Microsoft Store, and you can only browse with the Microsoft Edge browser using the Bing search engine. S Mode also disables most of the troubleshooting tools we introduce in Chapter 5. The upside to Windows 10 S Mode is that it is more secure, protecting a computer from malware, and generally faster since it does not allow apps to install startup tasks that can slow your computer.

Windows 10 S Mode is preinstalled with Windows 10 Home or Windows 10 Pro on computers for the education market. It is not something you can turn on and off at will. If you own a computer with Windows 10S Mode, you can disable S Mode through the Windows Store. There is no cost to doing this, which will give you a fully capable version of Windows 10. However, once disabled, you cannot enable it again.

Windows Hello

Windows Hello, a biometric sign-in feature, lets you sign in to your Windows 10 device with a biometric sign-in: fingerprint, facial recognition, or iris scan. It requires the existence of special hardware in the Windows 10 computer. To sign in with a finger-print, your computer must have a compatible fingerprint scanner. The facial scanning requires a special camera that uses infrared light to see features under the less-than-ideal settings, such as poor light conditions and users wearing makeup or having facial hair. Look for Windows Hello settings in the Settings app under Account protection.

Microsoft Passport

While Windows Hello allows you to log in to your Windows 10 device using biomet-rics, Microsoft Passport lets you securely sign in to network resources without send-ing a password or PIN over the network; the authentication is tied to the hardware. For greater security, combine the secure local authentication of Windows Hello with Microsoft Passport authentication to network resources. Presently, Microsoft Pass-port gives you access to resources, such as Microsoft's Azure Active Directory ser-vices, and Web servers, but there is limited support beyond Microsoft's products. That may change, as Microsoft is among many companies representing such industries as banking, software, hardware, and more who joined the industry consortium FIDO Alliance (Fast Identity Online) to contribute their technology and work together to develop solutions that will allow users to securely access online services and conduct financial transactions without using password authentication and to reduce the risk of fraud. Microsoft Passport is not available to Windows 10 devices that are not part of a Microsoft Azure AD or Microsoft Active Directory Domain Services enterprise.

> *Note:* Learn more about the FIDO Alliance at **https:// fidoalliance.org**.

Windows Security

Windows Security is really many security features that you manage through the Secu-rity page of Windows Settings, shown in Figure 4–38. From here you can quickly see the overall security status of your device, even if some of this protection is provided by third-party software. Installing a third-party security app replaces some features of Windows Security. Figure 4–39 shows the Virus & threat protection page of Windows Security after installing Bitdefender Antivirus.

Windows Firewall

Access the Windows Firewall and Network Protection status and settings (Figure 4–40) from the Windows Security page. This page contains links to firewall and network-related settings and tools.

FIGURE 4–38 Windows Security settings.
Source: Microsoft Corporation

FIGURE 4–39 The Windows Security Virus & threat protection page showing that a third-party antivirus is installed.
Source: Microsoft Corporation

Select Advanced settings (shown at bottom left in Figure 4-40) to open the Windows Firewall with Advanced Security management console, shown in Figure 4-41. This is a very advanced tool for a knowledgeable administrator. Using this console, you can set inbound and outbound rules for the traffic identified by its source or app name, allowing or blocking certain types of traffic.

Encrypting File System

The Microsoft NTFS allows you to encrypt selected files and folders (not an entire drive) through a feature called Encrypting File System (EFS). Turn on encryption through the Advanced button of the Properties dialog box of a folder residing on an NTFS volume, and then all files created in that folder become encrypted. Figure 4-42 shows the Advanced Attributes dialog that opens from the Advanced button on the Properties of a folder named Budget. Clicking the check box labeled Encrypt contents

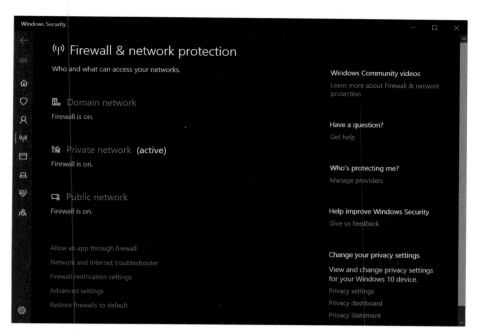

FIGURE 4–40 The Windows Security Firewall & network protection page.
Source: Microsoft Corporation

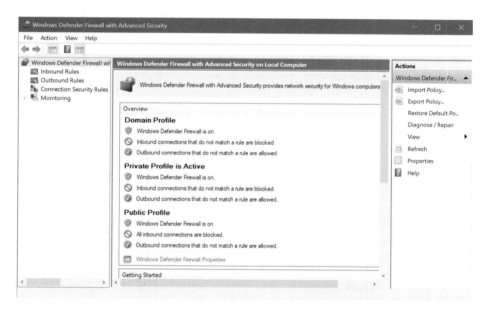

FIGURE 4–41 Windows Defender Firewall with Advanced Security.
Source: Microsoft Corporation

to secure data will turn on encryption for this folder. Anyone who is logged on with your credentials has access to EFS encrypted data. If you copy or move an encrypted file to another NTFS-formatted volume/drive, the encryption is maintained. If you copy or move an encrypted file to a volume/drive that is not formatted with NTFS, the file is saved without encryption.

While EFS is a useful tool, it is not without problems, including the risk that you will lock yourself out of your own files if you change your password. Only enable EFS if you have a knowledgeable administrator (such as at school or work) who will take certain precautions to ensure that someone can aid you in recovering your encrypted files should you be unable to access them yourself.

Encrypting with Windows BitLocker

BitLocker Drive Encryption is a feature of the Windows 10 Pro and Ultimate Editions. It allows you to encrypt an entire internal drive. You or anyone else who is logged on with your credentials has access to the encrypted drive. When using BitLocker in Windows 10, you can use a feature called **BitLocker To Go** to encrypt external hard drives and USB flash drives. When you create a BitLocker To Go volume, you select the method for unlocking. Because this is a portable drive, you can assign a password or a smart card to unlock the drive. See the BitLocker Control Panel in Figure 4-43.

User Account Control

Before Windows Vista, if you wanted to make changes to your system such as installing a new device or program, you had to log on as an administrator. This meant, if you were already logged on with an account that did not have administrative access, you would have to log off and log on again with an administrator account before you could perform a major system task. To avoid this annoyance, many people stayed logged on

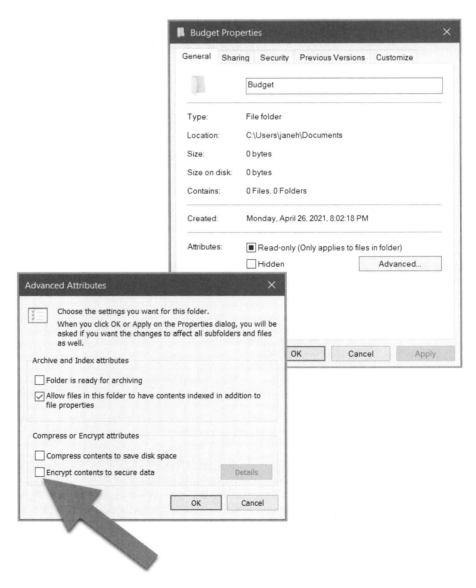

FIGURE 4–42 Turn NTFS Encryption on using Advanced Attributes.
Source: Microsoft Corporation

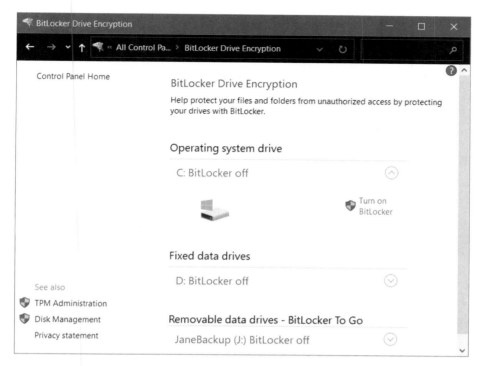

FIGURE 4–43 The Windows 10 BitLocker Control Panel.
Source: Microsoft Corporation

all day every day using an account with administrator access. This meant that if malware infected your computer, it would have full control over your computer because it would have the same level of access as the logged-on user. To prevent this, Microsoft introduced **User Account Control (UAC)** to prevent unauthorized changes to Windows even when you are logged on with an Administrator type account.

In Windows 10 configure this feature in User Account Control Settings, shown in Figure 4–44. There are four settings. The most restrictive will notify you whenever an app tries to install software or make changes and whenever you try to make changes to Windows settings. The next level (the default) will notify you only when apps try to

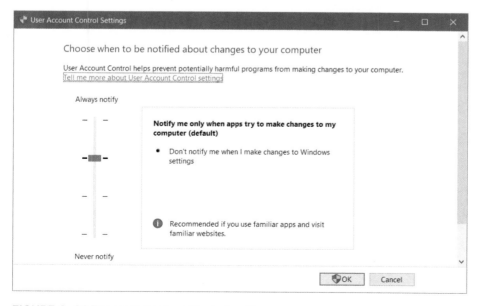

FIGURE 4–44 The User Account Control settings.
Source: Microsoft Corporation

make changes to your computer, but not when you make changes to Windows settings. The third level will notify you only when apps try to make changes to your computer, but it will not dim the desktop. The final, and least secure, level will never notify you when an app tries to install software or make changes to your computer or when you make changes to Windows settings.

UAC notifies you with one of two prompts—the Consent Prompt or the Credentials Prompt. When you are logged on as an administrator, you will be notified by the Consent Prompt, which only requires that you consent to the action. When logged on as a standard user, you will need to provide the computer administrator credentials in the Credentials Prompt.

Chapter 4 REVIEW

Chapter Summary

After reading this chapter and completing the exercises, you should understand the following facts about Windows 10.

Installing Windows 10

- The two retail editions of Windows 10 are Windows 10 Home and Windows 10 Pro.
- Windows 10 has operating modes that work on PCs, tablets, and two-in-ones.
- The minimum hardware requirements to install Windows 10 on a computer with Intel or AMD architecture are modest.
- Prior to upgrading, there are several things you should do:
  - Update Windows 7, Windows 8, or 8.1.
  - Back up your data.
  - Update the firmware, if an update is available.
  - Acquire updated drivers if the manufacturer has not automatically updated them.
  - Choose how you will sign in to Windows 10.
- Windows 10 comes "prekeyed" and will automatically provide the product key to Microsoft during the product activation process.
- If you purchase Windows 10 online, you can do a Web-based setup that requires very little interaction and is very fast.
- To do a traditional Windows setup, you must have the Windows 10 Setup files on bootable media.

Postinstallation Tasks

- Get acquainted with the Windows 10 Start menu.
- Quick links replace the previous shortcuts.
- File Explorer is the Windows 10 file management utility.

- Microsoft is the Windows 10 Web browser.
- Install drivers.
- Tweak the display settings from the Settings app, and make Windows more accessible with a long list of Ease of Access settings.
- Updates are mandatory in Windows 10. You can add updates for other Microsoft software.
- Remove bloatware from a computer that has Windows 10 preinstalled.
- Migrate or restore data.
- Back up both data and the system using either third-party utilities or the utilities available in Windows 10: Windows 7 Backup and Restore utility, File History, and image backup.

Working with Windows 10 Features

- Windows 10 default Desktop shows just the taskbar with the Start button, some other features, and the Recycle bin shortcut near the top left.
- On a computer with a keyboard, the Start menu opens in Desktop mode covering a small portion of the Desktop. Apps are windowed to make them easy to move around by keyboard, mouse, or touchpad.
- When Windows 10 wakes up on a tablet without an attached keyboard, the Start menu automatically opens in full-screen Tablet mode.
- The Continuum feature detects when the keyboard is attached so that Windows 10 will display the PC-style Desktop mode.
- Personalize the Start menu by adding Quick links to folders. Personalize the Desktop background and colors.

- Cortana, Windows 10's virtual assistant and enhanced search utility, includes a voice-activation option, Hey Cortana.

- When working in Desktop mode, you can launch an app from the Apps list and then pin it to the taskbar or create a shortcut on the Desktop.

- Windows Store apps run on all the devices this operating system supports, from the conventional PC to tablets and smartphones.

- Windows 10 Task view lets you quickly view your open apps. Access Task view by clicking or tapping the Task view icon.

- Windows 10 supports multiple Virtual Desktops. This is a great way to group your projects.

- The Windows Store requires a Microsoft account and offers services, software, games, music, movies, and TV. To make purchases through the Store, add a payment method through the Store. The Store requires a password for each purchase.

- Open the User menu from the User tile on the Start menu to change the user picture, lock the computer, or sign out.

Securing Windows 10

- When Windows 10 installs, it enables the most critical security features.

- Software and hardware designed to be used and managed by large organizations is part of enterprise computing.

- A computer not managed by an organization is protected by local security.

- Windows Hello lets you sign in to your Windows 10 device with a biometric sign-in type: fingerprint, facial recognition, or iris scan. It requires the existence of special hardware.

- Microsoft Passport lets you securely sign in to network resources without sending a password or PIN over the network. Once Passport authenticates you locally, it gives you access to resources, such as Microsoft's Azure Active Directory services and some Web servers.

- Windows Security has many security features that you manage through the Security page of Windows Settings.

- Windows Firewall and Network Protection is enabled by default. Select Advanced Settings on its settings page to open the Windows Defender Firewall with Advanced Security console.

- On an NTFS volume, use the Encrypting File System (EFS) to encrypt files and folders.

- Encrypt an entire internal disk drive with BitLocker Drive Encryption.

- Encrypt a removable drive with BitLocker To Go.

- User Account Control (UAC) prevents unauthorized changes to Windows.

Key Terms List

bloatware *(132)*

BitLocker and BitLocker To Go *(148)*

context menu *(126)*

Continuum *(137)*

Consent Prompt *(150)*

Cortana *(140)*

Credentials Prompt *(150)*

Desktop mode *(118)*

Device Manager *(122)*

Ease of Access *(128)*

Encrypting File System (EFS) *(146)*

enterprise computing *(144)*

FIDO Alliance (Fast Identity Online) *(145)*

File Explorer *(119)*

Hey Cortana *(141)*

jump list *(141)*

keyboard shortcut *(118)*

live tile *(136)*

local security *(144)*

Lock screen *(119)*

Microsoft account (MSA) *(109)*

Microsoft Edge *(121)*

Microsoft Passport *(145)*

Microsoft Product Activation (MPA) *(108)*

multitouch *(107)*

Out of Box Experience (OOBE) *(132)*

predictive notification *(141)*

Quick link *(119)*

shortcut *(118)*

Start button *(118)*

Tablet mode *(136)*

Task view *(142)*

upgrade *(107)*

Universal app *(141)*

User Account Control (UAC) *(149)*

User tile *(119)*

Virtual Desktop *(142)*

Web-based setup *(110)*

Windows 10 Home Edition *(106)*

Windows 10 Pro *(106)*

Windows Hello *(144)*

Windows Key *(118)*

Windows Preinstallation Environment (Windows PE) *(111)*

Windows Security *(145)*

Windows Setup *(110)*

Windows Store App *(141)*

Windows Update *(107)*

Key Terms Quiz

Use the Key Terms List to complete the sentences that follow. Not all terms will be used.

1. Although this sounds like you are greeting a female friend, _____ is a feature of Windows that lets you activate your personal assistant with your voice.

2. In _____ the Start menu covers the entire screen, and universal apps are full screen.

3. The _____ feature of Windows 10 lets you quickly view all open apps.

4. The _____ feature is similar to ones long available in OS X and Linux, in which you can organize your open apps into individual groupings, with one grouping on your screen at a time.

5. A Start menu _____ works like a shortcut with the added ability to display active content related to the app.

6. Sign in to Windows 10 with a/an _____ to have access to Microsoft services, as well as to programs and files on your local computer.

7. Windows 10 on a two-in-one device uses a feature called _____, by which it detects when the keyboard is disconnected and automatically changes to Tablet mode.

8. An example of _____ is when Cortana provides a notice in anticipation of a need it discovered by learning about you and your interests.

9. A/an _____ automatically runs full screen on a Windows 10 tablet, and windowed on a computer with a keyboard.

10. _____ is the biometric sign-in feature in Windows 10, requiring special hardware.

Multiple-Choice Quiz

1. This Windows 10 feature is very useful on a computer or device with a touch screen, preventing some unintended actions.
   a. Windows Defender
   b. Lock screen
   c. Continuum
   d. User tile
   e. Multitouch

2. Windows 10 introduced this new Web browser.
   a. Microsoft Edge
   b. Cortana
   c. Microsoft Passport
   d. Continuum
   e. Windows Defender

3. A feature of Windows that prevents unauthorized changes.
   a. Windows Hello
   b. Hey Cortana
   c. Windows Security
   d. Task view
   e. UAC

4. What is the name of the Windows 10 personal assistant?
   a. Microsoft Edge
   b. Cortana
   c. Microsoft Passport
   d. Continuum
   e. Windows Defender

5. This method for authenticating to network resources does not send passwords or PINs across the network.
   a. Microsoft Edge
   b. Cortana
   c. Microsoft Passport
   d. Continuum
   e. Windows Security

6. When working in Virtual Desktops in Windows 10, what feature will allow you to see a thumbnail representing each Virtual Desktop, as well as all open apps?
   a. Quick link
   b. Predictive notification
   c. Task view
   d. Windows Hello
   e. Jump list

7. This Windows 10 Settings pane is where you can manage many security features of Windows 10.
   a. Microsoft Edge
   b. Cortana
   c. Microsoft Passport
   d. Continuum
   e. Windows Security

8. Windows 10 includes this file management utility.
   a. Continuum
   b. Microsoft Passport
   c. Task view
   d. Cortana
   e. File Explorer

9. Which of these will be removed when upgrading a computer from Windows 7 to Windows 10? Select all correct answers.
   a. Windows Hello
   b. Windows Media Center
   c. Desktop gadgets
   d. Windows XP Mode
   e. Minesweeper

10. Click or tap this to open the Windows 10 Start menu. Select all correct answers.
    a. ⊞ KEY
    b. Start button
    c. Product key
    d. ⊞+I
    e. ⊞+C

11. Which of the following is the acronym for Microsoft's antipiracy tool?
    a. PIP
    b. OS
    c. MSA
    d. ISO
    e. MPA

12. Of the Windows editions available as retail products, which one is designed for very high-end (server) PCs?
    a. Windows 10 S
    b. Windows 10 Pro
    c. Windows 10 Pro for Workstations

    d. Windows Server
    e. Windows 10 Home

13. This is the type of security that is implemented solely on a desktop or laptop computer.
    a. Cortana
    b. Local
    c. Microsoft Password
    d. Windows Hello
    e. S Mode

14. Which retail edition of Windows 10 will you buy for your home PC if you need to use BitLocker To Go?
    a. Windows 10 Starter
    b. Windows 10 Education
    c. Windows 10 Enterprise
    d. Windows 10 Home
    e. Windows 10 Pro

15. If you want an app that runs well in Windows 10 on PCs, laptops, and tablets, use this type.
    a. Continuum
    b. Windows Passport
    c. Windows Defender Firewall
    d. Windows Store app
    e. File Explorer

Essay Quiz

1. Describe the User Account Control feature including the four settings options and how it protects Windows. Also describe what is different about how you respond to a UAC prompt when you are logged in as an administrator versus a standard user.

2. Describe Windows S Mode, when or how it is available, and both the advantages and inconveniences of this feature.

3. Describe and contrast Encrypting File System, Bit-Locker Drive Encryption, and BitLocker To Go. Be sure to explain when and how each is available.

4. Describe the differences between signing in with a local account and signing in with a Microsoft account.

5. Describe Windows Hello and Microsoft Passport and explain the relationship between these two features in making secure connections to network resources.

Lab Projects

LAB PROJECT 4.1

When Microsoft released Windows 10 as a free upgrade to many existing Windows computers, their hope was to replace old versions of Windows with one that would be continually upgraded as time went on. They also hoped

to gain market share of desktop and laptop computers. Research how successful this program was in terms of the market share of Windows 10 on all PCs worldwide.

LAB PROJECT 4.2

Research how to enable and disable a live tile. Then select a Windows Store app, such as the Mail App or Photos app, and turn the live tile for the app on and off. Then research how to size tiles and group them. Demonstrate the changes you made to your classmates and discuss your opinion of this feature.

LAB PROJECT 4.3

This chapter is a simple introduction and overview of Windows 10 and omits or only briefly mentions some features. Take time to explore one now. Research the Timeline feature to learn how to scroll through your Timeline of tasks performed on your Windows 10 computer and resume one or more of those tasks. Then, research how to enable or disable Timeline's tracking of activities associated with your Microsoft account across your devices. Write up your findings and share them with your classmates.

chapter

5 Supporting and Troubleshooting Windows

J.K2507/Shutterstock

Learning Outcomes

In this chapter, you will learn how to:

LO **5.1** Managing local accounts.

LO **5.2** Managing local data files.

LO **5.3** Define the role of the registry in Windows, and back up and modify the registry when needed.

LO **5.4** Describe the Windows user options and power options, and, given a scenario, select appropriate startup options.

LO **5.5** Troubleshoot common Windows problems.

As a user of Windows, no matter where you use this OS—at school, work, or at home— you may occasionally find yourself needing to manage and troubleshoot Windows. This chapter will guide you through a tour of some of the under-the-hood components and the tools for working with them. Begin by expanding your understanding of local accounts and file systems. Then explore the Windows registry and consider user options, power options, and various ways to start up Windows for resolving problems. Move on to the topic of installing and managing device drivers, and lastly look at methods for troubleshooting common Windows problems. This entire chapter is designed to give you the knowledge to both manage and troubleshoot your Windows computer. ❀

LO 5.1 | Managing Local Accounts

If your Windows computer is part of a Microsoft Active Directory Domain or some other enterprise service, the organization will centrally manage its security and other settings. A computer that is not part of an organization's network depends on the knowledge of the user to manage and secure it. Security implemented solely on a Windows device is local security. This Learning Objective describes how to administer local accounts.

Local User Accounts

On a Windows computer a local account, also known as an offline account, resides in the local accounts database, which is a part of the registry—a later topic in this chapter. A local account can only access the local data. Typically, only one person logs on locally to a PC or laptop. Therefore, most users have little or no experience managing local accounts other than their own, and those same users rarely need to make changes to their own local account. However, multiple local accounts can be created so that more than one user can interactively work with a computer at different times. Using different accounts allows each user to have their own desktop preferences and keep their own locally stored data safe.

Alternatively, if a locally managed computer has reliable Internet access the accounts that sign on to it can sign on with their Microsoft account (MSA), authenticating to Microsoft's servers. They can even sign on during occasional Internet outages. The author's four Windows computers (two desktops and two laptops) are not part of a corporate network but have Internet access. She manages the local security on those devices. While she could simply log into each with a unique local account, she finds it beneficial to sign in with her MSA. This allows her to use various Microsoft services on each device; her sign-in to Windows gives her access to those services as well to the local resources. She can also synchronize her personalized settings across devices.

When a user selects the option to sign on to their new computer using an MSA, Windows Setup creates a local user account based on the name supplied. The MSA authenticates through Microsoft, but it also signs on through the local user account with all its privileges. In turn that first local user account created during Setup is a member of a special local group named Administrators with the ability to perform system-wide tasks, such as changing computer settings and installing or removing software and hardware. This first user on a Windows computer, while a member of the Administrators group, is subject to the User Account Control (UAC) security and will be notified by the Consent Prompt when Windows detects software installing or some other significant change to the system. The action will not occur until the user approves it. A separate local user account—the built-in Administrator is all-powerful and not subject to the UAC security. Therefore, when the built-in Administrator account is logged on, the computer is more vulnerable to malware attack. This account is disabled by default and should normally remain so.

If you are using Windows 10 Pro, you can see and manage local accounts in the Computer Management console, shown in Figure 5-1. While you can open Computer Management in Windows 10 Home, the Users and Groups node does not display. The Users folder under the Local Users and Group node shows the local users on a Windows computer. Four of the accounts listed were created by Windows for special uses. Some local users and groups are created when new drivers and apps are installed. In Figure 5-1, the janeh user was created during installation from the name the user provided.

> *Note:* When sharing a computer with family members consider giving each their own account—whether it is strictly local or an MSA account. Then each user will have their own sign in, and their personal data will be unavailable to other family members. This protects documents, such as the family financial records, from accidental harm from activities of the family's gamer.

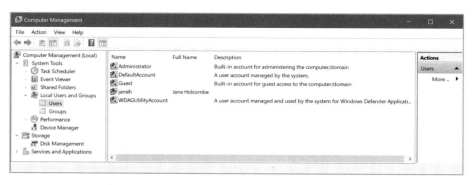

FIGURE 5–1 Computer Management displaying the list of local user accounts.
Source: Microsoft Corporation

For now, we will explore how to create and manage local user accounts. If you want to safely share your Windows computer with a roommate or family member when you are not using it, this section will show you how to create and manage local user accounts. You can also share your computer with those same users using their own MSA accounts. Indeed, you can have a mix of MSA and local accounts with local access to your Windows computer.

When you create a local user account after the first account, it is a standard user account, as described in Chapter 2. It is a member of the Users group. This is an ordinary user without administrator privileges. This type of account is also subject to UAC, but sees a different prompt, the Credentials Prompt, when a program attempts to make changes to the computer. In that case, the user will need to provide an administrator (first user) password. Create a local user account in Step-by-Step 5.01.

Step-by-Step 5.01

Creating a New Local Account in Windows 10

In this Step-by-Step, create a new user account for someone who is not a family member. To complete this exercise, you will need the following:

- A computer or virtual machine with Windows 10 installed.
- To be logged on with an account with administrative rights.

Step 1

From the Windows desktop select **Start | Settings | Accounts.** On the **Your info** page, shown in this example, notice that the Local Account janeh is an Administrator, which means this user is a member of the Administrators group but not the more powerful *Administrator* account. Confusing, but that is how it is.

Source: Microsoft Corporation

In the left pane select **Family & other users.** On the Family & other users page select **Add someone else to this PC.**

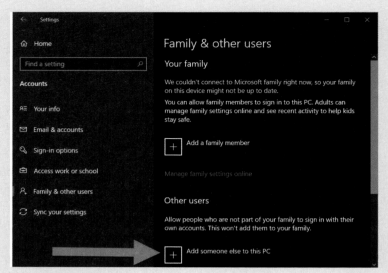

Source: Microsoft Corporation

The Microsoft account dialog for a new user displays. To create a local account select **I don't have this person's sign-in information.**

Source: Microsoft Corporation

When prompted to create a Microsoft account select **Add a user without a Microsoft account.**

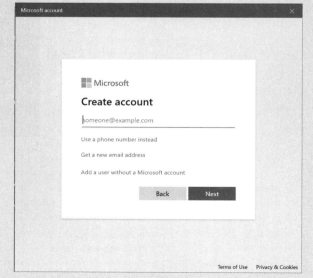

Source: Microsoft Corporation

The next Microsoft account dialog box prompts you to enter a user name and password. Until you enter a user name and type the password twice, only the first three text boxes display. Once those boxes are completed, several more boxes open in which you choose three security questions and supply answers. Once completed select **Next.**

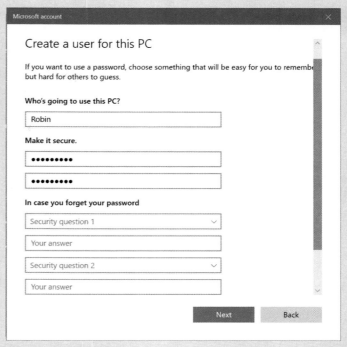

Source: Microsoft Corporation

Once the user account is created, it appears in **Settings | Accounts | Family & other users.** Notice that this account is described as a local account, meaning it is a member of the Users group, but not a member of Administrators. At this point, you can close out of Settings or select **Add someone else to this PC** to create another user account. For now, close the Settings window.

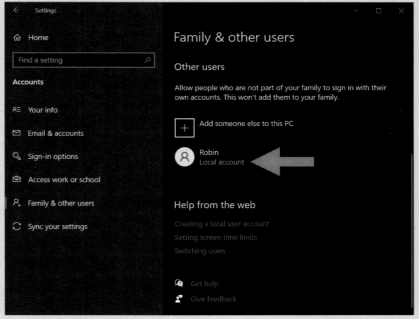

Source: Microsoft Corporation

Step 7

From the Desktop select **Start.** Then, click or tap on your user tile. In this example, the currently signed in user is janeh. Selecting the user tile opened the User options menu seen above it in dark gray. Selecting Sign out will close the current user session for janeh and a sign on screen will display. From that screen, you can select a user name and sign on as that user.

Step 8

After you sign on with the new user account, Windows Setup will prompt you to complete the initial setup of the new user, including services and a tutorial for using Windows Edge. If time permits, personalize the desktop. Finally sign out and sign in with your original account.

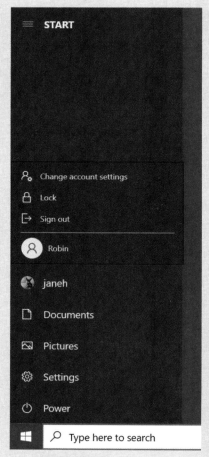

Source: Microsoft Corporation

Local User Groups and Special Accounts

The topic of Group Accounts was introduced in Chapter 2. User accounts in a group can be assigned permissions and privileges through their membership in a group, rather than to each individual. Windows contains built-in local groups, such as Administrators, Users, Guests, and groups that are created for other purposes. Figure 5-2 shows the Administrators Properties dialog box with just two members, Administrator and janeh. The try this! provides the steps for opening a local user's properties dialog box.

try this!

View the Properties of the First Local User

Use the Properties dialog. Try this:

1. In the taskbar Search box, enter "computer" and select **Computer Management** from the results.
2. The Computer Management console will open. There may be a slight delay.
3. In the navigation pane on the left click the Users and Groups folder.
4. In the contents pane, locate a user that shows a full name. Double-click this user to open the Properties dialog.
5. Click on the **Member Of** tab to display this user's groups.
6. Without making any changes, close the Properties dialog box and the Computer Management console.

LO 5.2 | Managing Local Data Files

Recall from Chapter 1 that a file system is the logical structure on a storage device for storing and managing files. The OS includes code to support certain file systems, and the OS creates the logical structure on the media through a process called formatting.

FIGURE 5–2 Only two users are shown as members of the local Administrators group.
Source: Microsoft Corporation

There are several types of file systems, and a different logical structure for each type of file system. In this section, we start with the object at the heart of a file system, a file. Then examine the user interface (UI) by which we manage files.

Understanding files and the types of files you may encounter, as well as the user interface that gives you access to files, may be all you need to know to manage and support files, but we go a bit deeper in this section, defining the file systems on desktops and laptops. In Chapter 12, we go beyond the desktop and laptop to working with files in the cloud—something you can do from any Internet-connected device.

File Management and the User Interface

A file is information stored as a unit on a storage device. A file is identified with a name and a short extension to identify the file type. Name and extension are separated by a period (.). There are many types of files. Think of a letter, spreadsheet, picture, or a program, each is stored in a different file type. The operating system and programs we use need to be able to identify the type of file to understand how to use the file. This all depends on some way to identify each file and to store and manage it, which brings us to the issue of the user interface (UI) and the tools in the UI for interacting with files. The typical user will do all their file management in the Windows graphical user interface (GUI) using File Explorer.

When viewing files in File Explorer, many file types can be identified by the icon to the left of the file name. Figure 5–3 shows File Explorer with a folder selected in the navigation pane; its contents displayed in the right pane. The list in the right pane shows three folders and several files. The folders are easily identified by the yellow folder icon. No problem there. From a user's perspective, anything that is not a folder is a file. In this case, there are three file types represented. When managing files, it helps to see the file name extensions. Turn this feature on in File Explorer using the

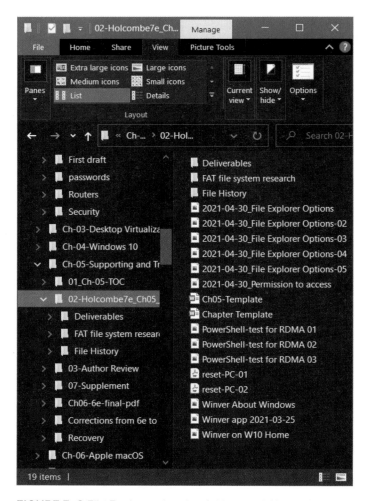

FIGURE 5–3 File Explorer showing folders and files with extensions hidden.
Source: Microsoft Corporation

Note: There is more to a file type than the file name extension. Just putting "exe" on the end of a file name does not make that file an executable. The contents of the file must be in a specific format for each file type.

File Explorer Options menu in Windows Control Panel. Figure 5–4 shows the File Explorer Options with extensions hidden. Clear this check box and click the Apply or OK button to make file name extensions visible the next time you open File Explorer, as shown in Figure 5–5.

The majority of the files listed in Figures 5–3 and 5–5 are in an image (or "graphic") file format. These image files are of the type called Portable Network Graphics (PNG). Image files can be read and edited using a variety of graphic viewing and editing apps. Another two files in Figure 5–3 have the Microsoft Word documents extension, DOCX. Open these files using Microsoft Word or another word processing app. Two of the files are in Adobe's Portable Document Format (PDF). Most printable documents available for download are in this format. They are printable, but not usually editable. Each chapter of this book is a PDF file. There are many apps that can read PDF files, and the most common one is Adobe Acrobat Reader. If you do not have this installed as a separate app, your browser will let you open and read PDF files, which is how you seamlessly open PDF documents on the Web.

The last file format we will discuss here is executable (EXE). While this is not the only file format and extension for executable files, this is the most common encountered in Windows. An executable file is a binary file that is loaded into memory and runs its instructions when certain actions are taken. The most obvious action is when you double-click an executable from the Windows GUI.

FIGURE 5–4 The File Explorer Options Control Panel with Hide Extensions for Known File Types selected.
Source: Microsoft Corporation

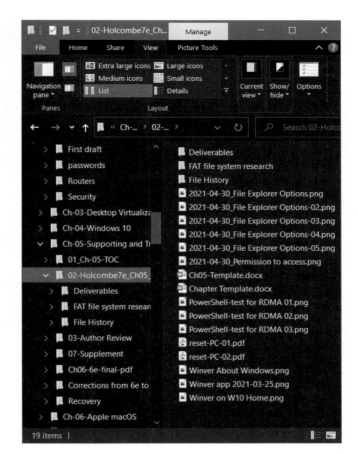

FIGURE 5–5 File Explorer showing folders and files with extensions visible.
Source: Microsoft Corporation

You can also manage files through a command-line interface (CLI), such as the venerable **Command Prompt** or the more advanced **Windows PowerShell**. Figure 5–6 shows the Windows PowerShell after the author entered commands to give the focus to the folder shown in Figures 5–3 and 5–5. Then the author entered the *dir* command to list the files in that folder. The author has the advantage of having worked with and taught DOS for several years. She first tries the old DOS commands in PowerShell. These work OK for simple tasks, but PowerShell has many more advanced commands. We will revisit PowerShell later in this chapter. Suffice it to say that (with some exceptions) even an experienced command-line person prefers to do file management tasks in the GUI.

The Windows Default File Hierarchy

During installation, Windows creates one set of folders for the operating system, another set for application program files, and an additional set, **personal folders**, for each local user account. The last set holds the user's data files. As users are added, Windows creates a new set of personal folders for each new user account. The file hierarchies of the 32-bit and 64-bit distributions of Windows differ only in the location in which they store programs. The 32-bit distributions of Windows store all programs in the Program Files folder, while the 64-bit distributions store only 64-bit programs in this folder and store 32-bit programs in the folder named Program Files (x86). The default location for the majority of the Windows operating system files is in C:\Windows. Figure 5–7 shows the folder hierarchy for a 64-bit installation of Windows. In the navigation pane on the left notice the four folders (Program files, Program Files (x86), Users, and Windows), all created on the root of drive C. Program Files is selected, and the contents of that folder are shown on the right.

Note: Most installations of Windows 10 are 64-bit. To learn the status of your installation of Windows 10, select the Start button, open Settings, System, About. Under Device specification, System type will show 64-bit or 32-bit.

FIGURE 5-6 Windows PowerShell CLI displaying the contents of the same folder shown in Figures 5-3 and 5-5.
Source: Microsoft Corporation

The default location for user data is C:\Users\<username> where <username> is the user name of a single user. In Figure 5-8, notice the folder for the user janeh. Within this folder are the personal folders created by Windows to hold various types of data or, as in the case of the Desktop folder, to hold files from a certain location in the Windows GUI. The Downloads folder holds files downloaded by this user using a Web browser.

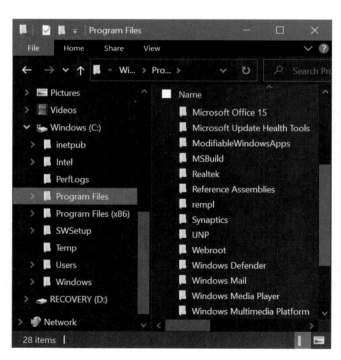

FIGURE 5-7 The Program Files folder created by Windows.
Source: Microsoft Corporation

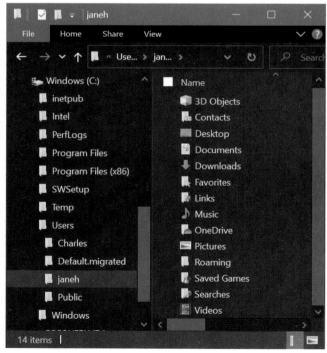

FIGURE 5-8 The folder janeh contains files and folders created by and for that user.
Source: Microsoft Corporation

Step-by-Step 5.02

Navigate File Explorer

In this hands-on exercise, use File Explorer to navigate and view the folders on your Windows computer. You may want to flip back to Figure 4-10 in Chapter 4 and review the File Explorer window components. To complete this exercise, you will need the following:

- A computer or virtual machine with Windows 10 installed.
- To be logged on with an account with local access to that computer.

Step 1

From the Windows taskbar, click or tap the **File Explorer** shortcut.

Source: Microsoft Corporation

Step 2

This example shows File Explorer on a new installation of Windows 10. The navigation pane on the left shows Quick access shortcuts to the currently signed-on user's personal folders. With Quick access selected, the contents pane on the right shows icons for the same list of folders. It shows individual folders, but not in their actual position in the personal folder hierarchy. This list will change as you work in Windows. Below the Quick access list are OneDrive (because the user signed in with a Microsoft Account), This PC, and Network.

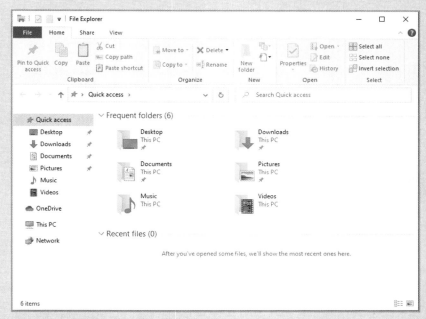

Source: Microsoft Corporation

Step 3

Select This PC in the navigation pane. Once again, the right pane includes the user's personal folder, but also shows devices and drives connected to the PC. This example is Windows running in a virtual machine, which will show virtual disk drivers (Floppy, DVD, and Local Disk). You may see an additional vertical pane on the right, the Preview pane.

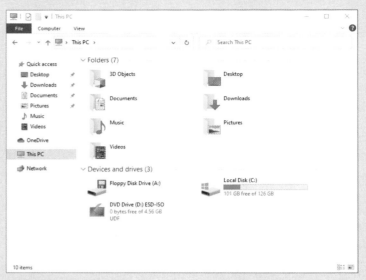

Source: Microsoft Corporation

Step 4

Double-click Local Disk. Notice the folders shown. Double-click the Users folder and then open the folder with your user name.

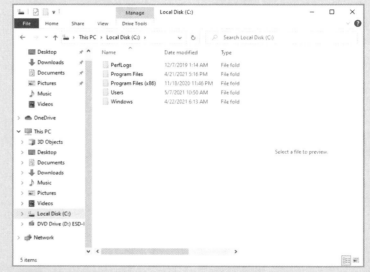

Source: Microsoft Corporation

Step 5

Notice various icons used to represent each of your default personal folders. Microsoft is updating icons—some of which remained much the same since the mid-1990s.

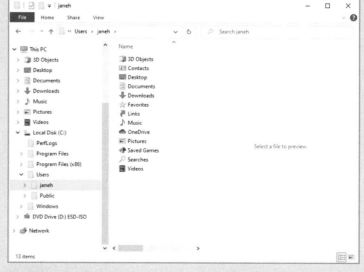

Source: Microsoft Corporation

You will not normally browse down through Local Disk | Users to access your data files. It is more convenient to use the shortcuts under Quick Access or This PC in the navigation pane. Return to This PC and click on each object in the contents pane in turn, watching the tab in the title bar change for some of the objects, providing appropriate toolbar tools. On a computer with a new installation of Windows, these folders will be empty, or will only contain other empty folders.

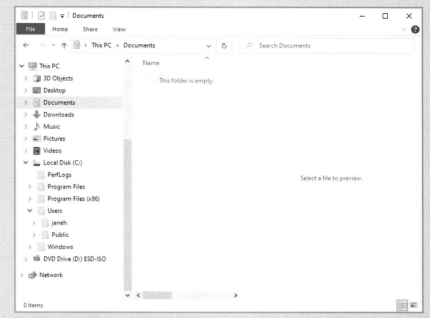

Source: Microsoft Corporation

Once you install apps and save data files, these folders will be populated, as shown here. Click or tap the View menu to change how the folders and files display in File Explorer. For instance, turn the Preview pane on and select files to view in the preview pane.

After exploring a bit with File Explorer, close it by clicking or tapping the Close (X) button on the top right of the window.

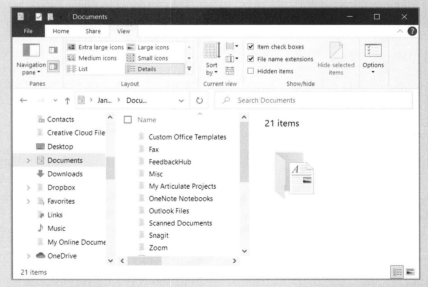

Source: Microsoft Corporation

The FAT File Systems

The **FAT file systems** include FAT12, FAT16, FAT32, and exFAT. Each has a logical structure that includes a file allocation table (FAT) and a directory structure. The file system gets its name from the FAT, which enables the OS to allocate space for files. Another logical structure, a directory, gives the OS a place for identifying information about each file. Early PCs using IBM's PC-DOS and Microsoft's MS-DOS used FAT12 on diskettes and FAT16 on most hard drives. Since then, the FAT32 and exFAT file systems were created to accommodate larger storage devices. The newest FAT file system, exFAT, was created for use on flash drives, SD cards, and solid-state drives (SSDs). The computing devices found in cars, appliances, and other everyday items that we don't think of as high-tech, often use a FAT file system because it is small and ideal for a device that does not need much space.

When you format a USB flash drive in Windows, the default file system is exFAT. The FAT file systems all lack file- and folder-level security, which are features of the New Technology File System (NTFS). In addition, the FAT file systems are not as resilient as NTFS. If you need to share a USB flash drive between a Windows PC and a Mac, your best option for compatibility is exFAT, which both operating systems can read and write.

File Systems for Optical Discs

Optical drives have all but disappeared from new PCs and laptops, but they have not disappeared from older systems you may use. Optical discs have their own file format and require special Windows file system drivers. The CD-ROM File System (CDFS) allows Windows OSs to read CD-ROMs and to read and write to writable CDs (CD-R) and rewritable CDs (CD-RW). The Universal Disk Format (UDF) is a file system driver required for Windows to read CDs and DVD ROMs and to read and write DVD-R and DVD-RW.

In addition to the original method for writing to optical drives (basically, a write once method called the Mastered disc format), Microsoft introduced a method for copying files to rewritable discs beginning in Windows Vista. This method, called Live File System, allows you to write to DVD-RW or CD-R optical discs, adding files at any time, as long as the disc has room. The upside to the older Mastered format is that it will work in other types of devices, such as DVD players, but Live File System is not compatible with those devices. Consider using the Live File System for discs you will only use on your Windows computers. You may not need to work with either of these file formats, due to the lack of optical drives in PCs and laptops manufactured in the last several years.

The Windows New Technology File System (NTFS)

NTFS is available in all versions of Windows beginning back in the 1990s with Windows NT, but excluding the Windows 95, Windows 98, and Windows Me versions. If you format an external drive in NTFS on a Windows PC, it will be readable by an Apple Mac, but the Mac will not be able to write to it.

Features of NTFS

The main NTFS logical structure is a master file table (MFT) that is expandable, and therefore Microsoft can add features in future versions. Windows uses a transaction processing system to track changes to files in NTFS. This adds a measure of transaction-level recoverability to the file system, similar to what your bank uses to track transactions. In both cases, incomplete transactions are rolled back.

From the beginning, NTFS provided file and folder security not available on FAT volumes. Today, in addition to file and folder security and transaction processing capability, Microsoft continues to improve this file system. NTFS is the preferred file system for hard drives in Windows and the default created when you install Windows.

File and Folder Permissions on NTFS

NTFS allows you to control who has access to specified files and folders by assigning permission to users and groups. These permissions restrict access to both local accounts, as well as network accounts. However, in the case of those connecting over a network, the share permissions (not related to NTFS permissions) take effect first and may block access to the underlying files and folders. Only NTFS volumes allow you to assign permissions to files and folders directly.

On a volume (drive) formatted with NTFS, each folder and file has a set of security permissions associated with it. Each file and folder on an NTFS volume has an associated Access Control List (ACL). An ACL is a table of users and/or groups and their permissions to access the file or folder. Each ACL has at least one Access Control Entry (ACE), which is like a record in this tiny ACL database. An ACE contains just user or group account name and the permissions assigned to this account for that file or folder. An administrator—or someone with Full Control permission for the file or folder, creates the ACEs.

To view the ACEs in an ACL for a file or folder in File Explorer, right-click on it and select **Properties** to open the Properties dialog box for that file or folder and select the Security tab. Figure 5–9 shows the Security page for the folder janeh, which is

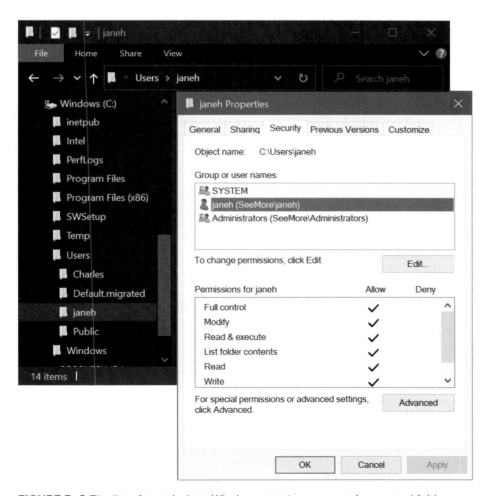

FIGURE 5–9 The list of permissions Windows creates on a user's personal folders.
Source: Microsoft Corporation

the top-level personal folders for the user janeh. These are the permissions Windows creates for a user's personal folders. Change the permissions on a file or folder in the Security page by selecting a user or group and clicking the Edit button.

LO 5.3 | Understanding the Registry

The registry is one of several features that make Windows so adaptable that we can add the hardware and applications to turn a Windows computer into the computing tool we need. Ironically, it is also one of the most complicated and least understood features of Windows. In this section, you'll learn about the registry—its role in Windows and how to modify it when needed.

The Definition and Purpose of the Registry

The Windows registry is a database of all configuration settings in one installation of Windows. It includes settings for:

- Device drivers
- Services
- Installed application programs
- Operating system components
- User preferences

Note: The registry contains only settings, not the actual device drivers, services, or applications to which the settings apply. Windows will not work as you expect it to if these other components are damaged or not available.

Windows creates the registry during its installation, and it continues to make modifications to it as you configure Windows and add applications and components. During startup, Windows depends on the registry to tell it what services, drivers, and components to load into memory, and how to configure each of them. The registry remains in memory while Windows is active.

Automatic Registry Changes

The Windows registry will automatically change when:

- Windows starts up or shuts down.
- Windows Setup runs (which occurs more often than you may think; for example, each time Windows gets updated).
- Changes are made through a Control Panel applet or the Settings tool.
- A new device is installed.
- Any changes are made to the Windows configuration.
- Any changes are made to a user's desktop preferences.
- An application is installed or modified.
- Changes are made to user preferences in any application.

Registry Files

Although considered only a single entity when Windows is running, the registry is stored in a number of binary files on disk. A binary file contains program code. The Windows registry files include the following:

- BCD
- default
- ntuser.dat
- sam
- security
- software
- system

TABLE 5-1 Locations of the Hives within the Registry

Hive File	Registry Location
BCD	HKEY_LOCAL_MACHINE\BCD00000000
default	HKEY_USERS\.DEFAULT
ntuser.dat (of the currently logged-on user)	HKEY_CURRENT_USER and HKEY_USERS
sam	HKEY_LOCAL_MACHINE\SAM
security	HKEY_LOCAL_MACHINE\SECURITY
software	HKEY_LOCAL_MACHINE\SOFTWARE
system	HKEY_LOCAL_MACHINE\SYSTEM

The portion of the registry represented in each of these registry files is a hive. Table 5-1 shows where the data from each registry hive is located in the registry. Hive files are the permanent portions of the registry, with all the changes saved from use to use. With the exception of ntuser.dat and BCD, these registry files are in a disk folder named config, located below C:\Windows\System32. You will see a warning box the first time you attempt to open the config folder. Once you click the **Continue** button you will have permanent access to the folder. Figure 5-10 shows the contents of the config folder in Windows 10. Look for the files that match the list above (except ntuser. dat and BCD). Notice that the registry files listed in the config folder have file names without file extensions. If you have File Manager configured to show hidden files, you will see other files in this location, including files with .log extensions that have file names that match the registry files. The operating system uses LOG files for logging transactions to the registry files. Other hidden files with matching file names and SAV extensions are backup copies of registry files created at the end of the text mode stage of setup.

try this!

View Hidden Files and Extensions in File Explorer

By default, Windows hides hidden files and extensions in the GUI. Make them visible in File Explorer. Try this:

1. Enter "control panel" in the Search box and select the result titled "Control Panel App."
2. In **Control Panel** select **File Explorer Options**.
3. In File Explorer Options select the **View** tab.
4. On the View tab enable the radio button labeled **Show hidden files, folders, and drives.**
5. Ensure that there is *no* check in the box labeled **Hide extensions for known file types.**
6. Click or tap the OK button.
7. Open Windows File Explorer and browse to the **config** folder, usually found at C:\Windows\System32. Extensions and hidden files are now visible.

BCD

The BCD file resides in the Boot folder in the hidden system partition. As with other registry files, it is a binary file. It contains the Boot Configuration Database (BCD) store used by Windows during the bootloader phase of startup, providing the bootloader with information it needs to locate and load the operating system files.

DEFAULT

The default hive is the user hive for the Local SYSTEM account. This hive has a security identifier HKEY_USERS\S-1-5-18. Programs and services that run as Local system use this hive.

WARNING!

In the try this, you disable a setting that hides protected operating system files. Only do this temporarily on a lab computer. Do not do this on a work or school computer unless you have technical support available.

Note: The Boot Configuration Database in the BCD file is used during the bootloader phase of startup.

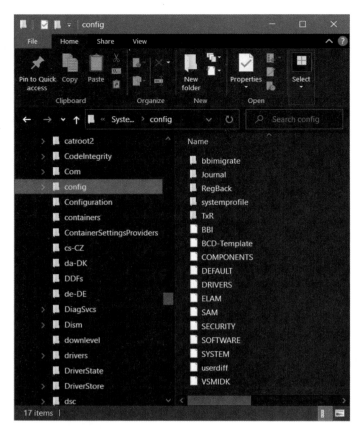

FIGURE 5–10 This view of the Windows 10 config folder shows most of the registry files.
Source: Microsoft Corporation

NTUSER.DAT

The ntuser.dat hive file contains the user profile for a single user. These settings include application preferences, screen colors, network connections, and other personal choices. Each user who logs on to the computer has a separate ntuser.dat file. During startup, Windows uses the other registry hives to load and configure the operating system. One of the last tasks of the operating system at startup is to request a user logon. When a user logs on, the settings from that user's ntuser.dat file apply and become part of the current registry. It saves the ntuser.dat file in the top-level personal folder for that user. It is a hidden file so it is only visible if your Folder Options are set to Show hidden files, folders, and drives.

Note: We described personal folders earlier in this chapter.

SAM

SAM is an acronym for Security Accounts Manager. This hive contains the local security accounts database. It is critical to user authentication because it stores user passwords.

SECURITY

The SECURITY hive contains the local security policy settings for the computer, including rules for password complexity and for how the system will handle numerous failed attempts at entering a password.

SOFTWARE

The SOFTWARE hive contains configuration settings for software installed on the local computer, along with various items of miscellaneous configuration data.

SYSTEM

The SYSTEM hive contains information used at startup, including device drivers to load as well as the order of their loading, and configuration settings, instructions for the starting and configuring of services, and various operating system settings.

The Temporary Portion of the Registry

The information stored in HKEY_LOCAL_MACHINE\HARDWARE is temporary information, gathered during the hardware detection process of the detect-and-configure-hardware phase of Windows startup. Windows does not save it to disk in a file, as it does other portions of the registry.

Viewing and Editing the Registry

View and edit the hierarchical structure of the active registry using the Registry Editor utility, Regedit. Its executable file, regedit.exe, is located in the folder in which the operating system is installed (by default that is C:\Windows), but it does not have a shortcut on the Start menu or other handy locations in the Windows GUI. This is for a very good reason: It should not be too handy. The try this! will walk you through opening Regedit and viewing the registry locations shown in Table 5-1.

The first time Regedit runs on a computer, it looks like Figure 5-11. Each folder represents a key, an object that may contain one or more settings as well as other keys. Each of the top five folders is a root key (also called a subtree in Microsoft documentation). Each root key is at the top of a hierarchical structure containing more keys. A key that exists within another key is a subkey. Each setting within a key is a value entry. When you click on the folder for a key, it becomes the active key in Regedit, its folder icon "opens," and the contents of the key show in the right pane, as you see in Figure 5-12. Table 5-2 gives an overview of the information stored within each root key of the registry.

> **WARNING!**
>
> Do not directly edit the registry with a tool such as Regedit unless it is absolutely necessary; there are many safer ways to make a change to the registry. For example, when you change settings in Control Panel or Windows Settings, the changes are recorded in the registry.

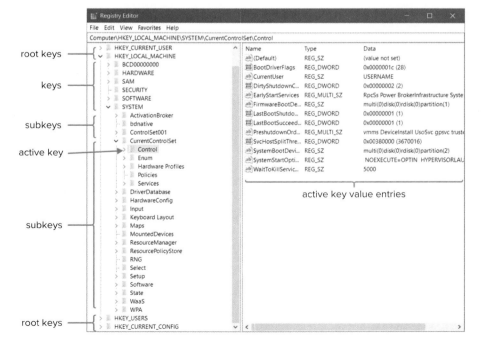

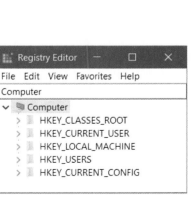

FIGURE 5-11 The registry root keys.
Source: Microsoft Corporation

FIGURE 5-12 Registry components as shown in Registry Editor.
Source: Microsoft Corporation

TABLE 5–2 Contents of Registry Root Keys

Root Key	Description
HKEY_CLASSES_ROOT	Shows relationships (called associations) between applications and data file types defined by file extension. Thanks to the information in this key, you can double-click on a data file and the correct application will open and load the file. This root key contains all the information located in HKEY_LOCAL_MACHINE\SOFTWARE\Classes.
HKEY_CURRENT_USER	Contains the user profile for the currently logged-on user, storing all the user settings that affect the desktop appearance and the default behavior of installed applications.
HKEY_LOCAL_MACHINE	Contains the system information, including detected hardware, application associations, and information for hardware configuration and device drivers.
HKEY_USERS	User profiles for all local user accounts, including the profile of the currently logged-on user (also shown under HKEY_CURRENT_USER), and profiles for special user accounts used to run services.
HKEY_CURRENT_CONFIG	Contains configuration information for the current hardware profile, which is a set of changes (*only* changes) to the standard configuration in the Software and System subkeys under HKEY_LOCAL_MACHINE.

In Regedit, each value entry appears in three columns labeled: Name, Type, and Data. The Type column shows a label that describes the format of the data in that registry value, also called data type. There are many data types in the registry; take a few minutes to study Table 5–3, which shows just a few registry data types, to give you an idea of how diverse the data in the registry can be. If you open the HKEY_USERS root key, notice the security ID (SID), a unique string of characters preceded by S-1-5 that identifies a security principal (an entity that can be authenticated) in the Windows security accounts database.

Backing Up the Registry

It is very important to remember that the last thing you should consider doing, even if your best friend or brother-in-law insists you do it, is to directly edit the registry using Regedit or a third-party registry editing tool. We strongly recommend that you not use the registry cleaning tools promoted on the Internet. While you should rarely (if ever) edit the registry, you should know how to back up the registry in case you decide that you have no choice but to use Regedit. Here are two methods for backing up the registry. The first, using System Restore, is a very broad approach that backs up the entire registry and more. The second method, backing up a portion of the registry with Regedit, is a more targeted approach.

Creating a Restore Point

Our favorite method is to simply create a restore point using System Restore. A restore point is a snapshot of Windows, its configuration, and all installed programs. If your computer has problems after you make a change, use System Restore to roll it back to a restore point. While Windows creates restore points on a regular basis, you can create one any time you want, knowing that you will have a snapshot of Windows at that point in time. Step-by-Step 5.03 will walk you through this process.

Note: Describing a registry location is similar to the way we describe file and folder locations on disk; we use a notation that shows the path from a root key down through the subkeys: HKEY_LOCAL_MACHINE\SYSTEM\CURRENT CONTROLSET\CONTROL.

try this!

Use Registry Editor to View the Registry

Open Registry Editor and explore the contents of the registry. Try this:

1. Press ⊞+R. This opens the Run box. Type "regedit" and click OK.
2. Respond to the User Account Control dialog to continue.
3. Once Regedit is open, be careful not to make any changes. Browse through the registry structure, much as you would navigate in File Explorer.
4. Notice the folders in the navigation pane and the various folders and settings in the contents pane on the right. Keep Registry Editor open as you read this chapter section.

TABLE 5-3 Windows Registry Data Types (The Short List)

Data Type	Description
REG_BINARY	Raw binary data. It shows some hardware data in binary. Ironically, it shows binary data in hexadecimal and might look like this: ff 00 ff ff 02 05.
REG_DWORD	A 4-byte-long number (32 bits), stored in binary, hexadecimal, or decimal format. It may look something like this in hexadecimal: 0x00000002.
REG_EXPAND_SZ	A single string of text including a variable, which is a value that an application will replace when called. An example of a common variable is %*systemroot*%, which, when Windows uses it, is replaced by the path of the folder containing the Windows system files. Example: A registry entry containing %*systemroot*%\regedit.exe becomes c:\windows\regedit.exe.
REG_MULTI_SZ	Multiple strings of human-readable text separated by a special NULL character that it does not display. Example: wuauserv gpsvc trustedinstaller.
REG_SZ	A sequence of characters representing human-readable text. It may use this data type when the data is quite simple, such as a string of alphanumeric characters—for example, ClosePerformanceData—or to represent an entire list: comm.drv commdlg.dll ctl3dv2.dll ddeml.dll.

Step-by-Step 5.03

Creating a Restore Point

In this step-by-step exercise, you will create a restore point. For this exercise you will need a computer running Windows 10. You will need to respond to a User Account Control (UAC) prompt. In which case, if you logged on as a standard account, you will need to enter an administrator password.

Step 1

Open the Run box in Windows using the keyboard shortcut ⊞ +R. In the Run box type "sysdm.cpl". Do not type the quotation marks! Click OK.

Step 2

This brings up the System Properties dialog. Select the System Protection tab. If the System Restore and Create buttons are disabled click the Configure button and enable System Protection. Then return to the System Protection tab in System Properties. To create a restore point click the Create button located at the bottom, as shown here.

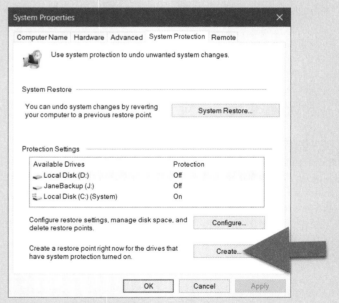

Source: Microsoft Corporation

Step 3

Type a descriptive name for the restore point. Then press the Create button.

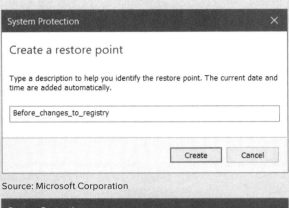

Source: Microsoft Corporation

Step 4

It will take a minute or two, during which a progress message will display in the System Protection box. When Windows has created the restore point, this message will display. Click the Close button.

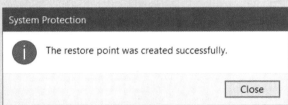

Source: Microsoft Corporation

Step 5

The System Properties dialog box from Step 2 will remain open to the System Protection page. To see the restore points, click the System Restore button. If a page displays with a recommended restore point, click Choose a different restore point. Then click the Next button. If a simpler page without the recommended restore point displays, as shown here, simply click Next.

Source: Microsoft Corporation

Step 6

Caution: you want to only view the existing restore points—you do not want to actually roll back to a previous restore point. Simply view the list of restore points, noticing the descriptions. Press Cancel to exit from System Restore. Press Cancel again in the System Properties dialog.

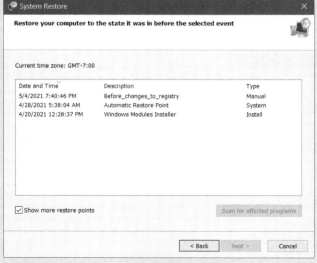

Source: Microsoft Corporation

Use Regedit to Back Up the Registry

Despite knowing the danger of directly editing the registry, you might find yourself in a position in which editing the registry is the only way to solve a problem. This may be the case when an administrator or help desk person has given you specific instructions for virus removal or some other necessary change. Do this only after eliminating all other avenues, including using system restore to restore your computer to a previous state or doing a total restore of your computer from a complete backup set.

If all else fails, and provided you know the exact change that you must make to the registry, first use Regedit to back up the portion of the registry you plan to edit. To back up a registry key, right-click on the folder for the key in Registry Editor and select Export, as shown in Figure 5–13. Provide a location and name for the file, and Regedit will create a .reg file. If you need to restore the file, simply double-click on it. Back up the entire registry by opening Regedit's file menu and selecting Export. As with a single key, you must provide a location and name for the file.

WARNING!

Many software utilities advertise on the Web promising to clean your Windows OS for you. Some specifically target the registry; others promise to clean both the files on disk and the registry. We do not recommend any of these products.

LO 5.4 | Windows User and Power Options

When it comes to managing and troubleshooting a Windows 10 computer, users are often confused by the terms for actions and how to locate the required action for a situation. This is not limited to novice users; even experienced users find it difficult to take the right action, even when they understand what they want to accomplish. Microsoft (and other software publishers) have not helped this problem with their changes to both the GUI and to the names assigned to certain actions. In this section we will survey some of the terms for necessary actions you need as well as how to find what you need in the GUI when you want to do several important maintenance and troubleshooting tasks. Start with options available from the User and Power tiles on the Start menu, look at how to modify these options, and how to change how your laptop behaves when you close the lid. Finally, learn about the Windows 10 boot process. This may seem a bit backward—talking about shut down before booting up—but it helps to understand something Windows normally does during shut down that enhances how it starts up again.

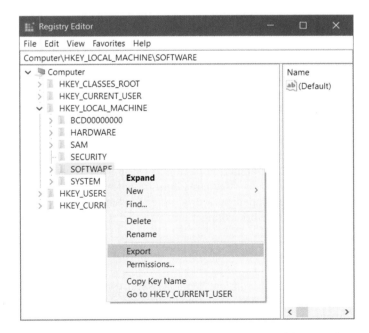

FIGURE 5–13 Back up a registry key and all its subkeys and values.
Source: Microsoft Corporation

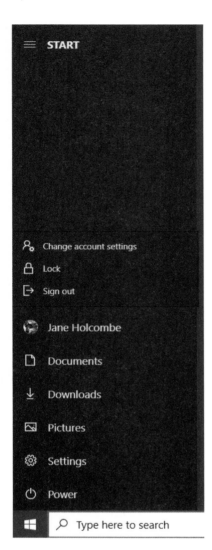

FIGURE 5–14 The Windows 10 User
options menu (above the user tile).
Source: Microsoft Corporation

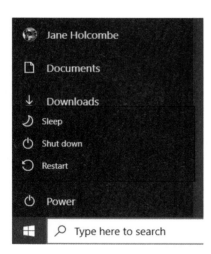

FIGURE 5–15 The Power options
menu.
Source: Microsoft Corporation

User Options

User options are available from the user tile. In Step-by-Step 5.01, Step 7, you opened the User Options menu by selecting Start, and then selecting the User tile. The options shown on the User Options menu in Step 7 included a tile for another local user as well as options to change account settings, lock the computer, and sign out.

Selecting the User tile for another user will switch users, meaning it will keep the current user's session in memory without closing any programs or files, and present the sign on screen with the second user's image. At the bottom left on this screen are tiles for other local users. Each user can sign on and run in a separate user session with their own user profile, files, and other resources, but they cannot access the first user's open session.

Selecting Change account settings opens the Your Info Settings page shown in Step 1 of Step-by-Step 5.01. From this page you can modify your account and, if you are an Administrator, you can add and manage other local accounts.

The Lock option on the User options menu will keep your session in memory but lock the screen. You will need to sign in to return to your Desktop. This resembles switch user, but it will be your user image in the center of the sign on screen.

The last option is Sign out, which closes your open session and returns to the lock screen. Figure 5-14 shows the Windows 10 User options menu with only one local account.

Power Options

The Windows 10 Power options menu, Figure 5-15, opens when you select Start and then select the Power tile. The default options are Sleep, Shutdown, and Restart. A fourth option, Hibernate, only appears in this menu if you enable it in Control Panel's Power Options. Understand the differences between Sleep and Hibernate, as we explore all four options.

Sleep

If you select the Sleep option, the computer stays on in a very-low-power mode; the system state (the OS and all its current settings and components) and user session (applications and data) are saved in RAM, and the screen turns off. Wake up your computer (resume) by clicking a mouse button, tapping a touch screen, or pressing keys. On some computers, you may press the power button to bring Windows out of Sleep mode, but try these other actions first. When the computer resumes from Sleep, you may need to enter your password before you are back in Windows with all your apps open and data intact.

When should you use Sleep? A common scenario is when you must interrupt your work on a laptop or tablet for a very short period of time, as when you board a plane. Select Sleep mode before boarding, and when you have settled in your seat, resume and continue working.

Do not use Sleep for a long period of time because when the battery runs down, Sleep mode ends. Microsoft has safeguards built in, but we have never been comfortable using Sleep for an extended period of time. We have seen problems with loss of data as well as with network connections after bringing a computer back from Sleep mode.

Hibernate

When you select the Hibernate option, Windows saves to local storage (disk or SSID) an image of the contents of RAM, including the OS, open apps, and all the associated data, in a file named hiberfil.sys, and then the OS sends the command to power down the computer. Hibernate does not require power.

When should you use Hibernate? If it is available, you may want to use it on a laptop or tablet when you would use Sleep. To resume, press the power button, and the

Lock screen or the Sign-in screen will greet you. The apps that were open before you hibernated Windows will be open with the data intact.

Note: A computer recovers more quickly from Sleep than from Hibernate, but Sleep requires power to maintain the system state, apps, and data in RAM. while Hibernate does not.

Windows 10 Hybrid Shutdown

When you select *Shutdown* from the Windows 10 Power menu it does a **Hybrid Shutdown**, during which Windows does the following:

1. Sends messages to all running apps to save data and settings, and then shuts down the apps.
2. Closes the session for each logged-on user.
3. Hibernates the Windows session and saves it in a file. It does not hibernate the User session (open programs and data).

Because the hibernate process saves an image of the system session to disk, the operating system does not have to reassemble all its parts every time it starts up.

Restart

When you select the *Restart* option, Windows does a full shutdown and a full system startup. This is important to know because a Restart will seem slower than a Shutdown followed by powering up your computer because it will not do the Hybrid shutdown described above, nor the Windows Fast Boot, described later. A Restart is often required when updating Windows or installing an app.

Note: By default, Windows does a Hybrid Shutdown when you select Shutdown from the Power menu, but it does a complete shutdown (not hibernating the system) when you select Restart from the Power menu.

Configuring What Happens When You Press the Power Button or Close the Lid

Do you know what happens when you press the physical power button on a PC or Laptop? What occurs when you close the lid on a laptop? As shown in Figure 5–16, the power button and the close lid actions can be configured for whether the device is on battery or plugged in. Manufacturers usually configure all four settings to Sleep. The drop-down menu for the lid setting offers four options: Do nothing, Sleep, Hibernate, and Shut down. The options for the power button include the same four, plus a fifth, Turn off the display. On a desktop system, the computer does not run on battery power, nor does it have a lid, so you will only see the options for the power button without mention of battery.

Figure 5–16 shows the **Power button and lid** settings on a laptop. Below these settings are the Shutdown settings. The first three settings affect the Power Options menu; the last one, Lock, is a User menu option. All four settings are grayed out, which means they are unavailable. The default settings are recommended. However, if you need to enable Hibernate as an option, select the option labeled **Change settings that are currently unavailable.** If you are a member of the Administrator group, selecting this will enable these options. If you are logged on with an account that is not a member of Administrator group, you will need to enter the password for the first user account (janeh in our example).

Windows 10 Boot Process

When you power on your computer, the CPU loads firmware programs into memory. Firmware is software installed in nonvolatile memory chips, which may be **read-only memory (ROM)**, **erasable programmable read-only memory (EPROM)**, or a similar technology. All computing devices contain firmware.

try this!

Explore the Power Options Settings

Windows offers power options for laptops and desktops. Look at what is available on your computer. Try this:

1. In the taskbar search box enter "Control Panel."
2. From the results list select the Control Panel app.
3. In Control Panel select **Power Options.**
4. In Power Options select **Choose what the power button does.**
5. Open the drop-down menu and select a different option and select the Save changes button.

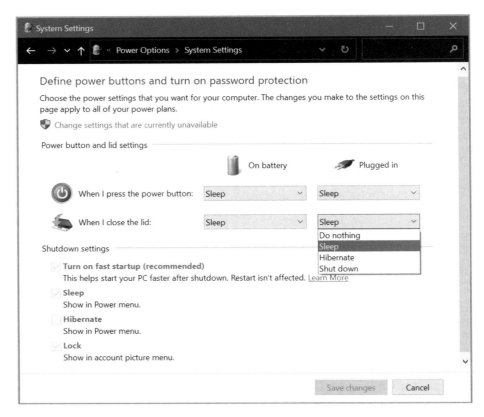

FIGURE 5–16 The Power Options Settings in Control Panel on a laptop.
Source: Microsoft Corporation

Legacy BIOS Firmware

PCs and laptops in the 1980s, 1990s, and some in the early 2000s were manufactured with firmware that is now simply called legacy BIOS, the long name for this legacy firmware is read-only memory basic input-output system (ROM-BIOS). It did the startup tasks beginning with checking out the hardware with the power-on-self-test (POST), and using a bit of firmware, the bootstrap loader, to look for a bootable device containing the bootloader program code, to begin the OS startup process. Legacy BIOS does not include protection from malware. The only protection comes into play after the Windows OS is in control, and that can be too late, allowing malware that can gain control and avoid detection from the OS.

Newer Unified Extensible Firmware Interface

New computers have more sophisticated and secure firmware, Unified Extensible Firmware Interface (UEFI), also called UEFI BIOS. Intel-based computers for several years included the newer UEFI BIOS with an optional legacy BIOS mode to support older peripherals and software. Beginning in 2020, Intel dropped support for legacy BIOS in UEFI BIOS. The most important thing to remember about UEFI BIOS is that it is more secure than legacy BIOS. Here are some of the features of UEFI BIOS:

- Measured Boot logs the boot process so that once the OS is fully loaded, antimalware software can analyze the log to determine if malware is on the computer or if malware tampered with the boot components.
- Secure Boot loads only trusted operating system boot loaders. A UEFI system with Secure Boot enabled will examine the digital signature on the boot loader to ensure it has not been modified.

- **Trusted Boot** examines each system file required for the boot process before it loads into memory. If one appears to have been altered, an unmodified version of the files is used.
  - **Early Launch Anti-Malware (ELAM)** works like Trusted Boot, only ELAM examines all device drivers before they load into memory.

The security features of UEFI BIOS and of the latest version of Windows, as well as the tasks of finding and loading all Windows components, might add more time to system startup, but Windows 10 compensates for this by using a feature called **Fast Boot**. Fast Boot takes advantage of the hibernated kernel of the Hybrid Shutdown, described earlier. Fast Boot simply brings the hibernated system session out of hibernation, saving all the work of the Windows Kernel Loading phase when the core OS components are loaded. Hybrid Shutdown is the default when you select the Shutdown option from the Power menu, and Fast Boot is the default when you power up your computer, following a Hybrid Shutdown.

Note: Yet another security feature of recent firmware is TPM, or Trusted Platform Module, which provides an additional layer of security for disk encryption and biometric sign-in with Windows Hello. Windows 11 requires the latest version of TPM as well as the other features described here.

Logon

After the firmware has done its part during startup, and Windows core components are in place, the Logon phase begins. More things happen during the logon phase than simply authenticating the user, and they happen simultaneously. They include the following:

User Logon. The key player in this phase is the Windows Logon service, which supports logging on and logging off, and starts the service control manager (services.exe) and the local security authority (lsass.exe). At this point, the sign on screen displays.

Program Startup. During program startup, logon scripts (if they exist) run, startup programs for various applications run, and noncritical services start. Windows finds instructions to run these programs and services in many locations in the registry.

Plug-and-Play Detection. Plug-and-play detection uses several methods to detect new plug-and-play devices, and when it detects a new device, it allocates system resources (memory and other OS resources) to the devices and installs appropriate device drivers.

Modifying System Startup

You can modify the system startup on your Windows computer in many ways. First, determine if you can make the change you want through the GUI, such as using System Properties, a Control Panel applet.

An advanced user may modify system startup by editing the Boot Configuration Database, a hidden part of the registry stored in a file named BCD and located in a hidden partition. The basic information stored in BCD provides locale information, the location of the boot disk and the Windows files, and other information required for the startup process. View the contents of BCD using the BCDedit program, a utility that runs from a Command Prompt or Windows PowerShell with elevated privileges, meaning that it runs with the privileges of a local administrator.

Note: Learn about special startup modes for troubleshooting later in this chapter.

The Command Prompt is a command-line interface (CLI) that you can launch from within Windows, from Safe Mode, or as a Recovery option. There are many commands that administrators use that run either in a Command Prompt or in Windows PowerShell. Both of these CLIs accept certain commands and can be used to run scripts that advanced technical people use to automate tasks, but Command Prompt is a much simpler and limited interface that only accepts text input. PowerShell accepts text input, but it also accepts objects, as defined by object-oriented programming. A software object has fields that define its state, and each object has a set of behaviors. Modern operating systems use object-oriented programming.

Step-by-Step 5.04 will walk you through making a change to BCD using the Startup and Recovery settings in the System Properties applet, and then you will use BCDedit to view the changes made to the BCD file. Another method for configuring Windows System Startup is to use the MSCONFIG utility, described later in this chapter under *Using Windows Troubleshooting and Recovery Tools.*

Step-by-Step 5.04

Using Windows Startup and Recovery Settings

In this step-by-step exercise, you will modify the system startup for Windows using the Startup and Recovery page of System Properties. To complete this exercise, you will need to be signed on to a Windows 10 computer as a member of the Administrators group.

Step 1

Use the keyboard shortcut ⊞+R to open the Run box. In the Run box, type "sysdm.cpl" (do not type the quotation marks). Click OK. In System Properties, click the Advanced tab.

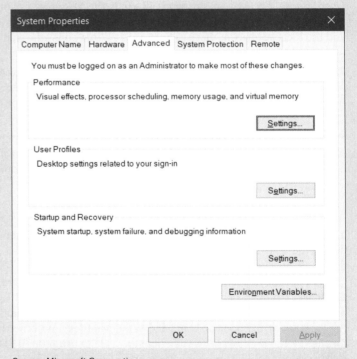

Source: Microsoft Corporation

On the Advanced tab of System Properties, locate the Startup and Recovery section near the bottom and click the Settings button to open the Startup and Recovery page. If your computer is a multiboot computer, you can choose the default operating system that it will select if you do not respond to the menu during the time that it displays the list of operating systems. Notice the time selected is 30 seconds.

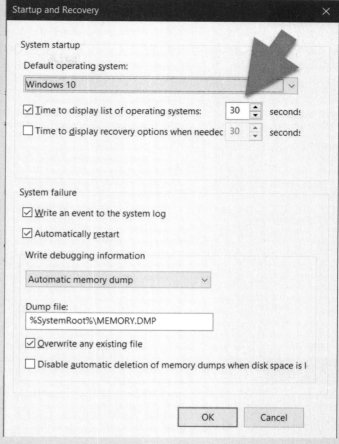

Source: Microsoft Corporation

Step 3

Even if the computer is not a multiboot computer, change the selected time to 35 seconds and click OK to close the Startup and Recovery page. Click OK again to close System Properties. Windows will save the changes in a file named BCD, and they will take effect the next time Windows starts.

Step 4

To see the changes you made, you will need to run BCDedit, an editor that will let you see the contents of BCD. Steps 5 and 6 will walk you through using this tool in either the Command Prompt or Windows PowerShell.

Step 5

Right-click on the Start button to open the Power User Menu. Select either Command Prompt (Admin) or Windows PowerShell (Admin). This will first open the User Account Control (UAC) box. After you respond to the UAC message, the Command Prompt or Windows PowerShell window will open.

Source: Microsoft Corporation

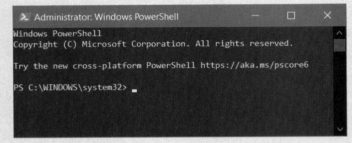

Source: Microsoft Corporation

Step 6

At the prompt in either window, type "bcdedit" and press Enter. The result should look something like the example here. Notice the Timeout setting, which you changed in the earlier steps.

Step 7

To close the Command Prompt or PowerShell windows, type Exit and press Enter.

Source: Microsoft Corporation

Managing Devices

While many devices (printers, mice, cameras, displays, and speakers) are automatically discovered and configured by Windows during Windows Setup or with setup apps, you may still need to install a new device that is not discovered. Occasionally, you will need to remove a device or change other settings. Beyond setup, Windows has two tools for adding and managing devices. They are the legacy Devices and Printers Control Panel, shown in Figure 5-17, and the Windows 10 Settings app. Figure 5-18 shows the Windows 10 Settings app with the **Devices** list on the left and the **Bluetooth & other devices** page on the right. You may be directed to use either of these apps when managing devices. Apps that are grayed out in Control Panel are not currently connected to the PC. This is proof of an important fact about Windows. Although you must be a member of Administrators to install devices, you do not need to be an administrator to use a device, even if it is disconnected and then reconnected. This is important for wireless devices that may not always be available, USB devices that may be removed, or devices that are turned off and on.

Virtual Printers

Figure 5-19 shows **Windows Settings** open to **Printers & scanners.** The first two items in the list, Fax and HP ePrint, represent special apps rather than physical printers. Fax is a Microsoft app or service that allows you to send a document from an Office app as a fax over the Internet. HP ePrint is a Hewlett Packard (HP) app, installed on this PC for use with HP printers. HP cloud resources act as a

try this!

Install a Plug-and-Play Device

Locate a plug-and-play USB device never before installed on your computer, such as a printer or wireless NIC. Try this:

1. Read the documentation for the device. If required, install the device driver before connecting the device.
2. Follow the instructions for the order in which you must power on and connect the USB device to a USB port. You may see a balloon by the notification area as Windows automatically recognizes it.

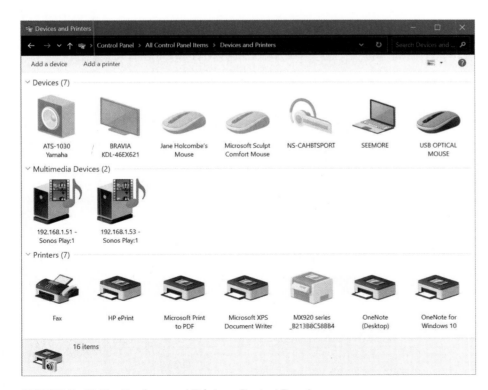

FIGURE 5–17 The **Devices and Printers** Control Panel.
Source: Microsoft Corporation

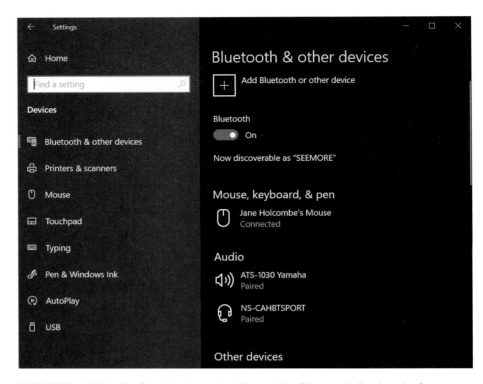

FIGURE 5-18 The **Devices** list is on the left, and the **Bluetooth & other devices** page on the right.
Source: Microsoft Corporation

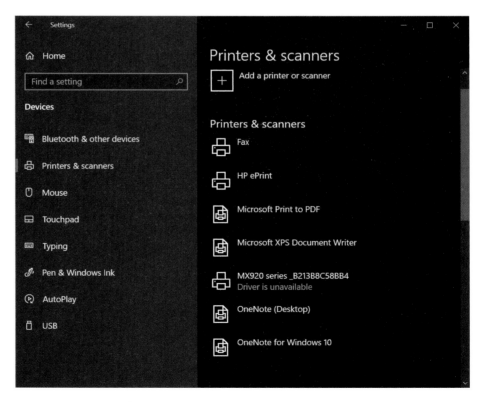

FIGURE 5-19 The **Printers & scanners** page shows several printers.
Source: Microsoft Corporation

sort-of router between the device and the printer. It is designed for laptops and other mobile devices. Four of the printers shown in both Figures 5–17 and 5–19 are virtual printers. When you select one of these printers from the Print menu in an app, the virtual printer saves the document to a file in a selected format, such as PDF, XPS, or OneNote formatted text.

Local Wired Printers

Because Windows and most printers are plug-and-play, installing a new local USB printer in Windows should be, and often is, a nonevent. Therefore, you simply follow the setup guide for the new printer, which will normally instruct you to install the driver before connecting the printer. In many cases, Windows will already have the printer driver and will install it without requiring a driver from the manufacturer. The advantage to using the manufacturer's setup is the access to documentation and the ability to install related apps, such as those for managing the scanning process, including selecting the document format in which the scanned document is saved: text, graphic, or PDF.

Network Printers

At school or work, if a printer is available on the network, an administrator will need to configure the printer with appropriate permissions and give you instructions for connecting. At home, a printer that is not directly wired to your computer can still be used if it has a wireless mode. This may be Bluetooth or Wi-Fi. Bluetooth is a well-established standard for connecting two devices directly over a short distance (same room). Wi-Fi is available over hundreds of feet (provided there are no obstructions to the signal). When you have a choice, select Wi-Fi over Bluetooth because, in addition to covering more distance, Wi-Fi is faster. There are two possible Wi-Fi options. One way is to connect to a printer via Wi-Fi through a Wi-Fi access point (also called router). Both the computer and the printer must be on the same Wi-Fi network. When configuring a printer, select the Wi-Fi network's SSID (name) and providing the password to connect.

There is another option that connects Wi-Fi devices directly to each other, much like Bluetooth, but with better security and greater range. This is Wi-Fi Direct. Using this option, your computer or the printer would host a temporary software access point during printer setup and use. Both the computer and the printer (or other device) must have this capability. Use the **Add Bluetooth & other devices** option from the **Bluetooth & other devices** Settings page to browse for wireless devices. When you select one, follow the prompts to connect your computer with the device.

Note: You may see some other Wi-Fi Direct devices, such as mobile phones and tablets, as well as smart TVs. If they use Wi-Fi Direct, they often have "Direct" in the name they broadcast on the network.

LO 5.5 | Using Windows Troubleshooting and Recovery Tools

Earlier, you worked with restore points, creating a restore point before making a change so that you could return to a restore point in the event that a change caused problems. In this section, explore other recovery tools.

For Startup Failures: The Windows Recovery Environment

In Chapter 4, we described the Windows Preinstallation Environment (Windows PE), the scaled-down Windows operating system that supports the Windows Setup GUI. It has limited drivers for basic hardware and support for NTFS, networks, and programs. However, this is still a very robust and specialized operating system, and when needed, it supports a powerful group of diagnostics and repair tools called the Windows Recovery Environment (Windows RE). Computer manufacturers who preinstall Windows have the option of adding their own repair tools to Windows RE.

If your Windows computer fails at startup, and if the damage is not too extensive, Windows RE will automatically start and load the Windows Error Recovery page with the options: Launch Startup Repair (Windows RE's built-in diagnostics and recovery tool) or Start Windows Normally. It is always worth trying the second option to see if the cause of the problem was something transient. Then, if it still doesn't start up normally, select the Launch Startup Repair and follow the instructions on the screen.

In situations where Windows starts, but you notice problems, you may want to use modified startups to troubleshoot and recover from the problem. We will look at them next.

Troubleshooting with Modified Startups

For those times when a Windows computer fails to start normally or behaves oddly after startup, Windows offers several methods for starting with certain components disabled. One way to access the Startup Settings menu is through Windows 10 Settings, as described in Step-by-Step 5.05. Before you access this menu, review the options you will see there.

Windows 10 Advanced Startup Options Menu

Enable Debugging. This is a very advanced, (dare we say) obsolete, option in which Windows starts normally, and information about the Windows startup is sent over a serial cable to another computer that is running a special program called a debugger.

Enable Boot Logging. While boot logging occurs automatically with each of the three Safe Modes, selecting Enable Boot Logging turns on boot logging and starts Windows normally. Boot logging causes Windows to write a log of the Windows startup in a file named ntbtlog.txt and save it in the systemroot folder. This log file contains an entry for each component in the order in which it loaded into memory. It also lists drivers that were not loaded, which alerts an administrator to a possible source of a problem.

Enable Low-Resolution Video. This option starts Windows normally, except the video mode is changed to the lowest resolution, using the currently installed video driver. It does not switch to the basic Windows video driver. Select this option after making a video configuration change that the video adapter does not support and that prevents Windows from displaying properly.

Safe Mode. Safe Mode is a mode for starting Windows with certain drivers and components disabled. Access Safe Mode from Settings, which we describe later. Safe Mode does not disable Windows security. You are required to log on in all variants of Safe Mode, and you can access only those resources for which you have permissions. If Windows will not start normally but starts just fine in Safe Mode, use Device Manager within Safe Mode to determine if the source of the problem is a faulty device. Run System Restore while in Safe Mode and roll back the entire system to a restore point from before the problem occurred.

Three Safe Mode variants are available:

- **Safe Mode** starts without using several drivers and components that it would normally start. It loads only very basic, non-vendor-specific drivers for mouse, video, keyboard, mass storage, and system services. Because network components are not started, plain Safe Mode does not support networking.
- **Safe Mode with Networking** is identical to plain Safe Mode, except that it starts the networking components. Use the following debug sequence with Safe Mode with Networking:
  - If Windows will not start normally but starts OK in plain Safe Mode, restart and select Safe Mode with Networking.

Note: If your computer does not actually fail, but shows other symptoms of instability, try a simple restart. Some problems go away after a restart, because restart reloads Windows components and gives you a fresh start. If the problem returns, look for a possible trigger, such as opening a certain app.

- If it fails to start in Safe Mode with Networking, the problem area is network drivers or components. Use Device Manager to disable the network adapter driver (the likely culprit), then boot up normally. If Windows now works, replace your network adapter driver.
- If this problem appears immediately after upgrading a network driver, use Device Manager while in Safe Mode to roll back the updated driver. When an updated driver is available, install it.

- **Safe Mode with Command Prompt** is Safe Mode with only a command prompt as a user interface. In a normal startup, Windows loads your GUI desktop, but this depends on the GUI shell to Windows. In place of this GUI shell, Safe Mode with Command Prompt loads a command prompt (cmd.exe) window. This is a handy option to remember if the desktop does not display at all. Once you have eliminated video drivers as the cause, corruption of the explorer.exe program may be the problem. From within the command prompt, you can delete the corrupted version of explorer.exe and copy an undamaged version. This requires knowledge of the command line commands for navigating the directory structure, as well as knowledge of the location of the file that you are replacing. You can launch some GUI administrative programs, such as the Event Viewer (eventvwr.msc), the Computer Management console (compmgmt.msc), or Device Manager (devmgmt.msc) from the command prompt.

Disable Driver Signature Enforcement. If you are unable to install a driver due to Driver Signing, and you trust the manufacturer, select this option, which will start Windows normally, disabling driver signature enforcement just for that startup.

Disable Early Launch Anti-Malware Protection. As described earlier, ELAM works like Trusted Boot, but ELAM examines device drivers before they load into memory. Caution, this option may put your system at risk from device drivers hosting malware, but consider doing this to see if boot up succeeds with ELAM disabled. Then dig deeper to investigate the drivers.

Disable Automatic Restart after Failure. The default setting for Windows is for it to restart after a system crash. However, depending on the problem, restarting may simply lead to another restart—in fact, you could find yourself faced with a continuous loop of restarts. If so, reselect the Disable automatic restart on system failure option. Windows will attempt to start normally (just once for each time you select this option) and may stay open long enough for you to troubleshoot. Do not attempt to work with any data file after restarting with this option because the system may be too unstable. If you are not able to solve the problem, then you will need to restart in Safe Mode to troubleshoot.

Step-by-Step 5.05

Restarting Windows 10 in a Troubleshooting Mode

If you have access to a computer running Windows 10 and can sign in with an administrator account for that computer, you can do this exercise.

Step 1

Open the Start menu and select Settings. In the Settings Home page, select **Update & Security**. On that page, select Recovery. Scroll down to see the options shown here. Then, locate **Advanced startup** and click the **Restart now** button below it.

Note: Another way to start in the Windows Recovery Environment is available from the Windows sign-in screen: press and hold the Shift, open the Power menu (from the icon on the bottom right), and select Restart. With either method, Windows Recovery Environment launches, as shown in Step 2.

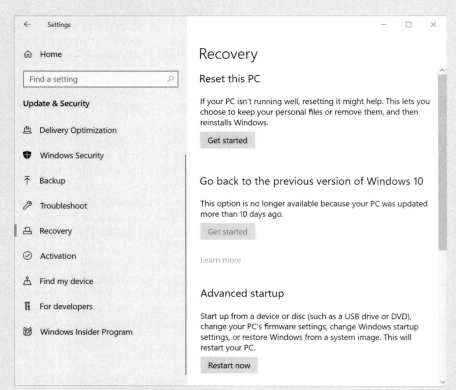

Source: Microsoft Corporation

Step 2

Windows Recovery Environment (Windows RE) launches. The resulting screen will resemble this, but it may have different options showing depending on the system and the Windows 10 version. To restart in a troubleshooting mode, select Troubleshoot.

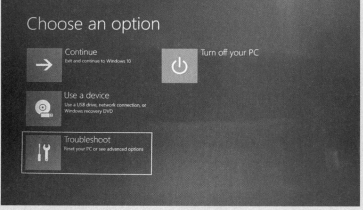

Source: Microsoft Corporation

Step 3

On the Troubleshoot screen, you will see these options, plus you may see one or more options added by the manufacturer of your computer. From this screen select **Advanced options**.

Source: Microsoft Corporation

Step 4

Again, the Advanced Options screen shown here may look different on your computer. From this screen select **Startup Settings**.

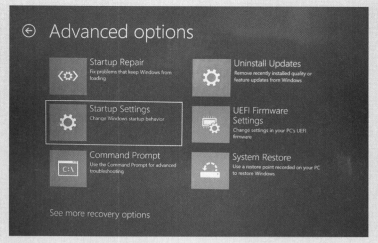

Source: Microsoft Corporation

Step 5

The Startup Settings screen shows the options coming up on the next screen, which will display after you click **Restart**. Select **Restart** now. The following screen contains a numbered list of Startup options. Press the 5 key to restart the computer in Safe Mode with Networking. At restart enter your password or PIN.

Source: Microsoft Corporation

Step 6

The desktop displays with a black background and the words *Safe Mode* in the corners of the screen, as shown here. If your network connection works, you can use the browser to search for a solution to your problem. Begin your search at support. microsoft.com.

Source: Microsoft Corporation

Spend a few minutes exploring more options available to you in Safe Mode. Just one way to do that is to right-click on the Start button to open the Power User menu to quickly access tools, such as Apps and Features, Power Options, Event Viewer, System, Device Manager, Network Connections, Disk Management, Computer Management, and PowerShell.

Source: Microsoft Corporation

When you are finished exploring the options in Windows Safe Mode, shut down or restart from the Power link on the Start menu or from the Power User menu, shown here.

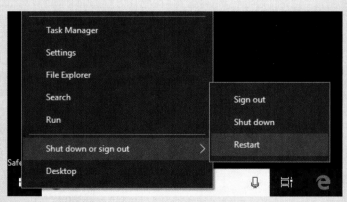

Source: Microsoft Corporation

Removing a Windows Update or Version versus Resetting

If one of the Advanced Startup options does not work, or if you are simply ready to have a fresh (or cleaner) Windows installation, consider (1) removing an installed Windows update, (2) going back to the previous version of Windows, or (3) resetting your PC.

Removing an Installed Windows Update

Of the three options we are considering here, removing an installed Windows Update is the quicker option, but not necessarily cleaner. The **try this!** exercise provides the steps to open the Uninstall an update Control Panel, shown in Figure 5-20.

Go Back to the Previous Version of Windows 10

Another option is when you have updated Windows 10 to a new version. Find this option on the **Settings | Update & Security | Recovery** page, shown in Step 1 of Step-by-Step 5.05. This option keeps your personal files and removes apps and drivers installed after the upgrade. It also removes changes you made to settings since the upgrade. Unfortunately, as shown in the image in Step 1, this option is not available if you updated more than 10 days prior to attempting this.

Note: Before the release of Windows 11 the author upgraded a Windows 10 Pro PC to a beta version of Windows 11. Days later she decided to install and test the beta on a different computer, so she used the "Go back" option to return the system to Windows 10 Pro. It worked, but this is only possible within ten days of an upgrade.

Reset this PC

Resetting your PC is an option that has been improved on over time. You can choose to keep your personal files or remove them. This is a bigger investment in time and patience because the reset takes considerable time, and you will need to reinstall all your apps after the reset completes. The benefit is a cleaner installation of Windows 10.

try this!

Uninstall an Update

If problems on your Windows computer began soon after an update installed, consider removing that update. Try this:

1. Select the **Start** button.
2. Select **Settings | Update & Security | Windows Update**.
3. Select an update (usually the latest) and select **Uninstall**.

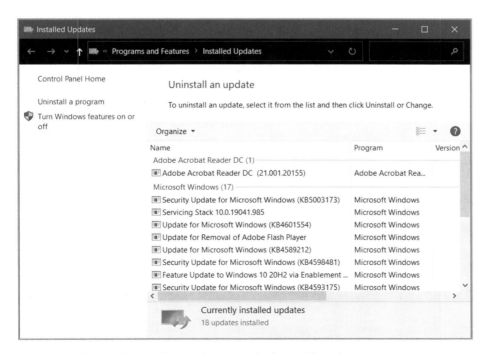

FIGURE 5-20 The Uninstall an update pane in Control Panel.
Source: Microsoft Corporation

However, if you have encrypted your storage device with BitLocker, you need the Bit-Locker key to reset your PC. Access the Reset option from one of these methods:

1. Reset your PC by using a recovery drive, booting from that drive, and selecting **Repair** or do a clean install.

2. Quickly access the **Reset** option from the Windows **sign on** screen by pressing and holding the **Shift** key while selecting the **Restart** option from the Power button on the bottom right of the sign on screen. This takes you directly to the **Choose an option** screen shown in Step 2 of Step-by-Step 5.05, then proceed as in Step-by-Step 5.06.

3. Begin Reset from **Settings | Update & Security | Recovery** page, shown in Step 1 of Step-by-Step 5.05. Then proceed as in Step-by-Step 5.06.

The author is presenting Reset in a Step-by-Step because it is the best way to discuss the actions, while providing images so that you know what to expect. The entire process can take hours, depending on the options you select and your Internet connection. It is doubtful that you will have time or resources to do Step-by-Step 5.06 in a classroom setting.

Note: The author recently tested this on several computers and did have Reset fail on one computer. It displayed the message: "There was a problem resetting your PC." Since this was only a test reset on this PC, we decided to wait and fight another day. In all the other tests, we found Reset improved over earlier versions of Windows 10, and it is greatly improved over pre-Windows 10 versions.

Step-by-Step 5.06

Reset Your Windows 10 Computer

In this Step-by-Step, reset your computer. To complete this exercise, you will need the following:

- A PC or laptop with Windows 10 installed. If using a laptop, keep it connected to power until the reset is complete.
- To be logged on with an account with administrative rights.
- The BitLocker recovery key if your device was encrypted with BitLocker.
- A reliable high-speed Internet connection.

Step 1

You can use one of the steps described above to start this. We begin here through the Windows Setting. From **Start** select **Settings | Update & Security | Recovery**. Under **Reset this PC** select **Get Started.**

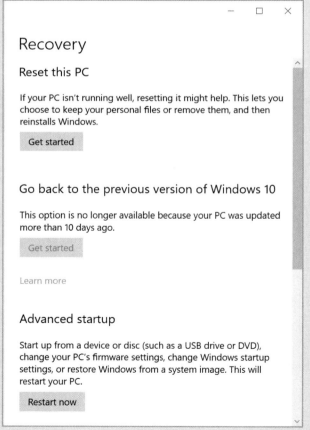

Source: Microsoft Corporation

Step 2

On the **Recovery** page select **Get started** under **Reset this PC.** On the Choose an option page choose either **Keep my files** or **Remove everything.**

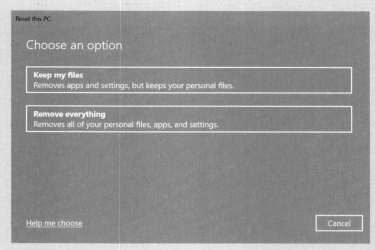

Source: Microsoft Corporation

Step 3

On this page decide how to reinstall. Select either **Cloud download** or **Local reinstall.**

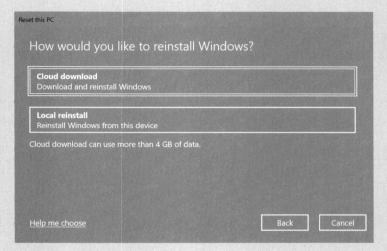

Source: Microsoft Corporation

Step 4

Depending on your selection in the last step, you will see one of these screens. If you are OK with your selection, click or tap the **Next** button. If you selected Download, you may see yet another "Are you sure?" type of screen.

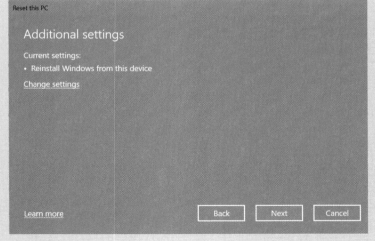

Source: Microsoft Corporation

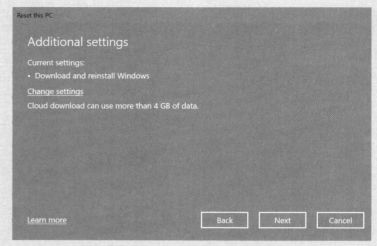

Source: Microsoft Corporation

Step 5

It will take several minutes with this screen showing with a progress spinner (spinning balls).

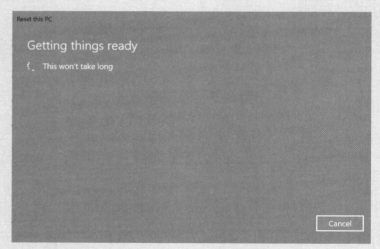

Source: Microsoft Corporation

Step 6

You have yet another chance to Cancel as well as a chance to review what apps will be removed. Click the link titled **View apps that will be removed.** This image shows that we selected **Cloud download,** but you will see a similar screen if you choose to reinstall from the local computer.

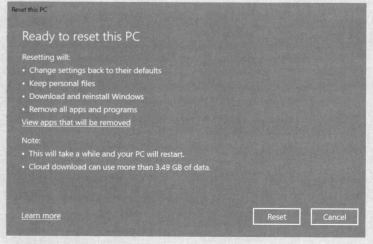

Source: Microsoft Corporation

Step 7

This is the list of apps to be removed on one of the computers we recently reset. After viewing this list, select the **Back** button to proceed.

Source: Microsoft Corporation

Step 8

It can take over an hour for the reset to complete. Then you will need to sign in. It will then install updates, if necessary. Then it goes through the last stages of Windows Setup, beginning with a Welcome screen. You can skip this by selecting **Remind me in 3 days.** Then select **Continue.**

Source: Microsoft Corporation

Step 9

You return to the Windows Desktop where you may be prompted to configure your browser.

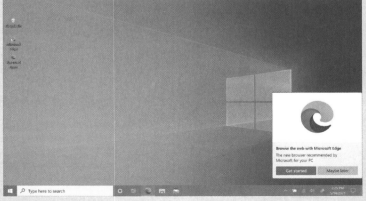

Step 10

But wait! There's more! You will need to reinstall your apps. Notice the link on the desktop to a list of Removed Apps. This is your chance to only install those apps you want to continue using.

Source: Microsoft Corporation

Troubleshooting with MSCONFIG and Task Manager

System Configuration, more commonly known by its executable name MSCONFIG, is a GUI tool for temporarily modifying system startup. The easiest method for starting MSCONFIG is to open the Run box (⊞+R), type "msconfig," and press enter. MSCONFIG allows you to modify and test startup configuration settings without altering the settings directly. Figure 5–21 shows MSCONFIG open to the General tab. Use the options on the MSCONFIG General and Boot tabs to restart Windows in various troubleshooting modes, including Safe Mode, offered on the Boot menu.

MSCONFIG gives you access to settings buried within the registry through a moderately friendly user interface and it allows you to make temporary changes to try to pinpoint the source of a startup problem. For instance, open the Services tab page and stop a service from launching at startup, restart Windows, and see if that solves the problem. If it does not, then go back into MSCONFIG, enable that service, and disable another. Repeat until you locate the problem. If disabling services does not solve the problem, then move on to the Tools tab, a list of tools and their descriptions. You can launch one of the tools from here. One of them is Task Manager. Task Manager allows you to disable programs that may be causing problems. Figure 5–22 shows Task Manager open to the Startup tab where you can select programs to disable. In previous versions of Windows, the MSCONFIG Startup had a list of programs loaded into memory as Windows starts up, but this list was moved to Task Manager, which is why all that remains on that tab is a link to Task Manager.

WARNING!

If you select the Safe option on the Boot page, it will also change settings on the General page. Therefore, any time you make changes, note the changes and be aware that before the system will restart normally, you will need to open MSCONFIG (either before a restart or from within Safe Mode) and return to the General page and select Normal startup.

try this!

Explore MSCONFIG

Open MSCONFIG and explore the option pages. Try this:

1. Open the Run box and type "msconfig" and press the Enter key or click or tap OK.
2. Explore the five tabs (General, Boot, Services, Startup, and Tools) of the System Configuration dialog box.
3. If you make any changes, make sure you remember them. Click Apply, then OK, and click the Restart button in the final message box.
4. After testing a modified restart, open MSCONFIG again and be sure to select Normal startup before restarting.

Note: Open Task Manager faster by using the keyboard shortcut: Ctrl-Shift-Escape.

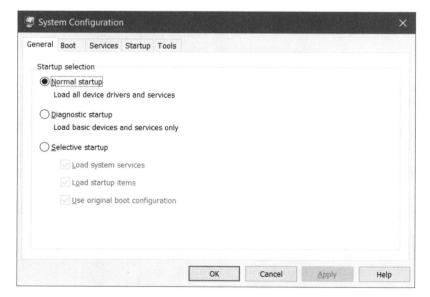

FIGURE 5–21 The Windows 10 System Configuration (MSCONFIG) General tab.
Source: Microsoft Corporation

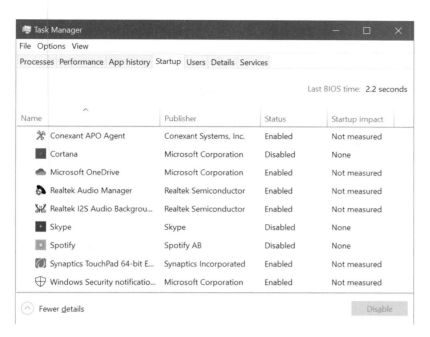

FIGURE 5–22 Use the Startup tab in Task Manager to disable/enable individual programs.
Source: Microsoft Corporation

CHAPTER 5 REVIEW

Chapter Summary

After reading this chapter, and completing the Step-by-Step tutorials and try this! exercises, you should understand the following facts about what is under the Windows desktop:

Managing Local Accounts

- Security implemented solely on a Windows device is local security.
- A local account, also known as an offline account, resides in the local account database.
- A local account can only access the local data.
- A user can sign on to a locally managed computer with a Microsoft Account (MSA), authenticating over the Internet to Microsoft's servers.
- When a user selects to sign on with an MSA during installation, Windows Setup creates a local user account based on the name supplied.
- The first user on a computer is a member of the local Administrators group.
- Any additional local accounts this user creates are standard accounts.
- Both the first user and standard users are subject to the User Account Control (UAC) security.

- Manage local accounts in the Computer Management console.

Managing Local Data Files

- A file is information stored as a unit. There are many types of files with different formats, identifiable by file name extension.
- File Explorer is Windows' file management tool.
- You can also manage files through a command-line interface (CLI), such as Command Prompt or Windows PowerShell.
- Windows default files hierarchy includes one set of folders for the operating system, another set for application program files, and an additional set, personal folders, for each local user account.
- The file systems supported by Windows are several versions of the FAT file system, file system for optical discs, and the NTFS file system. The last is the default installed with Windows. NTFS is expandable, secure, and recoverable.
- NTFS supports file and folder permissions.

Understanding the Registry

- The registry is a database of all configuration settings in Windows.
- Windows creates the registry during setup and modifies it any time a setup or installation program runs after that and during startup and shutdown as well as when device drivers and apps are installed.
- The permanent portion of the registry is in several files, called hives. They include system, software, security, sam, default, and ntuser.dat.
- View the registry in a hierarchical folder structure in Registry Editor.
- A registry key is a folder object that can contain one or more sets of settings as well as other keys.
- There are five top-level keys, or root keys.
- A key that exists within another key is a subkey.
- Settings within a key are value entries.
- Back up the entire registry by creating a Restore Point from System Properties.

Windows User and Power Options

- User options are available from the user tile. They include options to change account settings, lock the computer, and sign out.
- When the current user selects another user's tile, it causes Windows to switch users.

- Selecting Change account settings opens the Your Info Settings page where you can modify your account and, if you are an Administrator, you can add and manage other local accounts.
- The Lock option on the User options menu will keep your session in memory but lock the screen. Sign out closes your open session and returns to the lock screen.
- The default Power options are Sleep, Shutdown, and Restart. A fourth option, Hibernate, only appears in this menu if you enable it in Control Panel's Power Options.
- Use System Settings to add Hibernate to the Power menu.
- Configure what happens when you press the Power button or close the lid.
- The Windows 10 boot process is more secure with the UEFI BIOS.

Using Windows Troubleshooting and Recovery Tools

- Windows offers a variety of startup options, and some are well suited for troubleshooting.
- The Windows PE is a specialized operating system that supports the Windows Recovery Environment (Windows RE).
- Use modified startups, such as Safe Mode to troubleshoot and resolve problems.

Key Terms List

Key Terms Quiz

Use the Key Terms List to complete the sentences that follow.

1. A/an _____ is a portion of the Windows registry that is saved in a file.

2. Each file and folder on an NTFS volume has a/an _____ associated with it containing security permissions.

3. When viewed with a registry editor, a/an _____ is a registry key located at the top level.

4. Many things occur during some of the startup phases. For instance, during the _____ programs start and plug-and-play devices are detected.

5. A/an _____ is a snapshot of Windows, its configuration, and all installed programs.

6. _____ is the more advanced of the two command-line interfaces included with Windows 10.

7. A/an _____ contains program code.

8. The _____ utility is very handy for troubleshooting startup problems, allowing you to temporarily disable programs you suspect are causing problems.

9. _____ is a startup mode for starting Windows with certain drivers and components disabled.

10. A/an _____ is a unique string of numbers preceded by S-1-5 that identifies a security principal in a Windows security accounts database.

Multiple-Choice Quiz

1. Which of the following is not in the registry?
   a. Device driver settings
   b. Services settings
   c. User data files
   d. User preferences
   e. Application program settings

2. Any change to Windows or an installed application results in a change to this special database.
   a. Microsoft SQL Server
   b. Microsoft Excel
   c. ntuser.dat
   d. Registry
   e. Default

3. Most of the Windows registry files are stored in this location.
   a. *systemroot*\System32\config
   b. D:\Windows
   c. *systemroot*\System32\Registry
   d. *systemroot*\Windows
   e. *systemroot*\WINNT

4. If you select this option from the Power menu in Windows 10, both the system state and the user session are saved in memory, requiring a small amount of power.
   a. Fast Boot
   b. Hibernate
   c. Hybrid Shutdown
   d. Sleep
   e. Measured Boot

5. In Windows 10, the previous contents of the Startup tab page in MSCONFIG have been moved to this utility.
   a. System Configuration
   b. Task Manager
   c. BCDedit
   d. Windows RE
   e. PowerShell

6. Which statement is true?
   a. Only the Administrator may disconnect or reconnect an installed device.
   b. Only members of the Administrators group may disconnect or reconnect an installed device.
   c. Only members of the Guests group may disconnect or reconnect an installed device.
   d. Any member of the local Users group may disconnect or reconnect an installed device.
   e. No one may disconnect or reconnect an installed device.

7. What UEFI security feature loads only trusted operating system bootloaders?
   a. Fast Boot
   b. Secure Boot
   c. Measured Boot
   d. Trusted Boot
   e. Early Launch Anti-Malware (ELAM)

8. You are preparing a USB drive to be used in both a Windows PC and a macBook. What file system should you format onto that drive?
   a. NTFS
   b. exFAT
   c. CDFS
   d. FAT32
   e. FAT16

9. What registry hive does the bootloader use during startup to locate the operating system files it must load?
   a. BCD
   b. winload.exe
   c. bootmgr
   d. ntoskrnl.exe
   e. winlogon.exe

10. What page in System Properties would you open to modify the length of time the OS selection menu displays during Windows startup?
    a. Startup and Recovery
    b. Device Manager
    c. BCDedit
    d. Local Security Policy
    e. Computer Management

11. This powerful group of diagnostics and repair tools is supported by a specialized OS that has limited drivers, but supports the Windows Setup GUI.
    a. MSCONFIG
    b. Windows PowerShell
    c. Early Launch Anti-Malware (ELAM)
    d. Logon phase
    e. Windows Recovery Environment (Windows RE)

12. What is the acronym for the main logical structure of the NTFS file system?
    a. ACL
    b. ELAM
    c. EPROM
    d. FAT
    e. MFT

13. When Windows does this, it hibernates the Windows session and saves it in a file but does not save the user session.
    a. Sleep
    b. Hybrid Shutdown
    c. Switch user
    d. Restart
    e. Hibernate

14. You upgraded a device driver, and Windows immediately failed and restarted. The problem is that it seems to be in a continuous restarting loop. What boot startup option will restart normally and give you an opportunity to try to troubleshoot the problem after a normal reboot?
    a. Debugging mode
    b. Enable boot logging
    c. Safe Mode with command prompt
    d. Disable automatic restart on system failure
    e. Safe Mode with networking

15. Which of the following is the executable name for the GUI utility that allows you to temporarily modify system startup?
    a. SYSCON
    b. MSCONFIG
    c. SYSEDIT
    d. regedit
    e. BCDedit

Essay Quiz

1. Describe at least five actions that will automatically change the Windows registry.

2. Your Windows computer is having display problems. You suspect that the cause is a video driver update that you installed. You managed to log on at the first restart after the update, but then you found that, even though you had logged on, it was hopeless to try to work with the GUI. Describe how you would confirm that the problem is the video adapter and how you will correct the problem.

3. The first local account on a Windows computer is a member of two user groups. What are these groups? Describe the abilities given to that user by its membership in the more advanced of these groups.

4. Name the most powerful user account on a Windows computer and describe its default state and the reason for this.

5. Describe what boot logging does and how you would use it as a troubleshooting tool.

Lab Projects

LAB PROJECT 5.1

Your Windows 10 computer will not start, and you believe the cause is a network card you recently installed.

1. Describe the steps you will take to isolate the problem.
2. Demonstrate the steps to your instructor.

LAB PROJECT 5.2

A fellow student asked for your help because his Windows 10 computer is unstable. He is considering using Reset this PC. Describe the two options under Reset this PC and if possible do a reset of a Windows 10 computer. Be sure you have permission to do this, and do not use a production computer. After the refresh, go into Windows and describe any changes you found.

LAB PROJECT 5.3

You are having a problem with your Windows computer that is isolated to a single graphics editing program that you use every day in your work. When you described the problem to the customer service support person for this product, she told you that the only fix for it is to edit a key under HKEY-LOCAL_MACHINE\SOFTWARE. She has assured you that this fix will work without causing any problems, but you are wary of doing this.

1. Describe the steps you will take before making the suggested registry changes.
2. Demonstrate only the steps you would take before modifying the registry. Do not actually modify the registry.

chapter

6 Apple macOS on the Desktop

Iryna Gyrych/Shutterstock

Learning Outcomes

In this chapter, you will learn how to:

LO **6.1** Prepare and implement a macOS upgrade or installation, and list the postinstallation tasks.

LO **6.2** Navigate and manage macOS on the desktop, including working with features and settings.

LO **6.3** Manage files using Finder; backup local files, understand macOS file systems, and use the Disk Utility.

LO **6.4** Manage local security in macOS.

LO **6.5** Troubleshoot common macOS problems.

So far we have discussed operating systems in general, security for operating systems, virtualization of desktop operating systems, and the Windows operating system. Now we change our focus to Apple macOS, Apple's OS for their iMac desktops and Mac-Book laptops.

In this chapter, you will explore the macOS operating system beginning with installing and upgrading. Then move to navigating the desktop, working with files, and configuring local security. Finally, you'll learn the basics of local security in macOS on the desktop. ✸

LO 6.1 | Installing and Upgrading macOS

This section details the process of installing and upgrading macOS including the minimum hardware and software requirements, the installation process, and postinstallation tasks.

Plan Ahead

Before you begin, think about an Apple ID, a free account that identifies you as a customer of Apple for all their services and products. If you already have one, consider using it for your new device. There are many benefits to this. If not, consider creating one ahead of time before proceeding, although you can also create one during the installation process. There are three general scenarios for installing or upgrading macOS. They include (1) the first sign on after purchasing a new Mac, (2) an upgrade of an existing Mac to a new version of macOS, and (3) a clean installation of macOS. A new Apple Mac computer has macOS preinstalled, but not configured and personalized. When you upgrade to a new version of macOS, you have the older macOS installed and configured with all your apps and preferences. In contrast, a clean installation is most likely to be a reset of the same version to start fresh, reinstalling apps and services after the OS is installed.

Make Decisions and Gather Information

What the three scenarios have in common is the macOS Setup Assistant, which, like a Windows wizard, guides you through multiple tasks. In this case, macOS Setup Assistant steps through the configuration and personalization options. Figure 6-1 shows the initial screen, in which you select the language for the installation. Other than the very first screens, most of these options can be changed or enabled and configured later. Below is a list of screens displayed during an installation. You may see more screens, or fewer, depending on your response as you proceed.

- Language
- Country or Region

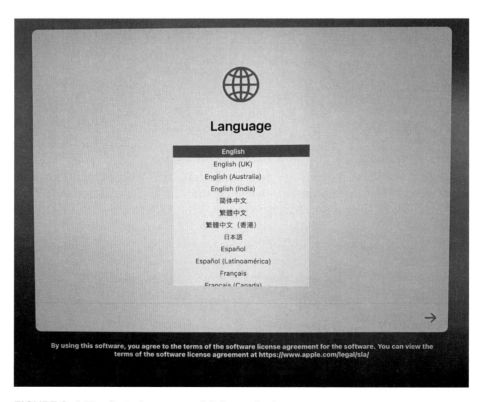

FIGURE 6-1 The first of many macOS Setup Assistant screens.
Source: Apple Inc.

- Accessibility—consider Apple's Vision, Motor, Hearing, and Cognitive options.
- Select Your Wi-Fi Network—provide the name and password of a Wi-Fi Network or select *Other Network Options* if an administrator has given you special instructions.
- Data &Privacy—click the *Learn More. . .* link to learn about Apple's data and privacy practices and policies.
- Migration Assistant—this is also available as an app in the Utilities folder after Setup is complete.
  - From a Mac, Time Machine backup or Startup Disk
  - From a Windows PC
- Sign In with Your Apple ID—choose to do this in order to seamlessly use iCloud, the App Store, and other Apple services. You can also select *Set Up Later.*
- Create a Computer Account—a local account. Consider selecting the option *Allow my Apple ID to reset this password.*
- Find My—enable Apple's Find My service for this Mac.
- Express Set Up (versus Customize Settings)—selecting this will allow some apps and services to gather and use location data and allows Apple to gather usage and other analytics from this Mac.
- Analytics—opt in or opt out to share crash and usage data with Apple and app developers.
- Screen Time—choose to set up now or later to help you manage your screen time.
- Siri—decide if you want to enable Ask Siri. This is followed by other screens concerning Siri and Dictation.
- Ask Siri, Dictation & Privacy—describes the types of data Siri (Apple's personal assistant) gathers, depending on your settings.
- FileVault Disk Encryption
  - Turn on FileVault disk encryption
  - Allow my iCloud account to unlock my disk
- Touch ID is Ready—for fingerprint authentication, if available on your Mac.
- Pay—add credit, debit, or store cards for use with Apple Pay with Touch ID.
- Choose Your Look—select an appearance now or after Setup.
- True Tone Display—enable or disable on Macs with this feature.

Check the Computer Model and macOS Version before Upgrading

Apple limits the length of time it will continue to support older hardware. It also limits the versions of macOS that can upgrade to the latest version. In general, be concerned if your current Apple computer is more than seven years old and your OS is more than five years old. Do a search of the Apple support site, **support.apple.com**, using a search string like "How to Upgrade to macOS <latest version>," substituting the name of the latest version. When checked recently, Apple Support listed multiple compatible models for each of their Mac products. There were almost two dozen listed under MacBook Pro, dating back seven years from the introduction of the latest macOS. They had similar, but shorter lists for the MacBook Air, MacBook, iMac, iMac Pro, Mac mini, and Mac Pro. We simply use the term "Mac" to refer to any of these. If you Mac is compatible, but the macOS on it is too old to upgrade, then upgrade to a version that can, in turn, upgrade to the latest macOS. Follow Step-by-Step 6.01 to check out the macOS version and hardware information.

Step-by-Step 6.01

Checking macOS Version and Hardware Information

It is simple to check the installed version of macOS as well as the model information for a Mac. This exercise will walk you through the steps for checking out this information and more. You need:

- A Mac running a recent version of macOS.
- The user name and password of an account for this computer.

Log on to the Mac. Click the Apple menu in the top-left corner of the screen and select *About this Mac*.

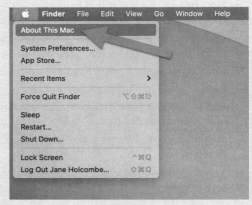

Source: Apple Inc.

The box that pops up displays the version of the installed macOS. It also lists the computer model and date of manufacturer and other basic information about the computer: processor, memory, and serial number. You may want to return to this window as you read the next section. Click the *System Report* button.

Source: Apple Inc.

A window opens with detailed technical information about the hardware, network, and software. Explore the three categories. When finished, close the open window.

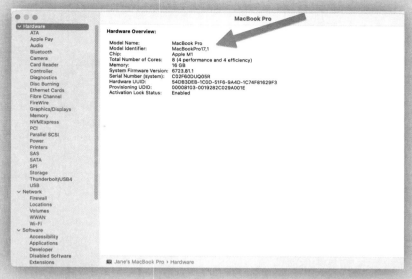

Source: Apple Inc.

Access a Fast Internet Connection

The latest macOS upgrade requires downloading a large file. If your Internet connection is metered, meaning you pay for a certain amount of data usage per month, then you may want to make a Genius Bar appointment at an Apple store near you and take advantage of their free fast Internet access to download the upgrade.

Note: When you exceed the data usage limit in a metered Internet connection, you are billed at a higher rate for the additional data.

Back Up Your Computer

Before installing or upgrading macOS, be sure to do a full backup. The best way to do this is to use an external drive and **Time Machine**, the backup software included with macOS since Snow Leopard (10.6). Time Machine requires a dedicated drive that is always available whenever the computer is on. This can be an external USB, FireWire, Thunderbolt drive, a networked drive, an internal drive (in addition to the startup drive), or a separate partition on a drive. If you have one of these drives available and connected to your computer, open the **Apple menu**, a drop-down menu that appears when you click the Apple icon on the far left of the menu bar; select System Preferences. In System Preferences, select Time Machine. Turn on Time Machine and follow the instructions. The first backup will take hours. Figure 6–2 shows the Time Machine app ready to setup and configuration. After selecting a backup disk, configure a complete backup.

Note: Select a drive or partition for Time Machine that is at least the size of the drive you are backing up.

Disable Disk Encryption

If you have encrypted your files with either FileVault or a third-party program, temporarily disable it or turn it off. This is just a precaution to avoid any possible incompatibilities during the upgrade process or delays caused by the process of unencrypting. After a successful upgrade, enable encryption, unless you are using a third-party program that the new macOS version no longer supports.

Decide Where to Install macOS

Normally, you install macOS as an upgrade over a previous version. You can also install macOS onto a separate drive or separate volume on the same drive as your present version. This allows you to dual-boot between the two versions. The drive

FIGURE 6–2 Select a disk for your Time Machine backups.
Source: Apple Inc.

or volume must be empty when you begin the installation. The last OS installed will be the one that boots up by default, but you can change this on the fly by pressing the Option key as you turn on your computer. That is a good way to temporarily boot to the alternate OS. If you wish to change the default, then open the Startup Disk option in System Preferences and the drive you select will be the default startup drive.

Prepare to Purchase the Upgrade Online

If you are upgrading an existing Mac, buy the latest version of macOS at the online App Store. You can no longer order it on DVD; you must do an online upgrade or, if you want to do a clean installation, download the installation image and burn it to a DVD or USB flash drive.

The Installation

There are rarely surprises with a macOS installation—whether it is a new mac or an upgrade. If you do an upgrade, then at the end of the upgrade, you should only need to log in with the account you used before the upgrade.

Even when you buy a new Apple computer, which always has the OS preinstalled, you get to experience the final stages of the installation the first time you start the computer. That is when the macOS Setup Assistant appears, with several screens to configure and personalize your computer.

> *Note:* Intel or M1 Mac? Whether you have an Intel Mac or an M1 Mac, macOS setup will proceed with the steps described here.

Postinstallation Tasks

A benefit of Apple's requirement that you purchase macOS through the online App Store is that the installation image you download includes the latest updates to macOS. This requirement eliminates the need to update macOS immediately after an upgrade or install. If you install macOS from an image you created days or weeks ago, you will need to check for and install updates, as described in the try this! on the next page. Other postinstallation tasks include installing apps into a clean installation, updating apps, and enabling disabled components. Once the macOS desktop appears, you will see helpful prompts to complete configuring some apps and services.

Installing Apps

If you signed in with your Apple iCloud account, your Apple services and apps will be available to you. Apple also makes it easy to reinstall other apps installed through the App Store.

Updating Apps

Apple does not include updates for your apps in the image, so you should check out available updates. An easy way to do this is by simply checking to see if a number appears on the top right of the App Store icon. When that happens, double-click the icon, the App Store window will open, as shown in Figure 6–3, and you can initiate the download and install the updates from there.

In another scenario, you open an app and a message displays stating that an update is available. Unless you know of a reason to not update the software, simply respond to messages to start the download, including one allowing incoming network connections from the update program. Then you may see a message box giving choices to accept or reject individual updates and to start the install. A progress message will display while the update downloads. After the download completes, respond to more messages to continue, to accept the license terms, to select a destination drive, and finally to install the update.

try this!

Install Software Updates

It is simple to install updates. Try this:

1. Click the Apple menu in the top-left corner of your desktop, select About this Mac, and click Software Update in the window that displays.
2. In the Updates page of the App Store, see if any updates are available and respond to any messages to begin the Install.
3. Click Agree on any License Agreement page that displays (if you agree, of course). There may be several.
4. Click Restart, if requested.
5. It can take several minutes for the updates to install.

The App Store icon on the Dock.
Source: Apple Inc.

Installing Apple Mobile Apps to M1 Macs and MacBooks

While there are thousands of apps for iOS and iPad OS, there are far fewer for the macOS. Most of us want to run the same apps on all our devices. While you cannot run iOS and iPad OS apps on an Intel Mac, you can run many of these in macOS on an M1 Mac.

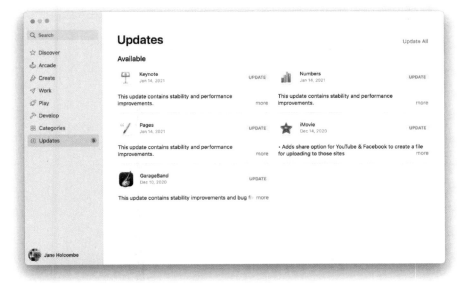

FIGURE 6–3 The Updates page of the App Store.
Source: Apple Inc.

Apple keeps track of apps we purchase for all our devices and lists them in the App Store on your Account page. If you have an iPhone or iPad with apps installed, then when you access the App Store on an M1 Mac there are two lists—*Mac Apps* (designed for macOS) and iPhone & iPad Apps (iOS and iPad OS apps). When you select the iPhone & iPad Apps tab the apps list displays. Below each app is the date the app was first installed on a device, plus a description, as shown in Figure 6-4. The descriptions you may see are *Designed for iPad* and *Designed for iPhone*. For those apps that are not verified by Apple as compatible with macOS on M1, the description will include *Not verified for macOS*.

Enable Disabled Components or Apps

If you disabled any components, such as FileVault, before upgrading macOS, enable them after completing the upgrade. We describe FileVault later in this chapter.

LO 6.2 | Navigating and Customizing the macOS Desktop

Navigating in macOS is much like it is in the Windows desktop. You move around by clicking graphical objects. Tasks include customizing the desktop, installing and removing applications, and adding a printer. You will learn how to set up system preferences, print, and create and manage user accounts. We also describe the features

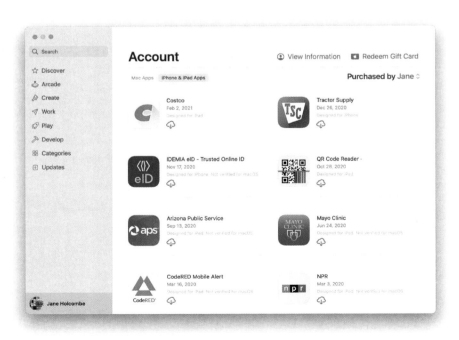

FIGURE 6–4 The *iPhone & iPad Apps* list on an M1 Mac.
Source: Apple Inc.

you use for your everyday work on a Mac, including launching programs and working with the newer macOS features.

Menu Bar, Dock, and Other Desktop Features

One of the biggest differences between the macOS GUI and the Windows desktop is that Windows has a Taskbar at the bottom of the screen with general functions and notifications, and each app has its own menu bar at the top of its window. But macOS has a menu bar across the top of the screen with general functions. It also contains drop-down menus for the current app, and a notification area on the far right that serves some of the same functions as the right end of the Windows Taskbar. Depending on how macOS is configured, the notification area displays the day and time and contains icons for features such as the **Spotlight** search feature. Spotlight is also at the top of every Finder window. Along the bottom of the macOS screen is the **Dock**, a floating tray that, much like the Windows Taskbar, holds icons for commonly used programs, as well as for open applications. Learn more about the Dock later in this chapter. Figure 6-5 shows the macOS desktop with key features labeled. COMMAND+SPACE BAR or a click of the magnifying glass icon, opens the Spotlight search box (Figure 6-6). Spotlight presents results as soon as you start typing because Spotlight does a live search. Spotlight searches everywhere, including the Web, and it is integrated into Safari. Another improvement in Spotlight is that you can ask natural language questions, as we have grown to expect to do with Apple's Siri.

Click on the Apple icon on the left of the menu bar to open the Apple menu shown in Figure 6-7. This menu has links to several handy tools (About This Mac, System Preferences, App Store, Force Quit). It includes power options (Sleep, Restart, Shutdown) and user options (Lock Screen and Log Out). Click Recent Items to see a list of recent apps and files.

> *Note:* The window for an app in macOS does not contain the menu bar, but it does contain buttons for accessing many of the same features available through the menu bar and the round window control buttons in the upper left corner for closing (red), minimizing (orange), and tiling or maximizing (green) the window.

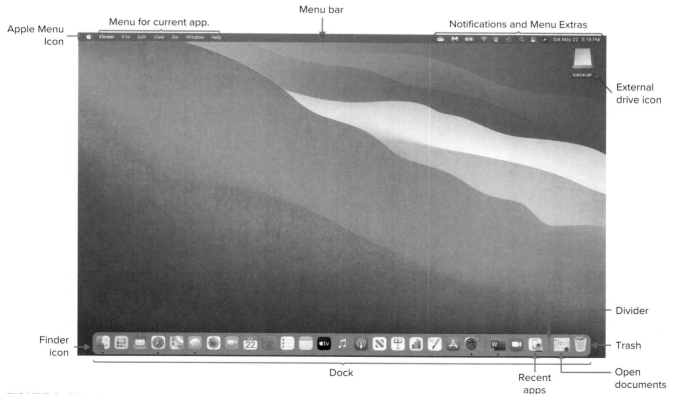

FIGURE 6–5 Key features of the macOS desktop.
Source: Apple Inc.

FIGURE 6–6 The Spotlight search box.
Source: Apple Inc.

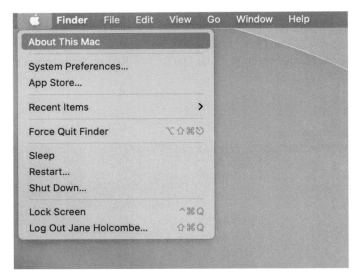

FIGURE 6–7 The Apple menu.
Source: Apple Inc.

Changing Settings in macOS

Open **System Preferences** from the Apple menu or from the Dock where its icon is a gray box containing a gear. Figure 6-8 shows the main System Preferences window. Notice the *Show All* button in the title bar; this will always return you to the main System Preferences window. The icons are in rows by category. The actual icons in each row depend on the installed features and devices. While any logged-on user can change some settings, others can only be changed by an administrator.

If you have trouble with the default organization of the System Preferences icons, you can sort them in alphabetical order by clicking the View menu (in the Menu bar at the top of the screen) and selecting *Organize Alphabetically.* When you do that, the settings in the System Preferences window are sorted, and the shading that previously separated the categories disappears. However, you don't really need to change the View;

The System Preferences icon on the Dock.
Source: Apple Inc.

Show All button

FIGURE 6–8 System Preferences organized by category.
Source: Apple Inc.

Note: Click the Show All button to return to the main Preferences window from any individual Preferences window.

Note: Press COMMAND+OPTION+D to hide the Dock. Press it again to unhide the Dock.

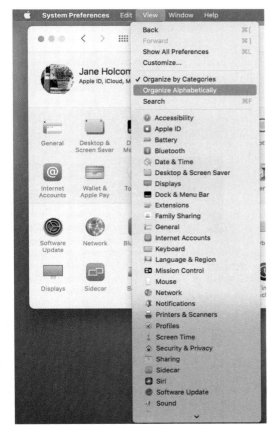

FIGURE 6–9 The View menu lets you change the appearance of the System Preferences folder.
Source: Apple Inc.

simply use the System Preferences Search box or select the setting name from the View menu, as shown in Figure 6–9. This is helpful when you know the name of a Preference pane but do not recall its category.

Launching and Switching between Apps with the Dock

Look more closely at the Dock in Figure 6-10 and notice that beginning on the left, are program icons for apps and features Apple expects you to use frequently. Also note the two vertical bars on the Dock. Apple automatically adds icons for open and recently opened apps between the two vertical bars. To the right of the Recent Apps, adjacent to Trash, is an area for open documents.

When you launch a program, a small dot appears under the app's icon on the Dock; simply click on one of these icons to quickly switch between tasks. The Trash icon sits on the Dock, waiting for you to drag unwanted files, folders, and apps into it. Add a file, folder, application, or Internet bookmark to the Dock by simply dragging it there. If you want to remove something from the Dock, just drag it off and onto the desktop until the word "Remove" appears over it, as shown in Figure 6-11; release the mouse button. The icon disappears, but the app and data are left intact.

Using the Heads-Up Program Switcher

In addition to Dock, another tool for switching between open apps is the Heads-Up Program Switcher. Simply press and hold the COMMAND key and tap the TAB key. The heads-up display of open app icons appears in the middle of the screen. Keep the COMMAND key down while you repeatedly tap the TAB key to cycle through the app icons. When the app you want is selected, release the COMMAND key.

The Heads-Up Program Switcher.
Source: Apple Inc.

FIGURE 6–10 Click an icon on the Dock to launch a program.
Source: Apple Inc.

try this!

Add an Icon to the Dock

Add a shortcut icon to the Dock. Try this:

1. Open the Application folder in Finder and select something not already on the Dock that you would like to add to the Dock.
2. Click the item's icon and drag it onto the Dock. Before letting go of the mouse button, move the icon over the Dock to position it between existing Dock icons.
3. Release the mouse button when you are satisfied with the position of the icon.
4. To remove the icon, drag it to the Trash.

View and Manage All Programs in Launchpad

Launchpad resembles the home screen on Apple iOS devices (shown in Chapter 10). Click the Launchpad icon on the Dock to open Launchpad. With Launchpad open, the menu bar at the top of the screen and objects on the desktop disappear, but the Dock remains visible. Now you can view all the apps installed on your computer and launch one with a single click. If you have more program icons than will fit on a page, scroll to see additional pages, just as in iOS.

Figure 6-12 shows Launchpad open with one page of app icons. When there are more apps than will fit on one page, Launchpad creates additional pages. The number of pages is indicated by dots positioned just above the Dock. Click a dot to move to another page. Customize Launchpad by clicking on an icon and holding the mouse button until all the icons in Launchpad start jiggling. Then drag the selected icon to different positions on the page or pages. If you drag an icon on top of another program icon (without releasing it), a horizontal band opens in the middle of the screen. Drop the icon into this band to group it into a folder with the other icon. When we dragged the Microsoft OneNote icon on top of the Microsoft Word icon, the band opened with

View and Manage All Programs in Launchpad
Source: Apple Inc.

FIGURE 6–11 To remove an icon simply drag it off the Dock until the word "Remove" appears, then release the mouse button.
Source: Apple Inc.

FIGURE 6–12 The Launchpad contains icons for all installed apps.
Source: Apple Inc.

FIGURE 6–13 Group apps that you use together in a folder in Launchpad.
Source: Apple Inc.

FIGURE 6–14 Add other apps to a Launchpad folder icon.
Source: Apple Inc.

the suggested folder name of "Productivity." When we dropped the Notepad icon, Launchpad created the folder and showed the suggested name above the band, as shown in Figure 6-13. After you create a grouping of apps in Launchpad, you can easily drag and drop more apps into the group, as shown in Figure 6-14. Each folder displays in Launchpad as an icon the same size as each icon representing a single app. This organizes and cleans up the Launchpad.

Declutter the Desktop with Mission Control

Mission Control is a window-management program for navigating among all open apps. Also use it to work with the **Spaces** features. A Space is a virtual screen; macOS supports up to 16 Spaces. Use Spaces for separating work, play, and school projects into virtual desktops.

Open Mission Control, Figure 6-15, by swiping up with three fingers on a trackpad; swipe down to exit Mission Control. The Mission control keyboard shortcut is usually CTRL+UP ARROW. Use it once to open Mission Control. Use it again to close Mission Control. Change Mission Control settings in its preferences pane, shown in Figure 6-16.

Note: A more generic term for Apple's Spaces feature is desktop, easily confused with the virtual desktops discussed in Chapter 2, but altogether different. Linux and Windows 10 each have features similar to Spaces.

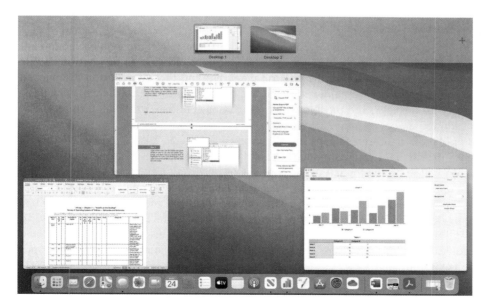

FIGURE 6–15 Mission Control.
Source: Apple Inc.

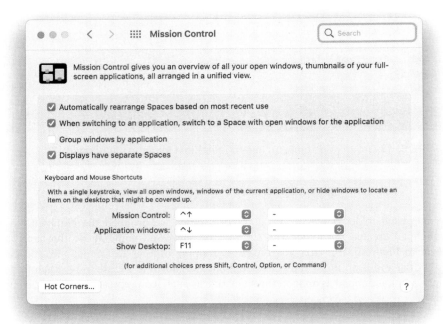

FIGURE 6–16 Change Mission Control settings in this preferences pane.
Source: Apple Inc.

Note: To see a list of all keyboard and mouse shortcuts for macOS open the Shortcuts tab of the Keyboard pane in System Preferences.

Note: Press CTRL+RIGHT ARROW key or CTRL+LEFT ARROW key to switch between Spaces.

When you open Mission Control, each window displays as a tile, and the Spaces bar is across the top with the current space or spaces identified as "Desktop 1," "Desktop 2," and so on. Move your cursor to the top of the screen and the bar will broaden, showing thumbnails for the current spaces, as shown in Figure 6–15. To add a space, simply click on the plus (+) at the top right and a desktop will be added showing a thumbnail. Drag an open window from below to another desktop on the bar. Switch between spaces by selecting a space within Mission Control or with the CTRL+RIGHT ARROW key or CTRL+LEFT ARROW key. The Spaces bar will also contain thumbnails for any Full Screen or Split View apps, described next.

Full Screen and Split View

Full Screen and Split View are accessed from the green button menu on the top left of an app window. Make an open app full screen by clicking on this button. While full screen, the app covers the desktop menu bar and the green button disappears. Exit full-screen view by moving the cursor to the top edge of the screen. The desktop menu displays, and the app window green button displays. Click it to return to windowed mode.

Make two full-screen apps share the screen, a feature called Split View. To begin, open the two apps you wish to have share the screen. In one of the apps click-hold the green button on the top left of the app window. A drop-down menu will appear with the options *Enter Full Screen, Tile Window to Left of Screen,* and *Tile Window to Right of Screen,* as shown in Figure 6–17. This is great when you need information from one app while working in another app. Figure 6–18 shows an example of Split View. To exit Split View, move the cursor to the top of the screen. This opens the menu bar and enables the window buttons. On one app window click the green button. Both apps will exit from Split View.

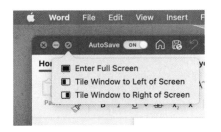

FIGURE 6–17 Select from the options on the drop-down menu.
Source: Apple Inc.

Notification Center

The Notification Center, as shown in Figure 6–19, displays important status messages, notifying you of events, such as a new email or text message or the availability of a new update. These messages pop out on the right of the Desktop. To open the

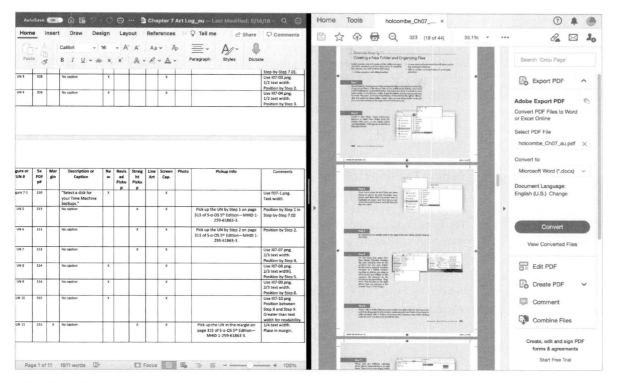

FIGURE 6–18 Full-screen apps can be viewed side-by-side in Split View.
Source: Apple Inc.

Notification Center click on the date and time at the far right of the desktop menu bar. In Figure 6-19 a single notification is at the top. Mini apps called widgets appear below Notifications and may take up most of the Notification area. Beginning with Big Sur, macOS supports the same widgets across devices—Macs, iPhones, and iPads. A widget uses few resources and can provide updated information, such as weather, stock prices, world clock, calendar, screen time, and more. To reposition a widget click and drag it. To change the size of each widget, scroll to the bottom of Notifications and select Edit Widgets. Manage notifications in the Notifications page in System Preferences.

Control Center

The Control Center, which first appeared on iPhones, is another example of the blending of the Apple mobile and desktop operating systems. The Control Center comes with some handy quick controls for changing settings—such as toggling between on and off states for your network connections. Open Control Center on your Mac by clicking on the Control Center button on the menu bar, as shown in Figure 6-20. Figure 6-21 shows Control Center.

Printing in macOS

No matter what type of printer you have, each macOS application manages the printing process in the same way, including giving you the ability to create an Adobe PDF document from any Print menu.

Installing a Printer

Installing a printer in macOS is a nonevent. You simply connect the printer, power up, and it installs without any fuss or obvious activity. The OS quietly searches for the driver, downloading it from the Internet if the computer has an Internet connection.

FIGURE 6–19 Open Notification Center to see all current notifications and widgets.
Source: Apple Inc.

FIGURE 6–20 The Control Center button on the menu bar.
Source: Apple Inc.

FIGURE 6–21 The Control Center.
Source: Apple Inc.

To verify that the printer did install, open Printers and Scanners in System Preferences. With the Print tab selected, installed printers are listed on the left. If your new printer is not listed, click the plus (+) button under the list (shown in Figure 6–22) to initiate the printer detection process. This is often necessary before macOS recognizes a printer over a Wi-Fi connection. If this doesn't work, contact the manufacturer for help finding a driver.

Most of your printer interaction takes place in the Print dialog box within applications. During printing, the Print Center icon appears in the Dock, allowing you to view, hold, or delete jobs.

Setting Printing Options

A printer has a variety of configurable options, which you may modify from the Print menu in any application's File menu (or the Printers and Scanners preferences pane). These options are specific to the printer model. You should explore these options for your own printer so that you are aware of its capabilities and can plan to take advantage of them.

Where to Find the Print Queue

When you are ready to send a job to the printer, simply open the Print menu in the application, select the printer, and if you need to change paper size, orientation, or scale, click the Page Setup button and make those changes. When you are ready to print, click the Print button. While a job is printing, an icon displays on the Dock, and if you're fast, you can open it in time to see the print queue, which closes when the print job is finished. Otherwise, you can find the print queue for an individual printer by calling up the Print and Scan preferences pane. Select a printer from the list on the left and double-click on any printer or click the *Open Print Queue* button to view its print queue, check the ink or toner level, print a test page, or open a printer utility that will let you do certain printer maintenance and testing.

Siri

Siri, Apple's voice-activated personal assistant, first appeared in iPhones. In the years since its introduction, Siri has gained functionality and become a popular feature of Apple desktops and laptops, thanks to support for Siri in macOS. When you install the latest version of macOS, the Setup Assistant prompts you to enable and configure Siri. If you decline, you can take time to do it later. When (or if) you are ready to do that, simply click the Siri icon in System Preferences.

Figure 6–23 shows the Siri Preferences after a user configured Siri. After enabling *Listen for "Hey Siri,"* you are prompted to give voice samples of some typical requests. Once Siri is configured, tap the Siri button on the menu bar or simply talk to Siri. Figure 6–24 shows Siri responding.

AirPlay versus AirDrop

Share videos, photos, music, and other content from you Apple device (iPhone, iPad, iPod touch, or Mac) with a variety of devices using **AirPlay**. Use AirPlay to connect to an Apple TV, which acts as an intermediary device for sending your iTunes songs, video, pictures, and other data from your computer to a high-definition (HD) TV via Wi-Fi. More capatiblities have been added in AirPlay 2,

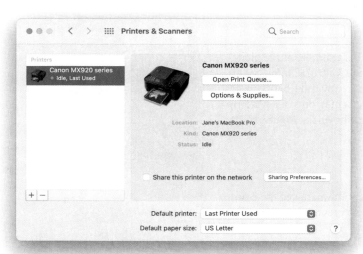

FIGURE 6–22 Click the plus (+) at the bottom of the list to add a new printer.
Source: Apple Inc.

including the ability to cast video directly to an AirPlay 2-compatible smart TV. You can also stream audio to multiple speakers. There is no central tool for managing AirPlay. It shows up on security prompts asking for an AirPlay Code sent when you first configure Screen Mirroring or another AirPlay-related service. While AirPlay allows for the sharing of video and music via Wi-Fi, **AirDrop** is a simpler feature, allowing two nearby devices to transfer files but both Wi-Fi and Bluetooth must be enabled.

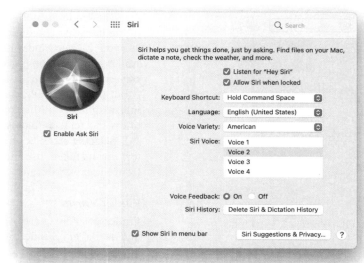

FIGURE 6–23 Enable and configure Siri in its Preferences pane.
Source: Apple Inc.

LO 6.3 | File Management

Like Windows, the macOS desktop has a file manager, **Finder**, as its foundation. When you launch macOS, Finder owns the desktop, as evidenced by the Finder menus at the top of the screen, but a Finder window is not open by default. Open Finder windows from the smiling Finder shortcut on the Dock or with the shortcut keys: Option+COMMAND+Spacebar. In the following sections practice file management tasks and explore the macOS folder structure.

Navigating in Finder

Your **Home folder** contains your personal folders. The keyboard shortcut (COMMAND+SHIFT+H) opens the Home folder (Figure 6–25), showing the user name in both the sidebar and the Finder window's button bar.

FIGURE 6–24 Tap the Siri button on the menu bar or simply talk to Siri.
Source: Apple Inc.

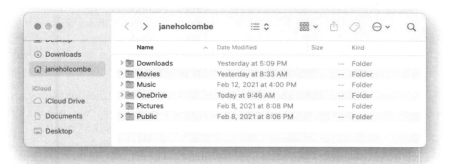

FIGURE 6–25 The Home folder is identified by the user name and contains the user's personal folders.
Source: Apple Inc.

Source: Apple Inc.

Note: COMMAND+SHIFT+D opens the Desktop folder.

The Finder icon on the Dock.
Source: Apple Inc.

FIGURE 6–26 The Finder menu.
Source: Apple Inc.

Note: Finder includes Finder Tabs, which act much like the tabs in Safari and other browsers. This reduces clutter by allowing you to have multiple tab pages in one window.

The Finder menus—Finder, File, Edit, View, Go, Window, and Help—offer a variety of file management and configuration tools. The Finder menu, shown in Figure 6-26, lets you manage Finder itself, as does the menu in this position for any open app. The About Finder option gives its version number. Since Finder is part of the OS, it has the same version number as the OS, but when you open the About option for an app that is not part of the OS you will see a different version number, and often, much more information about the app. The View menu arranges window views, and the Go menu offers shortcuts to folders used for storage both on the computer and out on a network.

Select Preferences from the Finder menu and personalize Finder's default behavior. For instance, use the Sidebar options (see Figure 6-27) to add or remove items from Finder's Sidebar.

Finder Views

Finder has four views or ways of displaying objects: as icons, as List, as Column, and as Gallery. Finder saves the preferred view of the first folder or disk opened in a new Finder window. The unifying factor in all four viewing modes in macOS is the ability to navigate the file and folder structure and to open files and folders by double-clicking them. If you are sitting at a Mac, experiment with the different views. You can set view options from the View menu, or from the View buttons on the top of the Finder window (Figure 6-28).

Icon View. In Icon view, shown in Figure 6-29, you simply see the icon for each object in the selected location. This example shows the Applications folder open in Icon view. macOS stores application executables in this folder; double-click an icon to launch its app.

List View. List view, shown in Figure 6-28, displays content as a descriptive list, showing details for each file or folder.

The List view offers a wealth of information about folders and files such as date last opened, date added, size, and kind (e.g., application or type of file). If you double-click a folder, that folder opens either in the same folder window or in a new window.

Column View. In Column view, shown in Figure 6-30, when you select a file by clicking it once, the file's icon or a preview of its contents, either text or graphics, displays in a column to the right. If you click on a folder, the contents display in the column to the right, and if you click on a subfolder, yet another column opens with that folder's contents. When a window is in Column view, you can change the size of columns by dragging the bottom of the column divider.

try this!

Sorting Files in List View

In List view, four columns offer information about your files: Name, Date Modified, Size, and Kind. The default view is an alphabetical sort by name. You can change that order. Try this:

1. Open a Finder folder by clicking the Finder icon on the Dock.
2. Browse to a folder that contains several files.
3. Click the title of any of the columns, and you will see your files sorted by that attribute. Sorting based on the size and date columns is useful when you want to recover disk space. Look for big, obsolete files this way.
4. Click the same title again to see the files sorted by that attribute in reverse order. Used most often with the Date column, this technique is effective when you want to search for recently changed or out-of-date files.

Gallery View. Gallery view, shown in Figure 6-31, opens a pane containing small images of each object in the currently selected folder. Below this pane is a list pane. Select a file or folder in this list and it will appear in the center of the Gallery.

Managing Files and Folders

Organize your documents and applications in the contents pane. Create a new folder to contain copied or moved files or folders by choosing New Folder from the File menu in the Finder or by right-clicking an area of the contents pane and selecting New Folder. Practice creating a new folder in Step-by-Step 6.02.

Copying, Pasting, and Deleting Files and Folders

Copy and paste files and folders into local or network locations.

- To copy, select the item and choose Copy from the Edit menu (or press COMMAND+C).
- To cut, select the item and choose Cut from the Edit menu (or press COMMAND+X) (Figure 6–32).
- To paste, first either copy or cut a file or folder. Then open the destination location and select Paste from the Edit menu (or press COMMAND+V).
- To delete, choose Delete from the Edit menu (or press COMMAND+DELETE). This moves the file or folder into the Trash. To empty the Trash, select Empty Trash from the Finder menu (or press COMMAND+SHIFT+DELETE).
- If you drag a file or folder and drop it onto a different drive, that operation is a copy, meaning that you have copied the file or folder to the new location and the original remains in the old location. To copy a file or folder onto the same drive with a drag operation, hold down the OPTION key as you let go of the file or folder. Otherwise, it will be a move (discussed next).

Moving and Renaming Files and Folders in Finder

If you drag a file or folder and drop it in a different folder on the same drive, that operation is a move, meaning that it is first copied to the new location and then automatically deleted from the old location. When you cut and paste a file or folder, it results in a move regardless of the locations. In Step-by-Step 6.02 you create a folder, and then drag files into the new folder.

Renaming Files and Folders in Finder

Open Finder and locate the file or folder you want to rename; click on it once to select it, and then after a short pause click again. This will highlight the name of the item and you will be able to edit the file name without changing the extension. (You should almost never change a file's extension.) When you are ready to save the item with the new name, either click away from the item or press RETURN.

FIGURE 6–27 Use Finder Preferences to add or remove items from the Sidebar.
Source: Apple Inc.

WARNING!

When you rename files, be careful not to change the file extension. This can keep the operating system from recognizing a file type and the OS would not know which program to use to open the file.

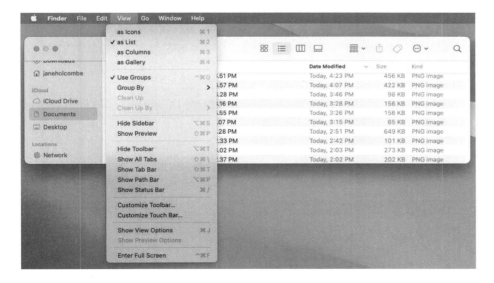

FIGURE 6–28 Change the view from the Finder View menu or by clicking one of the View buttons on the toolbar.
Source: Apple Inc.

Note: COMMAND+SHIFT+A opens the Applications folder.

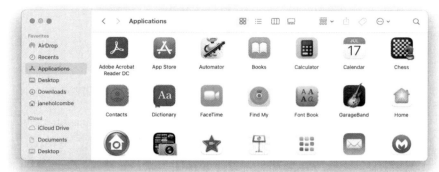

FIGURE 6–29 The Finder window with the Applications folder open in Icon view.
Source: Apple Inc.

FIGURE 6–30 The Finder window in Column view.
Source: Apple Inc.

FIGURE 6–31 The Finder window in Gallery view.
Source: Apple Inc.

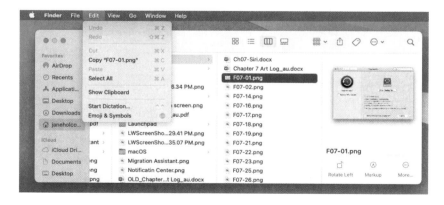

FIGURE 6–32 The Finder Edit menu.
Source: Apple Inc.

Step-by-Step **6.02**

Creating a New Folder and Organizing Files

In this exercise, you will create a folder within an existing folder, rename it, and copy files into it. To complete this exercise, you will need the following:

- A Mac computer with macOS installed.

- A user name and password that will allow you to log on to your computer.
- Files in at least one of the folders of your home directory.

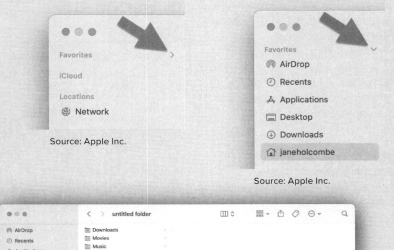

Source: Apple Inc.

Source: Apple Inc.

Step 1

Click the Finder icon on the Dock. If the Home folder is not visible in the Sidebar, first check Finder Preferences, and make sure there is a check by your Home folder. If it is still not visible, it may be hidden. Hover your mouse over the word "Favorites" at the top of the Sidebar. If the symbol points to the right, click it to unhide items. The Home folder will be visible. Ensure that the Finder window is in column view. Click on your Home folder in the left pane to see its contents on the right.

Step 2

Create a new folder. Press COMMAND+SHIFT+N or select New Folder from the Finder's File menu at the top of the screen. A new folder, called "untitled folder," will appear in the list of files and folders.

Source: Apple Inc.

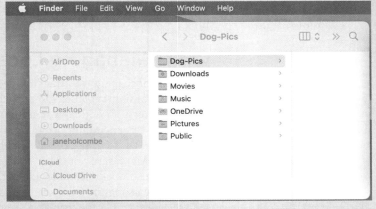

Step 3

Type a new name for the folder and press ENTER to save it. In this example, the folder is named Dog-Pics. Finder repositioned the renamed folder to comply with alphabetical sort order.

Source: Apple Inc.

Step 4

In the example, a column is open to the right. If a column is not already open to the right of the new folder, double-click on the folder.

Step 5

On the menu bar, select File, New Finder Window. Position the new window next to the window for the new folder. In the newly opened window, navigate to a folder containing files or folders you wish to copy to the new folder. In this example, the window on the left shows the new folder "Dog-Pics." The window on the right shows the selected folder, Dogs. Its contents are in the next column.

Source: Apple Inc.

Step 6

Select a file or folder by clicking on it. To select multiple files or folders, hold down the COMMAND key while clicking each until you have selected the ones you want.

Step 7

Press COMMAND+C to copy your selection. Then click in the folder area in the first Finder window. Press COMMAND+V to paste into the new folder. When you have completed the task, close all open windows.

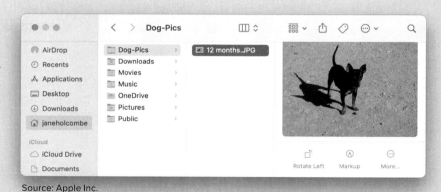

Source: Apple Inc.

LO 6.4 | Managing Local Security in macOS

Although most malware attacking desktop computers target Microsoft Windows, macOS is not impregnable, and anyone who connects to a network, plugs in a flash drive, or inserts an optical disc in their computer is vulnerable—not to mention the threats you can encounter browsing the Web and even in the messages you receive.

Apple is aware of the threats and has built in many security features that are on by default. Make sure you have updated your software, as described earlier in this chapter. It also doesn't hurt to add an antivirus program to your Mac. However, the greatest threats may be from scams and frauds, and your best defense against them is self-education and skepticism (even paranoia) when faced with messages that ask for information or require that you click on a link. In this section, we examine the macOS security features that do a pretty good job of protecting you from everything but social engineering.

So where do you begin? Start your relationship with your Mac by exploring the security features of macOS and ensuring that you are using every security option available to you.

Check Out the macOS Firewall

How does your Mac connect to the Internet? Is it through a broadband router at home, or through a Wi-Fi hotspot at the school cafeteria or the local coffee shop? However your computer connects—whether it is a network you trust (at home or school) or an untrusted network, such as many of the public Wi-Fi hotspots—you need to ensure that you have the macOS Firewall turned on. While the most recent versions of macOS turn it on by default, you should check it out and familiarize yourself with it.

To view and modify Firewall settings, open the Security and Privacy pane in System Preferences and click on Firewall. Ensure that the firewall is on. If it is not, turn it on. You may need to click on the lock icon on the lower left of the window to unlock the settings, in which case you will need to provide a password. Then click the button labeled **Turn on Firewall.** Figure 6-33 shows the Firewall turned on.

After ensuring that the firewall is on, you may need to click the lock icon (if not already unlocked) and provide a password. Now, click the Firewall Options button to view the settings. Figure 6-34 shows this page. This requires some explanation. You could block all incoming connections if all you are doing is simple Web browsing and sending and receiving email. During these operations, you initiate the connection to a Web server or mail server. The traffic that comes to your computer because of these actions is not seeking to initiate a connection to your computer; it is simply responding to your request for Web pages or email messages. Therefore, you could block all incoming connections, but still browse the Internet and send and receive email.

If you install or enable services on your Mac that require incoming traffic (not initiated from within), it will configure the Firewall to allow this type of traffic. However, if you do not plan to do any type of sharing and have not enabled any service requiring incoming traffic, Firewall will block all incoming connections and it will turn on stealth mode, which it will gray out so that you cannot disable it. If you later wish to use a sharing service, the installation will change the setting to allow incoming connections for that service.

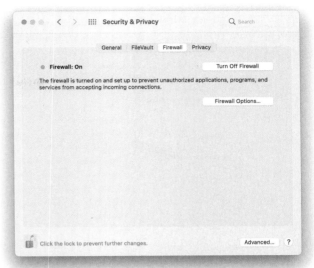

FIGURE 6–33 Firewall is on.
Source: Apple Inc.

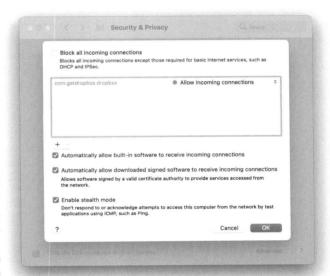

FIGURE 6–34 Incoming connections are allowed for sharing and for certain apps.
Source: Apple Inc.

Gatekeeper

Gatekeeper limits the online sources from which you can download programs. You will not find an icon labeled Gatekeeper, but you can configure Gatekeeper settings by selecting one of the options labeled *Allow applications downloaded from* on the General page of the Security & Privacy preferences pane. Here is a description of the settings shown in Figure 6-35:

1. **App Store**: Only install apps from the App Store. This is the most restrictive setting.

2. **App Store and identified developers**: Download and install apps that include a Developer ID signature as well as apps from the Apps Store which is less restrictive.

WARNING!

Anytime you unlock a settings pane, be sure to lock it again when you finish.

FIGURE 6–35 View and change the Gatekeeper settings by selecting one of the options under *Allow applications downloaded from.*
Source: Apple Inc.

FIGURE 6–36 FileVault is turned on and a recovery key has been set.
Source: Apple Inc.

Kernel ASLR

Using a security feature called address space layout randomization (ASLR), macOS loads the core operating system code, the kernel, into random locations in memory, rather than loading into the same memory addresses every time. This prevents malware from accessing operating system functions based on their known location in memory.

Digitally Signed and Sandboxed Apps

All apps available through the App Store are digitally signed. A digitally signed app will issue a warning if its code is modified. In addition, each app available through the App Store is sandboxed, meaning that it cannot access any code or device it is not authorized to access. It is in a virtual sandbox where it can only play with those "toys" it is permitted to access.

FileVault

FileVault is the macOS file and disk encryption feature. Recent versions of macOS FileVault encrypt everything on your startup drive every time you log out. With FileVault disk encryption turned on, your files are accessible only while you are logged on. Unless someone has access to your password, or you walk away from your computer without logging out, no one can open the encrypted files. Turn on FileVault on the FileVault page of Security preferences. Select "Allow my iCloud account to unlock my disk," and the system automatically generates a string of characters for security purposes called a recovery key. If you choose not to use your iCloud account, but to create a recovery key, it will be a local recovery key, created and displayed on the screen. Be sure to copy down the recovery key and store it in a safe place. You only need one recovery key on each computer. In Figure 6-36 FileVault is turned on.

Secure Virtual Memory

macOS uses a swap file, which is disk space the OS uses as if it is memory, so they call it virtual memory. All multitasking operating systems use virtual memory to allow you to have several applications open. While you are actively using your word processor, most other open applications are just waiting for you to switch back to them. Therefore, the operating system temporarily saves at least part of the code and data for these other apps to the swap file. Clever hackers can access the data in a swap file, so Apple includes a feature in macOS called Secure Virtual Memory, which encrypts the swap file.

Keychain

The keychain is part of a credentials management system using the name "keychain" as a metaphor for a physical keychain. The password to the keychain gives the user access to all the passwords or "keys" on that keychain. Each keychain is a secure database of a user's passwords, collected the first time it asks you to supply a user name and password to something, such as shared folders on your school or work network, at websites, FTP sites, and more.

Two default keychains, System and System Roots, belong to the OS. The first time you log in, macOS creates your first keychain, called login, using your account password as a master password for the keychain. Then as you go about your business, logging in to various servers to access email and other resources, as well as various websites, the credentials you supply are saved in your keychain, provided you respond to a prompt asking if you want to save the password. Although some websites have login programs that will not allow this, many do, and if you save the password for a website in your key chain, it will complete the login boxes (a process called AutoFill in Safari) each time you reconnect to one of these sites.

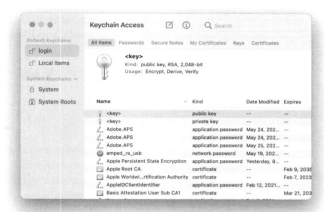

FIGURE 6–37 The Keychain Access utility.
Source: Apple Inc.

For most of us, the login keychain is sufficient for all our needs, but you can create multiple keychains, each with a separate purpose, such as for your online shopping or as a place to save your personal credit information. Create additional keychains if you need varying security levels. For instance, you can configure one keychain so that the keychain locks if there is idle time over a certain threshold. This is where you keep your keys for accessing online banking accounts. Then create another keychain that will not have such a restriction because it is for low-security activity, such as a website you access purely for entertainment, such as Pandora. To create multiple keychains for various purposes, use **Keychain Access**, a utility found in Finder | Applications | Utilities, shown in Figure 6-37.

There's more to this topic. Now that most of us work on multiple devices, we need a keychain that will work across those devices as we access the same networks and websites. Apple's solution is the **iCloud Keychain**. This is a keychain stored in iCloud and is accessible to all your devices that support it and that you have enabled. Turn on iCloud Keychain by opening System Preferences and selecting Apple ID. In the sidebar select iCloud. Scroll through the list of *Apps on this Mac using iCloud* and locate *Keychain*. If the check box is filled, it is enabled.

Managing Local User Accounts

macOS supports multiple local user accounts. At home, school, or work, you can set up a single computer with multiple accounts so that each person is restricted to their own home folder, preserving preferences from one session to another. As in Microsoft Windows, two users can be logged in to the same computer at the same time, but only one can have control of the "console," the keyboard, screen, and mouse, at any given time. macOS preserves each account's session in memory and users can switch back and forth using fast user switching. Alternatively, users can log in and log out when they finish working or step away.

Family Sharing

Family Sharing is a feature that replaces Parental Controls. Family Sharing is under Apple ID in System Preferences. Figure 6-38 shows the initial Family Sharing settings. On this page, you can add family members. On the left is the list of the services you can add and offer to members. Click the plus button to add someone. Once you add family members you can select the services to share with them, and you can control certain settings for family members, such as Screen Time.

FIGURE 6–38 The Family Sharing preferences page.
Source: Apple Inc.

Screen Time

If you have multiple Apple devices, Screen Time includes a group of settings to apply to your own usage of those devices. If you use Apple's Family sharing, you can use Screen Time for children (Figure 6-39). Enable Screen Time and then check out each of the areas. Begin by tracking device and app usage across all devices, and then decide if you need to set some limits. Apple's support site (**https://support.apple.com**) has articles to guide you through these and many other helpful settings.

Types of Users and Privileges

There are several types of user accounts; two of them, Administrator and Standard, are like the Windows account types of the same name. The others are Sharing Only, Guest account, and Root account. We describe the main functionality of the account types here.

Administrator Account. The Administrator account type, also simply called "admin," is for advanced users or for the person who will administer this computer. The first account created during installation is an Administrator. Open the Users & Groups preferences pane from System Preferences and view the local accounts on a Mac. Notice the description "Admin" on the left under the first account name in Figure 6-40. An Administrator account can do the following:

- Change all system preference settings and install software in the main application and library folders.
- Create, modify, and delete user accounts.

Standard Account. This account type is for ordinary users in an organization with tech support to take care of configuring and supporting computers. A Standard account type gets into far less trouble because of these restrictions:

- File access is limited to only the user's Home folder and the Shared folder (/Users/Shared/) that is accessible to other users without restriction.
- Access is denied to higher-level system preferences, such as network settings, sharing, software update settings, user setup, and date and time settings.

Sharing Only Account. You can create a Sharing Only account for someone who only needs to access shared folders on your Mac over a network. With a Sharing Only account type someone can connect remotely and log in with the local account but will not have her own set of Home folders on the local computer. A person with a Sharing Only account cannot log on locally at the computer where the Sharing Only account resides.

FIGURE 6–39 The App Usage page is one place to gather data after you enable Screen Time.
Source: Apple Inc.

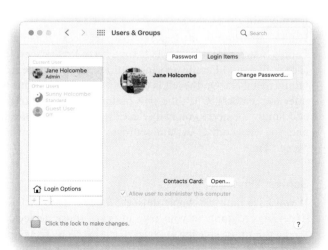

FIGURE 6–40 The Users & Groups preferences pane.
Source: Apple Inc.

Guest User. Guest is an account type with very limited access, but macOS no longer allows you to assign this account type to a new user. Instead, it creates a single Guest account, called Guest User. This account does not require a password, has access only to the Guest Home folder, and when a guest logs out, all files and folders created during that session in the Guest's Home folder are deleted. Enable the Guest Account in the Users & Groups preferences pane.

Root Account. The Root account, often called a super-user account, exists mainly for the use of the OS. It is not enabled for interactive users in the standard installation of macOS. Root is only for people familiar with the inner workings of UNIX, and changing things on your computer using this account can result in serious system dysfunction and lost data. We will not describe how to enable it. Root gives you complete control over all folders and files on the Mac.

Creating and Deleting User Accounts

The first user account is created when you install macOS, and it is automatically an administrator-type account. After the installation process is complete, you can create additional user accounts, as described in Step-by-Step 6.03. If it is not enabled, take an additional step and enable an option on the user account page for the first user labeled *Allow user to reset password using Apple ID.* This setting will make life easier for you if you should forget your password for this account.

Step-by-Step 6.03

Creating a New User/Deleting a User Account

In this exercise, you will add a new user to your computer and delete a user. To complete this exercise, you will need the following:

- A Mac computer with macOS installed.

- You must be logged on to the computer as an administrator.

Step 1

Open the Users & Groups preferences pane. Click the lock on the bottom left. In the box that opens enter your password and click *Unlock*. The lock icon will now appear unlocked.

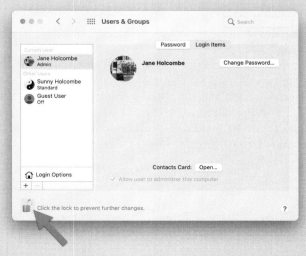

Source: Apple Inc.

Step 2

Back in Users & Groups, click the button with the plus sign at the bottom left. Enter a Full Name and press the Tab key. This will generate an account name based on the full name, by removing the space. At this point, you can change the account name, but once you create the user in the next step, the account name is permanent. Notice that we shortened the account name.

Source: Apple Inc.

Step 3

Create a password, and enter it in both the Password and Verify boxes. Enter a password hint, and then click Create User.

Step 4

The new user appears in the sidebar of Users & Groups, and the settings for that user display on the right. The new user in this example is a Standard User. If you want to change this account to an administrator-type account, click to place a check in the box labeled *Allow user to administer this computer* on this page. If the new user is a child, you may want to add the user to the list of family members and manage that user's settings.

Source: Apple Inc.

Step 5

To delete a user account you will need to ensure that Users & Groups is unlocked for changes. If the lock on the bottom left is locked, click it and enter your password. Then select the user account in the sidebar of Users & Groups and click the minus button (-) at the bottom of the sidebar. When prompted, select an option for saving or deleting the user's Home folder, and then click *Delete User*.

Source: Apple Inc.

LO 6.5 | Troubleshooting Common macOS Problems

In this section, you learn where to find basic help and a guide to the system utilities and keyboard shortcuts that can help you get out of trouble. You'll also learn how to handle the larger files that you'll encounter in today's computing environment.

Where to Find Help

When problems arise in macOS or within an application, where do you go to find help? Explore the options for solving problems and you may find that some of them direct you to the same sources.

Help with the OS

There are several ways to get help with macOS from within the OS itself, such as clicking on the help menu (Figure 6-41) and entering a search string or browsing through the other options. This is a good place to start if you are new to macOS.

With the improvements in Spotlight search and Siri, we rely more and more on simply asking a question in natural language and selecting a likely source for help among the results it produces. Or go directly to Apple's Support Center at **https://support.apple.com/**, select the product being used, and search there.

Alternatively, members of the network of Apple user groups around the world can get support from other users and learn more about their computers. For more information, see **www.apple.com/usergroups/**. Be prepared to broaden you search, as some groups lost membership and disbanded during the pandemic.

If self-help fails and your computer is still under warranty, contact Apple directly, using the information that came with your computer. Technical support is expensive if your computer is outside its warranty period. Novice users who use their computers enough to increase the likelihood of multiple requests for support should consider signing up for an AppleCare service and support package to keep technical support costs down. Find more information at the AppleCare site (Figure 6-42) at **www.apple.com/support/products/**.

Help within Applications

If a problem with an open application persists, click the Help menu from the Apple menu bar. In many cases, there will be a local help utility and an option to find online help for the application. Search through the help utility to find an answer to your problem or search the software publisher's website or the Web at large using a brief description of the problem or a part of the error message in the search string.

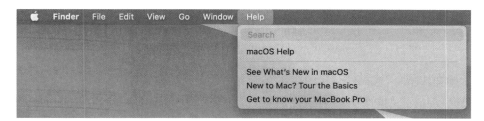

FIGURE 6-41 Begin a search for a problem solution by exploring the options on the Help menu.
Source: Apple Inc.

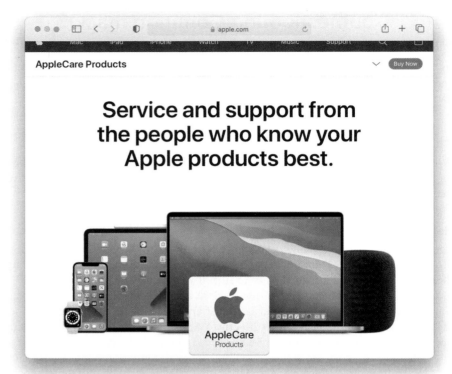

FIGURE 6–42 The AppleCare site.
Source: Apple Inc.

Note: COMMAND+Q quits the current app. COMMAND+OPTION+ESC opens the Force Quit Applications box for the current app.

FIGURE 6–43 An application's Quit option.
Source: Apple Inc.

When to Quit

When you finish working with an app, you can quickly quit the app by pressing COMMAND+Q or by opening the app's menu (shown in Figure 6-43), and selecting Quit. If an open application is behaving strangely—maybe it freezes, displaying the "busy" icon for no apparent reason—quit the application and restart it. This will resolve many transient problems.

Sometimes an application will not politely quit; that's when you must use Force Quit—either from the Apple menu or with the key combination of COMMAND+OPTION+ESC. This will bring up the Force Quit Applications box, shown in Figure 6-44. It shows you all the running applications, so you can select the correct one. A force quit allows you to safely remove an application from memory without requiring a restart of your computer and without adversely affecting the rest of the programs running in memory.

Sometimes, when you attempt to shut down, log off, or restart, you see a message similar to Figure 6-45, stating that you haven't been logged out because an application has failed to quit. Return to the app and close it out properly. If that does not work, use the Force Quit tool. If the application still refuses to quit, do a hard power-down by pressing and holding the power button for several seconds.

Forgotten Password

Most calls to help desks are for forgotten passwords. Here we describe your options for recovering from this minor disaster.

Resetting a Password in macOS Snow Leopard or Older

The first-created user account on your computer is automatically designated an administrator. If you happen to forget or lose the administrator password, and if you

FIGURE 6–44 Select the application from the Force Quit Applications box.
Source: Apple Inc.

have macOS Snow Leopard (10.6) or older, reset the password with the help of the installation disc. To do this insert the DVD and from the Install screen choose Utilities | Reset Password. Select the drive that contains the System folder, and use the first pop-up menu to select the name of your account. Enter your new password twice. You should keep the DVD in a safe place, because anyone with the macOS DVD can gain complete access to your system.

Resetting a Password

With macOS Lion (10.7) or newer how you reset a password depends on the scenario. We will look at each scenario next.

You are logged in with an administrator account. If macOS is running and you are logged in with an administrator account and wish to reset the password for another account, open System Preferences | Users & Groups. If the lock is in the locked position, click it and enter your password. Select the user in the Users and Groups sidebar, and then select *Reset Password*. Enter a password, verify it by entering it a second time, provide a password hint, and then click *Reset Password*.

You have forgotten your password and cannot log in and FileVault is off. If you cannot get into macOS because you have forgotten your password, and if you don't have FileVault turned on, then at the login screen when you enter a wrong password, the Password Hint box will pop up. If the hint doesn't help, or if there is no hint, click Reset password with Apple ID. The Reset Password box will display, and you can enter your Apple ID and password, and then click Reset Password. Follow the instructions from there.

You have forgotten your password and cannot log in and FileVault is turned on. If FileVault is enabled on your computer, you may be able to use the FileVault recovery key to reset your login password. For detailed instructions, you will need to go to another computer and search **support.apple.com** for the article titled "If you forget your login password and FileVault is on."

The article cited walks you through the necessary steps to attempt to login again with your Apple ID. If that fails, and you cannot reset the password using your Apple ID, select the option to "reset it using your Recovery Key." Then enter your recovery key and reset the password. Be sure to save the new password in a safe location. Or memorize it.

FIGURE 6–45 An application failed.
Source: Apple Inc.

Note: If you *change* a password, macOS lets you keep your login keychain and assigns the new password to the keychain. When you *reset* a password, macOS creates a new login keychain for that user, and you will need to manually enter passwords and allow them to be saved in the new keychain.

Note: There is a difference between the Change Password and Reset Password options in Users & Groups. The *Change Password* button appears on the account page for the currently logged-on user, and that user must provide their current password before entering a new password. When you choose *Reset Password,* which an administrator can do for another user, you need to provide only the new password.

Disappearing Sidebar Items

Our mantra is "Disaster is only a mouse-click away." We could write an entire book on the foibles of blithely moving objects around in any GUI. One minor but annoying problem we have had in macOS is the disappearance of Applications in the Finder Sidebar. If you have this problem, check out the Finder Preferences and/or unhide items, as described in Step 1 in Step-by-Step 6.02.

try this!

Help to the Rescue!

If you're in macOS and can't remember the keyboard shortcuts for escaping a program freeze or some other action, jog your memory with macOS Help Center. Try this:

1. Click the desktop or the Finder icon on the Dock to make sure you're in the Finder.
2. Select the Help menu.
3. Type "Freeze" in the Help Search box and press ENTER.
4. Choose Shortcuts for Freezes.

Useful System Utilities

The utilities described here for macOS are useful for basic troubleshooting. As with any situation, if you find yourself in deep water, seek expert advice. Here is a quick guide to macOS disk and network software utilities.

Disk Utility

Found in the macOS Utilities folder Disk Utility, shown in Figure 6–46, offers summary and usage statistics for all volumes attached to the computer. The utility also includes Disk First Aid, accessed from the button on the button bar, which enables you to verify or repair all volumes supported by macOS, including those on hard disks and solid-state drives (SSDs). In figure 6-46, Disk Utility uses the term Macintosh HD, although this computer uses an SSD.

When you explore Disk Utility, you will see information about the file system(s) on your Mac. Beginning in 2017, new Apple devices come preconfigured with the **Apple File System (APFS).** APFS is optimized for solid-state drive storage and supports advanced features. It also fixes problems with the previous file system, used for nearly 20 years and still in use on older systems. That is the Mac OS Extended file system, also known as Hierarchical File System Plus (HFS+). Apple still supports this older file system. Both APFS and HFS+ are only for use on Apple devices. If you need to share an external drive between a new Mac and an older Mac that cannot upgrade to a version that supports APFS, then format the external drive with HFS+ for compatibility with both systems.

There is also a solution for sharing between Windows and Mac. For compatibility when you need to use a removable drive in a Mac or Windows device, Apple supports the use of the Extended File Allocation Table

try this!

Take a Look at the Disks on Your Mac

The best tool for viewing and managing disks on a Mac is the Disk Utility. Become familiar with Disk Utility. See what file system resides on a disk and locate tools for fixing problems. Try this:

1. Open a Finder window and navigate to **Applications | Utilities.** Locate **Disk Utility** and double-click to open it.

2. In Disk Utility, notice the list of connected drives and mounted disk images in the sidebar. Click on one to select it.

3. If you are having stability problems with your device, click the **First Aid** button to run a check for errors on that volume.

4. After viewing the volumes on your Mac, simply press **Command+Q** or select Disk Utility from the menu bar and select **Quit Disk Utility.**

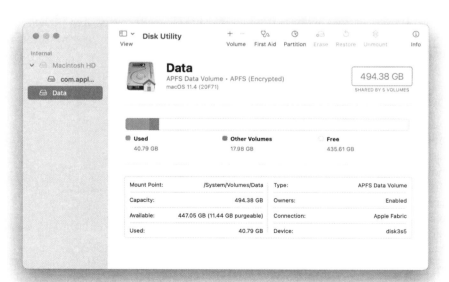

FIGURE 6–46 Disk Utility.
Source: Apple Inc.

(exFAT) and MS-DOS (FAT) file systems. Avoid the MS-DOS (FAT) file system and use exFAT whenever you need to use a drive between Windows and Apple systems.

In Figure 6-46 there is only one physical disk. At first, only that disk and a volume named **Data** were visible. Clicking on that disk (Macintosh HD) revealed another volume with a name beginning with **com.apple.** This is the operating system's bootable volume, not writable by users. In contrast, the Data volume is not bootable, but it is writable by users. Under the name of each volume, note the file system. In this case, it is APFS (Encrypted). The box to the right of the volume name gives the size of the disk, which is shared by five volumes. The three volumes not visible in Disk Utility are used by the operating system. They are named *PreBoot, Recovery,* and *VM.*

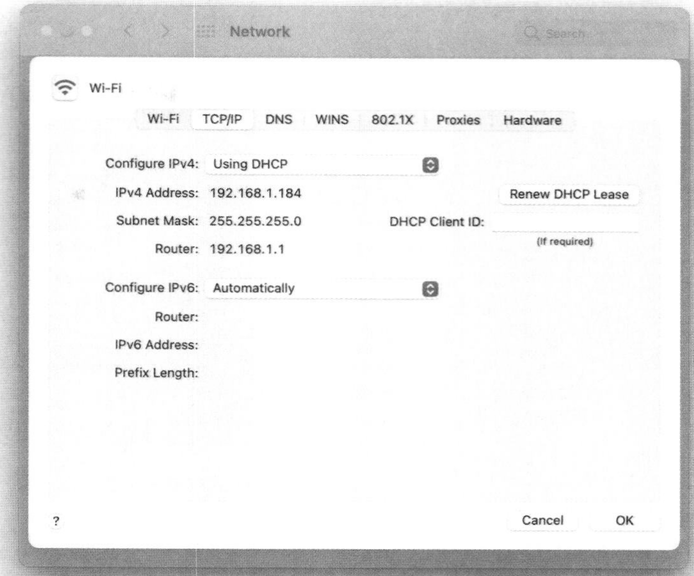

Network Preferences

Have you ever had a problem with your home Internet connection and found yourself talking to a help desk person from your Internet service provider (ISP)? The help desk often wants you to provide information about your network connection, such as the IP address and other configuration

FIGURE 6–47 Advanced page of the Network preferences pane.
Source: Apple Inc.

settings. To do that in macOS open the Network pane in System Preferences, select the network connection in the sidebar, and click the Advanced button, and then click the appropriate tab. For instance, the TCP/IP tab shows the IP configuration, while the Wi-Fi tab shows the network or networks to which your computer connects as preferred networks and the type of security used. Figure 6-47 shows the TCP/IP settings.

Using Terminal in macOS

Familiarize yourself with the macOS Command-line interface (CLI) Terminal, a window where you can get in touch with macOS UNIX roots, based on the core set of UNIX components known as Darwin. In this section, we give an overview of Terminal features and opportunities for you to practice using commands in Terminal. Terminal includes many of the same CLI commands as Linux, the topic of Chapter 7.

Launch Terminal

Launch Terminal from the Utilities folder located in the Applications folder. The first thing you will see is the character mode user interface, or shell. With a Terminal window open, add it to the Dock (Figure 6-48) so that it is easy to quickly launch.

Notice that the Terminal window bar contains the normal window control buttons on the top left, as well as the name of the current folder in the middle. By default, Terminal opens focused on the logged-on user's Home folder. In Figure 6-49 the first line shows when this user last logged in. The second line gives the folder name, the name of the device, and a prompt with a shaded rectangle. As you type, this rectangle travels along the line with your text. Figure 6-49 also shows the Terminal Shell menu open. From the Shell menu, you can open multiple Terminal windows or open multiple tabs in a single Terminal window.

FIGURE 6–48 Add the Terminal to the Dock.
Source: Apple Inc.

try this!

Open a Terminal Window in macOS

Explore Terminal in macOS. Try this:

1. Open a Finder window by clicking on the Finder icon on the Dock and browsing to **Applications | Utilities | Terminal.**
2. Double-click **Terminal** to launch it.
3. Leave it open as you read about Terminal.

FIGURE 6–49 The Terminal Shell menu.
Source: Apple Inc.

Note: For a short list of frequently used commands, see the *UNIX Command Summary* at **www. bsd.org/unixcmds.html**.

Note: UNIX-based macOS Terminal provides for the temporary use of the Root account security context when you precede a command with the sudo command and provide your password. This works only if you have logged in as an Administrator.

Shell Commands in Terminal

A shell command is a command entered through a CLI shell. Before you start typing commands at the prompt, understand that macOS Terminal is case sensitive and case aware, as are both Linux and UNIX. Commands are (mostly) in lower case, but options may vary, and whenever you type a directory or file name in Terminal, use the correct case. Like many other features, Terminal has changed in recent versions of macOS. The best thing to do before you get too far into the weeds is to use your browser to access the Apple Support site (support.apple.com) and search on the Terminal User Guide for the latest version of macOS. At this writing, the latest Guide is for macOS Big Sur. Note that the Guide is written for use by advanced users, who use Terminal's shell commands to manage many systems and servers. To get you started, Table 6–1 contains a short list of Terminal Shell Commands and Step-by-Step 6.04 will help you practice using Terminal.

Working with Manual Pages

Once you know the name of a command that you want to use, tap into the power of the **man** command to learn how to use that command. This command lets you view the manual page for a Terminal command, called a manpage, usually many "pages." Simply type the **man** command followed by the name of the command.

For instance, to see the manual page for the **ls** command type **man ls.** The documentation for the command will display one screen at a time. A colon (:) and a blinking cursor display on the last line of the window, indicating that there is more of the manpage to display. When you are ready to move to the next screenful of the

TABLE 6–1	A Short List of Terminal Shell Commands
Command	**Action**
ls	Show directory contents
logout	Logs out of the system
mkdir	Creates a directory
rmdir	Removes a directory
cd	Change current directory
man (command)	Show help (the manual) on a specific command
more (filename)	Views a file, pausing every screenful

manpage press the spacebar (or press RETURN to advance one line at a time). To go back up, press the up arrow. When it gets to the end of the manpage, "(END)" replaces the colon. You can quit a manpage at any time by pressing the **q** key. Practice in Step-by-Step 6.04.

Note: Whenever the screen gets too cluttered, simply use the clear command.

Step-by-Step 6.04

Using the man Command

Practice working in the macOS Terminal window. To complete this exercise you will need:

- A Mac with a recent version of macOS.
- To be logged on with an account that is an administrator.

Step 1

At the prompt type **man ls** and press ENTER.

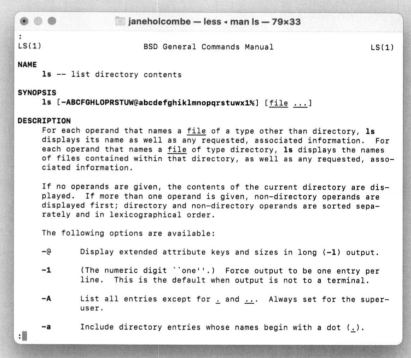

Source: Apple Inc.

Step 2

Notice what the manpage says will occur if no operands (options) are entered at the command line. Test this by opening a second Terminal window while leaving the one with the manpage open. To do this, click the **Shell** menu and then select **New Window.**

Step 3

In the new window, type **ls** and press ENTER. This displays a list of the nonhidden files and directories in the current directory.

```
● ● ●                    janeholcombe — -zsh — 80×8
Last login: Sat May 29 16:34:50 on ttys000
janeholcombe@Janes-MacBook-Pro ~ % ls
Desktop        Dog-Pics       Library        Music          Pictures
Documents      Downloads      Movies         OneDrive       Public
janeholcombe@Janes-MacBook-Pro ~ % ▊
```
Source: Apple Inc.

Step 4

Back in the first Terminal window, the first page of the **ls** manpage describes the **-a** option. In the second Terminal window, add the **-a** option to the **ls** command to see a list that includes both hidden and nonhidden files and directories. Type **ls -a** and press ENTER. All the normally hidden entries appear. They are the files and directories that begin with a period (.).

```
● ● ●                    janeholcombe — -zsh — 80×13
Last login: Sun May 30 13:11:58 on ttys002
janeholcombe@Janes-MacBook-Pro ~ % ls -a
.                      .zsh_history       Library
..                     .zsh_sessions      Movies
.CFUserTextEncoding    Desktop            Music
.DS_Store              Documents          OneDrive
.Trash                 Dog-Pics           Pictures
.cups                  Downloads          Public
janeholcombe@Janes-MacBook-Pro ~ % ▊
```
Source: Apple Inc.

Step 5

You know which entries are hidden and which are not, but so far, it is not clear which is a file and which is a directory. The second page of the **ls** manpage describes the **-F** option. To see all entries (as in step 4), and to also see directories identified with an ending slash (/), type **ls -aF** and press ENTER. Be sure to type the correct case.

Step 6

The output of the **ls** command with the **-aF** identifies all the directories with the forward slash (/). Notice the . and .. entries. The single period (.) represents the current directory and the double period (..) represents the parent directory—the directory above the current directory.

```
● ● ●                    janeholcombe — -zsh — 81×12
Last login: Sun May 30 13:12:29 on ttys002
janeholcombe@Janes-MacBook-Pro ~ % ls -aF
./                     .zsh_history       Library/
../                    .zsh_sessions/     Movies/
.CFUserTextEncoding    Desktop/           Music/
.DS_Store              Documents/         OneDrive/
.Trash/                Dog-Pics/          Pictures/
.cups/                 Downloads/         Public/
janeholcombe@Janes-MacBook-Pro ~ % ▊
```
Source: Apple Inc.

Step 7

In the window where you have been experimenting with the **ls** command, use the **cd** (change directory) command to move up to the parent directory. Type **cd ..** and press ENTER. This changes the current directory to the parent directory.

> Return to the Home directory: Type **cd ~** and press ENTER.
>
> Change to the Documents directory: Type **cd documents** and press ENTER.

```
● ● ●                    Documents — -zsh — 80×8
Last login: Sun May 30 13:33:01 on ttys003
janeholcombe@Janes-MacBook-Pro ~ % cd ..
janeholcombe@Janes-MacBook-Pro /Users % cd ~
janeholcombe@Janes-MacBook-Pro ~ % cd documents
janeholcombe@Janes-MacBook-Pro documents % ▊
```
Source: Apple Inc.

Step 8

To close out of a single Terminal shell session, type **exit** at the command prompt. This leaves the window open with the message "(Process completed)." When you are finished with Terminal app, use the **Quit Terminal** option from the Terminal menu, or use the Command+Q shortcut.

Chapter Summary

After reading this chapter and completing the Step-by-Step tutorials and try this! exercises you should understand the following facts about macOS:

Installing and Upgrading macOS

- macOS installs only on proprietary Apple hardware, which normally comes with the OS preinstalled.
- Before upgrading, check the version of the installed OS; you may need to upgrade to another version before upgrading to the latest version.
- You cannot upgrade some older Mac computers to the latest version. If the model is upgradable, check the firmware and make sure it has enough RAM and disk space.
- Disable disk encryption before upgrading.
- Install or upgrade macOS directly from the Apple Store as a download or download the installation image and burn it to DVD or USB flash drive.
- If you buy a new Mac, you complete the personalization of the installation with the macOS Setup Assistant.
- After the installation, enable OS components or apps that you previously disabled. If you did a clean installation, you will need to install and update apps and personalize the computer to your own preferences.
- Some iOS and iPad OS apps can be installed on an M1 Mac. Check the App Store to see if apps installed on your Apple mobile devices can be installed on your Mac.

Navigating and Managing the macOS Desktop

- The macOS desktop has a menu bar across the top containing general functions as well as the drop-down menus for the current app.
- The Apple menu opens when you click the Apple icon in the upper left of the macOS window.
- System Preferences is the macOS equivalent to the Windows Settings and Control Panel.
- Switch between apps using the Dock or the Heads-Up Program Switcher.
- Drag icons on and off the Dock and configure the Dock to be on the left side, right side, or bottom of the screen.
- See icons for all your installed programs using Launchpad. Group program icons together in folders.
- Declutter the desktop with Mission Control, which lets you create and manage desktop Spaces.

- Notification Center displays messages at the top right of the screen. It also contains helpful little apps called widgets.
- Most printers install automatically, appearing in the application's Print menu.
- Use AirPlay to share streaming media and audio and use AirDrop to share files with nearby devices.

Managing Files

- The Finder in macOS is the GUI face of macOS with a variety of file management tools.
- Each person who logs on to a macOS computer has a Home folder identified in the Finder window with a house icon and the user's name. The Documents folder in Home is the default location used by many apps for each user's data files.

Managing Local Security in macOS

- The macOS Firewall is enabled by default. If you install or enable services on your Mac that require incoming traffic, it will configure the Firewall to allow this type of traffic.
- Gatekeeper limits sources from which you can download apps. The most restrictive setting limits program downloads to the App Store. The App Store and identified developers setting is less restrictive.
- Using ASLR, macOS loads the kernel into random locations in memory.
- macOS apps are digitally signed and sandboxed, meaning that an app cannot access any code or devices it is not authorized to access.
- If you have important and sensitive information on your Mac, ensure that you securely encrypt your disk with FileVault.
- The keychain is a secure database of a user's passwords. By default, macOS creates a keychain for you the first time you log in.
- Create an iCloud Keychain to save your passwords across all your devices.
- macOS supports multiple local user accounts.
- The first user account in macOS is automatically designated an administrator.
- The types of user accounts in macOS are Administrator, Standard account, Sharing Only account, Guest account, and Root account.

- The Administrator account type can create new accounts, change all system preference settings, and install software in the main application and library folders.
- The Standard user account type can only access files in the user's home folder and the Shared folder (/Users/Shared/).
- The Sharing Only account type gives a remote user access to shared folders on the local computer, but this account cannot log on locally and does not have a local home folder.
- You cannot assign the Guest account type to any user other than the Guest User account created by macOS by default. It does not require a password, only has access to the Guest Home folder, and when the Guest logs off, the folder's contents are deleted.
- The Root account has complete control over all folders and files on the Mac. Only the OS uses this account and it is disabled for interactive users by default.

Troubleshooting Common macOS Problems

- When you need help with macOS, open the Help menu on the Finder menu bar. If you have narrowed the problem to one application, use that application's Help menu.
- If an application freezes, press COMMAND+OPTION+ESC to force it to quit.

- A user can change their own password using Users & Groups. If a user forgets a password, an administrator can reset the password, but the user will have a new, empty keychain associated with the new password. An administrator should configure their account so that they can reset the password using an Apple account.
- Use the Finder preferences pane to make folders display in the Finder sidebar.
- Erase and create volumes and repair a damaged disk with Disk First Aid in Disk Utility.
- The macOS CLI is the Terminal window where you can run macOS UNIX commands.
- Open a Terminal window from the Utilities directory.
- You can open multiple Terminal windows, and each window can have multiple tabs open.
- The default Terminal prompt includes the user name, the computer name, and a tilde (~) to represent the home directory.
- The Terminal window has a menu at the top of the macOS screen. Use the Shell menu to open new windows and/or new tabs within an open Terminal window.
- macOS Terminal is case-sensitive. Commands are usually in lower case, but options can vary.

Key Terms List

Key Terms Quiz

Use the Key Terms List to complete the sentences that follow:

1. Enter shell commands in the macOS _____.

2. To search for files, use _____, a feature found in the desktop menu bar and at the top of every Finder window.

3. A user's passwords for logging on to various servers and websites from a single computer are saved in a secure database called a/an _____.

4. At the core of macOS is a powerful UNIX system called _____.

5. The _____ displays icons for all installed apps.

6. The _____ account does not require a password, and any file or folder it creates is deleted when this user logs out.

7. _____ allows two full-screen apps to share the desktop.

8. The _____ is a GUI object on the macOS desktop that holds program icons for fast launching, as well as icons for open applications you can use for task switching.

9. The _____ limits the online sources from which you can download programs.

10. The _____ is accessed through a small icon at the extreme top left of the macOS screen, the name sounds like something the hostess hands you in a vegetarian restaurant.

Multiple-Choice Quiz

1. Use just one of these across all your devices in order to synchronize settings, access personal iCloud data, and use other Apple services.
   a. Gatekeeper
   b. Shared Folder
   c. Apple ID
   d. Time Machine
   e. APFS

2. This feature, adopted from Apple mobile devices, provides handy quick controls for changing settings.
   a. Cortana
   b. Gatekeeper
   c. Notification Center
   d. Control Center
   e. Mission Control

3. When you first power up a new Mac, what program starts automatically and prompts you for information?
   a. Dock
   b. Safari
   c. macOS Setup Assistant
   d. iChat
   e. System Preferences

4. Complete this sentence: In macOS forced quits of applications . . .
   a. often cause other applications to fail.
   b. always require a restart of the OS.
   c. is not an option.
   d. usually cause system crashes.
   e. rarely affect the performance of the rest of the computer's functions.

5. Where will you quickly find version information about your macOS installation?
   a. Recent items
   b. Window menu
   c. Help menu
   d. Apple menu
   e. Finder

6. Which of the following is one of the four views available in Finder windows?
   a. Date
   b. Columns
   c. Reverse
   d. Finder
   e. Jukebox

7. The Applications folder has disappeared from the Finder Sidebar. Where in the GUI can you go to put the Applications folder back into the Sidebar?
   a. System Preferences | General
   b. Utilities
   c. Sidebar | Preferences
   d. Finder | Preferences
   e. Window | Restore

8. In addition to having an upgradable version of macOS, you should also check to see if this is supported by Apple for an upgrade to a new version of macOS.
   a. Apple ID
   b. Video drivers
   c. Mac model
   d. FileVault
   e. Gatekeeper

9. Which all-powerful account is used by the operating system, but is disabled for interactive users?
   a. Standard
   b. Group
   c. Administrator
   d. Root
   e. Global

10. You have an external hard drive from another Mac, and you would like to remove all the data on it and use it as backup for your new Mac. What will you use to prepare this disk for use?
    a. Finder
    b. macOS Setup Assistant
    c. System Preferences
    d. Tools
    e. Disk Utility

11. What type of service should you disable as a precaution before beginning an upgrade macOS?
    a. Networking
    b. Launchpad
    c. Mission Control
    d. Sharing
    e. Disk encryption

12. What keyboard shortcut can you use to force an application to quit?
    a. COMMAND+POWER key
    b. SHIFT-ESC
    c. SHIFT-RETURN
    d. COMMAND-OPTION-ESC
    e. Press C during startup

13. A Sharing Only type of account is not allowed to do which of the following?
    a. Connect over a network.
    b. Access shared folders.
    c. Log in locally.
    d. Enter a password.
    e. Enter a user name.

14. This account is automatically created by macOS it does not require a password associated with it, has limited local access, and when this user logs out, the contents of its Home folder are deleted.
    a. Sharing Only
    b. Administrator
    c. Root
    d. Guest User
    e. Standard Account

15. Which of the following preference panes allows you to configure settings for Spaces?
    a. Finder
    b. Mission Control
    c. Desktop & Screen Saver
    d. Dock
    e. Notifications

Essay Quiz

1. Research the significance of the UNIX core of macOS and write a few sentences describing your findings.

2. Your Mac laptop has both personal financial information and files for all your in-process school projects, including data from research for a major project in one of your classes. This laptop is always with you at home, at school, and at work. Describe how you will ensure the security of your valuable data.

3. Your copy of Microsoft Word suddenly freezes midsentence. Describe the best way to regain control of your Mac.

4. You have signed up for Internet access with an new provider, and the setup instructions from your ISP request the hardware address (MAC address) of your Wireless network card. First research and then explain where you will find this information within the macOS GUI and describe how it represents this value.

5. Describe and demonstrate the purpose of the Dock.

Lab Projects

LAB PROJECT 6.1

One of the users on your network, Helen Bandora changed her name to Helen Moz.

While it is simple enough to log into macOS as an administrator and alter the long user name to reflect the name change, changing the short name is not possible in macOS because it was used to create the Home directory *hbandora*. The Home directory is not particularly full, with some Microsoft Word files in the Documents folder and some MP3s in the Music folder.

You decide to change both login names. What do you do to give the user a correctly named account?

You will need a computer with macOS installed on which you have administrator rights.

You will need to do the following:

1. Research the solution for setting up Helen with a correctly named account.
2. Find Helen's Home directory on the hard drive.
3. Implement your solution on the lab computer.

LAB PROJECT 6.2

macOS has a feature called Smart Folders that was not described in the chapter. Research Smart Folders and create at least one Smart Folder for yourself. Then, in your own words, write a short definition of Smart Folders, and describe a practical application of Smart Folders giving specifics.

LAB PROJECT 6.3

Research a feature called Sidecar and describe how it works, what is required, and how to configure it.

Summarize the feature and how to enable it, describing scenarios in which you would use Sidecar, provided you had the required devices.

chapter

7

Linux on the Desktop

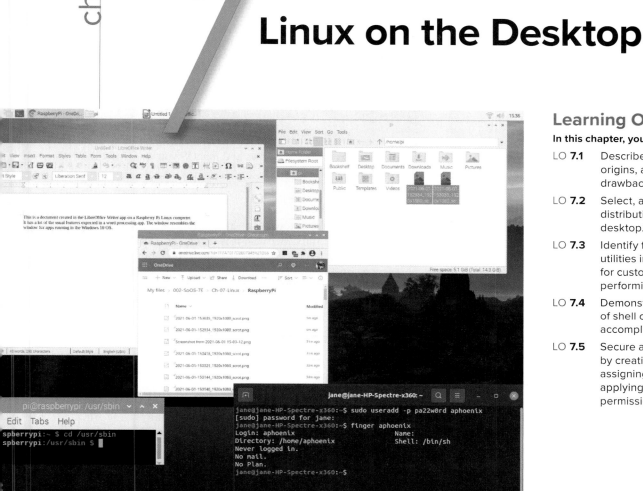

Ubuntu by Canonical, Raspberry Pi

Learning Outcomes

In this chapter, you will learn how to:

LO **7.1** Describe Linux and its origins, and list benefits and drawbacks.

LO **7.2** Select, acquire, and install a distribution of Linux for the desktop.

LO **7.3** Identify features and utilities in a Linux GUI for customizing it and performing common tasks.

LO **7.4** Demonstrate the use of shell commands to accomplish common tasks.

LO **7.5** Secure a Linux desktop by creating user accounts, assigning passwords, and applying file and folder permissions.

Linux, a free operating system with many of the same qualities as UNIX, has the potential to save corporations millions of dollars. To grasp how important a free operating system is, think of an operating system as the software engine of your computer. Then consider the engine in your car. An engine costs thousands of dollars, but if a company started making and distributing free engines, the cost of your new car would drop dramatically, requiring just the cost of the body and chassis, electrical system, radiator, passenger heater and air conditioner, radio, and many other components. Of course, the Linux community offers many of the additional software components for the OS free.

In this chapter, learn the basics of Linux on the desktop with one of the many graphical user interfaces (GUIs) available. Linux is far too broad a topic to give a detailed exploration here, but you will learn why Linux is growing in popularity. You will learn where to obtain Linux to test on your computer and basic configuration and navigation tasks in a Linux environment. If you have never worked with Linux before, this chapter will serve as an introduction to this OS and perhaps inspire you to study it further. 🌼

LO 7.1 | Linux Overview

Linux is an open-source operating system based on UNIX. In this section, discover why you should learn Linux, the features and benefits of Linux, and how and why Linux is used today.

Why Learn Linux?

Learning Linux can be very beneficial to your future career because of its growing importance on all types of computers. Like Windows and macOS you will find Linux on both desktops and servers.

Qualifying for a Job

If you are interested in a job in Information Technology (IT) or a related field, you should familiarize yourself with Linux. Because it is similar to UNIX, learning Linux prepares you for working with UNIX. Both Linux and UNIX are recognized as stable and used on servers worldwide. By learning Linux you are advertising your intelligence, initiative, and computer ability. A potential employer reviewing your résumé would see Linux knowledge as a big plus for an employee in many technology-related areas. Their reasoning is simple—if you can learn Linux, then you should quickly learn the idiosyncrasies of an organization's internal computer systems.

Improving Your Skills

Another reason to learn Linux is to improve your computer skills for working in a non-GUI environment, thus forcing you to be precise. Any OS is unforgiving when given the wrong instructions, but it doesn't take precision to browse a GUI and select the correct graphical object, which is how a GUI buffers users from the precision the operating system requires. The command-line interface (CLI) does not offer that buffer. In the IT networking environment, the typical router or switch is managed using shell commands in a CLI.

The Evolution of Linux

In the early 1970s, Ken Thompson, a developer working at Bell Labs, was criticized for playing a computer game on company equipment. He then found an unused computer and wrote an operating system that would run his game. This operating system became the foundation of UNIX, which has gone on to power the computers of many universities, corporations, and governments of the world. It is a powerful, stable, and fast system. While UNIX is not Linux, the latter does owe its existence to individuals who looked at what Thompson had done with UNIX and decided to create something similar. Below are just some of the important milestones in the evolution of Linux.

1984

In 1984, interested persons created the GNU organization to develop a free version of a UNIX-like operating system (GNU is a recursive acronym for GNU's Not Unix). Since its founding, GNU members have developed versions of Linux, as well as thousands of applications that run on UNIX and Linux platforms. Some of these apps are bundled with distributions of Linux.

Note: Learn more about GNU at **www.gnu.org**.

1988

In 1988, a group of UNIX licensees formed the Open Systems Foundation (OSF) to lobby for an "open" UNIX after AT&T formed a partnership with Sun Microsystems to develop a single proprietary UNIX. In response, AT&T and other licensees formed UNIX International to oppose the OSF. The trade press called the maneuverings of these two groups the "UNIX wars."

1991

In 1991, Linus Torvalds wanted to write a better, open-source version of MINIX, a UNIX-like operating system. Open-source software is distributed with all of its source code, which is the uncompiled program statements that can be viewed and edited with a text editor or special programming software. Linux is written in the C language as one or more text files, and then compiled, using a program called a C compiler, into binary object code. Object code is, essentially, an executable program in yet another language (machine language) that can be interpreted by a computer's CPU and loaded into memory as a running program. Object code cannot be edited.

Torvalds and a team of programmers succeeded in his original goal, but he receives no direct financial gain because he does not own Linux—just the name—and the open-source community could easily decide to rename it. But we don't believe that will happen because of Torvalds' fame and the very nature of the Linux community.

1994

Because the software was open source, many individuals and several companies modified the kernel. Two of the versions available in 1994 were the Slackware and Red Hat kernels, both written in the C++ language; both with TCP/IP functionality for communicating on the Internet as well as primitive Web servers. To obtain a copy, one simply went to an Internet site and selected the distribution to download. This is true today, with many more sources for the code.

> The World Wide Web (WWW) (also called the Web) is the graphical Internet consisting of a vast array of documents located on millions of specialized servers worldwide. Hypertext Transfer Protocol (HTTP) is the protocol for transferring the files that make up the rich graphical Web pages we view on the Web.

Linux Today

The open-source movement has gained credibility in part because vendors such as Novell and IBM integrated open-source software into their product mix. The notion of free and open software, with no one entity owning the source code, thrives today and has the support of many organizations that previously opposed it. Several vendors offer inexpensive Linux servers running the open-source Apache HTTP Server, often simply called "Apache." This Web server software was originally written for UNIX but also runs on Linux. Separate versions have been available for other operating systems, including Windows. Apache is one of the most widely used Web servers due to its stability, security, and cost (free).

try this!

Learn from the Linux Foundation

Explore what is happening in the world of Linux. Try this:

1. Point your browser to **www.linux.com**, a website sponsored by the Linux Foundation.
2. Click on the Search icon and type, "What is Linux?"
3. Read at least one article in the search results.

Linux Distributions

When you buy or download a version of Linux you get a distribution, sometimes called a "distro," that includes the Linux kernel and a whole set of programs that work together to make a functional version of Linux. Most distributions include a number of applications. A distribution targeting desktop users will include an office suite and other productivity apps, while a server distribution will include server-related tools. A good source of the latest information about Linux distributions is DistroWatch. This website has grown from a simple comparison of a handful of distributions to the go-to source for the latest information on Linux distributions. Learn more about Linux distributions in the try this!

Benefits of Linux

There are several benefits to using Linux on your desktop computer.

Linux Is Free

The first benefit of Linux is cost. You may freely download many versions of Linux from the Web. Many sites offer Linux distributions in convenient ISO images. If you don't want to download these distributions, you may purchase prepackaged versions of Linux online for modest cost.

Canonical is the company behind the open-source Ubuntu Linux distributions, updating the OS frequently. In addition, they are involved in other open-source projects and offer consulting services, which is how they pay their employees and keep the lights on and the servers running.

The Fedora Project is the organization founded in 2003 by Red Hat and other contributors. The resulting Fedora Linux distributions are open source, and also the basis for Red Hat's commercially available Red Hat Enterprise Linux (RHEL).

Linux Can Run on Old Equipment

In addition to being free or inexpensive, Linux can run on old equipment. A nonprofit organization can provide computers for its employees with donated or very inexpensive equipment. There are countless situations in which computers too underpowered to run even an outdated version of Windows continue to run reliably for years—as Web servers! The requirements for the latest version of the Ubuntu Linux Desktop Edition are:

- 2 GHz dual-core processor or better.
- 4 GB system RAM.
- 25 GB of free space on a hard drive, USB thumb drive, or external hard drive.
- A DVD drive or a USB port if using USB-attached installation media.

Linux Is Fast

While Linux runs respectably well on old computers, it is even faster on newer computers. This is because Linux programs are very lean and efficient. They use as few resources as possible, graphics use in Linux is optional, and many Linux applications use few, if any, graphics. Graphics can slow a system's response time, making it seem slower than it truly is.

Note: BASH is an acronym for Bourne-Again SHell. The BASH in use today (the default in most Linux systems) was written by Brian Fox for the GNU Project. It is an enhanced version of the original Bourne shell written by Steve Bourne for UNIX.

Linux Can Have a GUI

Unlike Windows, Linux was not intended to have a GUI, but rather just a text-only shell. A shell is the user interface to an OS; it accepts commands and displays error messages and other screen output. The traditional Linux shell is a command-line interface (CLI), such as BASH. The term "shell command" is most often applied to text commands entered through a CLI shell.

Many distributions of Linux, especially those for desktop computers, come with a GUI. Anyone familiar with the macOS or Windows GUI will adjust to these Linux

GUIs, as they have features we have learned to expect in a desktop GUI: windows, icons, menus, and a pointer, collectively referred to as WIMP.

Among the Linux GUIs available today are GNOME, KDE, Pantheon, and Deepin Desktop. GNOME, also called GNOME Shell, is the default desktop of Ubuntu. Figure 7-1 shows the Ubuntu desktop. Don't worry about the name of the GUI shell. If you have experience with other GUIs you can apply what you learned to navigate in a Linux GUI.

Linux Is Stable

Linux code is well written, which increases the speed at which Linux runs and improves the stability of the operating system. Linux is next to impossible to crash. If an application crashes, you can simply remove the program from memory and restart it (the program). This is why people use Linux on Web servers where stability is crucial.

Linux Is Secure

Linux is a secure operating system with all the appropriate security options, as well as the benefit of not being as much of a hacker target as Windows operating systems are. As open-source software, Linux has the advantage of having legions of programmers working to make it a better and more secure OS.

FIGURE 7–1 The GNOME GUI desktop in an Ubuntu installation.
Source: Ubuntu by Canonical

Linux Is Open Source

Finally, Linux is open-source software; users can read the source code and modify it as needed. This probably means little to the average user of the final version of a Linux kernel. However, during development, "beta" releases of the kernel are available to developers who download the code and test it thoroughly, searching for problems and correcting the code. This process helps to ensure an as-well-written-as-possible final release of the kernel.

Once they release a final version, developers can adjust the kernel as needed. For instance, some have modified the kernel to be more accessible. Being Open source makes it possible for developers to modify the Linux code as needed.

Drawbacks of Linux

Even though Linux is widely used on corporate servers, websites, and large-scale networking environments, you still won't find many people using it on their home desktop computers. There are several reasons for this.

Lack of Centralized Support

No system is 100 percent secure; however, both Apple and Microsoft products have extensive documentation and support. Both release service packs and frequent updates to fix discovered vulnerabilities. Because Linux does not have this centralized support, the support and documentation for free Linux can be spotty. A user who downloads Linux from the Internet may receive only a downloadable manual and access to online help pages. It is true that the Linux community is growing, and there are many active user groups, but one must search them out and expend considerable time and effort to get questions answered.

Choice of GUIs Is Confusing

The fact that you can choose from various GUIs is confusing. Users want what they know, and the Linux GUIs, while responding to some of the same mouse and keyboard shortcuts as Windows and macOS, are still different from both. Working in Linux requires some exploration and self-training. For instance, the desktop shown in the Ubuntu example in Figure 7-1 shows the GNOME desktop with a menu bar across the top, similar to macOS and a Dock bar along the side, unlike the GUIs for either macOS or Windows. But, both Ubuntu and Raspberry Pi (Figure 7-2) show the familiar Trash icon on the desktop. In Figure 7-2 Raspberry Pi does not have a dock bar along the side, but clicking the Raspberry on the far left of the menu bar opens the applications menu, which is just as handy without taking up desktop space. Figure 7-2 shows the Raspberry Pi desktop with multiple windows open.

Limited App Selection

There are important apps for Windows that are not available for Linux, so you need to check the software selection before moving to Linux on the desktop. But more titles are becoming available for Linux every year—even some very well-known titles. For example, consider Internet browsers. The most popular browsers, Mozilla Firefox, Google Chrome, and Microsoft Edge, are available for Linux, as are other browsers.

You are also limited in your choice of word processors. The most popular word processor is Microsoft Word. Various distributions of Linux have bundled excellent substitutions, including LibreOffice and Apache OpenOffice. Each of these is an applications suite that contains a word processor and other office productivity tools. However, although both are very nice products, an experienced Microsoft Office user would have to learn how to use one with the same level of proficiency.

Note: If you have a distribution of Linux with a GUI desktop, look for accessibility options in System Settings.

Note: Ubuntu documentation uses the terms "Dock" and "Dash" for the bar on left side of the screen. You may also see references to this as "Launcher" because it is used to launch programs. After throwing an imaginary dart at the documentation the author is using the term "Dock" for this Ubuntu GUI object.

Note: Note: There are third-party solutions for running Microsoft Office for the desktop in some distributions of Linux. Office for the Web will work in some browsers on Linux, but not all Office features will be available.

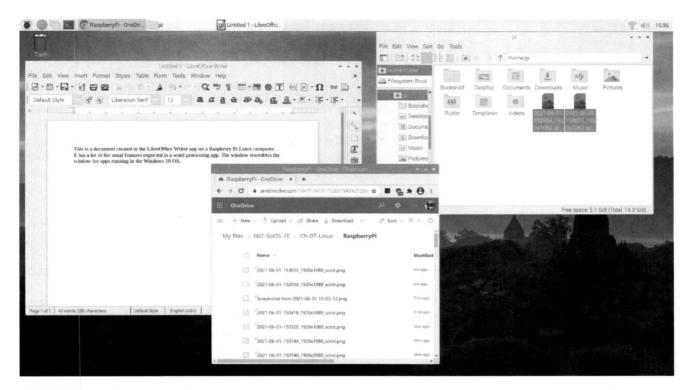

FIGURE 7–2 The Raspberry Pi OS desktop.
Source: Ubuntu by Canonical

Figure 7–3 shows the Ubuntu Software Center, where you can search for software for an Ubuntu installation. Three tabs labeled Explore, Installed, and Updates give quick access to the three general modes for working in the Software Center. You can browse for new apps (Explore), view a list of previously installed apps (Installed), and

Note: Versions of both LibreOffice and Apache OpenOffice are available for macOS and Windows as well as Linux.

FIGURE 7–3 The Ubuntu Software Center.
Source: Ubuntu by Canonical

update your apps (Updates). This is similar to what Apple and Microsoft offer for their OS platforms.

Limited Hardware Support

Not all hardware products work with Linux, but we see this situation improving. Linux vendors work very hard to support the more common devices by providing drivers for them. Having the correct driver is crucial. If you have a new or unusual device, you may need to search the Internet for a driver. Maybe the vendor has not created a Linux driver for your new device, but there is great support among Linux users who create drivers and make them available on the Internet.

Complexity

The last block in the wall between Linux and greater success as a desktop OS is Linux's difficulty of use at the command shell, which continues to be where advanced tasks must be done. Only a limited subset of users will invest the time and effort to learn its intricacies. Linux, like UNIX, assumes that you know what you are doing, and it assumes that you know the consequences of every command you type.

Even with the new, improved GUIs for Linux, it is not as easy to use as the more common operating systems. So if you implement Linux as a desktop OS, be prepared to spend time configuring Linux and providing training for other users who might need to use your computer.

Don't let this discourage you, however. By now, you have spent sufficient time working with operating systems so that you know the basic theory. You'll do fine in Linux. In this chapter, we will explore how to work in Linux in a GUI as well as the basics of working in the Linux terminal window.

LO 7.2 | Linux on Your Desktop

So now that you know some of the history of Linux and its benefits and drawbacks, how will you experience it? Do you have a computer to dedicate to Linux so that you can install it? Do you plan to install it in a dual-boot configuration and continue to boot into another OS? Do you have a computer with a hypervisor in which you can create a virtual machine for testing Linux? In this section, we will describe the sources of Linux distributions for desktop computers and test an option for experiencing Linux: a live image.

Acquiring Linux for the Desktop

There are many distributions of Linux, and many sources for them. The most important criterion to keep in mind before selecting one is the role you wish the Linux computer to play—will it be a server or a desktop? When selecting a source, select one that meets your support needs. Are you a developer who wants to participate in the further development of Linux and Linux apps? If so, you can join a community of like-minded people at one of many websites and social networking sites where they gather. Since this is a survey class, we will assume that most students reading this are only interested in getting acquainted with Linux to understand its place in the world.

Note: The term **burn** traditionally refers to the writing of digital data to a disc (CD-R, DVD-R, or DB-R).

Our criteria for a distribution to feature in this chapter was for a desktop version of Linux that we can use quickly and easily. We selected two: Ubuntu and Raspberry Pi OS (Raspberian). Learn more about each of these distributions at the following websites:

- **www.ubuntu.com**
- **Raspberrypi.org/software** or **www.raspbian.org**

FIGURE 7-4 Ubuntu offers many helpful tutorials.
Source: Ubuntu by Canonical

The Raspberry Pi OS used for this chapter came preinstalled on a new Raspberry Pi 400. In addition, the author selected Ubuntu Desktop Edition for installation on an existing lab computer and in a virtual machine. Ubuntu provides an ISO file that allows you to create a bootable flash drive or DVD disc. When you boot from either type of media, you have the option to install Linux onto the local computer or to boot into a live image of Linux. A *live image* is a bootable image of the operating system that will run from bootable media without requiring the OS be installed on the local computer.

The Ubuntu distribution we selected includes a complete software bundle: the GNOME GUI desktop and a number of GUI applications including LibreOffice, Firefox, and software selections for many other functions, such as email, chat, social networking, music streaming, photo management and editing, and more. The download for this edition is under 3 GB.

Please read all the information on the download page of the distribution you plan to install, paying attention to the system requirements for the installation. Usually, you have a choice of the very solid version that may be labeled LTS which stands for long-term support. In the case of Ubuntu Desktop, this support lasts up to five years and includes free security and maintenance updates. If you prefer to live on the bleeding edge, consider a newer version that has a shorter support window.

Step-by-Step 7.01 guides you through the process of downloading a distribution of Ubuntu Linux and creating a bootable DVD disc in Windows 10; it does not require special software. To create a bootable USB drive is another story; point your browser to https://ubuntu.com/download/desktop. Scroll down to *Easy ways to switch to Ubuntu*, shown in Figure 7-4. Follow the instructions for creating a bootable USB "stick" in the OS of your choice (Linux, Windows, or macOS). Following the instructions for Windows required downloading an app, Rufus, for creating the bootable USB drive.

Note: In discussions of Linux distributions, people often mention FreeBSD, but it is not a version of Linux. FreeBSD is an operating system based on the Berkeley UNIX distribution and is primarily used on servers, whereas Linux was designed for and focused on desktop architectures.

Step-by-Step 7.01

Downloading Linux and Creating Bootable Media

This step-by-step exercise takes you through downloading a distribution of Linux and burning the image to a disc, which you can then use in the remainder of the class. The instructions and illustrations are for using a Windows computer to download an Ubuntu Linux ISO file and to create a bootable DVD. You can complete this exercise using a different distribution of Linux, and the steps will be similar. Websites are frequently updated, affecting the screens and steps used here. To complete this exercise you will need:

- A Windows computer (if using another OS, the steps and screens will differ from those shown here).
- An optical drive capable of burning a disc.
- A blank DVD disc.
- Broadband Internet access.

Step 1

Use your browser to connect to **https://ubuntu.com**. Open the download menu and select the LTS button under Ubuntu Deskto Ubuntu Desktop.

Source: Ubuntu by Canonical

Step 2

On the Download Ubuntu Desktop page, the latest LTS distribution of Ubuntu is at the top. View the system requirements information on this page and scroll down for links to instructions on various options for downloading Linux and creating bootable media. Then return to the top of the page and click the *Download* button.

Source: Ubuntu by Canonical

Step 3

Your browser will now open a dialog box where you can select a location for saving the file. Select a location, such as Desktop or the Downloads folder on your computer. Then click OK.

Step 4

The Ubuntu *Thank you* page will display, and you can check on the progress which will display on the menu bar in some browsers or at the bottom of the window in others.

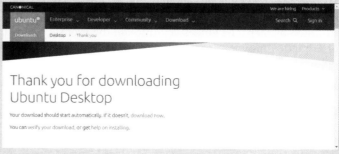

Source: Ubuntu by Canonical

Create the bootable disc by using the ISO image you downloaded. To do that in Windows, insert a disc in the drive, browse to the Downloads folder, right-click on the Ubuntu file, and select *Burn disc image*.

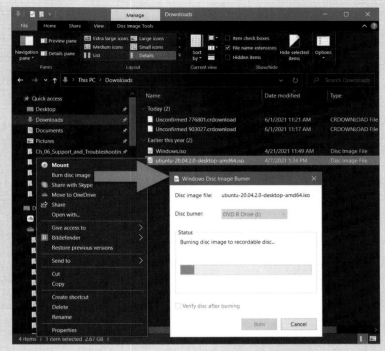

Source: Ubuntu by Canonical

Now test the disc by rebooting the computer with the disc inserted. After a brief delay during which you will see text on a black background, the Ubuntu Welcome screen displays. You have successfully downloaded Ubuntu Linux, created a bootable DVD, and are ready either to boot into Linux and explore it as a Guest or to proceed with an installation. Stay at this screen as you continue.

Source: Ubuntu by Canonical

Installing Linux or Using a Live Image

If you completed Step-by-Step 7.01, you should be at the Welcome screen. If so, select a language, and then click *Try Ubuntu* if you just want to try out Ubuntu without installing it, using the live image. If you run the live image, you will not need to log in, as you will be automatically logged in with the Guest account.

Only select the second option, *Install Ubuntu,* if you are ready to install it on the same computer. If you plan to install it to another location, click the System (gear) icon on the title bar in the upper right (see the illustration in Step 6), select *Shut Down* from the System menu and remove the disc before selecting *Shut Down* again in the confirmation box.

There are several possible scenarios for installing Linux. Just a few include a clean installation on a spare computer, a clean installation onto a second drive on a computer running another OS to create a dual-boot configuration, or an installation into a virtual machine. We installed Ubuntu Linux into virtual machines on Windows 10 computers and found Ubuntu worked well without tweaking it in the virtual machine. Installing Ubuntu onto a Windows computer and preserving the Windows installation

FIGURE 7–5 The Terminal window will open during installation to run certain shell commands.
Source: Ubuntu by Canonical

required installing onto a second partition, which the Ubuntu installation took care of during the installation, repartitioning the drive with a new partition for Ubuntu Linux. The computer chosen for this dual-boot installation was a seven-year-old HP Spectre Notebook with Windows 10 Home. Your experience may be different, as may the distribution you select.

You may want to run Linux in a virtual machine. If you completed the first three Step-by-Steps in Chapter 3, open Hyper-V Manager, and the virtual machine you created with Quick Create is still connected to the Default Switch, it will fail. To prevent that, open Hyper-V Manager and select the Settings for the Linux VM. Configure the network adapter to connect to the virtual switch with Internet access, created in Step-by-Step 3.02. Then select the Linux VM; open the Action menu and connect. When the VM opens, click Start to startup Linux. It should now open to the personalization screens for Linux.

For the remainder of this chapter, leave Linux open. If you are using a live image, you may not be able to do many of the activities. If you choose to install it, simply respond to each screen. Note that one screen has the option to install updates during the installation process. Be sure to select that option unless you are installing Linux in a school lab and have limited time. If you do not allow the updates to install during installation, you will be reminded of it after you restart. During the installation, Linux terminal windows will open, such as the one in Figure 7–5. This is because some components install using Shell commands. Do not try to interrupt them.

During installation, Ubuntu Linux prompts you to set up LivePatch, the security update utility for Linux. Livepatch automatically applies security updates that do not require a restart. To proceed, you will need to first authenticate with the username and password you provided for that installation. Then you need to sign in with an Ubuntu One Account. This is a free account for signing in and using Ubuntu services, such as LivePatch.

LO 7.3 | Exploring a Linux GUI

In this section, you will practice certain tasks in Linux using a GUI, beginning with logging in, exploring the GUI Desktop, locating tools for changing settings, modifying the desktop, and ending a Linux session.

Note: We recommend that you create a virtual machine for Linux, even if you plan only to boot into the live image because when you use a live image in a virtual machine you will still have access to your computer and can take notes, browse the Web, or take screen shots of the contents of the virtual machine.

Note: The Ubuntu user manual is available at **Ubuntu.com** for those who want to peruse it ahead of time. However, once Linux is installed, the manual is available through the Help utility. In the latest GNOME GUI used in this chapter, open Help from the question mark icon on the Dock.

Deciding How to Log In to Ubuntu Linux

In Linux, as in most modern operating systems, you are always logged in as a user—even when you do not see a login page and do not enter a username and credentials. When you run a live image of Linux, you are automatically logged in as the Guest, with limited privileges. However, if you opt to install Linux, the installation prompts you to create a username and password. You must do this, even if you plan to enable the Automatic Login option. If you choose that option, you will not need to enter a password to log in and will go directly to the desktop. However, if you make a significant settings change or install software, you will be prompted for the password for the currently logged in user.

Figure 7-6 shows the log in prompt. The user Jane Holcombe is the only user (other than Guest) on this installation, but if other accounts exist, they will also display here.

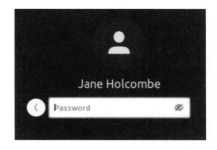

FIGURE 7–6 Log in to the Linux GUI.
Source: Ubuntu by Canonical

The Ubuntu GNOME Desktop

After logging in to Ubuntu Linux you will see the desktop. Notice the bar across the top, like the bar in macOS. The Activities button is on the left, and the date and time are in the middle of the bar. On the far right is a group of icons that opens the System menu. Figure 7-7 shows the open System menu from which you can adjust sound and light, check on network settings, toggle Bluetooth on and off, check battery state, lock screen rotation, access Settings, lock the computer, and log off or power off.

The Ubuntu GNOME desktop includes the **Dock**, a bar on the left side of the screen that serves as the application launcher. Simply pause the mouse cursor over one of the icons on the Launcher and a title will pop out. Figure 7-8 is a screenshot edited to show all the titles for the standard set of Dock icons.

Note: Note: The options shown in the System menu depend on the features of the device. Figure 7–7 shows this menu on a laptop. You will see far fewer options on Linux in a VM.

Searching in the Ubuntu GNOME Desktop

Use the search tool for finding apps and all types of files. To open it, click the Activities button at the top of the Dock or simply press the WINDOWS key (located next to the Ctrl key on many keyboards). A Search box opens at the top of the desktop, and below it the screen is covered with the Activities overview showing large icons for all running apps (even those that were minimized), as shown in Figure 7-9. To search for a file or app, enter a search string into the Search box.

The try this! exercise will walk you through a search.

Browse Directories in the GUI

Before browsing directories in either the GUI or the CLI, take time to learn about the Linux directory hierarchy. It contains two types of directories. The first type consists

Note: Every user on a Linux computer has a home directory with the exception of Guest.

FIGURE 7–7 The Ubuntu desktop with the System menu open on the right.
Source: Ubuntu by Canonical

of directories in which an ordinary user can make changes. We call these home directories. Every user has a **home directory**, the one place in Linux where a user has full control over files and directories without requiring elevated privileges. The second category consists of directories that the user cannot change: system directories, such as /etc and /bin, or home directories for other users.

To work with Linux directories, you should understand how to use paths. A **path** is a description that an operating system uses to identify the location of a file or directory. In Windows, a full path to a file or directory begins with the drive designator (letter plus colon) and you build it using the backslash (\) character as separators between the drive and root directory (first back-slash) and then between each of the subsequent directories in the path. Thus, one example of a Windows path is C:\Winnt\System32. In Linux, you do not use a drive letter in a path, you use a forward slash (/) at the beginning of a path to represent the root and a forward slash (/) to separate directories in a path. A valid path is **/etc/gtk**. In Linux, everything is a file identified within the file system. Files represent drives and other devices, as well as directories and files.

When you log in to Linux, your home directory becomes your current (working) directory. If you installed Linux with the defaults, your home directory path is **/home/*username*,** where *username* is the user name for the account you used to log in. The default installation includes several other directories. The **/bin** directory within your home directory contains many of the Linux commands. The **/usr/bin** directory

Note: While working in a GUI, you will not normally need to type in a path, nor will you often even see path notation in the GUI, but you should understand Linux paths as you navigate. You will need to understand paths if you decide to work in Linux at the CLI.

FIGURE 7–8 The Dock with icons labeled.
Source: Ubuntu by Canonical

try this!

Use a Linux GUI Search Tool

Whether you are using the Ubuntu GNOME desktop or another GUI, it will have a search utility. If it is not apparent to you how to open the Search utility, use the Help utility for your distribution of Linux, which should be readily available from a menu. Try this:

1. Locate and open the Search utility.
2. In the Search box, enter a search string and press the ENTER key.
3. What were the results? Did it find both apps and files that matched the search string?
4. Compare your results to others in your class.

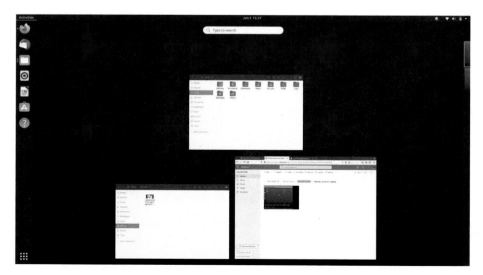

FIGURE 7–9 The Activities button opens a Search box at the top of the desktop and displays the Activities overview of open apps.
Source: Ubuntu by Canonical

TABLE 7–1 Linux Default Directories

Directory	Purpose or Contents
/	The top, or root, directory of a storage volume
/bin	Linux commands
/boot	Files to be loaded during Linux boot up
/dev	Files that represent physical devices
/etc	Linux system configuration files
/home	Home directories for each user
/lib	Shared libraries for programs and commands to use
/mnt	Mount points for removable devices
/opt	Optional (add-on) software packages
/proc	Current status of OS processes
/root	Root account home directory
/sbin	System commands and binary files
/tmp	Temporary files
/usr	Secondary hierarchy
/var	Several directories containing variable data

is an example of a symbolic link that points to another directory, in this case, **/bin**. Table 7–1 shows some of the default directories with brief descriptions.

Now that you know something about the directory structure on your Linux computer, find a tool in the Linux GUI for browsing the Linux directories and explore the directories on your computer. A big advantage of working in a GUI is that you do not need to carefully type the names of files and directories—a fact made more important, since Linux is case-sensitive, meaning that it preserves the case used in the characters of a file name when created, and requires that you enter the correct case to open or manage the file. Step-by-Step 7.02 will guide you through the process of browsing the Linux directory structure. Notice that some directories have upper and lower case. You will want to remember that later when you explore Linux directories from the CLI.

Note: While Linux is case-sensitive, Windows is case-aware, meaning that it will preserve the case used for the characters in a file name when you create it, but it does not require the correct case when retrieving or managing the file.

Step-by-Step 7.02

Browsing the Linux File System in a GUI

In this exercise, use a GUI to browse the Linux directory structure. You will need the following:

- A computer running Linux with a GUI.
- The username and password for a user account.

Step 1

Log in to a Linux installation with a GUI. In our case, we logged in to Ubuntu Linux with the GNOME GUI.

Step 2

Click on the Files icon in the Launcher and a window opens focused on the currently logged-on user's home directory. This home directory contains directories created during the installation of this distribution of Linux, as well as directories created by the user.

Source: Ubuntu by Canonical

Step 3

Browse through the directories in the home directory, then click the item on the left labeled Other Locations. In a dual-boot configuration, the result will show two drives: one labeled Computer, containing Linux, and one named for the other operating system. In this case, it is Windows. Otherwise, the first screen under Other Locations may resemble this second image. If the contents of Computer do not display from Other Locations, click Computer to view the contents.

Source: Ubuntu by Canonical

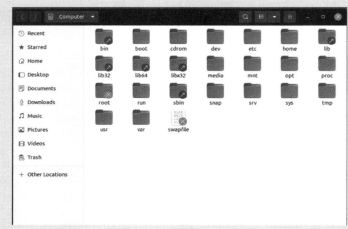

Source: Ubuntu by Canonical

Step 4

Double-click the *home* folder to open the top-level home directory. A home directory should display for each user. In this example, the only user is Jane. Notice that the Guest user does not have a home folder. When a Guest user logs in, they are given a Home folder, but it is deleted when they exit. Therefore, you will not see a Guest Home folder when you are logged in as another user.

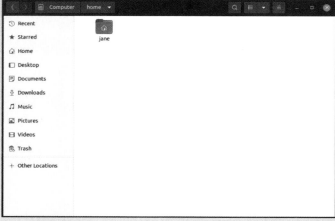

Source: Ubuntu by Canonical

Step 5

When you are finished browsing the directories, close the window.

Ubuntu Livepatch for Updating the OS

During installation, recent versions of Ubuntu install the Canonical Livepatch update utility. Once this is installed, Livepatch icon (a shield) displays on the right of the menu bar when LivePatch needs attention. Click this icon to open the LivePatch menu (Figure 7–10). Select Livepatch Settings to open the Software & Updates dialog (Figure 7–11).

System Settings

Click the small down arrow on the far right of the top bar to open the small drop-down System menu, shown in Figure 7–12. Locate the icon that resembles a gear. Tap this button to open Settings, shown in Figure 7–13. In Settings, work your way through the categories in the left column to configure your system settings.

Modify the Desktop

Modify the desktop to suit your personal tastes. Settings is the place to modify the Desktop using various categories in the left column, such as Background, Appearance, Displays, and Universal Access (accessibility). Step-by-Step 7.03 describes how to make changes to your Desktop.

FIGURE 7–10 The Livepatch menu.
Source: Ubuntu by Canonical

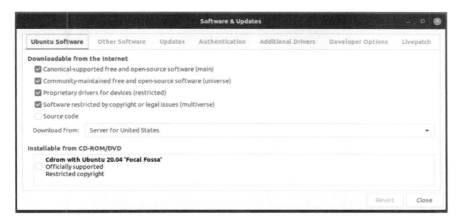

FIGURE 7–11 Software and Updates settings.
Source: Ubuntu by Canonical

FIGURE 7–12 The System menu.
Source: Ubuntu by Canonical

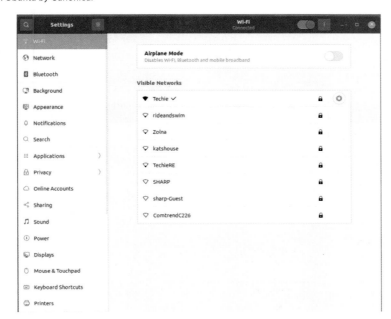

FIGURE 7–13 Open Settings from the System menu.
Source: Ubuntu by Canonical

Step-by-Step 7.03

Modifying the Desktop

You will need the following:

- A computer with Ubuntu installed. The steps are written for Ubuntu with the GNOME GUI.
- The username and password of an administrator account for this computer.

Step 1

Click the small down arrow on the far right of the top bar to open the drop-down System menu. Tap *Settings* to open Settings. In the left column select Background.

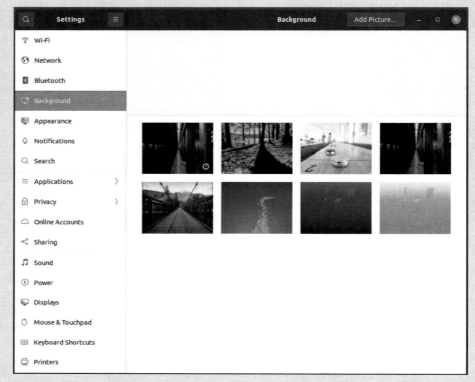

Source: Ubuntu by Canonical

Step 2

The Background control panel lets you change the background. If you want to add one of your own pictures, click the *Add Picture* button and browse for pictures to add to the selection gallery on the Background page. If you do not want to browse for a picture, click Cancel at the top left. When you are ready, select a new background from the Background page.

Source: Ubuntu by Canonical

Click on *Appearance* in the left column of Settings. This is where you can choose to change the window colors, auto-hide the Dock, change the icon size on the Dock, and select the position of the Dock: left, bottom, or right.

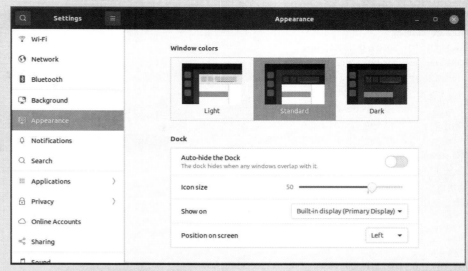

Source: Ubuntu by Canonical

No need to click an OK button; changes are made as soon as you select them. In our case, we selected a new background but did not change the behavior of the Dock.

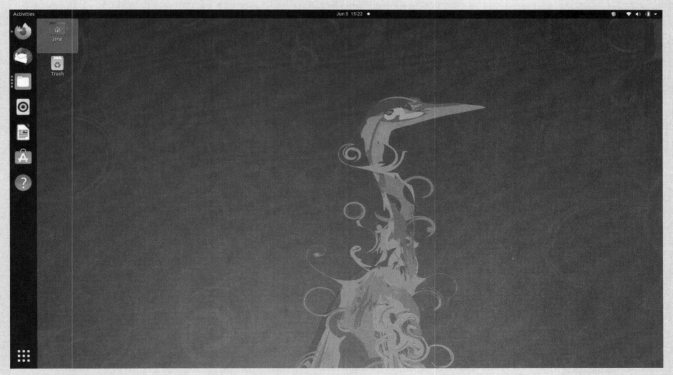

Source: Ubuntu by Canonical

Step 5

Return to Settings and open Displays. The Displays settings will vary depending on the capabilities of your computer. This window also has a tab, Night Light. Between the main Displays page and the Night Light page, you can select settings for Refresh Rate, Resolution, Scale, and Night Light (uses warmer screen color). Make desired changes and then return to the main Settings screen.

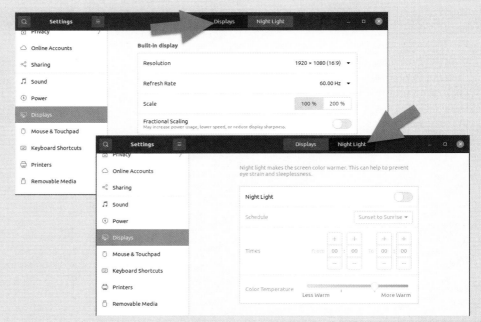

Source: Ubuntu by Canonical

Step 6

Return to the main Settings windows and select *Universal Access*. This is where you can customize this installation of Linux to make it more accessible to someone who needs adjustments made for viewing the screen, listening, typing, or using a pointing device. When you are finished close the window.

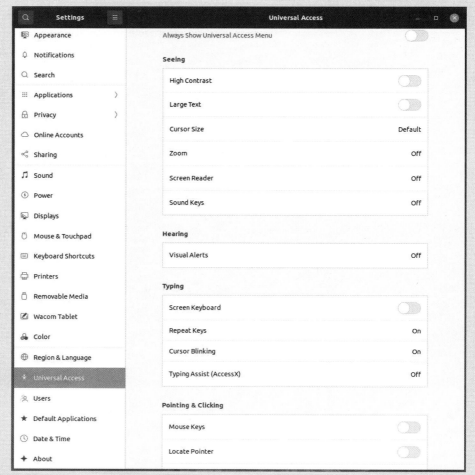

Source: Ubuntu by Canonical

Ending a Linux Session from the GUI

As with Windows and macOS, you have choices for ending your session in Linux. You can simply log out, which is a reasonable choice if you are sharing a computer with someone else. You can shut down, which will both log you out and shut down your computer. You can restart Linux.

Logging Out of a Linux GUI Session

When you log out of Linux it ends your session, giving you an opportunity to save files before closing down all apps (and your desktop if in a GUI), but does not turn off the computer. After logging out, another user can log in, using another account on that computer. How you log on or off a Linux GUI session depends on which GUI you are using.

If you are using the Ubuntu GNOME desktop, click on the System menu in the upper-right corner to open the System drop-down menu shown back in Figure 7-12. Then select *Power Off/Log Out* to open the menu in Figure 7-14. Finally, select *Log Out*. You will need to respond to the Log Out dialog box or allow it to occur within 60 seconds. Then the session will end; after a delay, a login page will display.

Switching Users

If you have multiple accounts on a Linux computer you can take advantage of switch users, a feature that allows the currently logged-on user to leave their apps and data open in memory, switching away so that another user can log in to a separate session. Each user's session is protected, requiring a password to access again.

To switch users in GNOME GUI in Ubuntu, select the Switch User option in the *Power Off/Log Out* menu in figure 7-14. This option is only available if more than one user account exists on the system. This opens a login screen where you can select a local account and enter a password to switch to another account.

Shutting Down, Restarting, or Suspending a Linux GUI

When you shut down a Linux computer, you are logged out and the operating system closes all files and powers off the computer. When you select restart on a Linux computer, you are logged out and the operating system closes all files and then issues a restart command to the computer, without turning the power off. The operating system is then restarted and the login screen displays.

To shut down a computer from the Linux GNOME GUI, Open the System menu and select *Power Off/Log Out*, shown in Figure 7-14, then select *Power Off*. Then the screen will dim and display the message shown in Figure 7-15. Here you have the choices *Cancel, Restart,* and *Power Off*.

LO 7.4 | Linux Command-Line Interface

The native Linux user interface is the command-line interface (CLI). Many installations of Linux, especially on servers, have only a CLI. Although there are great GUI options for working in Linux, system administrators still do much of the real work of supporting and managing Linux from the CLI, which forces you to be precise when entering commands. Any OS is unforgiving when given the wrong instructions, but it doesn't take precision to browse a GUI and select the correct graphical object, which is how a GUI buffers users from the precision required from a command prompt. Acquiring the habit of being precise now will help you succeed in future computer work.

To learn the commands, you must enter them at a Linux prompt. Sit at a Linux computer while reading the following sections because, as we examine various

FIGURE 7–14 From the System menu select *Power Off/Log Out*.
Source: Ubuntu by Canonical

Note: Note: The shortcut for opening the terminal window in Linux GUIs is **Ctrl+Alt+T**, including, but not limited to, Ubuntu GNOME and the Raspberry Pi 400 default GUIs.

FIGURE 7–15 Select *Power Off*.
Source: Ubuntu by Canonical

commands, you will have frequent opportunities to try them. Feel free also to experiment on your own. Note that your screen may not look exactly like the examples shown.

The Terminal Window in Linux

If you installed Linux with a GUI or are running it from a live image booted into a GUI, you can open a terminal window, equivalent to a macOS Terminal window, where you can experience the Linux CLI. How you do this depends on the GUI. For instance, in the Ubuntu GNOME GUI, click on Activities and type "terminal" in the Activities Search box (Figure 7-16). Then select the *Terminal* icon from the results list. That will open a terminal window, similar to the one shown in Figure 7-17. The Raspberry Pi GUI has a Terminal shortcut on the top menu bar. Figure 7-18 shows a terminal window open in Raspberry Pi.

When you open a terminal window you will see the **$ prompt**, which includes information, such as the name of the currently logged-on user and the computer name. These are separated by the @ sign, which in turn is followed by a tilde (~) representing the path to your home directory. When you start a session at the $ prompt, the current directory is your logged-on user's Home directory.

Later in this chapter you will learn how to use the **cd** command to change the current directory. If you make another directory current, the name of that directory will be included in the $ prompt. The appearance of the $ prompt may vary somewhat among Linux versions. The blinking cursor that follows the $ prompt, seen in Figures 7-17 and 7-18 as a white rectangle, indicates that it is awaiting your command.

Note: Type the **exit** command to leave (log off) the Linux CLI. If you are using a terminal window, this closes the window—only ending that session, it does not shut down the Linux GUI in which the terminal window resides. The command **sudo shutdown now** shuts down the computer from within the Terminal window.

FIGURE 7–16 Type "terminal" in the Activities Search box.
Source: Ubuntu by Canonical

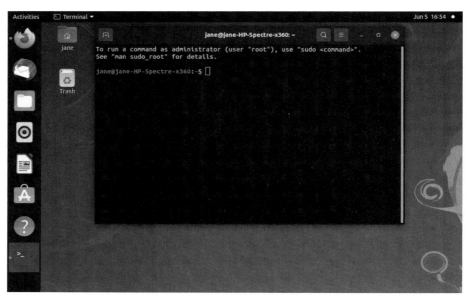

FIGURE 7–17 A terminal window in the Ubuntu GNOME GUI.
Source: Ubuntu by Canonical

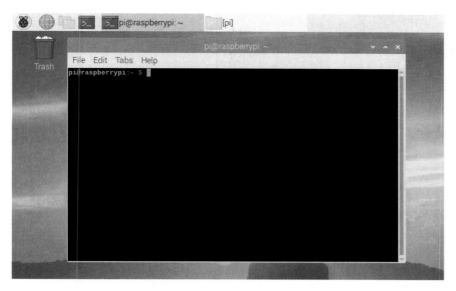

FIGURE 7–18 A terminal window in the Raspberry Pi GUI.
Source: Ubuntu by Canonical

Using Linux Shell Commands

The most important thing to learn and remember about working in the Linux shell (in a terminal window or in Linux without a GUI) is that it is case-sensitive. Commands are entered in lowercase, and so are most options.

Linux Shell Command Syntax

When working at the CLI, the Linux shell command syntax follows these rules:

- All lines start with a Linux command (the first string of characters).
- A space must follow the command.
- Next come options, specific to the command, that modify its behavior. Most options are short options using a single character, while more recent options may be long (more than one character).
- Order of options is usually of little importance.
- Use a space between each option.
- Short options are preceded by a hyphen (-d); long options are preceded by two hyphens (--help).
- If you want to use multiple short options for a command, you can combine them into one long option with a single hyphen at the beginning.
- Some commands are followed by a parameter, which is a file name, directory, or device name. A parameter is the object that the command action targets.

In general, the command syntax in Linux follows this format:

command option parameter

Combining Options

Now let's practice combining options. Consider the **ls** command, which lists contents of a directory, as shown in Figure 7-19, in which the command is run without any options or parameters.

try this!

Test Case Sensitivity in Linux

Test Linux case sensitivity while using the **man** command that, when entered correctly, opens the user manual page for the command you provide, such as the **list directory contents** command, **ls.** Try this:

1. At the Linux $ prompt enter the following command in all caps: MAN LS
2. Notice the resulting error message.
3. Now reenter the command in all lower case. The result is that the Linux user manual will open to the page on the command **ls.**
4. Use the SPACEBAR and UP and DOWN arrow keys to move through the manual page.
5. To quit a manual page, press **q.**

FIGURE 7–19 The **ls** command showing a simple listing of the current directory.
Source: Raspberry Pi

FIGURE 7–20 The **ls -a** command showing a listing of all items in the current directory.
Source: Raspberry Pi

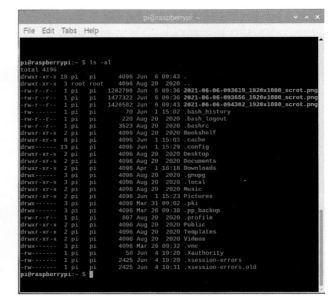

FIGURE 7–21 The **ls** command using two options (**-a** and **-l**) showing a listing of all items in the current directory and the "long" information on each item.
Source: Raspberry Pi

try this!

Using Multiple Options

Practice using **ls**. Run the command with a single option and then with multiple options. Try this:

1. Enter the command **ls.**
2. Notice that **ls** defaults to a column output (four across).
3. To get a long listing of this directory, enter **ls -l**. This runs the -l option on the current directory.
4. Now use multiple options. Enter **ls -la.** This provides a long listing for all files, including hidden files, in the current directory.

It has several options, two of which are **a** (all files including hidden files) and **l** (lowercase "L") for long format listing that will include permissions, owner, size, modification time, and more. Figures 7–20 and 7–21 show the use of each of these commands alone. To use **ls** with the **a** option enter **ls -a,** which will simply list the files, as shown in Figure 7–20, but give no information about them, other than the color coding for the type of file, explained later. To use both options at once, enter **ls -al** or **ls -la,** as shown in Figure 7–21. Either will work. When too much text displays for the size of the terminal window, a scroll bar appears on the side, and you can use it to scroll through the results.

The Help Manual

Help is always at hand in the form of the online user manual, accessed with the **man** command. Type **man** *command,* where *command* is the shell command you wish to learn more about. Figure 7–22 shows the result of entering **man ls**. This is the first page of the explanation for the **ls** command. Notice the instructions in white at the bottom of the screen. Press *h* to see an explanation of how to move through the manual. Press *q* to quit the **man** command. You can even see the documentation for the **man** command itself by entering **man man** at the $ prompt.

Command-Line History

Linux saves the shell commands you enter for the duration of the session (called command-line history), and you can scroll through these commands while at the $ prompt. Simply use the up and down arrow keys to move through the history. When you find the command you would like to reuse, you can edit the command by moving back and forth through it with the left and right arrow keys. When you are ready to use

Note: The screen (or terminal window) gets pretty cluttered. To clear the screen and return the $ prompt to the top of an empty screen, enter the **clear** command. If the screen has unusual characters on it that do not disappear with the **clear** command, use the **reset** command for a more thorough reset of the terminal window session.

the command, simply press ENTER. Linux saves these commands in a file called .bash_history, but you do not need to know anything about this file to take advantage of this feature.

Command Completion

As you enter a command at the $ prompt, experiment with the command completion feature. Enter the command name and a few more characters of the options, then press the TAB key. Linux tries to automatically fill in partially typed commands, and is especially clever at doing this when it looks like you are entering a directory name, indicated by the forward slash (/), but you need to give it more information than just the forward slash. For instance, when using the **cd** (change directory) command, if you enter **cd /e** and then press the TAB key, it will guess that you intended to type "etc/" and will complete it that way so that it reads **cd /etc/**. A more general term for this feature, when used in applications and search engines, is *autocompletion*.

FIGURE 7–22 Enter the **man ls** command to see the manual page for the **ls** command.
Source: Raspberry Pi

try this!

What Time Is It?

Practice entering the date and calendar commands. Try this:

1. Type the command **date** and press ENTER. This will display the current date, along with the day of the week and time.
2. Now type the command **cal** and press ENTER. This will display the calendar for the current month with the day highlighted.

Linux Feedback

When it comes to feedback, Linux commands are similar to Windows Command Prompt commands, in that they provide cryptic feedback, communicating with you only if there is a problem. A Linux BASH command does not report when it is successful, though you'll get an error message if the command is incorrect. In this example, we first tried to change to the documents directory using the command **cd documents**. The second line shows an error. We then ran the **ls** command (third line) to see the contents (fourth and fifth lines) that showed the directory was actually named "Documents." We entered it again (sixth line), using the correct case: **cd Documents**. No message resulted from this command, although it is clear that we changed directories because the dollar prompt on the seventh line now shows Documents as the current location.

Like Windows, Linux relies heavily on a directory structure that has several predefined directories created by default during installation. Some hold important system files, and others hold user data. Linux is very similar. It has several directories for system files and a home directory for each user. You have already been introduced to a few of the file and directory management tools: **ls** and **cd** while learning the basics of working with shell commands. In this section, you will use these and other commands to explore the default directories and learn more about working with Linux at the CLI.

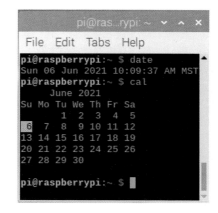

The date and cal commands.
Source: Raspberry Pi

Using Shell Commands for the Linux File System

A shorthand for the path, or location, of the Home directory both at the $ prompt and in a shell command is the tilde (~). Use the **ls** command to see other directories. Some have rather strange names.

In Linux everything is a file, even physical objects like a hard drive or other storage devices. Therefore, Linux shows each drive and other device simply as a part of the file system and gives it a path that begins at the root of the file system (/). Drives and other devices have assigned names, such as **/dev/sda0**, the first hard drive on an SCSI interface (indicated by **sda**); or **/dev/hda1,** the first hard drive on an IDE interface (**hda**).

A message appears only if a command causes an error.
Source: Raspberry Pi

Practice using shell commands to work with files and directories on your computer. Table 7-2 provides a list of basic file management commands for your reference.

You were introduced to the **ls** command earlier in this chapter, and Figure 7-22 showed the use of the **man ls** command to display the manual page for this command. Table 7-3 lists and explains the commonly used options for **ls**. Recall that Linux is case-sensitive, so pay attention to the case of each option. By itself, **ls** provides only the names of visible files in the current directory, and the **-a** option that you learned about earlier lists all files and directories, even hidden files. Hidden files have names that begin with a period (.).

Listing the Contents of a Specified Directory. If you do not specify the directory you want **ls** to work on, it uses the current directory. To point **ls** to another directory, use the directory name and the appropriate path as a parameter in the command. Figure 7-23 shows the result of typing **ls /etc.** The colors of the names tell you more about that file or directory.

- Blue = directory
- Green = program or binary data file such as jpeg
- Light blue or aqua = link to files in a different directory
- Magenta = image file
- White = text file
- Yellow = device

To view more details of the files in the **/etc** directory, enter the command **ls -l /etc;** the output will be similar to that shown in Figure 7-24. This listing does not include hidden files because we did not use the **-a** option to see hidden files.

In the results from using the **-l** option, the first column is 10 characters wide and lists the attributes on the file or folder, which you will examine a little later in this chapter. The next column indicates the number of links to a file. The next two columns list the owner (normally the user who created the file) and last modifier of the file, respectively. The next number indicates the size of the file. The next columns indicate the file creation date and time. Lastly, it shows the name of the file. If a file is a link, it next lists the link location; the file after the arrow is the original file. Figure 7-24 does not show any links.

TABLE 7-2 Basic Shell Commands for File Management

Command	Description
cd	Changes to another directory
chmod	Changes the mode or file permissions
cp	Copies a file
ls	Lists contents of a directory
mkdir	Makes a directory
more	Displays a text file, one screenful at a time
pwd	Prints the working directory
rm	Deletes a file

TABLE 7-3 Commonly Used Options for the ls Command

ls Option	Description
-a	Lists all files in the directory, including the hidden files. Files are hidden in Linux by making the first character a period, like this: **.bash_profile**
-l	Displays a long listing of the directory contents with all file attributes and permissions listed
-F	Classifies the listed objects. In particular, directory names have a / character after the name
-S	Sorts the output by size
-t	Sorts the output by time

```
pi@raspberrypi:~/Documents $ ls /etc
adduser.conf                    init                    pulse
alsa                            init.d                  python
alternatives                    initramfs-tools         python2.7
apache2                         inputrc                 python3
apparmor                        insserv.conf.d          python3.7
apparmor.d                      iproute2                rc0.d
apt                             issue                   rc1.d
avahi                           issue.net               rc2.d
bash.bashrc                     java                    rc3.d
bash_completion                 java-11-openjdk         rc4.d
bash_completion.d               kernel                  rc5.d
bindresvport.blacklist          ldap                    rc6.d
binfmt.d                        ld.so.cache             rc.local
bluetooth                       ld.so.conf              rcS.d
ca-certificates                 ld.so.conf.d            request-key.conf
ca-certificates.conf            ld.so.preload           request-key.d
ca-certificates.conf.dpkg-old   libaudit.conf           resolv.conf
calendar                        libblockdev             resolvconf
chromium-browser                libibverbs.d            resolv.conf.bak
cifs-utils                      libnl-3                 resolvconf.conf
console-setup                   libpaper.d              rmt
cron.d                          libreoffice             rpc
cron.daily                      lightdm                 rpi-issue
cron.hourly                     lighttpd                rsyslog.conf
cron.monthly                    locale.alias            rsyslog.d
crontab                         locale.gen              RTIMULib.ini
cron.weekly                     localtime               sane.d
cups                            logcheck                securetty
cupshelpers                     login.defs              security
dbus-1                          logrotate.conf          selinux
debconf.conf                    logrotate.d             sensors3.conf
debian_version                  machine-id              sensors.d
default                         magic                   services
deluser.conf                    magic.mime              sgml
dhcp                            mailcap                 shadow
dhcpcd.conf                     mailcap.order           shadow-
dictionaries-common             manpath.config          shells
dillo                           matplotlibrc            skel
```

FIGURE 7–23 A listing of the /**etc** directory.
Source: Raspberry Pi

```
pi@raspberrypi:~ $ ls -l /etc
total 1088
-rw-r--r--  1 root root    2981 Aug 20  2020 adduser.conf
drwxr-xr-x  3 root root    4096 Aug 20  2020 alsa
drwxr-xr-x  2 root root   12288 Mar 26 11:07 alternatives
drwxr-xr-x  3 root root    4096 Aug 20  2020 apache2
drwxr-xr-x  2 root root    4096 Aug 20  2020 apparmor
drwxr-xr-x  7 root root    4096 Jun  1 14:20 apparmor.d
drwxr-xr-x  7 root root    4096 Aug 20  2020 apt
drwxr-xr-x  3 root root    4096 Jun  1 14:20 avahi
-rw-r--r--  1 root root    1994 Apr 17  2019 bash.bashrc
-rw-r--r--  1 root root      45 Feb 11  2019 bash_completion
drwxr-xr-x  2 root root    4096 Aug 20  2020 bash_completion.d
-rw-r--r--  1 root root     367 May 13  2019 bindresvport.blacklist
drwxr-xr-x  2 root root    4096 May 11  2020 binfmt.d
drwxr-xr-x  2 root root    4096 Aug 20  2020 bluetooth
drwxr-xr-x  3 root root    4096 Aug 20  2020 ca-certificates
-rw-r--r--  1 root root    5989 Mar 26 11:07 ca-certificates.conf
-rw-r--r--  1 root root    5434 Aug 20  2020 ca-certificates.conf.dpkg
-old
drwxr-xr-x  2 root root    4096 Aug 20  2020 calendar
drwxr-xr-x  4 root root    4096 Mar 26 11:07 chromium-browser
drwxr-xr-x  2 root root    4096 Aug 20  2020 cifs-utils
drwxr-xr-x  2 root root    4096 Aug 20  2020 console-setup
drwxr-xr-x  2 root root    4096 Aug 20  2020 cron.d
drwxr-xr-x  2 root root    4096 Jun  1 14:14 cron.daily
drwxr-xr-x  2 root root    4096 Aug 20  2020 cron.hourly
drwxr-xr-x  2 root root    4096 Aug 20  2020 cron.monthly
-rw-r--r--  1 root root    1042 Oct 11  2019 crontab
drwxr-xr-x  2 root root    4096 Aug 20  2020 cron.weekly
drwxr-xr-x  5 root lp      4096 Jun  6 08:49 cups
drwxr-xr-x  2 root root    4096 Mar 26 11:08 cupshelpers
drwxr-xr-x  4 root root    4096 Aug 20  2020 dbus-1
-rw-r--r--  1 root root    2969 Feb 26  2019 debconf.conf
-rw-r--r--  1 root root       5 Mar 29 18:16 debian_version
drwxr-xr-x  2 root root    4096 Jun  1 14:20 default
-rw-r--r--  1 root root     604 Jun 26  2016 deluser.conf
drwxr-xr-x  2 root root    4096 Aug 20  2020 dhcp
-rw-rw-r--  1 root netdev  1777 Nov 13  2019 dhcpcd.conf
```

FIGURE 7–24 A listing of the /**etc** directory with more details.
Source: Raspberry Pi

Changing the Current Directory. The command to change the current directory in Linux is **cd**. The **cd** command was used in previous examples in this chapter to illustrate the command completion feature and the need to pay attention to letter case. Let's focus on this command for itself now.

The **cd** command requires one parameter: the directory to change to. If the directory is a child of the current directory, then you only need the name to change to this directory. For example, suppose that in your home directory you have a child directory called private. To change to this directory, you enter **cd private**. If the directory is not a child of the current directory, you will need to enter the path to the directory. An absolute path will start with **/** (the root directory). Each directory in the path is listed after the **/** and separated from the next by another **/**. For example, to change to the **sbin** directory under the **/usr** directory, you would enter **cd /usr/sbin**. It is called an absolute path because you clearly provide its location beginning with the top level, which in Linux is the root directory.

When you correctly use **cd** to change to a different directory, it rewards you with a change in your prompt. In Figure 7-25, the user started in the Home directory of the user, as indicated by the tilde (~) in the $ prompt, and changed to the /usr/sbin directory. The prompt changed to reflect the new directory. You can quickly change back to your personal home directory from any directory by entering **cd** ~ . Figure 7-26 shows the result of entering this command.

> ### WARNING!
>
> To avoid seeing error messages in place of results, whenever you need to use a shell command to perform an operation on a hidden file or directory, be sure to include the (.) at the beginning of the name.

FIGURE 7–25 Changing to the /**usr/ sbin** directory.
Source: Raspberry Pi

FIGURE 7–26 Changing to the Home directory using the tilde (~).
Source: Raspberry Pi

Use the **pwd** command to display the path to the current directory.
Source: Raspberry Pi

Where Am I? Unfortunately, the Linux prompt does not (by default) show the entire path to the current directory. If you are unsure of where you are, use the command **pwd,** which stands for print working directory. It does not send anything to your printer; rather it displays (prints) the path to the working (current) directory on your screen, as shown here where the **pwd** command shows the path to the current directory (/home/jane) on the second line and then returns to the $ prompt on the third line.

Relative Path. Linux allows you to use commands to navigate directories, using special symbols as shorthand for moving to directories that are relative to your current directory. For instance, the command **cd ..** will change the current directory to the next directory up in the hierarchy. If you are in your personal home directory, this command will move you to the home directory, one level up. In Figure 7–27, the first two lines show the **pwd** command and its result, showing that the /home/pi directory is current. The third line shows the command **cd ..** followed by the resulting $ prompt on the fourth line in which the /home directory is current. The /home directory is the parent directory of all the home directories on a Linux computer.

try this!

Display the Contents of a File

Use the **more** command to display the contents of a file on the screen. Try this:

1. If a terminal window is not open, open it now.
2. If the prompt does not include a tilde (~), enter **cd ~** to ensure that you are in the Home directory.
3. Enter the command: **more .bash_history.** This will display the contents of the hidden file .bash_history, pausing after the screen is full.
4. Press the ENTER key (repeatedly) to scroll one line at a time or press the SPACEBAR to scroll one screenful at a time. Continue to the end of the output.

Place the **..** characters between forward slashes (/) to move up additional levels. In addition, throw in a specific directory that exists at that level. For example, the command **cd ../../etc** moves up two levels and then to the etc directory. Be sure you know where you want to go, and remember, using one of these characters is supposed to save you typing. Rather than use the command string **cd ../../etc,** it is shorter to type **cd /etc**. Another special symbol is the single dot (**.**), which refers to the current directory.

try this!

Using Relative Path Statements

A little practice with relative paths is helpful. Try this:

1. Type the command: **cd ..**
2. Return to your home directory by typing: **cd ~**
3. Now move to the /etc directory using a relative path: **cd ../../etc**
4. Return to your home directory by typing: **cd ~**

Wildcards. Linux supports the use of wildcards. A wildcard is a symbol that replaces any character or string of characters in a command parameter. It is also supported in other CLIs for other OSs. The use of the asterisk (*) as a wildcard in a file name or directory name replaces all the characters from the point at which you place the asterisk to the end of the name. For instance, **ls bi*** would list all files or directories that begin with "bi."

Linux wildcard support is flexible. You can enter a range of characters as a wildcard. For instance, if you enter **ls [c-d]*** the **ls** command will display all files in the current directory that begin with the letters *c* through *d*. The bracket symbols (**[ ]**) are part of a Linux feature called regular expressions. Linux also allows you to use the dollar sign (**$**) to represent a single character within a file name, a feature also supported by DOS and the Windows Command Prompt. We considered ourselves very experienced DOS users (back in its heyday), and we found that using the dollar sign was rarely worth the bother.

When a parameter for the **ls** command is the name of a directory, the result will include the contents of that directory. Therefore, if you try the command in the example given in the previous paragraph from within the **/etc** directory, the **ls [c-d]*** command will result in a long listing because each of the items that begins with either a "c" or "d" that is also a directory will cause **ls** to list the contents of that directory. Figure 7–28 shows just a portion of the output from running this command with the

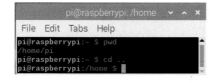

FIGURE 7–27 Use the command **cd ..** to move to the parent directory of the current directory.
Source: Raspberry Pi

/etc directory current. Each line that ends with a colon is for a directory and the following line or lines display the contents of that directory.

Creating Directories

Create a directory in Linux with the **mkdir** command, which requires at least one parameter: the name of the directory to create. For example, to create a directory called junk within the current directory, enter the command **mkdir junk.** Because Linux gives you no feedback after you create a directory, use **ls** to verify that it built the directory.

If you list more than one parameter, then it will create a directory for each. Therefore, to create two directories named "sales" and "marketing" with one command, enter the command **mkdir sales marketing** (see Figure 7-29).

Copying Files in Linux

The command to copy files is **cp.** We recommend you make a copy of a file before you change it. This allows you to recover from any changes you make.

The **cp** command requires two parameters. The first is the source file, which can be a file in the current directory or a file in another directory, as long as you provide the correct path. The second parameter is the target, which can be a target location to copy to and/or a name for the file. This makes more sense after you practice using the command.

As you can see in Figure 7-30, the file named hosts was copied from the /etc directory to the current directory. (The period at the end of the command represents the current directory.) This is just a copy, leaving the original hosts file in the /etc directory. Notice that Linux does not report that it copied a file. The figure also shows that we used the **ls** command to verify a successful copy of the file.

FIGURE 7–28 A portion of the results of the command **ls [c-d]*** when run from the **/etc** directory.
Source: Raspberry Pi

try this!

Using Wildcards

1. Change to the /etc directory (enter **cd /etc**).
2. Enter the command **ls e*.** You'll see all files that begin with the letter _e_.
3. Now enter the command **ls [c-d]* /etc.**

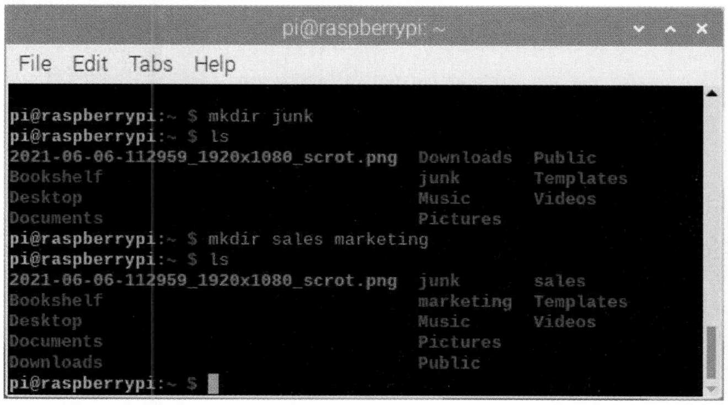

FIGURE 7–29 Use **mkdir** to create directories and **ls** to confirm that they were created.
Source: Raspberry Pi

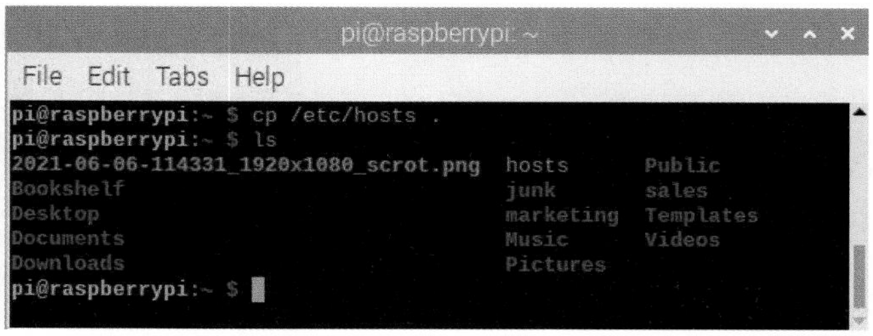

FIGURE 7–30 Copying the hosts file from the **/etc** directory to the user's home directory.
Source: Raspberry Pi

Create Directories

Create directories in your home folder. Try this:

1. Enter the command **mkdir data.**
2. Use the **ls** command to confirm that it created the data directory.
3. Make several directories by entering the **mkdir** command followed by two or more names for new directories.
4. Use the **ls** command to confirm that it created the new directories.

LO 7.5 | Securing a Linux Desktop

Linux is a very secure OS—whether you are using a GUI or a CLI. It is important to know how to configure a computer for the needs of its users. This includes managing user accounts and applying security to directories.

Keeping Linux Up-to-Date

Since security updates are an important part of updates to any software, ensure that your installation of Linux continues to get updates. The Software Updater app in the Ubuntu GNOME GUI will by default download and install updates; it requires interaction from the user to restart. This can cause delays in keeping your installation of Ubuntu up-to-date.

Ubuntu now includes Livepatch, an optional service that applies security updates without restarting Linux. We encountered this in recent versions of Ubuntu during the personalization stage. It has two requirements:

1. You must enter your user password for that installation of Linux (Figure 7–31). You will need to use your local password, even if you do not require a password to login.
2. You must sign in with an Ubuntu One Account, an online service requiring an email address and password (Figure 7–32). These credentials are usable and reusable across multiple instances. This gives you a single sign-on to Ubuntu services.

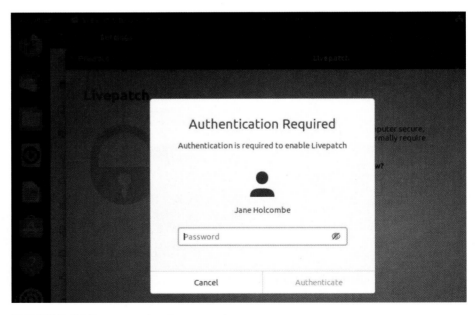

FIGURE 7–31 Enter your local password.
Source: Ubuntu by Canonical

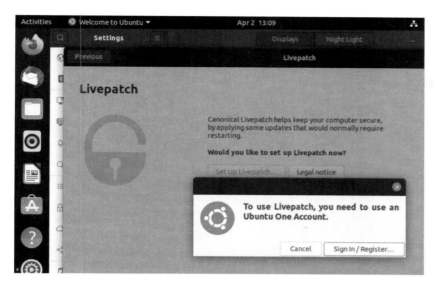

FIGURE 7–32 Sign in or register for an Ubuntu One Account.
Source: Ubuntu by Canonical

Managing Users

Linux allows several users to use one computer, but each user should have a unique account. When you create a user account, Linux also creates a home directory within the **/home** directory, using the user's name for the directory name. This is the place in the Linux file system where an ordinary user account has full control over directories and files. The user can both save files and create new subdirectories. Users can further protect files from other users by changing the permissions on files and folders in their home directories.

The Linux Root Account

Each installation of Linux has a root account, an all-powerful account that is only used when absolutely necessary to do advanced tasks. Ubuntu Linux comes with this account disabled in such a way that no one can log in directly with the account, but there is a way to temporarily use it whenever you need it for tasks, such as creating or deleting users. However, you must be logged on with an administrator-type account to do this. You can do this from within a GUI or at a CLI in Linux. You will practice this when you create a user account in the next section.

Creating a User Account in a GUI

Step-by-Step 7.04 describes how to temporarily take on the power of the root account and add a new user in the Ubuntu GNOME GUI. If you are using a different GUI, you will need to locate the GUI tool for administering user accounts. In GNOME for Ubuntu, this is User options in Settings.

Step-by-Step 7.04

Add a New User Account in GNOME for Ubuntu

If you are adding no more than a few users to a desktop installation of Ubuntu, a GUI tool is the easiest to use. In this example, we use the User Settings in GNOME for Ubuntu.

To complete this exercise you will need:

- A computer running Ubuntu with the GNOME GUI.
- The username and password of an administrator-type account for this computer.

Step 1

Open *Settings* in the Ubuntu GNOME GUI and select *Users* to open the Users pane in the Settings Window. Select *Unlock* in the top right.

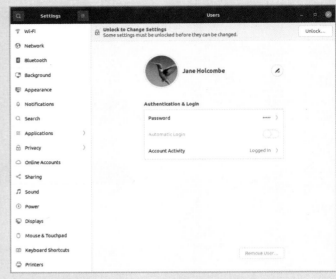

Source: Ubuntu by Canonical

Step 2

When prompted enter your password. The Users window now has a green *Add User* button.

Source: Ubuntu by Canonical

Step 3

Click *Add User.* This opens the Add User dialog box. Notice that you can choose to make this user a Standard user or an Administrator. If you wish to remain the sole administrator on the computer, be sure that Standard is selected, as shown.

Source: Ubuntu by Canonical

Step 4

Enter a full name for the new user. The system will generate a username from this full name. You may change it at this point, as we did, shortening the username. Leave the Password setting as is, so that the first time the user logs in they will need to create their own password. Then click *Add*.

Source: Ubuntu by Canonical

Step 5

The new user is added to the *Users* window. Notice that you can continue to create users one-by-one by clicking *Add User*. Once you close out of this window, when you return, it will be locked again, as it was before you unlocked it and created the user.

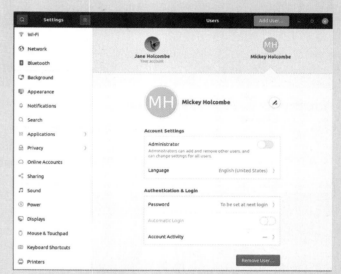

Step 6

The next time you log out or restart the computer, the sign-in screen will include the new user. When that user signs in, the dialog box will require that they create and confirm a password.

Source: Ubuntu by Canonical

Managing User Accounts with Shell Commands

When adding many users to either a Linux desktop or server, an advanced Linux administrator will add users by creating a special script that will create a list of users much faster than using a GUI. We believe that if you need to create only a few users on a few computers, it is easier to work through the GUI. However, if you need to manage users on a Linux computer without a GUI, you will need to know how to work with shell commands. Table 7–4 lists useful commands for managing users with shell commands.

> *Note:* When you enter a password in a Linux CLI, the characters you enter do not show on the line as you enter them. In fact nothing shows. The cursor does not move. Don't forget to press ENTER at the end of the password.

TABLE 7–4 Shell Commands for User Management

Command	Description
useradd	Adds a user to the system
userdel	Removes a user from the system
passwd	Changes a user's password
finger	Finds a username

When working from a Linux CLI, temporarily assign root account (also called Superuser) privileges to the currently logged-on user (who must be an administrator-type account) by preceding the command you wish to run with the sudo (Superuser Do) command. When you use **sudo** it will prompt you to enter your password (not the root password). Then, for the next five minutes (by default) you will be able to run **sudo** without requiring a password. After this time has passed, if you run **sudo** again, you will need to enter your password. The following includes examples of using the **sudo** command to run administrative commands, beginning with the installation of software to add a command to Linux.

The **finger** command allows you to look up user information, but some installations of Linux (including Ubuntu and Raspberry Pi) do not automatically install it. Therefore, if you want to experiment with the **finger** command, you must install the finger daemon. A daemon is a program that runs in background until it is activated by a command. Once installed, the **finger** daemon is activated by running the **finger** command. Install the **finger** daemon with this command: **sudo apt-get install finger**. This should result in the output shown in Figure 7-33.

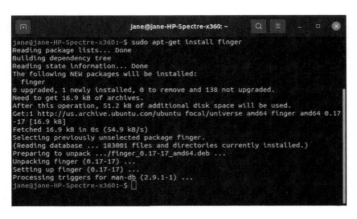

FIGURE 7–33 Installing the **finger** daemon.
Source: Ubuntu by Canonical

From the command shell, use the **useradd** command preceded by **sudo** to create a user. This command requires at least one parameter, the username you want to add. If you want to create a password for this user in the same operation, use the **useradd** option **-p** followed by the password. For instance, to create an account for Ashley Phoenix using the username of aphoenix with the password pa22w0rD, enter the command **sudo useradd -p pa22w0rD aphoenix.** To verify that it created the user account, use **finger aphoenix** (see Figure 7-34).

FIGURE 7–34 Create a user with the **useradd** command. Confirm its creation with the **finger** command.
Source: Ubuntu by Canonical

Changing User Passwords

Changing a user's password involves the command **passwd.** Entering **passwd** without any additional parameters will let you change your own password. Any user can change their own password, but only a user with root privileges can change the password on other user accounts. For example, enter **sudo passwd aphoenix** to change the password for the aphoenix account. The administrator doing this does not need to know the current password for the account before changing it to the new one, but can simply enter the new password twice. Note that, as always, Linux doesn't display passwords, but it does provide the useful feedback that the password was updated successfully.

try this!

Creating New Users

Practice creating user accounts for Ashley Phoenix (aphoenix), Jose Martinez (jmartinez), Kiesha Olson (kolson), and Beverly Chung (bchung). Try this:

1. Precede each command with **sudo.** Start by creating one user, Ashley Phoenix.
2. Enter the command **sudo useradd -p** *password* **aphoenix.** Provide a password in place of *password.*
3. Confirm that Linux added the account by entering the command **finger aphoenix.**
4. Now add accounts for the other three people.

Deleting Users

In any organization, employees leave. For security reasons, you should remove these accounts from the system shortly after the employee leaves. The command **userdel** allows you to remove a user from a Linux account, but you must run this command using **sudo.**

The syntax for userdel is similar to that for **passwd** and **useradd.** For example, you can remove the aphoenix account with the command **sudo userdel aphoenix.**

Recall that every user has a home directory in which to store their files. When you delete a user you do not remove this directory—you must remove these files manually. The long explanation for doing this is to delete the files contained in the user's home directory first; then delete the user's home directory itself. It will have the user's name. However, if a directory has subdirectories, you first need to switch into each subdirectory and delete all files in those as well. Once you have deleted the files, you change the directory to one level above and use the **rmdir** command. The syntax for **rmdir** is as follows: **rmdir** *directoryname*.

Now, we use the quicker method for deleting a directory and its contents. The **rmdir** command can only remove empty directories, but the **rm** command removes a file or a directory and its contents. Use the **rm** command with the -r (remove) and -f (force) type **rm -rf** *directory-or-file-name* to remove a directory and everything below it.

WARNING!

The **rm** command is very dangerous. Be very careful, and check your spelling before hitting the ENTER key.

File and Folder Permissions

To implement security for a file or folder, you must first understand Linux file and folder attributes. When you use the **-l** option with the **ls** command, you will see the attributes listed in a column of 10 characters on the far left. Each character is significant in both its placement (first, second, etc.) and in what each single character represents. The first character at the far left indicates whether the entry is a file (**-**), directory (**d**), or link (**l**). The next nine characters show the permissions on the file or folder for three different entities. Figure 7–35 shows a listing of a directory using the **-l** option to show all the attributes of nonhidden entries. To decode the permissions, use the following list:

r = read
w = write
x = execute
- = disabled

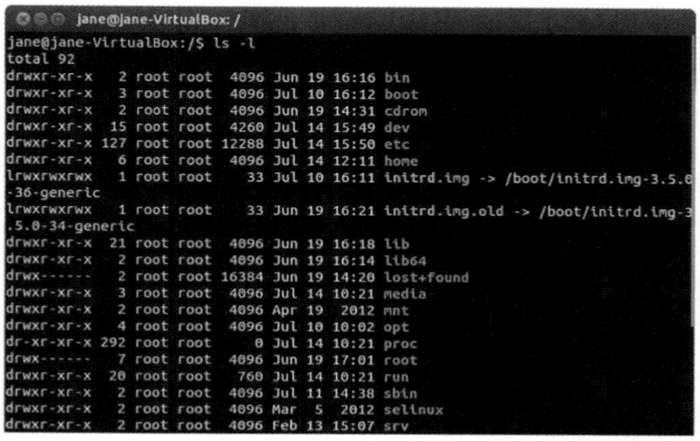

FIGURE 7–35 A sample listing showing attributes.
Source: Ubuntu by Canonical

Notice the set of permissions for the link named **initrd.img**. The attributes r (read), w (write), and x (execute) repeat three times. Linux is not repeating itself; it is listing permissions for three different individuals or groups. The first set of three permissions applies to the user who owns the files. Normally, if you create a file, then you are the owner.

The second set of three permissions applies to the group the user belongs to. We use groups to organize users, joining those with similar needs and access privileges. For example, a school may group all faculty members into a single group. This will allow instructors to create files that other instructors can read, but that students cannot read.

The third set of three permissions applies to all others. So the read, write, and execute permissions on initrd.img apply to the owner (root, in this case), the owner's group, and all others. Look at the permissions for the first entry, **bin**. The permissions on this directory are set so that the owner has read, write, and execute permissions, but the owner's group and all others have only read and execute permissions, meaning only the owner can change or delete the file.

The command to change a file's or a directory's permissions is **chmod** (called change mode). The **chmod** command requires two options. The first option is the access mode number. The second option is the file to change.

There is a small calculation to perform to determine the access mode number. In Figure 7–35, the link named **initrd.img** has access mode number 777, and the directory **bin** has access mode number 755. You can calculate this number by using the values in Table 7–5. Determine the permission for each user or group by adding the values together. Therefore, if the owner needs to read, write, and execute a file, the first number is 4 + 2 + 1 + 7. If the group is also to read, write, and execute the file, the second number is also 7. If a user has permission only to read and execute a file, the value is 4 + 1 + 5.

Note: To remember the order of the groups, think of the name UGO. UGO stands for User, Group, Other.

WARNING!

Always be sure the file owner has at least an access mode number of 6 for a file, which allows for read and write permissions. If the mode for the owner drops below 6, on some Linux installations any future access to this file is blocked. You should rarely have a file with permissions of 777 because it means that anyone can change the file.

TABLE 7–5 Access Mode Numbers

Permission	Value
Read	4
Write	2
Execute	1

Step-by-Step 7.05

Working with Directories

Imagine that a marketing firm that uses Linux as its primary OS hired you. You will work with a group of users. You need to create a series of directories that the group can see as well as a private directory that no one else but you can see. The following steps will allow you to create directories and set permissions on the directories. You will create these directories in your own home directory.

You will need the following:

- An account on a Linux computer with or without a GUI. If you log in to a GUI, open the terminal.
- Read access to the /etc directory.

Step 1

First create the directories needed to work. Use **mkdir** to create two directories, called wineProject and private, entering this command: **mkdir wineProject private.**

Step 2

Use the command **ls -l** to verify that Linux created the directories and to view the permissions assigned to the directories by default.

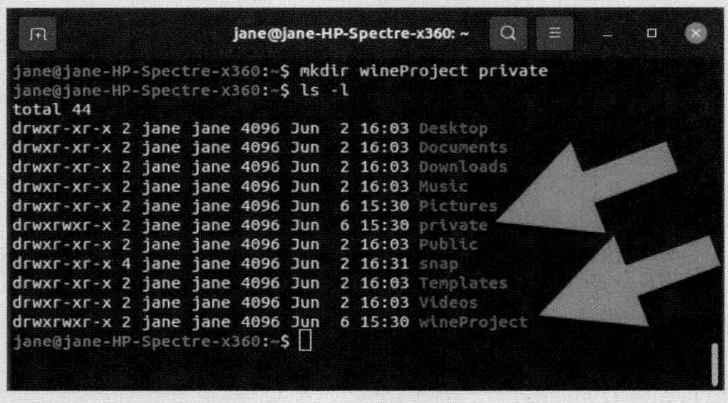

```
jane@jane-HP-Spectre-x360:~$ mkdir wineProject private
jane@jane-HP-Spectre-x360:~$ ls -l
total 44
drwxr-xr-x 2 jane jane 4096 Jun  2 16:03 Desktop
drwxr-xr-x 2 jane jane 4096 Jun  2 16:03 Documents
drwxr-xr-x 2 jane jane 4096 Jun  2 16:03 Downloads
drwxr-xr-x 2 jane jane 4096 Jun  2 16:03 Music
drwxr-xr-x 2 jane jane 4096 Jun  6 15:30 Pictures
drwxrwxr-x 2 jane jane 4096 Jun  6 15:30 private
drwxr-xr-x 2 jane jane 4096 Jun  2 16:03 Public
drwxr-xr-x 4 jane jane 4096 Jun  2 16:31 snap
drwxr-xr-x 2 jane jane 4096 Jun  2 16:03 Templates
drwxr-xr-x 2 jane jane 4096 Jun  2 16:03 Videos
drwxrwxr-x 2 jane jane 4096 Jun  6 15:30 wineProject
jane@jane-HP-Spectre-x360:~$ 
```

Source: Ubuntu by Canonical

Step 3

You are now the owner of these directories. Set the permissions on the private directory so that only you can access it, and on the wineProject directory give yourself read, write, and execute permissions, only read and write permissions to users in your group, and no permissions for others. To set the permissions appropriately enter these two commands: **chmod 700 private** and **chmod 760 wineProject.**

Step 4

Confirm the new permissions using **ls -l**.

Source: Ubuntu by Canonical

Step 5

Populate the wineProject directory by copying two files into it from your home directory, using the **cp** command. For instance, to copy the file named "letter" type **cp letter wineProject**. In this example, the two files copied are named instructor_letter.odt and busplan2025.odt.

Step 6

Change to the wineProject directory by entering the command **cd wineProject**. Confirm that the files are there and view the permissions on the files. They do not inherit the permissions of the directory. You will need to modify the permissions on the files if you wish permissions more restrictive than those assigned to the directory. However, any restrictive directory permissions will keep users from accessing the contents of the directory.

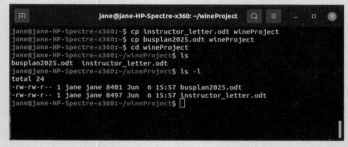

Source: Ubuntu by Canonical

Chapter 7 REVIEW

Chapter Summary

After reading this chapter and completing the Step-by-Step tutorials and try this! exercises, you should understand the following facts about Linux:

Linux Overview

- Linux, originally created by Linus Torvalds, is free, open-source software that is like UNIX in stability and function.
- Many versions of Linux exist for all types of computers, and it is used on many Web servers.
- Linux benefits include cost (it is free or inexpensively bundled), the ability to run on old hardware, speed, and stability.
- Drawbacks of Linux include lack of centralized support, choice of GUIs is confusing, limited software selection, limited hardware support, and complexity.

Linux on Your Desktop

- There are many sources of Linux distributions: just two are Ubuntu (www.ubuntu.com) and Raspberry Pi OS (rasberrypi.org).

- Software distributions are available with GUIs and a complete software bundle of apps.
- Download a distribution as an ISO file and create a bootable DVD or USB flash drive for installing. Popular distributions include a live image from which you can boot and run Linux without having to install it.
- Install Linux as a clean installation on a spare computer, in a dual boot configuration, or into a virtual machine.
- After installing Linux, initiate updates, as you would with Windows.

Exploring a Linux GUI

- If you boot into a live image of Ubuntu Linux, you are logged in as a Guest, but if you install Ubuntu Linux, you will log in with the username and password you provided during the installation.
- In a GUI, or at the CLI, Linux is case-sensitive.

- A Linux distribution with a GUI will have graphical objects similar, but not identical, to those in Windows and macOS.
- The Ubuntu Desktop bar displays at the top of the screen in the GNOME GUI.
- The Ubuntu GNOME desktop includes the Launcher, a bar on the left side of the screen.
- The Ubuntu GNOME desktop has a search tool for locating files and applications.
- Every user on a Linux computer has a home directory, the one place in Linux where a user has full control over files and directories without requiring elevated privileges.
- A path is a description that an operating system uses to identify the location of a file or directory. In Linux, you do not use a drive letter; you use a forward slash (/) character at the beginning of a path to represent the top level (root) of the file system.
- The path to a user's home directory is /home/username.
- The **bin** directory within each user's home directory contains many of the Linux commands.
- The **/etc** directory resides in the root of the file system and contains settings and configuration data for a Linux installation.
- It is far easier to browse the Linux directory structure in a GUI than in a Linux CLI.
- The GNOME GUI on Ubuntu includes an Update Manager utility for downloading and installing updates.
- Modify the GNOME Desktop using GUI tools similar to those in Windows and macOS.
- End a GNOME Ubuntu Linux session with the Shutdown command, which will log out the currently logged-on user and turn off the computer. You can also choose to restart or suspend.

Linux Command-Line Interface

- The Linux native user interface is the CLI, and many installations, especially on servers, only have a CLI.
- If you installed Linux with a GUI or are running it from a live image booted into a GUI, you can open a terminal window, where you can try the Linux CLI.
- You can combine short options and precede them with a single hyphen (-).
- Some options are followed by a parameter, such as a file name, directory, or device name that the command action targets.
- The command syntax in Linux follows this format: command -option parameter

- The **reset** command clears the screen and returns the $ prompt to the top.
- The **man** command gives you access to the Linux manual.
- Linux saves the history of the shell commands you enter for the duration of the session, and you can scroll through these commands while at the $ prompt.
- Linux has a command completion feature in which it tries to guess what you want to type next.
- The **date** command displays the day, date, and time. The **cal** command displays the calendar for the month with the current day highlighted.
- Linux gives very little feedback at the CLI, but it does issue error messages when you enter something wrong.
- Certain shell commands are useful when managing the file system. They are **cd, chmod, cp, ls, mkdir, more, pwd,** and **rm.**
- When you list the contents of a directory, the items are color coded to identify different types of entries.
- Linux allows you to use commands to navigate directories, using special symbols as shorthand for moving to directories that are relative to your current directory.
- The wildcard asterisk (*) is a symbol that replaces any character or string of characters, in a command parameter.
- Create a directory in Linux with the **mkdir** command, which requires at least one parameter: the name of the directory to create. Use multiple parameters to create multiple directories with one command.
- Use the **cp** command to copy files. It requires a parameter for the source file, and one for the target location and/or name of a file.

Securing a Linux Desktop

- If multiple people need to use one computer, each should have a unique account.
- When you create a Linux account, it also creates a home directory for the account using the user's name for the directory name.
- The **root account** is an all-powerful account that is only used when absolutely necessary to do advanced tasks. Linux comes with this account disabled in such a way that no one can log in directly with the account, but there is a way to temporarily use it.
- Create an account using a GUI tool or by using the **useradd** command at the CLI. The **userdel** command will delete specified users, **passwd** is used to change a user's password, and the **finger** daemon will confirm that a user has been created.
- Temporarily assign root account privileges to the currently logged-on user by preceding the command

you intend to run with the **sudo** command. **Sudo** will prompt you to enter your password (not the root password). Then, for the next five minutes (by default), you will be able to run **sudo** without requiring a password.

- The **rmdir** command can only delete empty directories, while the **rm** command will delete a directory and its contents. This is a very dangerous command.

- When you use the **ls** command with the **-l** option it lists files and directory details. The first 10 characters are attributes. The first character is the type of entry: file (**-**), directory (**d**), or link (**l**). The next nine characters show the permission on the file or folder for three different entities (owner, group, and others).

- The characters that represent permissions are **r** for read, **w** for write, **x** for execute, and **-** for disabled.

- The command to change a file's or a directory's permissions is **chmod**.

- Access mode values are 4 for read, 2 for write, and 1 for execute. These are added together to create the access mode number. If the owner, group, or other has read (4), write (2), and execute (1) permission to a file, the access mode number for that entity on that file is 7.

Key Terms List

$ prompt *(268)*

absolute path *(273)*

access mode number *(281)*

Apache HTTP Server *(249)*

BASH *(250)*

burn *(254)*

case-sensitive *(261)*

command completion *(271)*

command-line history *(270)*

daemon *(280)*

Dock *(252)*

distribution *(259)*

GNOME *(251)*

GNU *(248)*

home directory *(260)*

Hypertext Transfer Protocol (HTTP) *(249)*

Linux *(248)*

live image *(255)*

object code *(249)*

open-source software *(249)*

owner *(281)*

path *(260)*

Red Hat Enterprise Linux (RHEL) *(250)*

root account *(277)*

source code *(249)*

sudo *(280)*

switch users *(267)*

symbolic link *(261)*

terminal window *(268)*

Ubuntu *(250)*

Web *(249)*

wildcard *(274)*

World Wide Web (WWW) *(249)*

Key Terms Quiz

Use the Key Terms List to complete the sentences that follow. Not all terms will be used.

1. To access the CLI in the GNOME GUI, you open a _____.

2. When you create and save a file in Linux, you are the _____.

3. A/an _____ is a bootable image of the operating system that will run from bootable media without requiring that the OS be installed on the local computer.

4. When you create a user in Linux, the OS creates a _____ on disk for that user.

5. When you write digital data to an optical disc, you are said to _____ the disc.

6. A/an _____ is a program that runs in background until it is activated by a command.

7. The _____ organization was created in 1984 to develop a free UNIX-like operating system.

8. A/an _____ is a special symbol, such as an asterisk (*), that replaces a character or string of characters in a command parameter.

9. _____ is the uncompiled program statements that can be viewed and edited.

10. The most powerful account in Linux is the _____.

1. Linux is modeled on which operating system?
   a. Windows
   b. UNIX
   c. Chrome OS
   d. VMS
   e. CP/M

2. If the access mode number for the owner of a file or directory drops below this on some Linux installations, any future access to this file is blocked.
   a. 5
   b. 8
   c. 1
   d. 7
   e. 6

3. Who was the initial developer responsible for Linux?
   a. Ken Thompson
   b. Linus Torvalds
   c. Steve Jobs
   d. Dennis Ritchie
   e. Fred Linux

4. Which user has the most power and privileges in Linux?
   a. Administrator
   b. Admin
   c. Absolute
   d. Root
   e. Linus

5. What is the command a user invokes to log off when working at the Linux shell?
   a. **exit**
   b. **shutdown**
   c. **bye**
   d. **log off**
   e. **quit**

6. What is the Linux shell command to copy a file?
   a. **cpy**
   b. **rm**
   c. **mv**
   d. **copy**
   e. **cp**

7. What option for the **ls** command lists all files in a directory, including the hidden files?
   a. **-S**
   b. **-F**
   c. **-l**
   d. **-a**
   e. **-t**

8. What is the shell command (and option) to turn off a Linux computer immediately?
   a. **sudo down**
   b. **sudo shutdown now**
   c. **exit stat**
   d. **off now**
   e. **power off**

9. What feature preserves your open apps and data, but allows another user to log in to their own session on the same computer?
   a. Daemon
   b. Lock screen
   c. Live image
   d. Switch users
   e. Guest

10. What organization formed in 1988 to lobby for an "open" UNIX after AT&T formed a partnership with Sun Microsystems to develop a single proprietary UNIX?
    a. GNU
    b. Apache
    c. Ubuntu
    d. BASH
    e. OSF

11. Which shell command displays a text file one page (screenful) at a time?
    a. **mkdir**
    b. **more**
    c. **pwd**
    d. **cd**
    e. **rm**

12. What command can you use at the CLI to temporarily borrow the privileges of the most powerful account in a Linux system?
    a. **sudo**
    b. **root**
    c. **rm**
    d. **switch users**
    e. **chmod**

13. Which Linux command can you use to change file permissions?
    a. **cd**
    b. **ls**
    c. **more**
    d. **chmod**
    e. **rm**

14. Why would a Linux administrator use shell commands rather than a Linux GUI when creating many users at once?
    a. The shell commands are more intuitive.
    b. Linux GUIs are too cryptic.

c. Shell commands are faster.

d. The Linux CLI is more secure.

e. You cannot create users from a Linux GUI.

15. When in the terminal window, which command would return you to your Home directory, no matter what directory is current?

a. **cd ..**

b. **cd ~**

c. **cd /**

d. **chmod ~**

e. **cd.**

Essay Quiz

1. List and explain the reasons that Linux has not yet taken over the desktop OS market.

2. Discuss how your school or work could use Linux.

3. Discuss how open-source software can benefit an organization.

4. A charitable organization has asked you to set up its computer systems. The organization has a very limited budget. Describe how Linux can allow users to be productive while costing very little.

5. Explain the merits of **sudo,** as implemented in Ubuntu Linux.

Lab Projects

LAB PROJECT 7.1

The GNOME GUI includes workspaces, a feature not described in this chapter. Research the workspaces and write a few sentences describing the notion of workspaces in Linux.

LAB PROJECT 7.2

Research the open-source debate. Search online for recent articles on the open-source debate. Look at the arguments in favor of open source versus those in favor of proprietary operating systems. Determine which side of this debate you support and give your reasons.

LAB PROJECT 7.3

Research the Raspberry Pi and its value in education as well as its use by hobbyists. Describe scenarios for its use in education.

chapter

8 Chromebooks and Chrome OS

Source: Google LLC

Learning Outcomes

In this chapter, you will learn how to:

LO **8.1** Personalize Chrome OS on a Chromebook.

LO **8.2** Use the features of Chrome OS and Google.

LO **8.3** Install apps into Chrome OS.

LO **8.4** Manage files in Chrome OS.

LO **8.5** Configure security and Troubleshoot Chrome OS.

Chrome OS, the desktop operating system by Google, is based on their popular Chrome browser. Both the Chrome browser and Chrome OS have their roots in Linux. Earlier browsers were written in the 1990s to support how we experienced the Internet then, and they were added to as new uses and services evolved on the web. The Chrome browser, introduced in 2008, was created to support how we work on the web in the new millennium.

Similarly, the existing desktop operating systems have decades of added features and often contain code to support obsolete hardware and software. When Google announced their Google Chrome Operating System project in July of 2009, they described their vision: the new OS would be open source and "lightweight," meaning the software would be small and fast. They also promised "speed, simplicity, and security."

Competitors dismissed the idea of an operating system based on a browser. Google, perhaps more than other tech giants, appreciated that millions of people, especially millennials, spent most of their time on the Internet using a browser. So, they went ahead despite the naysayers. Now, the most popular vehicle for the Chrome OS, Chromebooks, have taken the education market by storm, squeezing out the more expensive Apple iPads, the longtime leader in the classroom. ✹

LO 8.1 | Getting Started with Chrome OS

What became known as the Chromium OS project moved quickly. Google released the Chrome OS source code, based on the Linux kernel, to developers late in 2009. By 2011, you could buy a Chromebook, a laptop with Chrome OS preinstalled. Chromebooks have also come a long way since their introduction. Several manufacturers produce them, and most of them come with a modified keyboard to support Chrome OS features. There are other types of computers that manufacturers sell with Chrome OS preinstalled, such as the Chromebox, a desktop computer, and the tiny Chromebit dongle that plugs into a TV or computer display's HDMI port. Add a wireless mouse and/or keyboard, and you have a Chrome OS computer. However, to keep things simple, and to focus primarily on the operating system, we will use the term Chromebook when discussing a computer manufactured to support Chrome OS. In this section, we begin with the out-of-box setup of a Chromebook. Your experience may be different, as both the Chrome OS and the hardware products that support it are quickly changing and often improving.

If you do not have a Google account, consider creating one before unpacking your Chromebook. This gives you some time and space to think of a unique username—a daunting task with so many Google accounts. Using any device with a browser, search on "create google account." From the search results select one that points to Google.com. In the Create your Google Account dialog, shown in Figure 8-1, enter a new username (a new gmail address) and create a new password. You will also be asked more questions in order to create a more secure method to sign in.

First Power Up and Sign In

As you prepare to unpack a new Chromebook, let's set expectations about what you will eventually see on the screen. If you are familiar with the publicity around the introduction of the Chromebook, you may expect what they promised at that time: "you can do everything on the web," "no programs," and "no desktop background (no rolling hills of green)." Chrome OS on Chromebooks has all those features that they promised would not be there. In addition to a full-screen mode, the Chrome browser can be resized, revealing a customizable desktop background. Oh, and you can choose to have that background be rolling hills of green or anything else you want. Chrome OS, while still a platform for working and storing your data completely in the cloud (if you wish), now allows you to access local files and devices. Many of us still have ties to the apps running on our desktops or mobile devices, as well as those devices sitting on our desks or local networks, and Chrome OS now supports apps created for the mobile Android OS. You might call this being "downward compatible."

Before unpacking and powering up a new Chromebook, ensure that you have Internet connectivity via a Wi-Fi network (unless your Chromebook can directly connect to a cellular network). You will need to know the network name and password. Then follow the manufacturer's instructions for unpacking, connecting to a power source, and turning on. After that, the steps are nearly identical across Chromebooks.

The Chromebook Keyboard

If this is your first experience with the Chromebook, note that it comes with a modified keyboard that includes different purposes for keys than those assigned to a standard PC keyboard. Perhaps the one that gets the most attention is the Everything button, located above the Shift key where a PC keyboard would have the Caps Lock key. This was formerly named Search. It still opens the Search box, which has been improved in recent editions with the ability to answer questions. This ability will expand; at this writing, it will answer math questions and provide local weather information. Another notable Chromebook key is the Refresh key, in the traditional F3 position. It refreshes a web page to update the content. The Immersive Mode key is in the F4 key position. Immersive Mode works in browsers to clean up the screen for better (immersive) reading. Also, the keyboard has a Switcher key (F5), which quickly displays all open windows on the desktop. Click or tap one to select it.

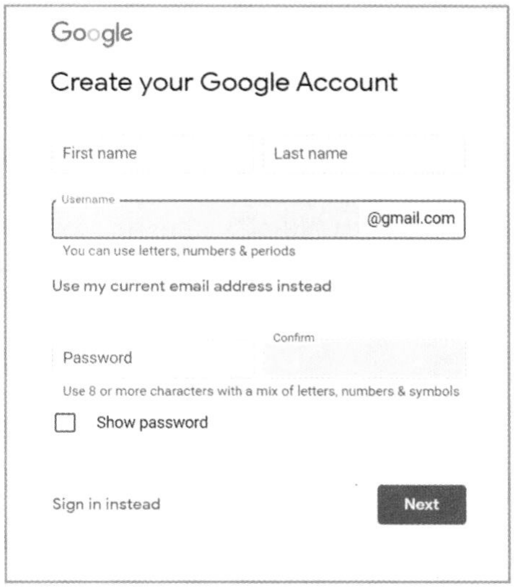

Initial Setup and Sign in with an Existing Google account

When you power up a new Chromebook, the first screen contains a Welcome window on a colorful background. Select your language, keyboard, and your Wi-Fi network and click the Continue button. Next review and accept the Terms of Use. After this, the Chrome OS updates, then it connects to Google, and the Google Sign-in prompt appears. If you already have a Google user account, a Google Account, sign in now by entering your username, selecting Next, and entering your password. If you do not have a Google account, you can create one at this point. The account you use for this initial sign in will be the owner of the Chromebook—the only account that can make significant changes to Chromebook settings.

FIGURE 8–1 Create a new Google account.
Source: Google LLC

Creating a Google Account

Google accounts are based on the Google Mail service with an email address ending in *@gmail.com*. A Google account gives you access to all the Google apps. Create a Google account from any device with a browser and Internet connection. Point your browser to **https://accounts.google.com/signup**. Figure 8–1 shows the Google dialog box for creating your own account. You will be required to enter your first and last names. These do not have to be unique because you will be giving Google other identifying information. What must be unique is your username, a name of at least 6 characters, but less than 30, that may include letters, numbers, and periods. When you enter your first and last names, Google will generate a possible username—one that is unique to Gmail. If you do not accept that username, you must create one that is unique.

Before you create a Google account be prepared with several options for your username. Google mail is so popular, the username you want to use may well be rejected because it belongs to someone else. Step-by-Step 8.01 will review some of the screens you will see during the initialization of your Chromebook.

Step-by-Step 8.01

Initializing a New Chromebook

In this hands-on exercise, walk through the enabling of Google features you encounter after the initial sign in to a Chromebook. Assuming you have already signed in, Step one is a Powerwash to return to "out of the box" state. Each screen in this exercise has a shutdown button on the far left that the author edited. If you use this, it will restart where you left off. To complete this exercise you will need:

- A Chromebook that has not been initialized or one you may reset with Chrome OS Powerwash to begin this process.

Step 1

If you are already signed on to a Chromebook and want to repeat the steps of initializing it, do the following: sign out, then press Shift+Ctrl+Alt+R to begin Powerwash. Respond to about a dozen screens, the last of which is the sign-in screen. After signing in, you will see this screen. Select Accept and continue.

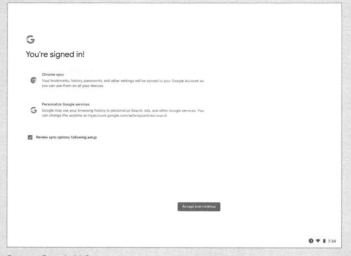

Source: Google LLC

Step 2

On this screen, you are asked to accept the Google Play apps and services. Google Play is used to install Android apps. Review the service. Select or deselect options, which may extend to multiple pages, and then click or tap the Accept button.

Source: Google LLC

Step 3

This page informs you that Google partners work with your Assistant to help you. This page varies if you have already set up Google Assistant on another device. Review the information and click or tap the I Agree or Continue button.

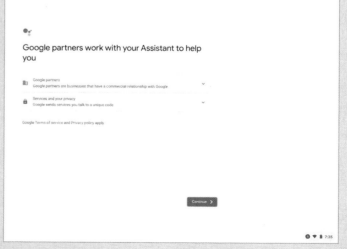

Source: Google LLC

Step 4

On this screen, you setup Voice Match for using the Google Assistant. Notice that you can Skip this and configure it later. You can teach the Assistant to recognize your voice. Click Next and learn that "Your Assistant is ready" and you can choose whether or not to allow Assistant to use information on screen to provide answers to you. On that screen (not shown here) click or tap the Done button.

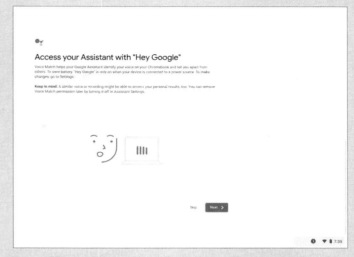

Source: Google LLC

Step 5

On this page you can connect your phone, if it is detected by Google. Here, an Android phone is detected and the user can choose connection features, based on the capabilities of the phone. Select either "No thanks" or "Accept & continue."

Source: Google LLC

Step 6

Click "Get started" to open the Chrome OS desktop on your Chromebook. If you chose to Review sync options following setup, Google Chrome Settings window will open on the desktop. Complete the sync settings or close this window.

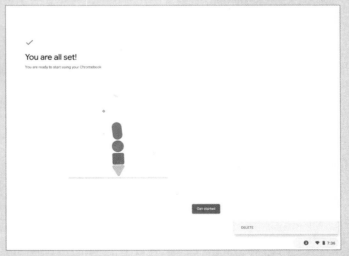

Source: Google LLC

First Look at the Chrome OS Desktop

After signing in to a new Chromebook, your first look at the desktop includes an invitation to take a tour (Figure 8–2). If you are new to the Chrome OS, take the time to do this. In this chapter, we will give a brief tour of some of the highlights to get you started in the Chrome OS, but there is much more to know about Chrome OS, and the services available to you. Google's tutorials are a great beginning.

The area along the bottom of the screen, as seen in Figure 8–2, is the shelf. Shortcuts to features and apps reside here. It acts much like the Windows taskbar. The shelf starts out with a few shortcuts, but as you use Chrome OS, you can choose to pin apps to the shelf to launch them directly from there. However, there are other ways to launch apps.

The shortcut on the far left of the shelf, resembling a white bull's eye, opens the Launcher, which scrolls up from the bottom of the screen like a vertical drawer behind the shelf. Click the Launcher shortcut to see shortcuts for recent apps, shown in Figure 8–3. The Launcher is more than an app launcher; it shows you all the apps installed into your Chrome OS. It has multiple pages, depending on how many apps are installed. A small button sits on the Launcher, just above the Search box, as shown in Figure 8–3. Click this to see more apps (Figure 8–4). Look carefully on the right side of this page of the Launcher to see the small buttons. The white one represents the current page of apps. Click on the second button to open another page. When you find an app you wish to launch, click on its shortcut in the launcher or on the shelf.

Any time you wish to learn more about your Chromebook and the Chrome OS, simply open the Explore app, a blue circle containing a rocket ship (Figure 8–5). On a new Chromebook, if the Explore app is not on the shelf, tap the Launcher and type "explore" in the Search box. This will open the app, and you can pin it to the shelf by right-clicking its shelf shortcut and selecting *pin*. It may depend on the screen size and resolution, but we found that once fourteen apps are pinned to the shelf, Chrome OS creates an additional row of shortcuts that only displays when you click an up arrow

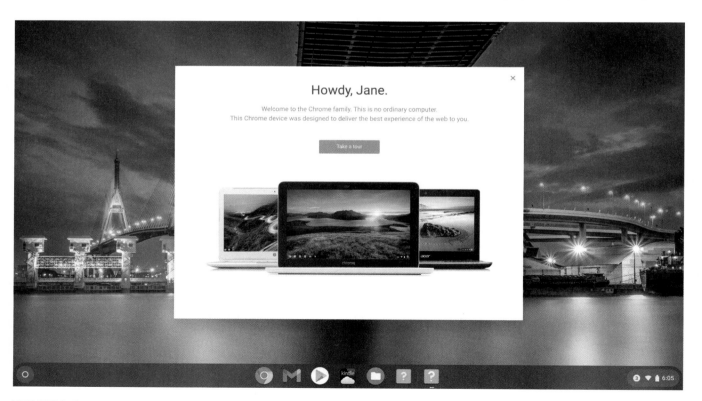

FIGURE 8–2 The Chrome OS desktop. Take a tour or open the Launcher from the button on the far left of the shelf.
Source: Google LLC

FIGURE 8–3 The Launcher showing recent apps. Click the button above the Search box to access more apps.
Source: Google LLC

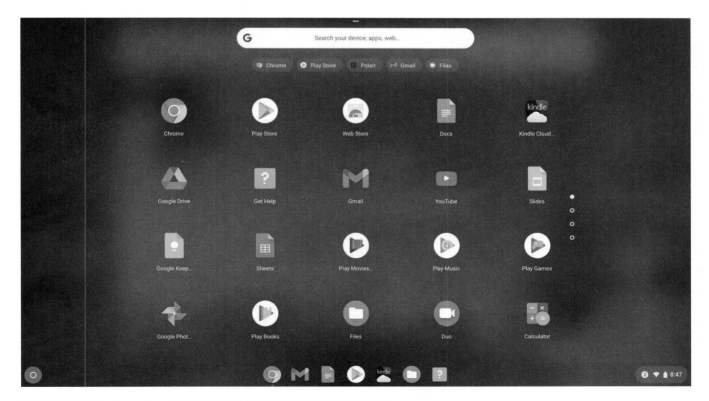

FIGURE 8–4 The Launcher displaying the first page of installed apps.
Source: Google LLC

FIGURE 8–5 Click or tap to open the Explore app.
Source: Google LLC

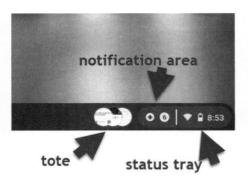

FIGURE 8–6 The tote, notification area, and system tray are on the far right of the shelf.
Source: Google LLC

added to the shelf between app shortcuts and the **tote**, a "holding space" for downloaded files and screenshots. To the right of the tote is a shaded area shared by two features: the **notification area**, containing shortcuts of apps that display notices, and the **status tray**. See Figure 8-6. Click anywhere in this shared area and a pop-up message box gives the current status of network connections, battery life, who is signed in, and more. A white box containing notices appears above the status information.

The Chrome OS Explore app is easy to use; the Welcome to your Chromebook page, shown in Figure 8-7, provides tutorials on using the desktop, managing your files, and how to work with other features.

try this!

Use *Explore* to Learn More about Chrome OS

Find out how to make your Chrome OS device the tool you need for work, school, or entertainment? Try this:

1. Locate the Explore shortcut and launch the app.
2. What do you need to know? Locate a category on the left that looks promising and click or tap it.
3. Continue to browse through categories, then, to exit Explore, use the close button (an "x") on the upper right of the window.

Options for Ending Your Chrome OS Session

OK, imagine you have been researching a paper or entertaining yourself with videos on your Chromebook. Now you need to go to lunch, exit from a commuter train, go out for the evening, or simply stop what you are doing for now. You can sign out, put Chrome OS (and your Chromebook) to sleep, lock the screen, switch users, or power off.

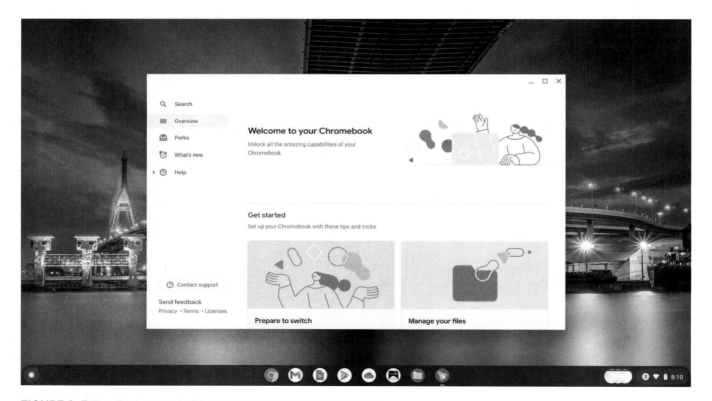

FIGURE 8–7 The Explore app's *Welcome to your Chromebook* page.
Source: Google LLC

Sign Out from Chrome OS

To sign out of Chrome OS, click or tap the Status bar and then in the pop-up (Figure 8–7) select *Sign out.* The Chrome OS ends your session and returns to the sign-in screen with the sign-in box in the center of the screen and a few other options along the bottom. From the sign-in screen, you can choose to browse as a Guest, add a user, shut down, or sign in with another Google account. You can also sign out of Chrome OS quickly using the Ctrl+Search+Q keyboard shortcut twice.

Put a Chromebook to Sleep

Put your Chromebook to sleep by simply closing the lid. That's it. At present, we are not aware of shortcut keys for this action. Sleep keeps your open apps and windows intact, keeps you signed in, and simply puts the computer into low power mode. If you are on battery power, do not leave it in sleep for a long time (over-night, days) or you could draw down the battery. Then you will not be able to bring it back up until you plug it in to power. To resume, simply open the lid and Chrome resumes with all your open apps and windows.

Lock the Screen

To lock the screen, click or tap the Status bar. Then, in the pop-up, select the Lock, as shown in Figure 8–8. The keyboard shortcut for locking the screen is Search+L. Locking the screen does not sign you out and leaves everything open, behind the sign-in screen. You are locked out until you sign in.

Switch Users

If you have added another Google Account to your device, you may choose to switch users to give the other user time on the Chromebook. To do this, sign out and click *Sign in another user.* Later we will look at how to add a user to your Chromebook.

Power off Your Device

To power off your Chromebook, click or tap the Status bar. Then, in the pop-up, select the Power button, to the right of Sign out in Figure 8–8. You can also do this by holding the physical power button on the device until it completely powers down to a black screen.

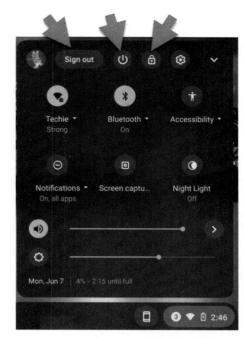

FIGURE 8–8 Sign Out, Power Off, or Lock the Screen.
Source: Google LLC

LO 8.2 | Getting Acquainted with Chrome OS and Google Features

In this section, learn how to find the Chrome OS version number, personalize the Chrome OS desktop, and prepare to print from Chrome OS.

Finding the Chrome OS Version Number

An important feature of Chrome OS is its automatic update. You might be thinking that we claimed this was true of all the other operating systems discussed so far, and you would be correct. Maybe the difference is that, for the most part, you don't know that Chrome OS is updating and, more importantly, you don't need to care what version is installed, but sometimes you want to know the version number of Chrome OS installed on your device. Perhaps someone on your favorite social media site boasted of doing things in the Chrome OS, but you can't seem to do those things.

What comes to mind is printing to the printer sitting on your desk. It was more challenging in earlier versions of the OS but has greatly improved. Some

try this!

Practice Leaving Your Chromebook Session

Experiment with different ways to leave and return to your Chrome OS desktop. Try this:

1. Sign out and sign in again. First sign out from the Status menu, sign back in and then sign out using the keyboard shortcut Search+Q (twice).
2. Log back in. Put the Chromebook to sleep by closing the lid. Wait for a few minutes, and then open the lid again and resume working.
3. Lock the screen by selecting the Lock from the Status menu. Sign back in.
4. Turn off your Chromebook.

FIGURE 8–9 The *Settings* button.
Source: Google LLC

users experienced it ahead of others because they participated in a preview program, but others may not have had that ability simply because their Chrome OS was a few days late in updating, compared to the computers of your social media friends.

To see the version of Chrome OS on your Chromebook, click or tap the Status bar and then in the pop-up (Figure 8-9) select Settings. In the sidebar of the Settings windows (Figure 8-10), scroll down and select About Chrome OS. In the contents pane the About information displays. Notice the version of Chrome OS on your computer. You can also check for updates, but Chrome is very good about keeping you up to date and notifying you if the Chromebook needs a restart to finish an update.

Personalizing the Desktop

Personalize Chrome OS by changing shelf settings, selecting wallpaper or a solid background.

Shelf Settings

Personalize the shelf of your Chrome OS desktop. The quickest way to access these settings is to right-click on an empty area of the desktop. This opens the context menu, shown in Figure 8-11. In this example, moving the pointer to Shelf position opened choices for that option. As with the Windows taskbar, you can move the shelf to either side or back to the default position on the bottom of the screen. Another choice allows you to autohide the shelf so that it is hidden until you move your cursor to its position, then it opens.

Wallpaper

The desktop setting with the most visual impact is *Set wallpaper.* As you can see in Figure 8-12, set wallpaper offers a variety of background wallpaper pictures in categories. You can also select a solid for the background or you can create a custom wallpaper from a file of your choice by selecting My Images at the bottom of the sidebar and browsing for one of your pictures.

FIGURE 8–10 The Chrome OS version information.
Source: Google LLC

More Chrome OS Settings

Beyond the Wallpaper settings, personalize Chrome OS with the Personalization settings. To do that, select the Settings button from the Status pop-up box (Figure 8-9). This opens the Settings window. Scroll down in the sidebar and select Personalization (Figure 8–13). Here you will see the *Wallpaper* option that was also available from the desktop context menu. Two other options are *Change device account image* and *Screensaver*. For some hands-on with *Personalization*, follow the instructions in the try this!

FIGURE 8–11 The *Shelf position* settings.
Source: Google LLC

Printing in Chrome OS

For several years printer manufacturers did not create Chrome OS drivers for their printers. Therefore, previous versions of Chrome OS printed via Google Cloud Print, a Google Cloud service that was retired on December 31, 2020. With the availability of Chrome OS printer drivers, Chrome OS now will print to a printer connected via USB cable or Wi-Fi. Bluetooth printing may be added by the time you read this. Step-by-Step 8.02 will guide you through configuring your Chromebook to connect to a Wi-Fi printer.

You may also directly connect your printer and Chromebook via USB, provided you have the correct connectors of the cable.

try this!

Use Personalization Settings in Chrome OS

Do you want to change the account image and screen saver? Try this:

1. In Chrome OS Settings, Personalization, select *Change device account image*.
2. A page of dozens of images display. Select a new image to represent your account on the Chromebook's sign-in screen. The default image is your first initial.
3. Click or tap the Status tray to open the Status menu and notice that your account image has changed.
4. Select Screen saver and set options for the Screen saver background and select Fahrenheit or Celsius for the weather information. Close Settings.

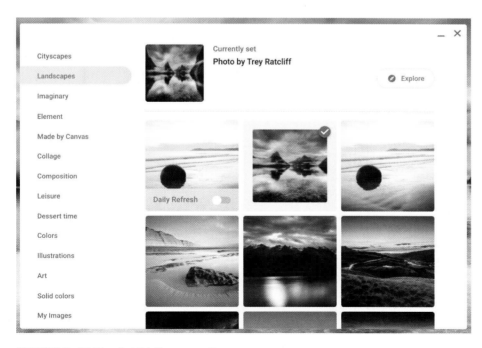

FIGURE 8–12 The *Set Wallpaper* options.
Source: Google LLC

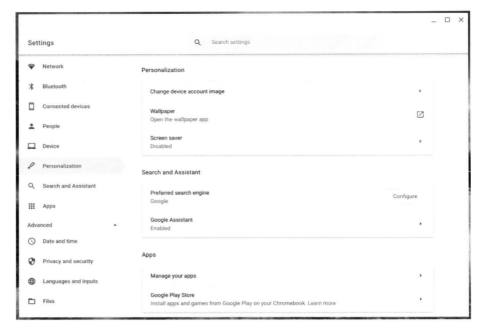

FIGURE 8–13 The *Personalization* category in Settings.
Source: Google LLC

Step-by-Step 8.02

Preparing to Print in Chrome OS

In this hands-on exercise, you will connect your printer and Chromebook to the same Wi-Fi network. To complete this exercise, you will need:

- A Chromebook that is up-to-date and connected to your Wi-Fi network.
- A printer connected to the same Wi-Fi network.

Step 1

Turn on your printer. Turn on your Chromebook and sign in.

Step 2

From the Status menu open Settings; from the Settings sidebar select Advanced. A list of advanced settings opens in the sidebar. Scroll down and select *Print and scan*.

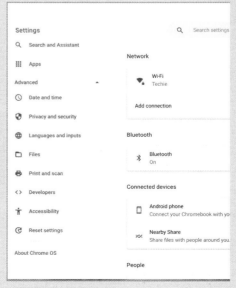

Source: Google LLC

Step 3

In the contents window under *Print and scan* select *Printers*.

Source: Google LLC

Step 4

If your printer name is displayed under *Your saved printers*, open an app (even the Chrome browser) and print to this printer to test it.

Source: Google LLC

Step 5

If your printer is not listed under *Your saved printers*, click or tap the Add printer button on the right. Follow the instructions for installing your printer. When you are finished close the open windows.

LO 8.3 | Installing Extensions and Apps

While all operating systems evolve and gain new features over time, Chrome OS seems to have evolved in leaps and bounds in its short lifetime, especially regarding the apps it supports. At first both the apps (web apps) and data resided in the Google cloud. A

web app runs from a website within the Chrome browser and is not installed into the operating system. In contrast, a browser extension adds features to the Chrome browser and is available while accessing various websites. Shop for web apps and browser extensions at the Google Web Store. This tethering to Google continues, but the OS has been beefed up to support more and more types of apps, including Linux apps.

In this section, we first look at adding browser extensions and web apps. Then we will look at installing such standard productivity tools as Microsoft Office. Finally, check out how Android apps are installed and run in Chrome OS.

Chrome Browser Extensions and Web Apps

Strictly speaking, a **browser extension** is not an app, but an add-on that adds features to the Chrome browser. Examples of extensions are password managers for storing your passwords and many aids to better and more secure browsing. Acquire Chrome extensions through the Chrome Web Store. Some extensions install a button on the far right of the Chrome browser toolbar.

To see what extensions are installed into your Chrome browser (in Chrome OS or in other operating systems), open the Chrome menu button on the far right of the toolbar, point to *More Tools,* in the drop-down menu select *Extensions.* The Chrome browser window will display all the installed extensions and web apps. as shown in Figure 8–14.

A web app runs within a browser, most of its program code is run from a website, and it is also acquired through the Web Store. A web app will be listed in the Launcher and launched as an app, albeit within a Chrome browser window.

You cannot add extensions or web apps to the Chrome browser using a school or business Google account. Those accounts and the systems on which they run are administered centrally by someone in those organizations, and individual users are limited in what they can change on their school or work computers. Step-by-Step 8.03 walks through the installation procedure for Chrome Browser Extensions apps.

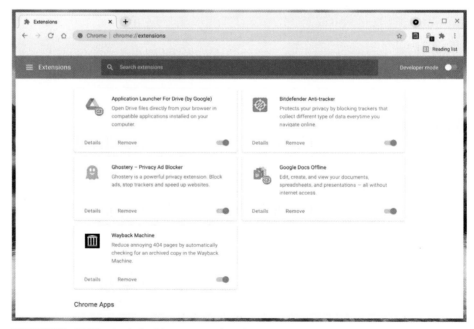

FIGURE 8–14 The installed browser extensions.
Source: Google LLC

Step-by-Step 8.03

Adding an Extension to the Chrome Browser

In this hands-on exercise, you will browse through the Google Web store and select an extension for installation into your Chrome browser. You cannot add extensions or web apps to the Chrome browser using a school or business Google account. To complete this exercise, you will need the following:

- A Chromebook or other device with the Chrome OS installed.
- You must be logged on to the Chromebook with your personal Google account.

Step 1

Locate the Web Store icon on the Chrome OS shelf or from the Launcher, and then click or tap it.

Source: Google LLC

Step 2

In the Web Store window, select Extensions in the sidebar, the right pane displays extension choices. From here, you can search or scroll down to browse for extensions.

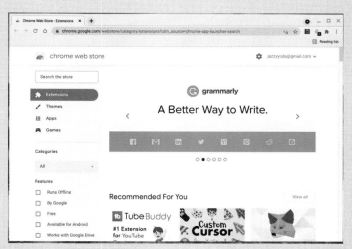

Source: Google LLC

Select an extension and read the information provided. Here we are looking at Earth View from Google Earth. Notice the tabs below the middle of the page labeled Overview, Privacy practices, Reviews, Support, and Related. We find the reviews very helpful—the more numerous the reviews the more we trust them. Once you decide on an extension, click the Add to Chrome button.

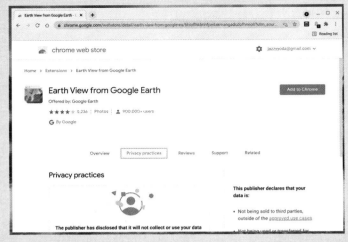

Source: Google LLC

Before Chrome installs the extension, it asks you to confirm that you want it and may give you a warning or other information about the extension. For instance, this is the dialog box that displayed for Earth View. Clicking the *Add extension* button installed Earth View.

Source: Google LLC

A confirmation appears that the extension was added to Chrome. Close this message box to return to Chrome.

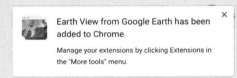

Source: Google LLC

In the Chrome browser, click the puzzle-shaped Extensions icon on the right. This opens the list of installed extensions. The gear icon on the bottom opens the Settings for managing extensions. Close the extension drop down.

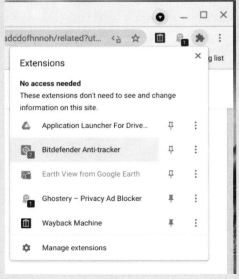

Source: Google LLC

Select and install Chrome web apps from the Web Store. Browse for them in the Apps category, as shown in Figure 8-15. Installed web apps are listed in the Launcher, and you can pin a web app's shortcut to the Shelf. Figure 8-16 shows the initial page of the Zoom app.

You can synchronize your apps and extensions across all devices on which you are signed-in. Chrome allows you to select just which type of data you want to sync, or you can choose to sync all data. Figure 8-17 shows a list of data types you can sync. Scroll down through this list to see all the data types.

try this!

Sync Apps and Extensions
You can sync your data across all your devices, selecting what type of data you want to sync. Try this:

1. Open the Status bar and select the Settings button.
2. In the People category, click or tap *Sync and Google service*. Then expand *Manage what you sync*.
3. Continue to browse through categories, then exit Settings.

Android Apps on Chrome OS

The type of app that runs on an Android phone is an **Android app**. There are thousands of Android apps available, and if you have both an Android phone and a device running Chrome OS (a close relative of Android), you want the same apps on both devices.

Installing Android Apps into Chrome OS

Android operating system and the apps that run on it use a small native screen size, so the transition from mobile devices to a different (but related) OS on a much larger screen was a challenge to Chrome OS developers, and perhaps to the Android app developers, but they succeeded. Beginning with Chrome OS version 53, you can install and run your favorite Android apps on your Chromebook. Let's say you use what you learned earlier about finding the version number of your Chrome OS, and you confirm

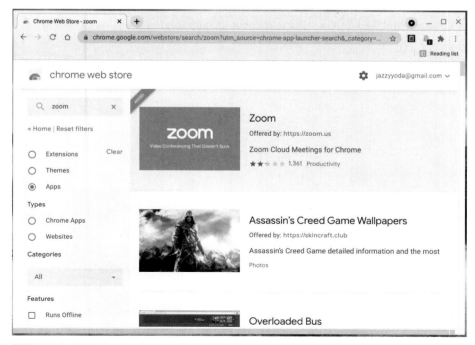

FIGURE 8–15 Select web apps from the web store.
Source: Google LLC

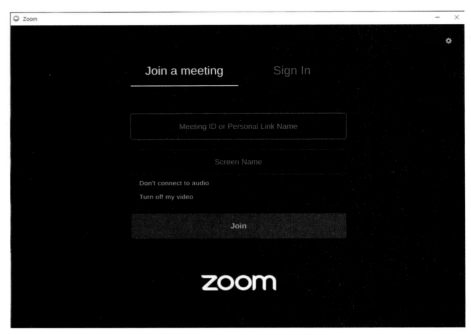

FIGURE 8–16 Zoom installed as a web app.
Source: Google LLC

that you have a Chrome OS version 53 or newer. So, you're all set and ready to install Android apps. Well, not quite.

Android apps are installed from the Google Play store. Look for the Play Store shortcut (Figure 8-18) on the Launcher. Then open the Play Store app (Figure 8-19) from the Launcher and browse for the apps you want and need for your Chromebook.

As you install and experiment with Android apps on your Chromebook, use the window maximize, minimize, and restore buttons that switch your window from full screen to minimized to a shortcut on the shelf, to a return to smartphone screen. There are presently some apps that only work in smartphone size. Sure, you can click the maximize button and the window will expand, but the app stays in smart screen mode.

FIGURE 8–17 Scroll down through the list of data types for syncing.
Source: Google LLC

FIGURE 8–18 Launch Play Store.
Source: Google LLC

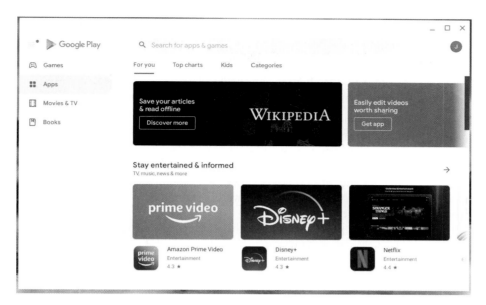

FIGURE 8–19 The Google Play Store app.
Source: Google LLC

As long-time users of Microsoft Office, we are pleased that the app we need the most, Word, works in both full screen and smartphone screen sizes. And full screen is resizable. Although it does not have all the advanced editing features that we like to use, it is certainly handy. Things are improving rapidly for many Android apps on Chromebooks, but some are not yet available, and some only let you view files, not edit them.

LO 8.4 | File Management in Chrome OS

In this section, we will explore file management in Chrome OS on the Chromebook. The Chrome OS Files app is your main tool for working with files, whether they are local to your OS device or in the cloud. Look on the Launcher or the Shelf for the round shortcut with a turquoise folder against a blue background (Figure 8–20).

Getting Started with the Files App

Because you sign in with a Google account, Google Drive appears in your Files app, as shown in Figure 8–21, as do other Cloud storage services. The Chrome OS Files app file management program supports several locations for files including:

- Local files on a Chrome OS device.
- Files on directly connected storage devices:
  - USB-connected hard drives and flash drives
  - USB-connected CD and DVD drives (read-only).
- Files in your Google Drive.
- Files stored in another cloud storage service, such as Microsoft OneDrive, Box, and Dropbox.

Location is just one of your concerns about your data files. The file format is very important, and Chrome OS supports many files formats including:

- Microsoft Office Files with these filename extensions: doc, docx, xls, xlsx, ppt (read-only), and pptx (read-only).
- Popular Media Files with these filename extensions: 3gp, avi, mov, mp4, m4a, mp3, mkv, ogv, ogg, oga, webm, and wav.

Note: Explore Google Drive and other cloud storage services in Chapter 11.

FIGURE 8–20 Launch the Files app.
Source: Google LLC

- Photos and other image files with these filename extensions: bmp, gif, jpg, jpeg, png, and webp.
- Compressed files with **zip** or **rar** filename extensions.
- Plain text files with the txt extension can be viewed but not edited.
- Portable document files with the pdf extension can be viewed but not edited.

The Files app is your Chrome OS tool for accessing, moving, copying, deleting, and otherwise managing files. Figure 8–21 shows the Files app opened and focused on the My Files folder. Notice that the sidebar includes two cloud storage services, Google Drive and OneDrive. At the very bottom, a USB drive named "data" is recognized by the Files app. Files can be easily copied among the locations in My Files, and the USB drive. In Chapter 11, practice working with files in various cloud storage services from your devices.

The Files app also previews files, as shown in Figure 8–22 in Thumbnail view in which the files appear as recognizable images. In some cases, the file type is recognized, but a preview is not shown. Other apps are required for opening a file for better viewing or for editing. By default, when you double-click (or double-tap) one of these files, Google will open the appropriate Google app for that file format. Some file types can only be viewed, not edited. This is also referred to as read-only. Many formats, such as most Microsoft Office file types, can be edited with Google apps or with other apps, including Microsoft apps, if installed. Yet, others can be launched, as in the case of media (video and sound) files. Again, these actions are done with the appropriate Google app for the file format.

Working Offline in Chrome OS

What happens when you do not have an Internet connection, but have a deadline and need to work offline on data normally stored in the cloud? Major Cloud providers saw this problem years ago, and each has a solution (usually an app) for that. In Google's

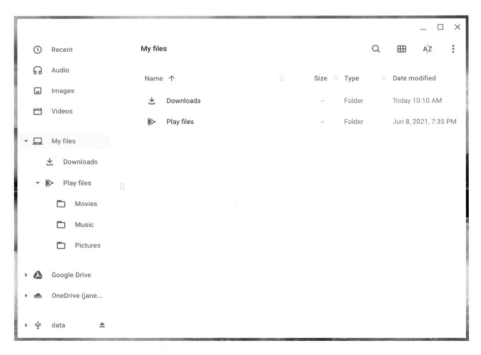

FIGURE 8–21 Manage local and cloud-based files in the Files app.
Source: Google LLC

FIGURE 8–22 The Files app showing previews of local files in the Research folder created by the user.
Sources: Google LLC

case, they have several offline file viewers so that you can view PDFs and play video or MP3 files offline, but the data must be downloaded beforehand. So, don't wait until you are confronted with that deadline-without-connectivity problem. Prepare.

Add an Extension for Google Drive

Google Docs Offline is the extension you need to work offline with your Google apps. You may already have this extension. To see if it is already installed, open Chrome and click on the *Extensions* icon on the far right. This opens the Extensions drop-down menu. Select *Manage Extensions*. The Chrome browser window will display all the installed extensions. If it is not installed, open the Web store and search on *google docs offline extension*. Then install the extension.

Working on Files Offline

With the Google Docs Offline extension installed, you are ready to turn on syncing between your Google Drive data and your local computer. To do that open Google Drive from the Launcher, which opens your Google Drive folders in a Chrome window. The first time you open Google Drive on your Chromebook, if sync is already turned on, you may see a message display, as shown in Figure 8-23. If so, simply close that message box. If this message does not display, and you want to ensure sync is turned on, then, look for the Settings button (a gear icon) located on the right of the Google Drive (not Chrome browser) button bar near the Help button (a question mark). Select the Settings button, and select Settings (again) from the drop-down menu. In the Offline category, click or tap the check box (if empty) to add a check mark and turn on Syncing of your Google Drive data to the local device. Now Google will automatically save your most recent files to your device for offline. Now you are ready to work with your data offline, as if you were still connected. When your device reconnects to the Internet, your offline data will be synced with Google Drive.

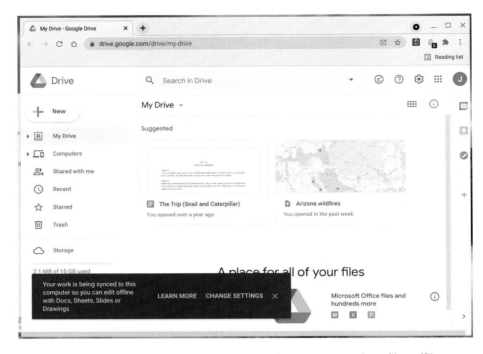

FIGURE 8–23 Be sure that sync is turned on so that you can work on files offline.
Sources: Google LLC

LO 8.5 | Configure Security and Troubleshoot Chrome OS

Troubleshooting and security go hand in hand because a computer that is behaving strangely could have malware installed. Also, Chrome OS is dependent on your Google Account. To keep your data safe when working in Chrome OS, secure your Google Account and make modifications to the Privacy and Security settings on your Chrome OS computer. Then, learn to use the Chrome OS Diagnostics tool.

Securing Your Google Account

The Google My Account home page is where you will find settings to make your Google account more secure, change your privacy settings, and manage your account preference.

Step-by-Step 8.04 explores security and privacy settings for your Google account. Among the tasks we will explore is Security Checkup, which enumerates devices from which you have logged in and used Google services, recent security activity, and whether or not you have 2-Step Verification turned on. Then check your settings for *Find Your Phone,* which can be enabled on any mobile device running Android or Apple iOS. Google already knows any device on which you have used your Google account. However, Google does not turn on the Find Your Phone service for each device; you get to decide if you want to do that.

The last task in Step-by-Step 8.04 is turning on **2-Step Verification**. It is Google's version of multi-step verification to add additional complexity to signing in beyond entering the correct password. When you enable 2-Step Verification, you give the online service a method of sending a one-time verification code back to you via a predefined method: email, voice message, or text message. The voice and text message options are also referred to as **Over the Phone (OTP)**. The default is Google Prompts; when you enter a password on another device, Google sends a notification to every phone to which you are signed in. Tap the notification and accept or reject the sign-in with a *Yes* or *No*. All of these require that you have a way of responding or retrieving the code at the time you are attempting to sign in. You can also have Google generate a list of Backup codes that you save to a file and/or print out and keep handy for those times when you cannot be directly verified, such as when you are traveling and need to sign in but do not have cellular service. There are even more options that you can explore in your Google Account's security settings.

Step-by-Step 8.04

Exploring Google Account Security and Privacy Settings

In this hands-on exercise, browse through your Google Account settings and determine the settings that will keep you more secure while allowing you to work within the Google environment. The exercise can be completed on any device that allows you to connect to Google and manage

your Account settings. We recommend the Chrome browser. To complete this exercise you will need:

- An Internet-connected device with a browser.
- Your personal Google account.

Step 1

From your browser, sign in to Google unless you are already signed in. In myaccount.google.com locate the Home tab for your Google Account.

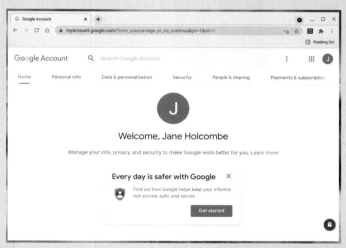

Source: Google LLC

Step 2

Scroll down and note the status of the four areas. In this example, the exclamation point shows that security issues were found. If you have a similar experience, click on it and follow the instructions to resolve the issue.

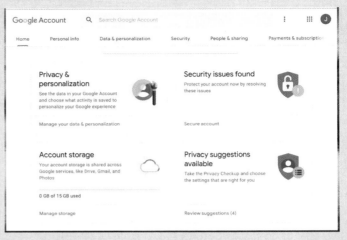

Source: Google LLC

Step 3

In the example, the security issue was an old Android device that was not removed from the account when the author discarded it months in the past. Clicking on Remove solved that problem. Make note of the number of signed-in devices at the bottom of your Security Checkup box.

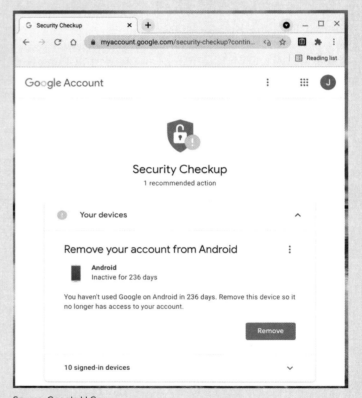

Source: Google LLC

Still in Security Checkup, scroll down. All areas are important for security. Be sure to enable 2-Step Verification, if you have not already. Once all areas show a white checkmark in a green circle, close out or continue to your Google Account.

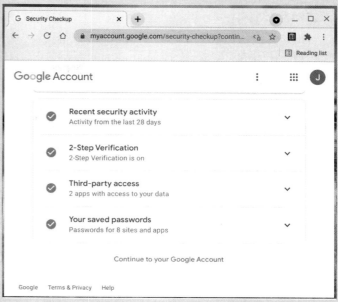

Source: Google LLC

Securing Chrome OS

In addition to securing your Google account, secure Chrome OS through the *Security and Privacy* settings, located in the Chrome OS Settings, which are separate from your Google Account settings.

Security and Privacy

Notice that the Chrome OS Settings app is a separate window (Figure 8–24), not to be confused with the Chrome browser settings. After taking care of your Google account settings via the Chrome browser, the Chrome OS *Security and Privacy* settings are

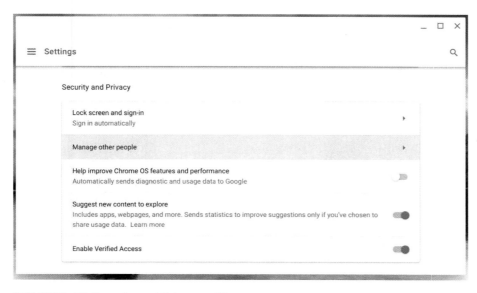

FIGURE 8–24 *Security and Privacy* settings.
Source: Google LLC

try this!

Explore Chrome OS Security and Privacy Settings

Check your Chrome OS Security and Privacy settings. Try this:

1. Open Chrome OS Settings from the Status menu.
2. Locate and open *Security and Privacy*.
3. Click or tap *Lock screen and sign-in*. Enter your password when prompted. Then decide if you want to lock the screen when waking from sleep.
4. Now select how to unlock the screen: *Password only* or *PIN or password*.
5. When finished, close the Settings window.

simple. They include settings for lock screen and sign-in; settings for allowing, or not allowing others to access your Chromebook, and three other sets of settings.

If you make changes to Security and Privacy settings, you are required to confirm your password, as shown in Figure 8–25. An important setting is *Lock screen and sign-in*, especially if you are using your Chromebook at school, work, or other public venue.

Troubleshooting and Repair

There are two important tools to use for troubleshooting and repair. They are the Diagnostics app and Powerwash.

The Diagnostics app is new and may not show in the Launcher pages. So, the first time you run it, you may need to tap the Everything Button to search for it. Once you locate it, launch it. Figure 8–26 shows the Diagnostics tool. The three areas it tests are battery, CPU, and memory. While these are all hardware measurements, they may give you clues to a problem beyond the hardware. For instance, you may have apps that are using more than their share of these resources.

Check the Battery health, shown as a percentage. As a battery ages, this percentage will go down, but a sudden drop may mean you have a problem with the battery and may need to have the Chromebook serviced. The CPU test may say more about the number and behavior of the apps you are running. The amount of memory also is about the number of programs you are running. Whatever you test, save the session log by selecting that option at the bottom of the window. You can send this log to a support person who may be able to help you resolve the problem.

When all else fails, and you are unhappy with the performance of your Chromebook, consider Powerwash. This option is available in Chrome OS Settings, but you need to expand Advanced, as shown in Figure 8–27. Scroll down in the Advanced settings and select *Reset settings.* This screen begs the question: Will there be more than one *Reset settings* option in the figure? For now, the only option is Powerwash, which

FIGURE 8–25 Confirm your password before making changes to *Security and Privacy* settings.
Source: Google LLC

FIGURE 8–26 The Chromebook Diagnostics app.
Source: Google LLC

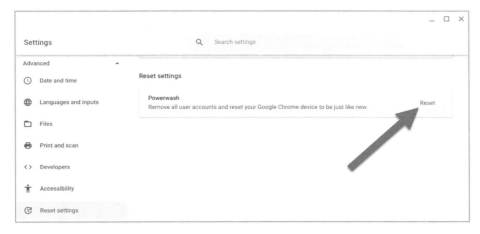

FIGURE 8–27 Reset a computer with Powerwash.
Source: Google LLC

we have used for several years. This is a great way to start over fresh for whatever reason. When Jane donated two Chromebooks to students in 2020, she simply did a Powerwash before packing them up. She also did Powerwash three time while writing this chapter to make sure she had not added something that distracted from the current topic. If Chromebooks are used in a class lab, Powerwash might be used daily. If the reason for doing this is to solve a slow computer, as you add things back in, you might discover what was causing the problem.

Chapter 8 REVIEW

Chapter Summary

After reading this chapter and completing the exercises, you should understand the following facts about the Chrome OS.

Getting Started with Chrome OS

- The Chrome OS operating system is based on the Chrome web browser.
- Chrome OS comes preinstalled on computers, such as the Chromebook, Chromebox, and Chromebit.
- Chrome OS supports Android mobile apps.
- Be ready to use or create a Google Account during the first power-on of a Chromebook. This first account is the owner of that device and the only person who can make significant changes to the Chromebook settings.
- The Explore app replaces the Help app. Search for answers and learn about features.
- Desktop objects include the Launcher, shelf, notification area, tote, status tray, and more.
- To end a Chrome OS session sign out, put the device to sleep, lock the screen, switch user, or power off the device.

Getting Acquainted with Chrome OS

- Find the Chrome OS version number in the About Chrome OS option on the main Settings menu of the devices Settings.
- Personalize the Chrome OS desktop by changing the wallpaper or background settings.
- The Personalization category in Chrome OS Settings gives more options, including browser themes and other settings that affect the browser.
- Print to USB as well as Wi-Fi printers.

Installing Extensions and Apps

- The Chrome Web Store is your source for Chrome browser extensions and web apps.

- Chrome browser extensions add features to the Chrome browser.
- A web app is not installed into the operating system and runs from a website within the Chrome browser.
- Android mobile apps can be installed into Chrome OS.
- The Google Play Store is your source for Android apps.

File Management in Chrome OS

- The Files app is the Chrome OS file management tool.
- Manage data stored in Google Drive as well as that stored locally.
- Google apps can view and/or open many file types. Some file types can only be viewed by Google apps, and require other apps to open them.

Configure Security and Troubleshoot Chrome OS

- Secure your Google Account by connecting to the Google My Account home page.
- The Security Checkup option will give you a quick snapshot of your Account security settings.
- Google is aware of any device from which you sign in to Google.
- Google's 2-Step Verification makes your account more secure.
- Secure Chrome OS through Settings accessed via the Status bar of the computer. Then open the *Security and Privacy* settings.
- Use the Diagnostics app to determine if you have a hardware problem.
- Use the Powerwash option whenever you need to return your Chromebook to its out-of-the-box state.

Key Terms List

2-Step Verification *(310)*

Android app *(305)*

Backup codes *(311)*

browser extension *(302)*

Chromebit *(290)*

Chromebook *(290)*

Chromebox *(290)*

Chrome OS *(290)*

Everything button *(290)*

Files app *(307)*

Google Account *(291)*

Google Mail *(291)*

Immersive Mode *(291)*

Launcher *(294)*

notification area *(296)*

Over the Phone (OTP) *(310)*

Refresh *(291)*

shelf *(294)*

status tray *(296)*

Switcher *(291)*

tote *(296)*

web app *(302)*

Key Terms Quiz

Use the Key Terms List to complete the sentences that follow. Not all terms will be used.

1. The _____, feature of the shelf, is a holding space for files and screenshots.

2. _____ is a dedicated key on a Chromebook keyboard that displays all open windows.

3. The _____ is a dedicated key on the Chromebook keyboard that opens the Search box.

4. _____, created to run on smartphones, are available for the Chrome OS through the Google Play Store.

5. The Chrome OS tool for folder and file management is the _____.

6. A/an _____ is a laptop that comes with the Chrome OS preinstalled.

7. A/an _____ is not an app, but an add-on that adds features to a browser.

8. The horizontal bar across the bottom of the Chrome OS desktop is the _____.

9. The _____ is based on the Linux kernel.

10. The _____ scrolls up from the bottom of the screen when you tap or click its button on the left of the shelf.

Multiple-Choice Quiz

1. The lightweight design of the Chrome OS is based on a certain Google app. What is that app?
   a. Gmail
   b. Google Drive
   c. Chrome
   d. Chromebit
   e. Explore

2. With this feature, you don't need to worry if your Chrome OS is running the latest version.
   a. Accessibility
   b. Wi-Fi
   c. Cloud storage
   d. Automatic update
   e. Launcher

3. This Google account security feature sends you a message with a code that you must enter, in addition to your correct password, when you attempt to sign in from a new device?
   a. Do Not Track
   b. Autofill
   c. 2-Step Verification
   d. Backup codes
   e. Password manager

4. When two or more users have accounts on a Chromebook, this option allows one to sign out, while preserving their work, so that another user may sign in.
   a. Lock the Screen
   b. Switch Users
   c. Sleep
   d. Automatic sign-in
   e. 2-factor authentication

5. The kernel of the Chrome OS operating system is based on which of the following?
   a. Linux
   b. Microsoft Windows
   c. macOS
   d. iOS
   e. Android

6. Which of the following locations is supported by the Chrome OS Files app?

a. Connected USB drives
b. Google Drive
c. Dropbox
d. OneDrive
e. Chromebook storage

7. Which of the following is the official source for Android apps?
a. App Store
b. Web Store
c. Play Store
d. Amazon
e. Google Drive

8. Which of the following is not found on the status pop-up?
a. Who is signed in
b. Network connection
c. Battery life
d. Google Docs Offline
e. Explore

9. Which of these is the extension that allows you to work offline with Google Drive files?
a. Gmail
b. Docs
c. Sync
d. Google Docs Offline
e. Explore

10. Running this on your Google account might reveal that you forgot to remove a device from your account.
a. Find Your Phone
b. Security Checkup
c. 2-Step Verification
d. Backup codes
e. OTP

11. This app tests Chromebook hardware components, providing a log of results you can give to a technical support person.
a. Status
b. Notifications

c. Tote
d. Explore
e. Diagnostics

12. This is required to sign on to a Chromebook.
a. Android phone
b. PIN
c. 2-Step Verification
d. Google Account
e. Touch screen

13. You have many windows open and you would like a snapshot of those windows. What feature of your Chromebook will do this for you?
a. Android app
b. Everything button
c. Refresh
d. Web app
e. Switcher

14. If you have 2-Step Verification enabled to send a text message, have Google create this handy list for those times when you cannot pick up a text message and you need to sign in on a device.
a. Chromebit
b. Backup codes
c. Google prompts
d. Calculator
e. Google+

15. If your account is configured for 2-Step Verification, add this app to your phone to greatly simplify the verification process when you sign in to your account from another device.
a. Chromebit
b. Backup codes
c. Google prompts
d. Calculator
e. Google+

Essay Quiz

1. Explain a significant difference between Google's 2009 vision of the user interface of the Chrome operating system and the Chrome OS GUI we see today.

2. Describe why early versions of Chrome OS were required to use Google Cloud Print to print to a local printer.

3. Compare and contrast browser extensions and web apps in Chrome OS and how you add them to your Chromebook.

4. Explain what an Android app is, why you would want one (or more) installed on your Chrome OS device, and the official source of Android apps.

5. Describe at least three scenarios in which Powerwash would be a good option.

Lab Projects

LAB PROJECT 8.1

Research significant changes in Chrome OS in the year immediately before you read this chapter. Are there more types of apps, or do web apps and Android apps have more abilities? Have there been more changes in security? Describe your findings.

LAB PROJECT 8.2

Research the term *Shadow IT* and how it relates to cloud computing. Something similar occurred in the 1980s after the IBM PC was available. See if you can find parallels to the Shadow IT caused by cloud computing to what happened in the first years after the IBM PC was introduced.

LAB PROJECT 8.3

One of many topics that could not be addressed in a single chapter on Chrome OS is the significance of something called Progressive Web Apps (PWAs). Research and describe PWAs and why they are significant.

chapter

9 Connecting Desktops and Laptops to Networks

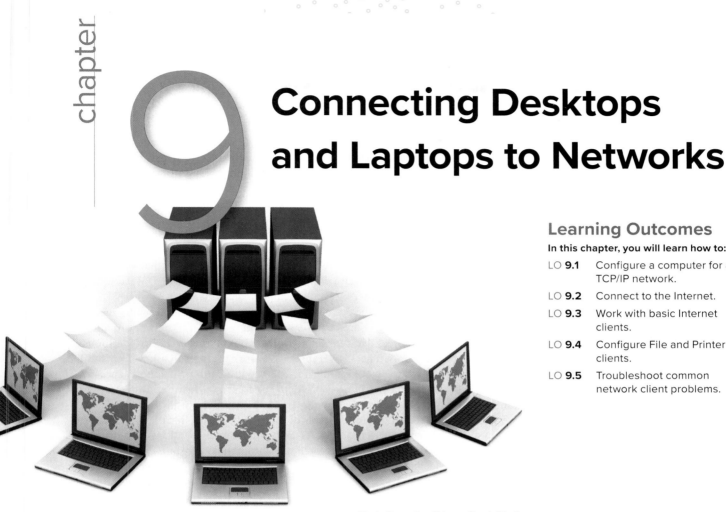

Yuriy Panyukov/Alamy Stock Photo

Learning Outcomes

In this chapter, you will learn how to:

LO **9.1**   Configure a computer for a TCP/IP network.

LO **9.2**   Connect to the Internet.

LO **9.3**   Work with basic Internet clients.

LO **9.4**   Configure File and Printer clients.

LO **9.5**   Troubleshoot common network client problems.

A stand-alone PC—one with no connection whatsoever to a network—is a rare thing today. Most of us can find some reason or need to connect to a network, whether it is a small home network, a corporate intranet, or the Internet. Without a network connection, a PC is like a remote island where the inhabitants have resolved to be isolated from civilization. And it does take resolve today to be so isolated because there are means by which a computer in the most remote location can connect to the Internet or another network. The heart and soul of all networks are the servers that provide the services we, as clients, seek on a network. These services are as simple as those that give us access to files and printers, Web pages, applications, and much more. Each of these services provides an important role on a network.

At work, at school, and at home, computer users depend on client software components that connect to services—whether for online research, playing games, engaging in a community through social media, using email, or downloading and uploading files.

In this chapter, you will study the client side of networking. Because a client computer cannot interact with network servers unless you properly configure it to communicate on a network, we begin with how to configure network connection settings on a client computer. Then we move on to the Internet, first examine methods for connecting to the Internet, and then look at the most common Internet clients for browsing and email. Finally, we practice methods for troubleshooting common connection problems. ✺

321

LO 9.1 | Configuring a Network Connection

In this section, we will briefly describe the TCP/IP protocol suite, the basics of the addressing scheme of the IP protocol, and how to view and configure the important IP settings on your devices.

Understanding the TCP/IP Protocol Suite

TCP/IP is a group of protocols that evolved from the work of the Defense Advanced Research Projects Agency (DARPA); the Internet Engineering Task Force (IETF) now oversees TCP/IP development. TCP/IP is the underlying protocol suite of the Internet and nearly all private networks, regardless of the network medium (wired or wireless). It is supported by all operating systems on desktops, servers, and common mobile devices.

Each software implementation of a component of TCP/IP is a protocol, regardless of whether it is a driver, a service, or an application. So, in computer networking, a protocol is both the set of rules for doing some task as well as the software that accomplishes it. In this section, we will work at understanding the TCP/IP protocol suite, software bundled together in what we call a protocol stack.

TCP/IP was developed for connecting networks to networks. For this reason it is routable, meaning that messages can be sent from one TCP/IP network to another through routers, the devices that connect networks. The Internet consists of millions of such connected networks. The TCP/IP protocols work together to allow both similar and dissimilar computers to communicate. You need this protocol suite to access the Internet, and it is the most common protocol suite used on private intranets. It gets its name from two of its many protocols: Transmission Control Protocol (TCP) and Internet Protocol (IP)—the core protocols of TCP/IP. If, during installation of an operating system, it detects a wired or wireless network adapter it will install a driver for that adapter card and the TCP/IP protocol will automatically install.

TCP/IP is a subject of epic proportions! We offer only an introduction to TCP/IP, in which we attempt to arm you with useful information, but not overwhelm you with detail. Our goal is to give you an overview of TCP/IP and familiarize you with the settings that you may need to enter or modify for your desktop or laptop computer. Of course, this knowledge should also help you with your mobile devices, the subject of Chapter 10. Most computers and mobile devices need little or no help in acquiring the address they need to connect to a network, but knowing more about how this works is very helpful when things don't work as they should.

<aside>
Note: For an entertaining and educational overview of TCP/IP and the workings of network devices (routers, switches, and firewalls), check out YouTube video *TCP/IP the Movie* (Parts 1 and 2).
</aside>

Transmission Control Protocol

Transmission Control Protocol (TCP) is the protocol responsible for the accurate delivery of messages, verifying and resending any pieces that fail to make the trip from source to destination. Several other protocols act as subprotocols, helping TCP accomplish this.

Internet Protocol

Internet Protocol (IP) is the protocol that delivers each IP packet (a small "package" containing chunks of data) from a source to a destination over a network on an Internetwork (a network of networks connected through routers). Special routing protocols use a destination IP address to choose the best route for a packet to take through a very complex internetwork. IP has subprotocols that help it accomplish its work, but we will not discuss the subprotocols.

Presently, there are two versions of Internet Protocol: IPv4 and IPv6, each with its own addressing scheme. Both protocols are present on the Internet, as it slowly transitions away from the older IPv4 (the standard since 1983) to IPv6. A lot of attention

<aside>
Note: What progress has the Internet community made in moving toward an IPv4-free world? Check out the website **https://pulse.internetsociety.org/technologies/** to see where things stand in the IP protocol world.
</aside>

is focused on the differences in addresses used by these two protocols, but there are many reasons for the Internet's move to IPv6.

The short list of reasons IPv6 is better than IPv4 includes:

- IPv4 has run out of addresses.
- IPv6 has many more addresses: 340 trillion trillion trillion unique identifiers.
- IPv6 works better with mobile devices using a subprotocol, Mobile IP.
- IPv6 automatically assigns addresses to devices in a very reliable and no-fuss way.
- IPv6 manages addresses better.
- IPv6 has subprotocols that support better security.

It is important for you to learn about IP addresses because you cannot participate on a TCP/IP network without a valid IP address.

IP Addressing Basics

Let's explore the basics of IP addressing. First, an IP address is not assigned to a computer but to a network interface card (NIC) on a TCP/IP network, whether wired (Ethernet) or wireless (Wi-Fi). A modem (whether it is a cable modem, DSL modem, or an old analog "dial-up" modem) also has an address when you use it to connect to the Internet. If your computer or mobile device has multiple network connection devices connected to different networks, such as an Ethernet network adapter connected to a LAN and a Wi-Fi or cellular connection, each must have an address when it connects to a network.

That is why you see the Internet Protocol, often shortened to "IP," as a component of a connection in Windows (see Figure 9-1). Windows supports both IPv4 and IPv6.

An IP address, along with a subnet mask (explained later), identifies both your network card (a "host" in Internet terms) and the network on which it resides. An IP address, when added to a message packet as the destination address, allows the message to move from one network to another until it reaches its destination. At the connecting point between networks, a special network device called a router uses its routing protocols to determine the route to the destination IP address, before sending each packet along to the next router closer to the destination network. Each device that directly attaches to the Internet must have a globally unique IP address. Both versions of IP have this much, and more, in common. Following are short explanations of IPv4 and IPv6 addresses.

IPv4 Addresses. IPv4 has been used on the Internet and other internetworks for nearly four decades. With 32-bit addressing, calculated by raising 2 to the 32nd power (2^{32}), IPv4 offers almost 4.3 billion possible IP addresses, but the way in which they were initially allocated to organizations greatly reduced the number of usable addresses, and we have now run out of IPv4 addresses.

An IPv4 address is 32 bits long in binary notation, but it usually appears as four decimal numbers, each in the range of 0–255, separated by a period. See examples of IPv4 addresses in Figures 9-1, 9-2, and 9-3.

In the macOS Network preferences pane, shown in Figure 9-2, the Wi-Fi device has an IPv4 address of 192.168.1.184. Figure 9-3 shows the Wi-Fi Network dialog box from Ubuntu's GUI with an IPv4 address of 192.168.1.30. Because this is a very simplified explanation, we will not go

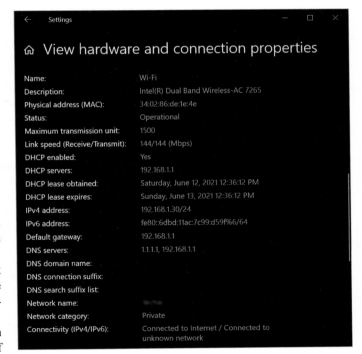

FIGURE 9-1 View hardware and connection properties in Windows 10.
Source: Microsoft Corporation

FIGURE 9-2 The macOS Network preferences pane.
Source: Apple Inc.

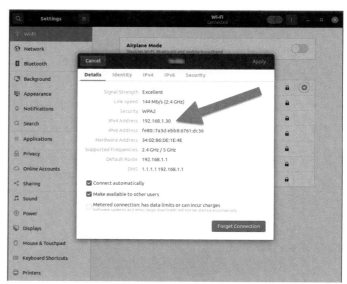

FIGURE 9-3 The Wi-Fi settings dialog box in the Ubuntu Linux GUI.
Source: Ubuntu by Canonical

into the exact rules for these addresses, just an overview. And, as you can see, there is more to an IP configuration than the address of the device itself, but we will tell you more about IP addresses before we discuss these other settings.

IPv6 Addresses. The Internet is currently transitioning to Internet Protocol version 6 (IPv6) with a new addressing scheme that provides astronomically more addresses. For many years, manufacturers and standards organizations worked toward the day when they could fully support IPv6 on the Internet. In fact, the World IPv6 Launch Day was June 6, 2012. On that day, however, the Internet world did not become an IPv6-only world. What did happen was that many important Internet service providers and websites became available to computers using either IPv4 or IPv6. They included Bing, Facebook, Google, and Yahoo!, and many more continue to join them. For the near future (perhaps decades), IPv4 and IPv6 will coexist on the Internet and on private and governmental internetworks of the world. Recent versions of operating systems and all new networking equipment come with support for both IPv4 and IPv6 built in.

Note: What happened to IPv5? An IPv5 standard was developed in the 1980s in an effort to better support nontext traffic, such as audio, video, and simulations. However, it did not replace IPv4, which was then still a recent standard.

IPv6 has 128-bit addressing, calculated by raising 2 to the 128th power (2^{128}), which supports a huge number of unique addresses—340,282,366,920,938,463,463, 374,607,431,768,211,456 to be exact. An IPv6 address appears as eight groups of four hexadecimal digits separated by colons. You will often see an IPv6 address shortened by eliminating leading zeros in a group, and if there are all zeros between a set of colons, the zeros won't show, and you will see just two colons together. If two or more groups of all zeros are adjacent, there will still only be two colons. In Figure 9-4, an IPv6 address is first shown in full hexadecimal notation, then with leading zeros removed, and finally as eight groups of binary numbers.

Which Addresses Can You Use?

While we described both IPv4 and IPv6 addresses above, our discussion here centers around IPv4 because it will be around for a while, and you are more likely to need help resolving a problem with an IPv4 address than with an IPv6 address. We doubt anyone other than a network administrator will be concerned about IPv6 addresses.

An IPv6 address in hexadecimal notation:

2002:0470:b8f9:0000:020c:29ff:fe53:45ca

The same address in hexadecimal notation with leading zeros removed:

2002:470:b8f9::20c:29ff:fe53:45ca

The same address in binary notation:

```
0010000000000010 0000010001110000 1011100011111001 0000000000000000
0000001000001100 0010100111111111 1111111001010011 0100010111001010
```

FIGURE 9–4 An IPv6 address expressed in both hexadecimal and binary notation.
Source: Jane Holcombe

There are billions of addresses, so how do you pick an address to use? Of course, the answer is—it all depends. Will you be using the address on a public network (the Internet) or on a private network? A central organization decides how to allocate all these addresses for use on the public Internet. They also understand that organizations need to use IP addresses within their private networks, and schemes were developed to slow down the depletion of addresses. One of those schemes involved dividing the possible IP addresses into two broad categories: public addresses and private addresses.

Public Addresses. Public IP addresses are designated for hosts directly connected to the Internet. A host is any computer or device that has an IP address. To communicate over the Internet, you must send your message from an IP address that is unique on the entire Internet, and your message must go to a unique IP address. The centrally responsible organization for allocation of public IP addresses is the Internet Assigned Numbers Authority (IANA). This organization allocates numbers to various Regional Internet Registries (RIRs), which have the task of allocating IP addresses to Internet service providers. The largest ISPs, in turn, allocate addresses to other ISPs. You or your school or employer receive addresses for each Internet connection from your ISP. The addresses provided are from selected portions of those many billions of possible addresses specifically used on the Internet.

Private Addresses. A private IP address is an address from one of three ranges of IPv4 addresses designated for use only on private networks, so they are unusable on the Internet. All the IPv4 addresses in Figures 9-1, 9-2, and 9-3 are private addresses. In fact, many organizations use the exact same addresses on their private IP networks, and you do not need to get permission to do so.

If a computer with a private address connects to the Internet, it will not be able to communicate because Internet routers will not forward packets with private addresses. Therefore, the same private address can be in use on millions of private networks, thus relieving some of the pressure on the limited supply of IPv4 addresses. Table 9-1 shows the three ranges used as private IPv4 addresses. All other IPv4 addresses either have specialized uses or are public addresses valid for computers and devices that are on the Internet.

If a user on a private network using private IP addresses wishes to connect to the Internet, a device between the local network and the Internet must intercept, repackage, and give a public IP address as its source address to each data packet before it

Note: Many home routers use IPv4 address 192.168.1.1 or 192.168.0.1. The examples given in Figures 9–1, 9–2, and 9–3 are from computers connected to a home router. In Figure 9–1, the address of the router to which a Windows computer connects is labeled "Default Gateway." In Figure 9–2, macOS uses "Router" for the label to this address. In Figure 9–3, the term "Default Route" identifies the router IP address.

TABLE 9-1 IPv4 Private IP Address Ranges

10.0.0.0 through 10.255.255.255
172.16.0.0 through 172.31.255.255
192.168.0.0 through 192.168.255.255

goes onto the Internet. Then, if there is a response, each returning packet will go through the same process in reverse before returning to the private address.

If you connect to the Internet from home, school, or work, there is a device between your computer and the ISP that substitutes (or translates) your actual IP address to a unique Internet IP address. There are a couple of methods for doing this. One involves a special network service called a proxy server, and another involves a special service called network address translation (NAT). These are services that your ISP or network administrator manages for your school or organization. Such services also exist in the devices called Internet routers, which allow home or small-office computers to connect to the Internet, usually through a cable or DSL connection. A cable provider or telephone company will normally supply this equipment along with the Internet service.

How Does a NIC Get an IP Address?

Recall from the earlier discussion under IP Addressing Basics that an address is assigned to a network interface card (NIC). A NIC gets an IP address in one of two ways: static address assignment or automatic address assignment. Automatic address assignment is the most common method used today and there are two ways automatic addresses are assigned.

Static Address Assignment. A static IP address is manually configured by an administrator and can, therefore, be considered semipermanent—that is, it stays with the NIC until someone changes it. Manually configuring an IP address involves entering the IP address and other necessary IP settings. Most organizations only use static IP addressing on servers, network printers, and network devices such as routers that are required to have static addresses.

Where will you find this information on your desktop or laptop computer? Actually, unless you are setting up your own TCP/IP network (a very advanced task!), you will be given the IP addressing information by a network administrator, if you are connecting to a LAN at school or work, or by your Internet service provider. But most ISPs automate all the configuration of home Internet connections.

If you need to manually configure an address, be sure to carefully enter the numbers given to you, and double-check them! In Windows, you will enter these in the TCP/IP properties found in the properties dialog box for the network connection (see Figure 9-5).

Automatic Address Assignment. One nearly universal method is used for assigning IP addresses to computers: automatic IP addressing. Another method is used as a sort of fail-safe: Automatic Private IP Addressing (APIPA).

- Most organizations use automatic IP addressing for their desktop computers. It requires a special server or service on the network, called a Dynamic Host Configuration Protocol (DHCP) server, which issues IP addresses and settings to computers configured to obtain an IP address automatically, thus making them DHCP clients. The news gets even better since the default configuration of TCP/IP in Windows, macOS, Linux, and Chrome OS is to obtain an IP address automatically. In Figures 9-1 and 9-2 you can see that DHCP is enabled.

- Do not confuse *automatic* with *automatic private*. Most operating systems will enable a feature of DHCP—Automatic Private IP Addressing (APIPA), whereby a DHCP client computer that fails to receive an address from a DHCP server will automatically give itself an address from a special range that has 169.254 in the first two octets of the IPv4 address. This is also called a link-local address, and IPv6 uses link-local addresses that begin with fe80. If a computer uses a link-local address, it will only be able to communicate on the local network segment, and then only with other devices and computers that use the same network ID. *When a computer is using an APIPA address, it continues to look for a DHCP server. Windows will check every 5 minutes.*

APIPA allows a novice to set up a small TCP/IP network without needing to learn about IP addressing. Each computer would use APIPA to assign itself an address, first testing that no other computer on the LAN is also using that same host ID.

IP Configuration Settings

If you must manually configure IPv4, you will need to understand the other settings to enter in addition to the IP address.

Subnet Mask. The subnet mask for an IPv4 address is as critical as the address itself because it takes what looks like a single address and divides it into two addresses by masking off part of the address. It is a little like your house address. The house number gives the address on the street, but you also need the street name. If a NIC with an IPv4 address of 192.168.1.132 has a mask of 255.255.255.0, the IP protocol knows that this network device has the host address of 132 (its house number) on network 192.168.1 (its street name). The host address is the host ID, and the network address is the net ID.

Let's take a brief look at how masking works. Technically, it is done using binary math (base-2 math that uses only 0s and 1s), but you do not have to be a binary math whiz to understand the concept of masking; just look at the IP address and the mask in its binary form. You can use the scientific setting of the Calculator program that comes with Windows to convert each octet (a group of eight binary digits) of an IP

> **WARNING!**
> An APIPA address can indicate that a router is turned off or faulty.

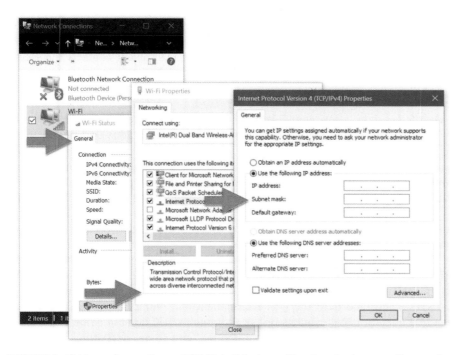

FIGURE 9–5 Manually configure TCP/IP in Windows 10 using the Internet Protocol Version 4 (TCP/IPv4) Properties dialog box.
Source: Microsoft Corporation

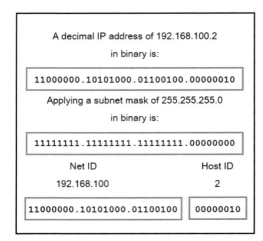

FIGURE 9-6 A subnet mask covers a portion of an IP address.
Source: Jane Holcombe

A decimal IP address of 192.168.100.2

in binary is:

11000000.10101000.01100100.00000010

Applying a subnet mask of 255.255.255.0

in binary is:

11111111.11111111.11111111.00000000

Net ID	Host ID
192.168.100	2

11000000.10101000.01100100 | 00000010

Note: The HTTPS that precedes the Fully Qualified Domain Name is a secure version of the Hypertext Transfer Protocol (HTTP), the protocol used to format and transfer data over the Internet. HTTPS was defined in Chapter 2.

address from binary to decimal or vice versa. As an example, if you convert an address of 192.168.100.2 to binary it looks like this:

11000000.10101000.01100100.00000010

If you convert the mask of 255.255.255.0 to binary, it looks like this:

11111111.11111111.11111111.00000000

If you lay the mask on top of the IP address, the ones cover (mask) the first 24 bits (short for binary digits). What falls under the ones of the mask is the network address, and what falls under the zeros of the mask is the host address. Figure 9-6 should make this concept clearer.

Default Gateway. The default gateway is the IP address of the router connected to your network. The router is the network device that directs traffic to destinations beyond the local network. The net ID of the gateway address should be identical to the net ID of your NIC. Without a properly configured router, as well as the correct address (Default Gateway) for reaching this router, you cannot communicate with computers beyond your network. In our example in Figure 9-1, the router connects network 192.168.1 to other networks. Anytime your computer has a packet destined for a network with a network address other than 192.168.1, IP will send the packet to the gateway address to be forwarded to a host on another network.

DNS Servers. Next in Figure 9-1 are addresses of Domain Name System (DNS) servers. DNS is a distributed hierarchical online database containing registered domain names mapped to IP addresses. Thousands of name servers on the Internet maintain this distributed database. When you attempt to connect to a website, such as https://www.mheducation.com, your computer's DNS client queries a DNS server to determine the IP address for that website.

You may enter two DNS addresses in the Properties dialog shown in Figure 9-5—a primary DNS server and a secondary DNS server. The primary DNS server is the server the DNS client on your computer contacts any time you make a request to connect to a server using a domain name rather than an IP address. The DNS server will attempt to resolve the name to an IP address. The DNS client contacts the second DNS server only if there is no response from the first DNS server.

"What is a registered domain name? When you point your browser to www.apple.com, you are using a Fully Qualified Domain Name (FQDN). It has four parts to it. On the far right, after "com" is the root domain, represented by a period (.). No period visible? That's fine. Your browser (and other apps) adds that period to the end. The next part is the Top Level Domain (TLD). In this case, it is ".com." The next element is the registered domain name, also called a second-level domain name: "Apple" in this example. To the far left is "www," which is the name of the host in that domain. This host name is associated with web servers, but it is often omitted by websites. Therefore, you may connect to some websites with or without the host name. When a portion of an FQDN is omitted, it is a Partially Qualified Domain Name (PQDN)."

The Internet Corporation for Assigned Names and Numbers (ICANN), a California nonprofit corporation, currently oversees the Domain Name System, after having replaced an organization called InterNIC. The U.S. government sanctions ICANN, which reports to the U.S. Department of Commerce. Anyone wishing to acquire a domain name contacts one of the roughly 200 domain name registrars of Top Level Domains (.com, .org, .pro, .info, .biz, and so on) accredited by ICANN. Once registered with ICANN, each domain name and its IP address go on the Internet Domain Name Servers so that users can access Internet services offered under those domain names.

Step-by-Step 9.01

Examine a Connection's IP Configuration in a GUI

In this step-by-step exercise, you will examine a connection's IP configuration in the Windows GUI. The illustrations are from Windows 10. You will need:

- A computer running Windows 10.
- An administrator account and password for the computer.

Step 1

In Windows 10 click or tap the *Start* button and select *Settings* (the gear). In Settings select *Network & Internet*.

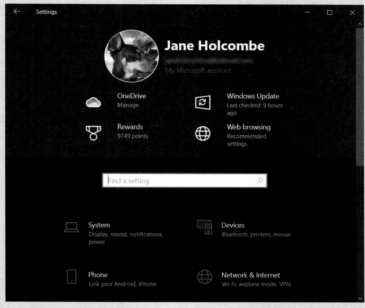

Source: Microsoft Corporation

Step 2

The Network & Internet page displays links to various settings. If you do not see both the sidebar and contents pane, widen the window until it resembles this. Select the *Properties* button.

Source: Microsoft Corporation

In the Properties page, the name at the top by the house icon depends on your NIC. In this office, the name is either the SSID (network name) of the Wi-Fi router or simply the word "Ethernet" for those computers connecting with Ethernet. In either case, to see the properties, scroll down to the bottom.

Source: Microsoft Corporation

The Properties listed in this example are for the Wi-Fi SSID identified at the top.

Source: Microsoft Corporation

Notice the *Copy* button at the bottom. Click this and the data under *Properties* is copied to the Windows Clipboard. You can then paste this data into an email, text editor, or word processor to send to a tech support person.

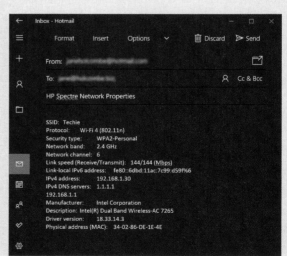

Source: Microsoft Corporation

Viewing an IP Configuration from a Command-Line Interface

View the IP configuration of a computer from the command-line interface (CLI) in all of the desktop operating systems included in this text. In Windows you have two options for a CLI. They are the Command Prompt and the PowerShell. Both were described in Chapter 5, and the commands we describe in this chapter for the Windows CLI work in both Windows CLIs. If you have a Linux or macOS computer, open a terminal window and run similar commands.

In either Windows CLI use the **ipconfig** command without any command-line switches to have it display only the IP address (both IPv4 and IPv6, when present), subnet mask, and default gateway for each NIC that is connected to a network. Using the command with the **/all** switch will display much more information for each NIC. For instance, without this switch no detail is listed under Windows IP Configuration, but with the **/all** switch, as shown in Figure 9–7, several lines display, beginning with the

```
C:\Windows\System32\cmd.exe                                    —    □    ✕

C:\WINDOWS\system32>ipconfig /all

Windows IP Configuration

    Host Name . . . . . . . . . . . . : SeeMore
    Primary Dns Suffix  . . . . . . . :
    Node Type . . . . . . . . . . . . : Hybrid
    IP Routing Enabled. . . . . . . . : No
    WINS Proxy Enabled. . . . . . . . : No

Wireless LAN adapter Local Area Connection* 1:

    Media State . . . . . . . . . . . : Media disconnected
    Connection-specific DNS Suffix  . :
    Description . . . . . . . . . . . : Microsoft Wi-Fi Direct Virtual Adapter
    Physical Address. . . . . . . . . : 34-02-86-DE-1E-4F
    DHCP Enabled. . . . . . . . . . . : Yes
    Autoconfiguration Enabled . . . . : Yes

Wireless LAN adapter Local Area Connection* 2:

    Media State . . . . . . . . . . . : Media disconnected
    Connection-specific DNS Suffix  . :
    Description . . . . . . . . . . . : Microsoft Wi-Fi Direct Virtual Adapter #2
    Physical Address. . . . . . . . . : 36-02-86-DE-1E-4E
    DHCP Enabled. . . . . . . . . . . : Yes
    Autoconfiguration Enabled . . . . : Yes

Wireless LAN adapter Wi-Fi:

    Connection-specific DNS Suffix  . :
    Description . . . . . . . . . . . : Intel(R) Dual Band Wireless-AC 7265
    Physical Address. . . . . . . . . : 34-02-86-DE-1E-4E
    DHCP Enabled. . . . . . . . . . . : Yes
    Autoconfiguration Enabled . . . . : Yes
    Link-local IPv6 Address . . . . . : fe80::6dbd:11ac:7c99:d59f%6(Preferred)
    IPv4 Address. . . . . . . . . . . : 192.168.1.30(Preferred)
    Subnet Mask . . . . . . . . . . . : 255.255.255.0
    Lease Obtained. . . . . . . . . . : Wednesday, May 6, 1885 12:11:10 PM
    Lease Expires . . . . . . . . . . : Sunday, June 13, 2021 12:40:32 PM
    Default Gateway . . . . . . . . . : 192.168.1.1
    DHCP Server . . . . . . . . . . . : 192.168.1.1
    DHCPv6 IAID . . . . . . . . . . . : 104071814
    DHCPv6 Client DUID. . . . . . . . : 00-01-00-01-28-30-9E-BB-34-02-86-DE-1E-4E
    DNS Servers . . . . . . . . . . . : 1.1.1.1
                                        192.168.1.1
    NetBIOS over Tcpip. . . . . . . . : Enabled
```

FIGURE 9–7 The output from running the command ipconfig /all.
Source: Microsoft Corporation

try this!

View Your IP Configuration from a Windows Command Prompt

Check out your current IP configuration using the **ipconfig** command. Try this:

1. Open a Command Prompt or the Windows PowerShell.
2. At the prompt type **ipconfig**.
3. After viewing the results of the command, type the command again with the **/all** switch: **ipconfig /all**.
4. Notice the additional information the **/all** switch provides.
5. Learn about other options for **ipconfig** using the **/?** switch.

Host Name. Then, for each adapter, in addition to the basic IP address, subnet mask, and default gateway, all the IP configuration information for each NIC displays. This includes the physical address, several lines of information pertaining to DHCP, and one or more DNS server addresses, if available, as well as the status of NetBIOS over TCP/IP, a protocol used for downward compatibility in networks with older Windows versions.

In both the macOS Terminal window and the Linux $ prompt, the **ifconfig** command is the equivalent of the Windows CLI **ipconfig** command. Open a Terminal window in macOS or access the $ prompt in Linux and enter the **ifconfig** command with the **-a** switch to see all information about network interfaces in that computer. The results for a macOS Terminal window are shown in Figure 9-8 and from the $ prompt in Linux in Figure 9-9. Notice that the information in macOS and in Linux is more difficult to decipher than it is in Windows. For instance, in both Figures 9-8 and 9-9 the lines labeled "inet6" refer to IPv6, while those beginning with "inet" refer to IPv4. You'll find the physical addresses of installed NICs in both figures on the lines beginning with "ether."

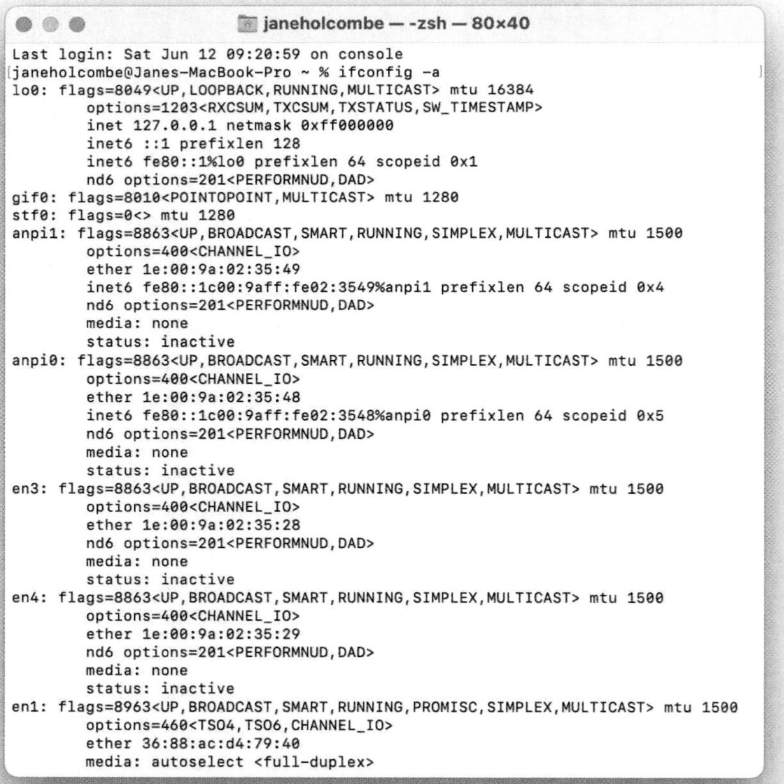
janeholcombe — -zsh — 80×40
Last login: Sat Jun 12 09:20:59 on console
janeholcombe@Janes-MacBook-Pro ~ % ifconfig -a
lo0: flags=8049<UP,LOOPBACK,RUNNING,MULTICAST> mtu 16384
options=1203<RXCSUM,TXCSUM,TXSTATUS,SW_TIMESTAMP>
inet 127.0.0.1 netmask 0xff000000
inet6 ::1 prefixlen 128
inet6 fe80::1%lo0 prefixlen 64 scopeid 0x1
nd6 options=201<PERFORMNUD,DAD>
gif0: flags=8010<POINTOPOINT,MULTICAST> mtu 1280
stf0: flags=0<> mtu 1280
anpi1: flags=8863<UP,BROADCAST,SMART,RUNNING,SIMPLEX,MULTICAST> mtu 1500
options=400<CHANNEL_IO>
ether 1e:00:9a:02:35:49
inet6 fe80::1c00:9aff:fe02:3549%anpi1 prefixlen 64 scopeid 0x4
nd6 options=201<PERFORMNUD,DAD>
media: none
status: inactive
anpi0: flags=8863<UP,BROADCAST,SMART,RUNNING,SIMPLEX,MULTICAST> mtu 1500
options=400<CHANNEL_IO>
ether 1e:00:9a:02:35:48
inet6 fe80::1c00:9aff:fe02:3548%anpi0 prefixlen 64 scopeid 0x5
nd6 options=201<PERFORMNUD,DAD>
media: none
status: inactive
en3: flags=8863<UP,BROADCAST,SMART,RUNNING,SIMPLEX,MULTICAST> mtu 1500
options=400<CHANNEL_IO>
ether 1e:00:9a:02:35:28
nd6 options=201<PERFORMNUD,DAD>
media: none
status: inactive
en4: flags=8863<UP,BROADCAST,SMART,RUNNING,SIMPLEX,MULTICAST> mtu 1500
options=400<CHANNEL_IO>
ether 1e:00:9a:02:35:29
nd6 options=201<PERFORMNUD,DAD>
media: none
status: inactive
en1: flags=8963<UP,BROADCAST,SMART,RUNNING,PROMISC,SIMPLEX,MULTICAST> mtu 1500
options=460<TSO4,TSO6,CHANNEL_IO>
ether 36:88:ac:d4:79:40
media: autoselect <full-duplex>

FIGURE 9–8 The result of running the **ifconfig -a** command in a Terminal window in macOS.
Source: Apple Inc.

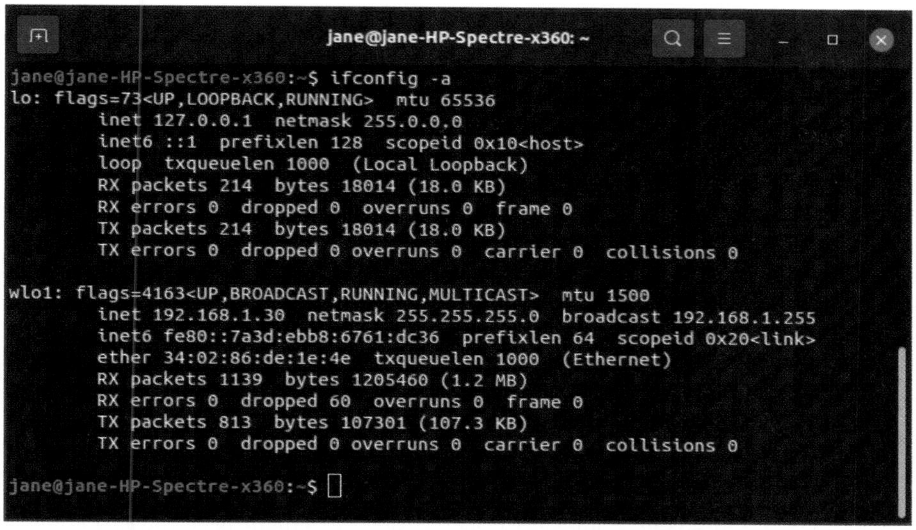

FIGURE 9–9 The result of running the **ifconfig -a** command at the $ prompt in Linux.
Source: Ubuntu by Canonical

LO 9.2 | Connecting to the Internet

A connection to the Internet is a wide area network (WAN) connection. A wide area network (WAN) is a network that covers a very large geographic area (miles). There are several WAN technologies to choose from. Some of these are wired technologies, and some are wireless. Most connection methods described here remain available 24/7, in which case, Internet access is as simple as opening your browser or social media app or sending an email. The connections include a wide range of speeds. In this section, we will compare the various means of connecting a network or computer to the Internet and discuss the most common methods for doing so from home or a small business so that you can decide for yourself. This will also help you to understand something about how you are connecting to the Internet from school or work, although we will not discuss the very expensive high-speed WAN services for connecting a large enterprise (commercial, government, or educational) to the Internet.

The choice of physical means of connecting to the Internet closely relates to your choice of an organization that will give you access to the Internet. This section includes an overview of these organizations first. Then you will learn about the technologies used at the connection point to the Internet, regardless of whether it is a single computer or a LAN connection.

Internet Service Providers

An Internet service provider (ISP) is an organization that provides access to the Internet for individuals and organizations. For a fee, an ISP provides connection service and may offer other Internet-related services, such as Web-server hosting and email. Some ISPs specialize in certain connection types. For instance, HughesNet and Dish are both ISPs that specialize in satellite Internet services. T-Mobile, Verizon, and AT&T all provide ISP services for their cellular customers; and your local telephone company may provide ISP services for dial-up, DSL, and cable customers. Virtually all cable TV providers also provide Internet service.

try this!

Find Internet Service Providers

You can use the Internet to find ISPs you might want to use. Try this:

1. Use your Web browser to connect to your favorite search engine, search on "Internet Service Provider."

2. To find ISPs that specialize in satellite connections, for example, search on "Internet Satellite Data Service Provider."

3. Browse through the results to see what is available in your area.

Computer-to-Internet versus LAN-to-Internet

A local area network (LAN) is a network that covers a building, home, office, or campus. It can be wired or wireless. The traditional wired network uses Ethernet connectors and cables; Ethernet connectors are still standard on many desktops and some laptops. A Wi-Fi network is a wireless LAN (WLAN) that complies with IEEE 802.11 standards. The maximum distance covered by WLAN signals or LAN cabling is measured in hundreds of feet. Almost any computer will first connect to a LAN or WLAN, which in turn connects to a router connected (directly or indirectly) to the Internet. There is usually at least one router between your computing device and the Internet. More likely, there are many routers.

At the point of connection at home, you will have some sort of modem (cable, DSL, or analog). One port of the modem connects to a WAN connection and through that to an ISP. The other port may connect directly to a computer or, most often, to a router that in many cases is also a wireless access point (WAP) and an Ethernet switch. Therefore, you are connecting via a WLAN (Wi-Fi) or LAN (Ethernet) to the Internet. This is also the case at school or work, only on a larger scale, because the LAN or WLAN ultimately connects through a router to a high-speed Internet connection. Figure 9–10 shows these two scenarios.

Wired Connectivity Technologies

Many wired WAN technologies for connecting to the Internet utilize the telecommunications infrastructure of the telephone system—either in its traditional state or with upgrades and equipment added to that infrastructure. Another private network often used for wired Internet connections belongs to the cable TV companies, which provide Internet access for their customers.

Dial-Up Connections Using Analog Modems

A technology that clearly takes advantage of the traditional phone system is dial-up, an inexpensive choice available to anyone with a standard phone line and an analog modem. At one time every laptop came with an internal analog modem.

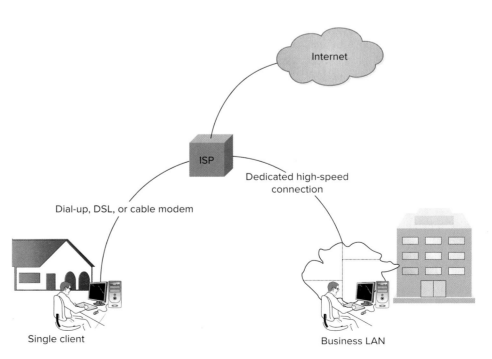

FIGURE 9–10 Connecting to the Internet from a single computer or from a LAN.

Analog modems as standard equipment in laptops have gone the way of the buggy whip. Never heard of buggy whips? That's our point. However, dial-up is the only low-cost means of connecting to the Internet in remote areas of the world, including some within the United States, and millions still use dial-up, so we will devote some space to this topic.

The longtime speed standard for dial-up is 56 kilobits per second (Kbps). The dial-up connection at 56 Kbps is very slow compared to a LAN running at 100 megabits per second (Mbps) or 1 gigabit per second (Gbps). In addition to a standard phone line (what we often call a "land line"), you also need to subscribe to an Internet connection service from an ISP. The cost of the ISP subscription should be your only cost in addition to your phone service. When using an analog modem, you may not use the phone line simultaneously for voice or fax.

In a dial-up connection to the Internet, your computer uses a modem to dial a telephone number provided by the ISP (hence the term *dial-up connection*). One of many modems maintained by the ISP at its facility answers your computer's call; a server maintained by the ISP for authenticating customers authenticates you, and then the ISP routes traffic between your computer and the Internet for that session. Like a voice phone conversation, the connection is only temporary and ends when either your PC or the ISP's server ends the call. Most ISP servers disconnect a dial-up connection automatically after a certain period of inactivity.

Note: Several ISPs advertise dial-up service, including (but not limited to) NetZero and EarthLink.

High-Speed Wired Access

If multiple users need to share an Internet connection, the connection between the network and the ISP must be adequate to simultaneously carry the traffic created by all the users at peak usage times. The author presently has a Wi-Fi router connected to a DSL modem. She connects 10 devices through that router. Many families exceed that number. For this you need high-speed WAN connections, such as the three wired options we describe here, or one of the wireless options detailed later.

Integrated Services Digital Network. Integrated services digital network (ISDN) is a digital telephone service that simultaneously transmits voice, data, and control signaling over a single telephone line. ISDN service operates on standard telephone lines but requires a special modem and phone service, which adds to the cost. An ISDN data connection can transfer data at up to 128,000 bits per second (128 Kbps). This seems extremely slow to most of us with faster options. While rarely used in homes in the United States, ISDN may be all that is available for a wired WAN connection in some areas, especially outside of the United States.

The benefits of ISDN (beyond the faster speed compared to a dial-up connection) include being able to connect a PC, telephone, and fax machine to a single ISDN line and use them simultaneously.

ISDN has fallen out of favor in many areas where there are higher performance options, such as cable and DSL. In remote parts of the world, another optional broadband service, satellite communications, may be a more viable option than ISDN because it does not require the wired infrastructure needed by ISDN.

Digital Subscriber Line. Digital subscriber line (DSL) service is similar to ISDN in its use of the telephone network, but it uses more advanced digital signal processing to compress more signals through the telephone lines. DSL requires component changes in the telephone network before they can offer it. DSL service can provide simultaneous data, voice, and fax transmissions on the same line. It gives you a dedicated circuit from your home or office to the central office and the service can usually guarantee consistent upload and download speeds.

Several versions of DSL services are available for home and business use. Each version provides a different level of service, speed, and distance, and each normally provides full-time connections. The two most common are asynchronous DSL

(ADSL) and synchronous DSL (SDSL). ADSL is the type of service normally available to home users. Other versions include high-data-rate DSL (HDSL) and very high-data-rate DSL (VDSL). The abbreviation often used to refer to DSL service in general begins with an *x* (*x*DSL), reflecting the varied first character in the DSL implementations.

Across the DSL services offered by various ISPs, data transmission speeds range from 128 Kbps for basic DSL service through 24 Mbps for high-end service. When describing DSL speeds, they usually refer to the speed of traffic flowing "downstream"—that is, from the ISP to your computer. For instance, the authors subscribe to a rural phone company's ADSL service, which provides a downstream speed of 15 Mbps, but an upstream speed of 1 Mbps. While SDSL provides the same speed in each direction, it is much more expensive and not widely available. Most home users only require the higher speeds for downloads (browsing the Internet, downloading streaming video, etc.), so SDSL service is only practical for customers who must upload a great deal of data.

Because servers must transfer a great deal of data in response to user requests, commercial Internet servers are normally hosted on much faster links than those discussed here.

Cable. Many cable television companies now use a portion of their network's bandwidth to offer Internet access through existing cable television connections. They call this Internet connection option cable modem service because of the need to use a special cable modem to connect.

Cable networks use coaxial cable, which can transmit data as much as 100 times faster than common telephone lines. Coaxial cable allows transmission over several channels simultaneously. Internet data can be on one channel while transmitting audio, video, and control signals separately. A user can access the Internet from his or her computer and watch cable television at the same time, over the same cable connection, without the two data streams interfering with one another.

The biggest drawback to cable modem service is the fact that the subscribers in a defined area share the signal. As the number of users in an area increases, less bandwidth is available to each user. Therefore, while cable providers advertise higher speeds than DSL, they cannot guarantee consistent speeds.

Wireless Connectivity Technologies

Like wired communications, wireless moved from analog to digital. Today, you can connect to the Internet through cellular networks, wireless wide area networks (WWANs), wireless LAN (WLAN) connections (if the WLAN ultimately connects to the Internet), and by satellite.

Smartphones support both voice and high-speed cellular data service, allowing users to surf the Internet from any location offering the required signal. Cellular Internet companies usually meter their connections, meaning that your plan allows only a predetermined amount of downstream data per month. Extra charges apply if you exceed the permitted amount.

In addition, modern smartphones also come with Wi-Fi. This allows users to configure their phones to use a Wi-Fi connection, when available, for connecting to a router that, in turn, is connected to the Internet, thus saving on connection and data charges from their cellular provider.

Tablets optionally have cellular communications features as well as Wi-Fi, allowing Web browsing and communicating by email and using a wide variety of services.

Wireless WAN Connections

A wireless wide area network (WWAN) is a digital wireless network that extends over a large geographical area. A WWAN receives and transmits data using radio signals over cellular sites and satellites, which makes the network accessible to mobile computer systems. At the switching center, the WWAN splits off into segments and then connects to a public or private network via telephone or other high-speed communication links. The data then links to an organization's existing LAN/WAN infrastructure (see Figure 9–11). The coverage area for a WWAN, normally measured in miles or kilometers, makes it therefore more susceptible than wired networks to environmental factors such as weather and terrain.

A WWAN is a fully bidirectional wireless network capable of data transfer at speeds in excess of 100 Mbps. Usually, basic WWAN services offer connection speeds between 1 and 10 Mbps. With dedicated equipment, the downlink speeds can reach 100 Mbps. The uplink speeds are less. A WWAN system requires an antenna tuned to receive the proper radio frequency (RF).

A cellular Internet connection is an example of a WWAN. Many cellular services offer Internet data service. In addition to using your smartphone or tablet on a cellular network, providers offer cellular hotspot plans, in which your smartphone or a separate hotspot device acts as a Wi-Fi router for your other computers and devices to access the Internet.

Satellite

Satellite connections are as suitable for large businesses as for small offices, cybercafés, individuals, homes, and the armed forces. Satellite is the WAN of choice when it is not possible or practical to use a wired connection and when cellular WAN services are not available or are too slow or costly. Satellite Internet providers offer several levels of service based on speed and they offer either stationary installations or mobile installations. The hardware cost for a mobile satellite installation is considerably higher than that for a stationary installation, and the ongoing service fees are higher, too.

Satellite Internet Connection Speeds. Like ADSL, satellite data communication is usually faster downstream than upstream. The discrepancy can be huge, as we found when we had our own mobile satellite system installed on our motor home in 2003.

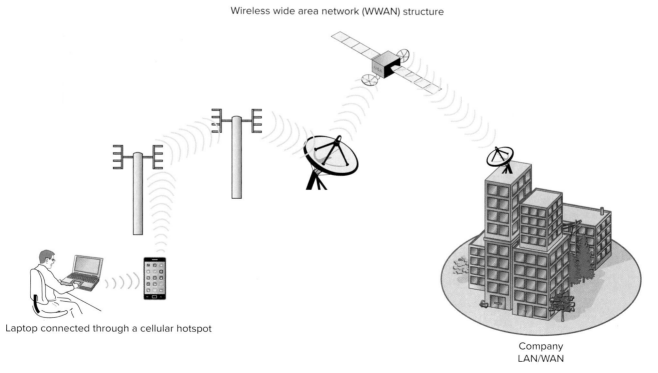

Wireless wide area network (WWAN) structure

Laptop connected through a cellular hotspot

Company
LAN/WAN

FIGURE 9–11 A WWAN includes devices that retransmit the wireless signal.

During our three years of living and working on the road, we often achieved download speeds of 400 to 800 Kbps (and occasionally more), but upload speeds were only in the range of 25 to 45 Kbps. While these speeds seem minimal compared to the mobile satellite options available today, the system worked well for us because, like most Internet users, our greatest need was for fast downloads as we browsed the Internet or downloaded files. At the time, cellular service was slow or simply did not exist in most locations, and so we found a mobile satellite connection was the best solution as long as we were careful not to park under trees or other obstacles to the satellite signal.

Satellite Internet Connection Costs. Today, the price of consumer-grade mobile satellite equipment and the basic monthly service fees are generally more expensive than they were in 2003. But the base plan speeds are much faster.

Satellite Internet Connection Latency. Satellite communications tend to have a higher latency, or lag. Think of watching a news broadcast that includes a foreign correspondent reporting over a satellite link. The news anchor in the studio asks a question, and you see the correspondent on the screen with a frozen smile while waiting to hear the question in its entirety. While it is barely noticeable when someone is reporting the news, such latency is very undesirable for real-time Internet applications, such as online games. Some IT professionals consider satellite connections unreliable, but it can be the best solution for Internet communications in remote areas.

When individuals or organizations contract with an ISP for stationary satellite service, they install an Earth-based communications station. It usually includes three parts: a transceiver (a combined transmitter and receiver), a device that for simplicity we call a modem, and the satellite dish on its mount. You place the satellite dish outdoors in direct line-of-sight of one of several data satellites in geostationary orbit around the Earth. The modem connects the other components to the computer or LAN. A mobile installation (on a land- or water-based vehicle) is generally much more expensive than a stationary installation because the mount must allow for moving the dish to align on the satellite, and therefore requires controlling circuitry and a costly motor-driven mount to achieve this with precision.

Because a satellite traveling in a geostationary orbit moves at the same speed as the Earth's rotation, it hovers over the same location on the Earth—therefore, you can align a satellite dish antenna precisely on the satellite. The satellite links the user's satellite dish to a land-based satellite operations center, through which the signal goes to the Internet (see Figure 9–12).

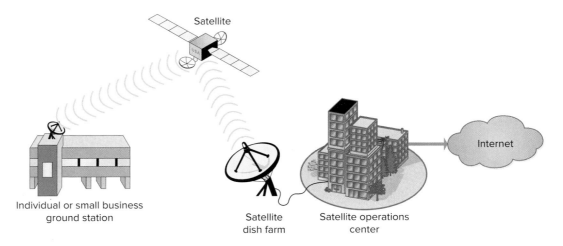

Satellite

Individual or small business ground station

Satellite dish farm

Satellite operations center

Internet

FIGURE 9–12 Accessing the Internet through a satellite WAN connection.

WLAN Connections

A WLAN is a local area network, usually using one of the standards referred to as Wi-Fi (for wireless fidelity). The Wi-Fi standards of the Institute of Electrical and Electronics Engineers include 802.11a, 802.11b, 802.11g, 802.11n, 802.11ac, and 802.11ax listed from oldest to newest. The maximum distance covered by a WLAN is a few hundred feet rather than miles. Therefore, this is not a technology that connects directly to an ISP (as a WWAN or satellite connection will) but can be used to connect to another LAN or device with a WAN connection. This is the technology of Internet cafés, wireless laptops, tablets, and smartphones. With enough wireless hubs, called wireless access points (WAPs), an entire community can offer wireless access to a shared Internet connection.

Many of us have one of the high-speed WAN technologies described above and connect multiple devices to them through a device that is both a wireless access point (WAP) and an Internet router. The author has a Wi-Fi router connected to an ADSL connection. Through that wireless router, several computing devices connect to the Internet.

The latest IEEE 802.11 standards are both faster and more secure owing to encryption technology. Therefore, we regularly replace our Wi-Fi devices with newer ones that are up to the new standards.

Using a Virtual Private Network

Mobile users and remote offices often need to connect to a corporate intranet through the Internet using any of the connection technologies discussed earlier. You can make such a connection more secure by connecting through a virtual private network (VPN), over an existing WAN connection. Think of a VPN as a simulated private network that runs inside a "tunnel" from end point to end point. When an individual connects from a computer or mobile device, we call this connection a remote access VPN (see Figure 9–13). One end is a computer connected to the Internet, while the other end is a VPN server in the private network. When two networks connect by VPN, we call it a site-to-site VPN.

The tunnel effect is the result of encapsulating each data packet sent at one end of the tunnel and removing it from the encapsulation at the receiving end. Because the encapsulation itself provides only a very small amount of protection, VPN providers apply other measures to protect the data, such as encrypting the data, and requiring authentication at both ends of the tunnel.

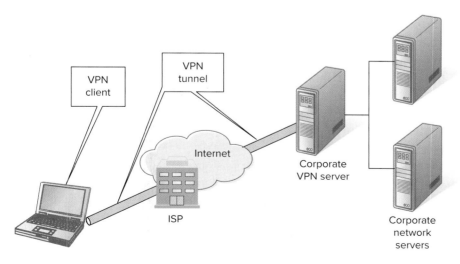

FIGURE 9–13 A remote access VPN.

Anyone who connects to the Internet while away from home, school, or work should consider using a VPN for secure access. Organizations often provide this service to their employees. Individuals can subscribe to VPN services targeted to consumers, such as Private Internet Access (PIA) or CyberGhost. This is not an endorsement of either of these services. If you are interested in protecting yourself while connected to public hotspots, research VPN services to find one that meets your needs and budget.

LO 9.3 | Using Internet Clients

The growth in the number and type of Internet services has increased the number of client types required to access those services. We will limit our discussion of Internet clients to Web browsers and email clients. Many services are accessible through Web browsers. Email may be the most important service on the Internet—many people, who have no other use for the Internet, use email.

Web Browsers

While the World Wide Web (the Web) is just one of many services that exist on the Internet, it alone is responsible for most of the huge growth in Internet use that began after the Web's introduction in the early 1990s. Web technologies changed the look of Internet content from all text to rich and colorful graphics, and made it simple to navigate the Web by using a special type of client called a Web browser. In this section, learn about common browser features and the most common browsers used on desktop and laptop computers.

Common Browser Features

The Web browser's ease of use hides the complexity of the Internet, as protocols help to transfer the content of a Web page to the user's computer. There, the Web browser translates the plain-text language into a rich, colorful document that may contain links to other pages—often at disparate locations on the Internet. Today, the popular free Web browsers come in versions for macOS, Microsoft Windows, and Linux. Beyond the desktop, you'll find versions of these and other Web browsers with scaled-down screens for smartphones and tablets. In short, just about any electronic device that can connect to the Internet and has a display includes a Web browser.

Popular browsers share many of the same features for both general browsing and security. General browser features found in most browsers include:

- Active search
- Add-ons
- Autofill
- Automatic updates
- Bookmarks
- Integrated search engine
- Password manager

- Reading mode
- Personalization
- RSS feeds
- Search within page
- Synchronization
- Tabbed browsing
- Zoom

Google Chrome

Google Chrome is software from the Chromium open-source project and other sources. It has a clean look with no menu bar, but a small button on the right called the Chrome button that opens the Customize and Control menu (shown in Figure 9-14). From this menu, you can access any feature you would find in a menu bar. The Settings option opens your personal settings page (saved with your Google account). The Help option connects to Chrome's online help.

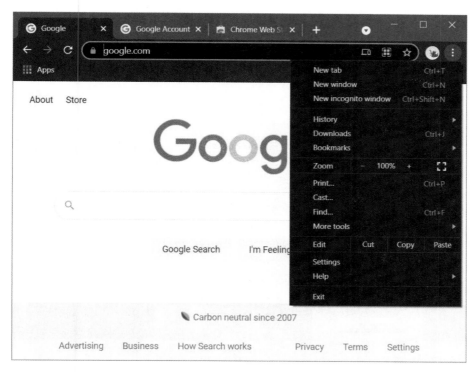

FIGURE 9–14 Google Chrome with three tabs open across the top and the Chrome menu open on the right.
Source: Google LLC

Mozilla Firefox

Mozilla Firefox is a product of the Mozilla Foundation. It has evolved as much as other browsers, with a look and features similar to them. Firefox also has a drop-down menu accessed from a button on the far right (Figure 9–15). It is available for Windows, macOS, Linux, Android, and iOS.

Internet Explorer

Microsoft introduced the Internet Explorer (IE) Web browser with the Windows 95 operating system. Microsoft retired this Web browser in 2021. It lasted as long as it did because many websites took advantage of its features, offering web extensions for it, but the world of browsers has moved on. Websites now use the features available in Chromium-based browsers.

Microsoft Edge

Microsoft Edge was introduced with Windows 10 as a replacement for IE. It is a Universal app, capable of adapting itself to all devices and screen sizes supported by Windows 10. Edge, like Google Chrome, is based on the code of the Chromium project. Like most browsers, Edge has a very clean look. It will be kept up-to-date with Windows Update. In addition to Windows, Edge is available for macOS, Android, iOS, and Linux. Figure 9–16 shows Microsoft Edge with the menu open on the right.

Other Browsers

Other browsers include Opera (**www.opera.com**) and Apple Safari (**www.apple.com/ safari**) for macOS. Unlike the other browsers discussed here, at this writing, Safari still has several drop-down menus with settings and features spread out among them.

FIGURE 9–15 Mozilla Firefox with the menu open on the right.
Source: Mozilla Corporation

FIGURE 9–16 Microsoft Edge with its menu open.
Source: Microsoft Corporation

Managing Privacy and Security

Rather than dive into the details of every security setting in your Web browser, we'll define certain security threats and describe how to manage them through modern Web browsers. Maintaining your privacy and security while browsing has become easier, because browsers now tend to turn on many critical protections. It has also become more complicated with all the added privacy and security features.

Cookies. As you learned in Chapter 2, cookies are good—mostly. Under some circumstances people can use them for the wrong purposes, but for the most part, their benefits outweigh the negatives. Normally, only the website that creates the cookies can access them. However, some advertisers on websites have the browser create so-called third-party cookies, which other sites that include this advertiser can use. Look for options to manage cookies when configuring a Web browser. Figure 9-17 shows the settings where you can change how Chrome handles cookies.

To check out the cookies settings for Firefox, click the menu button on the far right of the button bar. From the

try this!

Disable Third-Party Cookies in Chrome

Locate the settings for Cookies in the Chrome browser. Try this:

1. In the Chrome browser click the Chrome button on the far right of the menu bar to open the Chrome menu and select Settings.
2. On the Settings page scroll down to *Privacy and security*.
3. Select *Cookies and other site data*.
4. The *Cookies and other site data* category shows your current settings for cookies. If it is not enabled, turn on **Block third-party cookies.**
5. When you are done click the back arrow at the top of the page until you return to the Chrome browser page.

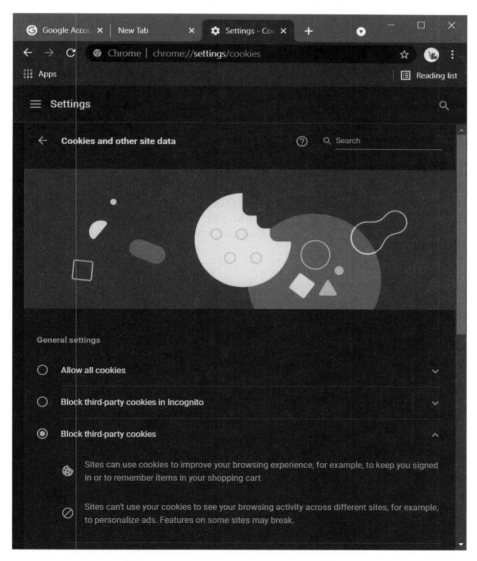

FIGURE 9–17 Chrome's settings for cookies are under the category *Cookies and other site data.*
Source: Google LLC

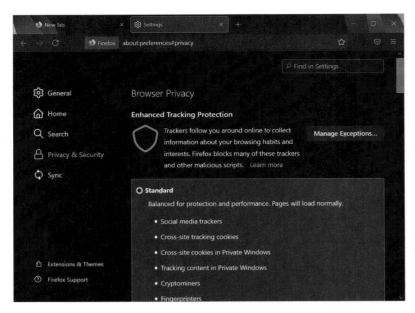

FIGURE 9–18 The Firefox *Privacy & Security* settings.
Source: Mozilla Corporation

drop-down menu select *Settings*. Settings should open with a sidebar on the left and a contents pane on the right. In the sidebar select *Privacy and Security*. Figure 9–18 shows just a few of the *Privacy & Security* options. Scroll down to see more. Firefox has grouped many settings together, offering two levels of privacy and security. They are *Standard* and *Strict*. Standard is a balanced approach that does not interfere with normal activities, but blocks trackers, cookies, and other threats from known sources. Strict is more secure but may interrupt your work. A third choice is *Custom* where you make your own decisions about tracking, cookies, cryptominers, fingerprinters, and more.

To change the Cookies settings in Microsoft Edge, click or tap the menu button on the far right of the button bar, select *Settings*. This opens the *Settings* tab with a sidebar on the left and content pane on the right. If both areas are not visible, drag the left or right edge of the window to widen it until they are both visible. In the Sidebar select *Cookies and site permissions*. In the content pane, locate and select *Manage and delete cookies and site data*. Figure 9–19 shows some of the settings. Notice that *Block third-party cookies* is turned on. To see other settings, scroll down.

Browsing History. Your browsing history is useful information to marketers and others who want to learn more about you. At the same time, some of their use of this information also makes life a bit easier for you when you return to favorite sites. While your browser does not divulge this information, a system compromised by spyware or malware could reveal this information to the wrong persons. Additionally, if you leave your computer unattended but logged on with your account, anyone with access to your computer could look at your browsing history; system administrators or others who

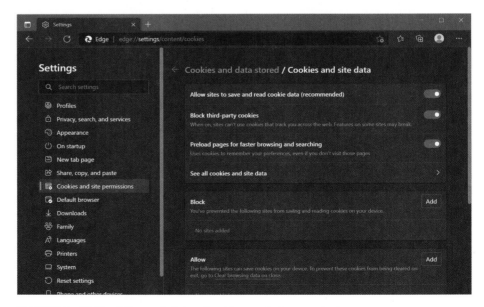

FIGURE 9–19 The Microsoft Edge *Cookies and site permissions*.
Source: Microsoft Corporation

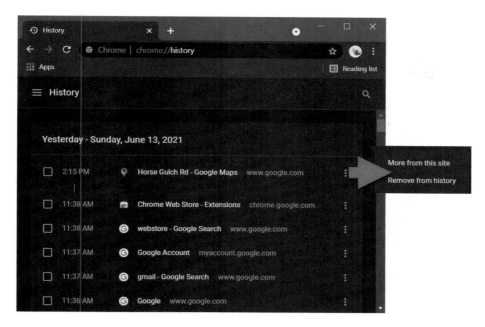

FIGURE 9–20 The Chrome History page.
Source: Google LLC

have administrative access to your computer can do the same. Once again, your security needs may be at odds with your need for convenience on the Web. Therefore, Web browsers allow you to manage your browsing history.

Access the Chrome browser History page with the keyboard shortcut Ctrl+H. Figure 9–20 shows the History page. From this page, you can search through the history, clear all browsing history, and select items using the check boxes to the left of each one. Or you can click the Actions button to the right of each item, which allows you to see more items from that site (searching) or remove the item from history.

In Firefox, the *History* settings are in the *Privacy & Security* pane, shown in Figure 9–21, where you can choose to have Firefox *Remember history, Never remember history*, or use *Custom settings*. If you select the Clear History button, you choose what type of history is cleared: *Browsing and Download History, Active Logins, Form and Search, Cookies, or Cache*). To see recent history in Firefox, open the drop-down menu from the button on the far right of the button bar and select History from the drop-down menu. This opens the History menu where you can view recently closed tabs, clear recent history, and see recent history of websites you visited in Firefox.

In Microsoft Edge, the CTRL-SHIFT-DELETE shortcut opens the browser settings to the *Clear browsing data* page, where you can clear selected browsing data stored by Edge. You can choose to clear data from the current device or across all your synced devices.

FIGURE 9–21 The Firefox History settings page.
Source: Microsoft Corporation

While a Chrome incognito window is open, this character on the right of the button bar watches over the window.
Source: Google LLC

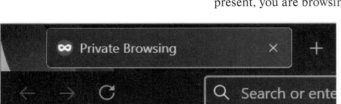

A white mask appears at the top of a Firefox Private Browsing window.
Source: Microsoft Corporation

Private Browsing. Private browsing is a browser security feature that allows you to browse the Web without saving any history on the local computer. All of the browsers discussed here offer private browsing. When you turn on private browsing you open a new window, and your protection exists as long as you remain in that window, even as you open new tabs within the window. Always use private browsing when you use a shared computer, as in a library or school lab.

Chrome's name for private browsing is incognito. To start a private browsing session in Chrome, select **new incognito window** from the Chrome menu or use the shortcut CTRL-SHIFT-N. Then notice the icon in the upper-right corner, shown here, resembling a man with glasses and hat peering down on your folders. As long as this is present, you are browsing incognito in Chrome.

Firefox simply calls the feature Private Browsing. To use it, click on the menu button on the right side of the button bar and select **New Private Window** or use the shortcut CTRL-SHIFT-P. The Firefox Private Browsing window is clearly marked, with a white mask on the top left of the window, as shown here.

The Microsoft Edge term for private browsing is InPrivate Browsing. In Microsoft Edge, click the menu button on the far right of the button bar and select *New InPrivate window*. When you open an InPrivate window, as shown in Figure 9–22, it opens a page that informs you that InPrivate is turned on and provides information about this feature. When you are ready to continue browsing, simply enter a universal resource locator (URL) or a search string in the address box.

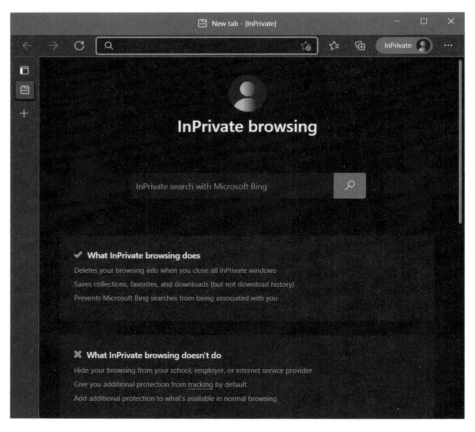

FIGURE 9–22 The Microsoft Edge InPrivate browsing window.
Source: Microsoft Corporation

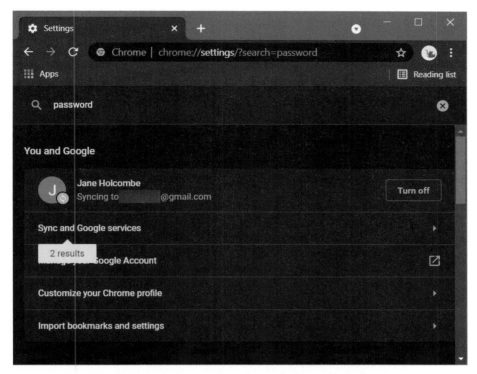

FIGURE 9–23 The Search results from searching **password** in Chrome Settings.
Source: Google LLC

Passwords. Do you like to have your browser remember your password to websites, or would you rather enter your user name and password every time you access a site? While it is convenient to have the browser remember passwords, this practice is a security risk if your computer is not protected with a strong password, or if you leave your computer unattended while you are logged in. It is also a great security risk if you are using a borrowed computer at a library or other public location. On your own computer configure the browser password settings that work best for you.

In Chrome, open the Chrome menu and select Settings. In Settings, enter **password** in the search box. The search results will resemble Figure 9-23, highlighting all the settings having to do with passwords in Chrome. The first one is for synchronizing your settings across your devices, a handy feature if you sign in to Chrome with a Google account and want all your Google preferences synchronized across your devices. There are several more password-related settings in Chrome. To see these, you need to scroll down in the window shown in Figure 9-23.

Manage passwords in Firefox using the Firefox Lockwise service. Begin by opening the Firefox menu and selecting *Passwords*. This takes you to the Firefox Lockwise window, shown in Figure 9-24. If you don't already have a sign-in, create one by clicking the *Sign in to sync* button. You can also import or export login information from other browsers by selecting the menu button on the right in this window.

In Microsoft Edge, open Settings. Under *Your profile* select *Passwords*. On the *Profiles/Passwords* page (Figure 9-25), browse through the settings and select those that work best for you. Scroll down to see a list of sites where you have allowed the browser to save passwords (knowingly or not). You can delete sites from this list or click on the Actions button to the right of each item, which gives you the options to copy, edit, or delete a password.

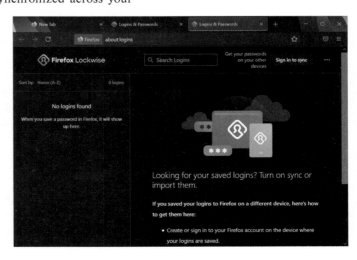

FIGURE 9–24 The Firefox Lockwise window.
Source: Mozilla Corporation

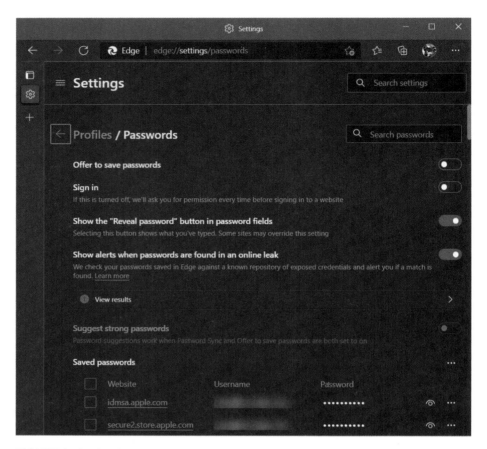

FIGURE 9–25 Configure the Edge browser's password settings on the Profiles/ Passwords page.
Source: Microsoft Corporation

Pop-Ups. We've all seen them. Those windows that pop up on top of your browser from a website advertising products, wanting to show you videos, or any number of excuses to get your attention and interrupt your stream of thought. We call them pop-ups, and not all pop-ups are bad. Some of our favorite websites use pop-up windows to open something we requested, such as a downloaded page or a login page, but the latest standard for creating Web pages discourages pop-ups because they do not work on all platforms and they interfere with assistive browsing technologies. Therefore, the use of pop-ups should wane in coming years. For the foreseeable future software that blocks pop-ups is necessary, but it also needs to be configurable so you can block pop-ups from all but the sites you trust.

To access the Pop-up settings for all of the browsers featured here, simply open Settings and type "pop-up" in the Search box. You will find that the default is to turn off Pop-ups. If you wish to make exceptions for websites you trust, simply open the Pop-ups option and add exceptions.

Email Clients

The scope of Internet email has made several major jumps in the past decades. It evolved from a service used by academics and government workers, through the period when early PC users accessed services such as CompuServ, to today's casual PC users, numbered in the billions, who joined the Internet since the advent of the World Wide Web in 1991. Because of the explosion in the use of the Internet, email has long been the most compelling reason to own a PC—but today you do not need to use a PC to send and receive email. Many people access their personal and business email from their mobile devices. Further, you do not need to own the device you use for Internet access.

An email client used in a school or corporate network may be specific to the private mail servers the user connects to, such as Microsoft Exchange, or the client may be one that you can use for different types of mail servers. Many users have access to email client software such as Microsoft Outlook, Apple Mail, or Mozilla Thunderbird. Users who subscribe to Web mail or free email services such as Gmail, Mailcom, Outlook.com, or ProtonMail can use a Web browser rather than special email client software. Regardless of the type of client software, they all accomplish the task of sending and receiving in the same way.

The client software will show a list of all the messages in the mailbox by displaying information it reads from the message headers. The message header is information added to the beginning of the message that contains details such as who sent it and the subject, and also may show the time and date of the message along with the message's size. Then the user may click on a message to open it and read the body of the email. Users can respond to the message, save the message, create a new message, add attachments, and/or send it to the intended recipient.

Email clients have become much easier to use, even to the point of automatically detecting and configuring the underlying settings for connecting to an email server, given your personal account information. They also will import your email and contact information from other accounts.

Email Protocols

There are three types of email accounts: POP, IMAP, and Web mail. The first two are protocols, while the third describes email that you access via a Web browser. When you configure an email client, you need to know the address and type of server, defined by the account type.

POP. Post Office Protocol (POP) is a protocol that enables email client computers to pick up email from mail servers, so that you can open it and read it in your email client. When it picks up a message, it deletes it from the POP server. The current version is POP3. This has been very popular with ISPs because it minimizes the amount of disk space required on the email server for each account. The user is responsible for maintaining and backing up messages. When the client computer does not connect to the email server, the user can still access all the locally stored messages.

IMAP. Internet Message Access Protocol (IMAP) is a protocol that will allow users to maintain the messages stored on an email server (usually on the Internet) without removing them from the server. This type of account allows you to log in and access your message store from any computer. Of course, the message store is not available to you when you are offline, and you may run out of allotted disk space on the mail server, at which point it rejects new messages.

Web Mail. Web mail is a generic term for using a Web browser (and therefore, HTTPS) to retrieve email, often replacing the traditional email client, such as Microsoft Outlook. In fact, this may be the method the tech support at school or work instructs you to use, allowing you to access your email from any browser on any device.

Configuring and Using an Email Client

Whether you use Outlook, Apple Mail, or one of many third-party email clients, you should be prepared with the information to configure your email client. This includes:

- The protocol used by the mail server you are accessing (POP3, IMAP, HTTPS, or HTTP).
- Your account name and password.

Note: A variation on a pop-up is a pop-under, a window that opens behind your browser window. Anytime you close a browser window and are puzzled to see a browser window (usually with an advertisement) lurking behind it, you have encountered a pop-under. These are also controlled through the pop-up settings for each browser.

Note: Don't confuse Microsoft Outlook, the email client, with Microsoft **Outlook.com**, the Web mail service.

- The DNS name of the incoming mail server.
- If you are preparing to connect to a POP3 or IMAP server, you will also need to know the name of an outgoing mail server.

If you do not have this information, ask your ISP, in the case of a private account, or ask a network administrator if your mail server is a school or corporate mail server. ISPs often provide email configuration information on their websites. Check this out before configuring your email client because it will help you avoid certain pitfalls. For instance, when configuring a client using a cell data connection, you may have to configure it to authenticate to a certain mail server in the home service area.

In Step-by-Step 9.02, we use Microsoft Outlook to demonstrate how to configure an email account. Although we stated that you need the information listed above, you might be lucky because email clients, such as Apple Mail and Outlook, can automatically configure some types of email accounts given just the user name and password. This is where you should start. Then, if that doesn't work, use the other information you gathered.

Step-by-Step 9.02

Adding an Email Account to an Email Client

To complete this step-by-step exercise, you will need a PC with an Internet connection and an email client. In this exercise, we use Microsoft Outlook in Windows 10. The basic steps are similar in other email clients. We assume you are adding an account and that the email client already has one account configured. If this is the first account for this email client, you may have introductory screens that will walk you through the process. To complete the exercise, you will need the first two items listed here for all accounts, and the last four only if the client fails to automatically connect to your account with the basic login information.

- The type of account.
- Your password, account name, and email address. The last two are often just the email address.
- The DNS name of an incoming mail server for POP3, IMAP, or HTTP.
- The DNS name of an outgoing mail server (SMTP).
- If using a provider, such as Gmail, you may need to change the settings for your Gmail account to allow IMAP access.

Step 1

Locate the option for adding an account. In Outlook select the *File* tab.

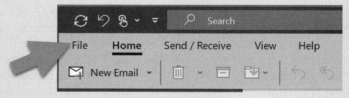

Source: Microsoft Corporation

Step 2

Under *Account Information* select *Add Account*.

Source: Microsoft Corporation

In this dialog box, enter the email address of the account and then select *Advanced Options*. Next, click to add a checkmark next to *Let me set up my account manually*. Then select *Connect*.

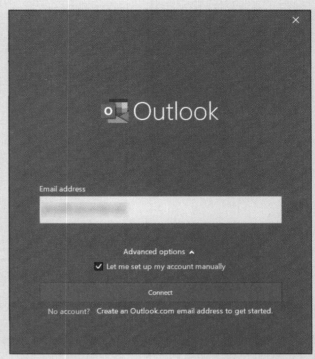

Source: Microsoft Corporation

On this screen, select the type of email service assigned to you by your administrator or instructor. We selected IMAP for our particular service because it is not one of the more popular email services, such as Gmail. It requires IMAP settings.

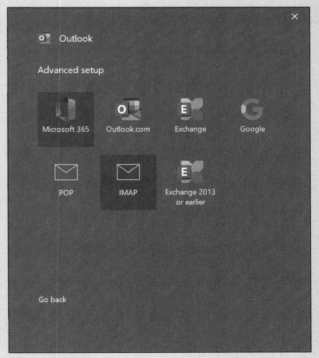

Source: Microsoft Corporation

Check the spelling of the email address. If it is correct, then enter the password and select *Connect*.

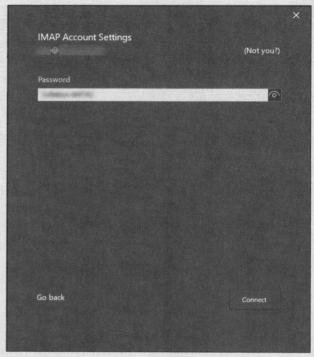

Source: Microsoft Corporation

Outlook asks for more settings to connect with your email service. In this example, the settings are for the IMAP type of service. Once you enter the settings, click Next.

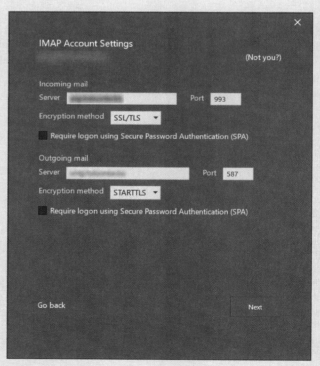

Source: Microsoft Corporation

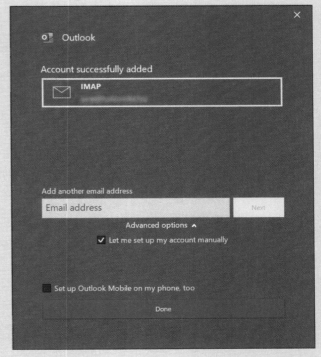

Step 7

The Account was successfully added to IMAP. At this point you can add yet another account or select *Done*, which will close this window. Microsoft will send a test message to the newly configured account. Outlook will open, and you can check that the test email was received.

LO 9.4 | Sharing Files and Printers

The file and printer sharing service allows users to share and access files and printers over a network. All the OSs discussed in this book have methods for allowing file and printer sharing. There are two sides to file and printer sharing: the server side and the client side, and before you implement either side of this equation, take a few minutes to understand how they interact. Both sides must use complementary file and printer services that can talk to each other. Then you can implement sharing on the server side (even on a desktop computer) and users can access it from the client side. For our examples, we'll use Microsoft Windows 10.

The Server Side of File and Printer Sharing

A **file and printer server** (often simply called a file server) is a computer that gives client computers access to files and printers over a network. The actual folder or printer being shared acts as a connecting point on the server and is called a **share**.

A share is visible as a folder over the network, but it is a separate entity from the disk folder or printer to which it points. Like other file-sharing services, the one installed with Windows allows you to share both files and printers. This service is installed and enabled by default, although it is up to you to decide how to use it. On a Windows desktop computer, look for File and Printer Sharing for Microsoft Networks in the Properties dialog box for a network connection, as shown in Figure 9-26.

try this!

Find Microsoft File and Printer Servers

Use File Explorer in Windows 10 to look for the file and printer servers on your network. Try this:

1. Open Windows File Explorer.
2. Select the Network folder in the navigation pane.
3. View the icons in the contents pane. The icons resembling a computer with a blue screen are file and printer servers.
4. If any file and printer servers are visible, double-click one to access it and browse. If you do not have permissions, you will see a Network Error message. If you have permissions to a server, you will be able to browse the folders to which you have permissions.

The Client Side of File and Printer Sharing

A file and printer client includes both the user interface and the underlying file-sharing protocols to access its matching file-sharing server service on a network server. The client for Microsoft file and printer sharing is installed and enabled by default. With the client installed, you can use the Windows GUI to see those Microsoft computers on the network that have file and printer sharing turned on. You can see both dedicated Windows network servers and Windows desktops that have this service turned on. Your ability to connect to any shares on those computers depends on the permissions applied to each share. Figure 9–27 shows one computer (Windows-10-Desk) with file sharing turned on and a multifunction device (MX920) with print sharing turned on. Other network devices are detected, including Sonos speakers and a Wi-Fi router (RT-N12D1).

With appropriate permissions, you will be able to browse to the shared folders on a server and perform file operations, such as copying, moving, deleting, and opening files in your locally installed applications.

FIGURE 9–26 File and Printer Sharing for Microsoft Networks is listed for a network connection.
Source: Microsoft Corporation

Note: As a rule, a desktop computer should not have File and Printer Sharing turned on, especially if the computer is a member of a domain and connects to dedicated servers for file and printer services. The exception to this is when a desktop computer is participating in a HomeGroup or work group and must share local files and printers with other computers. This is common in the small office/home office (SOHO) situation.

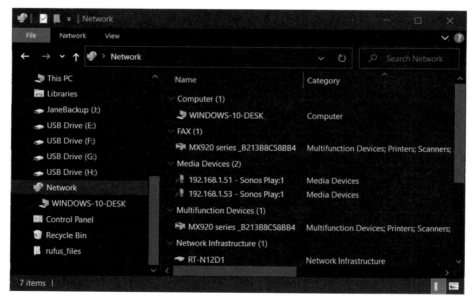

FIGURE 9–27 The computers and printer listed at the bottom under Network have File and Printer Sharing turned on.
Source: Microsoft Corporation

LO 9.5 | Troubleshooting Common Network Client Problems

If you are unable to access another computer on the network, several command-line utilities will help in pinpointing the source of a problem and arriving at a solution. In this section, you will learn to troubleshoot common client connection problems using each of these utilities, as indicated by the symptoms. Each utility provides different information and is most valuable when used appropriately. For instance, you should first view the IP configuration using the **ipconfig** or **ifconfig** utility and verify that it is correct for the network to which you are connected. If you discover any obvious problems when you view the IP configuration, correct them before proceeding. Then test the ability to communicate using the **ping** command. In Step-by-Step 9.03 you will use these commands and others to test connectivity.

Built-In Network Diagnostics

Each of the operating systems surveyed in this book has a variety of utilities for diagnosing network problems. From the command-line utilities discussed later in this section to GUI tools that combine the functions of several tools into one broad-stroke diagnostics tool, each generation of operating systems brings improvements in these tools. In Windows 10 use the *Network Trouble-shooter*, found under *Network & Internet* settings. Figure 9-28 shows the initial screen. Begin by selecting a network adapter; proceed through the Troubleshooter, answering questions. It will test the network and provide possible solutions.

The Network Utility in macOS, shown in Figure 9-29, requires more knowledge of the individual tools, but it does spare you from entering the commands from the macOS Terminal window.

Testing IP Configurations and Connectivity

When the TCP/IP suite is installed on a computer, it includes many protocols and many handy little programs that network professionals quickly learn to use. You should learn two right away, for those times when you find yourself sitting at your computer and talking to a network professional while trying to resolve a network problem. These are commands you enter at a command line. In Windows these commands are **ipconfig** and **ping**. In macOS and Linux they are **ifconfig** and **ping**. Learn about these commands below, and then do Step-by-Step 9.03, in which you will use both of these commands to test a network connection.

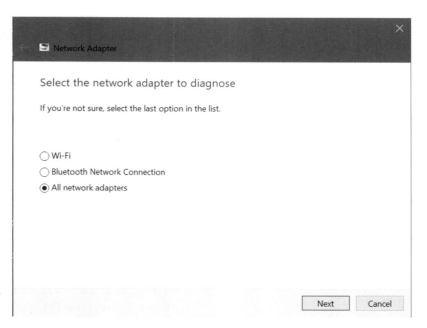

FIGURE 9-28 The Windows 10 Network Troubleshooter.
Source: Microsoft Corporation

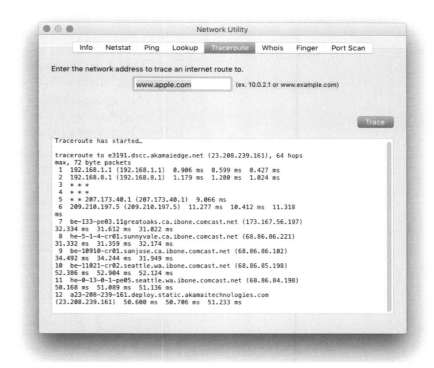

FIGURE 9-29 The macOS Network Utility at work (notice the various network diagnostic tools listed across the top).
Source: Apple Inc.

Verifying IP Configuration with ipconfig

The **ipconfig** command will display the IP configuration of all network interface cards, including those that receive their addresses and configuration through DHCP. Using this command shows whether the IP settings have been successfully bound to your network adapter. *Bound* means that there is a linking relationship, called a binding, between network components—in this case, between the network protocol and the adapter. A binding establishes the order in which each network component handles network communications. When troubleshooting network connectivity problems on an IP network, always use the **ipconfig** command to verify the IP configuration.

If the **ipconfig** command reveals an address beginning with 169.254, it is an APIPA address and a symptom of a failure of a Windows DHCP client to receive an IP address from a DHCP server (for whatever reason). Troubleshoot the DHCP server on your network (such as the DHCP service in a broadband router).

Troubleshooting Connection Errors with the ping Command

The **ping** command is useful for testing the communications between two computers. The name of this command is actually an acronym for packet Internet groper, but we prefer to think (as many do) that it was named after the sound of underwater sonar. Instead of bouncing sound waves off surfaces, the **ping** command uses data packets, and it sends them to specific IP addresses, requesting a response (hence the idea of pinging). This is a great test to see if you can access a certain computer.

To use the **ping** command, give it an address and it sends packets to the specified address, "listens" for a reply, and then displays the results.

1. Pinging the IP address of the computer's own NIC and receiving a successful response indicates that the IP protocol and the local address is working. Using the example in Figure 9–30, from Host_1-1 you would type: **ping 192.168.1.101** to ping the local NIC.

2. Then ping another computer on the same network to test the ability to communicate between the two computers. Again, from Host_1-1 you would type **ping 192.168.1.102** to ping Host_1-2, a computer on the same network.

3. Next, ping the gateway address to ensure that your computer can communicate with the router. Again, working from Host_1-1 in Figure 9–30, type **ping 192.168.1.1** to ping the gateway address for Network 1, which is the address of the router interface (NIC) connected to Network 1.

4. Finally, ping an address beyond your network, to test the router and the ability to communicate with a computer via the router. Using Figure 9–30, from Host_1-1 type **ping 192.168.2.101** to ping the address of Host_2-1 on Network 2.

Now the bad news about the **ping** command. First, a firewall can block specific types of traffic or configure an individual computer not to respond to a ping. Hence, you may not be able to ping a computer, even if you can communicate with that same computer in other ways such as by Web browsing or downloading email.

The reason firewalls or individual computers block or ignore the requests from a **ping** command is because people can use this command in malicious ways—most notoriously in a denial-of-service (DoS) attack, in which someone sends a large number of ping requests to an address, overwhelming the server so that it is unavailable to accept other traffic.

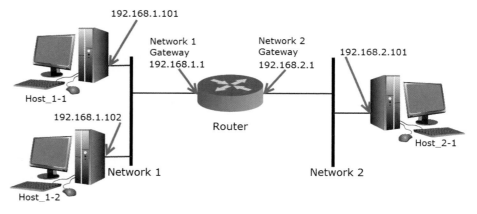

FIGURE 9–30 Two networks connected by a router.

Step-by-Step 9.03

Testing an IP Configuration

In this step-by-step exercise, you will first open a command-line interface (CLI) in Windows—either Command Prompt or Windows PowerShell. Then, you will run a CLI command to determine if the IP settings are automatic or static. Next, you will verify that you can communicate with a computer on your network and then test your connection to a router on your network. Finally, test to confirm that you can communicate with a computer beyond your network. To complete this exercise, you will need the following:

- A computer with Windows 10.

- A working connection to the Internet.
- The IP address of another computer on your local network (use this when a step asks for *NearbyIPaddress*). Enter this in the appropriate line in Step 3.
- The IP address of a computer beyond your local network (use this when a step asks for *RemoteIPaddress*). Enter this in the appropriate line in Step 3.
- The user name and password of an account that is a member of your computer's Administrators group.

Step 1

Begin by opening a CLI where you will run commands to view settings and test connectivity. First, right-click on the Start button to open the Power User Menu. Select either *Command Prompt (Admin)* or Windows Power Shell (Admin). This will open the User Account Control (UAC) message box. After you respond to the UAC message, the Command Prompt or Windows PowerShell window will open. At the prompt in the CLI type **ipconfig/all**.

```
Administrator: Windows PowerShell                                    —    □    ×

Windows PowerShell
Copyright (C) Microsoft Corporation. All rights reserved.

PS C:\WINDOWS\system32> ipconfig /all

Windows IP Configuration

   Host Name . . . . . . . . . . . . : SeeMore
   Primary Dns Suffix  . . . . . . . :
   Node Type . . . . . . . . . . . . : Hybrid
   IP Routing Enabled. . . . . . . . : No
   WINS Proxy Enabled. . . . . . . . : No

Wireless LAN adapter Wi-Fi:

   Connection-specific DNS Suffix  . :
   Description . . . . . . . . . . . : Intel(R) Dual Band Wireless-AC 7265
   Physical Address. . . . . . . . . : 34-02-86-DE-1E-4E
   DHCP Enabled. . . . . . . . . . . : Yes
   Autoconfiguration Enabled . . . . : Yes
   Link-local IPv6 Address . . . . . : fe80::6dbd:11ac:7c99:d59f%11(Preferred)
   IPv4 Address. . . . . . . . . . . : 192.168.1.30(Preferred)
   Subnet Mask . . . . . . . . . . . : 255.255.255.0
   Lease Obtained. . . . . . . . . . : Tuesday, June 15, 2021 5:27:54 AM
   Lease Expires . . . . . . . . . . : Wednesday, June 16, 2021 5:28:22 AM
   Default Gateway . . . . . . . . . : 192.168.1.1
   DHCP Server . . . . . . . . . . . : 192.168.1.1
   DHCPv6 IAID . . . . . . . . . . . : 104071814
   DHCPv6 Client DUID. . . . . . . . : 00-01-00-01-28-30-9E-BB-34-02-86-DE-1E-4E
   DNS Servers . . . . . . . . . . . : 1.1.1.1
                                       192.168.1.1
   NetBIOS over Tcpip. . . . . . . . : Enabled
```

Source: Microsoft Corporation

Step 2

If the current settings show an IP address other than 0.0.0.0, IP has successfully bound an IP address to the network adapter. If the current settings include DHCP enabled = **Yes,** and shows an IP address for a DHCP server, then your network adapter is configured to receive an address automatically and has received its address from the DHCP server whose address is listed. If your DHCP Enabled setting = **No** and your computer has a set of values for the IP address and subnet mask, then it has a static IP configuration that is successfully bound to the network adapter.

Step 3

Gather the information from the **ipconfig /all** command and fill in the first three lines provided below. Your instructor will give you the last two items, *NearbyIPaddress* and *RemoteIPaddress*. You will need these addresses in the following steps.

IPaddress: _____

Default GatewayIPaddress: _____

DNSServerIPaddress: _____

NearbyIPaddress: _____

RemoteIPaddress: _____

Step 4

At the prompt, enter **ping** *IPaddress,* where "*IPaddress*" is the address of your computer from Step 3. You should receive four replies if your computer is properly configured. If you receive an error message or fewer than four replies, report this to your instructor.

Step 5

At the prompt, enter **ping** *NearbyIPaddress,* where "*NearbyIPaddress*" is the address of another computer on your same network. You should receive four replies if your computer is properly configured and if the other computer is also powered up and properly configured. If you receive an error message or fewer than four replies, report this to your instructor.

```
Administrator: Windows PowerShell                             —    □    ×
PS C:\WINDOWS\system32> ping 192.168.1.3

Pinging 192.168.1.3 with 32 bytes of data:
Reply from 192.168.1.3: bytes=32 time=2ms TTL=128
Reply from 192.168.1.3: bytes=32 time=2ms TTL=128
Reply from 192.168.1.3: bytes=32 time=1ms TTL=128
Reply from 192.168.1.3: bytes=32 time=3ms TTL=128

Ping statistics for 192.168.1.3:
    Packets: Sent = 4, Received = 4, Lost = 0 (0% loss),
Approximate round trip times in milli-seconds:
    Minimum = 1ms, Maximum = 3ms, Average = 2ms
PS C:\WINDOWS\system32>
```

Source: Microsoft Corporation

Step 6

If the last test was successful, and if your computer has a gateway address, test this address now. Return to the prompt and enter **ping** *Default gatewayIPaddress,* where "*Default gatewayIPaddress*" equals the Default Gateway address recorded in Step 3. You should receive four replies if your computer is properly configured and if the default gateway is active on your network.

```
Administrator: Windows PowerShell                             —    □    ×
PS C:\WINDOWS\system32> ping 192.168.1.1

Pinging 192.168.1.1 with 32 bytes of data:
Reply from 192.168.1.1: bytes=32 time=1ms TTL=64
Reply from 192.168.1.1: bytes=32 time=1ms TTL=64
Reply from 192.168.1.1: bytes=32 time=1ms TTL=64
Reply from 192.168.1.1: bytes=32 time=2ms TTL=64

Ping statistics for 192.168.1.1:
    Packets: Sent = 4, Received = 4, Lost = 0 (0% loss),
Approximate round trip times in milli-seconds:
    Minimum = 1ms, Maximum = 2ms, Average = 1ms
PS C:\WINDOWS\system32>
```

Source: Microsoft Corporation

If your IP configuration includes the address of a DNS server, you should test connectivity to the DNS server now. Return to the prompt and enter **ping** *DNSServerIPaddress,* where *"DNSServerIPaddress"* equals the DNSServer address recorded in Step 3. You should receive four replies if your computer is properly configured and if the default gateway is active on your network.

```
Administrator: Windows PowerShell                      —    □    X

PS C:\WINDOWS\system32> ping 1.1.1.1

Pinging 1.1.1.1 with 32 bytes of data:
Reply from 1.1.1.1: bytes=32 time=20ms TTL=56
Reply from 1.1.1.1: bytes=32 time=18ms TTL=56
Reply from 1.1.1.1: bytes=32 time=20ms TTL=56
Reply from 1.1.1.1: bytes=32 time=20ms TTL=56

Ping statistics for 1.1.1.1:
    Packets: Sent = 4, Received = 4, Lost = 0 (0% loss),
Approximate round trip times in milli-seconds:
    Minimum = 18ms, Maximum = 20ms, Average = 19ms
PS C:\WINDOWS\system32>
```

Source: Microsoft Corporation

If you were given the address of a computer beyond your local network, test this address now by returning to the prompt and entering **ping** *RemoteIPaddress,* where *"RemoteIPaddress"* is the address of the remote computer.

Troubleshooting Connection Problems with tracert

You may have situations in which you can connect to a website or other remote resource, but the connection is very slow. If this connection is critical to business, you will want to gather information so that a network administrator or ISP can troubleshoot the source of the bottleneck. You can use the **tracert** command to gather this information. **tracert** is a command-line utility that traces the route taken by packets to a destination. When you use this command with the name or IP address of the target host, it will **ping** each of the intervening routers, from the nearest to the farthest, as shown in Figure 9–31. You see the length of the delay at each router, and you will be able to determine the location of the bottleneck. You can then provide this information to the people who will troubleshoot it for you. Consider a scenario in which your connection to the Google search engine (www. google.com) is extremely slow. You can use this command to run **tracert** and save the results to a file: **tracert** www .google.com > tracegoogle.txt.

Note: The equivalent command in Linux or macOS Terminal is **traceroute.**

try this!

Use tracert

You can use **tracert** to determine where a problem is occurring. Try this:

1. Open a Command Prompt or Windows PowerShell.
2. Type **tracert www.google.com**.
3. If the command runs successfully, you will see output similar to Figure 9–31, but with different intervening routers.

Troubleshooting DNS Errors Using ping, netstat, and nslookup

Have you ever attempted to browse to a Web page, only to have your browser display an error message such as "Cannot find server or DNS Error"? This may be a name resolution problem because the fully qualified domain name (FQDN) portion of a URL, such as www.google.com, must be resolved to an IP address before a single packet goes to the website.

Note: The file created when you run the command **tracert** www.google. com > tracegoogle.txt is saved in the current directory (C:-Windows\ system32 in Figure 9–31). Use the **type** command to see the contents.

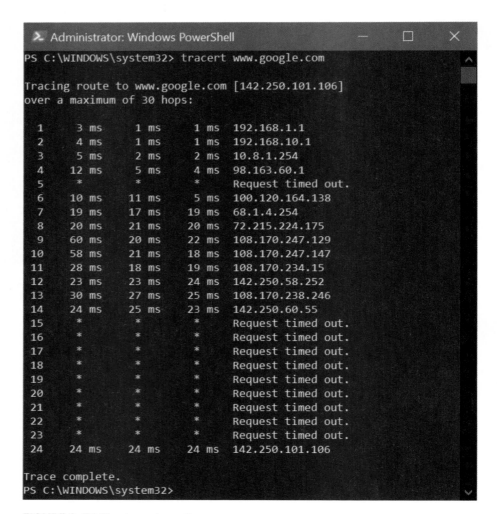

FIGURE 9–31 The tracert results.
Source: Microsoft Corporation

Using the ping Command to Troubleshoot DNS

One way to test if the problem is a connectivity problem or a DNS error is to first test for connectivity by either pinging the IP address of the website or using the IP address in place of the FQDN in the URL. If you cannot reach the website by using its IP address, then it is a connectivity problem and you should resolve it by contacting your network administrator or ISP and telling them the symptoms and the results of the **ping** test.

If you can reach the website by pinging the IP address but cannot access it through your browser, then it is a name resolution problem. A simple test to see if DNS name resolution is working is to ping the FQDN. Figure 9–32 shows the result of pinging the FQDN www.google.com. Notice that this displays the IP address of the website, confirming the DNS name-to-IP address resolution is working.

Troubleshooting with the netstat Command

When you are troubleshooting networking problems, it is very helpful to have a second computer that does not display the same problems. Then you can use the second computer to discover the IP address of a website by using your browser to connect. Once

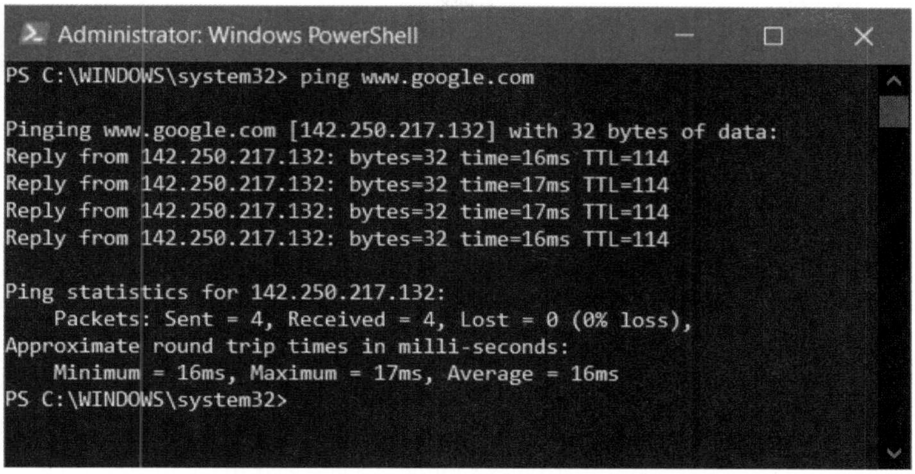

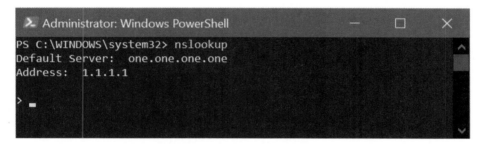

FIGURE 9–32 Pinging the FQDN **www.google.com** reveals the IP address.
Source: Microsoft Corporation

FIGURE 9–33 The **nslookup** command displays the address of the default DNS server.
Source: Microsoft Corporation

connected, you can use the **netstat** command to discover the IP address of the website. **netstat** displays network statistics, protocol statistics, and information about current TCP/IP connections.

Using the nslookup Command to Troubleshoot DNS

Finally, the classic command for troubleshooting DNS, used for many years on the Internet and other TCP/IP networks, is **nslookup.** The NS in this command name stands for "name server." This command allows you to send queries to a DNS name server directly and see the results. It is a very powerful command, but you can use it to test your DNS setting without learning all of its subcommands. Running **nslookup** in a Command Prompt without any additional command-line parameters will cause it to attempt to connect to the name server address in your IP configuration. Then it displays the **nslookup** prompt, a greater-than sign (>), as in Figure 9–33. You may enter subcommands at this prompt. If it cannot connect to the DNS server, it will display an error, "Can't find server name. . .". If you see this error, contact your network administrator or ISP. Type **exit** at the **nslookup** prompt to exit from the command. Then type **exit** again to exit from the Command Prompt or Windows PowerShell.

Chapter 9 REVIEW

Chapter Summary

After reading this chapter and completing the Step-by-Step tutorials and try this! exercises, you should understand the following facts about networking:

Configuring a Network Connection

- A protocol is a set of rules, usually formalized in a standard published by one of many standards organizations. A software implementation of a protocol is also called a protocol.
- TCP/IP is the protocol suite needed to access the Internet.
- Transmission Control Protocol (TCP) and Internet Protocol (IP) are the core protocols of TCP/IP.
- An IP address assigned to a network adapter or modem connects it to a network.
- IPv4, an old version of the protocol, is slowly being replaced by IPv6.
- Public IP addresses are for hosts on the Internet, and each address must be unique on the entire Internet.
- A private IP address is one of three ranges of IP addresses designated for use only on private networks.
- Computers on a private network using private IP addresses get access to the Internet through a specialized device, usually a router.
- Each host on a TCP/IP network must have an IP address. A host receives an address by two general methods: automatically as a DHCP client via a network DHCP server, or as a static address.
- In addition to the IP address there are several IP configuration settings including subnet mask, default gateway, DNS server, advanced DNS settings, and WINS settings.

Connecting to the Internet

- A connection to the Internet is a wide area network (WAN) connection.
- An Internet service provider (ISP) is an organization that provides access to the Internet.
- Common wired WAN technologies include dial-up, ISDN, DSL, and cable.
- ISDN is a digital telephone service that simultaneously transmits voice, data, and control signaling over a single telephone line.
- Digital subscriber line (DSL) service is similar to ISDN in its use of the telephone network, but it uses more advanced digital signal processing to compress

more signals through the telephone lines and is much faster than ISDN.
- Many cable television companies now offer Internet access through existing cable television connections using special cable modems.
- Wireless options for connecting to the Internet include cellular networks, wireless wide area networks (WWANs), wireless LAN (WLAN) connections (if the WLAN ultimately connects to the Internet), and satellite.
- Mobile users and remote offices often need to connect to the corporate intranet through the Internet using any of the connection technologies discussed previously, with the addition of a virtual private network (VPN) for security.

Using Internet Clients

- Web technologies changed the look of Internet content from all text to rich and colorful graphics using a special type of client called a Web browser.
- The top Web browsers are Google Chrome, Mozilla Firefox, and Microsoft Edge.
- Browsers have many configuration settings that range from GUI preferences to settings critical to protecting your privacy and maintaining security for your computer and personal data.
- An email service and client are defined by the protocols they use, which are POP3, IMAP, and Web mail (HTML protocol).
- While some email services require dedicated clients, some email clients can interact with a variety of email server types.
- To configure any email client you need a specific set of information. This includes:
  - The type of mail server you are accessing (POP3, IMAP, or HTTP).
  - Your account name and password.
  - The DNS name of the incoming mail server.
  - If you are preparing to connect to a POP3 or IMAP server, you will also need to know the name of an outgoing mail server.

Sharing Files and Printers

- A file and printer sharing protocol allows a computer to share files and printers with compatible clients.
- A file and printer client includes both the user interface and the underlying file-sharing protocols to access

a file-sharing system on a network file and printer server.

- Windows installs with both the server and client components for file and printer sharing.

Troubleshooting Common Network Client Connection Problems

- All the OSs surveyed in this book have GUI-based Network Diagnostics that combine many functions.

- Several command-line commands help in diagnosing and solving network client connection problems. These utilities include:
  - **ipconfig**
  - **ifconfig**
  - **ping**
  - **tracert**
  - **netstat**
  - **nslookup**

Key Terms List

automatic IP addressing *(326)*

Automatic Private IP Addressing (APIPA) *(326)*

cellular hotspot *(337)*

default gateway *(328)*

dial-up *(334)*

digital subscriber line (DSL) *(335)*

Domain Name System (DNS) *(328)*

Dynamic Host Configuration Protocol (DHCP) server *(326)*

file and printer server *(353)*

fully qualified domain name (FQDN) *(328)*

host ID *(327)*

integrated services digital network (ISDN) *(335)*

Internet Protocol (IP) *(322)*

Internet service provider (ISP) *(333)*

IP address *(323)*

IPv4 *(322)*

IPv6 *(323)*

local area network (LAN) *(334)*

net ID *(327)*

octet *(327)*

packet *(322)*

private browsing *(346)*

private IP address *(325)*

protocol *(322)*

protocol stack *(322)*

public IP addresses *(325)*

registered domain name *(328)*

remote access VPN *(339)*

router *(328)*

share *(353)*

site-to-site VPN *(339)*

static IP address *(326)*

subnet mask *(327)*

TCP/IP *(322)*

Top Level Domain (TLD) *(328)*

Transmission Control Protocol (TCP) *(322)*

virtual private network (VPN) *(339)*

Web browser *(340)*

Web mail *(349)*

wide area network (WAN) *(333)*

Wi-Fi network *(334)*

wireless LAN (WLAN) *(334)*

wireless wide area network (WWAN) *(336)*

Key Terms Quiz

Use the Key Terms List to complete the sentences that follow:

1. The IP addresses designated for hosts connected directly to the Internet are _____.

2. _____ is the version of the Internet Protocol that is slowly replacing the version that has been in use since 1983.

3. A/an _____ uses encapsulation to protect data sent over a public network. Encryption makes the data more secure.

4. An IPv4 address beginning with 169.254 is a/an _____ address.

5. A/an _____ is not used for hosts on the Internet.

6. A/an _____ is an organization that provides individuals or entire companies with access to the Internet.

7. In an IPv4 address, each grouping of decimal numbers is called a/an _____ because it represents eight bits.

8. Among IP configuration settings, the _____ is the IP address of the router used to send packets beyond the local network.

9. _____ is a term for a group of wired high-speed technologies offered through the phone company, and capable of much greater speeds than ISDN.

10. Most organizations use a _____ to assign IP addresses to desktop computers.

1. The IPv4 address 192.168.30.24 is an example of one of these.
   a. DNS server address
   b. Public IP address
   c. Private IP address
   d. Automatic private IP address
   e. IPv6 address

2. This protocol has 340 trillion, trillion, trillion unique identifiers.
   a. DNS
   b. IPv6
   c. DSL
   d. DHCP
   e. IMAP

3. In the chapter, which form of DSL is described as having the same speed upstream as downstream?
   a. ADSL
   b. *x*DSL
   c. VDSL
   d. HDSL
   e. SDSL

4. Your neighbor tells you that his Internet connection at home is much slower than the connection he enjoys at work—and he is disconnected if there is a period of inactivity. From his description, which type of connection would you assume he has?
   a. ISDN
   b. Dial-up
   c. ADSL
   d. SDSL
   e. Cable

5. When you connect to the Internet through a service at an airport or coffee shop, you are using a/an _____.
   a. Cellular hotspot
   b. Default gateway
   c. Public hotspot
   d. Remote access VPN
   e. Domain Name System (DNS)

6. Which of the following is obviously *not* a valid IPv4 address?
   a. 192.168.100.48
   b. 10.0.33.50
   c. 172.300.256.100
   d. 30.88.29.1
   e. 200.100.99.99

7. You connect to Wi-Fi from your smartphone or laptop in public places, such as airports and coffee shops. What type of service should you use to protect your communications?
   a. VPN
   b. Firewall
   c. Private browsing
   d. IPv6
   e. Private IP address

8. What command can you use to view the status of current connections, including the IP address and protocol used for each connection?
   a. **ipconfig**
   b. **cmd**
   c. **ping**
   d. **netstat**
   e. **tracert**

9. Which of the following is an example of an IPv6 address with the leading zeros removed?
   a. 2002:0470:b8f9:0000:020c:29ff:fe53:45ca
   b. 192.168.1.1
   c. 10.0.0.1
   d. 2002:470:b8f9::20c:29ff:fe53:45ca
   e. 0.0.0.0

10. Which command would you use as a test to see if a DNS server will respond to a request to resolve a name?
    a. **ping**
    b. **nslookup**
    c. **ipconfig**
    d. **netstat**
    e. **tracert**

11. This IPv4 configuration setting defines the two parts of an IP address: the Host ID and the Net ID.
    a. Gateway
    b. Subnet mask
    c. DNS
    d. DHCP
    e. Host name

12. What collection of information reveals your online activities?
    a. First-party cookies
    b. Incognito
    c. Google account
    d. Browsing history
    e. Private browsing

13. Your neighbor, a retiree on a modest fixed income, has asked your help in acquiring an Internet connection for his computer, a desktop computer running Windows 10. His only interest in Internet access is to use email to keep in touch with his children, who live in other

states. He has a reliable phone connection. Based on this information, which service will you recommend?

a. Cable

b. ISDN

c. Dial-up

d. DSL

e. Satellite

14. If you wanted to see the IP configuration from the Terminal window on a macOS or Linux system, which command would you use?

a. **ipconfig**

b. **netstat**

c. **nslookup**

d. **ping**

e. **ifconfig**

15. What protocol is responsible for the accurate delivery of messages, verifying and resending pieces that fail to make the trip from source to destination?

a. Internet Protocol (IP)

b. Transmit Control Protocol (TCP)

c. Secure Sockets Layer (SSL)

d. Virtual Private Network (VPN)

e. Transmission Control Protocol (TCP)

Essay Quiz

1. Your computer was recently connected via a network adapter to a LAN that includes a router through which traffic passes to the Internet. You know the adapter was configured to use TCP/IP, and you need to test its ability to communicate with computers on the LAN and on the Internet. In your own words describe the steps you will take.

2. After reviewing Web browsers in this chapter, do you see a commonality in the user interface and in the less obvious features of these different apps? Describe your observations.

3. In a large western state, an agency that dispatches mobile units to disaster areas to monitor the disaster sites for hazardous chemical and biological contamination requires reliable Internet access for these units

from any location in the state. They need to be up-to-date with technical information via postings on federal websites and to upload their data to state and federal sites. Which Internet connection option is the best fit for their needs? Explain your answer.

4. Most email clients have a setting for when messages should be deleted from the mail server. Consider how you would configure your email clients on several devices connecting to the same email service, including an explanation of why you would (or would not) configure all your clients to delete messages as soon as they are picked up.

5. Explain subnet masking in simple terms, including why a subnet mask is required when an adapter is configured with an IP address.

Lab Projects

LAB PROJECT 9.1

Research VPN services for individuals and answer these questions.

1 How do the various VPN services differ?

2 What is the advantage of the feature called geo-shifting?

3 What does it mean when a provider says that they do not keep logs?

4 Why is it important to know where the VPN servers are located when selecting a VPN service?

5 Why would someone want the feature that makes it appear that they are connected from a different country?

6 What are the advantages to hiding the type of content you are downloading?

LAB PROJECT 9.2

This project requires the use of a Windows, Linux, or Mac computer that has Internet access. Using methods you learned in this chapter, find the answers to the following questions:

1. How is an IP address assigned to the lab computer?

2. Record the IP configuration settings for the lab computer below:
   a. IP address
   b. Subnet mask
   c. Default gateway
   d. DNS server

LAB PROJECT 9.3

Interview the IT staff at your school, place of work, or another organization and determine what Internet services they offer to students (Web pages, email, etc.). The list will usually go beyond the basic services studied in this chapter. Create a list of these services and the clients they require.

chapter

10

Mobile Operating Systems: iOS and Android

Learning Outcomes

In this chapter, you will learn how to:

LO **10.1** Describe the benefits and challenges of BYOD in the workplace.

LO **10.2** Configure accounts for mobile devices.

LO **10.3** Configure wireless connections on mobile devices.

LO **10.4** Configure email, apps, and synchronization on mobile devices.

LO **10.5** Secure mobile devices.

Source: Apple Inc. and Google LLC

Chapter 1 introduced mobile devices and mobile operating systems. Before reading this chapter, we urge you to review the Chapter 1 section titled "Today's Mobile Operating Systems." The coverage includes a description of the hardware features of popular smartphones and tablets. In this chapter, we first explore the issues surrounding employees using their personal mobile devices at work, then we describe common features and configuration tasks for your mobile device, and finally we look at security for mobile devices. ✳

LO 10.1 | From Luggable to BYOD

Mobile computing was once something only certain business travelers did using computers that were just luggable versions of the PCs they left at the office. Mobile computing has evolved, and in just the last decade the mobile computing market has been flooded with tiny and powerful mobile devices. Now consumers in every walk of life practice mobile computing, children carry smartphones to preschool, and teachers uncrate boxes of iPads preloaded with student coursework. The "mobile" aspect seems to mean that we are not tethered to power and data lines, as we practice mobile computing everywhere.

In this section, you'll peek at the past of mobile computing, which wasn't very mobile, rarely connected, and involved little computing power. Then you'll examine the issue of using personal mobile devices in the workplace.

Mobile Computing Then and Now

In a span of 30 years, mobile computing devices went from a few heavy underpowered devices to today's large number of mobile devices that fit nicely in the hand and whose weight is measured in ounces rather than in tens of pounds. Hence, personal mobile devices are rarely out of reach of their owners, who have come to depend on them at home, school, work, and play. Some of us have lived through this history.

Sometime in the mid-1980s, our friend Amber was waiting in the baggage area of an airport as a gray plastic bin rose into view at the center of the baggage carousel and made a precarious slide down to the moving stainless-steel track. She recognized its clattering contents as the components of a Compaq portable computer, its cracked case the size of a suitcase.

Obviously, some road warrior had wearied of lugging 28 pounds of technology and checked it as baggage. Amber smugly snatched up her own suitcase and placed it on top of her luggage cart that already contained her carry-on: a 16-pound Zenith Data Systems Z-180 Portable PC. She had spent the flight with her feet resting uneasily on the portion of the laptop that did not fit under the passenger seat in front of her, while the luggage cart rode in the overhead compartment. There was no way she could actually put the laptop on her lap and get real work done. Computer professionals like Amber, rather than the typical consumer of the time, were the target market for portable computers. To quote the Welcome page of the Zenith Data Systems Z-180 Owner's Manual:

> This Owner's Manual is for you, the new computer user. In the first part of this manual, you will learn how to set up and operate your new computer for the first time. In the second part, you will learn about the firmware of the computer and how to program it. In the third part, you will learn about the hardware and how to use the programmable registers in the computer.

Programmable registers? Times have changed. Three decades later we no longer expect or need a technical manual for a new tablet or smartphone. Another big change is that modern mobile devices are almost always connected to one or more wireless networks, whereas the old devices did not connect to any network while in transit. Amber had to wait until she arrived in a classroom with a connection to a local area network (LAN) or hotel room that included a "modem line" for a slow dial-up connection. The more expensive the hotel, the more they charged for this service. Today's travelers demand that hotels provide free high-speed Internet access. A majority of people with mobile devices have cellular data plans in order to connect to the Internet 24/7.

The Home screen on an iPhone.
Source: Apple Inc.

And consider what they do with those connections! Mobile device users collectively upload and share hundreds of millions of photos every day. They upload an estimated 500 hours of video to YouTube per minute. And this type of traffic is increasing as more and more mobile users stay in touch, sharing their thoughts and opinions via social media, and keeping up with work and personal email. This pervasiveness of mobile devices has led to a phenomenon in the workplace that we explore next.

Mobile Devices and BYOD

Smartphones and tablets present a challenge for schools and employers because many people come to school or work armed with a pocket or a backpack full of technology. And they don't care to spend any time separated from these devices. Many demand to be able to use their personal devices for accessing work email, text messages, and data. This practice is called bring your own device (BYOD), and it occurs in many organizations, whether or not they officially condone it.

There are variations of policies (or lack of them) governing BYOD in the workplace. Here are just a few examples:

- Companies may reimburse an employee who uses their own device for cellular voice and data usage. This is important, because cellular voice charges are usually by the minute, and cellular data services are metered, with the cost going up with the amount of data downloaded. Charges can quickly mount up for someone using their personal device for work.
- In a form of shared ownership, an employer subsidizes the purchase of an employee's personal mobile device, giving the employee the option of buying a more expensive device than budgeted.
- An employer may allow or require use of personal mobile devices but not compensate the employee or have any clear policies regarding how to protect work data.

The Home screen on an Android smartphone.
Source: Google LLC

Advantages of BYOD to Employers

BYOD has certain advantages for employers:

- Quicker response by the employee using email and text messaging.
- It saves the employer the cost of the device.
- Some jobs require, or at least benefit from, the use of mobile devices.
- Acceptance of employees' use of mobile devices attracts tech-savvy people.
- Employees are inclined to work outside of normal work hours.
- You can deliver important job training to mobile devices that employees can use when needed.

Disadvantages of BYOD to Employers

There are risks to allowing employees access to email and corporate data using their personal mobile devices. A few of the issues include:

- Personal mobile devices can significantly increase the load on the employer's network infrastructure.
- It may conflict with corporate security policy.
- It may violate government regulations for employees to have certain data on their mobile devices.
- If a device is lost or stolen, it puts the employer at risk.
- Employees may leave a job and still have sensitive work-related data on their personal devices.

The Home screen on an iPad.
Source: Apple Inc.

- Normally, intellectual property created as part of a job belongs to the employer. It is unclear who owns the intellectual property if it is created on the employee's device.

Risks of BYOD to Employees

There are risks and concerns for the employee. Consider these issues:

- Who will pay for the cost of the device?
- Who will pay for added voice and data usage due to business use?
- What protects the employees if the employer's policy mandates monitoring BYOD devices?
- Can an employer or law enforcement agency confiscate an employee's device for any work-related reason?

Basic BYOD Policies

Basic BYOD policies should address these areas:

- Who owns intellectual property created on an employee's device—the employee or the employer?
- What security requirements should there be and how should they be enforced, including but not limited to passwords, encryption, and remote wipe (remotely deleting data from a lost or stolen device)?
- How and when does the employee back up the employer's data?
- Will video- and audio-recording features in BYOD devices be allowed in the workplace?
- Will the employer take advantage of location services on devices to monitor an employee's location during working hours? A location service is one that allows an app to track your location, using one or more methods, often with the help of the Internet.

Managing BYOD

Managing BYOD begins with company policies covering work behavior, security, and employee reimbursement. Existing policies may cover the use of personal devices in very broad terms and need updating. Employers have many options for managing BYOD to protect themselves and their employees. They also want to make the mobile devices more useful to the employees.

Employers' awareness of BYOD and the need to manage it varies. Therefore, some experts on security and BYOD promote a bottom-up approach, seeking to educate the employees so that they will be aware of the risks to themselves and request more clarity in BYOD policies from their employers.

In addition to modifying policies for BYOD, employers can enforce those policies and manage mobile devices using a category of software called mobile device management (MDM). Companies such as Citrix, VMware, Sophos, MobileIron, Acronis, and Microsoft offer MDM products—sometimes integrated into existing suites of products. Mobile device management is a broad term for the variety of features offered and the different approaches by the vendors of this type of software.

To isolate work apps and data from personal apps and data, some employers use products that include some form of virtualization. That may be in the form of a virtual machine running on the remote device or some variation of application virtualization—with processing occurring either on the mobile device or on the remote servers.

Others prefer to create a Web-based portal to work apps and data, making this available to a wider range of devices, since the only required client software is a browser.

> *Note:* In an interesting twist on BYOD, some cellular providers now advertise "Bring your own Device" or "Bring your own Phone." What they are offering is switching your existing mobile device from another provider to their service, with incentives.

Hardware Features in Mobile Devices

Today's tiny mobile devices contain many hardware features, such as cameras, radios that support several wireless standards, and a surprising array of sensors. Briefly consider the vast amount of hardware in these small packages.

Sensors

Our mobile devices can sense what is happening around you, even things you are unaware of. Your mobile device may include all or some of these sensors:

- Accelerometer
- Ambient light
- Barometer
- Compass
- Gyroscope
- Magnetometer
- Proximity
- Autofocus
- Fingerprint

Buttons and Ports

A mobile device still has buttons, such as power, volume control, and fingerprint touch. Although their use is dwindling, look for a speaker or headset jack and a charging port. An Android device might have a SIM and microSD card tray.

Touch screens, Cameras, Flash, and Speakers

Let's not forget those features that appeal to our senses, such as touchscreens, cameras, flash, microphones, and speakers. Although some of us still use desktop computers at home or work, mobile devices are our constant companions. The touch screen is your doorway into your mobile device and beyond. Many users interact with friends, family, and coworkers via visual means: text, social media, virtual meeting platforms, and even the old standby, email. A greater portion of our communication is done by these means than by phone calls. I may not speak for everyone, but this is definitely a thing now. So, the clarity and brilliance of a screen and speakers are critical to this experience, as is the ability to simply tap and gesture on a screen to accomplish many things. And then there is the real companion behind those screens and microphones: Apple's Siri, available on all Apple devices, and Google Assistant on Android devices.

Wireless Radios

Wireless communication is what untethered us from our offices and homes. Your mobile device has several wireless radios. They include cellular, Wi-Fi, Bluetooth, and more. Consider the apps and services that use these wireless features. For instance, Personal Hotspot uses two wireless standards because it acts as a router between your device and the Internet.

LO 10.2 | Configure Accounts for Mobile Devices

There are two or more accounts associated with each mobile device. First, there is the credit account with the cellular provider. It is the account we set up and forget until we see our monthly statement. Then there is the account associated with the operating system on the device. Beyond that, many of us have one or more other accounts for additional cloud services we use on that device. Of course, we also need wireless

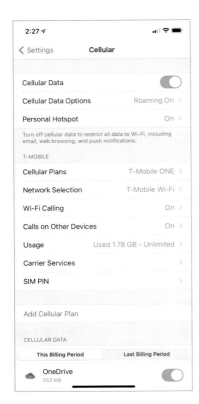

FIGURE 10-1 Cellular settings on an iPhone.
Source: Apple Inc.

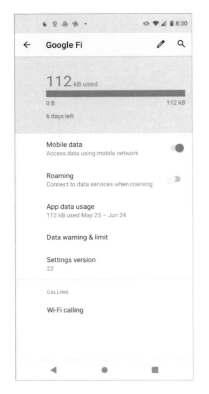

FIGURE 10-2 Cellular settings on an Android phone.
Source: Google LLC

connections for these mobile devices. That's what makes them mobile. The accounts and the connections are equally important, so the question is, which to address first? Other than the credit account with the cellular provider, the other accounts can be created and configured before or after you purchase your mobile device. After all, you are probably already using cloud services through your employer or school and/or have a personal account with Google, Microsoft, DropBox, or other cloud services. Then there are the social media accounts (Facebook, Twitter, and many more). For that reason, we will consider the accounts first, using the account associated with your mobile OS as an example. The security settings you create for this account affect your privacy and safety on your device. Later, in this chapter, we will return to the topic of security and the settings you can configure on the device itself to further secure your data privacy.

Mobile Provider Accounts

When you purchase a smartphone or cellular-enabled tablet (one with an internal cellular modem) at one of Verizon's, AT&T's, T-Mobile's, or any cellular provider's brick-and-mortar store, they check your credit and you provide a payment method for the monthly charges, all associated with your account with them. They then program the device for their cellular network. This activation process often includes inserting a card called a Subscriber Identity Module (SIM). If you purchase the device over the Internet, the SIM card may come with the device, with instructions for installing it and activating the phone yourself. Beyond the personal billing and contract information tied to this account, configure settings that affect your usage of that service on each mobile device included in your plan to keep from incurring more costs. To see the cellular provider for an iPhone, as well as how an iPhone is using cellular data, open *Settings* and select *Cellular,* as shown in Figure 10-1. On an Android device, open *Settings* and select the *Network & Internet* category and tap *Mobile Network* to open the page shown in Figure 10-2.

Accounts Tied to Mobile Operating Systems

You also have an account tied to the operating system on each mobile device. The most common are Google accounts for Android devices and Apple IDs for Apple mobile devices. A tablet may or may not include a cellular modem, but it will have Wi-Fi. And yes, you may have a cellular-enabled tablet running Microsoft Windows, or a Wi-Fi-only Windows tablet. In that case, the account associated with the operating system is a Microsoft Account (MSA), which you will want to use on a Windows device if you use Microsoft services. You can configure the account associated with the operating system before purchasing a mobile device and we recommend that you do so. If you already have the account for the operating system, this is an opportunity to examine the security settings for that account. See Chapter 4 for information on creating and configuring a Microsoft Account.

On your device with Apple iOS, Google Android, or Windows, you can also subscribe to any of the other cloud services available: Apple services on Windows or Google devices, Google services on Apple or Windows devices, and Windows services on Apple or Google devices. There are many more cloud services that we have not mentioned here, and you can have multiple cloud providers on each device. What you learn here configuring an Account for Apple or Google services generally applies to other cloud services.

Sign in with a Google Account

When you power up a new Android smartphone or tablet, you must sign in with a Google account. The account you use for this initial sign in will be the owner of the device—the only account that can make significant changes to device settings. A Google account is free, including the use of many Google apps, but some of the services, such as Google Drive space over the 4GB free service limit, are fee-based. If you are unfamiliar with Google accounts, review the information on this topic in Chapter 8. Learn more about Google accounts and the cloud services available from Google and other providers in Chapter 11.

Sign in with an Apple ID

When you power up a new iPhone or iPad, you must sign in with an Apple ID, your customer account for all Apple services and products. The Apple ID includes an email address you provide when you create the account. The basic account is free, and you can opt for additional, fee-based services. Your payment information for those services is saved with your account. Your Apple ID you use for the initial sign in to an Apple device will be the owner of the device—the only account that can make significant changes to device settings.

Note: Your Apple ID credentials include an email address (any working email address) and a password you create just for the Apple ID—*not* the password for using the email account.

Step-by-Step 10.01 will walk you through the process of logging in with an existing or new Apple ID. It includes instructions on creating a new Apple ID and retrieving an Apple ID after you have forgotten the Apple ID or password.

Step-by-Step 10.01

Sign in with Your Apple ID or Create a New One

In this hands-on exercise, you will use a browser to sign in with your existing Apple ID or create a new one.

- A computer or mobile device with an Internet connection that is not signed in to an Apple account.
- The username (email address) and password for your existing Apple ID, or

- One or more possible usernames and a complex password of eight or more characters with a mix of letters, numbers, and symbols.

Step 1

Point your browser to **appleid.apple.com**.

If you do not have an Apple ID, and wish to create one, select *Create Your Apple ID* (at the top right of the window) and proceed to Step 2.

If you do have an Apple ID, sign in now. Your Apple Account page will open. Skip the remaining steps of this exercise and move on to the section titled *Exploring your Apple ID Account Settings.*

If you do have an Apple ID, but have forgotten either the Apple ID or the password, skip to Step 3.

Source: Apple Inc.

Step 2

On the *Create Your Apple ID* page fill in all the information, scrolling down to complete the form. Tap *Next* as you complete each page. In addition to a password, you will also need to choose three security questions. At this point Apple sends a single-use verification email to you. You need to pick up this email and enter the code on the website. Apple creates your Apple ID. Once you successfully create your Apple ID, you have completed this exercise. Skip the remaining steps. Stay signed in to your account, which we will explore in the section titled ***Exploring your Apple ID Account Settings.***

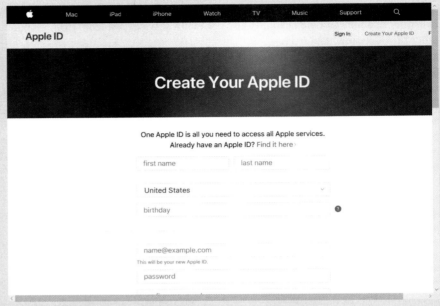

Source: Apple Inc.

Step 3

If you have an existing Apple ID, but cannot sign in, look for this link on the bottom of the Apple ID page: *Forgot Apple ID or password.* Click or tap it to open this page and enter your email address or look it up and then tap Continue.

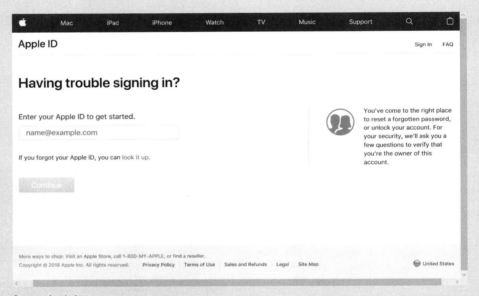

Source: Apple Inc.

Once you provide an email address, and it is confirmed to be a valid Apple ID email, Apple will send a password reset email. When you receive that email, follow the instructions which take you to a Web page where you can provide confirming information and create a new password. Once you are signed in, keep the Apple Account page open and move on to the section titled *Exploring your Apple ID Account Settings.*

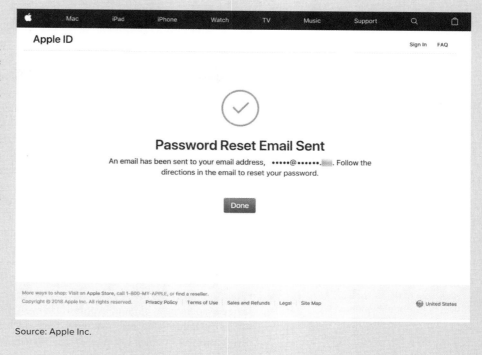

Source: Apple Inc.

Exploring Your Apple ID Account Settings

After signing in to your Apple ID, check out the account settings and make a few decisions about securing your account and Apple devices. On your Apple ID settings page (Figure 10–3), verify that the information in the Account section is correct. If you find

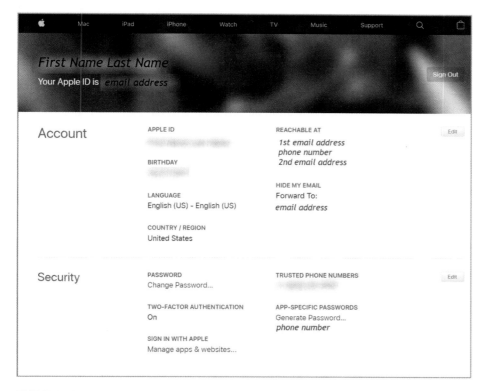

FIGURE 10–3 Manage your Apple ID settings.
Source: Apple Inc.

an error, or wish to change something in any section, click or tap the Edit button at the top right of the section and make the changes.

Now explore the Security section. This is where you can change your password, add a rescue email, change the security questions, and configure additional security for your Apple ID. We will leave the password and security questions for now, assuming they are recent, and look at the other options for securing your account.

If you have a second email that you frequently check, use it as your rescue email and to reset your password and security questions. To add a rescue email, simply select *Add a Rescue Email* and provide the email address.

Apple has two extra security options with similar names: Two-Step Verification and Two-Factor Authentication, a newer more secure option.

> *Note:* Other online services, such as Microsoft and Google, offer two-step verification or multifactor authentication. The name may be the same (or it may just be similar), but the implementation varies, and most of these services now have enhancements to two-step verification.

Two-Step Verification. Apple added the Two-Step Verification to Apple accounts several years ago and it is still available in the Apple ID Security settings for a new account. When you enable this feature, you must register at least one device that can receive a verification code via an Apple push notification or text message (SMS). In addition to that device, you can provide a phone number for a voice message. Apple can also contact you through Find My iPhone. When you turn this on, Apple provides a Recovery Key for use in the event you forget your Apple ID password or lose the device associated with your Apple ID. Save this Recovery Key in a file and/or print it out. In both cases, be sure you have quick access to the Recovery Key. Once Two-Step Verification is enabled, whenever you sign in to your Apple account using a device that is not trusted by your account, you will need to enter your account password after which a dialog box will open into which you must enter a single-use code sent by Apple to the registered device. Therefore, you need access to both devices. If you do not have access to the trusted device, you will need your Recovery Key.

FIGURE 10–4 Select *Don't Allow* or *Allow.*
Source: Apple Inc.

Two-Factor Authentication. Apple has a newer implementation of multifactor authentication they call Two-Factor Authentication. This feature is not available in your Apple ID settings until you register at least one device running iOS 9 or greater or OS X 10.11 (El Capitan) or greater. Once you have a qualifying device registered with your account, Two-Factor Authentication is available in your Security settings. With this enabled, when someone attempts to sign in with your account from an unknown (to your Apple account) device, you will receive two dialog boxes on the trusted device. The first, shown in Figure 10–4, informs you that your Apple ID is being used to sign in to a new device, giving a location and a map, and you can allow or disallow this attempt. If you allow it, a second dialog box provides the single-use verification code, shown in Figure 10–5. Enter this code on the new device.

LO 10.3 | Configure Wireless Connections on Mobile Devices

When preparing to buy a smartphone, first shop for the cellular provider, such as Verizon, AT&T, T-Mobile, or others, and look for the best service and options in your area. If you live in an area with multiple providers visit several stores or websites to compare plans and costs before making your final choice. There are many plans and a great deal of competition among providers, especially in metro areas. These

FIGURE 10–5 Enter this single-use code on the new device.
Source: Apple Inc.

include plans with a flat rate for a certain amount of cellular data usage or even unlimited data. The data portion of the plan is important if you are using your smartphone for services other than just voice, and most of us use our smartphones all day long for various types of data—email, text messaging, browsing the Internet, and social media.

After selecting the carrier and the plan you would like, select the device. Once you have selected the device that fits your needs and budget, you normally sign a contract for a certain level of service and for a credit account with the provider. Before you receive the phone, the cellular service provider will program it for your cellular account. This process often includes inserting a card called a Subscriber Identity Module (SIM) into the device. If you purchase the device over the Internet, the SIM card may come with the device, with instructions for installing it and activating the phone. If you purchase a smartphone in a brick-and-mortar store, you will usually configure the cellular connection while still in the store, or the salesperson may do it for you.

> *Note:* When it comes to device options, the author found that going directly to Apple, rather than the cellular provider, gave her more choices in device model and features. This was true for the last two iPhones she purchased, as well as for an Apple Watch. The provider she selected, T-Mobile, had a limited selection of both. Apple configured the T-Mobile connection before shipping the device to her.

Connecting to Cellular Networks

The first time you power up a new smartphone that has not been prepared or one that has the basic configuration but still needs your personal settings, a setup screen will display and lead you through the process. This will include accepting a language and terms of use. You will also have an opportunity to read a privacy statement and then go through steps for setting up your phone.

Cellular data communications is optional in a tablet, adding a premium to the cost of the device because of the required internal cellular modem as well as the ongoing cost for the cellular data plan. As with a smartphone, the cellular provider will either configure the device or give you special instructions. The device may come preconfigured for connecting to the cellular network, and the first time you start it up, you personalize it by moving through screens where you answer questions.

Cellular Data Settings

An important money-saving feature is enabled by default in most mobile devices with both cellular and Wi-Fi connections. When the device is connected to a Wi-Fi network with a good signal, it will use that rather than the cellular network for data. Look back at Figure 10-1, which shows the cellular settings on an iPhone with Cellular Data turned on. If you have a limited data plan and are often connected to a trusted Wi-Fi network, turn cellular data off, or turn it on and scroll down to the list of apps using cellular data and turn off the use of cellular data in those apps that are not critical.

Sharing Your Cellular Connection

A mobile hotspot is a generic term for sharing a cellular connection with nearby devices connected by Wi-Fi, Bluetooth, or USB. The device at the core of the mobile hotspot is a cellular wireless router within the device. This may be a smartphone or tablet with cellular access or a dedicated mobile hotspot device. Figure 10-6 shows the mobile hotspot setting on an iPhone, where it is referred to as *Personal Hotspot*. A password is provided for devices that connect via Wi-Fi. Connecting via Bluetooth or USB does not require the Wi-Fi password. Your cellular provider may charge extra for a hotspot, or may offer two levels of hotspot service: one free with restrictions on the speed and amount of data, and another level with upgraded access for an additional fee. Once you have arranged for this service with your provider, you would turn on Personal Hotspot.

Similarly, Android has settings for sharing a cellular connection, which is called Wi-Fi hotspot, as shown in Figure 10-7. To enable this, locate the

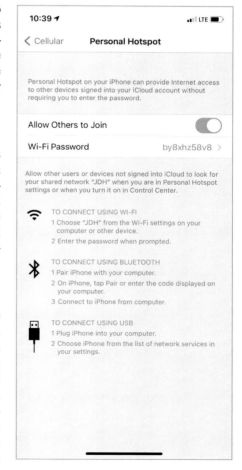

FIGURE 10-6 Personal Hotspot settings on an iPhone.
Source: Apple Inc.

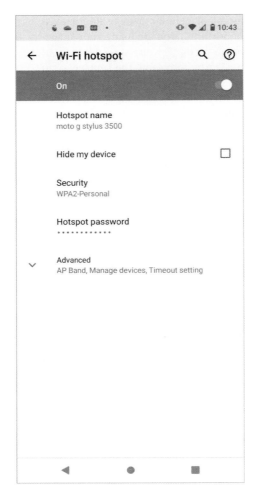

FIGURE 10–7 Wi-Fi hotspot settings on an Android phone.
Source: Google LLC

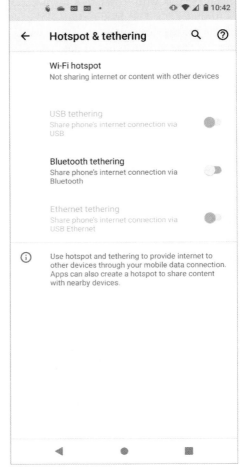

FIGURE 10–8 Tethering settings on an Android phone.
Source: Google LLC

Hotspot & Tethering settings under Network & Internet. Open it and select *Wi-Fi hotspot*. If the Wi-Fi hotspot is enabled, this page will show that it is on. If it is not, tap it to enable it. You can opt to hide your hotspot by tapping *Hide my device*, which will place a checkmark in the box. If it is not hidden, you only need to provide the password to the hotspot to allow another device to use it. If it is hidden, the device attempting to connect needs to enter both the hotspot name and the password. To see the password, tap Hotspot password.

Android makes a distinction between connecting to a Wi-Fi hotspot via Wi-Fi and connecting via a Bluetooth, USB, or Ethernet connection. The term **tethering** is used for non-Wi-Fi connections to the device itself. Only Bluetooth tethering is available on the device shown in Figure 10–8. A Bluetooth connection to a hotspot requires that you pair the devices.

Connecting to Wi-Fi Networks

To connect to a Wi-Fi network for the first time, open the Settings app on your device. Then select the option for Wireless (or Wi-Fi) and turn on Wi-Fi, if necessary. It will then scan for Wi-Fi networks and list detected Wi-Fi networks, using the SSID of each network. A **Service Set ID (SSID)** is a network name used to identify a wireless network. Consisting of up to 32 characters, the SSID travels with the messages on a Wi-Fi network, and all wireless devices on a WLAN must use the same SSID to communicate.

In the list of available Wi-Fi networks, select one and enter the required password. The device will remember this network and the password, maintain a list of Wi-Fi networks it has successfully connected to, and automatically provide the password you entered when you first connected to that network. Figure 10-9 shows an iPhone Wi-Fi Settings page with a successful connection to a Wi-Fi network named Techie. The Android Wi-Fi settings page is shown in Figure 10-10.

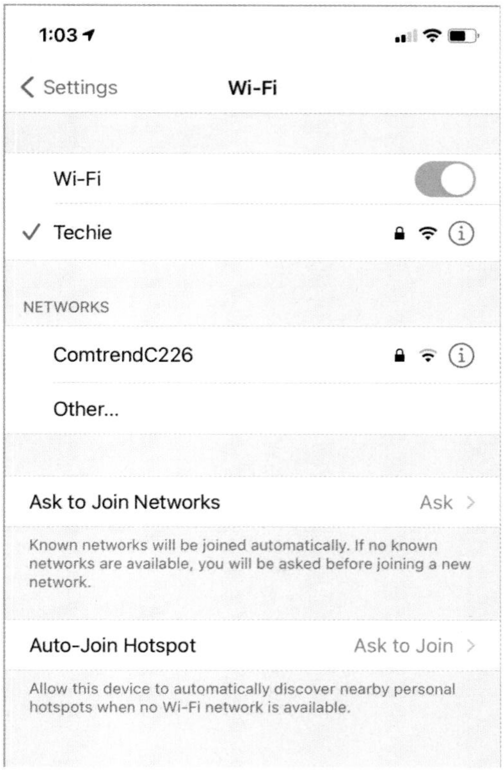

For additional security, the network administrator may turn off broadcasting of the SSID, so the network name will not show in the list of networks displayed when your device attempts to connect. In that case, the administrator gives authorized users the name of the network and the password to enter. On an iOS device, select *Other* (shown in the list of networks in Figure 10-9) to open the dialog box and manually enter the network name and password.

Wi-Fi Calling

Wi-Fi calling is a feature supported on Android and iOS devices. With Wi-Fi calling enabled, outgoing and incoming calls, texts, and video calls will use a Wi-Fi connection rather than cellular. This is a valuable feature when the cellular network is unavailable or unreliable at your location, but you have Wi-Fi access to the Internet. Wi-Fi settings are found under your cellular provider settings. Refer to Figure 10-1, showing the Cellular settings on an iPhone. Wi-Fi calling is in the middle of the list, and it is turned on. Android settings for the Google Fi cellular provider are shown in Figure 10-2. The Wi-Fi calling option is at the bottom of the page. Select this to enable or disable Wi-Fi calling.

FIGURE 10–9 The iPhone Wi-Fi settings page.
Source: Google LLC

Connecting to Bluetooth Devices

Bluetooth is a wireless standard originally used for communicating over short distances. Both the standard and its implementation in devices have improved. You can connect a Bluetooth headset or keyboard to your mobile device, connect your smartphone to your car stereo, or connect your phone or tablet to a PC or Mac to synchronize data. Bluetooth consumes battery power, so it is disabled by default. To connect devices via Bluetooth, first open the Settings app on your mobile device and enable Bluetooth. When connecting to a device without a user interface, such as a headset or keyboard, Bluetooth is enabled on that device every time you turn it on, so you simply use the Bluetooth settings on your mobile device to detect the device and select it. The connection between two Bluetooth devices is a **pairing**. Figure 10-11 shows the confirmation message on an Android phone for pairing with a Bluetooth speaker. In this case, we did not allow access to contacts and call history, because access is not needed for a simple speaker. At this point, simply tap *Pair*.

Bluetooth connections have improved, allowing a device to remember multiple pairings, and rarely requiring your intervention. When required, you will need to respond to a prompt on your mobile device. Check on Bluetooth connections in Bluetooth Settings.

Always test connectivity between devices. We have found that just entering the pairing code on a Bluetooth keyboard is not enough confirmation

WARNING!

Nothing is free. Never connect to a Wi-Fi router/hotspot that does not require a password. Hotspots that require a password encrypt communications between your device and the hotspot. On a free or "open" hotspot, communications are not encrypted and your data is at risk.

try this!

Enable or Disable Wi-Fi

If you have a mobile device, it will have a setting for enabling or disabling Wi-Fi networking. Try this:

1. Open the Settings utility on your mobile device.
2. Search for the Wi-Fi settings.
3. Enable or disable Wi-Fi.
4. Test the setting by opening an app that requires Wi-Fi access.
5. Return the Wi-Fi setting to its previous configuration.

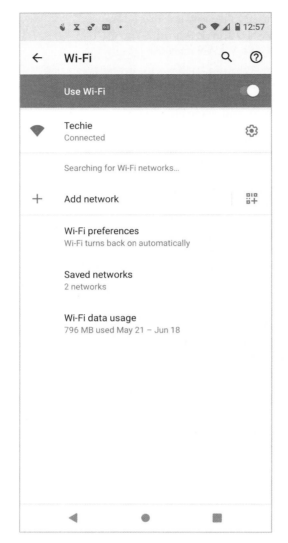

FIGURE 10–10 The Android Wi-Fi settings page.
Source: Google LLC

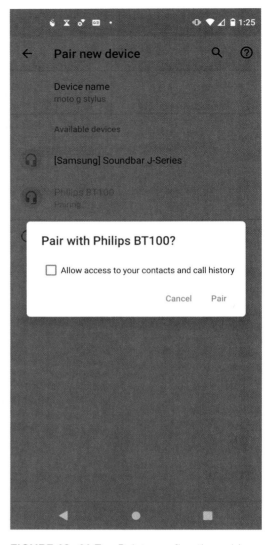

FIGURE 10–11 Tap *Pair* to confirm the pairing.
Source: Google LLC

that the connection is working, so we open an app that accepts keyboard input and start typing on the keyboard. If it does not work, you may not have confirmed the pairing on both sides (not usually necessary). A failure to connect may simply be a case of impatience, so a short wait is in order. If the pairing problem persists, disable Bluetooth on both devices and start over again.

try this!

Pair Two Devices with Bluetooth

Connect your mobile device to a computer or peripheral using Bluetooth. Try this:

1. Open the Settings utility on your mobile device.
2. Locate the Bluetooth setting and turn it on.
3. Turn on your Bluetooth device.
4. The mobile device should show that it is searching, connecting, and pairing.
5. If it is a keyboard, enter the code that appears on the mobile device.
6. Test the connection: for instance, play music to test a Bluetooth headset.
7. Disable Bluetooth when you are finished if you do not need it.

Making Bluetooth Easier

While pairing Bluetooth devices is not difficult, it usually requires opening the Settings app on your mobile device. In the future, that may not be necessary. For instance, Google's **Fast Pair** feature scans for nearby Bluetooth signals and displays a prompt identifying the device. Tap the box, and your phone connects to the device. Following that first connection the user is prompted to download an app, providing one is available for the device. Fast Pair is relatively new, and it will take time for manufacturers to provide a Fast Pair companion app for their devices. When this or other solutions become common, we will avoid having to go into the Settings app to connect to Bluetooth devices.

Combining Bluetooth and Wi-Fi

Apple, Google, Microsoft, and other tech companies offer enhanced Bluetooth capabilities or combine Bluetooth with other technologies. Apple requires that Bluetooth be enabled on their devices for AirDrop, AirPlay, and location services, even when the service uses other wireless types of signals. In addition, their AirDrop service uses Bluetooth or Wi-Fi to transfer files between Apple devices (Mac, iPad, iPhone, iPod Touch). Apple AirPlay, originally designed for audio data, is Apple's technology for streaming several types of data (audio, video, and photos) between Apple devices using both Wi-Fi and Bluetooth.

Connecting with Other Short-Range Wireless Methods

Some mobile devices include the ability to use Near Field Communication (NFC). With this enabled, you can position your phone very close to another device that also has NFC enabled and share data and even pay for purchases at location using this type of device. Apple uses NFC technology for their Apple Pay, Wallet, Touch ID, and Face ID services.

Airplane Mode

When traveling by commercial airliner you may be required to turn off all wireless signals (Wi-Fi, cellular, Bluetooth, NFC) on mobile devices. This may be only during takeoff and landing or during the entire trip. Some airlines allow Wi-Fi use via their provided in-flight Wi-Fi service, and some offer cellular service. The policy concerning wireless devices on airliners varies by airline company and by country. Modern devices have airplane mode to turn off the wireless features without the need to power off the device, so you can continue to do other tasks that do not require wireless connections.

Airplane mode is useful beyond its use on airlines because it prevents your device from repeatedly attempting to connect while you are out of range. Similarly, when you are traveling (especially by air), it may deplete your battery as it repeatedly attempts to detect cell towers as you fly over the landscape. Look for *Airplane Mode* in Settings, as shown in Figure 10–12, the *Settings* screen on an Android smartphone containing the switch for enabling or disabling airplane mode. When enabled, an airplane icon will display in the notification bar at the top of your device.

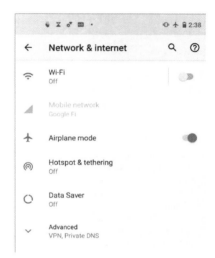

FIGURE 10–12 The *Airplane Mode* setting on an Android phone.
Source: Google LLC

try this!

Enable or Disable Airplane Mode

If you have a mobile device, experiment with enabling or disabling Airplane Mode. Try this:

1. Open the Settings utility on your mobile device.
2. Locate the *Airplane Mode* settings.
3. Turn Airplane mode on.
4. Test Airplane mode by opening a browser and attempting to connect to a website.
5. When you have tested it, turn Airplane mode off.

Note: Radio frequency (RF) is the general term for wireless technologies that use radio signals, as do those in this chapter.

LO 10.4 | Email, Apps, Wallets, and Synchronization

Once you know how to work with your mobile device's connection settings, you will want to configure email, acquire new apps, and enable synchronization.

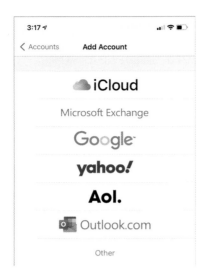

FIGURE 10-13 Mobile OSs offer many types of accounts for email and social networking.
Source: Apple Inc.

Note: Both Apple iOS and Google Android offer control centers for quickly enabling and disabling features, such as wireless connections and airplane mode. On an iOS device, swipe down from the top right edge to open the full-screen control panel. On an Android device swipe down from the top to open a screen that contains both the control center and notifications.

FIGURE 10-14 The settings for an IMAP email account.
Source: Apple Inc.

Configuring Email

In order to use your mobile device to access your email, begin by adding the email account. Mobile devices support several types of accounts for email, social networking, data backup, and more. You can configure a single device to use several accounts. Mobile operating systems know the basic connection information for many types of accounts. Therefore, for many accounts, you only need to provide your personal login information to the account, which is usually an email address and password. Figure 10-13 shows a list of account types supported on an iPhone or iPad. Chapter 9 described email account types as well as the settings required to connect to an email account.

Web Mail Accounts

For Web mail accounts, such as Hotmail or Gmail, you do not have to specify a sending and receiving server. All you need to enter is your user name and password. All the mobile OSs described here work with Web mail accounts.

Accounts Requiring IMAP, POP, or SMTP Settings

If you want to use an account type other than a Web mail service, you will need server names for the incoming and outgoing mail servers. Obtain these from your mail server administrator. To receive mail you will need a name for a Post Office Protocol 3 (POP3) or an Internet Message Access Protocol 4 (IMAP4) server that receives your incoming mail and forwards it to you. An email client uses one or the other of these. To send email you usually need the name of your Simple Mail Transfer Protocol (SMTP) server that accepts your outgoing email and forwards it to the recipient's mail server.

A POP3 name will simply be the name of a mail server in an Internet domain and may resemble this: **pop.domainname.com**; while the name for an IMAP4 server might look something like this: **imap.domainname.com**. Then, we probably don't need to say this, but the SMTP name might look like this: **smtp.domainname.com**. These are just examples, and you need to get the names for these servers from your email administrator.

Armed with the needed information, locate the email settings on your mobile device and carefully enter the information. On an iPhone or iPad, open the Settings app and tap *Mail*. Then, tap *Accounts* and on the Accounts page tap **Add Account** (see Figure 10-13). Does the list include the type of email account you need to use? If it does, tap it and continue. If not, tap **Other** at the bottom of the list and then tap **Add Mail Account.** The **New Account** dialog box will display, along with the virtual keyboard (unless you have an external keyboard connected). Enter your name (not a user account name), email address, password for that email account, and a description for the email account that will identify it for you in the list of accounts. Tap **Next,** and follow the instructions, using the addresses you obtained from your mail server administrator. Figure 10-14 shows the settings for an IMAP account.

On an Android device, you will have a Google account for accessing Google services and Gmail. To add another type of account in Android, open **Settings.** Then under **Accounts** tap **Add an Account** (located at the bottom). This opens the **Add an Account** screen (Figure 10-15) listing a variety of account types, not just email accounts but social networking sites, photo sharing sites, data backup sites, and other accounts added as you install certain apps.

From the **Add an Account** screen, scroll through the list of account types and select the type of account you wish to add. Then enter the appropriate information for that account type.

Configuring an Exchange Client

Many organizations use internally maintained Microsoft Exchange mail servers for employee email accounts and for email within the organization as well as over the Internet. Also, many hosting services for Internet domain names offer Exchange email hosting services to their clients. Exchange gives the organization full administrative control, while providing users with a central location for their email history, contacts, tasks, and many collaborative tools.

The organization owning the Exchange server and domain, such as a company or university, centrally manages and owns all Exchange accounts stored in one Exchange accounts database. Due to the complexity and cost of managing large numbers of email accounts, organizations are increasingly outsourcing email services to companies like Google and Microsoft.

Mobile Apps

Apps are what make your mobile device the high-tech version of a Swiss Army knife. All mobile devices come with some built-in apps, but everyone installs more apps. Whatever mobile OS you select, you can choose from among hundreds of thousands of mobile apps. Apps are OS specific, so you must find apps that work with your OS and device. The Home screen on a mobile device will normally have an icon for connecting to an online retail site for buying apps for that mobile OS and (sometimes) device type.

When you find an app that sounds like what you need, read through the description, paying close attention to the requirements. An app may require certain services in order to work as advertised. For instance, you may need to give the app full control of your device or turn on the location service and/or global positioning system (GPS) service.

Apps for Android

Play Store is an Android app that connects you to the Google Play online app store, the official source for Android apps, but since this is an open OS, there are other sources in the open-source market. Pay very close attention to the specs for an app, as there are many versions of Android, with features that are only supported on some devices. Figure 10-16 shows a small sampling of the Android apps at the Google Play store.

Apps for Apple iOS

Apple's online App Store or the brick-and-mortar Apple stores are the only app sources for Apple devices of any type. They sell only Apple-sanctioned software from many publishers. Because of the screen size differences some apps display best on the device for which they were written. Tap the App Store on the home page of your iOS device to connect to the App Store; the first time you connect from a device you will need to provide your Apple ID and password. Figure 10-17 shows the App Store. Update apps through the App Store, and when one or more updates are ready, the number of updates will appear on the App Store icon. When you open the App Store, the updates will display, and if you decide to update or download an app, you will need to enter your Apple ID and password (or use *Touch ID* or *Face ID*) before continuing.

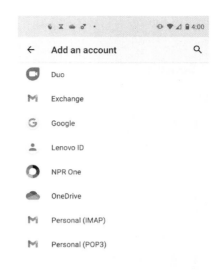

FIGURE 10–15 Select the account type from the list in the Android **Add account** page.
Source: Google LLC

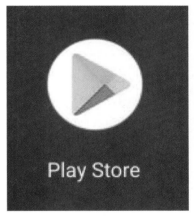

Source: Google LLC

Source: Apple Inc.

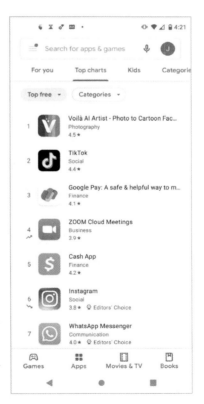

FIGURE 10–16 A small sampling of apps in the Google Play online app store.
Source: Google LLC

Apple's solutions to the dizzying array of app shortcuts stored on multiple pages on iPhones and iPads are somewhat helpful. First, there is the horizontal line of dots below the shortcuts that you can swipe like a scroll bar. Next, you can create folders for related apps to save screen space. The latest aid is the **App Library** (Figure 10-18), accessed by moving to the last page of shortcuts and swiping in from the right. When the App Library needs more room, it scrolls vertically.

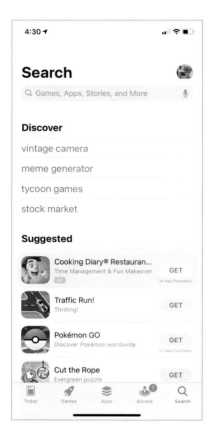

FIGURE 10–17 The Apple online App Store.
Source: Apple Inc.

Replacing Your Wallet with a Mobile Device

If you still carry a stack of plastic to pay for purchases, consider checking out one of the virtual wallets available to you for your mobile device. Both Apple and Google offer payment services that are accepted at a growing number of brick-and-mortar locations, as well as online.

Google Pay

Google Pay is the combined and renamed Android Pay and Google Wallet services. It uses payment methods saved in your Google Account. Use this service to pay anyone via their email address or phone number. Store loyalty membership cards and movie tickets in Google Pay. Do you commute to work in London, Chicago, Las Vegas, or Portland? Store your transit tickets in Google Pay and then use your phone as a ticket before you board. This service is available in other cities, too. Figure 10-19 shows the Google Pay app description opened from the Google Pay icon on the home page of a new Android device. From here (or from the Play Store), download, install, and configure it with one or more payment methods.

FIGURE 10–18 Apple's App Library.
Source: Apple Inc.

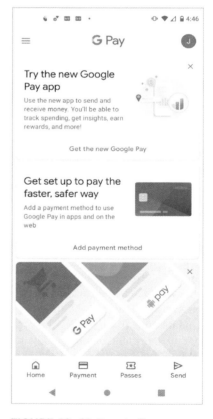

FIGURE 10–19 Google Pay.
Source: Google LLC

Apple Pay and Wallet

Wallet is an Apple iOS app for storing (in digital form) those plastic cards overflowing your physical wallet. Wallet does more than store those cards—it lets you use them for making payments and even for other purposes. For example, you can store and use coupons, boarding passes, tickets, credit cards, student IDs, and much more, using them just like the physical cards with other services that accept them. This data is stored online with your Apple ID and can be used from any of your iOS devices with Wallet enabled.

Apple Pay allows you to use credit and debit cards stored in Wallet to make purchases with Apple Pay. Turn on Apple Pay and configure it with payment sources by opening *Wallet & Apple Pay* in iOS Settings.

Synchronization

Some of us have multiple computing devices. With so many devices it is a challenge to keep track of our data. Therefore, we synchronize certain data between devices. When data is synchronized between two locations, the files are examined and newer files replace the older files—sometimes, but not always, in both directions so that the contents match. Synchronizing can be to another computer or mobile device or to a cloud-based service to ensure against data loss if the device is lost or stolen.

> *Note:* Depending on the device and the options available to you, you can synchronize data using four connection types: USB cable, Wi-Fi, Bluetooth, or cellular data network.

Connecting Mobile Devices for Syncing

You can synchronize your smartphone or tablet with your computer, using a USB cable, Wi-Fi, Bluetooth, or over the Internet using a cloud-based service. If you choose a cable, use the USB cable that came with the smartphone; it is usually attached to an alternating current (AC) adapter for charging. Disconnect it from the AC adapter and connect the end previously connected to the power supply (usually a standard USB connector) to the computer and connect the other end to the device. On smartphones, this will usually be a micro-USB connector; on older iPads and some other tablets, it was a proprietary 30-pin connector. Recent Apple devices come with Lightning or USB C connectors. On some devices, this connection will cause two programs to run on the PC—one from your cellular provider (if the device has cellular service) for configuring your online account (if you already have one, you simply log in). The second program will be device-specific to aid in transferring files.

Syncing Android Devices

When you connect an Android device to your computer it is treated like an external drive, and you can copy files back and forth once you figure out the directory structure and locate the files you want to copy or back up. Strictly speaking, this isn't syncing. There are individual solutions for various types of data. For instance, when you create a contact in Android it asks you to pick an account to store (or back up) the contact information. The choices are Google or one provided by your cellular carrier. Select Google and they will be automatically backed up and synced to Google over the Internet, either through a cellular connection or via Wi-Fi. Who do you expect to have the longest relationship with, Google or your cellular provider? We use Google to back up our contacts on Android devices because it will be available to use if we cancel the contract with the cellular provider.

There are apps, such as Coolmuster Android Assistant, for syncing Android devices with a PC. It is designed to work with Samsung devices, but may work with devices from other manufacturers. Microsoft has the *Your Phone* app that works with a companion app, *Link to Windows*, installed on an Android device. This app is not specifically a backup app, but it allows you to access data and apps on both the Android device and the PC. The one caveat is that it may not work with all Android versions or devices.

Syncing an Apple Mobile Device with a Mac or PC

Use Apple iTunes for syncing an iOS device with a Mac with macOS Mojave or earlier or with a PC. Apple iTunes comes with all Apple computers and is a free download from the Microsoft Store for Windows PC. You can synchronize apps, several types of audio content, books, contacts, calendars, movies, TV shows, photos, notes, documents, and ringtones.

If you have a Mac, you may still need to update to the latest version of iTunes.

There are other requirements for playing music and video through iTunes on a PC, but we are only concerned with the requirements to synchronize your contacts, email, pictures, music, and videos from the device to the Mac or PC. You cannot copy files from the Mac or PC to the mobile device.

Once you have configured iTunes to backup your device when connected to your Mac or PC, you can setup Wi-Fi sync. Then, whenever the device is plugged in to power and on the same network as the computer, it will sync.

Another option that is more of a backup than a synchronizing option is iCloud, an Apple Internet-based service for backing up your data from any Apple device to the iCloud service. This data is available to all devices from any location with Internet access.

Step-by-Step 10.02

Synchronize an Apple Mobile Device with a Windows PC

This step-by-step exercise goes through the steps for synchronizing your Apple mobile device data using iTunes. The steps are written for using a direct connection via a USB cable, but you can also synchronize using Wi-Fi. To complete this exercise, you will need the following:

- The latest version of iTunes on your Mac or Windows PC.
- An iPhone or iPad as well as the USB cable that came with the device.

Step 1	

Open iTunes on your Mac or Windows PC and sign in, if prompted. Connect the USB cable between the Apple mobile device and the computer. The first time you do this on a Windows PC, there will be a slight delay while Windows installs the driver. Then you will need to sign in to the iTunes Store.

Source: Apple Inc.

Step 2

The iTunes app will open. When the device is recognized, the device button will appear near the left of the iTunes window. Tap it. The iTunes windows will now focus on the device. Notice that the device button is no longer on the bar, but now a blue button with the name of the device centered on the bar. On the left is an image of the device with status information. More information is in the main panel.

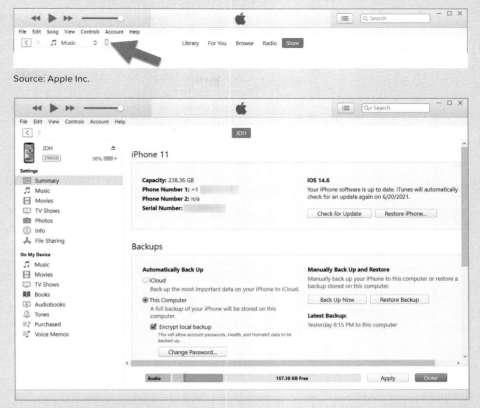

Source: Apple Inc.

Step 3

Configure sync/backup settings for your device. In the sidebar under Settings, select each type of data to configure backup or sync. In the example by Step 2, *This Computer* is selected for backups, as is *Encrypt local backup*.

Step 4

Scroll down to *Options*. Here two options are selected. After making changes tap the *Apply* button. Once the changes are made, the *Apply* button becomes the *Sync* button. Tap it when you want to manually sync. The first time backup runs you will need to create a password for the backup.

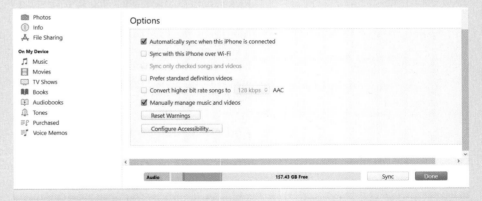

Source: Apple Inc.

Step 5

When iTunes is backing up or syncing your device, do not interrupt it. When it is complete, close the iTunes window.

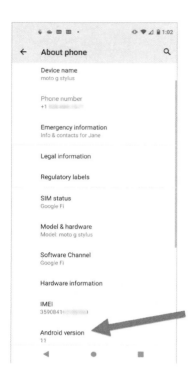

FIGURE 10–20 Android *About phone* showing one screen of information.
Source: Google LLC

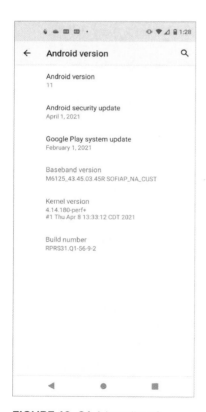

FIGURE 10–21 A long list of information about your Apple device.
Source: Google LLC

LO 10.5 | Securing Mobile Devices

How do you protect a mobile device from malware? How do you keep the wrong people from logging on to a device they stole or found? How do you keep mobile operating systems up to date? How can you find lost devices? Mobile operating systems have many built-in security features. In this section, we describe the steps you can take to make your mobile device more secure using those built-in features, as well as features tied to your Google or Apple ID accounts for protecting your devices.

Patching and OS Updates

As with any computer, you need to keep your device updated with operating system patches and security updates to protect it from malware and other threats. The mobile OSs described here update automatically. You can check on the status for each OS.

Android Updates

Android has updates turned on by default, but the cellular carriers control what updates download and install on specific phone models. Check out the status of updates on your Android device by opening **Settings.** Scroll down and tap **About tablet** or **About phone**. This opens a list of information about your device, as shown in Figure 10–20. Locate and tap *Android version* to see the status of updates (Figure 10–21). On some devices, you can disable or enable updates. We recommend that you leave it turned on.

iOS Updates

On an Apple iOS device, open **Settings,** tap **General,** and then tap **About.** This opens a page of information (Figure 10–22) about your device, such as the cellular network it uses, what types of data and apps are using local storage, and how much available space is left. In this list, **Software Version** shows the version number of iOS installed on that device. To check the status of updates, open Settings, tap General, and on that page locate Software Update, which will show the numeral 1 inside a red circle if an update is available. Configure **Automatic Updates** to both download and install.

Securing Lock Screens on Mobile Devices

A mobile device has a lock screen that keeps you from accidental touch actions, such as inadvertently "pocket dialing" your boss when you are at lunch. By default, the lock screen displays when you first start up your device or after a period of inactivity on the device. Mobile devices usually have an optional setting for a passcode lock that keeps the lock screen in place until you perform some action, such as entering a code or password or using a biometric sign-in, such as Apple's Touch ID or Face ID. Without a passcode lock a simple swipe closes the lock screen and gives anyone access to the device. Android, iOS, and Windows include this feature, although they use different terms to describe it as well as different options.

Android Screen Lock

Android's settings for screen lock range from the least secure (*None* or *Swipe*) to *Pattern*, *PIN*, and *Password*. Biometrics (fingerprints and face recognition) are only available on devices that have hardware support for those features. Before selecting a biometric option, you must have another way to unlock your phone, selected from *pattern, PIN,* or *password.*

iOS Passcode, Face ID, and Touch ID

Apple offers several options for securing the lock screen, depending on the vintage of the device. Of course, on all Apple devices, you can still opt to have no security on the lock screen, "unlocking" it with a simple swipe, or you can use a passcode. On certain

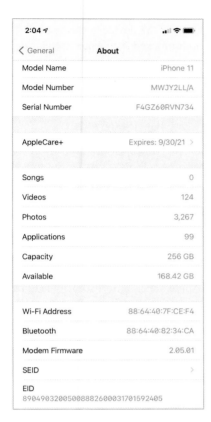

FIGURE 10–22 The first of three pages of information about an iPhone.
Source: Apple Inc.

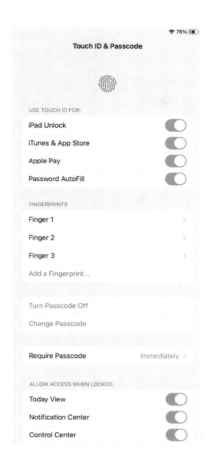

FIGURE 10–23 *Touch ID & Passcode* settings on an iPad.
Source: Apple Inc.

devices you can use one of Apple's biometric methods—either Touch ID or Face ID. As for which devices have these features, Apple introduced **Touch ID** on the iPhone 5S, and it is on newer iPads and iPhones that have the Home button with its special sensors. Face ID was introduced with the iPhone X, which does not have a Home button. As with Android devices, you must have a passcode in place and enter it before you can enable one of the biometric authentication methods or make any changes to these settings.

Touch ID When you first enable Touch ID (using *Touch ID and Passcode* settings), you go through the process of having a finger scanned several times, moving it slightly before each scan. You can add multiple fingers, which is a very good idea. Figure 10-23 shows the *Touch ID & Passcode* Settings page on an iPad.

Face ID Apple uses infrared facial recognition for its **Face ID** feature, but it does not support Touch ID and Face ID on the same device. In Settings look for *Face ID & Passcode*. When you first enable Face ID, follow the instructions for moving your head while the device uses infrared light and an infrared scanner to scan your face creating a mathematical model that is stored in the device. Then, when someone attempts to unlock your phone with Face ID, it scans the face and compares it to the stored mathematical model, unlocking the phone if there is a match.

With either Touch ID or Face ID, you still need to remember your passcode because there are situations when you are required to use it rather than Touch ID or Face ID. These scenarios include:

- After turning off and restarting the device.
- After the device has been locked for over 48 hours.

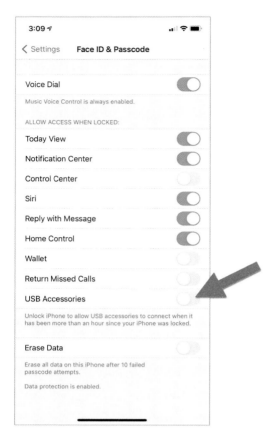

FIGURE 10-24 *When the USB Accessories setting is disabled on an Apple device, USB Restricted Mode is enabled.*
Source: Apple Inc.

- If the passcode has not been used to unlock the device in the last 6.5 days, and Touch ID or Face ID has not unlocked the device in the last 4 hours.
- If the device received a remote lock command.
- After five unsuccessful attempts to unlock with Touch ID or Face ID.
- After a power off/Emergency SOS.

Use any of the three methods—Passcode, Touch ID, or Face ID—to authenticate yourself for purchases made in iTunes or the App Store or through many other sources using Wallet or Apple Pay. Enable the use of Touch ID and Passcode for Apple Pay and for Wallet by locating each of these under *Touch ID & Passcode* in iOS Settings. Until you do this, you will need to authenticate with your Apple ID.

USB Restricted Mode A serious security vulnerability in iOS devices has been exploited by unauthorized persons to bypass Apple's security using a special USB accessory plugged into the iOS device's USB port, the Lightning port. Beginning with iOS version 11.4.1, Apple added a new security feature, USB Restricted Mode, that is enabled by default. But presently, you won't find it by searching on "USB restricted mode" in Settings. The setting for this mode, titled *USB Accessories,* is located under *Touch ID and Passcode* or *Face ID and Passcode,* as shown in Figure 10-24. In reverse logic, when USB Accessories is disabled, USB Restricted Mode is enabled meaning that a USB accessory cannot make a data connection to the device if it has been more than an hour since it was locked. In this mode, you can charge the phone via the Lightning connector, but not access data. When USB Accessories is enabled, USB Restricted Mode is disabled, and a USB connection can be used to both charge the phone and access data.

Location Settings

Applications that track the location of your device have a variety of uses, such as allowing you to find your lost or stolen mobile device from another device or computer, plotting driving directions from your current location, and much more. For these apps to work enable a location service on your device. Apps that use location services are expected to inform you, and once you turn on location services for a device, you should be able to enable or disable it for individual apps in all operating systems. The Emergency 911 (E911) location service is enabled by default on mobile phones and cannot be disabled.

try this!

Enable or Disable Location Services

If you have a mobile device, it should have a setting for enabling or disabling location services. Try this:

1. Open the Settings utility in your mobile device.
2. Look for a setting for location and tap it.
3. If you do not see a setting for location, look for "privacy."
4. Once you find it, disable it and test it by opening a mapping program and trying to find your location. It will fail if you turned the location service off, and it will succeed if you turned it on.

Android Location Services

On an Android device, Location settings, shown in Figure 10-25, shows the Location Service enabled. Here you can see what apps have recently accessed the location of the device. You can also turn Location service on or off for individual apps. Wi-Fi and Bluetooth scanning are needed for a variety of apps and features, such as the ability to find your device.

iOS Location Services

On an Apple device, open **Settings,** select **Privacy,** and then tap **Location Services** to open the list of settings shown in Figure 10-26. Notice that you can enable or disable location services for various components and apps on this device.

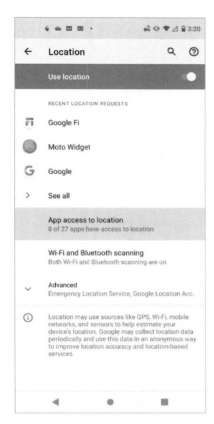

FIGURE 10–25 Android location settings.
Source: Google LLC

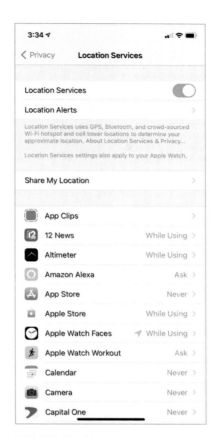

FIGURE 10–26 Apple location settings.
Source: Apple Inc.

Lost or Stolen Devices

Mobile devices are easily stolen or lost. Therefore, take steps ahead of time to protect your data and to help you locate the lost or stolen device. This will usually involve enabling a locator service on the device that tracks its location. Then enable the device-finding service on the device. These services for your Apple devices are associated with your Apple ID account. Similar services for Android devices are associated with your Google account.

Google Find My Device

When you sign in to Google from any mobile device (regardless of the OS), Google adds it to your list of devices in your Google Account. However, when it comes to Google's Find My Device service, it is designed for your Android devices, not for Apple devices. If an Android device has this service enabled on the device and it is lost or stolen, sign in to your Google Account in the browser of any device. On the Google Account page, locate *Find your phone* under *Sign-in & security* (Figure 10-27). Select your phone or tablet from the list of detected devices. You will need to sign in again and tap *Next*.

Figure 10-28 shows the Google page with a map showing the device's approximate location. On this page select the most appropriate option, based on the location. If it is very close to you, select *Play Sound*. Otherwise, you may want to select *Secure Device* or *Erase Device*.

Apple iCloud Find My iPhone

On an Apple device you can enable a feature that uses iCloud to locate a lost or stolen device and then select from several actions, including a remote wipe if your device is lost or stolen. Find my iPhone is a service associated with your Apple ID. On the device, open Settings, tap your Apple ID, and select *Find My* to open the page shown

FIGURE 10–27 Select a device in Google *Find your phone*.
Source: Google LLC

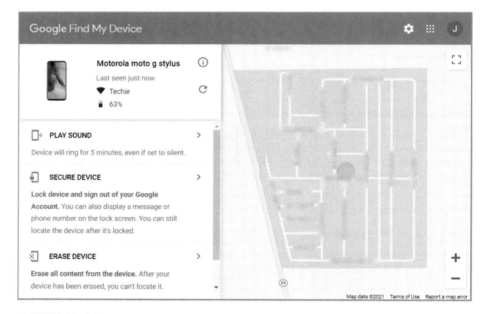

FIGURE 10–28 Once your Android device is located, decide what action to take.
Source: Google LLC

in Figure 10-29. Then select Find My iPhone to open the Find My iPhone page. Then enable **Find My iPhone**, **Find My network**, and **Send Last Location,** as shown in Figure 10-30. Tap **Allow** in the confirmation message that displays.

Once enabled, you can connect to **www.icloud.com** from another device and log in with your Apple ID. On the iCloud home screen (Figure 10-31), select **Find iPhone** (i.e., the name of this service, whether you have an iPhone or not). You may be prompted to sign in again. Then on the next screen, a map will display with the location of your devices.

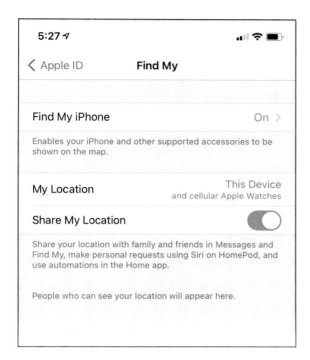

FIGURE 10–29 The *Find My* settings page shows that *Find My iPhone* is turned on.
Source: Apple Inc.

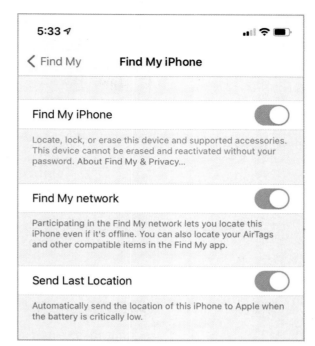

FIGURE 10–30 The *Find My iPhone* page.
Source: Apple Inc.

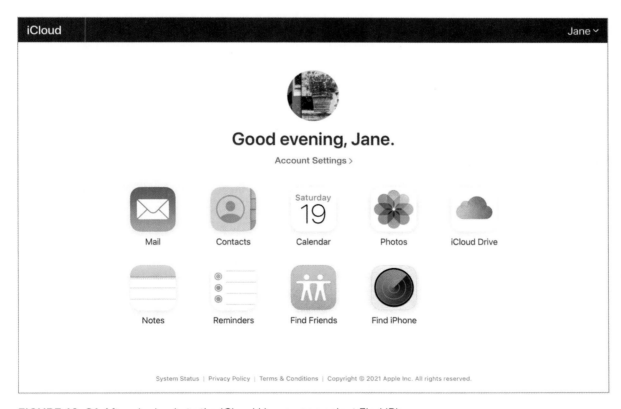

FIGURE 10–31 After signing in to the iCloud Home page select Find iPhone.
Source: Apple Inc.

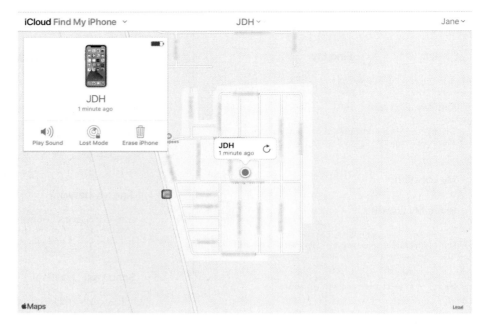

FIGURE 10-32 Select the actions for a lost device.
Source: Apple Inc.

Select All Devices at the top center of this page to open a menu of your devices. Select the lost or stolen device, and the title **All Devices** changes to the name of the selected device and a box opens for that device, as shown in Figure 10-32. This box tells you the battery life of the device (see the upper-right corner of the box) and lets you take some action. Clicking **Play Sound** causes a sound on the device, and it will display the message "Find My iPhone Alert" on the device. This is very handy when your device is hiding under a pile of papers in your office. Select **Lost Mode** and enter a passcode to lock the device (this appears if the device does not already have a passcode). Once someone enters the passcode on the device itself, it is no longer in Lost Mode and can be used. The last option is **Erase iPhone.** Select this if you are convinced it is stolen.

Chapter 10 REVIEW

Chapter Summary

After reading this chapter and completing the step-by-step tutorial and Try This! exercises, you should understand the following facts about mobile operating systems.

From Luggable to BYOD

- Just 40 years ago, mobile computing involved lugging heavy computers that could not connect to a network when in transit.
- Today's mobile devices are popular consumer devices that are tiny, powerful, and connected 24/7.

- People bring their personal mobile devices to school and work, a practice called bring your own device (BYOD).
- Most employers do not have an adequate policy for BYOD to address the many issues of security, ownership, and cost.
- Mobile device management (MDM) is a category of software for managing mobile devices.
- A typical mobile device has a large array of sophisticated hardware in a tiny package.

Configure Accounts for Mobile Devices

- A cellular mobile device needs a credit account with the provider that you use for paying the monthly fees.
- All popular smartphones and tablets require a user account associated with the operating system.
- An Android device has a Google account associated with it for accessing Google services.
- An Apple ID is a customer account for accessing Apple services and products.
- Configure accounts for additional cloud services you use on the device.
- The security settings on the account associated with the device OS affect your privacy and safety on all your devices.

Configure Wireless Connections on Mobile Devices

- A smartphone requires a cellular connection from a cellular provider.
- A cellular connection is an extra option for a tablet, adding a premium to the cost of the device, plus requiring a cellular data plan.
- All popular mobile devices offer Wi-Fi connections, which you can enable and connect to hotspots using appropriate credentials.
- A mobile device with a cellular connection may be able to share that connection, turning the device into a mobile hotspot.
- Tethering is a feature that allows you to share your smartphone's cellular data connection.
- Near Field Communication (NFC) is a special chipset in some mobile devices that allows you to position your device close to another that also has NFC enabled and share data, use some services, or pay for purchases.
- Airplane mode is a feature of mobile devices that, when enabled, turns off all wireless signals.

Email, Apps, Wallets, and Synchronization

- Any popular mobile device can support multiple accounts of different types at once.
- Mobile operating systems understand the basic connection information required for some email providers, so you may only need to enter the personal login information for the account and it will attempt to connect.
- Sometimes when configuring an email account you may have to provide more information, such as the name of POP, IMAP, or SMTP servers.
- Replace your physical wallet with Google Pay or Apple's Wallet and Apple Pay.
- Each mobile OS has some service for synchronizing data between the mobile device and other devices or to the cloud.

Securing Mobile Devices

- Mobile OSs have many security features built in.
- By default, mobile operating systems have updates enabled, so that security patches and updates of the OS are downloaded and installed automatically.
- A mobile device has a lock screen to prevent accidental touch actions. You can protect a lock screen with various security measures so that a simple swiping gesture does not give the wrong person access to the device.
- Enable location services on your mobile device then use settings to control which apps can use it.
- Google *Find your phone* is a free service from Google that will help you locate and manage a lost or stolen device, remotely wipe the device, and cause it to ring.
- Apple iCloud has the free Find My iPhone service. Enable it through settings on your device.

Key Terms List

airplane mode *(381)*

App Library *(384)*

Apple Pay *(385)*

Bluetooth *(379)*

Face ID *(389)*

Fast Pair *(380)*

Google Pay *(384)*

Lightning port *(390)*

location service *(370)*

mobile device management (MDM) *(370)*

mobile hotspot *(377)*

Near Field Communication (NFC) *(381)*

pairing *(379)*

passcode lock *(388)*

Service Set ID (SSID) *(379)*

Subscriber Identity Module (SIM) *(377)*

synchronize *(385)*

tethering *(378)*

Touch ID *(389)*

Two-Factor Authentication *(376)*

USB Restricted Mode *(390)*

Wallet *(385)*

Wi-Fi calling *(379)*

Key Terms Quiz

Use the Key Terms List to complete the sentences that follow:

1. If you turn on the _____ feature of an Android device, other devices can connect via USB, Bluetooth, or Ethernet and use the Android device's mobile hotspot.

2. Turn on _____ to turn off all radios in your mobile device.

3. The list of available Wi-Fi networks that display on your device or computer are each identified by a/an _____.

4. An Apple solution to the multiple pages of app shortcuts is yet another multi-page feature called _____.

5. Its name implies that it is associated with rainstorms, but a _____ is a proprietary USB connection on an Apple device _____.

6. A connection between two Bluetooth devices is called a _____.

7. Some organizations use a type of software called _____ to manage mobile devices used by their employees.

8. When in an area where you cellular service is unreliable, consider enabling _____.

9. A/an _____ secures the lock screen on a mobile device.

10. _____ is a service offered by Apple on their devices that have both Touch ID and NFC, allowing the user to pay for purchases wirelessly.

Multiple-Choice Quiz

1. Which of the following is *not* true concerning BYOD?
   a. Employees may personally incur higher voice and data costs when they bring their own devices to work.
   b. A lost or stolen device can put the employer at risk.
   c. It is unclear who owns intellectual property created.
   d. An employee's private data on their personally owned device may be at risk.
   e. Most organizations have adequate policies in place for BYOD.

2. Which of the following is not a type of wireless communications?
   a. NFC
   b. USB
   c. Wi-Fi
   d. Cellular
   e. Bluetooth

3. Which of the following is an account required for using an Android smartphone?
   a. Apple ID
   b. Microsoft account
   c. Yahoo!
   d. Google account
   e. Hotmail

4. Which type of connection is the primary connection type for a smartphone?
   a. NFC
   b. USB
   c. Wi-Fi
   d. Cellular
   e. Bluetooth

5. Which type of connection is an option for a tablet that adds cost to the hardware as well as a fee for data usage?
   a. NFC
   b. USB
   c. Wi-Fi
   d. Cellular
   e. Bluetooth

6. Which of the following is not a sensor found in mobile devices?
   a. Fingerprint
   b. SIM
   c. Proximity
   d. Gyroscope
   e. Compass

7. Which mode turns off all radio frequency (RF) signals on a device?
   a. Tethering
   b. Mobile hotspot
   c. Airplane mode
   d. Synchronization
   e. USB Restricted Mode

8. What wireless connection feature, if available in your phone, would allow you to pay for purchases by simply positioning the device very close to another device with this feature?
   a. NFC
   b. USB
   c. Wi-Fi
   d. Cellular
   e. Bluetooth

9. Without this type of feature on a mobile device, a simple swipe gives anyone access to the device. What is the term for this feature?
   a. Location service
   b. Passcode lock
   c. Updates
   d. Screen saver
   e. Device manager

10. This wireless connection option is often used to connect keyboard and headsets to mobile devices.
    a. NFC
    b. USB
    c. Wi-Fi
    d. Cellular
    e. Bluetooth

11. What free Google service is available to all Google accounts, allowing them to locate their lost or stolen Android mobile devices?
    a. iCloud
    b. Find Your Phone
    c. Web apps
    d. Find My iPhone
    e. Google Play

12. Use this Apple service to synchronize your iOS device with a Mac or PC.
    a. iCloud

    b. Apple ID
    c. Find My iPhone
    d. iTunes
    e. iMac

13. What Apple service allows you to back up your data from any Apple device so that it is available to all your devices?
    a. iCloud
    b. Apple ID
    c. Find My iPhone
    d. iTunes
    e. iMac

14. What type of card inserted into a mobile device programs it for a user's cellular account information?
    a. NFC
    b. SSID
    c. MDM
    d. SIM
    e. Flash

15. This name identifies a Wi-Fi network.
    a. NFC
    b. SSID
    c. MDM
    d. SIM
    e. Flash

Essay Quiz

1. Describe your ideal mobile device, whether it exists or not.

2. What options do you have for cellular service in your area? Write a paragraph listing the cellular providers who service your area and which one you would choose if you were shopping for a mobile device today. Explain your choice.

3. Take a poll of your fellow students or coworkers. What mobile operating systems are on their mobile devices? Record the results of your poll and compute the percentage between Android and iOS devices.

4. What is the U.S. Federal Aviation Administration policy for the use of electronic devices on an airliner? If you live or travel outside the United States, research the policy of the equivalent agency in another country. Does this policy allow for Airplane mode?

5. Research how mobile devices are being used in both virtual reality (VR) and augmented reality (AR) scenarios for education and on-the-job training. Find some free VR or AR apps and experiment with them on a mobile device.

Lab Projects

LAB PROJECT 10.1

Research mobile device management (MDM) software products by searching for recent product reviews and answer the following questions.

1. What mobile operating systems did the majority of the MDM products you found support?

2. How many of the reviewed products included support for desktop OSs in addition to mobile OSs? List the OSs and the number of MDM products you found that supported them.

3. How many of the MDM products reviewed included a feature that would block devices from accessing email if MDM policies were violated?

LAB PROJECT 10.2

An organization that hosts email services for clients does not need to view the content of the messages in order to provide this service. They can deliver messages by simply examining the header information of the packets that comprise each message. Storing email messages on servers also does not require scanning the content.

Two popular email service providers, Microsoft (**hotmail.com** and **outlook.com**) and Google (Gmail), both include advertising next to your messages in their Web-based email GUIs. Research this practice by these two providers and see if you discern any difference in their use of advertising. Write up your findings and share them with your instructor or class.

LAB PROJECT 10.3

What do you see as the most significant change in mobile devices over the last five years? Is it a new type of mobile device or a revolutionary new app? Is this change a law concerning mobile devices? Discuss this change with your classmates, and tell why you believe it is the most significant change.

11 File Management in the Cloud

Learning Outcomes

In this chapter, you will learn how to:

LO **11.1** Identify consumer-level data storage services in the public cloud, and describe how these services fit into the larger picture of cloud services.

LO **11.2** Create a Dropbox account, and install and use the Dropbox app.

LO **11.3** Create a Google Drive account, and install and use the Google Drive app.

The COVID-19 pandemic brought with it a huge increase in remote work and video conferencing. More students had to access cloud-based apps for online learning, completing projects and labs, submitting papers, collaborating with other students, and taking exams. As we confront the new normal, many are returning to the office or in-person learning, but we continue to depend on online services. Outside of school and the workplace, we use online services for entertainment, for managing our finances, and for shopping, researching vacation destinations, and for storing our personal data. Chapter One introduced the most basic terms associated with cloud computing. In this chapter, we examine how to manage data stored in the cloud. ☀

LO 11.1 | Data Storage in the Public Cloud

In this section, we consider some of the reasons for storing your data in the cloud and why it is important that a cloud storage service has an app compatible with your desktop or mobile operating system.

Data Storage before the Cloud

Where do you keep your personal digital data? If you were born after the year 2000, you may not give this much thought, simply storing your music, photos, videos, and more in the most logical place for anyone whose coming-of-age included a personal mobile device. If you were born prior to this century, then you may have had a longer journey in which you made several transitions in personal data storage from the diskettes of the 1980s to the cloud of the 21st century. And now we find ourselves using our mobile devices for tasks people previously only did sitting at their PCs or laptops. For many of us that means we need to access our data from multiple devices and multiple locations. Therefore, the data must be stored in the cloud.

Private Cloud versus Public Cloud

Cloud storage services are provided by many sources for all sizes and types of data storage needs. We distinguish between two types of cloud storage services, based on who can access them. They are private cloud and public cloud. The reality is much more complicated, but this is one way to begin exploring cloud services.

Private Cloud

A private cloud is an intranet that is owned or managed for the benefit of a single organization and offers a variety of services to members or employees. A private cloud may physically reside on the organization's computers and networks, or it may be hosted by a service provider who charges by the number of users and the services used. These services are not available to the general public. Service providers offer private cloud services to businesses or educational organizations. Your school or employer may use one of these services. A very short list of the largest private cloud providers includes Amazon Web Services (AWS), Microsoft Azure, IBM Cloud, Google Cloud, and Oracle Cloud.

Public Cloud

The term public cloud describes the hosting of a variety of free and/or fee-based services over the Internet available to anyone who enrolls in the service. The short list of public cloud storage services include Apple iCloud, Microsoft OneDrive, Google Drive, Box, and Dropbox.

Why Use Cloud Storage?

There are compelling reasons for millions of individuals to use cloud storage. Now that mobile devices have acquired more capabilities, more people are untethered from desktop computers and use mobile devices. Some are using only mobile devices for computing, and others are using both desktop and mobile devices. Therefore, two benefits of cloud storage seem to be the most compelling to users: access to data from multiple devices and access to the same data from any location. Another benefit is the ability to easily share your data. With cloud services you can simply share your data for others to view, or you can allow others to make changes to that data and collaborate on projects. Cost is another reason to move to cloud storage. Basic storage is free to individuals from many providers and upgrading to more storage space is usually inexpensive.

Access Data from Many Devices and Many Locations

For the author the move to the cloud happened as she found herself needing to access her data from multiple computers and devices in her home office as well as from two other locations. With a cloud-based account, she connects to her cloud storage from practically any computing device and from almost anywhere in the world. Most of her personal and work data are stored in Microsoft OneDrive, but she uses two other data storage services to share work files, and she uses yet another storage service as a volunteer to a nonprofit.

When managing data in the cloud, there are a few terms we need to keep straight. The first two are upload and download. When you select the option to upload one or more files to the cloud, you are sending it from storage on your device to the cloud. A download involves bringing data from the cloud down to your device. Most activity on the Internet involves downloading of files during browsing. This is activity we don't think much about. However, there are times when you are more aware of initiating a download. For instance, you have read this term several times in this book as you downloaded apps to your device. The same term applies when you are using cloud storage.

Two other terms you encounter when working with cloud storage are online and offline. When a file is stored online, it remains online until you download it to work on it. When you save an online file, it is stored in your cloud storage. This has the benefit of not using storage on your local device, but you can only work on online files while you have an Internet connection to the cloud service. When you designate a file in cloud storage as offline, it is downloaded from the cloud storage to storage on your local device. The advantage of this is that you can work on this file when you do not have Internet access. When you make changes to the file, it is stored locally, but synchronized with your cloud storage the next time the device is connected to the cloud storage service.

Collaborate with Others

The increase in remote workers requires that they work in the cloud with collaboration services, which allow two or more people to work together on documents and entire projects. Simple collaboration services are available at the consumer level through file and folder sharing. More sophisticated collaboration services are part of most business-level cloud services.

Consider the Apps You Use

And then, there are the apps associated with popular cloud storage providers. The author uses productivity apps from a handful of sources, but most of her time is spent using Microsoft's suite, especially Word, Outlook, PowerPoint, and Excel. Therefore, as Microsoft moved from selling prepackaged versions of their apps to providing them as part of their cloud service, she enrolled in what is now Microsoft 365. This gives her 1 TB of OneDrive cloud storage and the suite of apps, installable on all her devices.

Basic Public Cloud Storage Is Free

Once you are motivated to consider cloud storage you can try it for free. Dozens of providers in the public cloud offer basic public-cloud storage plans for free. For a fee you can upgrade each of these plans to gain more storage space.

In the world of cloud services, as in other technical areas, things are changing rapidly, so you will need to research which cloud storage service best suits your needs. If your desktop or laptop is a Mac or MacBook, and your phone is an iPhone, the cloud storage that works the best in a pure Apple environment is iCloud Drive. If you primarily use Google services for email and apps, you are already using Google Drive. Those of us dependent on Microsoft Office apps use OneDrive. If you don't comfortably fit into the Apple, Google, or Microsoft mold, consider Dropbox, Box, or one of many other services. And you aren't required to stick with one cloud storage provider,

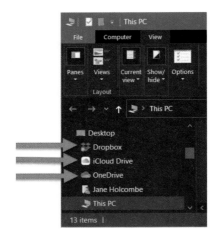

FIGURE 11–1 Windows File Explorer with folders for three different cloud services.
Source: Microsoft Corporation

although it can get chaotic if you are using more than one from the same device. In fact, only backup and synchronize files from a local computer/device to one cloud storage service. Make a choice and stick to it. There can be other reasons for using more than one cloud storage service, but for most people, one cloud storage service is sufficient.

The Operating System Connection

You may question what cloud storage has to do with operating systems. After all, you have heard that all you need to connect to cloud services is a browser. Not entirely true. You can access the data storage services we review here with a browser, but to have data from your device synchronize with the cloud, you must install client software (an app) that is compatible with the operating system on that device. The app interacts with the local file system and appears as a folder in your file management utility. Windows File Explorer in Figure 11-1 shows folders for three cloud storage services: Dropbox, iCloud Drive, and OneDrive. In Figure 11-2, the Apple Finder app displays the OneDrive folder under the user's home folder, while the sidebar shows the iCloud Drive for the same user.

try this!

Which Public Cloud Storage Meets Your Needs?

What are your options for consumer-level cloud storage? Search for one that meets your needs. Try this:

1. On a Mac, PC, or mobile device open a browser.
2. In the Search box enter "public cloud storage reviews."
3. Carefully select links in the search results, looking for recent reviews on public cloud storage services.
4. After reading at least three sets of reviews, decide which service sounds appropriate for you.

LO 11.2 | Dropbox

Dropbox is a cloud storage service that doesn't have a big name like Google associated with it. Dropbox is compatible with Windows, macOS, and Linux, as well as most mobile operating systems. The Dropbox Android app gives access to Dropbox services on Chromebooks.

Free Dropbox Storage

Dropbox Basic is a free plan for a single user with up to 2 GB of storage. There are ways to earn more free storage, such as referring people to Dropbox. Figure 11-3 shows a comparison of Dropbox plans *for individuals* at the time of this writing. This comparison scrolls down for several pages, so to see the complete list search for "Dropbox plans for individuals." Currently, computer backup is part of the Basic plan, but Smart Sync is not. Also, the Basic plan includes camera uploads

WARNING!

Be very suspicious and cautious of each link you encounter on the Web and in email, because there are many imposters posing as legitimate sites. Many of these sites are littered with ads and links to malicious sites.

FIGURE 11–2 Apple's Finder displays two cloud storage services.
Source: Apple Inc.

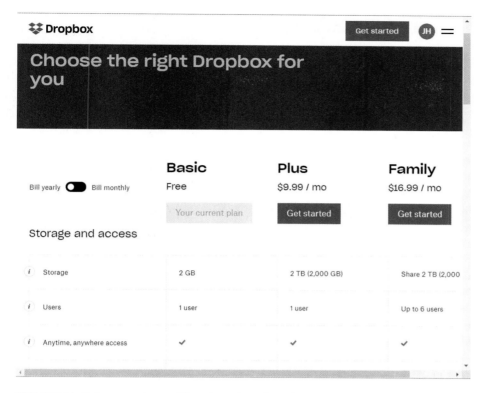

FIGURE 11–3 A comparison of Dropbox plans for individuals.
Source: Dropbox, Inc.

only with the desktop app installed and its use is limited to just three devices. Anyone seriously considering Dropbox Basic should keep in mind that the free storage space will soon be used up if you store photos and videos on Dropbox. Therefore, consider the features and cost of upgrading to one of their other plans. The **Dropbox Plus** plan allots up to 2 TB to a single user, while **Dropbox Family** allows a single user to share 2 TB of access with up to 5 other users. Each upgrade includes other additional features.

Installing the Dropbox app on your computer creates a Dropbox folder in the file system of the OS. Copy or move files and folders into the Dropbox folder, and Dropbox will automatically synchronize them to the Dropbox cloud storage servers, and save versions every time you make changes to files in the Dropbox folder. Your data is available from all your computers and devices.

> *Note:* Recall that in Chapter 10 you learned that the term synchronize means to match the contents of two locations. When you apply that definition to your use of a single cloud storage account, if a file is changed on one device and then synchronized with the cloud storage, the new version will eventually be synchronized to all devices using that account and running the cloud storage app.

Working with Dropbox on a Desktop or Laptop

Once you select a storage plan that fits your needs, sign in from a desktop or other device and install Dropbox. Installing Dropbox Basic is quick and easy. Step-by-Step 11.01 describes how to create a new Dropbox account, install Dropbox on your desktop or laptop, and move a folder from your local computer to your Dropbox folder. A word of caution. With every interaction Dropbox offers enticements to commit to one of their fee-based plans. Figure 11–4 is an example of a message received while installing the Dropbox Basic app on a Windows desktop. It took a moment to realize that clicking *Continue with Basic* was the option for Dropbox Basic. That action was immediately followed by an "Are you sure?" box, which required clicking yet another button to continue. The Dropbox Basic plan is the only one that remains free.

> *Note:* You can associate any email account with Dropbox. You do not need to have an email with one specific provider.

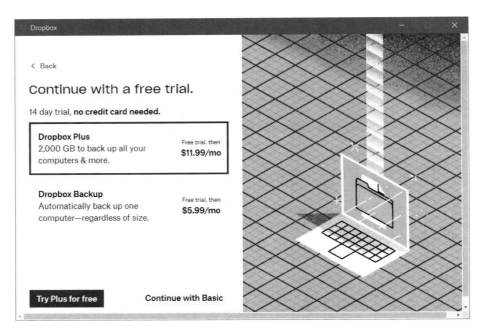

FIGURE 11–4 Dropbox often suggests upgrading.
Source: Dropbox, Inc.

Step-by-Step 11.01

Getting Started with Dropbox

In this hands-on exercise, create a Dropbox account, download the Dropbox app to your computer, and move files or folders from your local computer to your Dropbox folder. The steps and the screenshots were created on a MacBook. You can also easily complete these tasks in Windows, following the instructions from the Dropbox website. To complete the steps, we recommend the following:

- A Mac or a Windows PC or laptop.

- If you do not already have a Dropbox account, be prepared to provide an existing email address and to create a user name and password for a new Dropbox account.
- Create a folder on the Mac or Windows computer and copy a few files into it before starting this exercise. Be sure that the folder contains less than 2 GB of data.

| Step 1 |

Point your browser to **www.dropbox.com/basic**. Click on the button labeled *Sign up for free*.

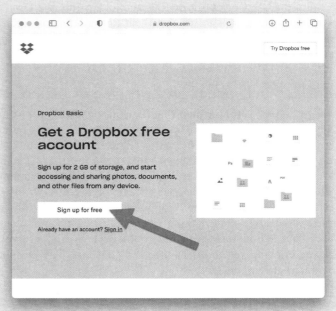

Source: Dropbox, Inc.

On the next page enter your first name, last name, and email address. Then create a new password for Dropbox, click to place a check in the box labeled *I agree to the Dropbox terms.* Then click *Create an account.*

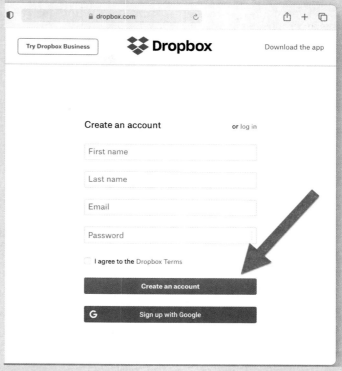

Source: Dropbox, Inc.

Dropbox displays a suggestion that you get a free trial of one of the fee-based plans. Scroll to the bottom and select *Or continue with 2 GB Dropbox Basic plan.* A confirming email is sent to the address you provided, but in our tests, we did not open the email until after DropBox was installed, so it may not be significant.

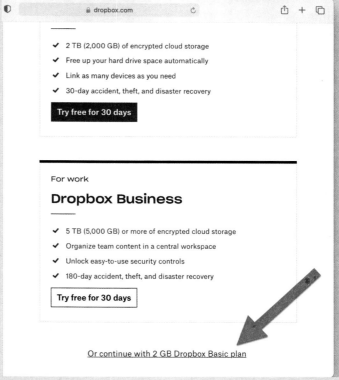

Source: Dropbox, Inc.

Step 4

On the next screen click *Download Dropbox* to download the Dropbox installer.

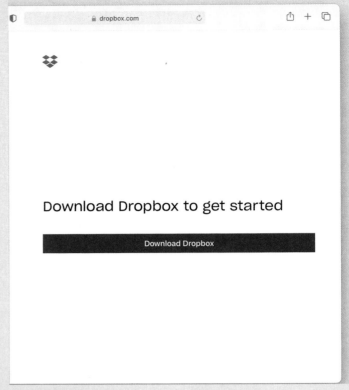

Source: Dropbox, Inc.

Step 5

A message will display when download completes. In Windows, select *Open* to run the installer app. In macOS, you may need to search for the installer app, DropBoxInstaller.DMG. In the past, the installer was saved on the desktop. If it is not on the macOS desktop, locate it in the Applications folder. Once you locate it, double-click to launch it. When the dialog box shown here displays, click the *Open* button. This is followed by more downloading as the Dropbox installer downloads and installs Dropbox.

Source: Dropbox, Inc.

Step 6

At this point, you have the opportunity to allow Dropbox to text or email a link to install the Dropbox app on your mobile device.

Source: Dropbox, Inc.

Step 7

Dropbox is installed. Click *Next* to learn more about Dropbox. Exit when you are ready to move a folder from your computer to Dropbox.

Source: Dropbox, Inc.

Step 8

Locate the Dropbox folder in the file manager on your computer. In the macOS Finder, open the user's Home folder and locate the Dropbox folder. In Windows File Explorer, locate the Dropbox folder under Desktop, as shown back in Figure 11–1.

Source: Apple Inc.

Step 9

Locate the local folder you created before beginning this Step-by-Step. Drag and drop it onto the Dropbox folder.

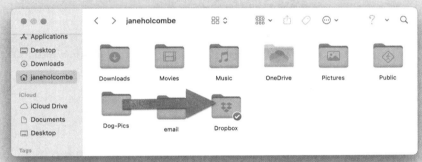

Source: Apple Inc.

Step 10

The Dropbox folder will open as you drop the local folder onto it. Keep Dropbox open as you continue through this section of the chapter.

Source: Apple Inc.

Working in Dropbox Using a Web Browser

You can either use the Dropbox folder installed on your computer in Step-by-Step 11.01 or point your browser to **dropbox.com**. Either way, you can add files and folders from your computer to Dropbox, create all types of data files, and save them to Dropbox as easily as saving them to your local computer. Of course, the storage limit of your Dropbox plan may limit the size of file you can upload.

After creating a Dropbox account, suppose you need to upload some files from your computer to Dropbox. You can do this, even on a computer that does not have Dropbox installed. You simply use the browser to connect to Dropbox. Step-by-Step 11.02 walks through this process.

Step-by-Step 11.02

Working with Dropbox in a Web Browser

In this hands-on exercise, connect to Dropbox from your browser and upload files from your local computer to Dropbox. Any browser will work. To complete the steps, as shown, we recommend the following:

- A Mac (desktop or MacBook) or Windows PC or laptop.
- If this is a different computer or browser from the one you used to create your Dropbox account, be prepared

for a first-time sign in from that browser to the Dropbox account.

- Identify one or more files on the local computer that you will upload to Dropbox. Be sure that the file will not cause your Dropbox folder to exceed 2 GB of data.

Step 1

Point your browser to **https://www.dropbox.com** and sign in to your account. If you completed Step-by-Step 11.01, the folder you moved into Dropbox will show under All files.

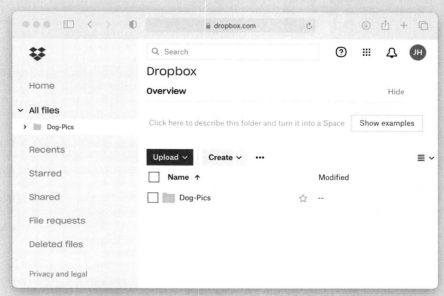

Source: Dropbox, Inc.

Step 2

Click the *Upload* button and select *Files*.

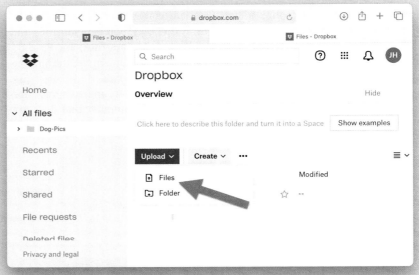

Source: Dropbox, Inc.

Step 3

The local file manager (macOS Finder or Windows File Explorer) will open. Browse the local computer and select one or more files to upload.

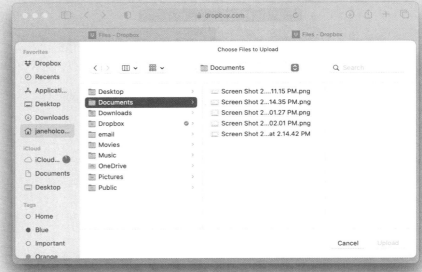

Source: Dropbox, Inc.

Step 4

After selecting files click the *Upload* button.

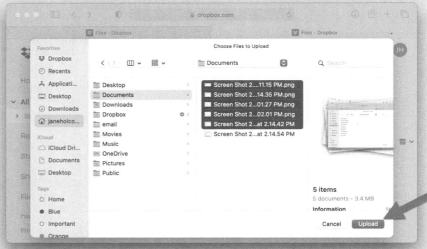

Source: Dropbox, Inc.

Step 5

A status bar opens to show the progress of the upload. Once the upload completes, the status bar indicates how many files were uploaded. Click the *View details* button.

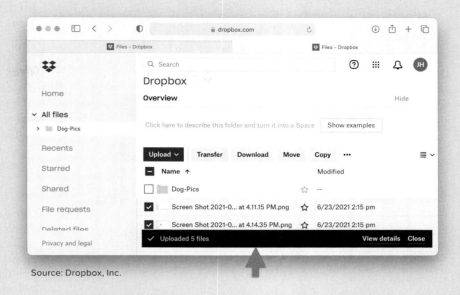

Source: Dropbox, Inc.

Step 6

From the *Upload details* dialog box, you can add more files to the upload. When you have completed the upload, click the *Done* button.

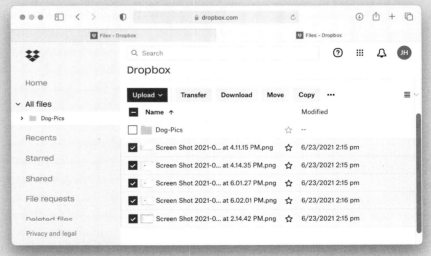

Source: Dropbox, Inc.

Step 7

Dropbox displays the list of uploaded files.

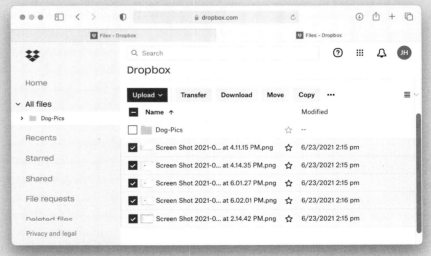

Source: Dropbox, Inc.

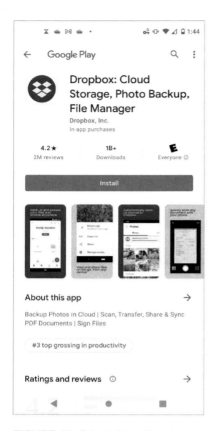

FIGURE 11–5 Install the Dropbox Android app from Google Play.
Source: Google LLC

FIGURE 11–6 Download and install the Dropbox app from the Apple App Store.
Source: Apple Inc.

Note: As mentioned earlier, the free Dropbox Basic only allows up to three connected devices.

Installing the Dropbox App on a Mobile Device

Installing the Dropbox App on your mobile devices gives you access to your files in the cloud from almost anywhere. On an Android device, open Google Play and search for "dropbox." Figure 11-5 shows that the Dropbox app is ready to install. Clicking the Install button resulted in a brief wait for the installation to complete. Once the app installs, click the Open button and sign in or sign up.

If you have an Apple mobile device, connect to the App Store, the source of apps for those devices. When prompted, enter your Apple account credentials. In the App Store search for the Dropbox app. Figure 11-6 shows the Dropbox page in the App Store.

On Apple or Android devices, follow the prompts to sign in to Dropbox, but do not commit to uploading and backing up just yet. For instance, if you elect to backup your Photos folder to Dropbox, it may soon use up your 2 GB of free storage. As for syncing, that is not supported for the free Dropbox Basic plan. We will look at uploading files using a mobile app in Step-by-Step 11.03.

Accessing Dropbox from a Mobile Device

After installing Dropbox on a mobile device, consider how you will use Dropbox from that device. Do you want to download files from Dropbox to your smartphone or tablet? Do you want to upload files from your mobile device to Dropbox? You will likely do both as you learn your way around Dropbox and find more uses for its abilities.

In our case, we wanted to select certain files from an iPhone to upload to Dropbox, and we decided that we would keep files uploaded from the iPhone separate from other files in Dropbox. With that in mind, we created a folder on Dropbox to contain the files. Step-by-Step 11.03 will walk you through creating a folder in Dropbox and selecting and copying files from a mobile device to Dropbox.

Step-by-Step 11.03

Uploading Files from a Mobile Device to Dropbox

In this hands-on exercise, connect to Dropbox, create a folder in Dropbox, and then select files from a mobile device and upload those files into the new folder on Dropbox. The steps and screenshots were recorded using an iPhone, but because most of this occurs within Dropbox, the steps are nearly identical to how you would do these tasks from any device. To complete the steps, as shown, we recommend having the following:

- A Dropbox user account.
- A mobile device running iOS, iPad OS, or Android.
- The Dropbox app installed on that device.
- Be prepared with a folder name to use in the beginning steps.
- Be prepared to select files from your device to upload to Dropbox.

Step 1

If you are not already signed in to Dropbox on your mobile device, locate the Dropbox app and tap it to open it. Provide your email address and Dropbox password. When prompted to upgrade to Dropbox Plus, tap *Cancel.*

Step 2

On the Welcome to Dropbox page select *Skip.* If prompted to Allow notifications, tap *Don't Allow.*

Source: Dropbox, Inc.

Step 3

On the bottom of the Home page tap the *Files* icon.

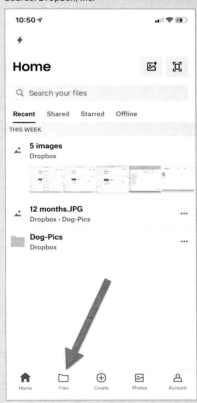

Source: Dropbox, Inc.

On the Files page tap the *Folder* button. On the New folder page (not shown here), note that it will be saved to Dropbox and presently only you can access it. Tap *New Folder*. On the Rename folder page, enter a folder name ("Drafts" in this example) and tap *Done*. On the New folder page (not shown here), leave the Save to location as *Dropbox*. Tap *Create*.

Source: Dropbox, Inc.

Source: Dropbox, Inc.

Dropbox opens the new folder. Shown here is the folder named Drafts. Notice the actions available. That is not all you can do. The only upload option shown is *Upload photos*. To upload other types of files, tap the *Create* button at the bottom of the page.

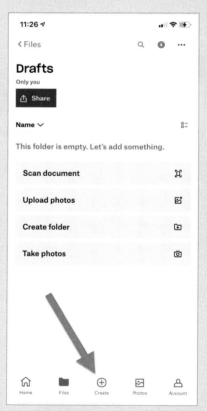

Source: Dropbox, Inc.

Step 6

A pop-up menu offers many choices, but to do a simple file upload select *Create or upload file*.

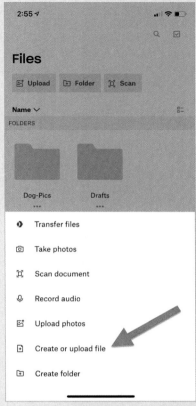

Source: Dropbox, Inc.

Step 7

A new menu of options for creating or modifying a file pops up. If you are uploading from the mobile device, select *Upload file*.

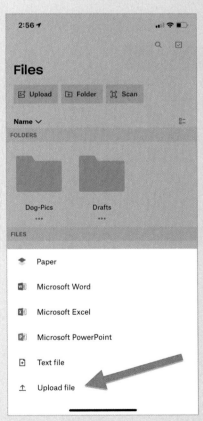

Source: Dropbox, Inc.

If the *Recents* page displays, select *Browse* at the bottom. Then, on the *Browse* page, shown here, select *On My iPhone* (or whatever mobile device you are using).

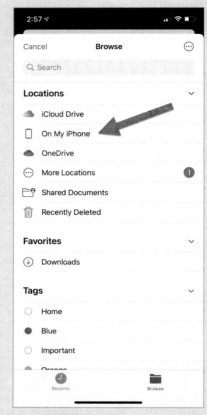

Source: Dropbox, Inc.

If no files or folders are shown on this page, return to Browse and select another location. In this case, there are two folders, so we opened one and tapped the file named Welcome.

Source: Dropbox, Inc.

Step 10

Once the file is selected the *Upload file* page opens. This is where you select the target folder on Dropbox for this file. Once you have selected it, then tap Upload.

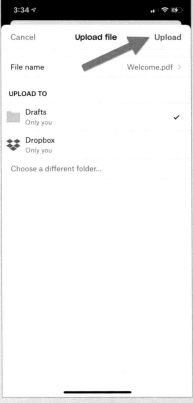

Source: Dropbox, Inc.

Step 11

The uploaded file is listed in the selected folder on Dropbox.

Source: Dropbox, Inc.

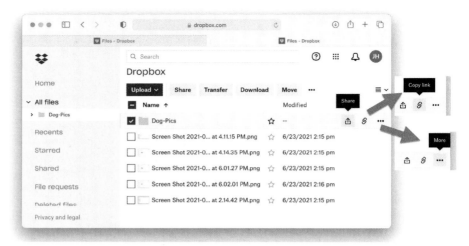

FIGURE 11-7 Share or copy a link.
Source: Dropbox, Inc.

Sharing

Share a file or folder from any device using either the app or browser to connect to **dropbox.com**. When you want to share a folder or file in Dropbox, click or tap the file or folder and three buttons will appear on the right, as shown in Figure 11-7. Use the *Share* option to share with other Dropbox members. When you share a file, you invite people. You can assign the **Can Edit** permission, allowing them to edit the contents of a file or folder. Alternatively, you can assign the **Can View** permission to a shared file or folder, restricting access to simply viewing the contents. The *Copy link* option is more universal. It creates a copy of a link to the file or folder that you can send via email or message to anyone, including nonmembers, but they only have the *can view* permission. The *More* button opens a menu of these and other options. With the Dropbox Basic service, anyone with the link to the share can view or download the file or a folder's contents and the link never expires. A shared file does not impact the storage space limit of a person given access to the share by the owner.

LO 11.3 | Google Drive

Google Drive, like Dropbox, is an online storage service for keeping your files, photos, stories, designs, drawings, recordings, videos, or anything you need to store where you can access it from any device. As you would expect, you can give others access to just what you want them to be able to see or use. Google, like other cloud services, offers plans for individuals as well as for businesses.

Getting Started with Free Google Drive Storage

Your individual Google account gives you 15 GB of free online storage shared by Google Drive, Gmail, and Google Photos. In addition to Gmail and Google Photos, you have free use of the Google Web apps, productivity apps similar to Microsoft's free Web apps. Google Drive can store individual files up to 5 TB in size, as long as they do not exceed the total storage available for your account. It's important to understand the following about how the type of data you store impacts your Google Drive storage limit:

- Your Gmail messages and attachments (both sent and received) count against your storage limit.
- All PDFs, images, and videos stored in My Drive count against your limit.
- If you use the **Original** format option for files saved in Google Photos, they count against your limit and are saved without compression in their original

format. You may quickly run out of space using this option, especially if your camera is set to save in the **RAW** format preferred by professional photographers and some hobbyists. RAW saves all the unprocessed data for an image and creates very large files.

- Before June 1, 2021, any files you created with the Google productivity apps (Docs, Sheets, or Slides) did not count against your limit. Since then, those files do count against your storage limit, and any files created before that date and modified since then count.

- Before June 1, 2021, photos and videos saved or backed up in what was formerly called **High Quality** did not count against the storage limit, but any files modified and saved after that date do count. Since June 1, 2021, the new name for this Google Photos format is **Storage saver**. The resolution of the images must be 16 megapixels or less and videos must be 1080p or lower. Any photos or videos that exceed this limit will be compressed when synced to the original device that uploaded them.

- The storage space for shared files only counts against the owner's limit.

You can store files, save email attachments, and back up photos directly to Drive. Google Drive works with Microsoft Windows operating systems and with Mac operating systems. It currently does not have support for Linux operating systems, although there is a work around for adding it to the Ubuntu File Manager. See the article on this topic posted at https://vitux.com/. Google Drive also works with Android and Apple's mobile operating systems. Google Drive and the Google Apps work with the major browsers, including Chrome, Firefox, Microsoft Edge (on Windows only), and Safari (on macOS only).

Creating a Google Account

To use Google Drive you need a free Google account. Google accounts are based on the **Google Mail** app with an email address ending in *@gmail.com*. A Google account gives you access to all the Google apps. Google Drive is just one of the apps. Before you create a Google account be prepared with several options for names. Google mail is so popular you may well have the user name you want to use rejected because it already belongs to someone else.

You will need a Google Account to complete Step-by-Step 11.04. If you need to create one, point your browser to **https://accounts.google.com/signup**, then enter your information in the *Create your Google Account* dialog, shown in Figure 11-8. The *Create your Google Account* page asks you to prove you're not a robot. Google uses several types of challenge/response tests to ensure that automated software, a **bot**, is not attempting to create an email address to use for sending out spam. The type of program often used for these tests is a **CAPTCHA (Completely Automated Public Turing Test to Tell Computers and Humans Apart)**. LC Check generates and grades the tests to determine that it is interacting with a human before Google will create an account. You may need to type what you see in a picture or what you hear in an audio message into the answer box.

After you sign in to Google in your browser, notice the bar across the top of the page. It includes a tiny three-by-three grid of dots near the right side, as shown in Figure 11-9. This is the *Google Apps* menu button; click this to open a menu of the Google apps, including Google Drive.

Transitioning from Backup and Sync to Google Drive Desktop App

If you want to sync or backup files between your Windows or Apple Mac desktop, Google offers **Google Drive for desktop**, an improvement and replacement for **Backup and Sync**, the previous option for individuals. The biggest difference between the two is that *Google Drive for desktop* streams all files and folders from the cloud, while *Backup and Sync* stored your My Drive files on the local computer, backing up and syncing to the Web. Google was still offering both apps until they completed the

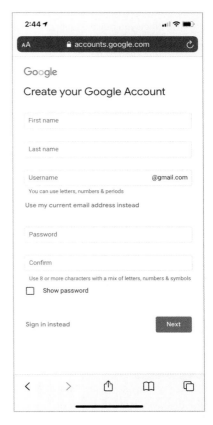

FIGURE 11–8 Create your Google Account.
Source: Google LLC

Note: Bots are used for a variety of simple, repetitive tasks that can be automated. They are often used in malicious attacks and for gathering data, such as email addresses from websites.

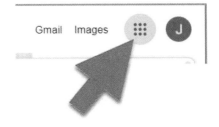

FIGURE 11–9 The *Google Apps* menu button.
Source: Google LLC

transition to Google Drive for desktop in the fall of 2021. There are more differences. In Step-by-Step 11.04 see a comparison of these two apps, and download the new and improved Google Drive for desktop to your Windows or Apple Mac desktop. You may need to take different actions to find and download the app, and you may see different screens. At this writing, the desktop app integrates well into the operating system, but it is not clear how to access all the features of the app.

Step-by-Step 11.04

Installing the Google Drive for Desktop App

In this hands-on exercise, download and install the Google Drive for Desktop app to your computer. The screenshots were created in Windows 10. You can also easily complete these tasks in macOS on a Mac, allowing for the differences in appearance between the Windows and macOS GUIs.

To complete the steps, as shown, we recommend the following:

- A Windows PC or laptop.
- Be prepared to sign in with an existing Gmail account.

Step 1

To see a comparison of the old app for desktops and the new one, point your browser to "**support.google. com.**" In the search box type "compare backup and sync." From the results select *Compare Backup and Sync & Google Drive for desktop.*

Source: Google LLC

Step 2

Read the article to understand the differences between these two apps.

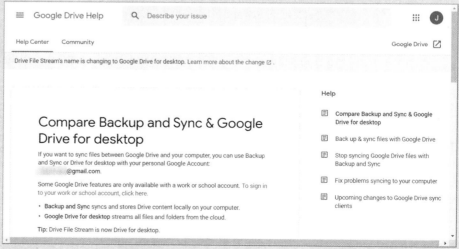

Source: Google LLC

Step 3

Scroll down to see the comparison table. Then click the button labeled *Download Google Drive for Desktop*. If this is not available to you, sign in to Google in your browser and open the Google Drive page. There may be a link on that page for downloading the app. Otherwise, proceed with these steps.

	Backup and Sync	Google Drive for desktop
Use files in My Drive	Yes	Yes
Use files in shared drives	No	Yes
Sync only selected folders in My Drive*	Yes	Yes
Sync only individual files in My Drive*	No	Yes
Use native apps, like Microsoft Office & Photoshop	Yes	Yes
See who's editing with real-time presence in Microsoft Office	No	Yes
Integrates with Microsoft Outlook, Meet scheduling	No	Yes
Sync other folders, like Documents or Desktop	Yes	No
Use with your personal Google Account, like _____@gmail.com	Yes	Yes
Use with your work or school Google Account	Yes	Yes
Upload photos and videos to Google Photos	Yes	No

*With Google Drive for desktop, you can make selected files or folders 'Available offline' to sync them to your computer rather than an online stream.

DOWNLOAD BACKUP & SYNC   DOWNLOAD GOOGLE DRIVE FOR DESKTOP

Source: Google LLC

Step 4

On the next page scroll down until you see the two buttons for downloading. Click the button for your operating system. Note that the downloaded file for Windows will be GoogleDriveSetup.exe and the file for Mac will be GoogleDrive.dmg. When the download completes, locate the file and launch the installer. Follow the prompts to complete the installation.

≡ Google Drive Help   Q Describe your issue

Get started with Google Drive for desktop

You can find and open your files from Google Drive on your computer with Google Drive for desktop. You can:

- Save specific files and folders offline, including shared drives.
- View and organize your files in your computer's file system without using storage space.
- Open files on your computer.

Download & install Google Drive for desktop   ^

You might not be able to use Google Drive for desktop, or your organization might install it for you. If you have questions, ask your administrator.

To download Google Drive for desktop:

DOWNLOAD FOR WINDOWS   DOWNLOAD FOR MAC

1. On your computer, open:
   - **GoogleDriveSetup.exe** on Windows
   - **GoogleDrive.dmg** on Mac

2. Follow the on-screen instructions.

Watch video tutorials

To get the latest tips, tricks, and how-to's, subscribe to our YouTube Channel.

Source: Google LLC

Step 5

When this window displays, click *Sign in with browser*.

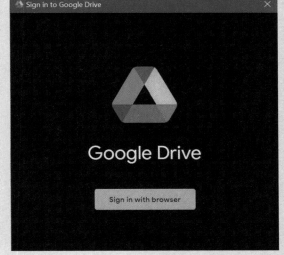

Source: Google LLC

Step 6

There will be a brief delay while Google installs drivers for your operating system. The browser will open and this message will display. If you are sure you downloaded the app from Google, click the *Sign* in button.

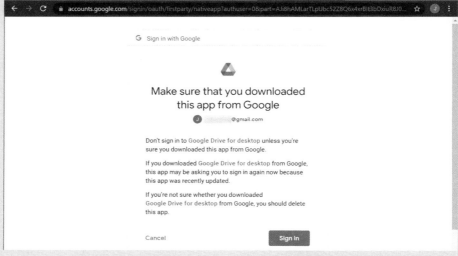

Source: Google LLC

Step 7

The *Welcome* to *Google Drive* window displays, offering several pages of introduction to the features of Google Drive.

Source: Google LLC

Step 8

On the last page of Welcome to Google Drive, click the button labeled *Open Google Drive folder*.

Source: Google LLC

Step 9

The file manager for your operating system opens. In this case it is Windows File Explorer. Notice the new Google Drive icon in the sidebar under *This PC*. Now you can copy and move files between this computer and Google Drive, just as you manage files between other folders on your computer.

Source: Google LLC

Step 10

Explore other options the Google Drive app provides for working with your files. In Windows right-click on the My Drive folder to open the context menu. From here you can open Google Drive on the Web or configure Offline access. For now, select *Open with Google Drive*.

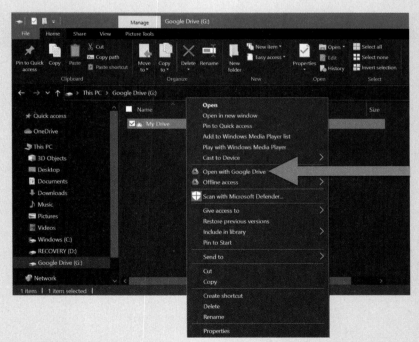

Source: Google LLC

Step 11

When the browser opens, sign in to Google and click *Next*.

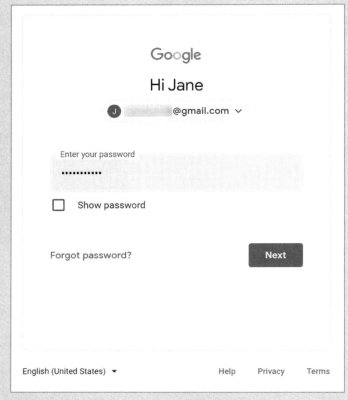

Source: Google LLC

Step 12

Google Drive opens in the browser. Select *Computers* in the sidebar. Once sync is enabled for a computer it will be listed here.

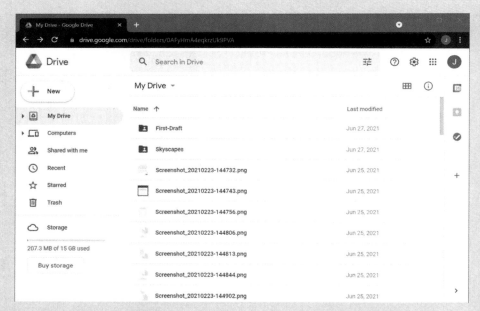

Source: Google LLC

Return to the file manager (in this example, File Explorer) and locate *My Drive*. Double-click to open *My Drive*. Notice the cloud icons on each file listed here, indicating that the file is stored online.

Source: Google LLC

Right-click on one of the files to open the context menu, shown here. Notice the many Google Drive options in the list. Select *Available offline*. The icon for the selected file changes to a green offline icon. When you edit an offline file, it is saved to Google Drive the next time you have an Internet connection.

Source: Google LLC

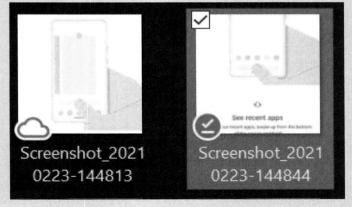

Source: Google LLC

Now locate a folder in the open My Drive folder. Right-click on that folder to see the Google Drive options available for folders, as shown here. Then close the current window.

Source: Google LLC

Securing Your Google Account

The Google *My Account* home page (Figure 11–10) is where you will find settings to make your Google account more secure, change your privacy settings, and manage your account preferences. Refer back to Chapter 8, Step-by-Step 8.04, *Exploring Google Account Security and Privacy Settings*.

WARNING!

Always provide the minimal personal data to any online service: name, email address, and phone number (for two-factor verification). Date of birth is valuable information that you should keep to yourself unless absolutely necessary. For instance, you need to provide your birth date (and more) when you have an online account with a legitimate financial or health care organization.

Note: Presently Google requires JavaScript for the Security Checkup, Privacy Checkup, and other wizard-type features that guide you through steps for configuring settings. If you have disabled JavaScript, you will see a message, and you can enable your browser's JavaScript or choose to run an "alternate version" of the Account Settings. This means that you will not be helped through the steps and will have a simpler interface to the settings.

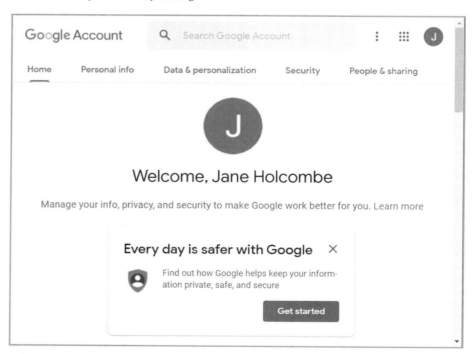

FIGURE 11–10 The settings for security, privacy, and preferences are available through the *My Account* home page.
Source: Google LLC

Uploading Files to Google Drive

It is now possible to simply "work in the cloud," creating your files using the free Google apps, such as *Docs, Sheets,* or *Slides,* and saving all your data from those cloud apps to your cloud storage. In Step-by-Step 11.05 you will practice the basic skill of uploading files from a folder on your local computer to a folder you will create in Google Drive.

Step-by-Step 11.05

Uploading Files to Google Drive

In this hands-on exercise, open your My Drive page in Google on the Web, create a folder, and copy files from your local computer into the new folder. The screenshots were created in Windows 10. You can also easily complete these tasks in a browser in macOS.

To complete the steps, as shown, we recommend the following:

- A Windows PC or laptop.
- A Gmail address and password to sign in to Google.
- Identify a folder on the local computer that you will move to Google Drive. Be sure that the folder will not cause you to exceed the limit of 15 GB of data.

Step 1

Point your browser to **https://drive.google.com/**. If you are not automatically signed in, then enter your username and password. You may need to enter a verification code if you have enabled two-step verification. When the My Drive page opens in Google Drive click on the *New* button and select *Folder.*

Source: Google LLC

Step 2

In the *New folder* box enter a name for the folder. In this example it is named *Skyscapes.* Press the *Create* button.

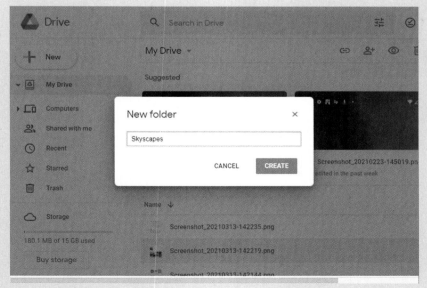

Source: Google LLC

Step 3

Your new folder appears in your **My Drive** page.

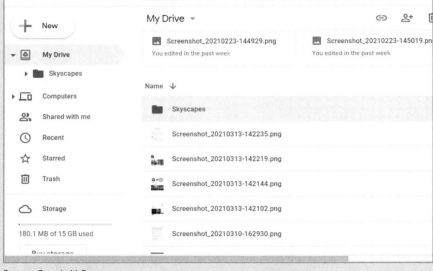

Source: Google LLC

Step 4

Double-click the folder to open it.

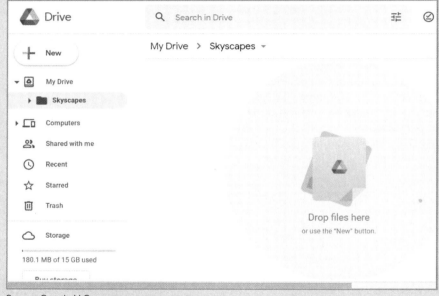

Source: Google LLC

Step 5

Click or tap the New button, and select *File upload* from the menu. A dialog box opens in which you can browse to a local folder. Select one or more files and then click or tap *Open*.

Source: Google LLC

A small *Uploading* box will open in the bottom of the Google Drive page, showing the progress of the upload. When it completes, the title changes to *Uploads completed*. Close the browser window when you are finished.

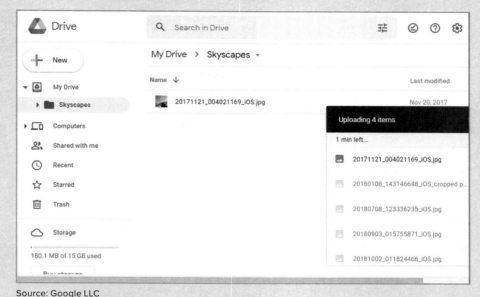

Source: Google LLC

Sharing Files and Folders from Google Drive

Share a file or folder in your Google Drive via email invitation, or by using Link sharing. You can initiate sharing from your *Google Drive* folder on your computer (if you installed the app), from your *My Google* page on Google Drive on the Web, or from the Google Docs, Sheets, or Slides app.

Sharing with Other Google Subscribers

To begin sharing from Google on the Web, first sign in and open Google Drive. In *My Drive* select a file or folder to share and click or tap the Share button (Figure 11-11). Enter the email address of one or more people then click the down arrow to the far right and select the permission. Figure 11-12 shows the drop down box with the permissions. You can give people three levels of permission to the file or folder, Viewer, Commenter, or Editor. These permissions are also called "Roles." A Viewer can only view a file or folder, A Commenter can add comments but cannot edit, while an Editor can edit a file. The owner of a file or folder has full control over it, including the ability to assign permissions/roles to a share or link. Permissions apply to the user or group when they are accessing the share.

Once you select the permission, the drop-down menu closes and you can click the *Done* button. If you wish to send a message to someone with whom you are sharing a file or folder, select *Notify people* (shown in Figure 11-13) and type a message. Then click the *Send* button. Figure 11-14 shows a message regarding a shared folder.

FIGURE 11–11 The buttons on your *My Drive* page in Google Drive on the Web.
Source: Google LLC

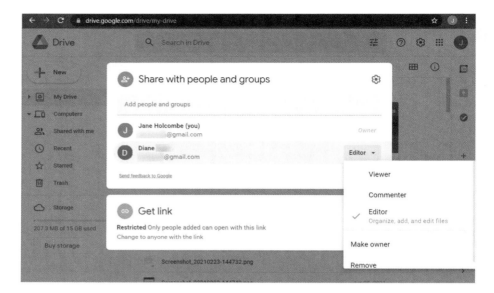

FIGURE 11–12 Select people or groups to share a file or folder and assign permissions.
Source: Google LLC

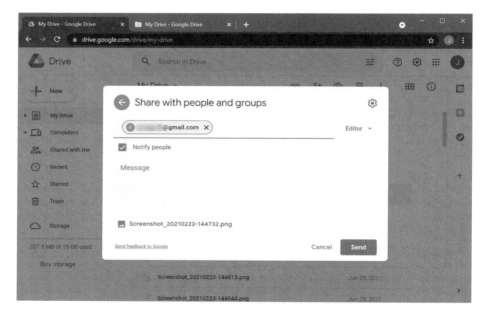

FIGURE 11–13 Type a message and click or tap *Send*.
Source: Google LLC

Link Sharing

Link sharing is a bit different from the more direct sharing of files and folders with other Google subscribers. One important difference is that the permission is assigned to the link, and therefore, to anyone using the link. If you select the *Restricted* option, only someone you explicitly add can open the link and only as a Viewer. If you select the *Anyone with the link* option, the obvious occurs: anyone who has access to the link can open it, but you can assign the same permissions/roles (Figure 11-15) to an unrestricted link as you can to shared files and folders. After selecting the option, copy the link and send the link.

FIGURE 11–14 An email received by a sharing recipient.
Source: Google LLC

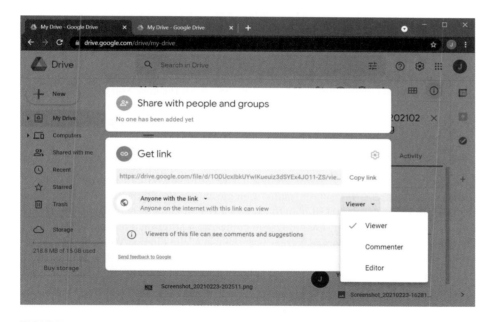

FIGURE 11–15 Select the permission for a link.
Source: Google LLC

Installing Google Drive on a Mobile Device

A compelling reason for subscribing to Google Drive, or any cloud storage service, is the benefit of accessing your data using your mobile devices. To that end, let's look at installing Google Drive on your tablet or smartphone.

Using your smartphone or tablet, point the browser to **https://accounts.google.com/** and sign in with your email address and password. If this is the first time you have signed in to Google Drive on this device, and if you have two-factor verification enabled, you will then have to respond to a message similar to the one shown in Figure 11-16.

Once you sign in tap *More* on the Google bar to open the Google menu. Then tap Drive to open your My Drive page. If this is your first time signing in from your smartphone or tablet, a small notice will pop up suggesting that you install the Google App. If you do not want to install it, tap *No thanks* to close the box, and you can simply

FIGURE 11–16 A confirming message sent after a new sign in to Google from a new device.
Source: Google LLC

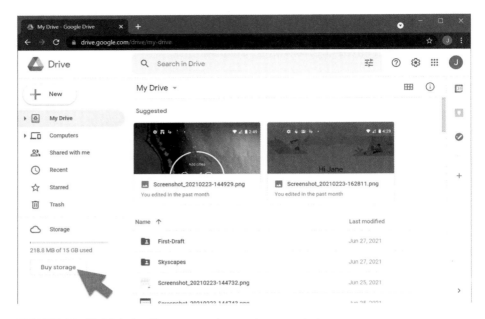

FIGURE 11–17 Click the *Buy storage* button to upgrade to Google One.
Source: Google LLC

continue to access your My Drive page in Google on the Web. If you decide to install the app, follow the instructions to download and install the app. You can create a new folder in Drive, upload files, use the device's camera to take a picture and upload to Drive, or you can create new documents with Google Docs, Sheets, or Slides.

Upgrading Your Google Drive Account to Google One

If you need more than 15 GB of Google Drive Storage you can upgrade to one of Google's fee-based Google One plans. Google currently offers three Google One plans for individuals, a 100 GB plan for $19.99 a year, a 200 GB plan for $29.99 a year, and 2 TB for $99.99 a year. Each upgrade comes with additional features. With all of them the first 15 GB of storage is free, as is the use of the Google Web apps.

To change your storage plan from My Drive on Google on the Web, simply click or tap the *Buy Storage* button in the navigation panel, shown in Figure 11–17. This opens the Google One page where you can select a plan and arrange for payment.

Chapter 11 REVIEW

Chapter Summary

After reading this chapter and completing the exercises, you should understand the following facts about file management in the consumer cloud.

Data Storage in the Public Cloud

- The term *cloud* now encompasses all the services offered over the Internet and on intranets.
- Cloud computing is the use of Internet or intranet-based services.

- Cloud storage is a common cloud-based service.
- A private cloud is an intranet that is owned or managed for the benefit of a single organization and may offer a variety of services. Private cloud services are not available to the general public.
- A public cloud hosts a variety of free and/or fee-based services over the Internet to anyone enrolled in the service.

- A short list of public cloud service providers includes Apple iCloud, Microsoft OneDrive, Google Drive, Box, and Dropbox.
- People use cloud services to access their data from multiple devices and various locations.
- Another motivation for using cloud services is to collaborate with others on documents and entire projects.
- Basic public cloud storage is free to individuals. This includes a storage limit from 2 GB to 15 GB, depending on the provider.

Dropbox

- Dropbox cloud storage service is compatible with Windows, macOS, Linux, and most mobile operating systems.
- Dropbox Basic offers 2 GB of storage for free. You must provide an existing email address and assign a unique password to your Dropbox account.
- Dropbox Basic allows you to share files or folders using a link or to invite Dropbox members to share a file or folder with assigned permissions.
- Install Dropbox on a PC or Mac, and it creates a Dropbox folder in the file system.
- Copy or move files and folders into the Dropbox folder, and Dropbox will synchronize them to the Dropbox cloud storage servers.
- Select and upload multiple files to Dropbox.

- Install the Dropbox app on your mobile device using the appropriate app source, such as *Google Play* for Android and the *App Store* for iOS.
- If the free storage is inadequate, consider upgrading.

Google Drive

- The Google Drive online storage is tied to a Gmail account.
- A Google account gives you access to several free Google Apps.
- The Google Drive online storage service offers 15 GB of storage for free, but Gmail and other data count against that storage limit.
- Save your photos and videos from Google Photos using the *Storage saver* option.
- To create a Google account you must prove that you are not a bot by completing an interactive test that automated software cannot pass.
- The type of program used for many of these tests is a CAPTCHA.
- Use the settings available from your Google Account page to make Google more secure and to help you recover your account if you forget the password.
- If you need more Google Drive storage than the 15 GB available for free consider the fee-based Google One plans.

Key Terms List

Amazon Web Services (AWS) *(400)*

Backup and Sync *(419)*

bot *(419)*

Can Edit *(418)*

Can View *(418)*

CAPTCHA (Completely Automated Public Turing Test to Tell Computers and Humans Apart) *(419)*

collaboration services *(401)*

Commenter *(429)*

download *(401)*

Dropbox *(402)*

Dropbox Basic *(402)*

Dropbox Family *(403)*

Dropbox Plus *(403)*

Editor *(429)*

Google Cloud *(400)*

Google Drive *(418)*

Google Drive for desktop *(419)*

Google One *(432)*

High Quality *(419)*

IBM Cloud *(400)*

Microsoft Azure *(400)*

offline *(401)*

online *(401)*

Oracle Cloud *(400)*

Original *(419)*

private cloud *(400)*

public cloud *(400)*

RAW *(419)*

Storage saver *(419)*

upload *(401)*

Viewer *(429)*

Key Terms Quiz

Use the Key Terms List to complete the sentences that follow. Not all terms will be used.

1. When you transfer files over a network from your local computer, it is a/an _____.

2. _____ is a photo-saving option on cameras that creates very large files because it includes a great deal of preprocessed image data.

3. Free or fee-based services available over the Internet to anyone who signs up are said to be in the _____.

4. _____ allow two or more people to work together on documents and entire projects.

5. The _____ plan is a fee-based plan for individuals that allows you to share your Dropbox storage with up to five family members.

6. When you move a file from a remote computer to your desktop computer, it is a/an _____.

7. A/an _____ is an automated program that performs certain functions, such as gathering data from websites or creating multiple email addresses for the use of spammers.

8. Some online services use a/an _____ program for challenge-response tests to determine that they are interacting with a human, not with an automated program.

9. A privately owned or managed intranet hosting services for the benefit of a single organization is a/an

_____.

10. If you save files using the _____ option in Google's Photos app, the photos and videos will count against your Drive storage limit, but will be compressed by Google if they exceed certain resolution limits.

Multiple-Choice Quiz

1. What permission is assigned to a Google Drive restricted link?
   a. Viewer
   b. Owner
   c. Editor
   d. Upload
   e. Offline

2. Which of the following is not among the largest public cloud services in the world?
   a. Dropbox
   b. Google Cloud
   c. IBM Cloud
   d. Amazon Web Services (AWS)
   e. Microsoft Azure

3. You should enable this account security feature in Google and other online services that send you a message with a code that you must enter in addition to the usual user name and password when you attempt to sign in from a new device.
   a. CAPTCHA
   b. Storage saver
   c. Two-step verification
   d. Private cloud
   e. AWS

4. In Google Drive, assign this option to a file you want to edit when you do not have an Internet connection.
   a. Cloud storage
   b. Available offline
   c. Download
   d. Editor
   e. High Quality

5. Consider this fee-based Dropbox service if you need more than 2 GB of storage, but do not wish to share your cloud storage with others.
   a. Dropbox Plus
   b. Dropbox Business
   c. Dropbox Basic
   d. Dropbox Family
   e. Dropbox Enterprise

6. Which of the following is not a Google Drive share permission/role? Select all correct answers.
   a. Storage saver
   b. Owner
   c. Commenter
   d. Editor
   e. Viewer

7. What is the official source for the Dropbox app for your Android device?
   a. App Store
   b. Dropbox Store
   c. Google Play
   d. Dropbox Pro
   e. CAPTCHA

8. This Dropbox service allows an individual to share their Dropbox storage limit with up to five other people.
   a. Dropbox Basic
   b. Dropbox Plus
   c. Dropbox Family
   d. Dropbox Business
   e. Dropbox Enterprise

9. Which of these Google apps negatively impacts an individual's Google Drive storage capacity? Select all that apply.
   a. Gmail
   b. Docs
   c. Photos
   d. Sheets
   e. Slides

10. If you set a digital camera to save files in this format, preferred by professional photographers, it saves all the unprocessed data for an image, creating large files.
    a. Original
    b. RAW
    c. High Quality
    d. Enhanced
    e. Storage saver

11. To synchronize files between a cloud service and your computer, you must install a client app for that service that interacts with this function of the operating system.
    a. Video
    b. Email
    c. Network service
    d. Security
    e. File system

12. Of the following choices, which are reasons for using cloud storage? Select all that apply.
    a. Collaboration
    b. Access from many locations
    c. Security
    d. Unlimited free storage
    e. Access from many devices

13. Which of the free cloud storage services described in this chapter offers the least amount of storage?
    a. Dropbox Basic
    b. Dropbox Plus

    c. Google Drive
    d. Dropbox Family
    e. Google One

14. Which of the following allows someone to make changes to a shared Google Drive file?
    a. Viewer
    b. Online
    c. Link
    d. Commenter
    e. Editor

15. What will integrate Google Drive with your file system on a PC or Apple Mac?
    a. Viewer
    b. Gmail
    c. Google Drive for desktop app
    d. Storage saver
    e. Google Cloud

Essay Quiz

1. Compare the free Dropbox Basic service with the free Google Drive service.

2. Compare and name two fee-based services from Google and Dropbox that allow an individual to share their storage and other features with family members. What other features do these services offer?

3. Research how you can determine what devices have used your Google account. Then describe what you can

do if you see a device you no longer own is still signed in to your account.

4. Describe the permissions an owner can assign to a Dropbox share versus permissions assigned to a Dropbox link.

5. Explain how a Dropbox shared folder impacts the Dropbox members who are given access to the folder.

Lab Projects

LAB PROJECT 11.1

Amazon is more than an online retailer. It is also one of the world's largest cloud services providers with its Amazon Web Services (AWS). Amazon even provides a free service, the Amazon Web Services (AWS) Free Tier. Consider what you have learned about the free cloud services for consumers from the providers featured in this chapter, research the AWS free offering, and answer the following questions:

1. Is this service aimed at consumers? Provide justification for your answer.

2. Is this service one you would consider for your personal data in the long term? Why?

3. This service requires certain information not required by the free services featured in this chapter. Describe what this information is and your reaction (if any) to this requirement.

LAB PROJECT 11.2

Research public cloud services not mentioned in this chapter. Find at least two that are targeted to specialized needs or interests and describe them.

LAB PROJECT 11.3

Consider what you would do as a subscriber to a cloud service who believes the provider is experiencing downtime. Research and then describe how you would confirm this.

Glossary

The number at the end of the entry refers to the chapter where the term is introduced.

2-Step Verification Google's version of multi-factor verification for authenticating a user with more than a user name and password, but sending a code or using an authentication app. (8)

$ prompt (Pronounced "dollar prompt.") The command prompt displayed in a Linux CLI. (7)

absolute path A directory path that begins with the top level. In Linux, an absolute path begins with a forward slash (/) to indicate the root directory. (7)

accelerometer A component of a mobile device that detects the physical tilt and acceleration of the device, allowing the device to change the screen orientation for readability. (1)

Access Control Entry (ACE) An entry in an Access Control List, containing just one user or group account name and the permissions assigned to this account for that file or folder. (5)

Access Control List (ACL) A table of users and/or groups and their permissions to access the file or folder associated with the ACL. (5)

access mode number A value assigned to a file permission in Linux. The user (owner), group, and others each have a different access mode number calculated using the following values: read = 4, write = 2, and execute = 1. (7)

address space layout randomization (ASLR) A security feature of macOS that loads the kernel, into random locations in memory, rather than loading into the same memory addresses every time. (6)

administrator account type An account type in an OS that can perform system-wide tasks. (2)

adware A form of spyware downloaded to a computer without permission. It collects information about the user. (2)

AirDrop An Apple service that uses Bluetooth or Wi-Fi to transfer files between Apple devices. (6)

airplane mode A feature of mobile devices that turns off all wireless communications (cellular, Wi-Fi, Bluetooth, and NFC) without powering off the device. (10)

AirPlay A feature for connecting an iOS or macOS device to an Apple TV, which acts as an intermediary device for sending iTunes songs, video, pictures, and other data from the computer to a high-definition (HD) TV via Wi-Fi. (6)

Amazon Web Services (AWS) Amazon's cloud services. (11)

Android app An app created for the Google Android operating system and available at the Play Store. (8)

Apache HTTP Server Open-source Web server software, originally written for UNIX, runs on Linux. (7)

Apple File System (APFS) Introduced in 2017, APFS fixes problems with the older file system and is optimized for solid-state drive storage. (6)

Apple ID A free account that identifies the holder as a customer of Apple for all Apple services and products. (6)

App Library The last page in an iPhone Home Screen containing shortcuts to every app on the device organized into folders, such as Productivity and Social. (10)

Apple menu A pop-up menu opened by clicking on the Apple icon in the upper left of the macOS desktop. (6)

Apple Pay An automatic payment system for Apple Watch and iPhones that uses NFC wireless technology. It can also be used from a Mac computer. (10)

application (app) Software that allows a user to perform useful functions such as writing a report or calculating a budget. (1)

application virtualization Virtualization of an application whereby a user connects to a server and accesses only the application rather than an entire desktop environment. (3)

augmented reality (AR) Viewing something in real time through a smartphone or special eyeglasses while the image (or other input) is digitally modified. (3)

authentication Validation of a user account that occurs before the security components of an OS give a user access to a computer or network. (2)

authorization The process of both authenticating a user and determining the permissions that the user has for a resource. (2)

automatic IP addressing A method by which a host can be automatically assigned an IP address and all the additional configuration settings. (9)

Automatic Private IP Addressing (APIPA) A method by which a DHCP client computer that fails to receive an address from a DHCP server will automatically give itself an address from a special range that has the value 169 (base-10) in the first octet (eight binary digits) of the IP address. (9)

avatar An animated computer-generated being used in a virtual world to represent an individual. (3)

back door The use of software to bypass security and gain access to a computer or other device. (2)

Backup codes Codes generated by Google for use by a user when that user cannot be directly verified. (8)

Backup and Sync Google's former app for syncing files between an individual's Google Drive folders and Windows or Apple Mac desktops. (11)

BASH An acronym for Bourne Again Shell; the Linux component (shell) that provides the character-mode user interface for entering and processing commands, issuing error messages, and other feedback. (7)

binary file A file that contains program code, as opposed to a file containing data. (5)

BitLocker A Windows 10 Pro or Enterprise edition feature for encrypting disk drives. (4)

BitLocker To Go An enhanced feature of BitLocker that includes encryption of removable devices. (4)

black hat hacker Someone who breaks into computers (hacks) to do harm. (2)

bloatware Slang for the software added to a computer when it is purchased with Windows preinstalled. Some of these programs are useful, but most are annoying or may be free trial software that you can try, but must purchase to use after the trial period (often 30 days) expires. (4)

bluesnarfing The act of covertly collecting information broadcast from wireless Bluetooth devices. (2)

Bluetooth A wireless standard for using radio waves to communicate over very short distances between devices. (10)

bot Automated software that performs tasks, often malicious tasks. (11)

bootloader OS startup code that must be loaded into early in the startup process. The Windows bootloader is a file named BOOTMGR. (5)

bootstrap loader A firmware program that uses hardware configuration settings stored in nonvolatile memory, to determine what devices can start an OS and the order in which the system will search these devices while attempting to begin the OS startup process. It then loads the bootloader program. (5)

bot herder Someone who initiates and controls a botnet. (2)

botnet A group of networked computers that, usually unbeknown to their owners, has been infected with programs that forward information to other computers over the network (usually the Internet). (2)

bring your own device (BYOD) The practice of using personal mobile devices at work. (1)

browser extension An add-on to a browser that adds features. (8)

browser hijacking Malware installed on a computer that causes the browser home page to always point to a specific site, often advertising something. (2)

burn To write digital data just once to a CD or DVD disc. (7)

can edit A Dropbox file permission that allows a person to edit a shared file. (11)

can view A Dropbox file permission that allows a person to only view a shared file. (11)

CAPTCHA (Completely Automated Public Turing Test to Tell Computers and Humans Apart) A test to prove that you are not a robot when creating or modifying an online account. (11)

case-sensitive In an operating system, a feature that allows the OS to preserve the case used for the characters in a file name when creating it, and requires the correct case to open or manage the file. (7)

cellular hotspot A service offered by cell providers in which a customer's smartphone or a separate device acts as a Wi-Fi router to allow other computers and devices to access the Internet. (9)

central processing unit (CPU) An integrated circuit (chip) that performs the calculations, or processing, for a computer. See also *microprocessor.* (1)

Chromebit A dongle containing the Chrome OS that plugs into a TV or computer display's HDMI port. (8)

Chromebook A laptop with the Chrome OS preinstalled. (8)

Chromebox A desktop computer with the Chrome OS preinstalled. (8)

Chrome OS Google's OS based on their Chrome browser. (8)

click bait Content in an email, web page, social networking page, or any online app, designed to lure the user to click on it and its associated link. (2)

client A software component on a computer that accesses services from a network server. (1)

cloud All services offered over the Internet and on intranets. (1)

cloud computing The use of services offered in the cloud. (1)

cloud storage Services offering data storage in the cloud. (1)

collaboration services Cloud-based services that allow two or more people to work together on documents and projects. (11)

command completion A feature of Linux and UNIX (and macOS Terminal) that completes what is entered at the command line with a command name or file or directory name. (7)

Command Prompt In Windows, the command-line interface that is launched from within Windows or in Safe Mode or as a Recovery option. (5)

command-line history The Linux and UNIX (and macOS Terminal) feature that saves command-line history in a file named bash_history. (7)

command-line interface (CLI) A user interface that includes a character-based command line that requires text input. (1)

Commenter A Google Drive permission (also called a role) that allows a person to add comments to a shared file, but not edit it. (11)

computer A device that calculates. (1)

Consent Prompt Part of the Windows User Account Control security feature, this prompt appears when a user is logged on as an administrator and a program attempts to perform a task requiring administrative permissions. (4)

content filter Software that blocks Web content based on predetermined rules. (2)

context menu In Windows, a menu that displays when you right-click (or press on) an object in Windows. Not all objects have context menus, but many do. (4)

Continuum A feature of Windows 10 that senses when a keyboard is attached versus when a keyboard is removed and presents the appropriate desktop for each configuration. (4)

cookies Very small text files an Internet browser saves on the local hard drive at the request of a website. (2)

Cortana An intelligent search system and personal assistant in Windows 10. (4)

Credentials Prompt Part of the Windows User Account Control security feature, this prompt appears when a user is logged on as a standard user and a program attempts to perform a task requiring administrative permission. The user must provide an administrator password to continue. (4)

cursor In a command-line interface (CLI), a marker for where the next character you type on the keyboard will appear on the screen. In a GUI the cursor is replaced by both an insertion point as well as by a graphical pointer that can have a variety of shapes. (1)

cybercrime Illegal activity performed using computer technology. (2)

cybercriminal A person who breaks laws using computer technology. (2)

cyberterrorism A computer-based attack that wreaks havoc on victims. (2)

cyberterrorist A person who commits a computer-based attack that wreaks havoc on victims. (2)

daemon In Linux, software that runs in background until it is activated. (7)

Darwin The name of the core operating system on which macOS is based. A product of the open-source community. (6)

data type In the Windows registry, a special data format. There are several registry data types, such as REG_BINARY, REG_DWORD, and so forth. (5)

data wiping The permanent removal of data from a storage device. (2)

default gateway The IP address of the router connected to your network. (9)

Desktop mode A feature of Windows 10 that displays the desktop and apps appropriately for a computer with a keyboard attached. (4)

desktop virtualization The virtualization of a desktop computer into which you can install an operating system, its unique configuration, applications, and user data. (3)

device driver Software that is added to an OS to control a physical component (device). (1)

device management An OS function that controls hardware devices through the use of device drivers. (1)

Device Manager A Windows recovery tool that aids in troubleshooting device problems. (4)

dial-up An inexpensive WAN option available to anyone with a phone line and a standard analog modem (the longtime standard runs at 56 Kbps). (9)

digital certificate A special file stored on a computer that may hold a secret key for decrypting data. (2)

digital subscriber line (DSL) A WAN service similar to ISDN in its use of the telephone network, but using more advanced digital signal processing to compress signals through the telephone lines. (9)

directory A special file on a storage device that can contain files as well as other directories. In a GUI a directory is represented by a file folder image. (1)

distribution A bundling of the Linux kernel and software—both enhancements to the OS and applications—such as word processors, spreadsheets, media players, and more. (7)

DMZ A network between a private network and the Internet with a firewall on both sides. (2)

Dock A floating bar on the macOS desktop that holds icons for commonly used programs, as well as icons for open applications. A single click on an icon launches the program. (6)

Dock The launcher bar, also called "dock," found in the Ubuntu GUI. (7)

Domain Name System (DNS) A distributed online database containing registered domain names mapped to IP addresses. (9)

download Both the action and result of moving data from a remote location to a local device. (11)

drive-by download A program downloaded to a user's computer without consent. (2)

Dropbox A public cloud service provider. (11)

Dropbox Basic A free public cloud service. (11)

Dropbox Family A fee-based public cloud service allowing an individual to share the cloud services with family. (11)

Dropbox Plus A fee-based pubic cloud service giving an individual more storage and other features than the free Dropbox Basic. (11)

dumb terminal A device consisting of little more than a keyboard and display with a connection to a host computer and having no native processing power of its own. (3)

Dynamic Host Configuration Protocol (DHCP) server A server that issues IP addresses and settings to computers that are configured to obtain an IP address automatically, thus making them DHCP clients. (9)

Early Launch Anti-Malware (ELAM) A security feature, introduced in Windows 8, that examines all device drivers before they are loaded into memory, preventing suspicious drivers from loading. (5)

Ease of Access A group of Windows settings for audio and visual aids. (4)

Editor A Google Drive permission (also called a role) that allows a person to edit a shared file. (11)

email spoofing Forging of a sender's address in the email message's header so that an incorrect address appears in the "from" field of an email message. (2)

embedded OS An operating system stored in firmware, as in a mobile device (1)

Encrypting File System (EFS) An NTFS file encryption feature for encrypting selected files and folders (not entire drives). (4)

encryption The transformation of data into a code that can be decrypted only through the use of a secret key or password. (2)

enterprise computing A term for software and hardware used and managed by large organizations. (4)

erasable programmable read-only memory (EPROM) A type of nonvolatile memory chip containing firmware. (5)

Everything button A special key, formerly named *Search*, on the Chromebook keyboard that opens the Chrome OS Search bar. (8)

exploit A malware attack. (2)

Face ID Apple's infrared facial recognition technology introduced on the iPhone X. (10)

Fast Boot A feature of Windows 8 and newer in which startup takes advantage of the hibernated kernel (if the last shutdown was a Hybrid Shutdown), bringing the hibernated system session out of hibernation, saving all the work of the Kernel Loading phase. (5)

Fast Pair A Google Android feature that scans for nearby Bluetooth signals, displaying a prompt identifying the device. Tap the box, and the phone connects to the device. (10)

FAT file systems Several related file systems based on the original FAT file system. They include FAT12, FAT16, FAT32, and exFAT. Each has a logical structure that includes a file allocation table (FAT) and a directory structure. (5)

FIDO Alliance (Fast Identity Online) An industry consortium that works together on solutions that will allow users to securely access online services and conduct financial transactions without using password authentication and reduce the risk of fraud. (4)

file Information stored as a unit on a storage device and identified with a name and an extension to identify the storage type. (5)

file and printer server A network server that gives client computers access to files and printers. Also simply called a file server. (9)

File Explorer Previously named Windows Explorer, the name of the Windows file management tool. (4)

file management An operating system function that allows the operating system to read, write, and modify data and programs organized into files and directories. (1)

file system The logical structure used on a storage device for the purpose of storing files, as well as the code within an operating system that allows the OS to store and manage files. (1)

Files app The Chrome OS file management app. (8)

FileVault A feature in macOs that, in earlier versions, encrypted the Home folder. In recent versions, it encrypts the entire startup disk. (6)

Finder The foundation of the macOS GUI and the equivalent to File Explorer, the Windows file management tool. (6)

firewall A software or physical device that rejects certain traffic coming into a computer or network. The two general types of firewalls are network-based firewalls and personal firewalls on individual computers. (2)

firmware Software resident in integrated circuits. (1)

first-party cookie A cookie that originates with the domain name of the URL to which you directly connect. (2)

folder A special file that can contain files as well as other folders. This term is often used with GUI operating systems, while *directory* is often used in a CLI. (1)

forged email address A false address that appears in the "from" field of an email address. This type of forgery is also called *email spoofing*. (2)

formatting The action of an operating system when it maps the logical organization of a file system to physical locations on the storage device so that it can store and retrieve the data. (1)

fraud The use of deceit and trickery to persuade someone to hand over money or other valuables. (2)

fully qualified domain name (FQDN) The human-readable name corresponding to the TCP/IP address of a host, as found on a computer, router, or other networked device. It includes both its host name and its domain name. (9)

Gatekeeper A security feature of macOS that limits sources from which you can download apps. (6)

GNOME An acronym for GNU network object model environment, a Linux GUI that uses the Linux X Windows system. (7)

GNU An organization created in 1984 to develop a free version of a UNIX-like operating system. GNU develops applications that run on UNIX and Linux platforms. Many are distributed with versions of Linux. (7)

Google Account A free account that gives the account holder access to basic Google services. (8)

Google Cloud Google's fee-based cloud services offered to businesses and educational organizations. (11)

Google Drive Google's online file storage service. (11)

Google Drive for desktop Google's improved replacement for Backup and Sync for syncing files between an individual's Google Drive folders and Windows or Apple Mac desktops. (11)

Google Mail Google's electronic mail service. (8)

Google One Google's fee-based plans for individuals offering different storage capacity levels and features. (11)

Google Pay Google's virtual wallet that stores a variety of membership cards, movie tickets, transit tickets, and other card information. It uses payment methods stored with a Google Account. (10)

graphical user interface (GUI) A user interface that takes advantage of a computer's graphics capabilities to make it easier to use with graphical elements that a user can manipulate to perform tasks. (1)

group account A security account that may contain one or more individual or group accounts. (2)

guest account A special account used when someone connects to a computer but is not a member of a security account recognized on that computer. That person will have limited permissions assigned to the guest account. (2)

guest OS An operating system running within a virtual machine. (3)

Guest User An account created by macOS (and other operating systems) that does not require a password, has access only to the Guest Home folder, and when this account logs out, all files and folders created during that session are deleted. (6)

hacker Someone with a great deal of computing expertise. One who does no harm is a white hat hacker. One who does harm is a black hat hacker. (2)

header The information that accompanies a message but does not appear in the message. (2)

Hey Cortana The voice activation options for the Cortana feature of Windows 10. (4)

hibernate A Windows power or shutdown option that, if enabled, saves both the system state and the user session in a file named hiberfil.sys. (5)

High Quality The former name for Google Photos *Storage saver* option. (11)

hive The portion of the Windows registry represented in one registry file. (5)

home directory In Linux, a directory created for a user, using the user's login name, and located under the /home directory. This is the one place in Linux where an ordinary user account has full control over files without logging in as the root account. (7)

Home folder A folder created by macOS for a user that displays in the Finder when that user is logged on, identified in the sidebar by a house icon and the user's name. (6)

honey pot A server created as a decoy to draw malware attacks and gather information about attackers. (2)

host ID The portion of an IP address that identifies the host on a network, as determined using the subnet mask. (9)

host key A key or key combination that releases the mouse and keyboard from a virtual machine to the host OS. (3)

host OS The operating system installed directly on a computer. (3)

hotspot A Wi-Fi network that connects to the Internet through a router. (2)

Hybrid Shutdown The default when you select Shutdown from the Windows 10 Power menu: Windows closes the session for each logged-on user, and hibernates the Windows session, saving it in a file. (5)

Hypertext Transfer Protocol (HTTP) The protocol for transferring the files that make up the rich graphical Web pages we view on the World Wide Web (WWW). (7)

hypervisor The software layer that emulates the necessary hardware for an operating system to run in, creating a virtual machine within which a guest OS can run. (3)

IBM cloud One of the largest private cloud providers. (11)

iCloud keychain A database of user names and passwords to various locations stored in a user's iCloud and accessible to all devices that support it and that have been enabled by the user. (6)

identity theft The collection of personal information belonging to another person and the use of that information to fraudulently make purchases, open new credit accounts, or even obtain new driver's licenses and other forms of identification in the victim's name. (2)

Immersive Mode A special key on the Chromebook keyboard that opens the Chrome OS Search bar. (8)

input/output (I/O) Anything sent into a computer (input); anything coming out of a computer (output). (1)

integrated circuit (IC) A small electronic component made up of transistors (tiny switches) and other miniaturized parts. (1)

integrated services digital network (ISDN) A digital telephone service that simultaneously transmits voice, data, and control signaling over a single telephone line. An ISDN data connection can transfer data at up to 128,000 bits per second (128 Kbps). (9)

Internet A public internetwork that spans the entire world. (1)

Internet of Things (IoT) Not really a separate Internet, but a term that describes the trend to have devices such as appliances connected to networks—even to the Internet. (1)

Internet Protocol (IP) The core TCP/IP protocol that delivers communications in chunks, called packets. It uses a logical address called an IP address. (9)

Internet service provider (ISP) An organization that provides individuals or entire organizations access to the Internet. (9)

internetwork A network of interconnected networks. (1)

intranet A privately owned network of networks. (1)

IP address The logical address used on a TCP/IP network to identify a network interface card (NIC). (9)

IPv4 The version of the Internet Protocol in use since 1983 (with updates). (9)

IPv6 The latest version of the Internet Protocol that is gradually replacing IPv4. (9)

ISO file A copy of the entire contents of a CD or DVD that can be easily transferred to a writable CD or DVD with ISO image copy software. (3)

job management An operating system function that controls the order and time in which programs are run. (1)

Jump List In Windows, a list of recently opened items such as files, folders, and websites that appear when you right-click on a program on the Start menu or taskbar. (4)

kernel The main component of an operating system that always remains in memory while a computer is running. (1)

key In the Windows registry, a folder object that may contain one or more sets of settings as well as other keys. (5)

keyboard shortcut A key combination that performs an assigned action, saving you several mouse or keyboard actions. (4)

keychain A database in which macOS saves encrypted passwords for a single computer. The first keychain, login, is created for each user and associated with the user's login password. (6)

Keychain Access The macOS utility for managing the keychain. (6)

keylogger See *keystroke logger.* (2)

keystroke logger A hardware device or a program that monitors and records a user's every keystroke, usually without the user's knowledge. Also called a keylogger. (2)

killer app An application that is so useful or otherwise desirable that customers buy a device in order to use that app. (1)

Launcher A GUI object (a bar) on the left side of the Ubuntu Unity desktop that serves the same purpose as the macOS Dock and the pinned items feature on the taskbar on the Windows Desktop. This same term is used in Chrome OS. (8)

Launchpad A feature in macOS that resembles the home screen on Apple iOS devices. It consists of one or more screens holding icons for all installed apps. Apps can be grouped together and/or launched from the Launchpad. (6)

legacy BIOS The recent name for firmware installed in PCs of the 1980s, 1990s, and early 2000s. Originally labeled read-only memory basic input-output system (ROM-BIOS) (5)

Lightning port The USB port on an iOS device used for charging the device, as well as for file transfer. (10)

Linux An open-source operating system based on UNIX that was developed by Linus Torvalds and others beginning in 1991. (7)

live image A bootable image of the operating system that will run from disc or other bootable media without requiring that the OS be installed on the local computer. (7)

live tile A rectangle on the Windows 10 Start screen that when, tapped with a finger or clicked with a mouse launches an app. The "live" part of the name is due to each tile's ability to display active content related to the app without requiring that you launch the app. (4)

local account A user account that resides in the local accounts database. (5)

local area network (LAN) A network that covers a building, home, office, or campus. It can be wireless or wired. (9)

local security The security options available and limited to a local computer. In Windows, this includes local security accounts and local security for files and folders, Windows BitLocker drive encryption, Windows Defender antispam protection, and Windows Firewall. (5)

location service A service on a computer or mobile device that allows an app to track your location, using one or more methods, often with the help of the Internet. (10)

Lock screen A screen that displays at startup of a Windows computer, when Windows is locked, or when a period of inactivity triggers the screen saver. (4)

logon phase A phase of Windows startup during which a user is authenticated, the service control manager starts, logon scripts run, startup programs run, and noncritical services start. Plug-and-play detection occurs during this startup phase. (5)

Mac The product name for Apple's desktop and laptop computers. (1)

macOS Setup Assistant In a new computer with macOS preinstalled, the OS is not configured, so the first time it is powered up, this program prompts you for the user preferences information. (6)

malware A shortened form of "malicious software" that covers a large and growing list of threats such as viruses, worms, Trojan horses, and spam. (2)

manpage In Linux, UNIX, and the macOS Terminal window, a manual page is the documentation for a command, accessed with the **man** command. (6)

master file table (MFT) The main logical structure of the NTFS file system that is expandable and uses transaction processing to track changes to files. (5)

Measured Boot A UEFI firmware feature that logs the startup process. Antimalware software can analyze this log to determine if malware is on the computer or if the boot components were tampered with. (5)

memory The physical chips that store programs and data. There are two basic types: random-access memory (RAM) and read-only memory (ROM). (1)

memory management An operating system function that manages and tracks the placement of programs and data in memory. (1)

microcomputer A computer built around a microprocessor. (1)

microprocessor An integrated circuit (chip) that performs the calculations, or processing, for a computer. Also called a processor or central processing unit (CPU). (1)

Microsoft account (MSA) A free account with Microsoft that gives the subscriber access to Microsoft services. (4)

Microsoft Azure Microsoft's fee-based private cloud services for organizations. (11)

Microsoft Edge The Internet browser introduced with Windows 10. (4)

Microsoft Passport A feature that securely signs in to network resources without sending a password or PIN over the network. (4)

Microsoft Product Activation (MPA) Microsoft's method of combating software piracy, intended to ensure that each software license is used solely on a single computer. Many other software vendors require activation. See *activation*. (4)

MiFi Novatel's trademarked name for the hotspot device they manufactured. It stands for "my Wi-Fi." (10)

Mission Control A screen in macOS where you can create and organize Spaces. (6)

mobile device A device that uses wireless technologies and offers a variety of functions to the user. (1)

mobile device management (MDM) A category of software for enforcing policies and managing mobile devices. (10)

mobile hotspot A mobile device that shares its data cellular connection with nearby devices connected via Wi-Fi. (10)

motherboard The central circuit board of a computer to which all other devices connect. (1)

MSCONFIG The System Configuration Utility, a Windows tool for modifying system startup, allows you to modify and test start-up configuration settings without having to alter the settings directly. (5)

multitasking Two or more programs (tasks) running simultaneously on a computer. (1)

multitouch The ability of a device to interpret multiple simultaneous touch gestures on a screen, touch mouse, or touch pad. (4)

Near Field Communication (NFC) A technology that supports a short-distance wireless standard that requires two devices to touch before communicating. (10)

net ID The network portion of an IP address, as determined through the subnet mask. (9)

network virtualization A network addressing space that exists within one or more physical networks, but which is logically independent of the physical network structure. (3)

New Technology File System (NTFS) The Windows file system that includes many advanced features, such as file compression, file encryption, file and folder security, and indexing. (1)

notification area In Chrome OS, an area on the shelf located to the right of app shortcuts and to the left of the status bar. (8)

Notification Center A macOS feature that displays important status messages, notifying the user of important events, such as a new email or text message or that an update is available. Windows, Linux, and Chrome OS also have this feature. (6)

object code An executable program, the result of compiling programming statements, that can be interpreted by a computer's CPU or operating system and loaded into memory as a running program. (7)

octet A group of eight binary digits. (9)

offline A cloud storage term for a file remains available on the local device, even when there is no Internet access. It will be synchronized with cloud storage the next time the device is connected. (11)

online A cloud storage term for a file stored online and not available when the device is not connected to the Internet. (11)

open-source software Software distributed with all its source code, allowing developers to customize it as necessary. (7)

operating system (OS) A collection of programs that provides a computer with critical functionality, such as a user interface, management of hardware and software, and ways of creating, managing, and using files. (1)

Oracle Cloud One of the largest private cloud providers. (11)

Original An option for files saved in Google Photos that counts against your Google storage limit. (11)

Out of Box Experience (OOBE) A feature on a new computer with Windows preinstalled. When you take it out of the box and turn it on, it runs the last phase of Windows installation where you personalize the GUI and configure how you will sign in. (4)

over the phone (OTP) The use of voice or text for sending a verification code for sign in. (8)

owner In Linux, the user account that creates a file or directory. This term is also used in Windows. (7)

packet A piece of a message packaged by the Internet Protocol. Each packet includes a header that contains information including the source address (local host address) and the destination address. (9)

pairing A connection between two devices using the Bluetooth wireless standard. (10)

partition An area of a physical hard disk that defines space used for a logical drive. (1)

passcode lock A string of characters (or gestures) that a user enters to close the lock screen and access a device. (10)

password A string of characters that a user enters (along with a user name) in order to be authenticated. (2)

password cracker A program used to discover a password. (2)

password manager Software that creates and remembers passwords, and can manage your use of passwords across all your devices. (2)

path A description that an operating system uses to identify the location of a file or directory. (7)

permission A level of access to an object, such as a file or folder, that is granted to a user account or group account. (2)

personal computer (PC) A microcomputer that complies with the Microsoft/Intel standards. (1)

personal folders A set of folders created by Windows for each user account to hold user data files. (5)

phishing A fraudulent method of obtaining personal financial information through Web page pop-ups, email, and even paper letters mailed via the postal service. Phishing is a form of social engineering. (2)

plug-and-play (PnP) The ability of a computer to detect and configure a hardware device automatically. To work, the computer, the device, and the OS must all comply with the same plug-and-play standard. (1)

pop-up An ad that runs in a separate browser window you must close before continuing with the present task. (2)

pop-up blocker A program that works against pop-ups. (2)

pop-up download A program that is downloaded to a user's computer through the use of a pop-up page that appears while surfing the Web. (2)

power-on self-test (POST) Tests of system hardware that runs from firmware when a computer starts up. (5)

predictive notification A feature of Cortana by which it provides a notice or other information in anticipation of a need. (4)

private browsing A security feature available in browsers that allows you to browse the Web without saving any history on the local computer of the sites visited. (9)

private cloud An intranet that is owned and managed for one organization, offering a variety of cloud services. (11)

private IP address An address from one of three ranges designated for use only on private networks. The private IP address ranges are 10.0.0.0 through 10.255.255.255, 172.16.0.0 through 172.31.255.255, and 192.168.0.0 through 192.168.255.255. (9)

processes Components of a program active in memory. (1)

protocol In computer technology and networking a set of rules, usually formalized in a standard published by one of many standards organizations. This is also the term for the software that implements a certain set of rules. (9)

protocol stack A group of bundled programs based on networking protocols and designed to work together. (9)

public cloud The hosting of a variety of free and/or fee-based services over the Internet available to anyone who enrolls in the service. (11)

public IP addresses IP addresses assigned to hosts on the Internet. (9)

Quick link The name for a shortcut on the Windows 10 Start menu. (4)

random-access memory (RAM) Memory in a computer that acts as the main memory for holding active programs. (1)

ransomware Malware that threatens to do damage or lock a user out of a computer unless the user pays a "ransom." (2)

RAW A photo file format, generated within a camera, that saves all unprocessed data for an image, creating a very large file. (11)

read-only memory (ROM) Nonvolatile memory chips containing firmware. (5)

read-only memory basic input/output system (ROM-BIOS) The original firmware in PCs that provided basic support for the hardware. (5)

recovery key A code generated by macOS when it encrypts the start disk with FileVault. (6)

Red Hat Enterprise Linux (RHEL) Red Hat's commercially available version of Linux. (7)

Refresh On a Chromebook keyboard, the key in the traditional F3 position that refreshes a Web page. (8)

registry A database of all configuration settings in Windows. (5)

registered domain name An Internet domain name registered with the Internet Corporate for Assigned names and Numbers (ICANN). It is also called a second-level domain name. An example of a registered domain name is "Apple," registered as "Apple.com." (9)

remote access VPN A connection between an individual computer or mobile device using a VPN over a WAN connection. (9)

restore point A snapshot of Windows, its configuration, and all installed programs. If your computer has problems after you have made a change, you can use System Restore to roll it back to a restore point. (5)

robocall An automated, unwanted, and annoying phone call from an unknown source. (2)

root account In Linux, an all-powerful account that is used only when absolutely necessary to do advanced tasks. (7)

root key In the Windows registry, each of the top five folders is a root key, sometimes called a subtree in Microsoft documentation. Each of these root keys is the top of a hierarchical structure containing folders called keys. (5)

rootkit Malware that hides within the OS code or another program running on the computer. (2)

router A network device that sits between networks and directs (routes) traffic to destinations beyond the local network. (9)

Safe Mode A start-up mode in which Windows starts without using all of the drivers and components that would normally be loaded. Use Safe Mode when your Windows computer will not start normally. (5)

Safe Mode with Command Prompt A start-up mode in which Windows starts without using all of the drivers and components that would normally be loaded and opens an Administrator Command Prompt window against a black background with the words "Safe Mode" in the four corners of the screen. Use Safe Mode when your Windows computer will not start normally. (5)

sandboxed A feature in macOS that isolates an app so that it cannot access any code or device it is not authorized to access. (6)

scareware A vector technique that uses threatening messages. (2)

screen rotation A feature of mobile operating systems that takes advantage of the built-in hardware accelerometer by rotating the image on the screen to accommodate the position and allow you to read the screen. (1)

secret key A special code that can be used to decrypt encrypted data. (2)

Second-Level Address Translation (SLAT) A feature of many newer Intel and AMD CPUs, required by some hypervisors. (3)

Secure Boot A UEFI firmware feature that loads only trusted operating system bootloaders. This is one of the UEFI security features required on computers that come with Windows 8 preinstalled. (5)

Secure HTTP (HTTPS) A form of the HTTP protocol that supports encryption of the communications. HTTPS uses the Secure Sockets Layer (SSL) security protocol. (2)

Secure Sockets Layer (SSL) A security protocol for encrypting network data. (2)

Secure Virtual Memory A macOS feature that encrypts the swap file (virtual memory). (6)

security An operating system function that provides password-protected authentication of the user before allowing access to the local computer. (1)

security account In a security accounts database, a listing of information about a user, group, or computer. A security account is used for authentication. (2)

security ID (SID) A unique string of numbers preceded by *S-1-5* that identifies a security principal in a Windows security accounts database. (5)

server A computer that plays one or more of several roles on a network, providing services to other computers (clients). (1)

server operating system An operating system that includes server protocols in its integrated network support. (1)

server virtualization The hosting of multiple virtual servers on a single computer. (3)

Service Set ID (SSID) A network name that identifies a Wi-Fi network. (10)

share A connecting point to which network clients may connect. Visible as a folder over the network, it is a separate entity from the disk folder to which it points. (9)

Shared folder A folder created by macOS in each user's Home folder. It is accessible to other users without restriction. (6)

Sharing Only account In macOS, an account that allows a user to log in remotely and access shared folders, but that does not have a Home folder and cannot be used to log in locally on that computer. (6)

shelf In the Chrome OS desktop, a bar on the edge of the screen containing shortcuts to features and apps. (8)

shell The operating system component that provides the character-mode user interface—processing commands and displays error messages and other feedback. (6)

shell command A command entered through a CLI shell. (6)

shortcut An icon that represents a link to an object, such as a file or program. Activating a shortcut (by clicking on it) is a quick way to access an object or to start a program from any location. (4)

shoulder surfing The gathering of information by reading information on a screen as a user works on the device. (2)

site-to-site VPN A VPN connection between two networks. (9)

Sleep A Windows power down option that leaves the computer in a very-low-power mode in which the system state and user session (applications and data) are saved in RAM, but the screen turns off. (5)

smartphone A cell phone that connects to the Internet and runs a variety of apps for entertainment, education, and work. (1)

social engineering The use of persuasion techniques to gain the confidence of individuals—for both good and bad purposes. (2)

social media A service (Internet-based or other) that provides a place where people can interact in online communities, sharing information in various forms. (2)

social networking The use of social media. (2)

solid-state drive (SSD) A storage device that uses integrated circuits, which are faster than conventional hard disk drives and optical drives. (1)

source code The uncompiled text program statements that can be viewed and edited with a text editor or special software. (7)

Spaces A macOS feature in which a space is a virtual screen; macOS supports up to 16 Spaces. Use Spaces for separating categories of files, such as those for work, play, and school projects. (6)

spam Unsolicited email. This includes email from a legitimate source selling a real service or product, but if you did not give permission to send such information to you, it is spam. (2)

spam filter Software designed to combat spam by examining incoming messages and filtering out those that have characteristics of spam. (2)

spear phishing Targeted phishing attacks that often target high-value individuals. (2)

spim An acronym for Spam over Instant Messaging; the perpetrators are called spimmers. (2)

Split View A feature introduced in macOS 10.11 El Capitan that allows two full-screen apps to share the screen. (6)

Spotlight A macOS search utility that, much like Search in Windows, is a live search, presenting results as soon as you start typing. (6)

spyware A category of software that runs surreptitiously on a user's computer, gathers information without permission from the user, and then sends that information to the people who requested the information. (2)

Standard account In macOS an account type that can only access files in that user's Home folder and the Shared folder and is denied access to higher-level system settings. (6)

standard user account An account for an "ordinary" user without administrator status. (2)

Start button A button on the Windows taskbar that opens the Start menu. (4)

static IP address An IP address that is manually configured for a host and can, therefore, be considered semipermanent in that, it stays with the device until someone changes it. (9)

status tray A bar on the far right of the Chrome OS shelf that opens a pop-up with the current status of network connections, battery life, who is signed in, and more. (8)

Storage Saver The new (since 2018) name for Google Photo's High Quality file format that compresses images and videos that exceed a certain resolution. (11)

storage virtualization Multiple networked hard drives functioning as a single logical drive. (3)

subkey In the Windows registry, a key that exists within another key. (5)

subnet mask An important IP configuration parameter as critical as the address itself, because it divides what looks like a single address into two addresses by masking off part of the address. (9)

Subscriber Identity Module (SIM) An integrated circuit card that, when inserted into a mobile device, programs it for a customer's use on a cellular network. (10)

sudo In Linux, the command that temporarily allows an administrator-type account to perform administrative functions from the command line. (7)

switch A hardware network device that connects multiple devices in a network, reviewing the packets of data and sending each packet to the correct device on that network. (3)

switch users A feature of most operating systems that allows the currently logged-on users to leave their apps and data open in memory, switching away so that another user can log in to a separate session. (7)

Switcher On a Chromebook keyboard, the key in the traditional F5 position that quickly displays all open windows. (8)

symbolic link In Linux, a string of characters, such as **/usr/bin**, that points to another directory. (7)

synchronize To match the contents of two locations, sometimes in both directions, so that the contents match. (10)

system firmware Software resident in integrated circuits that contains program code for interacting with the hardware. (1)

system-on-a-chip (SoC) A term used to describe a microchip containing all or most of the electronic circuitry for a small computing device, such as a smartphone. (1)

System Preferences The macOS settings utility. (6)

tablet A mobile computing device with a touch screen and no integrated keyboard, and it is larger than a smartphone but more portable than a laptop. (1)

Tablet mode The Windows 10 mode for displaying the desktop and applications when no keyboard is attached to a device. (4)

task management An operating system function in multitasking OSs that controls the focus. (1)

Task Manager A Windows utility that allows you to see the state of the individual processes and programs running on the computer and to stop one, if necessary. (5)

Task view A feature of Windows 10 that lets the user quickly view all open apps. (4)

TCP/IP A suite of protocols that work together to allow both similar and dissimilar computers to communicate. It is needed to access the Internet and is the most common protocol suite used on private intranets. (9)

Terminal A window in the macOS GUI that provides a command-line interface (CLI) for entering UNIX shell commands. The default Terminal shell is BASH. (6)

terminal client Software that establishes a connection to a terminal server. (3)

terminal services Software running on servers to which users connect from their desktop PCs using terminal client software. (3)

terminal window A window in a Linux GUI that provides a command-line interface (CLI) for entering Linux shell commands. (7)

tethering A feature that allows you to share your smartphone's cellular data connection with another device. The connection between the smartphone and the computer, laptop, or tablet can be via USB cable, Wi-Fi, or Bluetooth. (10)

thin client A minimally configured network computer. (3)

third-party cookie A cookie that originates with a domain name beyond the one shown in the URL for the current Web page. (2)

Time Machine An macOS backup utility that automatically backs up files to a dedicated drive that is always available when the computer is turned on. (6)

token A physical device that can be used in authentication, either alone or together with a user name and password. (2)

Top Level Domain (TLD) A special Internet domain name that appears on the right of a registered domain name, just to the left of the root domain. An example of a TLD is ".com." (9)

tote A "holding space" for downloaded files and screenshots. It resides to the left of the notification area on the shelf. (8)

Touch ID A feature in iPhone 5s and newer incorporating a fingerprint scanner into the Home button for authentication. (10)

Transmission Control Protocol (TCP) The protocol responsible for the accurate delivery of messages, verifying and resending pieces that fail to make the trip from source to destination. (9)

Trojan horse A program that is installed and activated on a computer by appearing to be something harmless. This is a common vector. (2)

Trusted Boot A feature of Windows 8 and newer that examines each of the system files loaded during the boot process before it is loaded into memory. (5)

Two-Factor Authentication In an Apple ID account, a security service that adds an extra layer of protection to an account. It differs from Two-Step Verification in that it first sends a message stating that someone is attempting to access a device. (10)

Type I hypervisor A hypervisor that can run directly on a computer without an underlying host operating system—sometimes called a bare-metal hypervisor. (3)

Type II hypervisor A hypervisor that requires a host operating system. (3)

Ubuntu A group of Linux distributions supported by a company named Canonical. (7)

UEFI BIOS System firmware that includes important security features. (5)

Unified Extensible Firmware Interface (UEFI) The specification for system firmware that replaced ROM-BIOS. (5)

Universal app A type of app, introduced in Windows 10, that adapts to the screen size and type so that it displays in both desktop mode and tablet mode. (4)

upgrade An installation of an OS installed directly into the folders in which a previous version was installed, preserving preferences and data. (4)

upload Both the action and result of moving data from a local device to a remote location over a network. (11)

USB Restricted Mode An Apple security feature that prevents a USB accessory from making a data connection to a device if it has been more than an hour since it was locked. (10)

user account A record in an accounts database that represents a single person and that is used for authentication. (2)

User Account Control (UAC) A security feature that prevents unauthorized changes to Windows. A user logged on with an administrator-type account only has the privileges of a standard account until the user (or a malicious program) attempts to do something that requires higher privileges. (4)

user interface (UI) The software layer, or shell, through which the user communicates with the OS. (1)

user right The privilege to perform a systemwide function, such as access the computer from the network, log on locally, log on from the network, back up files, change the system time, or load and unload device drivers. (2)

User tile A small image representing the user. A user tile appears in various places in Windows: in the Start menu in Windows 7 and Windows 10 and on the top right of the Start screen in Windows 8.x. Beginning in Windows 8, click or tap the User tile to open User settings. (4)

value entry A setting within a Windows registry key. (5)

vector A mode of malware infection, such as email, code on websites, Trojan horse, searching out unprotected computers, sneakernet, back doors, rootkits, pop-up downloads, drive-by downloads, war driving, and bluesnarfing. (2)

Viewer A Google Drive permission (also called a role) that allows a person to only view a shared file. (11)

Virtual Desktop A feature of Windows (and other OSs) that supports multiple unique instances of the desktop. (4)

virtual desktop infrastructure (VDI) Hosting and managing multiple virtual desktops on network servers. (3)

virtual keyboard An onscreen image of a keyboard with labeled keys that you can tap. (1)

virtual machine (VM) A software simulation of a computer. (3)

virtual machine monitor (VMM) Another name for a hypervisor. A software layer that emulates the necessary hardware for an operating system to run in. (3)

virtual printer Software that behaves like a printer, but saves the print output to a file, rather than sending it to a physical printer. (5)

virtual private network (VPN) A virtual tunnel created between two end points over a real network or internetwork. (9)

virtual reality (VR) A virtual environment that includes three-dimensional images and involves other senses, giving the participant a feeling of actually being present in that time and space. (3)

virtual switch A virtual version of a physical network switch. See *switch*. (3)

virtual world An online simulated communal environment within which users, often using an animated computer-generated human (avatar), can interact with one another and create and use various objects. (3)

virtualization The creation of an environment that seems real, but isn't. (3)

virus In the broadest sense, malware, a program that is installed and activated on a computer without the knowledge or permission of the user. (2)

Wallet The Apple app that holds credit and debit card data for use with Apple Pay. It also digitally stores other data normally carried in a physical wallet, such as tickets, boarding passes, and student IDs. (10)

war driving The act of moving through a neighborhood in a vehicle or on foot, using a Wi-Fi sensor to exploit unsecured Wi-Fi networks. (2)

Web A shortened version of the term World Wide Web (WWW). (7)

web app An app that runs entirely within a browser and resides on a website. (8)

Web-based setup An online installer, available through the Microsoft website for installing Windows 10. (4)

Web browser A special type of client software used to navigate the Web. (9)

Web mail A generic term for Web-based email services such as Hotmail, Gmail, and Yahoo! that keep your messages stored on the Internet, allowing you to access them from any computer via a Web browser. (9)

white hat hacker A hacker who is not a cybercriminal. (2)

wide area network (WAN) A network that covers a very large geographic area (miles). (9)

widget A mini app in Apple desktop and mobile device OSs that uses few resources, but provides updated information. (6)

Wi-Fi calling A feature of mobile devices the allows outgoing and incoming calls, texts, and video calls to use a Wi-Fi connection rather than a cellular connection. (10)

Wi-Fi network A wireless LAN (WLAN) that complies with IEEE 802.11 standards. (9)

wildcard A symbol that replaces a character or string of characters as a parameter in a CLI command. (7)

Windows 10 Home Edition A Windows edition targeted to consumers. (4)

Windows 10 Pro A Windows edition targeted to people who need advanced features. (4)

Windows Hello A Windows 10 biometric sign-in feature that uses fingerprint scanning, facial recognition, or iris scanning. It requires special hardware. (4)

Windows key (⊞) A key located near the bottom left of most keyboards that displays a Windows logo and is used in combination with other keys to create keyboard shortcuts. (4)

Windows PowerShell A Windows CLI scripting environment for advanced users and administrators. (5)

Windows Preinstallation Environment (Windows PE) A scaled-down Windows operating system. Windows PE supports the Windows Setup GUI, collecting configuration information. (4)

Windows Recovery Environment (Windows RE) A powerful group of Windows diagnostics and repair tools that runs in the Windows Preinstallation Environment (Windows PE). (5)

Windows Setup The traditional program for installing and upgrading Windows. (4)

Windows Store app The official source of software for Windows. (4)

Windows Update A Windows program that can automatically connect to the Microsoft site and download and install updates. (4)

wireless LAN (WLAN) A local area network using one of the standards referred to as Wi-Fi (for wireless fidelity). The distance covered by a WLAN is measured in a hundreds of feet rather than miles. (9)

wireless wide area network (WWAN) A digital wireless network that extends over a large geographical area. (9)

World Wide Web (WWW) The graphical Internet consisting of a vast array of documents located on millions of specialized servers worldwide. (7)

worm A self-replicating computer virus. (2)

zero-day exploit A software vulnerability in an operating system or application that is unknown to the publisher of the software. (2)

zombie An individual computer in a botnet. (2)

Index

Note: Page numbers followed by *f* or *t* represent figures or tables, respectively.